THE COLUMBIA ANTHOLOGY OF

MODERN JAPANESE DRAMA

J. THOMAS RIMER,
MITSUYA MORI, &
M. CODY POULTON

EDITORS

THE COLUMBIA ANTHOLOGY OF

MODERN JAPANESE DRAMA

COLUMBIA UNIVERSITY PRESS *NEW YORK*

*Columbia University Press wishes to express its appreciation
for assistance given by The Pushkin Fund
toward the cost of publishing this book.*

Columbia University Press
Publishers Since 1893
New York Chichester, West Sussex
cup.columbia.edu

Paperback edition, 2017

Library of Congress Cataloging-in-Publication Data
The Columbia anthology of modern Japanese drama / edited by J. Thomas Rimer,
Mitsuya Mori, and M. Cody Poulton.
pages cm
Also includes historical, critical commentaries.
Includes bibliographical references.
Summary: "An anthology of modern Japanese drama from the mid-nineteenth century to
the early twenty-first century" — Provided by publisher.
ISBN 978-0-231-12830-8 (cloth : alk. paper)—ISBN 978-0-231-12831-5 (pbk. : alk. paper)—
ISBN 978-0-231-53713-1 (e-book)
1. Japanese drama—19th century—Translations into English. 2. Japanese drama—
20th century—Translations into English. 3. Japanese drama—21st century—
Translations into English. 4. Japanese drama—19th century—History and criticism.
5. Japanese drama—20th century—History and criticism. 6. Japanese drama—21st century—
History and criticism. 7. Theater—Japan—History—19th century. 8. Theater—Japan—
History—20th century. 9. Theater—Japan—History—21st century. I. Rimer, J. Thomas, editor.
II. Mori, Mitsuya, 1937– editor. III. Poulton, M. Cody, 1955– editor.

PL782.E5C65 2014
792.0952—dc23
2013027559

Columbia University Press books are printed on permanent
and durable acid-free paper.
Printed in the United States of America

COVER IMAGE: Akita Unaku, *The Skeletons' Dance.*
(Courtesy of The Tsubouchi Memorial Theatre Museum Waseda University)
COVER AND BOOK DESIGN: Lisa Hamm
With the exception of figures 2, 4, 5, and 7, which are in the public domain,
all figures not otherwise credited are courtesy of Teatro, Corporation Chamomile.

To Donald Keene

an inspiration to us all

CONTENTS

PART II. THE TSUKIJI LITTLE THEATER AND ITS AFTERMATH

J. THOMAS RIMER

PART III. WARTIME AND POSTWAR DRAMA

J. THOMAS RIMER

PART V. THE 1980S AND BEYOND

M. CODY POULTON

PART VI. POPULAR THEATER

MITSUYA MORI

PREFACE

When we began compiling *The Columbia Anthology of Modern Japanese Drama*, our purpose was to introduce English-speaking readers to the richness and depth of modern Japanese drama, from early experiments to the contemporary period, a span of nearly one hundred years. Now that this compilation is complete, however, we see that its significance may well reach beyond our original conception, for in fact, this anthology can be read in several ways.

First, of course, each play can, and should, be read on its own, either in or out of chronological order, simply for the intellectual and aesthetic pleasure we believe that each provides. Second, with the help of the introductions to each section, this anthology offers a history of modern spoken drama in Japan, from its beginning in the early twentieth century to almost the present. Inevitably, however, the anthology is incomplete, since we could not include all forms of twentieth-century theater. In addition, most of the plays—in the various social, intellectual, and theatrical frameworks in which they were written—can be regarded as works of artistic ambition rather than simple entertainment.

One of the sections, on popular theater, contains examples of modern kabuki, a scene from a Takarazuka musical, and a scene from a play written for the *shinpa* theater that flourished in the early twentieth century. These, we hope, will give the reader a glimpse of yet another aspect of modern Japanese theater.

Another feature of the modern period in Japan is the participation of women in theatrical productions, as both performers and playwrights, even though men occupied most of those roles. Accordingly, besides some examples of the few dramas written by women, we offer a short history of the women playwrights during this period, by Yoshie Inoue, a leading scholar on modern Japanese theater.

Finally, the plays in this anthology exemplify both the vicissitudes and the accomplishments of larger issues in modern Japanese culture during this period. In a sense, they also provide another kind of history of modern Japan, which, though connected to politics and social issues, produced its own, evolving traditions. The progression of these plays thus reveals a trajectory similar to those found in other artistic endeavors in Japan at this time, ranging from the development of modern fiction and poetry to architecture, painting, sculpture, and printmaking. This progression has three phases: first, a response to the stimulus of imported Western culture; second, an attempt to work creatively within the perceived possibilities of these new modalities; and last, a transcendence into something both truly Japanese and truly contemporary. In a larger sense, then, the theater points to the ways in which Japan, after centuries of isolation, found a secure and respected place in world culture.

These larger significances are, at best, implicit in the individual works in this anthology, and they should not be sought at the expense of the reader's pleasure in discovering the artistic, social, and theatrical accomplishments of each play.

Some issues this anthology cannot address, particularly the important matter of stage language. Read in translation, these plays have necessarily been stripped of the beauty of the original Japanese dialogue. The central issue of creating an authentic modern stage speech, in a theatrical tradition far more attuned to a rhetoric of illusion and stylization, cannot be illustrated through translated texts. Indeed, in one sense, when read in the original, many of these plays can be seen as a series of experiments, a succession of attempts to create a kind of spoken realism—personal, political, social—that was not present in the Japanese theater until the twentieth century. Reading these plays in English, therefore, may allow the reader to imagine these experiments but not to experience them. Nonetheless, we believe that this anthology offers a sustained look at a rich and diverse century within a long and vibrant theatrical tradition.

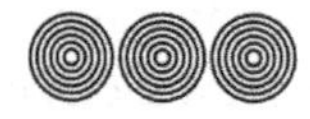

So many friends and colleagues have given help and advice to us while compiling this anthology that would be impossible to list them all. We begin, however, with our heartfelt appreciation to the support shown us by Jennifer Crewe at Columbia University Press, whose enthusiasm has sustained us from the beginning of this project a decade ago. Our editors, Irene Pavitt and Margaret B. Yamashita, have been both patient and forthcoming in helping us make these translations as readable as possible. Paula Locante, at the University of Pittsburgh, was generous with her help in preparing early versions of the manuscript. Joanna Kriese, at the University of Victoria, was essential to preparing the final manuscript. Among those who have given us wise counsel and good suggestions are Dennis Kennedy, Mark Oshima, Yoko Shioya, John Gillespie, Kevin Wetmore, and Carol Sorgenfrei, as well as those who read the original manuscript and recommended it to the press.

Finally, we want our readers to know that we compiled this anthology with the enthusiasm we feel for the accomplishments of modern Japanese theater. It is our greatest hope that our readers will have the same feeling.

A NOTE ON JAPANESE NAMES

Japanese names follow the customary manner of family name first and given name second. Although authors are usually referred to by their family name, until around the beginning of the twentieth century, literary figures customarily took special names, called *gō*. Tsubouchi Yūzō, for example, chose the name Shōyō, so most of the time he is called Tsubouchi Shōyō, or even just Shōyō. Likewise, we refer to Mori Rintarō as Mori Ōgai, or just Ōgai. This is the same when referring to kabuki actors: Ichikawa Danjūrō IX, for example, is called Danjūrō IX. Some writers used *gō*, and others did not. Therefore, Shimamura Hōgetsu and Osanai Kaoru appear side by side as the founders of *shingeki*, but the former is referred to as Hōgetsu and the latter as Osanai.

In the translations of the plays, names are presented in the Japanese fashion, family name first and personal name second. The names of the Japanese contributors to the anthology, however, are listed in the Western way, personal name followed by family name. In addition, the text occasionally refers to era names (*nengō*). The dates for those in the modern era are as follows:

Meiji	1868–1912
Taishō	1912–1926
Shōwa	1926–1989
Heisei	1989–present

NOTE ON JAPANESE NAMES

THE COLUMBIA ANTHOLOGY OF

MODERN JAPANESE DRAMA

INTRODUCTION

The Prelude to Modern Drama in the Meiji Era (1868–1912)

In the mid-nineteenth century, Japan, plagued by political and economic corruption, began modernizing its politics, technology, and society. In addition, the Tokugawa government (shogunate) was being pressured by the West to abandon its seclusion policy, according to which it had maintained only limited contact with the Netherlands and China since the early seventeenth century. The United States, Britain, and France demanded that Japan sign a series of unfair trade treaties, and the shogunate had no choice but to agree, faced with the overwhelming power of the West's iron "black ships" (*kurofune*). Furthermore, Japan was well aware of China's defeat in the Opium War in 1842. The emperor and the court council, however, did not support the shogunate's slavish attitude toward the Western powers, and young nationalistic samurai even resorted to terrorist acts under the slogan of *sonnō jōi* (revere the emperor, expel the barbarians). Consequently, Japan fell into chaos and was rescued only by the so-called Meiji Restoration (Meiji ishin).

When the new Meiji government was established in 1868, top government officials, who had wanted to expel the foreigners, now reversed to *fukoku kyōhei* (enrich the country, strengthen the military). In this way, the Meiji government began trying to Westernize the government and institutions, as well as industry and the common people's everyday life, through a process called *bunmei kaika* (civilization and enlightenment). The goal was reached, for good or ill, with miraculous speed, and by the turn of the twentieth century, Japan was generally recognized as the most modern country outside Europe and North America.

The theater in Japan was modernized as well, with the first notable move in 1872 when the Tokyo municipal government issued a directive stipulating that the theater become more sophisticated and the plays be based on historical fact. In the same year, the municipal government also issued a decree liberalizing theaters in Tokyo, thereby annulling the shogunate's earlier regulations licensing only four—later reduced to three—kabuki theaters in a segregated area of Edo (modern-day Tokyo) close to the Yoshiwara licensed quarters. This was the first effort to recognize the theater (then synonymous with kabuki) as a legitimate cultural activity, which in the past had sometimes even been associated with prostitution.

Morita Kan'ya XII (1846–1897), the owner of one of the licensed theaters, the Moritaza, responded to this decree by opening a new kabuki theater in Shintomi-chō in downtown Tokyo. This theater, later called the Shintomiza, was, in many respects, modeled on Western theaters. For instance, chairs were installed for foreigners, and the stage was entirely Western style except for the *hanamichi* (flower way), the ramp extending from the main stage to the back of the auditorium, which was used as a performance space.

Kan'ya, a progressive young producer of kabuki, used the Meiji period's two most acclaimed kabuki actors, Ichikawa Danjūrō IX (1838–1903) and Onoe Kikugorō V (1844–1903), in an effort to reform the plays. Danjūrō wished to make period plays (*jidaimono*) historically accurate and to perform them in a realist style without many of the conventional patterns of acting. He thus asked the most popular kabuki playwright of that era, Kawatake Mokuami (1816–1893), to write what were called "living history plays" (*katsurekimono*). Kikugorō, in contrast, was more interested in plays about contemporary lives and behavior, known as "crop-haired plays" (*zangirimono*), in reference to the Western hairstyle then in vogue. Mokuami wrote the first original *zangirimono*, *Tokyo Daily* (*Tokyo nichinichi shinbun*), in 1873.

In 1878, Itō Hirobumi (1841–1909), one of the Meiji period's most prominent politicians, made a point of telling Kan'ya and four actors in his company (Danjūrō, Kikugorō, Nakazō, and Sōjūrō) about the Western theater performances he had seen as a member of the official diplomatic mission that had traveled around the world from 1871 to 1873, led by Foreign Minister Iwakura Tomomi (1825–1883). The purpose of the Iwakura mission was to negotiate with Western countries a revision of the unequal treaties, but it was not successful. Consequently, it turned into a fact-finding mission in almost every field that would promote Japan's modernization.

Many of those close to Kan'ya sensed that at one point he was ambitious enough to want to make his Shintomiza Japan's national theater. The culmination of his enthusiasm for Westernizing kabuki was the visit in 1879 by the former president of the United States, Ulysses S. Grant, to the Shintomiza. In the same year, Mokuami's *The Strange Tale of a Man Adrift: A Western Kabuki* (*Hyōryū kitan seiyō-kabuki*) was performed at the Shintomiza. This play was about the various experiences in the United States and Europe of a Japanese man who had been shipwrecked and rescued by an American ship. In one of the scenes, kabuki actors played the Americans, and foreign actors appeared in a scene set in Paris.[1] The play, however, was a box-office disaster, and Kan'ya's passion to Westernize kabuki quickly cooled. Mokuami also returned to conventional kabuki dramaturgy. His play in the old style, *Kōchiyama and Naozamurai* (*Kumo ni magou Ueno no hatsuhana*), was a great success in 1881 and is still a popular kabuki play.

Since the theater people were no longer interested in modernizing the theater, in 1886 representatives from the university, business, and government established the Theater Reform Society (Engeki kairyōkai). (In this context, "theater" meant kabuki; no one thought of modernizing nō or the bunraku puppet theater.) The Theater Reform Society included quite a few university intellectuals, politicians, and businessmen as supporting members, but no kabuki actors or producers. Many of them had visited Western countries and been invited to theaters there, so they felt that Japan also should have a theater elegant enough for foreign guests.

The driving force behind the Theater Reform Society was Suematsu Norizumi (1855–1920), who had served for several years as a secretary at the Japanese embassy in London and had studied at Cambridge University. He later became a son-in-law of Itō Hirobumi, who was prime minister at the time and was one of the society's major supporting members.

The society's manifesto had three goals in mind: (1) to produce good theater in Japan, (2) to make the profession of playwriting honorable and respectable, and (3) to build playhouses suitable for not only theater performances but also music concerts and song recitals. Suematsu himself made his opinions clear in a public lecture, which later was published. He suggested, for example, abandoning the *hanamichi* and eliminating *onnagata* (female impersonators), a convention foreign to modern Western theater. Another member of the society, Toyama Masakazu (1848–1900), a professor at Tokyo Imperial University, published similar opinions.

Their views elicited a backlash. Tsubouchi Shōyō (1859–1935), a professor of English literature at Waseda University, and Mori Ōgai (1862–1922), a medical officer in the army and also a poet, novelist, and critic, were in the vanguard of the attack on the society. Both Shōyō and Ōgai, the two most respected literary figures in Japan in the Meiji period, insisted that what Japanese theater needed most was good drama suitable for a modern society. To be fair, Suematsu and Toyama wanted good drama as well. But in any event, their call for a theater building similar to the Paris Opera received more attention, as they clearly were more interested in the material conditions of performance.

In 1887, the year after the society was founded, a special event at which Emperor Meiji would enjoy kabuki performances was planned. He was invited to a celebration of the opening of the teahouse in the garden of Inoue Kaoru, the minister of foreign affairs. As part of the celebration, the emperor also watched Danjūrō, Kikugorō, Sadanji, and other kabuki actors perform classical plays, including *The Subscription List* (*Kanjinchō*) and

1. Harue Tsutsumi, "Kabuki Encounters the West: Morita Kan'ya's Shintomi-za Productions, 1878–1879" (Ann Arbor, Mich.: UMI Dissertation Services, ProQuest [BA76372061], 2005).

SUEMATSU NORIZUMI

. . . The purpose of theater reform is to make theater enjoyable for middle- or upper-class people. But I do not mean that it is made understandable only for them and not for lower-class people. As stated earlier, ideally speaking, theater should be made easy for everyone to understand and should elevate everyone's artistic sensibility. But this is the final goal, and for the time being, theater should be directed to middle-class people.

Then, how should we find actors? Some people have the crazy idea that actors in the reformed theater should be recruited in London or Paris. But it would be more to the point to employ Japanese actors. Even though some reformers are against Japanese actors, they are not inferior to Western ones. On the contrary, they are quite good. Unfortunately, however, their style of acting is different. It is as if the reason for doing a good thing were employed for doing a bad thing. A lot of misleading discussions are taking place now because of the wrong way of doing things. Acting style is something that should be reformed gradually. The style of Japanese actors is, in short, based more on their outer movements than on their inner mind. Their speaking style is artificial. . . .

I have been talking about male actors so far. You may be ready to accept the idea that I am going to propose now, but most people will be surprised to hear it. It is only that female roles should be played by female actors. There is no question about it. Without female actors, theater is not real. Therefore, the reformed theater must use female actors. Where to find and how to educate them, I have not yet considered. So I will not talk about that today.

FROM SUEMATSU NORIZUMI, "ENGEKI KAIRYŌ IKEN" (OPINIONS ABOUT THEATER REFORM), NOVEMBER 1886.

The Village School (*Terakoya*). This event was arguably the sole positive achievement of the Theater Reform Society, elevating the social status of kabuki and its actors, who had been treated as being even below the lowest of the social classes in the Edo (also known as the Tokugawa) era.

The Theater Reform Society was reorganized twice, and even Shōyō and Ōgai joined the later organization. But nothing new came of it. Kabuki returned to its old, conservative style and gradually began to lose its relevance to modern life. Because of this reversion, however, kabuki acquired the status of classical theater and remained accessible because it continued to be regularly performed year around. In Japan, the theater had to be modernized outside the kabuki world.

MORI RINTARŌ (ŌGAI)

What is theater? It is actors enacting a drama on the stage. Drama precedes theater. The former is the primary, and the latter, the secondary. Some say that drama is made for theater. But if this idea gained ground in society, both drama and theater would decline. The reason is that drama is the best of poetry. We Japanese traditionally do not respect drama. But abroad, it goes without saying that drama stands at the center of poetry. . . .

I am not satisfied with the theater in Japan today. It may have been acceptable in premodern times when theater was called *shibai*. But today, in the nineteenth century, we should have certain kinds of theater buildings. Theaters should be securely built. We should not permit theaters made of wood, as they burn easily. Theaters should be clean: people's health should not be affected by bad air in theaters. The stage should be simple. I do not mean that it should be like a nō theater or a Chinese theater. What I mean is that exaggerated makeup and the miming of horseback riding or rowing a boat only by physical gestures should not be accepted. Wave boards or wave curtains should be changed. A lantern signifying the moon also should not be allowed. I am afraid that these attract the audience's attention entirely by their attempting to be as real as possible.

Drama requires a simple stage. This is not my personal opinion. Great critics in the West have been suggesting the like in order to correct prejudices in society. Not a few are critical of the exaggerated stage sets of big theaters in Paris. They not only criticize them but also are trying to build simpler stages. According to a German newspaper, *Grenzboten*, a public theater in Munich has tried to restore the old style of stage sets. [Here] a play by Shakespeare opened with a Shakespearean-style set. Despite the simple set, the audience thoroughly enjoyed the play. Although there is much to be said about Shakespearean stage sets and their restoration, we should reserve discussion of that for another day.

FROM MORI RINTARŌ (ŌGAI), "ENGEKI KAIRYŌ RONJA NO HENKEN NI ODOROKU" (SURPRISED BY THE PREJUDICE OF THEATER REFORMISTS), *SHIGARAMI-ZŌSHI*, OCTOBER 1889. REPRINTED IN *ŌGAI ZENSHŪ*, VOL. 22 (TOKYO: IWANAMI SHOTEN, 1973).

At the end of 1887, the government passed a law expelling antigovernment "agitators" (*sōshi*) from the Tokyo region. Many fled to Osaka, and one of them, Nakae Chōmin (1847–1901), a progressive political thinker, advised the agitators instead to criticize the government in theater performances. One of them, Sudō Sadanori (1867–1907), followed Nakae's advice and produced a piece of agit-prop in Osaka in 1888, the year after Emperor Meiji's attendance at the kabuki performances. This agit-prop was called "agitators' theater" (*sōshi shibai*) and was political theater, all of whose performers were amateurs with almost no theatrical experience. Other agitator groups followed Sudō's example. Kawakami Otojirō (1864–1911), who boasted that he had been arrested more than a hundred times because of his denunciations of the government, started his agitator's theater in 1891 in Sakai, near Osaka, with the productions of *Useful Stories of Nation Building* (*Keikoku bidan*), an adaptation of the story of Thebes's revolt against Sparta in ancient Greece, and *The True Story of an Attack on Mr. Itagaki* (*Itagaki-kun sōnan jikki*). (Itagaki was the leader of the opposition party.) In bringing these productions to Tokyo later the same year, Kawakami became famous for being the first performer of agitators' theater there. He thus came to be regarded as the pioneer of a new theatrical form (later called *shinpa* [new school]), even though Sudo Sadanori had always claimed to be the creator of this genre.

What Kawakami himself preferred to call *shin-engeki* (new theater) immediately became popular as a new type of theatrical performance. The audience was particularly attracted to the actors' inflammatory speech, which was addressed directly to them, and the realistic fighting scenes between the opposing political sides, in addition to Kawakami's popular finales of politically and socially satirical songs, called *oppekepe*.

Other new theater people were not so politically minded but instead were eager to pursue a new style of theater outside kabuki. One such actor, Ii Yōhō (1871–1932), produced a new play, *A Lady's Chastity: A Useful Story of Political Parties* (*Seitō-bidan shukujo no misao*), written by the critic and playwright Yoda Gakkai (1833–1909), right after Kawakami's Tokyo debut. In this production a female actor, Chitose Beiha, a former geisha, appeared together with male actors. This was the first mixed-gender theater performance since the Tokugawa government in 1629 banned female actors from appearing together with male actors on stage. Later, Ii Yōhō became one of *shinpa*'s most important actors.

Kawakami, however, gradually jettisoned his political radicalism as his popularity increased, and he even began to support the government. When the Sino-Japanese War began in 1894, Kawakami staged a nationalistic play, *The Sublime, Exhilarating Sino-Japanese War* (*Sōzetsu-kaizetsu Nisshin sensō*), which was a great box-office hit. Eventually, the Kawakami Company went on tour to America and Europe, from April 1899 to January 1901 and again from April 1901 to September 1902.[2]

2. The Kawakami troupe's tour in abroad is meticulously documented in Joseph L. Anderson, *Enter a Samurai: Kawakami Otojirō and Japanese Theater in the West*, 2 vols. (Tucson: Wheatmark, 2011).

Kawakami Otojirō and his wife, Sadayakko (1872–1946), charmed Western audiences with traditional dance and pseudo-kabuki acting. Sadayakko had been a geisha before she married Kawakami, so she had had some training in traditional dance. But she had never appeared on stage as a professional actress before the American and European tour. At first, she only accompanied her husband on this tour, but in San Francisco, where the Kawakami troupe first landed in the United States, she was urged by the producer to appear onstage to satisfy the curiosity of American audiences.[3] Sadayakko continued to perform on tour, and her dancing became the talk of the town in New York and Paris, even attracting such prominent artists as André Gide and Pablo Picasso. André Antoine, the founder of Théâtre libre, greatly praised Otojirō's sensational *seppuku* (ritual suicide), which actually had little relevance to the play he was in.

In contrast, the Kawakami Company's pseudo-kabuki performances looked phony and absurd to the Japanese who saw them in Europe. Consequently, the company's activities abroad were not seriously studied in Japan for a long time. But recently, some Western and Japanese scholars have begun to argue that Kawakami stimulated a new theater movement of symbolism and neo-romanticism in fin-de-siècle Europe.

In 1903, the year after he returned to Tokyo, Kawakami staged three Shakespearean plays: *Othello*, the court scene from *The Merchant of Venice*, and *Hamlet*. Both *Othello* and *Hamlet* were set in Japan, so, for example, in *Othello*, Cyprus became Taiwan, a Japanese colony at the time. But most of the characters' lines were faithful translations of the original, and the title of the play remained *Othello*. In these productions, Sadayakko played the heroine, marking her debut as an actress on the Japanese stage. The same year, 1903, two of the best-known kabuki actors, Ichikawa Danjūrō IX and Onoe Kikugorō V, died, and another, Ichikawa Sadanji I, died the following year. Many people felt that this was the end of traditional kabuki and that *shinpa* would come to dominate the Japanese theater scene.

This turned out to be only half true, however. At the beginning of the twentieth century, *shinpa*—the offspring of the Kawakami Company's and Ii Yōhō's new theater—gained great popularity with new melodramas that were adaptations of popular novels, such as *Demon Gold* (*Konjiki yasha*, 1897–1902) by Ozaki Kōyō (1867–1903), *Cuckoo* (*Hototogisu*, 1898–1899) by Tokutomi Roka (1868–1927), *Foster Sisters* (*Chi-kyōdai*, 1903) and *My Crime* (*Ono ga tsumi*, 1899–1900) by Kikuchi Yūhō (1870–1947), and *A Woman's Pedigree* (*Onna keizu*, 1907) by Izumi Kyōka (1873–1939). By the end of the Meiji period, however, *shinpa* began to lose ground to a more modern theatrical style, called *shingeki*. Today *shinpa* is performed only sporadically, in contrast to kabuki, which still is popular.

Today some critics try to credit Kawakami, if not *shinpa*, with the creation of *shingeki*, but *shinpa* was not entirely modern drama. Although Kawakami did call his Shakespearean

---

3. This is the legendary story of how Sadayakko became an actress in America. But in preparation for the tour, Sadayakko did perform a kabuki dance piece on stage in Osaka. Some critics therefore assumed that Kawakami had foreseen an occasion on which Sadayakko would appear on stage in the United States.

productions "straight drama" (*seigeki*), he removed most of the soliloquies, for he had no idea how to deliver them properly. He died in November 1911, at the age of forty-seven.

In the year that Kawakami died, Henrik Ibsen's *A Doll's House* was performed in translation in Japan by the Literary Society (Bungei kyōkai), led by Tsubouchi Shōyō. The first Ibsen production in translation had been staged two years earlier, in 1909: *John Gabriel Borkman*, staged by the Free Theater (Jiyū gekijō), founded by Osanai Kaoru (1881–1928), a Tokyo Imperial University graduate, and Ichikawa Sadanji II (1880–1940), a progressive young kabuki actor. In this way, a new kind of modern drama in Japan was introduced.

LITERARY AND PERFORMATIVE THEATER

Theater can be divided into two aspects, variously termed "inner" and "outer," "literary" and "performative," or "text" and "performance." In premodern times in both the West and the East, the text of a play and its performance were not as distinct as they are today. At that time, if a text was published, it was almost always after the performance, and the playwright always belonged, or was closely related, to a theater company. Only in modern times was a play written without being necessarily connected to a performance. (As we shall see in part IV, this premodern, or postmodern, relationship between text and performance has been reappraised in recent years.) Even though kabuki and *shinpa* cannot strictly be called modern because their texts are closely linked to performance conventions, new types of plays were tried early in the Meiji era.

Examples are the "living history plays" (*katsurekimono*) and the "crop-haired plays" (*zangirimono*), mentioned earlier. Kabuki and *shinpa* adaptations of Western stories also were a great box-office draw, as were adaptations of Shakespeare's plays. When *All That Matters Is Money in the Time of Cherry Blossoms* (*Sakuradoki zeni no yononaka*) was performed by kabuki actors in Osaka in 1885, it was promoted as an adaptation of Shakespeare's *The Merchant of Venice*.

As the number of adaptations of Western plays to kabuki and *shinpa* increased, however, there was a tendency to conceal as much as possible the play's foreign origin. That is, a work was regarded as successful if it appeared to be completely Japanese. This tradition continued into the twentieth century, and sometimes the playwright was even accused of stealing plots from foreign literature.

The version of Ibsen's *An Enemy of the People* by Hanabusa Ryūgai (1872–1906) is an example. It was performed in Tokyo in 1902 with Ibsen listed as the original author, the first performance in Japan of a play attributed to him. But the plot, about farmers protesting river pollution caused by the Ashio Copper Mine in Tochigi Prefecture, had almost nothing to do with Ibsen's original story.[4] Clearly, although Hanabusa was a progressive

4. The Ashio Copper Mine, located in Ashio, Tochigi Prefecture, was the cause of serious pollution in the 1880s, which was severely criticized by Tanaka Shōzō, a Diet member.

HANABUSA RYŪGAI

I have heard that legislation regarding the theater will be submitted to the Diet this year. I think that a law to encourage theater would have no effect on its artistic development. Although I do not know the details, I read a report of it in this paper. I remember that the legislation includes a rule stipulating that more than one new play be staged each year. I would say that this is a ridiculous rule. No matter how many new plays might be staged, there is no merit in staging only superficially new plays. To demand that the ignorant producers of the current theater world to do so would be meaningless. The best way to reform the theater is to produce excellent actors and playwrights. The first step for that is to establish a theater that does not depend on financial profit. In this theater, the playwrights should be given enough time to develop. Elizabethan theater was formed with the support of the king. This also would be the best model for Japan's imperial theater, although building it now would be too difficult, for a variety of reasons. Therefore, first, a theater managed by the municipal government should be built, and top-notch writers should be supported, regardless of economic profit. Because the theater includes every kind of art form, it would take more than several decades to reach this final goal without such support. To hasten this process, public support would be the most effective. People have long tired of the current, tasteless, immature theater, and they complain of the lack of real pleasure in going to the theater. Nonetheless, the public pays attention to the material aspects of an enterprise, not its spiritual value, which has a profound effect on forming the character of Japanese people. I urge the authorities to consider this seriously.

HANABUSA RYŪGAI, "SHIRITSU GEKIJŌ WO KENSETSU SEYO!" (ESTABLISH MUNICIPAL THEATERS!), *YOMIURI SHINBUN*, NOVEMBER 29, 1903.

playwright, he seems to have been more interested in attracting audiences through the use of Ibsen's name rather than his choice of what to perform.

Likewise, as mentioned earlier, Tsubouchi Shōyō severely criticized the Theater Reform Society and advocated a kind of new drama. In 1894, he wrote *A Paulownia Leaf* (*Kiri hitoha*) as an example of the kind of new historical play that he had been advocating. The play is set at the start of the seventeenth century, in the final stage of the fall of the house of Toyotomi. This was a crucial turning point in Japanese history, and Shōyō's goal was a modern psychological portrayal, especially of the main characters: Yodogimi and Katagiri Katsumoto. *A Paulownia Leaf* was one of the earliest original plays written by an outsider for kabuki or *shinpa*, although it was not staged until 1904, ten years later.

TSUBOUCHI SHŌYŌ

. . . Now, what I believe is fundamentally lacking in our historical plays can be neatly summarized in three points. These three are nothing particular; perhaps most theatergoers have already noted them. . . .

These three are

1. The forms of epic and drama should be distinguished.
2. The unity of interest should be observed.
3. Characters should be the main cause for action.

. . .

The above-stated three points all are based on the apparent difference between epic (or fiction) and drama. This common observation is my first proposal for the future historical play. It is true that reform of the theater has been proposed repeatedly since the Meiji Restoration. Indeed, it has been carried out to a small extent. But no substantial step has been taken in this direction. A few attempts toward theater reform were made in the so-called living history plays [*katsureki-geki*] or agitators' theater [*sōshi-geki*] and in some plays by those authors who do not belong to established theaters. Likewise, some efforts have been made to reform ideas regarding stage directions, sets and costuming, new styles of speaking, and characterization. Nevertheless, they have generally neglected to make clear this fundamental distinction between epic and drama, nor have they made characters the main cause for dramatic action, and they have failed to create consistent interest for an entire play.

FROM TSUBOUCHI SHŌYŌ, "WAGAKUNI NO SHIGEKI" (OUR COUNTRY'S HISTORICAL DRAMA), *WASEDA BUNGAKU*, APRIL 1894.

A Paulownia Leaf, together with Shōyō's other historical plays, was nonetheless written in the style of kabuki. Such works were labeled *shinkabuki* (new kabuki), which came to be recognized as a particular type of this classical theater. Besides Shōyō, there were other *shinkabuki* playwrights in the late Meiji era, such as Enomoto Torahiko (1866–1916), Oka Onitarō (1872–1943), and Okamoto Kidō (1872–1939), and, in the Taishō era, Mayama Seika (1878–1948) and Hasegawa Shin (1884–1963). Kidō's *The Tale of Shuzenji* (*Shuzenji monogatari*, 1911) remains one of the most frequently performed kabuki plays. But regardless of their popularity, such plays did not mark the origin of modern drama in Japan because they are not entirely free from kabuki's performance conventions.

KITAMURA TŌKOKU

. . . What is unique to Japanese plays is the symmetrical harmony throughout a play. In music, sound effects, speeches, movements and behavior, dance, chanting, and in many other things, harmony is the core. Song is accompanied by movements of the legs and gestures by the hands, followed by various complicated demands. One part cannot be the whole, and the whole cannot be expressed by one part. Thus, our plays are in the service of symmetrical harmony. Without it no beauty would emerge. . . .

There would be no complaints if poetic drama could attract enough readers outside the theater world. But if it is staged, such drama often has problems. Should, then, future writers of poetic drama be familiar with the inner situation of the theater world before they write a play? That would not be the way to produce a great dramatic poet. Such a rule instead would transform a great poet into a small poet. If the poets outside the theater world and the poets inside (conventional playwrights) are to work in different ways—the former being engaged only with writing dramas and the latter with putting them on the stage—a contradiction between the two would be unavoidable. I have come to realize that there is no way to eliminate the defective convention of symmetrical harmony in Japanese drama. [Therefore,] Japanese drama will have much difficulty in the future.

FROM KITAMURA TŌKOKU, "GEKISHI NO ZENTO IKAN?"
(WHAT IS THE FUTURE OF POETIC DRAMA?) *BUNGAKUKAI*, DECEMBER 1893.

At the same time, many young writers, mostly poets, felt compelled to express, in the form of drama, their deep and complex feelings toward the new modern age. They wrote first under the influence of European, especially German and English, Romantic poets such as Goethe, Schiller, Byron, and Shelley. Christianity also had a great impact on many young writers at that time. In 1892, Kitamura Tōkoku (1868–1894) wrote a dramatic poem, *Mount Hōrai: A Play* (*Hōraikyoku*), that mixed Romantic and Christian ideas. In the poem, the young son of an aristocratic family wanders in the mountains seeking a place to die and, in death, finds the woman of his dreams. This dramatic poem was not intended to be performed and, indeed, was not staged until 1964. But it is regarded as the first attempt, under the influence of modern Western literature, to portray a genuinely modern character, here patterned after Byron's *Manfred* (1817).

Tōkoku's *Mount Hōrai: A Play* was the inspiration for Shimazaki Tōson's (1872–1943) play *The Biwa Player: An Elegy* (*Hikyoku biwa-hōshi*, 1893). Tōson started out as a poet, and his first anthology, *Seedlings* (*Wakanashū*, 1897), was praised as a prime example of Japanese romanticism. After the turn of the century, however, Tōson began to write naturalist novels and became much interested in Ibsen. It is said that Tōson recommended Ibsen's *John Gabriel Borkman* to Osanai Kaoru for the Free Theater's opening play in 1909. Mori Ōgai, the translator of *John Gabriel Borkman*, also wrote original drama. His romantic *River Ikuta* (*Ikutagawa*, 1910) draws on a story from classical literature about a girl who, courted by two men, dies because she cannot choose between them. The story is based on a legend in the *Man'yōshū*, the earliest collection of Japanese poetry. Furthermore, Kan'ami, who created the artistic form of nō in the fourteenth century, is thought to have dramatized this story in the nō play *Motomezuka*. But Ōgai's drama, unlike *Motomezuka*, ends before the girl commits suicide, thus suggesting a new life for her. This short one-act play, whose dialogue is simple and poetic, could be said in retrospective to be a forerunner of Mishima Yukio's modern nō plays written after World War II.

In Europe, a new strain of romanticism emerged at the end of the nineteenth century, mitigating to some extent naturalism's dominance in literature. But naturalism and neoromanticism were introduced into Japanese literature almost simultaneously, so from the outset modern Japanese drama was tinged by both romantic and naturalist styles. A typical example of a playwright who was influenced by both is Iwano Hōmei (1973–1920), who advocated "mysterious semianimalism" (*shinpiteki han-jū-shugi*) and wrote a play about a lustful woman, *Tongues of Flame* (*Honō no shita*, 1906).

Nevertheless, it was naturalism, or realism, that opened a totally new vista for modern drama in Japan. Productions of Ibsen's *John Gabriel Borkman* and *A Doll's House* in 1909 and 1911, respectively, prompted young writers in this field to turn to drama as a literary form. It was also at this time that a political event shocked the general public. In 1910, a number of leftists and their sympathizers were suddenly arrested for plotting to assassinate the emperor. The political philosopher Kōtoku Shūsui (1871–1911) and several others were sentenced to death and hastily executed in January 1911, even though many of the accused clearly were innocent. This so-called high treason case (*taigyaku jiken*) had a great impact on young writers.

The Ibsen productions spawned an amazing number of works that can be seen as forerunners of modern realist drama. Examples are a pseudo-Ibsen play about hereditary sickness, *A Fiend for Pleasure* (*Kanraku no oni*, 1910) by Nagata Hideo (1885–1949); a family play, *Izumiya Dye House* (*Izumiya somemonoten*, 1911) by Kinoshita Mokutarō (1885–1945); a play about Robespierre and the ghost of Danton, *An Incorruptible Madman* (*Fuhai-subekarazaru kyōjin*, 1911) by Kōri Torahiko (1890–1924); and plays by the first two female playwrights in Japan, *One Afternoon* (*Aruhi no gogo*, 1912) by Hasegawa

Shigure (1879–1941), about a strong-willed country girl, and *The Boxwood Comb* (*Tsuge no kushi*, 1912), about a comb maker and his wife, by Okada Yachiyo (1883–1962). (See "Japanese Women Playwrights" in part II.) Among these plays, *Izumiya Dye House*—whose author was a scientist and well known for his lyrical poems—was perhaps the first to allude to the high-treason case. All these playwrights were young, and none of them was connected to either the kabuki or the *shinpa* world. Their plays thus forecast the truly modern drama of the Taishō era, which began in 1912.

THE COMPOSITION OF THIS ANTHOLOGY

Most of the plays in *The Columbia Anthology of Modern Japanese Drama* are *shingeki* and its successors in the twentieth century. The book has six parts. Part I contains plays in the period from the first Ibsen productions to the Great Kantō Earthquake of 1923, covering most of the Taishō era (1912–1926). During this time, many young writers became interested in playwriting and helped establish modern Japanese drama (*shingeki*), although many of their plays were performed by kabuki or *shinpa* actors.

Part II covers the period from 1924 to 1940. In 1924, a year after the Great Kantō Earthquake, the Tsukiji Little Theater (Tsukiji shōgekijō) was founded and produced genuine *shingeki*, which dominated modern Japanese theater until around the 1970s. During this period, proletarian theater also became popular, reflecting the worldwide leftist theater movement after the Russian Revolution. By the 1930s, however, this movement was severely suppressed by the government as Japan became increasingly militaristic.

Part III deals with plays during and after World War II. Because of their leftist tendencies, however, most *shingeki* companies were forced to disband during the war. Then, after Japan was defeated in 1945, the Occupation forces (dominated by the United States) made Japan into a democracy, and the *shingeki* companies were again allowed to do what they wanted. This was *shingeki*'s golden age. Even so, its theatrical form and stance did not change much and continued to follow Western theater in both drama and performance.

The plays in part IV are from the period beginning in the late 1960s, when *shingeki* had become orthodoxy and was being viciously criticized by the newly emerging avant-garde theater. This backlash against *shingeki* is called *angura* in Japanese, an abbreviation of "underground." The *angura* movement was clearly antirealist and is usually divided into first, second, and third generations, roughly corresponding to the 1960s, 1970s, and 1980s.

Many of the playwrights in these three generations, including those of orthodox *shingeki*, continued to be active during this period. But in the last decade of the twentieth century, a new wave of young playwrights suddenly emerged. They could not be called *angura* playwrights, for most of their plays seemed to return to the realism of everyday life. Their plays are in part V. They still are at the forefront of theater activities in Japan, although even newer types of plays have been appearing in the first decade of the twenty-first century.

Finally, although the history of theater usually focuses on new theater movements and trends and often neglects popular theater (*taishū engeki*), popular theater is, in fact, the mainstream in regard to the size of the audiences it draws. Accordingly, we offer examples of modern popular theater in part VI.

MITSUYA MORI

PART I

THE AGE OF "TAISHŌ DRAMA"

The productions of Henrik Ibsen's *John Gabriel Borkman*, by Osanai Kaoru's Free Theater in 1909, and of *A Doll's House*, by Tsubouchi Shōyō's Literary Society in 1912, marked the birth of modern drama and theater in Japan. This birth may have taken a longer and more convoluted course than that of fiction in Japan, but it would be a mistake to overlook its impact on Japanese culture. Early productions of Ibsen and other European playwrights in the first decade or so of the twentieth century brought about not just the modernization of Japanese theater but (in the words of one playwright, Mafune Yutaka), the very "theatricalization of the modern spirit."[1] By the time of his death in 1906, Ibsen was already the subject of intense interest and debate in the Japanese intelligentsia, and his works had spawned a new movement, naturalism, that had shaken Japanese literature to its foundations, informing the work of such novelists as Tayama Katai and Shimazaki Tōson. Ibsen's influence impressed on a generation of Japanese the idea that theater and drama could create a ground for the exchange of artistic, social, and political ideas. Toward the end of the Meiji era, the audiences for Ibsen's plays in Japan represented almost a *Who's Who* of the country's intellectuals, both men and also many of the "new women" (*atarashii onna*), for whom characters like Nora had become the subject of much debate. This was also a movement led by the young: Osanai Kaoru, one of its spearheads, was

1. Quoted in Gioia Ottaviani, "The Shingeki Movement Until 1930: Its Experience in Western Approaches," in *Rethinking Japan*, vol. 1, *Literature, Visual Arts, and Linguistics*, ed. Adriana Boscaro, Franco Gatti, and Massimo Raveri (New York: St. Martin's Press, 1990), 178.

a mere twenty-nine years old when his Free Theater opened with *Borkman*. Shōyō, like Mori Ōgai, represented an older generation, but it was their students, people like Osanai and Shimamura Hōgetsu, who were to determine the direction for the culture of the Taishō era (1912–1926).

THE IMPORTANCE OF THE PLAYWRIGHT

In the final years of the Meiji period (1868–1912), drama came into its own as a literary genre, paving the way for what Japanese critics have called the age of "Taishō drama." Although Japan could boast a great tradition of works written for the stage, drama remained largely just a pretext for performance. Ibsen showed, however, that drama could be a medium for the personal expression of its author.

Morita Sōhei's (1881–1949; pen name of Morita Yonematsu, a novelist and translator of Western literature) impressions were typical of many other writers of his generation. The

MORITA SŌHEI

I heard spectators criticize the performance for lacking something, that the acting was weak, but none of that troubled me at all. That the actors were poor or deficient in any way was no concern of mine because I could make up for that. Rather, it would have been a problem if they were good. Were they too good, their personalities would have got in the way of what I imagined, breaking the illusion I had created of them in my own mind. That was my impression. particularly of the actors who played Forder and Erhart; the others acted, I thought, to the best of their abilities.

But that's enough about the actors. I am no critic of good or bad acting, nor do I take any pleasure in speaking about it. But I expected worse, so it was good enough. Perhaps I am wrong in thinking it was good enough. But it's not worth talking about the actors here. Theater stands or falls on its script, so do not go on about the art of acting to me. [. . .]

And so I say the Free Theater's first production was a great success, far more than anticipated. And this was thanks to neither the acting nor the setting, but all due directly to Ibsen himself. Credit thus should go to the two men who brought Ibsen's drama to Japan: to Osanai Kaoru and Ichikawa Sadanji.

FROM MORITA SŌHEI, "HAIYŪ MUYŌRON" (NO NEED FOR ACTORS), *TOKYO ASAHI SHINBUN*, DECEMBER 12, 1909.

Free Theater's production of *Borkman* inspired nearly every writer of this time (including Izumi Kyōka and Kikuchi Kan, whose works are featured in part I, and Yamamoto Yūzō) to try their hand at writing plays. Indeed, the critic Ōyama Isao listed as many as eighty professional playwrights active in the first four decades of the twentieth century. The leading literary magazines of the day—*New Tides of Thought* (*Shinshichō*), *The Pleiades* (*Subaru*), *Central Review* (*Chūō kōron*), *Literary Annals* (*Bungei shunjū*), and *New Fiction* (*Shinshōsetsu*), to name a few—published plays, and several new magazines appeared that were devoted almost exclusively to theater and drama, including *Kabuki*, *Entertainment Illustrated* (*Engei gahō*), *New Entertainment* (*Shin-engei*), and *New Tides in Theater* (*Engeki shinchō*). These journals' publication of new drama and fiction certainly helped determine the length of new works, so short stories and one-act plays flourished during this period. The pace of modern life also was reflected in the brevity of such forms. Kikuchi Kan, the most successful playwright of this time, noted that not only do truly dramatic events occur rarely in life and are brief in duration but modern audiences cannot spend long hours in the theater, "making it all the more essential that the playwright gets his point across in as little time as he can."[2] Accordingly, the one-act became the quintessential form of the modern age.

DRAMA AND PERFORMANCE

For Morita Sōhei and most of his contemporaries, modern drama, even in performance, could be an essentially literary experience that put the audience in direct touch with the author. The performer could either facilitate or get in the way of this experience, but in any case, the reception of the new drama revealed a new critical hierarchy in which the playwright was the god, the director his priest, and the actor the servant to the written message.

Although many plays written during this period remained on the page as essentially literary forms of expression (for example, Izumi Kyōka's original plays were never performed during his lifetime), the new drama led to an interest in and, indeed, demanded new techniques for realization on stage. Indeed, the modernization of Japanese theater was a far more complicated task than simply publishing a new work in a literary magazine. New drama required a new theater. It required theater buildings, a cast and crew of artists, and an audience that could support the considerable financial outlay needed to produce the plays. Despite the government's efforts to spearhead theater reform in the 1880s, there was no real public support for it in Japan until well after World War II. Although a host of theater companies sprang up to perform these new plays, with kabuki and *shinpa* actors eager to stage both Japanese and translated drama, it increasingly was

2. Kikuchi Kan, "Ichimakumono ni tsuite," *Engeki shinchō* 1, no. 2 (1924): 3.

KOMIYA TOYOTAKA

Since the actors of the Literary Society have no background in either kabuki or *shinpa*, they are obliged to create new *forms* [*kata*] as a style of self-expression—this is cause for the actor's freedom, his joy and his pain. For at the same time that he is attempting to invent a new theater, in order to give life to his interpretation of the stage character, he also must create a *kata* flowing with a life that is a distillation of the relationship between his own sensibility and the form and voice of what he aims to express. I am sad to say, however, that the *kata* that most of these gentlemen have chosen—the relationship between *form* and *feeling*, in other words—is incomplete; it lacks luster and individuality. Maybe they will be all right in the future, but right now they cannot stand comparison with the actors of the Free Theater; they have failed to achieve a match of intent with expression. They have created no better than a dead *form*, a shallow stereotype that falls short of their interpretation.

FROM KOMIYA TOYOTAKA, "JIYŪ GEKIJŌ TO BUNGEI KYŌKAI" (THE FREE THEATER AND THE LITERARY SOCIETY), *SHINSHŌSETSU*, JUNE 1912.

felt that kabuki and *shinpa*, with their use of such conventions as *onnagata* (female impersonators), were anathema to the more realist aesthetic of the new theater. The actors' training was especially an issue for the two companies credited with being the vanguards of new drama in Japan: Osanai's Free Theater and Shōyō's Literary Society.

Should we attempt to train rank amateurs or, instead, use professional actors and hope that they adapt to the new style of acting? Osanai addressed this question in an open letter to Ichikawa Danko,[3] the actor who played Erhart in *Borkman*:

> The most urgent tasks in the theater today are, on the one hand, to "make amateur actors into professionals" and, on the other, to "make professional actors into amateurs." It seems that Dr. T. [Tsubouchi] and S. H. [Shimamura Hōgetsu] are aiming at the first course. We will pursue the second. These two alternative courses should progress strictly in parallel, without ever converging. The degree of despair at present-day actors must be the same, in both those who aim at the first and those who pursue the second. . . .
>
> Recently, in answer to a statement of mine that "drama is not all pleasure," you wrote in a letter, "But surely it is not all pain, either?"—quite a natural question. Challenges like this have come from many quarters, not only from you.

3. Later known as Ennosuke, this actor also played the title character in Kikuchi Kan's *Father Returns*.

> I thought I had explained this by distinguishing between purely pleasurable entertainment and artistic entertainment. I meant to say that it was not a function of drama to provide purely pleasurable entertainment; it was the function of drama to provide artistic entertainment. Entertainment is, of course, entertainment, but artistic entertainment is not as easygoing as purely pleasurable entertainment.[4]

For some, like Osanai, the greatest challenge for the New Theater was training actors, but for others, like the playwright Mayama Seika, there would be no revolution in the theater until play texts of sufficient quality were produced. In truth, both were essential, but this "chicken and egg" debate over text versus performance exercised the minds of Japanese intellectuals from at least the 1880s until the late 1920s, with dramatists like Ōgai and Seika advocating "first the play, then the performance," while directors like Osanai reversed this formula in stressing acting and direction over script. Indeed, the debate over text versus performance is perennial, as we have seen since the 1960s with the interest in performance studies, or in the reaction against *shingeki*'s "overly literary" tendency.

TRANSLATED VERSUS NATIVE DRAMA

The paradigms of modern drama, just like those for Japan's modernization, were imported and, indeed, even felt by some to be as much an imposition on the Japanese people as the unequal trade treaties. It is no surprise, then, that translations of drama played a crucial but also ambivalent role in transforming Japan's theater in the Meiji and Taishō eras. Ibsen may have led the way, but he was accompanied by translations of a host of other European playwrights, including William Shakespeare, Anton Chekhov, August Strindberg, Gerhart Hauptmann, Hugo von Hofmanstahl, Maurice Maeterlinck, Frank Wedekind, Oscar Wilde, John Synge, and George Bernard Shaw. Mori Ōgai, who played a key role in the modernization of Japanese culture, published two volumes of translations of one-act plays in 1909 and 1910, following up with a third volume of his own one-acts in 1912. Mafune Yutaka remarked that these anthologies were considered a bible for the young Japanese playwrights of that day.

By the end of Meiji, the European works translated by Ōgai and others give us an idea of the incredible variety of Western drama that suddenly became accessible to Japanese. With so much—and from so many periods, languages, cultures, and genres—flooding into Japan around this time, just as Japanese were becoming accustomed to one style or idea they were struck by yet another. It thus was inevitable that Japanese readers and audiences were, for the most part, oblivious of these plays' historical and social context and the artistic debates that they sparked in Europe. What had been a diachronic

4. Osanai Kaoru, "Letter to Actor D," *Engei gahō*, January 1909.

SHIMAMURA HŌGETSU

The value of translated drama has been discussed time and again, and people have come to more or less a consensus on the matter. Theater circles in Japan cannot go on worshipping translated drama forever. The Japanese must create their own modern drama in opposition to translated drama; they must overcome it. This is needed not only from an artistic standpoint but also for patriotic reasons. Even in foreign countries, a nation's art arises in concert with patriotic movements in politics and society. In Germany in the past, and Ireland at present, movements to liberate art have gone hand in hand with movements for the liberation of politics and language. So, considering that such external and extracultural forces have an impact on creation, the Japanese can draw much artistic material from their own society. I refer here not simply to such superficial matters as distinctions in dress or deportment. Such distinctions between Japanese and foreigners regarding their thoughts and feelings today are no real barrier; indeed, people have largely forgotten about such things, regarding them as matters of individual differences. Rather, what I mean here are those aspects that, over and above what has already been mentioned, make a Japanese work of art feel somehow more congenial to us. Were we to take only fiction as an example, it would be readily apparent that it is more a question of the work's being pleasing to us that we feel close to its sensibility, rather than a matter of its being superior or inferior in aesthetic terms. And the same must apply to a play as well. Unfortunately, however, in a very real sense modern drama has not yet been staged in Japan. Thus we have not even had a chance to experience such a sense of identification with any work for the theater. I wish that we could soon experience the like, and for that reason, I hope to soon see a flourishing of native Japanese drama. When I talk about identification with a work, what I mean is a feeling that one's desire to see oneself has been fulfilled, that the Japanese people have been able to see themselves portrayed onstage. It is the feeling of satisfaction, of intimacy in seeing oneself. It goes without saying that this ability to see oneself has been a major feature of all modern art, but when a person, a Japanese, attempts to discover himself in a work of art from a foreign country, one has the sense of being overwhelmed by strangers on all sides.

FROM SHIMAMURA HŌGETSU, "ATARASHII GEKIDAN NO RONGI" (DEBATES OVER THE NEW THEATER), *KABUKI*, JUNE 1913.

development in Europe became flattened into a confusing homeostasis in which contesting forms—lyric and spoken drama, romanticism, naturalism, realism, symbolism, and expressionism—came to coexist in Japan. The sheer force and volume of these translations were such that European culture could no longer be altered to suit a stable Japanese culture but instead became the agent for the transformation of Japanese culture. By the Taishō era, the modernization of theater had passed from an age of freewheeling adaptations (*hon'an*) of Shakespeare and other Western playwrights' works to one in which faithful translations (*hon'yaku*) of European drama were slavishly performed with an eye to being as "authentic" as possible.

In a very real sense, in Japan the history of *shingeki* became a history of the performance of *foreign* drama. To the extent that *shingeki* was a social and political as well as an artistic revolution, there was an expectation that not only theatrical conventions but also traditional thought and behavior would be abandoned for modern, supposedly more "civilized," European values and ways of life. If the model for modernity was increasingly a Western one, it created nearly insurmountable challenges, both artistic and existential, for the Japanese. Can foreign modes of feeling, thought, behavior, and speech ever be assimilated? Should they? What happens to our own identity when we attempt to be someone else, especially someone of another race? How can a modern theater portray contemporary Japanese if everyone on stage is supposed to be a Westerner?

Even as a purely artistic project, Japanese could not learn to emulate the Western masters overnight. For Osanai, Japanese playwrights were still incapable of writing "social dramas" (*shakaigeki*) of the caliber of Ibsen, and in his open letter to Danko, he called for a "true age of the foreign play in translation." As we shall see, Osanai once again favored foreign over domestic drama in his inauguration of the Tsukiji Little Theater in 1924, earning considerable enmity from many of his compatriots and colleagues. Two-thirds of the productions by both the Free Theater and the Literary Society were of European drama, and this proportion rose to as much as 80 percent with the Tsukiji Little Theater fifteen years later, at a time when drama was flourishing as a literary genre in Japan. The frustration of Japanese playwrights, whose own work was repeatedly snubbed for productions of foreign drama, can be well imagined.

THE ELEMENTS OF MODERN DRAMA

Kishida Kunio, considered by many as Japan's greatest playwright of the early twentieth century, claimed in 1923 that his country's playwrights "were able to acquire almost nothing of substance from the influence of foreign drama."[5] Certainly, the "anxiety of

5. Kishida Kunio, "Taiwa saseru jutsu," quoted in Saitō Yasuhide, "Gikyokuron kara mita kindaigeki," *Higeki kigeki* 43, no. 8 (1990): 30.

KIKUCHI KAN

What's that? You're telling me that the plot of Kikuchi Kan's play *Father Returns* resembles a one-act play by Gilbert Canna? You censure me! Yet your example needn't range so far afield as that. There is another one much closer at hand. It's the novel by my friend Mizumori Kamenosuke, *The Father Who Returns.* He describes there the human circumstances in which a mother takes her two sons and her daughter, in order to wait for their dissolute father, who has left their home, presenting a situation understandable all around the world. And if someone here in Japan thinks that such circumstances could arise only in another country, so that if a Japanese playwright were to use such a topic, peculiar rumors could circulate about a work that he or she has only half digested, insisting that "it's just a copy!" well, *there's* a situation that in fact could occur only in Japan.

Wanting to put an end to all this, let me repeat this one more time. The same is true for a play or for a novel: the subject matter and the circumstances presented do not by themselves constitute the purpose. It is the theme that arises from these that is important. It is this theme that can reveal the writer's understanding, his outlook on life, and his conception of human feelings, which the writer can freely make use of through his artistic technique. Such constitutes the true substance of his accomplishment. To articulate such things is scarcely necessary for those who have at least some understanding of the arts. To make an issue of the plot of a novel or play, or such things, is to set up a straw man.

FROM KIKUCHI KAN, "GEKI NO SUJI OYOBI KYŌGŪ"
(THE PLOT AND THE SITUATION IN DRAMA), *SHINBUNGAKU*, APRIL 1921.

influence" delayed, and even distorted, the direction that modern Japanese drama would take, but its features were, at the very least, inspired by translated drama from the West. Ibsen and his contemporaries taught Japanese playwrights that drama could be an author's forum for illustrating social problems and exploring ideas and possible solutions. To do so required a strong theme and well-constructed plots, with psychologically delineated characters in conflict with their feelings, their peers, and their social environment.

As Kikuchi Kan's remarks indicate, the themes of modern drama spoke to all people, regardless of race or culture, especially in their growing experience of modernity. In the drama of this period, the family typically stands for a society under stress, and all the plays presented in part I deal with marital or intergenerational discord. In *Father Returns*, we see the inability of an older generation to adapt to the radical changes of modern society, as well as the increasing distrust of the patriarchy of Meiji Japan when a son rejects his feckless father. In their exploration of sexual desire and adultery, the plays by Izumi Kyōka are representative of the growing cynicism and taste for decadence among many writers of this generation. A major development in works of this period—indeed, one of the hallmarks of modern literature—is a growing interiority and complexity in characterization. The aim of traditional theater had been to present types—representative members of different social classes, ages, and genders; paragons of heroism and virtue; or caricatures of vice—engaged in melodramatic displays of public struggle in which good usually triumphed over evil. The new drama, however, just like the society it reflected, was more morally ambivalent. People, portrayed for the first time as individuals, had to stand or fall on their own judgment and resources in a world in which old certainties and values no longer supported them. The rising urban middle class was a favorite subject for this theater, not least because these characters were close to the experience of the young intellectuals who wrote and saw these plays, but also because more and more members of the working class and provincials were included.

Realism may have become the mark of modernity in drama as in fiction, but it was not a stable expressive mode. For decades, the increasing focus on psychological characterization presented both artistic and ideological challenges for playwrights. On the one hand, the Ibsenesque "social dramas" advocated by people like Osanai pointed to a more politically committed theater that regarded psychological family dramas as bourgeois. On the other hand, many playwrights were finding that naturalism and realism failed to adequately describe the depths of human experience. The exploration of personal relationships and extreme emotions promoted styles of drama inspired by the symbolist and expressionist experiments of European playwrights like Maeterlinck, Strindberg, Georg Kaiser, and Ernst Toller. Whether projected against society or inward on oneself, conflict is often considered a sine qua non of drama. But as many have noted, Japanese society typically avoids conflict whenever it can, so many Japanese playwrights in the early twentieth century felt the focus on discord in European drama as somehow unnatural. Maeterlinck's *drames statiques*—plays more like still lifes, quiet portrayals of mental states—were found by many like Ōgai, Kinoshita Mokutarō, and Yoshii Isamu to be a more congenial form than Ibsen's argumentative plays. If many Japanese stage characters seemed not to change or undergo a fundamental awakening of consciousness, this might have been less a failure on the dramatist's part than an assertion that such reversals and recognitions were not an accurate picture of what life really was like.

Kikuchi Kan and Yamamoto Yūzō have been credited with being the greatest innovators of theme and structure in modern Japanese drama. A third feature that made the plays of this period "new" was language, requiring dramatic diction to be reformed before the theater of this period could be called modern. The rhetoric of modernity was resolved by being divided into two forms, confession and dialogue. Confession became the model for the "I-novel," the "pure" literature of early-twentieth-century Japanese fiction, and spoken dialogue became the medium of modern drama. As was the case with *genbun itchi* (the unification of the spoken and written languages) in Japanese fiction, such fundamental reform took decades. We have seen that the first move in this direction was the call for "straight drama" by people like Kawakami Otojirō and Mori Ōgai. For such reformers, modern drama required the eradication of narrative, lyrical, musical, or choreographic elements in favor of spoken dialogue as almost the sole medium of expression. Few languages in the modern world have undergone such radical change as Japanese has over the past century or so. The language of kabuki, for example, was not standard Japanese but a local dialect of the Edo (present-day Tokyo) urbanite, nor was it how people actually spoke but, rather, a highly rhythmic and patterned style of declamation created expressly for the theater to accentuate the force and beauty of its actors. We see in the translations of Shakespeare and the original plays by Shōyō, Ōgai, and others during the Meiji era their attempts to discover a modern idiom for the stage. Intriguingly, these attempts trace the development of the Japanese language of drama from the traditional theaters of nō and *kyōgen*, through *jōruri* and kabuki, to something that began to echo how modern Japanese people actually spoke. Initially, translated drama was the model of the new dramatic idiom as well, but increasingly playwrights realized that Japanese people did not speak in the same way as did the characters in Ibsen's, Chekhov's, or Shaw's plays. Instead, the characters in many early Taishō plays often speak stiffly, as if laboring under the influence of their European models or the effort to express their creators' ideas, but in the best work of this period we begin to hear the living voices of people not so different from ourselves.

M. CODY POULTON

Izumi Kyōka, *Kerria Japonica*, directed by Nakamura Takao, Parco Part 3, September 1992.

KERRIA JAPONICA

IZUMI KYŌKA
TRANSLATED BY M. CODY POULTON

Known for his rich and poetic prose style, Izumi Kyōka (1873–1939) wrote romances and fantasies that challenged the work of his contemporaries and that, with the rise of naturalism as a literary movement, tended to be simpler, more direct and realistic, and even autobiographical. Kyōka's inspiration came from predominantly traditional sources—folklore, nō and kabuki theater, the illustrated fiction of the Edo era—but his literature already anticipated the decadent turn in Japanese culture in the Taishō era. He attracted an avid following of younger writers like Tanizaki Jun'ichirō and Kawabata Yasunari, and, even later, Mishima Yukio, Kara Jūrō, and Terayama Shūji. In fact, from as early as the mid-1890s, the *shinpa* theater adapted many of Kyōka's novels to the stage. (See his *Nihonbashi* and a discussion of *shinpa* theater in part VI.) Primarily a novelist, as were many of his contemporaries, Kyōka also wrote many plays, mostly during the Taishō era. Many of these original works, like *Demon Pond* (*Yasha ga ike*) and *The Castle Tower* (*Tenshu monogatari*), are unbridled fantasies with supernatural characters and elements drawn from ghost stories and legends. Although most of them were never performed in his lifetime, thanks to revivals since the 1960s by the kabuki actor Bandō Tamasaburō V and various avant-garde stage artists like Ninagawa Yukio and Miyagi Satoshi, these plays have become the favorites of Kyōka's works and are, in many respects, more accessible to a modern Japanese public than his fiction, which is difficult to read.

Kerria Japonica (*Yamabuki*, 1923) is an exception to much of Kyōka's original work for the stage, in that all the characters are human, yet the play displays touches of the grotesque and decadent that can be found in his wildest fantasies. A favorite of Mishima Yukio, who said of it that all the people it portrays are in fact monsters, the play is a study of obsessive love. It was first staged in 1978.

How like a lovely woman fresh from her bath (her dark eyebrows, faint mountain crescents) are the white blooms of the kerria rose, strikingly pale against their deep green leaves damp with rain!

Time: The present. A morning in late April.
Place: A back alley in Shuzenji hot spring. Later, also in Shuzenji, a shortcut in the woods to the road to Shimoda.

Characters

An ARTIST, Shimazu Tadashi, forty-five or forty-six years old
A LADY, Nuiko, Viscountess Koitogawa, formerly the daughter of the proprietor of the restaurant Yukari, age twenty-five
A traveling PUPPETEER, Heguri Tōji, age sixty-nine
A YOUNG BOY and GIRL, festival pages. A SHOPKEEPER of a general store. A GROOM. Fourteen or fifteen VILLAGERS

SCENE 1

A general store. On one side are three double-petaled cherry trees in full bloom. Inside the closed glass doors of the store are a variety of products for sale: cotton batting, paper, bolts of cloth, dried shiitake mushrooms, patent medicines, soft drinks, and the like. In the earthen entrance, with its door open, are some chairs and a table laid with beer, juice, a keg of saké covered in straw matting, and a bottle of shōchū. *Right beside the store is a rice paddy.*

To the other side of the store is a hedge of cedar over a low stone wall, beneath which flows a small stream. Saffron flowers and weeds grow in the wall. Behind the hedge is a willow in fresh green leaf, its branches drooping over the path. A purple magnolia in blossom would also look good in the background. There is a path between the store and the hedge. The rice paddy, which has not yet been tilled, is covered with green waterweeds. Here and there bloom milk vetch and mustard blossoms. Following the path along the hedge, farther on is a bamboo grove and a tall zelkova tree, in whose shadows the path disappears up the mountain.

The PUPPETEER *is seated, his back to the audience, at the squalid-looking table at the earthen storefront. As he speaks, he rubs his upper lip.*

PUPPETEER: Master—Kind master! Pour me another, won't you?

SHOPKEEPER (*Enters the storefront from behind the glass partition*): Why, there ain't no need to be calling me "kind"! A simple sir will do me fine. (*Smiles wryly.*) Don't you think the sun's high enough yet, old man? How do you expect to make a living if you drink like that?

PUPPETEER: Hah, hah, hah. I've done with work for the day already. Pardon me for saying so, but once I'm through here, I'll just stagger off to my little nest in the woods.

SHOPKEEPER: You needn't tell me how unsteady your legs will be, but it's a bit too early to be heading back to that nest of yours! —I have to mind the store today on me own, but this side of the bridge to the public baths don't see much traffic compared to the crush of visitors in Shuzenji. Now's when you ought to be making money.

PUPPETEER: Right you are. First the locals, then the pilgrims from all over the country—aunties and grannies, grandpas with their grandkids, swarms of them, black as the smoke rising from the ritual bonfires, undaunted by cloudbursts like the monsoons of summer. —And then, the boom! boom! of festival drums have drowned out the tinkle-tinkle coming from the little sideshow tents—why would anybody want to come way over here? Cross the bridge, and so long customers! Hah, hah! —I can ply my trade come evening and make some money, but I've earned enough right now for a drink or two, and I don't need no more than that. —And if worse comes to worst, well then, just let me die here. (*Bows deeply, bumping his head hard against the glass pane.*) —Kind master, pour me another drink!

SHOPKEEPER: You're just like a dying sailor begging Davy Jones to give him water. Maybe that's where the expression "bottomless cup" came from. . . . Drink as much as you like. It's my business, after all. (*Wipes the neck of the bottle.*) —Just don't go smashing the merchandise there, old man.

PUPPETEER: Let me die in peace. (*Gulps down the drink and laps up what's left on the palm of his hand.*) Besides, it's the anniversary of the Saint's death. —Reverend Kōbō, come pick me up and take me away in your automobile with its shiny gold trim!

SHOPKEEPER: It won't be the saint that comes and takes you away, but the town hall, and there'll be hell to pay for that. Easy with the alcohol there. (*Starts to go inside.*)

PUPPETEER (*Shouting*): Kind master, pour me another!

SHOPKEEPER: It's the Feast of Saint Kōbō, so I won't have my spuds turn into stones on account of you.[1] . . . I hate to be stingy, so be my guest, drink as much as you like. But are you sure you finished the last drop of the one I just gave you?

PUPPETEER: So far, I knocked back five cups. I drank to the snow . . . and now I drink to the blossoms. . . . Kind master, three cherries grow under your eaves. . . . Young trees but in full bloom. . . . There ain't another house in Shuzenji that can boast such

---

1. Saint Kōbō (Kūkai, 774–835) was the founder in Japan of Shingon (Mantrayana) Buddhism, an esoteric sect. He is reputed to have established springs, wells, and reservoirs all over Japan, including Shuzenji hot spring. A folktale has him turning potatoes into stones, to punish stingy farmers who refused to give him alms.

blossoms. —And it costs me nothing to look at 'em. The drink costs me dear, but still this is a fine sight. Damn, that's good!

SHOPKEEPER: Don't spout nonsense. You're drunk, old man. . . .

PUPPETEER: Why, just the occasional cup or two is a libation for the cherries, to ensure they blossom better. A blessing from Saint Kōbō himself!

SHOPKEEPER: Cut the cheap compliments. —It's awful how nobody passes this way. . . . Just two children a while back, in a procession over the mountain from Tatsuno, and nobody else since then, not even a horse and his groom. —It's such a bore having to mind the shop. —Ah, I can hear the drums!

(*The drums are the kind held up on a pole by two musicians who beat them in turn on both sides. The sound—boom! baboom! boom!—can be heard dimly in the distance.*)

PUPPETEER: The pipes and flutes, men in formal jackets and *hakama.* —An escort of firemen and pages. In fore and aft, monks burning incense and chanting sutras. The procession of young men in court caps from the Inner Sanctum, carrying the portable shrines. —Hail to the Great Teacher, Diamond of Universal Light! Both right and left of the path are thick with men and women. Offerings fall like rain. . . . The young ladies of town have come to pray in their best kimonos with their flowing sleeves. An old lady leaps out of the Vajra Bath stark naked![2] —Ah, hah, hah, hah! Bet Saint Kōbō would've been pleased if it were a young 'un instead!

SHOPKEEPER: Shut up! You'll pay for such profanity. (*Goes inside.*)

PUPPETEER: Hail to the Great Teacher, Diamond of Universal Light! (*Sipping his saké, slumps down.*)

(*Enter the* LADY, *Nuiko, holding a handbag and a folded umbrella downward by the handle. Her hair is held up with a comb, and her obi is simply tied. She is wearing wooden clogs. She gazes at the late, double-petaled cherry in blossom.*)

LADY: My, how lovely! —Such work for such beauty— (*Pause.*) . . . You ought to be thanked for it. —You really are so lovely. Such blossoms! (*So speaking, she follows the path along the little stream. Gazing at the saffron flowers growing on the wall, her attention is turned to the water.*) Why, it's a carp! Such a big one! —Dear me! He's dead.

(*A longish pause. As the* LADY *steps aside to avoid the carp, she stops in front of the puppet that the* PUPPETEER *has left propped against the wall. It is a beautiful and elegant figure of a* shirabyōshi *dancer, attached by strings to bamboo sticks.*[3] *The* LADY *studies it carefully, saying nothing. The sound of rain.*)

LADY: Ah, it's started to rain. (*The Japanese umbrella she opens has the insignia of an inn, the Igiku, or Well-Side Chrysanthemum.*) There are dewdrops on the doll's eyelashes, as if she were weeping. . . . (*She holds the umbrella over the puppet as if to protect it.*)

---

2. Vajra bath (*tokko no yu*) is the hot spring created by Kūkai when he struck his *vajra* staff against a rock.

3. *Shirabyōshi* refers to a type of female dancer in the Middle Ages who danced in a man's cap and costume.

(*The* PUPPETEER *sticks his head out of the shop curtain to stare at the* LADY. *His mouth is large, his brow is furrowed, his face wrinkled and flushed with liquor and pockmarked with a grizzled five o'clock shadow. Covered in a headscarf, he looked mild mannered, but now he is without it, and with his boxy forehead and gray hair, he is a fright to behold.*)

(*Enter the* ARTIST, *wearing a thin cape and fedora. His face is long and narrow, elegantly thin, his hooded eyes a little sleepy looking. He sports a slender and well-trimmed moustache that is dappled with gray. His complexion is a little pallid, his expression mild, yet dignified. He is shod in borrowed clogs from the inn he is staying at, and heedless of the rain, he carries only a walking stick. He stops to gaze at the cherries. The* PUPPETEER *turns back and flops down at the table.*)

ARTIST (*As if unconcerned about the* LADY*'s presence*): A puppet, I see.

LADY: Sir? —Excuse me, but she doesn't belong to me.

ARTIST (*Only now seeming to have noticed her*): Excuse me, Madame. Actually, I never thought it was yours. It's just a strange sight to see in this day and age. —In Tokyo, you hardly see such a thing nowadays, not even in the little shrine or temple fairs off the beaten track.... This would be Lady Shizuka, right? Turn her around and there's bold Benkei, with his halberd. . . .Turn Benkei around and you've got yourself an octopus, sporting a red bandanna, who'll dance you a jig.[4] But this one doesn't seem rigged out for such tricks. (*Nonchalantly leans in under the umbrella that the* LADY *is holding.*) Nope, this one is just the dancing girl. Ah, but she's a real work of art. —Take a look, see how fine the workmanship is! . . . Who's the owner? Who'd leave a lovely thing like this out in the rain?

LADY: The puppeteer, I believe, is over there. —(*Modestly indicating and lowering her voice.*) . . . The old man's been drinking.

ARTIST: I bet he's a master.... Shall we have him perform a bit for us?

LADY: Please don't, sir.... He's had rather a lot to drink, it seems.

ARTIST: I see. It would be a bother if the man's as drunk as he looks. Ah, but this puppet is truly a work of art! — If you'll excuse me, Madame. (*Half muttering.*) Maybe we'll meet again on my way back. (*Coolly saunters off in the direction of the mountain path.*)

LADY (*Following a few steps behind him*): Sir! Uh, sir . . . Which way would you be going?

ARTIST (*Again, as if noticing her for the first time. Speaking softly*): Please. (*Pause.*) . . . Don't call me "sir." The town's in such pandemonium that I thought I'd take myself to the mountains for a bit. —Excuse me, Madame. (*Gazing at her with his sleepy eyes.*) I failed to notice you before, but would you be staying at the same inn as me?

LADY: Yes, near you.... In back, downstairs. Uh . . .

ARTIST: Is that so? Then, you'll excuse me. (*Again, makes to go.*)

---

4. Lady Shizuka was the mistress of Minamoto Yoshitsune (1159–1189), the famous general in the war between the Genji and Heike clans, and Benkei was his loyal retainer. Yoshitsune was eventually hunted down and killed on the orders of his brother Minamoto Yoritomo (1147–1199), who became the first shōgun of the Kamakura period. Many tales and plays hail Yoshitsune's exploits.

LADY (*Following a step behind*): Sir, on your way here, did you happen to run into a manservant wearing a jacket with the inn's insignia?

ARTIST: Yes I did.

LADY: Did he say nothing?

ARTIST (*Slowly crossing his arms*): Well . . . just as I was about to cross the bridge over to the Kikuya and Nodaya inns, on the railing, attached to a long pole, was a straw raincoat. —Seems they were selling a lot of them in the market for the Saint's Day. It was an advertisement of sorts for it, but it looked for all the world like a scarecrow. I stood there looking at it and had to laugh. —I look like a scarecrow myself, mind you. (*Smiles.*) Thought of buying one, but it'd have just weighed me down. That was when the manservant from the inn passed me.

LADY: Then what happened?

ARTIST: Ah, yes. (*Uncrosses his arms.*) . . . "The lady went that way," said the man, then passed me. . . . I see, he must have been talking about you. I suppose he thought we were a couple and went out together. —If you'll excuse me.

LADY: Well, sir. We're separate now, but late last night we arrived together, you know.

ARTIST: With you?

LADY: Yes.

ARTIST: I know nothing about that.

LADY: In Ōhito . . . We came in separate cars, but at the same time. . . .

ARTIST: I shared a car. —Ah, come to think of it . . . there was someone I think who called for the cab, with the most modish hairstyle parted on the side . . . (*Half to himself.*)

LADY: A woman . . . (*Breathing heavily.*) That woman, as soon as she got to the inn, sir, she shaved her eyebrows.[5] (*Looks up, suddenly embarrassed.*) Her hair was done up in curls, like this.

ARTIST: Ah hah. (*Growing more suspicious, yet acting nonchalant.*)

LADY: Sir. (*Holding out her umbrella, hangs her head. Snow could not be whiter than the nape of her neck.*) None other than I was the lady the manservant from the inn was talking about. (*Rather excitedly.*) He meant your wife.

(*Pause.*)

ARTIST (*Quietly*): . . . Meaning?

LADY: Last night, as soon as I arrived at the inn with you, I told the innkeeper I'm with Mr. Shimazu. You see, I, uh, . . . (*Haltingly, pausing a moment.*) I know you from your photographs, your exhibitions. —"I'm Shimazu's wife," I told the innkeeper. "I followed him on the same train in secret, so he wouldn't see me," I said. Of course, what I said didn't make much sense, but I said it. . . . And the reason I gave was my husband was having an affair and was meeting a woman there.

ARTIST: *I* was.

LADY: Yes, you being my, uh, husband.

---

5. Although outlawed as a practice in 1870, shaved eyebrows traditionally indicated that a woman was married.

ARTIST: That was quite impertinent of you! (*Smiles wryly.*)

LADY: Please forgive me, sir. —"Book me next door to him in secret, so I can spy on him. I'll make myself look different in case we run into each other in the hallway and I get caught," I said. . . . And right then and there, in front of the mirror stand, I shaved my eyebrows, rearranged my hair, shook off my *haori*, and retied my obi this way (*Lissomely turns around and gazes at the bow.*) loosely, telling him, "For heaven's sake, keep this a secret." Then in the register, after your name I wrote "his wife."

ARTIST (*Frowns slightly, but then generously*): One comes to a place like this for rest, so I'll indulge a prank like that, I suppose. . . . Well, you'll have to excuse me—

LADY: Please, sir, don't be angry with me.

ARTIST: What? Have somebody's beautiful wife play a joke on me? —You never know, I might be pleased. —But I really must go.

LADY: What'll I do? Sir, this was no joke I was playing.

ARTIST: What do you mean by that? (*Speaking sharply for the first time.*)

LADY (*Upset, trembling slightly*): I beg you, look. I have something to show you. (*Pulling forcefully at the sleeve of his cape, she draws him back toward the edge of the stream.*) Look there. (*She points at the dead carp. It still is invisible to the audience.*)

ARTIST: That is awful! How frightful!

LADY: Sir, I feel like that carp. I'm at death's door myself. (*The* ARTIST *says nothing. Pause.*) There are men after me. If they find me, they'll have to take me away. —I happened to recognize you and followed you as far as the inn, then I took it in my mind to do something unpardonable. I was desperate and made up my mind to die. —Anyway, I shaved my eyebrows, changed the way I look, and pretended to be your wife. I was lost, at my wit's end, at that busy inn. Please forgive me. . . . Never in my dreams would I ever play a trick on you.

ARTIST: I suppose there's nothing I can do.

LADY (*Reluctantly, as if unsatisfied with his response*): Can you forgive me? . . . I know this sounds as if I'm taking advantage of your kindness, but . . . would you please let me join you on your walk? I'll even follow behind you. If you grant me this wish, no one will notice me, I'm sure. —Sir! (*Ever so slightly coquettish.*) Please, let me come with you.

ARTIST (*Firmly*): You'd be in the way.

LADY: Ah . . . but, no. You see, even if I went with you, I'd go only so far as it took to make up my mind to become like that thing there. (*Points at the dead fish.*)

ARTIST: We can't have that happen to you! I have no idea what your situation may be, but you mustn't end up like that.

PUPPETEER (*Lying face down, then bolting up suddenly*): Master! Gimme another drink! Master!

ARTIST (*Hearing, but trying to pay him no attention*): I consider it my duty to see that at the very least you do not turn out that way. —If you'll excuse me. (*Steps away and heads toward the path into the mountains.*)

LADY (*As the* ARTIST *disappears into the trees, she hastily runs after him, then holds back, watching him go*): Nothing lasts, does it? (*She looks around, ashamed of her own voice. She opens her umbrella, though there is no rain, as if to hide her embarrassment, then dejectedly heads into the grove of trees along the same path the* ARTIST *took.*)

PUPPETEER: Master! Another drink!

SHOPKEEPER: Tch! You are a troublemaker, aren't you? (*Pours him another.*)

PUPPETEER: But this drink—hah, hah, hah—I dedicate to the moon. When the clouds come out, the full moon hides his face. (*Drains the glass in one gulp.*) Aaah, whew! . . . The bill, sir. . . . (*Sloppily pulls out a change purse from a string around his neck and tosses down some coins.*) For Saint Kōbō and the moon as well. These coins, too, shine like the diamonds of universal dharma. Oof! (*Stands. He is tall, staggering on a pair of scrawny shins poking through torn gaiters. The* SHOPKEEPER, *paying him no mind, clears off his table and goes indoors.*) Oof! (*Tipsily staggers over to the puppet.*) My dear Lady Shizuka! (*Suddenly respectful, he practically collapses to the ground to prostrate himself before the doll. Pause. His drunken eyes take in the dead carp.*) Ah, brother, you lie there still. Did an otter bite you? A weasel take a nip out of you? Somebody's surely taken a chunk out of you—look at them teeth marks—and now the maggots are making off with what's left. Any stray cat or dog that saw you here would have taken one sniff and left you to rot. Even a dog wouldn't eat you. You had it in you to become a dragon, but some ill karma fell on you that your carcass should be exposed here, food for the worms. Poor thing! —Let me give you a proper funeral. (*Pulls out the bloated, rotten corpse of the carp. Now the audience can see it.*) But I don't know what to say for your last rites. How 'bout this: "A curse on all who think ill of you! Go haunt the lot of them, even charge an admission fee! Amen!" (*Wraps the carcass in the headscarf tied around his neck with his change purse, straps it to his waist, and kneels down again.*) Ah, Lady Shizuka! (*Unties the ragged cloth around his throat and wraps it over his mouth, like a gag. He has done this so as not to offend the beautiful woman with his breath, stinking of stale alcohol. He raises the doll on its bamboo pole high over his shoulder and heads toward the mountain path.*) Oof! (*Tipsily staggers from side to side.*)

(*The* LADY *steps out slightly from the shadow of the trees, watching this scene.*)

PUPPETEER: Oof! (*Staggers.*) Oof! (*Staggers.*)

LADY (*Slowly steps from the shadows and crosses the* PUPPETEER*'s path, as if turning back the way she came, and accosts him*): Grandpa, grandpa!

(*The* PUPPETEER, *tall and red faced, looks eerily at her as if he were possessed.*)

LADY (*Boldly strides up to him*): I no longer have any wishes for this world, nothing holding me back, so please, if there's anything I can do to make your wish come true, I'll do it for you. Please make me a wish, grandpa. (*The* PUPPETEER, *still silent and gazing at her as if to consume her with his eyes, eventually picks up a rope lying under a bale of rotten straw by the roadside. He approaches her, with it dangling, swinging limply from his hand.*) Ah! (*She steps back. The* PUPPETEER *sneers at her.*) I thought it was a snake! —Oh, so what if it is a snake? What are you going to do? —What will you do to me?

(*Saying nothing, the* PUPPETEER *merely stretches out his wrinkled hand and beckons her. Beckoning her, he backs again into the shadows of the trees.*)

LADY: What will you do to me? What are you planning to do? (*She follows him into the trees.*)

(*For a while the stage is empty. Five white ducks waddle through the rice paddy in a line, hunting for grub. It is, as it were, a portent of spring's passing.*)

GROOM (*Leading a horse, emerges from the trees, gazing back the way he came. There are two sacks of rice on the horse's back, donations to the temple. The sacks bear labels on which are written: "White Rice. Hail to the Great Teacher, Diamond of Universal Light!"*): There was a sight to chill your blood! Why, makes me wonder whether now, even in the noonday sun, this rice I'm carrying hasn't turned to sand. (*Wets his brows with spittle and fishes out a few grains from one of the sacks.*) Still safe. (*Listens to the beating of festival drums.*) —Thanks be to Saint Kōbō! Still, it was awful! Damned devils, they were, scared the life out of me!

THE STAGE REVOLVES

SCENE 2

On one side a steep hill where alternate rows, two to three feet wide, of mustard flowers and barley grow. On the brow of the hill bloom bushes of Kerria japonica, *a wild rose. Below in a ravine where the foot of the mountain has deeply eroded away, is an expanse of grass where mulberry saplings grow here and there, small and spindly as stalks of rattan.*

On the other side is a wooded mountain with stands of evergreen oak, some trees tall, others shorter, their boughs so thick they seem black with leaf, roiling like eddies of black clouds, in stark contrast to the brightness of the scene on the other side.

A narrow path wends its way down the hanamichi *and between the hills. In the distance looms the Izu mountain chain.*

Alone, halfway up the slope between the kerria roses growing on the cliff and the mustard flowers below, the ARTIST *quietly takes a swig from a flask of whiskey. —The call, far off, of a bush warbler. Two, three sharp cries of a cockerel, then, farther away, the belling of a deer. He stands there for some time, seemingly surprised. Then, as if spying on someone, he hides himself among the leaves and flowers.*

The LADY *enters. In one hand she holds her umbrella; in the other she clings to one end of the rope. She is leading the* PUPPETEER, *his headscarf tied like a monkey's bit. Strapped crosswise to his back is a black, Western-style umbrella and, vertically, his Shizuka doll. His arms, which hold the puppet's bamboo staff, are tied behind his back with the* LADY'*s rope. Head down, his shoulders slumped, it is as if he were being led to slaughter. Still drunk, stumbling on unsteady legs, he steps forth into the shadows of the deep ravine at the foot of the mountain. The* LADY *releases the rope, and it falls to the ground. In fact, he wasn't bound at all, it only appeared that way. He props his puppet against the trunk of a mulberry and kneels in prayer. Thus, at some distance from the* LADY, *he unties the headscarf.*

PUPPETEER: Lady, honor your promise and grant me what I beg of you. (*He rises on his hands and legs and grovels face down into the grass.*)

LADY: Are you sure, grandpa?

PUPPETEER: Could I make up such a lie? Please, thrash me as hard as you can.

LADY: Strike you? Are you sure?

PUPPETEER: Thrash me till you draw blood, till I can't breathe no more. I beg you!

LADY: Really hit you? You're sure, are you?

PUPPETEER: Please, don't trifle with me! I can't wait no longer.

LADY: . . . I won't trifle, in case later you resent what I do. —Well, in that case, since I made a promise, I'll really beat you. Bear with it. (*She strikes him three, four times with her Japanese umbrella, then five, six more times to follow.*)

PUPPETEER: No good! No good at all!

LADY (*Whipping him*): Like this? —Like this?

PUPPETEER: Too weak! (*Twisting around to look at her.*) Let me really have it! Like you were giving me what for.

LADY: Like I, uh, was giving you what for —

PUPPETEER: That's why it's not good enough! Hang on a sec. (*He removes his padded vest together with his worn and filthy crested jacket, baring his skinny, wrinkled back. He totters to his feet and embraces the tree with his back toward her. He turns around and glares at her.*) Rip off the parchment so the staff and ribs are exposed. If you just continue swatting me the way you were, you won't even scratch me.

LADY (*Sighing*): Ah!

PUPPETEER: You'll never be able to put any muscle into it if you keeping thinking I'm just some old, drunken beggar. Surely, lady, there's somebody you hate in this world, someone you'd like to thrash the living daylights out of. A mother-in-law, a father-in-law, a brother-in-law, some relative, some stranger, even a friend. You needn't hold back.

LADY: Ah!

PUPPETEER: Think of those bastards and give me what for. All right? Are you ready?

LADY: Ah!

PUPPETEER: Pull yourself together!

LADY: Ah, all right, then! (*Growing aroused, she begins ripping the parchment off the umbrella, and in so doing, she cuts herself. Her fingers and arms grow pink with the flow of blood to her extremities. —She grasps the umbrella again.*) —You beast! You beast! You beast! You beast, you!!

PUPPETEER: Unh. (*Groaning faintly.*) Unh, yeah, right there, uh huh, that's better now. Oh, yeah.

LADY: Is that how you like it? Huh? You beast!

PUPPETEER: No, it ain't enough for you just to whack me 'cross the rump or back that way. Smack me 'cross the head, box my ears, as hard as you can!

LADY: You beast! You beast! You beast! (*Losing all control of herself, as if possessed, she leaps and dances around, her hair flying, her face growing pale. Beating and thrashing him for all she is worth, she begins to run out of breath.*) Ah! For pity's sake, I can't take it anymore!

PUPPETEER: Can't take it anymore? Good! That's the spirit! Keep it up!

ARTIST (*Following the embankment, descends into the ravine. Though calm, he hastens to stop them*): —Madame!

LADY: Why, sir! (*On seeing him, her frail arms freeze, her legs turn to jelly, and she sinks down and falls half into a faint.*)

ARTIST: This is whiskey. —To revive you. —What on earth has been going on here? (*In shock, the* PUPPETEER *writhes around on the ground. The* ARTIST *observes him.*) I've no idea what this is about, but I do know anything taken too far is wrong.

LADY (*Gasping for breath*): What have I done? I've exposed you to something so base, something no human should ever see, let alone do. Oh, what am I to do? (*Begins weeping hysterically.*)

ARTIST (*At a loss to stop her, he rubs her hands, her back, in an effort to soothe her*): Please, calm yourself.

PUPPETEER (*Wraps his bloody flesh in his jacket and, panting, bows on hand and knee in the grass*): Ah . . . This must be, er, er, your husband. Would it, ma'am?

ARTIST: I'm no one to this lady, particularly. Call me an acquaintance.

PUPPETEER: Then let this old man tell the gentleman—her acquaintance, if you will—what's happening here. Yes, er, forgive me my impertinence—this ain't an easy story to listen to. . . . In short, this dried-up, decrepit ruin, slimy and black as a strip of eel jerky, was once a young man, and long ago committed a great sin. All for a woman. I was a snake that wound itself around an angel on some high balcony. No, rather, I was a lizard who'd gobbled up a frog in a pond. I'm at a loss for metaphors. . . . I sucked the very lifeblood out of her. —And when I awoke from my dream, the sin I committed terrified me. There was nowhere I could go. . . . Exposing myself to the elements, risking life and limb to lose myself, to disappear, I met a traveling monk on the pilgrim's road in Shikoku—surely it was Saint Kōbō himself—who left me this mysterious gift. This doll attached to this bamboo pole is the image of a lovely woman. I'm sure she's offended every time the old man gets drunk, so I bite on this kerchief to protect her from the fumes from my foul-smelling mouth. . . . This beautiful young lady is a goddess for these ancient eyes, so every time I see her I'm reminded of my old sin. Were someone able morn and night to punish me, to beat and torture me, then perhaps I could rid myself of at least some of the sin I've piled up. I'm not afraid neither of going to hell in the afterlife. My load of suffering in this life is not enough, so I long for nothing else in all the world. I'd have old wives and women, the kind who'd lie with me in seedy flophouses or under the verandas of village shrines, kick and beat me, but it was never enough. It was a beautiful lady who lost her precious life, all due to the recklessness of this here beggar. So, if I'm not punished at the hands of a young and beautiful woman like her, my flesh and blood scarcely feel a thing. —And when such a wish, the veritable prayer of a ghost or vengeful spirit, comes from someone with my face, anybody in his right mind would run away. . . . You'd have to be a saint or a genius, a fearless hero or a man of peerless virtue, to listen to a tale like mine! —This ruin you see before you was born sixty-nine years ago, and it's forty-one years to the month and day today that he made this vow. —And here it was just now that this beautiful lady accosted this beggar, called to me, promising me she'd grant me any wish I had, whatever it might be. —I may be no expert, but it's my trade, after all, and I made the most fearsome face I could, but I could see she was afraid of nothing, no ghost or demon crying for vengeance. I told her my wish, a wish I'd borne so long, that I wanted to be exposed like some common criminal on the execution ground. And so we came here, on the roadside to be sure, but in a hidden place in a gully where the mountain has washed away, where I could submit to this blessed beating, this exquisite torture. . . . Master. —Thank you, lovely lady, thank you most kindly!

LADY (*For the first time, calm*): Does it hurt you, sir?

PUPPETEER: Why, lady, this pain brings as much joy to this besotted face as the caress of a spring breeze, or the sweet nectar proffered by Kannon herself from the tresses of a willow.[6] . . . And that it was a beauty like you, ma'am—better yet, somebody like one of them Buddhist she-demons—makes me worship you even more, like you was some kind of angel or goddess. Surely, thanks to the pain you inflicted on me, my flesh and bones have grown soft and supple, my blood courses fast like I was twenty-years old again, and I can live another blessed day with joy in my heart.

ARTIST (*Cocking his head as he listens, he casually lights up a gold-tipped cigarette*): Old man, care for a smoke?

PUPPETEER: Why, sir, if saké is holy water, then tobacco is incense burned for a dead man.

ARTIST: Have a smoke, then. (*Holds out a cigarette case encrusted with pearls.*)

PUPPETEER: Now don't it shine like Saint Kōbō's staff? 'Tis a sin. (*Crawls out and lights one of the gold-tipped cigarettes.*) There'll be hell to pay for this. 'Tis a sin, to be sure. I'll fly up on a waft of this here purple smoke and sail off to paradise.

LADY: I have to leave now, sir. . . . Are you sure all you wanted was to be beaten?

PUPPETEER: Even if the Katsura River turned round and flowed back the other way, I'd tell you no lie.

LADY: Ask me a favor. I feel I still owe you.

PUPPETEER: Had I anything left to ask, it'd be for you to beat and punish me again, another time, three times more.

6. Kannon is the bodhisattva Avalokitesvara, sometimes called the goddess of mercy.

LADY: Anything else?

PUPPETEER: My utmost desire would be for you, my lovely lady, to beat me day after day and day and night, till my body was pummeled to dust. —But I've sobered up now. Enough of this nonsense. —By day I avoid others, but just like the badgers and otters and goblins, none can begrudge my coming on this mountain trail to Shuzenji, bedding down in a flophouse in Tatsuno along the way, to enjoy a dip in Saint Kōbō's springs. —Today, I'll let my feet take me somewhere down the road to Shimoda. I spoke of clouds and water, but Heaven's River[7] and the runoff in a ditch each have their separate courses, so here's where you and I must part and I'll never see the likes of you again. May the two of you prosper till the end of time. —Lady Shizuka, aye, I'll keep you company.

LADY: Sir, wait. (*Having made an important decision, she steels herself.*) I'll follow you down that muddy course for ten years, a hundred even, to make your wish come true each morn and night. (PUPPETEER, *by his visage, wordlessly expresses shock.*)

Master—I left home. I'm the wife of another man. So he won't drag me back, I'd hide myself anywhere, no matter how out of the way it was. As it is, I've nowhere to go. —When I saw that dead carp in the ditch, how dreadful it was, I made up my mind I'd drink poison or drown, commit suicide somehow, no matter how ugly my corpse would look. But maybe it was just out of impatience with me that you said you'd never let me end up that way. . . . In any case, because of what you said to me back then, I decided not to kill myself.

Sir—I am the wife of Koitogawa, a family with a title but no money.

ARTIST: Ah, the viscount's?

LADY: What should I say? Why . . . it was some years ago, back when you had just returned from Europe. With your friends and fans, you used to come often, to Nihonbashi . . . (*Gazes at the* ARTIST *ecstatically.*)—Have you forgotten me? I'm Nui, the daughter at the Yukari Restaurant.

ARTIST: Ah, so you're O-Nui? . . . The little sister, right? I heard folks say how pretty the younger one was.

LADY (*Wistfully*): Yes, master. I'm sure my mention made no more impression on you than someone commenting on how cold it was on a chilly day. I was so shy about being seen by you that I wouldn't even dare stray past the threshold of a room you were in, but I stayed close enough that I never missed a single word of what you had to say at any of your parties. When you held court in the room downstairs, I'd lie face down on the floor above and listen in. And when you were in the room at back, I'd hide out in the bathhouse in the courtyard behind, pressed naked against the wall, listening. Whatever room they put you in, like a mouse, I'd find a spot to hide myself, my heart like a moth drawn the light of your heart. Nobody, not the hardworking

7. The Milky Way.

maids nor even my worldly sister, ever guessed how I felt about you. My heart was true. My gestures, my whole demeanor, betrayed nothing; I never spoke a word of this to anyone. Only love shames one. That's why from that time on—I wonder if I wasn't even hysterical—people said I was a little strange. . . . Please, sir, understand what I say. . . . I truly went a little crazy. When you married, for a whole year all I could do was weep; my hair grew long and wild. It wasn't as if they locked me up, but I just lay there like an empty shell while they tended to me. It annoyed me that I couldn't die. . . . I felt wretched that I couldn't simply disappear, and so somehow I went on living.

—When I came to my senses, I was already twenty-three. My mother, who had so spoiled me in that big house, had passed away. When blind love dies, the world grows dark. Having been able to have my way so long made me feel obligated to crush that selfish nature of mine. Still, I stayed selfish. —I turned down all the suitors that my brothers and sisters and relatives picked out for me—keen merchants, savvy businessmen, every one—and married into the family I did.

There was the mother-in-law and two sisters-in-law, one divorced—three women. It's the family tradition, they said, for a wife to serve her husband, so I had to go fetch the water from a well, the house being located in the suburbs. . . . I cut vegetables. Evenings I went out with the mother-in-law to shop for groceries—I didn't mind those household chores. For savories for supper and sweets for snacks, the boys from the restaurant brought them by bicycle, all the way from my home in Nihonbashi, cases of food, pails of fish, every single day. My mother-in-law would berate the chef, saying the fish wasn't fresh or the omelet hadn't set, that they were feeding us the restaurant customers' leftovers, and sometimes she'd even kick the trays of dishes. At first, knowing I was still so inept, I swallowed my anger, my bitterness, but when this went on for a year, two years, I learned how they really felt. — My husband, for starters . . . well, they all had their eyes on my money, that is, my share of the family business. The monthly interest—how shall I say it?—it was enough for living costs, but it was never enough for them. Every time a niece had a suitor, or a cousin got married, I lost some heirloom, like a formal kimono or ornaments for my hair. My brocades and white underthings, my black satin and crepe—every single bolt of cloth for my kimonos was sold for summer and year-end gifts, presents to pay off the people they knew with some favor or other. The chest of drawers I brought with me when I married was practically empty by then. . . .

And what did my husband do for a living? He wrote poetry, both classical and in the modern style; he wrote plays; he sent letters to the editors of newspapers.

ARTIST: It must have been hard on you. But surely he still has prospects.

LADY: But no! His prospects were my inheritance, and they bullied me unless I brought my inheritance to them. If I coughed or complained of a headache, all the in-laws would huddle together and mutter lines like you'd hear in a play or movie, that it was "that lung disease" and for the sake of the family they had no choice but to send me back home. —"Put up with it! Put up with it!" was all my husband ever said, but I'd have died before I'd finished putting up with what they had in store for me. Finally I came down with a cold that kept me in bed for three days. Then in the hall on the way to get some water to drink, I heard my mother-in-law say, "Now's our chance.... What say we send her home?" That cut me to the quick.

ARTIST: Cruel, for sure.

LADY: Cruel? Was that all it was? —I was so mad, my cold cleared up completely and I said to my husband, "Even if I have to fight for it, I'll go home and bring you back my inheritance. But I want you to do something for me, just once—take your mother and throw her out of my room, then grab your one sister by her ponytail and slap the other one hard across the face!" . . .

PUPPETEER (*Slithering out*): That's the spirit! That's the spirit!

ARTIST: Hah, hah, hah! Bet that made you feel better! Hardly meek, mind you.

LADY (*Furious, then smiling as if all were forgotten*): Hardly.

ARTIST: Not then, anyway.

LADY: "You're a demon!" my husband suddenly shouted, and he flung me out of the room, grabbed me by the hair and slapped *me* hard across the face. That night was last night? No, the night before last—had I left that night it would have been too obvious. Sir, if I was as good as a goldfish or quiet as a houseplant, then the house where I was born or one of my relatives would surely take me back, but I have my pride.... Ready to die because there was no place for me, I've found a place to go now. (*With resolution.*) I'll follow this old gentleman. —This man understands the sin of making a woman suffer, and now he wants to pay for it by being beaten night and day. I'll become all the women of this world to avenge ourselves on this one man. —He worships this doll of Lady Shizuka as if she were human. He'll offer me the pride and blessing of having been born a woman, and in return, he can have my weak and discarded body, like the carcass of that dead carp he saved from its fate.

ARTIST (*Sometimes nodding, sometimes cocking his head doubtfully*): Madame. I mean, O-Nui.

LADY (*Happy, laughs guilelessly*): Ye-es!

ARTIST: Is there nothing I can do to change your mind?

LADY: No, sir. Unless you take me by the hand, back to the inn . . .

PUPPETEER: That's right! That's right!

(*The* ARTIST *is silent.*)

LADY (*Turns around*): Sir.

ARTIST: Madame, you are ill, you're sick. But I'm no doctor and I cannot tell you what to do. —I can't fathom your reasoning, but then again, I don't claim to understand the ways of other people. I've nothing to teach you. Whether it's right or wrong to take you back with me, I can't say at the moment. I'm not leaving you out of cowardice. I'm preoccupied with my own work right now and haven't the freedom to pass judgment on you. —I'm sorry to say I'm weak, and I can do nothing for you. But if you could wait for a month or even a fortnight, then I'd find it in me to do something.

LADY: Master, in the course of just one night I've changed the way I look. My destiny can't wait any longer.

ARTIST: Understood. (*As if no longer able to look her in the eye, he turns to the* PUPPETEER.) —Old man, promise to keep her company.

PUPPETEER: I'll be her dog— (*He picks up the* LADY, *then gets down on all fours. The* LADY *mounts his back. The* ARTIST *takes her hand so she will not fall.*) I'll be her horse and take her wherever she wants to go.

ARTIST: Madame. . . . May all go as you desire.

LADY: Please give us your whiskey, sir. . . . Then be witness to our union. (*Saying nothing, the* ARTIST *takes out the bottle, pours a cup, and offers it her. The* LADY *drains the cup in one gulp, then takes a deep breath.*) Grandpa, we need something to go with the toast.

PUPPETEER: I could sing a ditty in place of a formal speech . . .

LADY: No, bring out that rotten carp you rescued.

PUPPETEER: Surely not!

LADY: Take it out. Have you a knife?

PUPPETEER: I always carry a knife, to fend off dogs and whatever else may come my way. (*From a bowl wrapped in his waist he pulls out a rusty blade.*)

ARTIST: Surely, Madame!

LADY: We'll be traveling together. —I'll have to get used to eating this sort of fare. . . .

PUPPETEER: Now you're talking! I'll have some, too.

(*Shocked, the* ARTIST *turns his head away. From far off, voices chant "Hail to the Great Teacher, Diamond of Universal Light! Hail to the Great Teacher, Diamond of Universal Light!" A young* BOY *and* GIRL *enter, in procession.*)

CHILDREN (*Innocently*): Hail to the Great Teacher, Diamond of Universal Light!

(*The two* CHILDREN *at first enter slowly, the* GIRL *with her hair tied in a ponytail with purple cloth, the* BOY *with his hair formally tied back with a long white ribbon. Then, noticing the* PUPPETEER, *the* LADY, *and the* ARTIST, *they suddenly become afraid and hastily race past them, running down the* hanamichi. *As if they have come to an understanding, the* LADY *and the* ARTIST *both turn and look their way. The* PUPPETEER *also gazes after them, beckoning. The scene created by this ensemble is truly eerie. The two* CHILDREN *return, as if pulled back.*)

ARTIST: Fine children! We need your services.

LADY: Aren't they sweet?

ARTIST (*Removes his cloak and lays it on the grass*): Madame, please seat yourself down next to grandpa here.

LADY: Surely we don't deserve this.

ARTIST: Of course you do. But if you're sick, then maybe I've fallen a bit ill myself. —Now, seal your oath with a toast.[8]

8. In a traditional Japanese wedding, rather than using rings, a marriage is sealed by an exchange of cups of saké.

(*The* LADY *and the* PUPPETEER *sit down side by side. The two* CHILDREN, *as if in the service of demons, take turns pouring the whiskey. Silence. A cloud passes over, darkening the stage. A bush warbler cries impatiently. Distant sounds of court music. Then, gradually, the cries of "Hail to the Great Teacher, Diamond of Universal Light!" draw nigh, and some dozen or so* VILLAGERS, *old and young, men and women, enter chanting.*)

VILLAGER 1: Hey! Why are you children here?

VILLAGER 2: You're Saint Kōbō's emissaries. That's why we keep a respectful distance from you.

VILLAGER 3: We follow you reverently. —You mustn't play tricks on us.

VILLAGERS 4, 5, 6 (*In turn*): Come! Come! (*Surrounding the* CHILDREN.) Hail to the Great Teacher, Diamond of Universal Light! . . . (*Thus they exit off the wings.*)

LADY (*Takes the cloak, brushes off the dust, and drapes it over the* ARTIST'*s shoulders*): It was only once—perhaps you don't remember? You were drunk and put your hand on mine. This one. . . . Please take my hand, once more, in memory of me. I wish for no more. (*Kneels on the grass and bows to him.*) Dear sir. If only it could be otherwise.

ARTIST: And if I could do anything else.

LADY: Grandpa, let's be going.

PUPPETEER: Aye, aye . . . Farewell, sir!

LADY: Let's go! (*As they start off, it begins to rain in earnest.*)

ARTIST: Wait! (*Rushing after them, he holds out an open umbrella.*)

LADY: Sir, what about you?

ARTIST: A little rain won't hurt me.

LADY: Thank you kindly. (*Takes the umbrella.*) Oh, to hell with them! (*She kicks off her clogs and, barefoot, hikes up the skirt of her kimono, exposing fetching scarlet petticoats underneath. She pulls hard on the* PUPPETEER'*s hand.*)

PUPPETEER (*Follows on tottering legs*): Hail to the Great Teacher, Diamond of Universal Light!

LADY (*Halfway down the* hanamichi, *she turns back. The* ARTIST *sees her off*): Master! . . . Farewell! Pay my respects to the world.

ARTIST: Take care of yourself.

(*Wrapping the* PUPPETEER'*s wrinkled arm around her own, the* LADY *leads him, holding high the umbrella, toward the curtain at the end of the* hanamichi. *The* ARTIST *watches them. From offstage, the* PUPPETEER'*s voice is heard chanting, "Hail to the Great Teacher, Diamond of Universal Light!" Then we hear the* LADY *also chant, "Hail to the Great Teacher, Diamond of Universal Light!"*)

ARTIST: Ah, are we in hell? Or surely, this is a dream. No, it's real. —(*Sees the* LADY'*s clog.*) Should I throw it all away, I wonder? My name, everything? (*Takes the clog in his hands, looking distressed.*) But no, I've got my work. (*Throws the clog away.*)

(*The sound of the rain stops. The vesper bell of Shuzenji Temple rings.*)

CURTAIN

Kikuchi Kan, *Father Returns*, 1920s.

FATHER RETURNS

KIKUCHI KAN

TRANSLATED BY M. CODY POULTON

As a novelist, playwright, critic, and book and magazine editor, Kikuchi Kan (1888–1948) was one of the most powerful figures in Japanese letters before the war. A student of Irish literature at Kyoto University, his early work as a dramatist during the Taishō era was strongly influenced by George Bernard Shaw and John Synge. His plays, as well as his editorship of *New Tides in Thought* (*Shinshichō*) and *New Tides in Theater* (*Engeki shinchō*), helped spark the thirst for theater and drama in the first and second decades of the twentieth century. Kikuchi's first hit as a playwright was with a production in 1919 of *The Loves of Tōjūrō*, about the seventeenth-century kabuki actor Sakate Tōjūrō and starring Nakamura Ganjirō I, the inheritor of the realistic acting style innovated by Tōjūrō. This success was followed the next year by a production of *Father Returns* (*Chichi kaeru*), featuring another popular kabuki actor, Ichikawa Ennosuke II (1888–1963), in the title role. (Ennosuke II, formerly called Danko, was the "Actor D" whom Osanai addressed in his open letter, quoted in the introduction to part I.) Together with Morimoto Kaoru's *A Woman's Life* (*Onna no isshō*) and Kinoshita Junji's *Twilight Crane* (*Yūzuru*), *Father Returns* has been one of the most popular Japanese plays of the twentieth century.

Kikuchi preferred one-act plays that were critically incisive and realistic and that presented a powerful social message. "The spirit of modern theater, regardless of where it is from," he wrote, "is a reaction against and attack on existing customs and morals. Here in a country like Japan, customs and morals have latched like a scab onto our social lives. The work of a modern dramatist must be to peel off this scab."[1] Adapted from *The Return of the Prodigal* by the minor playwright St. John Hankin, the work has been called a textbook for one-act plays because of its strong dramatic structure, economic dialogue, and psychological realism. On stage, *Father Returns* lasts no longer than about thirty minutes, but its impact was profound, moving to tears even the confirmed cynic and novelist Akutagawa Ryūnosuke. With great economy, it shows what happens to a family when their father, who had abandoned them some twenty years earlier, comes home. As can be seen in such fictional works as Natsume Sōseki's *And Then* (*Sorekara*) and Shiga Naoya's *Reconciliation* (*Wakai*), intergenerational conflict and the decline of the Meiji patriarchy was a theme of many writers' works in this period.

A six-mat tatami room in a modest middle-class house. Upstage center is a chest on which sits an alarm clock, and downstage is a long wooden charcoal brazier where a kettle is steaming. A low dining table has been set out. KEN'ICHIRŌ *has just returned from his work at City Hall; he has changed into a kimono and is relaxing, reading the newspaper. His mother,* OTAKA, *is sewing. It is early October, around seven in the evening, and already dark outside.*

Time: Around 1907.
Place: A town on the coast of Shikoku.[2]

Characters

KURODA KEN'ICHIRŌ, age twenty-eight
SHINJIRŌ, his brother, age twenty-three
OTANE, their sister, age twenty
OTAKA, their mother, age fifty-one
SŌTARŌ, their father, age fifty-eight

KEN'ICHIRŌ: Where's Otane gone, Mum?
OTAKA: Off to deliver some sewing.

---

1. Kikuchi Kan, "Engeki zuihitsu," quoted in Oyama Isao, *Kindai Nihon gikyokushi* (Yamagata: Kindai Nihon gikyokushi kankōkai, 1968), 2:514.
2. *Nankaidō no kaigan ni aru shō tokai*: literally, "a small city on the Nankaidō coast." Nankaidō refers to the old provinces adjoining the eastern region of the Inland Sea, from modern Wakayama Prefecture to Hyōgō Prefecture along the Honshū coast and including the islands of Awaji and Shikoku. Kikuchi no doubt is alluding to his birthplace, Takamatsu, in Kagawa Prefecture.

KEN'ICHIRŌ: Don't tell me she's still doing that. Surely she doesn't have to anymore.

OTAKA: Yes, but she'll need a decent kimono when she gets married.

KEN'ICHIRŌ (*Turning over a page of the paper*): What became of that offer you told me about?

OTAKA: They kept begging me to give her away, but it seems she didn't fancy the man at all.

KEN'ICHIRŌ: He had money. Would have made a fine match.

OTAKA: Maybe so, but one can have a small fortune and spend it all and, when all's said and done, still have nothing to show for it. Why, our house had some twenty, thirty thousand yen in bonds and real estate when I first came, but your dad blew it all away living high off the hog. He might just as well have fed it to the wind. (KEN'ICHIRŌ *says nothing, as if recalling unpleasant memories.*) I learned the hard way, so I'd rather Otane married for love than money. Even if her husband's poor, so long as he's got a good heart, life shouldn't be too hard on her.

KEN'ICHIRŌ: Ah, but how much better it'd be if he had both.

OTAKA: And if wishes were horses . . . Otane may be pretty, but we're hardly well to do. . . . Besides, the smallest wedding outfit these days will easily cost you a couple of hundred yen.

KEN'ICHIRŌ: Otane's had a hard time of it ever since she was a kid, and all because of dad. We ought to make sure at least she's married off properly. Once we've got a thousand saved up, I suggest we give her half of it.

OTAKA: That's hardly necessary—even three hundred would do. I'll feel even more relieved when you get yourself a wife. Everyone says I had bad luck with a husband, but good luck with kids. I didn't know what I was going to do when your dad left us. . . .

KEN'ICHIRŌ (*Changing the subject*): Shin's late.

OTAKA: That's because he's on duty tonight. Shin said he's getting a raise this month.

KEN'ICHIRŌ: Is that so? He did so well in high school I'd imagine he's not happy staying a primary school teacher. There's no telling how far he'll go if he sets his mind to it and studies some more.

OTAKA: I've had someone on the lookout for a wife for you too, but so far no luck. The Sonoda girl would be a good match but her family's more respectable than ours, so they may not want us to have her.

KEN'ICHIRŌ: Surely we can wait a couple more years at least.

OTAKA: In any case, once Otane's married off we really do have to get you a wife. That'd fix everything. When your dad ran off, I was left with three babes in arms, wondering what on earth I was going to do.

KEN'ICHIRŌ: There's no sense dwelling on the past. What's done is done.

(*The front door rattles open and* SHINJIRŌ *returns. For a mere primary school teacher, he is an impressive-looking young man.*)

SHINJIRŌ: I'm back.

OTAKA: Welcome home.

KEN'ICHIRŌ: You're dreadfully late tonight.

SHINJIRŌ: I had so much to do I was at my wit's end. My shoulders ache something awful.

OTAKA: We've been holding supper for you.

KEN'ICHIRŌ: You can have a bath after you've eaten.

SHINJIRŌ (*Changing into a kimono*): Where's Otane, Mum?

OTAKA: Went to deliver some sewing.

SHINJIRŌ: Hey, Ken'ichi, I heard something interesting today. Principal Sugita told me that he'd seen somebody who looked like Dad in Furushinmachi.

KEN'ICHIRŌ and OTAKA: Eh!?

SHINJIRŌ: Mr. Sugita was walking down the street in Furushinmachi—you know, where all the inns are—when he saw someone ahead, about sixty years old. The man looked vaguely familiar, so he caught up to him and had a good look at him from the side. He could almost swear it was Dad, Mr. Sugita said. If it's Sōtarō, then sure as you're born, he'll have a mole on his right cheek. If so, I'll hail him, he thought, but when he got closer, the man slunk off down that side street by the Water God's shrine.

OTAKA: Mr. Sugita was an old friend of your dad's—the two took lance lessons together in the old days—so, if anybody ought to know him, it'd be him. Even so, it's been some twenty years now.

SHINJIRŌ: That's what Mr. Sugita said. It's been twenty-odd years since he'd seen him, so he couldn't be sure, but then again, this was somebody he'd chummed around with since when they were kids, so he couldn't swear he was completely mistaken.

KEN'ICHIRŌ (*An uneasy light in his eyes*): So Mr. Sugita didn't call out to him then.

SHINJIRŌ: He said he was ready to say something if the man had a mole.

OTAKA: Well, I suppose Mr. Sugita was wrong after all. If your dad had come back to this town, then there's no way he wouldn't stop at the old homestead.

KEN'ICHIRŌ: He'd never dare set foot in this door again, let me tell you.

OTAKA: Anyway, as far as I'm concerned, he's dead. It's been twenty years.

SHINJIRŌ: Didn't you say somebody ran into him in Okayama? When was that?

OTAKA: Why, that was ten years ago already. That was when the Kubo boy, Chūta, made a trip to Okayama. Your dad had brought some lions and tigers to town for a show, he said. He treated Chūta to dinner and asked about us. Chūta said he wore a gold watch on his *obi* and was all decked out in silk—cut a real figure, he did. But that's the last we've heard of him. That was the year after the war, so I guess it must be twelve, thirteen years ago already.[3]

SHINJIRŌ: Dad was quite the eccentric, wasn't he.

3. Otaka is referring here to the Sino-Japanese War of 1895/1896.

OTAKA: Ever since he was young, he had no taste for the family studies[4] but preferred to spend his time prospecting for gold and whatnot. So it wasn't just the high life that got him in debt. He lost a small fortune exporting patent medicines to China.

KEN'ICHIRŌ (*Looking even more perturbed*): Let's eat, Mum.

OTAKA: Yes, yes, let's eat. I clean forgot. (*Leaves for the kitchen. From offstage.*) Mr. Sugita must've been mistaken. If he was still alive he'd be getting on. Surely, he would've sent us a postcard at least.

KEN'ICHIRŌ (*More seriously*): When was it Mr. Sugita ran into that fellow?

SHINJIRŌ: Last night about nine, he said.

KEN'ICHIRŌ: How was he dressed?

SHINJIRŌ: Not very well, apparently. Didn't have a coat on.

KEN'ICHIRŌ: That so?

SHINJIRŌ: How do you remember him?

KEN'ICHIRŌ: I don't.

SHINJIRŌ: Surely you do. You were eight then. Even I have a foggy memory of him.

KEN'ICHIRŌ: I don't. I used to, but I made a point of forgetting.

SHINJIRŌ: Mr. Sugita talks about Dad a lot. Says he was quite good looking when he was young.

OTAKA (*Bringing supper out of the kitchen*): That's right. Your dad was very popular. When he was a page for his lordship, one of the ladies-in-waiting gave him a chopstick box with a love poem inside.

SHINJIRŌ (*Laughing*): Why the hell would she do that? Hah hah hah hah.

OTAKA: He was born in the Year of the Ox, so that'd make him fifty-eight now. If he'd stayed put here he'd be enjoying his retirement now. (*Pause. The three begin to eat.*) Otane should be home soon. It's getting quite cold out, isn't it?

SHINJIRŌ: I heard a shrike today, mum, in that big elm at Jōganji. It's autumn already.... Oh, I've got some news for you, Ken. I've decided to get my English certificate. There aren't any good math teachers, you know.

KEN'ICHIRŌ: Good idea. So you'll be going to the Ericsons'?

SHINJIRŌ: That's what I thought. They're missionaries, so I don't have to pay them anything.

KEN'ICHIRŌ: In any case, if you want to show the world you can stand on your own two feet, you know you can't rely on your dad's reputation. So hit the books. I was thinking of taking the senior civil service exam myself, but they've changed the rules, and now you have to be a high school graduate, so I've given up the idea. You graduated from high school, so you've got to give it your best shot.

(*The front door opens and* OTANE *returns. She is a pale-complexioned young woman of above-average good looks.*)

---

4. *Ie no gakumon* is the Confucian learning that would have been a tradition in a samurai family like theirs.

OTANE: I'm home.

OTAKA: You're late.

OTANE: They had more work for me. That's what held me up.

OTAKA: Have some supper.

OTANE (*Sits. Looking rather worried*): When I got back to the house just now, Ken'ichi, there was this strange old man loitering across the road, just staring at our doorway. (*The other three start.*)

KEN'ICHIRŌ: Hm.

SHINJIRŌ: What did he look like?

OTANE: It was so dark I couldn't tell for sure, but he was tall.

(SHINJIRŌ *goes over to the window and looks outside.*)

KEN'ICHIRŌ: Anybody there?

SHINJIRŌ: Uh uh. Nobody. (*The three children are silent.*)

OTAKA: It was the third day after Obon when he left home.

KEN'ICHIRŌ: I'd rather you didn't bring up the past anymore, Mum.

OTAKA: I used to feel as bitter as you do, but as I get older, my heart's not as hard as it used to be.

(*All four eat their supper in silence. Suddenly, there is a rattling at the front door.* KEN'ICHIRŌ*'s and* OTAKA*'s faces register the greatest emotion, but the nature of that emotion differs radically.*)

MAN'S VOICE: Hello?

OTANE: Yes? (*She makes no move to rise, however.*)

MAN'S VOICE: I wonder—is Otaka there?

OTAKA: Yes! (*Goes toward the front door as if sucked toward it. Henceforth, we can hear only their voices.*)

MAN (*Offstage*): Otaka, is it you?

OTAKA (*Offstage*): It's you! My God . . . how you've changed.

(*Their voices are filled with tears.*)

MAN (*Offstage*): Well . . . you look . . . well. The children must be all grown up by now.

OTAKA (*Offstage*): Indeed. They've turned into fine young grownups. Come see for yourself.

MAN (*Offstage*): Is it all right?

OTAKA (*Offstage*): Of course it is.

(*Returning home for the first time in twenty years, the haggard father,* SŌTARŌ, *is led into the living room by his old wife.* SHINJIRŌ *and* OTANE *stare at their father, blinking in disbelief.*)

SHINJIRŌ: Is this Father? I'm Shinjirō.

SŌTARŌ: Why, what a fine young man you've become! When I left, you were hardly a toddler.

OTANE: Father, I'm Otane.

SŌTARŌ: I'd heard there was a girl, but, my, you're a pretty one.

OTAKA: Well, my dear . . . where to begin? It's a fine thing the children have turned out so well, don't you think?

SŌTARŌ: They say kids'll grow up even without their parents' help, and I guess they're right, aren't they? Hah hah hah. (*Laughs.*)

(*But no one joins him in his laughter.* KEN'ICHIRŌ *remains silent, leaning on the table.*)

OTAKA: Dear. Ken and Shin have both turned into fine young men. Ken passed the regular civil service exam when he was only twenty, and Shin here never fell lower than third place in middle school. The two of them now pull in about sixty yen a month. And Otane, well, as you can see, she's a fine-looking girl. We've had proposals from some fine places, let me tell you.

SŌTARŌ: Why, that's a fine thing indeed. I myself was doing quite well till about four, five years back. Had myself a troupe of some two dozen, touring the country. Then, when we were in Kure, our show tent burned down and we lost everything. After that nothing went right and before I knew it, I was an old man. I started to miss my old wife and kids, so that's why I crept back here. Be good to me, 'cause I don't expect I'll have much longer to live. (*Looks at* KEN'ICHIRŌ.) What d'ye say, Ken'ichirō? Won't you pass the cup to me? Your dad's not much used to drinking the good stuff these days. Ah, but you'd be the only one to remember my face, wouldn't you?

(KEN'ICHIRŌ *does not respond.*)

OTAKA: Come, Ken. Listen to your dad. It's been years since the two of you met, so you ought to celebrate.

SHINJIRŌ (*Takes the saké cup and offers it to* SŌTARŌ): There you go.

KEN'ICHIRŌ (*Abruptly*): Stoppit. You've no right to give it to him.

OTAKA: What are you saying? Ken!

(SŌTARŌ *gives him a sharp look.* SHINJIRŌ *and* OTANE *hold down their heads and say nothing.*)

KEN'ICHIRŌ (*Goading him*): We have no father. How could *that* be our father?

SŌTARŌ (*Barely restraining his rage*): What did you say!?

KEN'ICHIRŌ (*Coldly*): If we had a father, then Mum wouldn't have led us all by the hand to the breakwater and made us jump in with her. I was eight then. Luckily, Mum picked a spot that was too shallow, otherwise we'd have all drowned. Had I a father, I wouldn't have had to go work as an errand boy when I was ten years old. It's because we had no father our childhood was so miserable. Shinjirō, have you forgotten how, when you were in primary school, you cried because we couldn't afford to buy any ink and paper? Or how you cried when we couldn't buy the textbooks you needed and your classmates made fun of you because you'd brought handwritten copies to school? How could we have a father? A real father wouldn't have let us suffer like that!

(OTAKA *and* OTANE *weep;* SHINJIRŌ *fights back the tears. Even the old man begins to lose his rage and succumb to grief.*)

SHINJIRŌ: But, Ken, see how much our mum's willing to forgive. Surely you can find it in you to let bygones be bygones.

KEN'ICHIRŌ (*Even more coldly*): Mum's a woman, so I don't know what she thinks, but if her husband's my father, then he's my enemy. When we were kids and times were bad or we were hungry and complained to Mum, she'd say, "It's all your dad's fault. If you're looking for somebody to blame, then blame your dad." If that man's our father, he's the one who's given us nothing but grief since when we were just kids. When I was ten and running errands for the prefectural office, our mum was at home making matchboxes to make ends meet. One month she didn't have any work and the three of us had to go without lunches. Have you forgotten? The reason I studied so hard was so I could show that bastard. I wanted to get back at the man who abandoned us. I wanted to prove to him that I could lose a father and still grow up to be a man. Do I remember him ever loving me? I don't think so! Till I was eight, he spent all his time out drinking, thanks to which he got up to his head in debts, then ran off with another woman. The love of a wife and three children still didn't amount to any more than that one woman. And when he disappeared, so did the passbook with sixteen yen in it that Mum had put away for me.

SHINJIRŌ (*Holding back his tears*): But brother! See how old Dad's become.

KEN'ICHIRŌ: It's easy enough for you, Shin, to glibly call him "Dad"! Just because some stranger you've never seen before comes crawling into our house and says he's our father, you suddenly feel sorry for him?

SHINJIRŌ: But Ken, we're his own flesh and blood. No matter what happens, our duty's—

KEN'ICHIRŌ: To look after him, you say? Off he went and had the time of his life. Now he's old and can't get by any longer, he says, so he comes home. I don't care what you say. I haven't got a dad.

SŌTARŌ (*Indignantly, but his anger is entirely feigned and carries no power or conviction*): Ken'ichirō! How dare you speak like that to your own father!

KEN'ICHIRŌ: You may be my father, but you sure didn't raise me! You threw away the right to be my father when your children died, there on the breakwater, twenty years ago. Whatever I am today I made myself. I don't owe anybody anything.

(*Everyone falls silent. Only* OTAKA*'s and* OTANE*'s quiet sobbing can be heard.*)

SŌTARŌ: Right then, I'll leave. I've been a man of some means, I'll have you know. I made a small fortune in the past, and no matter how far I've fallen I'm still able to feed myself. Well, sorry for the trouble I've caused you all. (*Indignantly makes to leave.*)

SHINJIRŌ: Wait, please. I'll look after you, even if my brother won't. Ken'ichi's your own flesh and blood, so even he'll come 'round soon enough, I'm sure. Wait! I'll do whatever I can to look after you.

KEN'ICHIRŌ: Shinjirō! What has this man ever done for you? I still bear the scars of his beatings, but what have you got to show for him? Nothing. Who paid for your primary school? Have you forgotten it was your big brother who paid for your tuition out of the wretched salary I made as an errand boy? The only real father you ever had was me. All right, go ahead and help that man out if that's what you want. But if you do, I'll never talk to you again.

SHINJIRŌ: But—

KEN'ICHIRŌ: If you don't like it, you can leave. And take that man with you.

(*The women continue to cry.* SHINJIRŌ *says nothing.*)

KEN'ICHIRŌ: Thanks to the fact we had no father, I scrimped and saved, working late into the night, just so my little brother and sister didn't have to suffer like I did. I put you both through middle school.

SŌTARŌ (*Weakly*): Say no more. I must've put you all out by coming back. I won't trouble you again. I've got enough wits about me to figure out how to fend for myself. I'll be off, then. Otaka! Look after yourself. I guess it's a good thing I left you, after all.

SHINJIRŌ (*Following his father as he attempts to leave*): Have you got enough cash on you, sir? Surely you haven't had supper yet.

SŌTARŌ (*His eyes shining as if appealing to him*): No, no. Thanks anyway. (*He stumbles at the entranceway and collapses on the lower step.*)

OTAKA: Be careful!

SHINJIRŌ (*Helping him up*): Do you have some place to go?

SŌTARŌ (*Remains seated, dejectedly*): Who needs a home? I'll die on the road. . . . (*As if to himself.*) I'd no right to come beating on your door, but still, I got older and weaker and found my feet naturally wending their way back to where I was born. It's been three days since I came back to town, and every night I'd stand outside the door here, but I couldn't bring myself to cross this threshold. . . . All said and done, I'd have been better off if I hadn't come. Anybody would make a fool of a man who came home penniless. . . . When I turned fifty, I started to long for my old home again, and I figured I'd bring back a thousand or two at least and beg your forgiveness, but when you're older it's that much harder to make a living. . . . (*Stands up.*) No matter, I'll make do somehow. (*He weakly gets to his feet and, turning back, gazes at his old wife before opening the door and leaving. The other four family members remain silent for some time.*)

OTAKA (*Appealingly*): Ken'ichirō!

OTANE: Brother!

(*There is a tense pause that lasts some time.*)

KEN'ICHIRŌ: Shin! Go, find Dad and bring him back.

(SHINJIRŌ *flies out the door. The other three wait anxiously.* SHINJIRŌ *presently returns, his face pale.*)

SHINJIRŌ: I took the street south and looked for him, but there was no sign of him. I'll go north this time. Come with me, brother.

KEN'ICHIRŌ (*Anxiously*): How could you have lost him! He can't be lost!

(*The two brothers madly rush out the door.*)

CURTAIN

Akita Ujaku, *The Skeletons' Dance*, directed by Uchiyama Jun, Mingei, 1983.
(Courtesy of The Tsubouchi Memorial Theatre Museum Waseda University)

THE SKELETONS' DANCE

AKITA UJAKU
TRANSLATED BY M. CODY POULTON

The Skeletons' Dance is a remarkable dramatic testimony to a dark event in Japan's modern history: the Great Kantō Earthquake of 1923 and the slaughter of several thousand resident Koreans by vigilante groups during the ensuing chaos. At the time of the earthquake, Akita Ujaku (1883–1962) had been on a lecture tour of the Tōhoku region. Quickly returning to Tokyo, he was harassed by both the police and vigilante groups. He remained in Tokyo, touring the worst-hit places, for a few days before returning to his native Aomori Prefecture for his own safety. Ujaku's leftist sympathies were no doubt known to authorities, and the suspension of civil liberties after the earthquake led to the murders of several activists, including anarchist Osugi Sakae and the leftist playwright Hirasawa Keishichi.

Ujaku was a student of English literature at the Tokyo senmon gakkō (the precursor to Waseda University). His Waseda contacts introduced him to Shimamura Hōgetsu and Osanai Kaoru, and he became one of the founding members of Osanai's Free Theater in 1909. His first successful play, *Buried Spring* (*Umoreta haru*), was written for Sawamura Sōjūrō's Art Theater (Bijutsu gekijō) in 1913. His early plays are romantic, poetical; their idealism later found expression in a more direct political engagement, which led to his joining the Japan Socialist League (Nihon shakaishugi renmei) in 1921. He was also a regular contributor to the foremost leftist journal of the day, *The Sower* (*Tanemaku hito*). Although Ujaku's dramatic production, like that of many Taishō writers, declined after the late 1920s, he continued to be active in the theater, in 1934 as the secretary of the Shinkyō gekidan, one of the leftist spin-offs from the Tsukiji Little Theater, and as the editor of

Teatoro magazine. Like several hundred other *shingeki* artists, he was arrested in the 1940 purge of leftist theater people.

The Skeletons' Dance does not portray the earthquake but, rather, its aftermath. It is set in a town, possibly Morioka, to which survivors of the earthquake have been evacuated. A young man bravely defends one of the evacuees, who may be Korean, when vigilantes threaten him. The play is an early example of expressionist theater in Japan, its style inspired by playwrights like August Strindberg, Georg Kaiser, and Ernst Toller. As its notes indicate, Ujaku conceived its staging in the style of Mavo artists like Yanase Masamu and Murayama Tomoyoshi, who designed many productions for the Tsukiji Little Theater and other stages in the 1920s. Ujaku's play miraculously escaped censorship when it was first published in *New Tides of Theater* (*Engeki shinchō*) in April 1924, but authorities quickly confiscated issues of the magazine when they realized its content. The play was not performed professionally until 1982.

Place: Inside the tent of a first-aid station. (Cubist staging could be employed here. It might be interesting to try the "Mavo" style.)

Characters

A YOUTH
An OLD MAN
A NURSE
A DOCTOR
A KOREAN
VIGILANTES (later, SKELETONS)
A LADY
Various EVACUEES
OTHERS

OLD MAN: Excuse me . . .
YOUTH: Are you talking to me?
OLD MAN: Sorry to disturb you at your sleep, but what is this place?
YOUTH (*Raising his head and glancing at the* OLD MAN): This is M Station. Where are you going?
OLD MAN: I was headed for Hokkaido, but it's M Station, you say? . . . What time is it?
YOUTH: It's past two already.
OLD MAN: Will it be dawn soon, then?

YOUTH: Not for another couple of hours.

OLD MAN: Is that so?... What a disaster!... For this to happen, and at my age.... What was that sound?

YOUTH: Nothing, just a train. When did you get here?

OLD MAN: Last night.... Late last night.... Why did this have to happen? It's crazy.

YOUTH: You had a bad time of it, then, in Tokyo, did you? We were both unlucky, I guess.

OLD MAN: "Bad time" hardly begins to describe it.... I lost my daughter and my grandchildren.... Besides, I was sick and hardly in any state to be making a trip anywhere.

YOUTH: Is that so? I'm sorry for you.... Where was it your daughter and grandkids died? Honjo?

OLD MAN: No, Mukōjima.... I've been living in Mukōjima for some thirty years, now.... I heard from a neighbor that my daughter fled with my grandchildren to the embankment. They were pushed into the river by the crush of people....

YOUTH: That's terrible. I heard that happened to a lot of people there. But luckily you managed to get away....

OLD MAN: I'd have been better off dead.... What have I got to look forward to now, with my daughter and grandchildren gone?

YOUTH: You've a right to feel that way.... But in this world of ours, we've got to hang on. If we do, something will turn up.... Mind you, I can't see any light at the end of the tunnel myself... but so long as one's alive, one's got to live.

OLD MAN: Is there somebody sleeping next to me? It feels like somebody's lying on top of my right arm.... Sorry to bother you, but could you have a look for me?

YOUTH: Yes, there is.... You can't move your right arm?

OLD MAN: I haven't been able to for some three years now.

YOUTH: How did you ever manage to come this far?... You should've stayed in Tokyo.... Hello? Could you please move your head there? You're lying on top of a sick man's arm. Please move.

(*The* MAN *raises his head, opens his eyes and looks at the other two. He appears to want to say something but simply smiles sadly at them and shifts over, then falls asleep as before, lying face up. Two or three other* MEN *raise their heads and gaze at the* YOUTH *and* OLD MAN.)

OLD MAN (*Breathing deeply*): Thank you.... That feels a lot better now.... You must be tired.... I think I'll try to catch some sleep myself before morning.... Hey, what is that racket?... Is there a fire someplace?

YOUTH (*Laughing*): That's no fire. It's a locomotive. We're five hundred miles away from Tokyo here. No earthquakes or fires are going to get you here.

OLD MAN: That so?... But aren't they saying the Koreans are going around lighting fires?... It's really frightening.

YOUTH (*Firmly*): You believe it too? We should have a bit more faith than that. I'm doing what I can to find out the truth.

OLD MAN: Really? But if it's a lie, it's a terrible one. . . . Is it true that because of the rumors a lot of Koreans have been killed along the railroad tracks?

YOUTH: It is. I've seen a lot since yesterday myself. . . . I'm sick to my stomach of the Japanese. I thought we were a people with a bit more sense than that, but I feel completely betrayed by what's happened. And deeply disappointed.

(*During this speech, a* MAN *in back raises his head and looks at the two. His eyes shine strangely.*)

OLD MAN: I know nothing about what happened, but if the Koreans didn't do anything, I feel sorry for them. . . . Why did they have to take it out on them again?

YOUTH: Because people have no faith. All they do is go around smugly wearing somebody else's clothes. I'm disappointed in the Japanese as citizens, but I won't lose my faith in them as human beings. It doesn't matter where they're from—all humans are, deep down, good and innocent.

OLD MAN: That may be, but I'm Japanese, and I think the Japanese are fine people.

YOUTH: Yes. I too want to think that, but I saw what the Japanese did last night and I didn't want to think that my own countrymen could do such a thing. . . . If you didn't see what I saw, there's no way you could understand how I feel.

OLD MAN: In any case, it's turned into a nasty world, that's for sure. . . . Where are you headed from here?

YOUTH: I'm going back to Aomori. I've got brothers there. . . .

OLD MAN: Is that so? . . . If you don't mind my asking, have you got a job?

YOUTH (*Laughing*): Me? . . . Why, I'm still a student. . . .

OLD MAN: Is that so? . . . Still studying, are you? . . . Good for you. . . .

YOUTH: And what line of work were you in?

OLD MAN: Me? . . . Nothing special. . . . I worked for a foundry. . . .

YOUTH: A foundry? You mean, like casting sculptures?

OLD MAN: Well . . . I was really just a tradesman, after all. . . . Nothing to write home about. . . .

YOUTH: I know quite a few sculptors myself. There was Y, a poor fellow who was eking a living casting medals and statues of Daikoku. He was living in Mukōjima too, I think.

OLD MAN: Y . . . I think I've heard that name before. . . . Hey, it sounds like there's some kind of noise. Ever since the fire, my hearing's not what it used to be. . . .

YOUTH (*Listening carefully*): It's nothing. You're just upset. You should try to relax.

NURSE (*To a first-aid station* ATTENDANT): Nishimura-san, go to the headquarters and get us some more cotton batting. (ATTENDANT *exits right without speaking.*) Is there anyone here who doesn't feel well?

EVACUEE: Nurse, call me a doctor. . . . My stomach hurts so bad I don't know what to do. . . .

EVACUEE: Nurse, bring me a glass of water. . . .

EVACUEE: Nurse, can I board the boat in my state? . . .

EVACUEE: Nurse, will this ticket let me board the boat for free?

NURSE: Quiet, everybody, please! I can't do anything for you if you all talk at once. (*To the* OLD MAN.) Are you getting on the boat tonight?

OLD MAN: I wanted to ask you . . . Would it be impossible for me to stay here a bit longer? . . . I hurt so bad, I'm not sure I can go anywhere. . . .

NURSE: Is that so? The doctor will be coming tonight, so I'll have him take a look at you.

EVACUEE: I want a glass of water. My body feels like it's burning all over. . . .

NURSE (*Drawing a glass of boiled water from a large bucket and handing it to him*): There you go. Drink.

EVACUEE: Nurse, me too . . .

EVACUEE: Me too . . .

EVACUEE: Me too . . .

NURSE: You'll just have to wait your turn.

EVACUEE: You're mean . . .

EVACUEE: A spiteful nurse. . . . Really stuck up.

EVACUEE: I should never have come here in the first place. . . . Never in my life have I been treated so badly before.

EVACUEE: Yeah, they were so ever much nicer at O Station. . . . They can't understand how we feel 'cause they didn't get burned.

EVACUEE: Nurse, could you take this bandage off? . . . Ever since you put it on, it's been hurting something awful. . . . Ow! . . . It hurts!

NURSE: That shouldn't be. It may hurt a bit now, but in no time you'll be feeling better.

EVACUEE: Ah, it hurts! . . . Ah, it hurts! . . . I'd sooner be dead than hang around in a place like this.

EVACUEE: Quiet there, you! . . . This child here is deathly ill.

NURSE: Now, please try to be quiet. . . . I'm afraid she hasn't long.

EVACUEE (*To the other* EVACUEE): Shut up, you old bag! . . . We ought to kill you instead. . . . Can't you see this child's going to die? . . . We're all suffering here. . . .

NURSE: Now, now. I know how you all feel, but try to quiet down now.

LADY (*Enters tent carrying a basket filled with various things*): Good evening, everyone. You must all be tired.

NURSE: Good evening, madam. Thanks for coming. But why at such an hour as this?

LADY: I was up all night last night at Headquarters with the bureau chief's wife. You know? Even the bureau chief's wife stayed up with us!

NURSE: Is that so? Well, we appreciate it.

LADY (*Looking at the scene inside the tent*): Quite a few have left already, it seems. These are gifts from Headquarters.

NURSE: Why, thank you very much. I'm sure they'll all be delighted.

YOUTH: Won't you try to sleep?

OLD MAN: How can I sleep with all this racket? . . . I don't need anything. . . . I just want to have a decent rest. . . . But when I think of my daughter and the grandkids . . .

EVACUEE: Who is that woman?

EVACUEE: Her? She's brought something. . . . Get a load of the rock on the ring she's wearing! . . . Maybe I should ask her to give it to me. . . .

EVACUEE: White collar, crested jacket . . . A real looker. . . .What d'ya think? Used to be a professional woman? . . .

LADY: You must all be very tired, surely. . . . Please tell me if there's anything you need. Don't be shy, now.

NURSE: This is the wife of the mayor, everybody. . . . She's been working very hard for us all since the fire. . . .

LADY (*Laughs youthfully*): My, but you flatter me! It's such a poor town, I'm ashamed to say that it's more than I can manage. But if it's in my power, I'll do all I possibly can, so do please speak up and tell me.

EVACUEE (*To himself*): Speak up? Isn't it obvious without our telling you? We don't have anything.

LADY: Anyone hungry?

EVACUEE: I'm not hungry, but I'm dying of thirst here.

LADY: Is that so? Here's a soft drink for you.

EVACUEE: I'm thirsty too, ma'am! I'm thirsty too! . . .

LADY: I've only five bottles of soft drink here. You'll have to share them among yourselves. (*The* EVACUEES *all swarm around the* LADY *like beggars, attempting to grab bottles of soft drink. The* LADY *blushes and tries to prevent all the bottles from being taken. The* EVACUEES *press in on her from all sides.*)

NURSE: Let me handle this, madam. . . . It's dangerous for you. . . . Now, settle down everybody! If you don't settle down you'll have to give back what you've got. Are you listening?

EVACUEE: Quiet, everybody! . . . I've got no need for any soft drink. . . . Let's give them to the ladies. . . .

EVACUEE: Yeah, give them to the ladies! . . .

NURSE (*Taking the basket from the* LADY): Yes, why don't you do that? I'll give you men some apples instead. (*She gives the women the bottles of soft drink and apples to the men. The* EVACUEES *stretch out their arms to receive the gifts.*)

LADY: It's quite a task, isn't it, handing out rations? I feel I understand for the first time how much you all suffered.

NURSE: It's nothing once you get used to it, my lady. Thank you so much. They're all just like children. But I suppose they have a right to be.

YOUTH: You're not hungry?

OLD MAN: No . . . not much. . . . I just don't feel like eating. . . .

YOUTH: It's unpleasant having to receive things, but there's something even uglier about the spirit of those who are doing the giving.

LADY: Well, I'll be taking my leave of you all now. Please, do look after them. Farewell.

NURSE: Are you going? Thank you so much, madam. Please give my regards to the people at Headquarters.

LADY (*Heading out of the tent with her empty basket*): It looks like tomorrow will be another fine day.

NURSE: Is that so? Good-bye, my lady!

ATTENDANT (*Enters the tent with a box of cotton batting*): Terrible news, Miss Yamada! Some Koreans have been killed in front of Headquarters!

NURSE: Were they up to something, the Koreans?

ATTENDANT: They say the Koreans were launching an all-out attack on the home guard.

EVACUEES (*Practically all the men stand up as one*): Koreans!

EVACUEE: The Koreans are here. I might have known it!

EVACUEE: The Koreans are beasts!

NURSE: Now, try to settle down, all of you! . . . The doctor will be here soon. . . . It's nothing to worry about. . . .

EVACUEE: Nothing to worry about? . . . The Koreans want to slaughter us all! . . . Kill the Koreans! . . .

NURSE: Miss Nishimura, quickly call the doctor here. Everybody—I'm here to look after you, so settle down until the doctor gets here.

EVACUEE: Let's wait till the doctor gets here. . . .

EVACUEE: Yeah, good idea! Good idea! . . .

EVACUEE: What should we do, nurse? Will the Koreans kill me? . . . My house got burned down. . . . Never would have I imagined we've run into trouble here too, of all places. . . . Ah, what should we do? . . .

OLD MAN: Is it true the Koreans are going to attack us?

YOUTH (*Laughing*): Why do they think that? That's a pretty bizarre notion of them attacking the home guard, surely. The Koreans don't have any weapons. How can a people who have been given no weapons dare carry out such a thing? I met yesterday a staff officer from U division, and he told me none of the Koreans had any weapons or bombs or anything.

OLD MAN: Really? . . . But why, then, would such a rumor be spread?

YOUTH: Because the Japanese have no faith!

EVACUEE: Who is that guy?

EVACUEE: He's a Korean!

EVACUEE: A Korean! . . . A Korean! . . .

EVACUEE: Get him! Get the bastard!

OLD MAN (*Rising halfway up*): Really, everyone! You're not making any sense. . . . This nonsense about Koreans is all a terrible mistake. . . . You have to tell them. . . .

YOUTH: No, there's no point trying. . . . They'll all know soon enough.

EVACUEE: Know what? . . . What will we know?

NURSE: Now, settle down, everyone. The doctor's coming.

DOCTOR (*Wearing the uniform of a military doctor*): What's going on here?

NURSE: They're all upset over the rumors about the Koreans.

DOCTOR: Hm, what could the Koreans do? Gentlemen! Do you doubt the power of the heroic Imperial Army? Fear not, Gentlemen! The home guard division in this city is awaiting its marching orders as we speak. . . .

EVACUEE: A division! . . . A whole division!

EVACUEE: Awaiting marching orders as we speak! . . .

DOCTOR: I understand all too well your selfless love for the state. . . . You yourselves have sent so many devoted soldiers to serve in our forces. . . . But fear not, Gentlemen! . . . The Imperial Army would not let them lay a finger on you. . . . So long as you're here and in my charge, Gentlemen, you must follow my orders. . . .

EVACUEE: That's right! The army's here! We've got the army!

DOCTOR: Good thinking, lads. (*To the* NURSE.) How are the patients?

NURSE: Well, that one says ever since we bandaged him up, he's hurting terribly.

DOCTOR: Hm, so long as it hurts he's fine. If the treatment doesn't hurt, then it's not working. . . . And the others? . . .

NURSE: Well, that child over there is not in very good shape at all. . . .

DOCTOR: Hm, that won't do. . . . We'll move him to Headquarters in the morning. . . . She was a fool to board the train with a child in that condition. . . .

NURSE: Is there anything we can do for her right now? . . .

DOCTOR: It's too late. . . . (*The cries of an* EVACUEE *can be heard.*) There's still time before morning. Don't worry, lads. Get some rest. . . . You mustn't make a fuss. . . .

NURSE: Relax, everyone, and get some rest. . . . You mustn't cry there. . . . Your child will be fine. . . . We're taking her to the hospital first thing in the morning. . . . So sleep till morning comes. . . . The rest of you too, get some sleep. . . .

(*The* EVACUEES *all return to their places and lie down. The sound of the wind whipping the tent can be heard and, far off, the barking of a dog. Then the sound of a marching line of soldiers.*)

DOCTOR: I'll be at Headquarters. Let me know if there's anything that needs doing. You mustn't give the patients anything to worry about. . . . And don't let them have their way. . . . Do you understand?

NURSE: Yes, sir. I understand.

(*The* DOCTOR *leaves the tent, his saber making a rattling noise. The* NURSE *silently makes her way among the lines of sleeping patients. At the back of the tent, an* ATTENDANT *begins to nod off. Two, three barks of a dog.*

—A longish pause. A group of VIGILANTES *enter the tent. They are dressed in a variety of costumes, some in the uniform of reservists, others in old-fashioned tabards, some wearing bandannas, and still others in school uniforms. The one in command is wearing armor and brandishing a sword. They all carry some kind of weapon: a spear or sword or saber.*)

ARMOR (*Gazing around inside the tent*): Here?

TABARD: Yeah, here. . . . This was the place. . . . Come on in, everyone.

ARMOR: Bring the lantern, bring the lantern.

BANDANNA (*Enters the tent holding the lantern*): Where is he?
STUDENT: Be careful. He might be carrying a bomb.
RESERVIST: You think a bomb or two is going to make me shit my pants?
ARMOR: Hush! . . . Nurse, good evening!
NURSE: What do you want? . . . You can't come in here. . . . What on earth is going on here?
ARMOR: Actually, nurse, we're looking for somebody. If you'd be so kind, let us in the tent. . . .
NURSE: I can't allow it. The patients are asleep. . . .
BANDANNA: Surely you don't have to say no to everything we ask. . . . Come on, let's go in and have a look. . . .
NURSE (*Her lips trembling*): You mustn't! . . . I forbid it!
ARMOR: The fact is, nurse, there's a Korean bastard hiding out here. . . . Somebody saw him get off the train. . . . For the sake of the fatherland, we have to kill the Koreans. . . .
TABARD: That's right! For the fatherland! . . . For the peace of our citizens! . . .
RESERVIST: That's right! For the peace of our citizens! . . .
BANDANNA: Quit your muttering and get in there, look for him! . . . Get the bastard! . . .

(*The* VIGILANTES *barge among the patients, shining the lantern in their faces. Ashen faced, the* NURSE *follows after them, looking pale.*

One of the VIGILANTES *stands over a man who is squatting like a puppy behind the* OLD MAN *and the* YOUTH.)

BANDANNA: Here he is! . . . We've got him! . . . Bring the lantern over! . . . Look at his face! . . .
MAN (*Apparently a laborer in his mid-twenties*): I haven't done anything!
STUDENT (*Imitating him*): I haven't done anything! . . .
TABARD: Get him!
ARMOR: Don't rough him up. . . . I'll interrogate him. . . . Hey, dog! You're a Korean, aren't you? Lying to us won't get you anywhere, you know. . . .
MAN: I'm Japanese. . . . What are you doing?
STUDENT: "I'm Japanese!" . . . Would any Japanese ever say that?
ARMOR: Quiet! . . . What's your name?
MAN: Kitamura Yoshio. . . .

(*The* VIGILANTES *laugh.*)

ARMOR: Hm! Kitamura Yoshio, eh? . . . How old are you?
MAN: Twenty-four.
ARMOR: So, what year were you born?[1]
MAN (*Nonplussed*): I . . . er . . . I . . .

(*The* VIGILANTES *all laugh.*)

1. A trick question to catch out a foreigner: a Japanese would readily answer the reign year (*nengō*) in which he was born—in this case, Meiji 32 (1899).

YOUTH (*Suddenly standing*): Stop this! On what authority are you asking these questions? Who gave you the authority to do this?

OLD MAN (*Flustered*): Stop this! . . . Please, stop! . . .

ARMOR (*Looking at the* YOUTH): Who the hell are you?

YOUTH (*Quietly*): I'm a human being. . . .

ARMOR: Of course, you're human. . . . I'm not asking whether you're man or beast. I'm asking you what kind of man you are?

(*The* VIGILANTES *thrust out their lanterns at the* YOUTH*'s face and mutter among themselves.*)

YOUTH: I'm a student. . . . And who are you, to come barging into a tent of evacuees and rough people up at this hour of the night?

ARMOR: Rough people up? Have we roughed anyone up?

YOUTH: If that isn't roughing people up, then what is? Barging into a tent where evacuees are being treated, disturbing their sleep asking for identification. What right have you to ask where people are from?

TABARD: Right?

ARMOR: Yeah, we've got a right. . . .

YOUTH: Who gave you the right to do this? . . . As far as I'm aware, no one but the army and the police have such a right. . . .

OLD MAN: For heaven's sake, be quiet, man! Talk it over later—I'm sure they'll understand.

RESERVIST: You've got a lot of nerve asking us. Our authority comes from the most reliable of sources. Why, even the prefectural police have given us their stamp of approval.

ARMOR: Besides, we're not going to let a few little laws get in our way. . . . What I'm saying is, we operate under the higher dictates of our loyalty to the state.

YOUTH (*Laughing*): Ha! The state? The state exists somewhere outside the rule of law? . . . Now, isn't that interesting! So, what is this state you're talking about?

BANDANNA: Who is this upstart? . . . You've got no business spouting off here, so shut your trap! . . . We're not going to put up with any nonsense out of you! (*Thrusts his spear at him.*)

YOUTH:

No business, you say? Oh, yes, I do,
You're the ones who have no business here,
We've got the army, we've got police.
Look at you all!
In your armor, tabards, *judo-gi* . . .
Don't you have anything better to wear?
(*The* YOUTH *looks at the* MAN.)
Come, stand up tall.
Stand up, my man,

Maybe you're right,
Maybe this man is Korean,
But the Koreans aren't your enemy.
Japanese, Japanese, Japanese,
What have the Japanese done to you?
Who have made the Japanese suffer?
Not the Koreans, but the Japanese themselves!
It's a simple fact—can't you fellows understand?
(*The* YOUTH *takes the* KOREAN*'s hand and lays his arm on his shoulder as if to protect him.*)
Look at this man!
He's a human being.
Look on his face!
Could he have killed innocent people?
Or poisoned your wells?
This man has enemies too,
But he doesn't hate you.
You all understand nothing.
You know nothing,
Nor do you even try.
Your comrades took his friends,
Men without sin, who bore no arms,
Men as obedient and innocent as leaves,
Your comrades cut them down without reason, killed them!
Look at this man!
What this man now has,
The only thing nature ever gave him,
Is his life.
Here is your true human being!
And who the hell are you?
All you fellows have
Are dead, moldering morals.
Your armor, that tabard,
Might have had some value as antiques.
But what good are they for a living human being?
If there's any blood coursing in those hearts of yours,
Then you should be wearing your own clothing!
Take off that armor!
Take off that jacket!
You're all marionettes with no life of your own!
Bloated corpses!

Mummies!

Skeletons!

BANDANNA: Japanese traitor!

TABARD: Fanatic!

STUDENT: Enemy of the state!

ARMOR: Get them both!

OLD MAN: Stop it, please! I'll take responsibility for this. . . . Please, you really must apologize to them all. . . . This is outrageous. . . .

(*The* EVACUEES *run around inside the tent. The* WOMEN EVACUEES *weep.*)

NURSE (*To the* EVACUEES): Everyone, please leave the tent this minute! You mustn't hurt anyone!

YOUTH (*To the* KOREAN):

Come, my friend, take my hand,
If you're to be killed, then I'll die too!
Oh Death!
How many hundreds, how many thousands,
In hundreds and thousands of years,
Have been slaughtered for their beloved countrymen?
We weren't born to fawn and
Toady to our stupid compatriots,
We were born to struggle and to die!
For the sake of righteousness, for friendship,
We will die! . . .

(*The* VIGILANTES *begin to move about violently. Brandishing their weapons they press in on the two from both sides. Holding aloft his sword,* ARMOR *faces the* YOUTH; TABARD *faces the* KOREAN, *with the* OTHERS *closing in on either side.*)

YOUTH (*Speaking quietly but with force; this must not be confused with the notion of heroism*):

Behold a new mystery!
From strength and friendship
A new mystery gives birth
To the founding of a new race of men!
Rise up and wash away
The dead and ugly mold you hide!
Tear off your mask
Your false, contemptible ancestor worship,
Your heroism,
Your racism,
And dance the dance of hideous skeletons!
Wait, orchestra!
You hideous skeletons,

Turn to stone!

Turn to stone,

You hideous skeletons!

Hideous skeletons,

Turn to stone!

(*With his sword still held aloft,* ARMOR *turns to stone.* TABARD *similarly freezes, sword held high.* BANDANNA *freezes with his spear thrust out.* STUDENT *freezes, holding his bamboo spear.* OTHER VIGILANTES *all turn to stone. The* DOCTOR, *just about to enter the tent, similarly turns to stone.*)

YOUTH: Dance, skeletons!

(*A sudden blackout puts the tent into darkness. A phosphorescent light illuminates the inside of the tent, revealing ten* SKELETONS *standing in the same attitude as the* VIGILANTES *previously.* [Note: *The* SKELETONS *may be played by the same actors, who can do a quick change of costume.*])

YOUTH: Orchestra! Strike up a waltz for these skeletons! . . .

(*The* TEN SKELETONS *begin to dance. Together with the* OLD MAN *and the* KOREAN, *the* YOUTH *stands by, watching.*)

YOUTH: A "death fantasia" to comfort the blameless ones, those who died before us . . .

(*The* TEN SKELETONS *dance a fantasia. Two or three* SKELETONS *begin to weaken. . . . Suddenly, on either side of the* YOUTH *is heard sharp laughter.*)

YOUTH:

Oh, dead ones,

How right it is for you to laugh!

Orchestra!

A round dance to bid farewell . . .

To you hideous skeletons.

Dance and dance till you fade away!

(*The* SKELETONS *begin dancing in a circle faster and faster until the circle is broken and their limbs snap off and fall in pieces to the ground. Sharp laughter. Blackout. The lights slowly come up, vaguely illuminating the tent's interior. The sound of weeping* WOMEN EVACUEES.)

NURSE (*Quietly lifting her head*): Poor thing. . . . But it was meant to be. . . .

CURTAIN

PART II

THE TSUKIJI LITTLE THEATER AND ITS AFTERMATH

Writing from Paris in 1913 and flush with his own fresh encounters with contemporary European theater, the eminent Japanese novelist Shimazaki Tōson (1872–1943) described the excitement he found among those artists, writers, and intellectuals in his generation seeking a new future for Japanese culture in which Japan could join the larger world:

> Just look at the way in which, so long as it promises to be profitable or to help in the development of humanity, our people will not hesitate to recognize the excellence of anything—the passion that the French show toward art, or the philosophy of the Germans, or the Naturalism and the Religion of the Russians or whatever. The fantasies of Maeterlinck, the self-indulgence of D'Annunzio, the labors of Gorky or the cold tears of Chekov—they all touch our young people; they laugh together with them, they sigh together with them. Thus were the dramas of Ibsen greeted; thus was the philosophy of Nietzsche greeted. Some people, observing this, have laughed at our frivolity and lack of clear-cut opinions, but I do not think that is correct. Far from revealing any frivolity and lack of clear-cut opinions among the Japanese people, it is instead proof of their rich endowment of warm sympathy.[1]

1. Shimazaki Tōson, "Waga kokuminsei no ketten," in *Shinkatamachi yori, zenshū* (Tokyo: Chikuma shobō, 1987), 6:8–9. The translation is from William E. Naff, *The Kiso Road: The Life and Times of Shimazaki Tōson* (Honolulu: University of Hawai'i Press, 2011), 384.

The kind of enthusiasm that Tōson identifies did much to propel the various theatrical experiments undertaken in the Taishō period (1912–1926). Ten years after he made these remarks, a defining moment for prewar Japanese theater came on September 1, 1923, when an enormous earthquake destroyed most of the significant performing spaces in Tokyo. And indeed, for significant experimentation in the contemporary Japanese theater during that period, Japan *was* Tokyo. The renewed theatrical efforts that soon followed brought about the establishment of a new framework in which the contemporary Japanese theater could continue to grow. When examining the work of the playwrights active between 1924 and 1945, we must base much of our judgment on the play texts that remain. Although we have reviews, diaries, photographs, set and costume sketches, and the like, we can only imagine the problems, both financial and artistic, that faced the generation trying to create a truly contemporary theater and then move forward.

OSANAI KAORU'S VIEW OF THE THEATER

Perhaps the best way to understand these issues is to examine the declaration by Osanai Kaoru (1881–1928), a kind of manifesto of his views of the state of the theater in 1924. His remarks were composed and published in the context of the construction of the Tsukiji Little Theater (Tsukiji shōgekijō), a thoroughly up-to-date performance space with some five hundred seats and equipment as sophisticated as could be found in Europe at the time. The project was made possible though the enthusiasm and financial support of Hijikata Yoshi (1898–1959), a peer and the son of a millionaire.

Read in retrospect, three of the major issues that Osanai raised in his manifesto reveal more of the range of problems facing the theater than a simple reading of the dramas themselves might suggest, divorced as they are from the context in which they were performed.

Osanai first distinguishes between drama on the page and drama in performance. He undoubtedly is correct when he says that "theaters do not exist for literature," although his own preference was often for "literary" plays by Anton Chekhov and Henrik Ibsen. From the vantage point of today's readers, however, the playwriting skills shown by a number of writers active in this period was gratifyingly high. But performance skills were not as well developed, at least for those plays performed in the *shingeki* repertory. The significance of this issue is perhaps difficult for contemporary theatergoers in the United States to fully comprehend. These days, well-trained acting talent is abundant, but significant playwrights are not. In the Japan of 1924, however, the *shingeki* actors—as several of the writers cited later point out—were often too young, not sufficiently sophisticated, and relatively unskilled in the necessary means needed to deliver their dialogue with appropriate energy and nuance. Performers in kabuki and *shinpa*, with longer performing traditions, were highly skilled at presentational performance, although they often seemed less so when they attempted to perform in the representational mode, in which they faced similar challenges. Nevertheless, some of the experimental performances in various types of contemporary drama by kabuki and *shinpa* actors were well received.

Osanai's second conviction was that his new theater should work for the future of Japanese theater, serving as a kind of "laboratory." In ways that perhaps Osanai did not altogether anticipate, however, the "future" of Japanese contemporary theater fractured over issues important in the larger society and, in particular, over the increasing spread of Marxist thought in the arts of the period. (Here there are certain parallels with Europe during the same period.) Contemporary theater in any culture, must, of necessity, gain authenticity and presence through an ability to reflect, at least in some measure, on issues salient in the surrounding society. In Japan, the political, economic, and social stresses already captured by certain earlier playwrights were now becoming even more apparent.

Part of Osanai's concept of a "laboratory" doubtless led to his decision to produce only imported plays in translation, a policy that continued through his first two seasons. In effect, he wanted to introduce the contemporary theater of the world to Japanese audiences.

Osanai's personal point of reference was the Moscow Art Theater, where he saw performances during his visit to Europe and Russia in 1912/1913. He shared directorial duties with two others, who maintained their own artistic points of view. One, Aoyama Sugisaku (1891–1956), became interested in theater while he was a student at Waseda University and both directed and acted for the company. His acting career, incidentally, extended into the postwar period, and his performances can be seen in such classic Japanese films as Mizoguchi Kenji's *Ugetsu* (1953) and Kurosawa Akira's *Scandal* (1956). Apparently Aoyama's chief interest was in productions of high artistic standards, and he maintained no particular political point of view. Hijikata, the third of the triumvirate, now back from Berlin and, briefly, Moscow, where he witnessed the expressionist experiments of Georg Kaiser, Ernst Toller, and Vsevolod Meyerhold, had in mind quite a different progressive political model. These competing visions of what might constitute a theater relevant to its time brought about the breakup of the company after Osanai's death in 1928 into what might be seen as two competing camps, literary and political.

Not only did the Tsukiji Little Theater company attract aspiring actors and (once Osanai started to stage Japanese plays) playwrights, but several gifted stage designers also began their impressive careers during this period. Itō Kisaku (1899–1967), the elder brother of the actor and director Senda Koreya (Itō Kunio, 1904–1994), designed the stage sets for several of the company's most popular productions, including Maurice Maeterlinck's always popular *Blue Bird*, in 1925, as well as the settings for the first Japanese drama staged by the company in 1926, *En the Ascetic* (*En no gyōja*), by the dramatist and Shakespeare scholar Tsubouchi Shōyō (1859–1935). Itō continued his design work for Senda's Actors' Theater (Haiyūza) troupe and other groups in the postwar period.

Perhaps the single most striking contribution was the design for the 1924 production, directed by Hijikata, of Georg Kaiser's expressionist play *From Morn to Midnight*, created by the artist and playwright Murayama Tomoyoshi, whose work is discussed later in

OSANAI KAORU: FOR WHAT DOES THE TSUKIJI SHŌGEKIJŌ [LITTLE THEATER] EXIST?

FOR DRAMA

Tsukiji Shōgekijō, like all other theaters, exists for drama. Tsukiji Shōgekijō exists for drama. It does not exist for plays.

Plays are literature. Literature has its own organs—newspapers, magazines, books—things that are printed.

Theaters do not exist for literature.

The best place to appreciate plays—literature—is a quiet study.

Theaters are organizations which present drama.

Theaters are not places where plays are introduced.

Tsukiji Shōgekijō will look for plays to benefit drama. It will not look for plays to benefit plays.

Tsukiji Shōgekijō earnestly hopes to present something that has value as drama. As regards the value of the plays which Tsukiji Shōgekijō will use, we will leave this to the literary critics to determine.

The value of Tsukiji Shōgekijō will be the value of the drama it presents.

It will not be the value of the plays it uses.

FOR THE FUTURE

Tsukiji Shōgekijō exists for the future.

For future playwrights, for future directors, for future actors—for future Japanese drama.

Tsukiji Shōgekijō does not exist for the plays it is using now, for the directors who are engaged in their work now, for the actors who are treading the boards now—it is not for us that it exists.

It exists for those who come after us. If it does not exist for us, it is not us as we are now but as we shall be in the future.

The reason for Tsukiji Shōgekijō using only Western plays for a certain period is not a love of novelty. It is not adulation of the West. It is not despair of Japanese plays.

Tsukiji Shōgekijō is working hard to create a future dramatic art for future Japanese plays.

The problems of presentation in present-day Japanese plays—in particular, those of established playwrights—can be solved by the training in pictorial technique associated with kabuki and *shinpa*. The proof of this is surely in the fact that kabuki and *shinpa* actors who have a smattering of the new knowledge to perform such plays without much difficulty and are even achieving great success.

The future Japanese plays for which we are waiting and hoping must contain problems beyond the scope of kabuki and *shinpa*.

For the sake of these future plays we must develop our new dramatic art.

Let kabuki tradition remain kabuki tradition.

Let *shinpa* tradition remain *shinpa* tradition.

Let the inheritors of their traditions remain such.

The mission of the Tsukiji Shōgekijō lies completely apart from these traditions.

In order to set ourselves apart we must acquire a deep knowledge of these traditions.

In this sense we will never neglect the study of kabuki or the investigation of *shinpa*.

This is our path at the present time.

There may be those who cannot agree with it—this is inevitable.

We will have our work observed only by those who can.

We exist for the future.

Tsukiji Shōgekijō does not exist for the Tsukiji Shōgekijō of the present.

It exists for the Tsukiji Shōgekijō of the future.

FOR THE PEOPLE

Tsukiji Shōgekijō does not exist for *litterateurs*. It does not exist for the "literary world." It does not exist for the privileged classes.

Tsukiji Shōgekijō exists for all ordinary people for whom drama is as necessary as food. It exists to make ordinary people happy, to give them strength, to instill them with life.

Tsukiji Shōgekijō is undoubtedly a study center for us.

But this is said only in reference to us, not in reference to the general public.

(Every kind of theater serves as a study center for those who work in it. If it does not, it is no true theater.)

For the general public, Tsukiji Shōgekijō will above all be a center where drama is presented and performed.

Tsukiji Shōgekijō will be a "little theater" that welcomes all ordinary people.

Tsukiji Shōgekijō is not isolated in the Japanese theater world. It stands in opposition to the Imperial Theater, Kabukiza, Hongōza, and Shōchikuza.

FROM BRIAN POWELL, "JAPAN'S FIRST MODERN THEATER: THE TSUKIJI SHŌGEKIJŌ AND ITS COMPANY, 1924–26," *MONUMENTA NIPPONICA* 30, NO. 1 (1975): 69–85.

this book. Often cited as the first constructivist stage design in the history of Japanese theater, the set provides vivid angular images that, even in photographs, provide striking evidence of a whole new kind of abstract stage space.

Finally, in his manifesto, Osanai defines his putative audience. His theater should not perform for the literary world or for the privileged classes but should exist "for all ordinary people for whom drama is as necessary as food." This was perhaps the most difficult task that he assigned his troupe. At that time, there certainly were popular audiences in Japan, but their loyalties were to kabuki, *shinpa*, and films. In contrast, the Tsukiji audiences were largely drawn from the intelligentsia and increasingly from the progressive intelligentsia, who were enthralled with the efforts of the Japanese stage to join the larger world community dedicated to a contemporary, committed theater. But more general audiences would not follow them in any large measure until after World War II, and then in a considerably different context.

INFLUENCES ON THE JAPANESE THEATER

For a committed intellectual and playwright like Akita Ujaku (1883–1962), the opening of the Tsukiji Little Theater was an epoch-making event. Although many shared his view, few of them could be categorized as "ordinary people." Furthermore, many who were familiar with these plays knew them from the printed page. Most of the plays in part II were written for publication in high-quality journals, rather than composed for immediate production. In that sense, their connection to the literary world remained very close.

In many important ways, then, the developments in the theater of this period can be categorized as various responses to Osanai's challenges.

The Tsukiji Little Theater was born amid a larger array of performances available in Tokyo, Osaka, and elsewhere. From an examination of the play texts alone, it immediately is clear that all forms of theater during this period were heavily influenced, either directly or indirectly, by European models. In the same way, Japanese painters during the period chose either the medium of *yōga* (Western style) or *Nihonga* (Japanese style) for their work, yet both were influenced by the powerful example of contemporary Western art and its long heritage. Both kabuki and *shinpa* began to incorporate attempts at psychological depth, and, indeed, some kabuki performers themselves began to experiment with newer dramatic forms. One famous instance was the hugely successful performance of Ichikawa Ennosuke II (1888–1963) in Kikuchi Kan's *Father Returns*, discussed in part I. Ennosuke had traveled to Europe and the United States in 1919, which inspired him to extend his skills beyond the normal range of the kabuki traditions.

An expansion of the dramatic range of *shinpa* can also be seen in the work of a playwright like Masamune Hakuchō (1879–1962). Hakuchō, a friend of Osanai and a highly respected literary critic and novelist, set out to look more closely at his society, and without undue sentimentality. To the familiar elements of melodrama, inherited partly from

AKITA UJAKU

From the darkness, the thick and heavy darkness, comes flickering up in a flash the production at the Tsukiji Little Theater of Reinhardt Goering's *A Sea Battle* (*Seeschlacht*); and the joy with which we witness this performance is much like the excitement we felt at the moment when the Free Theater presented Ibsen's *John Gabriel Borkman*. Our lives, both during that period when *Borkman* was produced and now, when *A Sea Battle* has been staged, have received—at least so far as I am concerned—a powerful inspiration. The period during which *Borkman* was performed represents the moment when naturalism was imported onto the Japanese stage, while *A Sea Battle* marks the occasion when expressionism came to our stage, and at precisely the time when our youthful artistic circles reached a standstill, a moment when a call habitually goes out to signal our craving for a new subjectivity. If we think even of the changes that have come to us young people since that earlier period some ten years ago or more, the pent-up excitement we now feel, both in terms of history and of our own subjectivity, comes welling up inside us.

AKITA UJAKU, *YOMIURI SHINBUN*, JUNE 19, 1924.

those in Meiji kabuki's traditional domestic dramas, he added a complexity of characterization and an irony of expression that expanded the possibilities of the genre. The influences of Ibsen and August Strindberg are evident.

The dramas written for *shingeki* performance were, of course, intended from the start to be close in spirit to the ideas of nineteenth- and early-twentieth-century European drama. These reference points ranged from Ibsen and Chekhov for those Japanese writers attempting to stress the importance of psychological elements in their dramas to political models, which, for those Japanese writers interested in writing left-wing political drama, were often from such post–World War I political playwrights as Frank Wedekind, Ernst Toller, and Georg Kaiser. (Bertolt Brecht's work, however, except for one production of Senda Koreya's adaptation of *The Threepenny Opera* in 1932, was not widely known in Japan until after World War II.) By the same token, those dramatists, like Kishida Kunio, who were interested in portraying the psychological states of their stage characters, were not altogether devoid of concern for social significance, although these concerns or anxieties were often expressed indirectly.

Enchi Fumiko (1905–1986), who rose to great fame as a novelist after World War II, was active as a playwright in this period and was, in fact, one of the few significant women playwrights with a certain "literary pedigree" to have her work produced at the Tsukiji Little Theater. She, like so many others in her generation, was inspired by her early contact with Osanai, who published a number of her plays in his journal. The play included here, *Restless Night in Late Spring* (*Banshun sōya*), was one of the very last productions staged by the company before Osanai's death. The characters are sketched effectively, and the pull between a dedication to art and a dedication to politics reflects what so many *shingeki* dramatists grappled with in trying to compose dramas portraying the tensions in their contemporary society.

KISHIDA KUNIO AND THE JAPANESE THEATER

Kishida Kunio (1890–1954), who spent several formative years after World War I in France, placed emphasis on the delicacy of gesture and the poetry of language, characteristics, and possibilities of the modern theater that he admired in the work of the great French director Jacques Copeau in Paris. Kishida's plays often deal with the psychic gaps between Japanese and Western culture. Although his lack of direct political involvement was heavily criticized at the time, in retrospect his characters often capture the confusions and hesitations of his generation. At his most eloquent, Kishida produced a snapshot, if not a critique, of his culture. The annual prize for drama in Japan, the Kishida Kunio Award, is named in his honor.

Having seen superior theater in Europe, Kishida was quick to point out that the power of Western theater—at least the styles of theater with which he was familiar from his time in France—rested on the interplay between dialogue and movement. Well known as a drama critic, he often stressed their intertwining purposes. But again, the gap between the potentialities of a text and its successful performance in *shingeki* repertory was not completely closed in Japan until the 1950s and after. Given the long history of stylized acting in the various Japanese traditions, the kind of subtly and suggestive realistic movement sought by Kishida and some of his colleagues remained the greatest challenge for Japanese performers of his generation and was not overcome in his lifetime.

THE LEFT WING AND THE THEATER

Shingeki plays offering a more direct political statement became more and more important, at least until the government's increasing censorship and control halted them before the war. Yet the rise in popularity of such left-wing plays suggests that Osanai's desire for productions for ordinary people remained unfulfilled. Instead, the political plays were productions for and attended by the intelligentsia and dealt with ideas and social critiques rather than a broad spectrum of human emotions. This aspect of the Tsukiji Little Theater's activity was supported and encouraged by Hijikata Yoshi, mentioned earlier,

KISHIDA KUNIO

1929

On their part, the audience may be foolish enough to look only for a "story" on the stage. Their expectations when the curtain goes up are aligned with the idea of "what will happen." Yet the words of the characters and their gestures give rise to a piling up of images resulting in a harmony like that of notes of music. For the lines delivered by the actors are not merely a means to tell the story but are each in itself a theatrical moment.

1934

Compare the relative attraction of words and movement on the stage. Whatever else can be said about movement, it is surely mechanical and simple. The training to master movement is not difficult. Words, however, are on an altogether higher level. The training necessary to speak well on the stage *is* very difficult. Until one masters the act of delivering lines on the stage, one is not really an actor, and the art of speaking remains the most important of an actor's professional necessities.

FROM J. THOMAS RIMER, *TOWARDS A MODERN JAPANESE THEATRE: KISHIDA KUNIO* (PRINCETON, N.J.: PRINCETON UNIVERSITY PRESS, 1974), 136 (1929), 140 (1934).

whose enthusiasm for Vsevolod Meyerhold, Georg Kaiser, Ernst Toller, and others whose work he had seen in Germany and the Soviet Union led him to regard political drama as helping raise the larger society's consciousness of social justice and future political action. In this conviction he had an ally in Senda Koreya, a gifted actor and director who also spent time in Germany from 1927 until 1931. Both became central figures in early postwar theatrical activity and are discussed in more detail in part III.

The history of the left-leaning, sometimes overtly proletarian, theater in prewar Japan is complex, filled with both opportunities and discouragement. After the demise of the Tsukiji Little Theater company, works of varying political intensity were performed in the Tsukiji auditorium and in various small performance spaces in Tokyo. But by the middle of the 1930s, government censorship had nearly ended political theater. By 1940, left-wing theater companies were forced to disband, and the only professional repertory company permitted to perform on a regular basis was the Literary Theater (Bungakuza), founded by Kishida Kunio and two colleagues, which had opened in 1938.

To examine the lasting significance of the left-wing theater within the larger prewar *shingeki* spectrum, we next look at the activities of two of its central figures. The first is

MURAYAMA TOMOYOSHI

Japan's *shingeki* is facing a grave crisis now. I would like to think over the ways in which we can escape from this situation.

Shingeki has its roots in the struggle against concepts of art built on old feudalistic attitudes and capitalistic morality. It has been developed on the basis of liberalism, but such liberalism has not been able to grow properly and remains in a very primitive state in Japan today. Here I include the proletarian theater within the larger *shingeki* movement. As for the proletarian theater movement itself, although it reached the height of prosperity some two years ago after struggling for ten years since its beginnings, it, too, has fallen into a miserable situation, since those involved in the proletarian theater have no ability to adapt themselves to social changes. Their playwrights cannot create plays that truly mirror the present situation of society, and since directors cannot find worthwhile plays to direct, they retreat to the commercial theater. Actors have lost any sense of the proper standards of performance, and the public has abandoned the theater, either by its own volition or by force. The proletarian theater is not going forward; indeed, it is going backward. . . .

How can we overcome this crisis?

First of all, we have to make clear just what kind of theater we should be performing. Even if a new theory of drama is established, this does not mean that effective dramatic works based on that theory can simply spring into being. In general, the nature of the form and content of art is shaped to a great extent by those who make up the audience, who experience the art. At present, the intelligentsia undoubtedly appreciate most of what we produce. Although we cannot expect any organization to enlighten its workers in the near future, what the workers do appreciate is artistically quite different from what we wish to produce. Some say that we should create a highly artistic theater that is firmly based on the principles of socialist realism, a theater that always aims to be appreciated by the workers. But this kind of formula has not succeeded. On the contrary, it has been harmful. . . .

Therefore, I propose that for now, we present a theater that is both progressive and on an artistically high level and that we not try to compromise with the audience. (I am not, to be sure, rejecting workers as an audience. We will heartily welcome them to this kind of theater if they come.) But if we wish to have the general mass of workers as our audience, we must have different repertories and theatrical organizations. We can achieve such results only when we have gained the ability to bring them about. . . .

Therefore, I can think of only one solution: we must dissolve all the *shingeki* companies and unite them in one professional company. This company is not to be under the thumb of any capitalist sponsor or to be forced to go from one producer to another, seeking a chance to perform. Any restrictions on theatrical activities, no matter what they are or how small they may be, will destroy the art.

FROM MURAYAMA TOMOYOSHI, "SHINGEKI NO KIKI"
(THE CRISIS OF *SHINGEKI*), *SHINCHŌ*, JULY 1934, 126–31.

the playwright and director Murayama Tomoyoshi (1901–1977). Murayama was a kind of Renaissance man, difficult to categorize, as he was at once a brilliant avant-garde artist, set designer, director, critic, and playwright. He understood many of the anomalies in the theater of his time. Based on his experiences in Germany in 1922 and 1923, he, too, felt the weaknesses in contemporary Japanese performance, and his sharp social sense allowed him to articulate—in some ways more sharply than Kishida did—the problems involved.

In his own plays and theatrical adaptations, Murayama sometimes chose what may have seemed exotic subjects to his well-educated audiences (Catherine the Great, Chinese railway workers, striking factory employees, and the like) in order to manifest his Marxist sympathies. For many theatergoers, his work represented the most eloquent efforts of the proletarian theater in the 1920s and after.

The second central figure is the playwright Kubo Sakae (1901–1958), who was able, in both his plays and his critical writing, to look beyond the merely doctrinaire for a more sophisticated rapprochement between art and politics. His conviction that true social criticism must come from a close observation of society, rather than simply imposing a doctrine on those realities, gives his plays a depth that has helped his work, and his example, to outlive his time.

Finally, from the point of view of readers now, particularly in the United States, certain implicit parallels can be observed concerning the influence of European theater in both New York and Tokyo during this interwar period. The often parochial theatrical world in both countries continually responded to the powerful presence of one wave after another of brilliant European theatrical experiments in playwriting, directing, and acting technique, all three of which eventually helped transform theater in the United States and Japan alike. The crucial difference was that many of the celebrated Europeans who brought about these changes and set these new standards often came to the United States and even brought their troupes for performances in New York and other large cities. A few Japanese intellectuals were able to learn, for example, who the great Austrian director Max Reinhardt was and to see his productions in Berlin or Vienna; New York audiences were able to watch his celebrated production of the play *The Miracle* (1911) in 1924. Many of the great stars, particularly in the English theater, performed regularly in the United States, and with the coming of the Nazis, a number of important figures, including some of the same men and women who were so admired by Hijikata and Senda, found themselves working as exiles in New York, Chicago, and Los Angeles. Even one great director of the Weimar period in Germany, Erwin Piscator, opened an acting school in New York in 1939 and counted among his students Marlon Brando, James Dean, Shelley Winters, and Tony Curtis.

None of this more or less direct fertilization was possible in prewar Japan, however. Besides the language barrier between Europe and Japan was the prohibitive cost of international travel. A few Japanese—Osanai, Hijikata, Murayama, and Senda—managed to visit Europe, but their students and disciples in Tokyo had to depend on their reports

KUBO SAKAE

First, it must be said that the term "socialism," as employed in this "new realism," does not by any means refer to "socialism" in its more expansive meaning. It certainly differs from those theories of a socialistic art suggested by the writings of Marx and Engels. This is because during the period in which they were writing, the kind of socialism that involves the connections between the producers of goods [that have existed in the Soviet Union since 1929] had not as yet come into existence in Japan. . . .

As long as such connections are not yet established, as my friend Moriyama Kei has emphasized, it is clear that the word "socialist" cannot yet be applied to the kind of "realism" currently possible here in Japan, since we have not yet reached that stage in our own evolution. And it is not simply a question of misunderstanding the meaning of the word "socialism" itself. As Gorky remarked, when a certain writer referred to Gogol as a "socialist-style realist," such a comment represented nothing more than the absurd expression of various literary concepts stuck together in an arbitrary fashion. In the Russia of that period of *Dead Souls* and *The Inspector-General*, the characteristics of any real socialism could not as yet have made their appearance. The kind of realism that we know, created under the variety of capitalism in which we now live, is a realism in which censorship prevails, an "XX realism"; so if we want to avoid these blanked-out words, perhaps we should simply say an "anticapitalist" realism. . . .

While among those who support the proletarian theater, there are some who experience a stuffy confusion of concerns over the nature of "realism"; others, in the relatively calm environment created by the so-called Hikōkan dramatists, create works that exhibit a kind of "social realism," which allows these dramatists to discreetly maintain their integrity. Among those who have modestly graced the footlights, such works as Mafune Yutaka's *The Weasel*, Taguchi Takeo's *Kyoto Third Avenue*, Kawaguchi Ichirō's *Apartment 26*, Tanaka Chikao's "*Old Bag*," and Igayama Masashi's *Noise* can be identified here. . . .

This group of young playwrights, in sketching out in their plays the details of episodes from the social life of our times, have now taken a first step in this effort. But they should not be permitted to simply continue on too long in this fashion. This is because a continual repetition of a "preponderance on social issues" will inevitably weaken the deep artistic impression their work should make. Writers, in some sense or other, must now find the means to seek out a still stronger theatricality. Such is the fork in the road that awaits them all.

FROM KUBO SAKAE, "MAYOERU REARIZUMU" (MISGUIDED REALISM), *MIYAKO SHINBUN*, FEBRUARY 20-23, 1935.

in order to absorb, secondhand, some knowledge of the true potential for an authentic modern theater and Japan's place in it.

Osanai spoke of the Tsukiji Little Theater as a "laboratory," which is an adequate description of the activities carried out by these small, brave bands of largely young people dedicated to the theater. There were disappointments, and occasional triumphs, but some of the graduates of this sometimes painful process emerged in the postwar period, still enthusiastic and considerably more resilient.

J. THOMAS RIMER

Masamune Hakuchō, *The Couple Next Door*, Hatanaka, 1924.

THE COUPLE NEXT DOOR

MASAMUNE HAKUCHŌ

TRANSLATED BY JOHN K. GILLESPIE

The Couple Next Door (*Tonari no fūfu*), a three-act play by Masamune Hakuchō (1879–1962) published in 1925, is one of more than twenty dramas that the author composed between 1924 and 1928. Although he had written a few plays before that time, and would write a few more in the early postwar years, this particular period reveals his strong interest in the artistic potential for dramatic situations. This new enthusiasm developed at a time in Hakuchō's career when, over a period of some twenty years, he had already earned a considerable reputation as a critic and a writer of fiction in the naturalist mode, often defined as disguised autobiography, which then was popular with his generation of Japanese writers. In his plays, however, his situations are imagined and, of course, carried out only in the dialogue.

The play was first published in *Chūō kōron* and was first staged in the same year, 1925, by the Shingeki kyōkai (New Theater Society) company, already well known for productions of works by Anton Chekhov and August Strindberg, as well as other plays by Hakuchō. The somewhat melodramatic happenings of the narrative line soon encouraged another production in 1927, this time by *shinpa* performers.

Characters

MIDONO SHŌICHI, twenty-seven, freeloads off the YOSHIMURAS. Unappealing appearance, with a rather menacing look
ISHIKAWA SADAKICHI, about the same age as MIDONO, a delicate-looking writer
YOSHIMURA TORAZŌ, forty-two, plain looking and thin, a market speculator
TAMIKO, thirty, YOSHIMURA's wife, looks older than her age

ACT I

Evening in late October. An overstuffed recliner chair sits on a rather wide veranda of a small country cottage. Stage rear is a room in the cottage from which every decoration has been removed, and the room is empty. MIDONO *steps into the garden, stands near a wooden fence, and appears to look up toward the second floor of the neighboring house.*

MIDONO: Mr. Ishikawa!
ISHIKAWA (*Voice only*): Hey . . . You seem to have been really busy lately.
MIDONO: Yeah, well it's a big mess here. Today I'm really bored. How about dropping over for a visit?
ISHIKAWA: If I won't bother you, I'd be happy to.
MIDONO: Great.
(MIDONO *leaves the wooden fence and returns to the cottage. He gets another chair from inside and brings it out to the veranda.* ISHIKAWA *enters slowly from the path by the garden and looks around affably.*)
ISHIKAWA: Been a while since it's as clear as today.
MIDONO: Yep. Very nice weather. Have a seat. (*Puts his hands on the chair.*)
(ISHIKAWA *steps up onto the veranda and stands there looking into the desolate room.* MIDONO *looks in the opposite direction, into the garden.*)
MIDONO: I've neglected the garden, just left it messy as is. Plucked all the cosmos flowers and gave them to the neighborhood kids. A little riper and the persimmons on the tree out back would have been ready to eat. I was really looking forward to that, but last night, they stole them all. I wasn't vigilant.
ISHIKAWA (*Not paying attention*): Have you finished cleaning up inside?
MIDONO: Yep.
(*The two face each other and sit down.*)
MIDONO: Night before last in that steady drizzle, it was about 2:00 A.M. when we packed up in a great hurry, loaded the truck, and sent it on. It was a little bit like a war. I was completely worn out—slept all day yesterday.

ISHIKAWA: That night I hardly slept, kept getting up, opening the window, checking on all that commotion. I heard Yoshimura's agitated voice now and again. Did his business fail? Is it true?

MIDONO: This time it really looks like it. (*With deep feeling.*) Look, business is business, so you could probably expect such a terrible thing to happen at some point. It was bad for him just now, so he might not be able to rebuild his business. This cottage, too, even though he's been putting on a proud face living here, it's not his. Even this one small house is tangled up in odd circumstances—the ins and outs of his business are so complicated we've got no idea what's going on. What's happening in the family, that's between the two of them, but it's been a strained relationship recently. He's now in double trouble. Like this empty house. It's a joke I'm actually here as a caretaker in a house he doesn't really own, but that may be the mixed-up mental state of someone gone belly up. The land is owned by a liquor store called "Ume-ya," and the house is registered under the name of Sakamoto, a Tōyō Bank director, who's the key guy behind the bankruptcy. On pure speculation, he threw away the bank's money on the market. So Yoshimura then puts me here as watchdog, swindles the transfer fee out of the owner, and apparently schemes to wheedle funds out of Sakamoto on some pretext or other. Well, he schemed for sure. Sakamoto's a crafty guy himself, and when his bank failed, I think he conspired with Yoshimura to minimize his losses by hiding his assets.

ISHIKAWA: What a con man! Even now a year after the bank closed, everything's still up in the air. The local people here are pretty pissed off.

MIDONO (*In a plausibly serious tone*): What the bank did was, of course, inexcusable, but these cunning country folk tend to be easily taken in. Yoshimura often said that. In his own store, he still rips off the bumpkins behind their backs, however shrewd they may be.

ISHIKAWA (*Not really listening closely, he looks back into the empty room*): You've taken away all the plush furniture and things.

MIDONO: Yep. Did it, but it was like I was in a fog. Had to hurry out of fear that the creditors would come tomorrow to take possession. Yoshimura was out of his head. He was on my case like a mad man. With all the rain, the important stuff probably got damaged. (*Suddenly looks at the recliner chair he's sitting on.*) Take a look at this. I begged his wife to leave it. Yesterday, I took an all-day nap right here. These cushions are soft, great for sleeping.

ISHIKAWA (*Finally drawn in by* MIDONO'*s words, looks over at the recliner*): Looks like it. His wife often sat there and read the paper.

MIDONO (*As if making an excuse*): Well, it wasn't just for her. When her husband was here once a week, he'd relax by lying right here and dozing off. My guess is he was thinking up his business tricks. In the first place, even when he's here at Ōiso, he never goes swimming, never takes a walk; god forbid he'd ever read even a single page of a book. Asleep or awake, he's always thinking about money. A real animal.

ISHIKAWA: That's a bit harsh. (*Smiling.*) I hear he often spends time with geisha.

MIDONO: You saying he's obsessed with them? (*With a questioning look.*) Who'd you hear that from?

ISHIKAWA: No one in particular. That's the rumor.

MIDONO: Isn't that just a figment of your imagination? (*Lets slip a knowing laugh.*) Everybody knows that market speculators visit geisha and that geisha commonly sponsor actors. So I'd venture to say there's no need to count on the imaginative power of someone with your good sense. But Ishikawa, the imagination is interesting, don't you think? Nothing at all bad about indulging yourself on an autumn day, lying down on such soft cushions, drifting off.

ISHIKAWA: Absolutely. I myself have wanted this kind of plush recliner.

MIDONO: Aha! A completely stable frame of mind is good, you know. Here, sit down and give it a try.

(MIDONO *stands and has* ISHIKAWA *sit down on the recliner, then sits in the chair where* ISHIKAWA *was sitting.*)

MIDONO: Look, the Yoshimuras left the recliner for me, so you can't bad-mouth them. A market speculator is hardly going to be a virtuous gentleman, but the actual guy's relatively indifferent to women. For the strong desire for money to flourish, the desire for women has to weaken. Or, uh, maybe not. (*Falls into deep thought.*)

ISHIKAWA: So how long are you going to look after the place? Must be lonely being here all by yourself.

MIDONO: No, I've been alone only since yesterday, so I'm not feeling lonely yet. But I'm not going to be here long like this. Got here to Ōiso at the beginning of July, and I've been living off the Yoshimuras for the four months since, so I was thinking that even if his business hadn't failed, I'd lay out my own course of action and get out of here. By the way, Mr. Ishikawa, please listen to this one insider story about him. When I was at your place recently, I saw on your desk something you'd written, called "The Couple Next Door." Let me give you more stuff about them.

ISHIKAWA: What you saw—that's not about this couple here.

MIDONO: Doesn't matter. I'd like you to listen to me. This morning I lay down on this recliner. I was looking at the autumn sky after the rain let up, and a number of interesting thoughts swirled around, even in a dunderhead like me. Say, I just remembered—in packing up all that fine stuff day before yesterday, I spirited away one bottle of wine. Why not open it and drink up, as a kind of listening fee?

(MIDONO *heads inside. Just as* ISHIKAWA *stretches out comfortably on the recliner chair,* YOSHIMURA*'s wife,* TAMIKO, *dressed plainly and looking older than her age, enters. Her simple, crepe clothes appear to have been soiled by the rain.* ISHIKAWA *doesn't notice her at first.*)

TAMIKO: Mr. Ishikawa, did you come for a visit? (*Her tone is warm and charming.*)

(*Surprised,* ISHIKAWA *jumps up and greets her with an embarrassed look.*)

TAMIKO: What nice weather it's become! When I stepped outside, it's even a bit too warm.

(*She steps up onto the veranda, looks silently into the room, and, with pursed lips, is immersed in deep feeling.* MIDONO *returns, carrying the bottle of wine and two cups.*)

MIDONO (*Surprised*): Oh, Missus, is something wrong? Are you alone? (*He speaks quickly.*)

TAMIKO (*Casually*): I suddenly had an errand to do here, so I came alone. I was just thinking, you know, about how exhausting the other night was, and all the baggage we brought home. When we got there, they hardly said they were expecting us when they repossessed everything, just like that. So, as I thought, we should've settled the situation here. How stupid we were!

MIDONO: So you made a fool of yourself.

TAMIKO: Oh, you found a bottle of wine? How nice! I'll have some later. Serve some to Mr. Ishikawa. I'm just going to go in and take a look first.

(TAMIKO *goes inside.* MIDONO *gives a cup to* ISHIKAWA *and pours the wine.*)

MIDONO: With her here, got to restart my thinking of this morning.

ISHIKAWA (*Not listening, sips the wine and puts down his cup*): I need to go. How about dropping by this evening?

MIDONO: Too bad, because I really want you to hear what I was thinking. But OK, I'll bring the bottle over tonight, and we can have a leisurely drink.

(MIDONO *watches* ISHIKAWA *leave through the garden, then pricks up his ears toward the inside of the house, pours himself more wine, drains his cup, and sits down on the recliner. He keeps his attention focused on the interior of the house.* TAMIKO *returns, her attitude more animated than before.*)

TAMIKO: Where's Mr. Ishikawa?

MIDONO: Out of deference to you, he decided to go home.

TAMIKO: Deference? Because he thinks I don't want to be regarded by others as down on my luck? Silly deference. And yet for all that, he seems interested in us. Whenever he comes over, he looks the place up and down. Renting a room alone, as he does, maybe he's envious of this kind of lifestyle or something.

MIDONO: He's even been envious of my situation.

TAMIKO: He's about the same age you are. But he's really quite different physically. It's a pity that in the bloom of youth he has bad lungs. Probably won't live all that long.

MIDONO: Could be. Did you come to look for something important that you forgot?

TAMIKO: That's right.

MIDONO: Did you find it?

TAMIKO: Yes, indeed. I wonder if you could help me with it.

MIDONO: How can I be of any use?

TAMIKO: Unlike the night when we packed up and fled and with you being just a caretaker, you too may find something worth doing for yourself.

MIDONO (*Leaning forward*): What would that be?

TAMIKO: You'll find out later. (*Sits down on the recliner.*) I'm exhausted. Will you treat me to some of that wine? (*Takes off her black* haori *and tosses it aside.*) This was something we really messed up—even my clothing got taken away—this rain-soaked one piece of clothing is all I've got left. The way Yoshimura is down in the dumps is bad enough, but how shabbily dressed I must look to you. I came here not having slept last night, didn't even have a bath, and barely was able even to wash my face.

(*Silently,* MIDONO *steals a glance at* TAMIKO'*s face and pours her some wine. She happily drains her cup.*)

TAMIKO: You're thinking, aren't you, how much my circumstances have changed since the other day and how despicable someone is who's been ruined? . . . I'm too exhausted today to have any troubling thoughts, so I'm not going to toss any puzzles your way or put up any smoke screens. Let me say what's actually on my mind. . . . You haven't understood my feelings all along, but I've specifically prepared for this kind of thing, anticipating it at any moment. (*She appears to be calmly enjoying her own words.*) Yoshimura has, as a matter of course, purchased a geisha's freedom and kept her, but in money matters, he's very shrewd. And people say he's not a guy who any woman can make a fool of and that he's gotten quite conceited about it. But there's something really stupid about him. Clever guys might appear to be clever, but actually it's not so. See, that's why he had to go through this bankruptcy, but I went about tending to my livelihood as always. Whatever reasons there may be, truth be told, I married him for money, so when it ran out, it's only to be expected there'd be a rift in our relationship. Yoshimura lost interest in me long ago, but I haven't been a big impediment to him, and we've kept up appearances and he's gone out of his way not to stir up trouble. I've been a wife in name only. If I left his house, I wouldn't be able to find someone who would take care of me. So if he allows me just to stick around like this, that's to my advantage—it's how I've put up with things till now. (*Suddenly looks up.*) Are you listening to me?

(MIDONO'*s facial expression shows that he is.*)

TAMIKO: I'm not talking just for fun. Please listen closely. . . . It's with the sense that it was an advantage only with my playing around, not being asked to do anything, that I've endured all this up till now as his wife. It's because I'm a weird woman that I think that way—I don't think ordinary wives are like this. . . . Mr. Midono, either way you want to think about it is OK. Now I'm leaving Yoshimura and will stand on my own two feet. How about standing with me? I've got a little money. (*She is quiet for a moment, looking at* MIDONO'*s face as if seeking something.*) Yoshimura's a sharp cookie when it comes to money—he'll even get right into your breast pocket; he well knows the amount of money in my bank account, not to mention my rings and my wardrobe. When it's necessary, he makes me transfer funds for his business use. It makes sense, doesn't it, that it won't do to keep all this hidden from him? But look, I'm pretty remarkable, don't you think? Unbeknown to Yoshimura, I've squirreled away 20,000 or 30,000 yen.

(MIDONO *listens with interest, becoming excited and fixing his gaze on her face when he hears about the amount of money.*)

MIDONO: Where do you have such a large sum of money? (*Reproachfully.*) Because Yoshimura couldn't get hold of 20,000 yen to complete one of his makeshift deals, he's as depressed as if the toy balloons he's kept all this time burst, isn't he? Why wouldn't you give up such an amount of secretly kept money to help your husband in a crisis? First off, if Yoshimura's shop goes bankrupt, wouldn't that really hurt you, too?

TAMIKO (*Unperturbed, though with more intensity*): Are you offended that I'm a woman lacking in wifely affection? Blaming me for that is laughable.... Look, it's not that I didn't think laying out all the money here and now wouldn't make Yoshimura happy, but the moment was a tipping point, and I'm not going back. Are you blaming me for having such deeply rooted feelings?

MIDONO: What's in it for you to become so adamant? You're a married couple, aren't you, not like enemies.

TAMIKO: No, of course, not enemies. Would a mortal enemy buy me things like diamond rings and the most fashionable clothes? (*Falls silent for a moment, then is irritated.*) Probably not. How can I make other people understand what I'm feeling? Maybe if I borrow some of Mr. Ishikawa's intelligence, I could find some good words.

MIDONO: I've never heard your husband say bad things about you.

TAMIKO: Is that so? . . . Well, Yoshimura thinks that with women, you just give them money, so for a woman to run out on him because he's bankrupt—it's only natural that he reaps what he sows. If I'd run out on him last year or the year before when he was sitting pretty, he would have seen it only like one of the cats had disappeared and would've quite routinely picked up another woman with the power of his money. So I've intentionally put up with everything all along, but now he'll finally realize what's what.

MIDONO: That's cruel. Even if you're enemies, kicking him when he's down is cowardly, don't you think?

TAMIKO (*Smiling derisively*): Anyone can say that to maintain a superficial sort of public propriety. Come on, Mr. Midono, what about the sleeping comfort of this soft recliner chair that I coaxed Yoshimura to have especially made? (*Flirting with him.*)

MIDONO (*Losing composure*): Nice and soft, yes. But so what?

TAMIKO: You attack me for being cowardly, but you, a man, you're the real coward. You feign ignorance, but I know the truth. (*Savoring her own words.*) It's clear to me you have no intention of becoming Yoshimura's henchman or trying to pick up on his market speculation. One might think you could work for a company someplace else—you're not a guy who can't work—so why come to my house as a freeloader? Why have you worked here just as an errand boy or caretaker? And why have you come here to Ōiso for these three or four months leisurely whiling away your days? To recuperate from some physical weakness? Some other lie? You're not like Mr. Ishikawa, are you, what with your robust body. I understand only too well what's in your belly.

(MIDONO, *feeling awkward in her presence, hangs his head and says nothing.* TAMIKO *smiles wholeheartedly.*)

TAMIKO: No need to hold back any longer. I'm going to be straight with you. From the start, I disliked you. I had weird feelings about you, so I tried to badger Yoshimura into getting rid of you. Among the various men going in and out of the house, you were the only one not stuck on himself. Once I knew you wanted to be on my side, I felt this odd attraction to you. It's the first time in my life I'd met someone like you, so I feel I can confide in you even what's locked in my heart of hearts. If you can disparage what I've been saying, then I've missed the mark with you.

MIDONO: Your line of reasoning can't be helped, but there's no way I can dishonor this man who usually helped me. (*Enunciating deliberately, with pauses.*)

TAMIKO (*Unexpectedly angry*): So does that mean you'll let Yoshimura know what I've been sharing with you? You going to tell him I've got money stashed away?

MIDONO: Not at all, I have no desire to tell him such unnecessary stuff. I'm not sympathetic enough to tell a nasty guy, who'd extort a moving fee from a landlord and homeowner, about the whereabouts of money he could grab. (*Gathering more confidence, he raises his eyes, heretofore averted, to look directly at* TAMIKO.)

TAMIKO: Unsympathetic, maybe, but you're afraid of him, of the flat-broke Yoshimura. . . .

MIDONO: You're the one I've gotten uneasy about.

TAMIKO: You think that would happen because you got mixed up with me? (*Suddenly laughs.*) That's real funny. Haven't you been on my side all along? Even assuming I'm a bad person, you listened to my requests, you lent me strength, and it wasn't like an imposition for you. It doesn't stand to reason that ordinary people would suddenly reject you. And now you're under orders to take on a role that goes against your nature and hurts your reputation. In religiously sticking to those orders, aren't you a miserable caretaker here? Or else maybe in a strange way you were thinking about dealing with me as my ally. Just because I've left Yoshimura and become free doesn't mean I'd try to tempt you. Make no mistake about that, please; it was just an innocent feeling to try to connect to you. Leaving even a man like Yoshimura is, for a woman, somehow like being at loose ends.

(*Speaking in honeyed tones unbefitting her age, she puts her whole body into flirtatious mode.* MIDONO, *still with his bad thoughts, averts his eyes.*)

MIDONO: . . . Anyway, are you putting this large sum of money you've hidden from your husband in a bank or something?

TAMIKO (*Shakes her head*): With Yoshimura, you put your money in a bank, but it won't always stay secret. The guy can even sniff out the smell of bills in the house. I spent none of the money I received from him on things like dressing up and looking nice and generously scattering it among close friends. He well knows that.

MIDONO (*His curiosity piqued*): Well, then, Missus, how did you raise such a big sum, and where are you keeping it?

TAMIKO: "Big sum, big sum"—you even appear shocked at amounts of 20,000 or 30,000 yen. Couldn't that make you rich in the future?

MIDONO: Taking my future so rashly to such lengths would get me into trouble. . . . For your husband, wasn't 20,000 yen the amount that would decide whether his shop would sink or swim?

TAMIKO: For me, that sum of money is the basis of my life. . . . That's why I wouldn't carelessly reveal its whereabouts to someone I can't trust and who won't listen to my requests. (*She sleepily appears to notice* MIDONO*'s passionate attitude.*) I'm so exhausted, I can hardly keep from falling asleep right this minute. How about if I nap here on the recliner? Meanwhile, can you please order some tasty items from the Praying Dragon Pavilion so I can eat as soon as I wake up? The wine's made me sleepy, can't stay awake for love nor money.

(*She stretches out on the recliner, puts her handkerchief to her face, and closes her eyes.* MIDONO *approaches her.*)

MIDONO: Where in Tokyo is Mr. Yoshimura?

TAMIKO: Where? Except for his mistress's place, he's got nowhere to stay. She's probably been trying to repay him for his kindness in feeding her up till now. Good for her! (*Speaking in a sleepy voice.*)

MIDONO: And you're OK with that and can just fall asleep? And the 20,000 yen, it's all right for you to have that much money?

TAMIKO: Wouldn't that be bad enough, you yelling this and that about the 20,000 yen, but what if a thief or some debt collector overheard you saying this? (*Appears to fall asleep.*)

(*At that point, a voice announcing "telegram" is heard through the front gate.* MIDONO *responds and disappears into the garden.*)

TELEGRAM MESSENGER'S VOICE: Is Itō Tamiko here?

MIDONO'S VOICE: Itō Tamiko? Haven't you got the wrong house? . . . Oh, right! It's care of Yoshimura. Right here, right here.

(MIDONO *returns, eyeing the telegram.*)

MIDONO: Missus, it's a telegram. (*He says it again. When* TAMIKO *does not open her eyes, he shakes her shoulder.*) Missus, a telegram has arrived.

TAMIKO (*Still lying down, in a drowsy voice*): Who from? Can you read it, please? . . . Isn't it from Sawai?

MIDONO (*Cuts open the telegram envelope*): It says, "Come back now. I'm waiting at the usual place. Umeura." And it's addressed to Itō Tamiko.

TAMIKO: Umeura? Hm . . . I understand. Thanks.

MIDONO (*Stands beside the recliner*): So does that mean you'll go back to Tokyo now?

TAMIKO: I'm not sure. (*Falls back asleep.*)

MIDONO: Who's this person Umeura? It's a name I've never heard.

TAMIKO: Really? I'll introduce you, and you can see for yourself. He's not important.

MIDONO: Missus, have you already given up Yoshimura's family name?

TAMIKO: . . . That's why I'm no longer "Missus."

MIDONO (*Changing his mind*): Let me order some food. No need to answer the telegram?

(TAMIKO *falls asleep without responding.* MIDONO *sits down in the other chair and stares fixedly at the telegram. Finally tossing it aside, he steps into the garden and disappears. The silence is broken by the sounds of cars and horse-drawn carts. The sliding paper doors in the rear open. A remarkably haggard-looking* YOSHIMURA *enters, wearing a suit and a felt hat tilted at an angle. He virtually collapses into the chair where* MIDONO *had been sitting. After a few moments, he sees the sleeping* TAMIKO. *Finally, he gets up and shakes her. She doesn't awaken right away, so he shakes her harder. Opening her eyes slightly,* TAMIKO *looks at* YOSHIMURA *as though in a dream and listlessly wakes up.*)

TAMIKO: Sleeping so soundly. (*Grouchily.*) —What're you doing here?

YOSHIMURA: I also came home to Ōiso to sleep. Not a wink of sleep the last two nights running.

TAMIKO: Well, relax over there. Drink some wine.

YOSHIMURA (*Sees the wine bottle for the first time*): This is good stuff to have. (*Pours wine into a glass and drains it.*) When did you get here?

TAMIKO (*Shaking off her sleepiness*): Just got here. . . . You followed after me, right?

YOSHIMURA: Not so. After leaving you yesterday morning, I was running around here and there settling things, felt I was stripped stark naked, and determined to start doing some kind of small operation. I'm so totally worn out that I suddenly decided to come here and get some sleep. . . . Maybe it's my long-standing nervous exhaustion acting up, so no way I could sleep in a noisy place like Tokyo. Couldn't sleep on the train, either.

TAMIKO: But don't you have a home in Tokyo where you can relax? I don't have a place like that anywhere where I can relax and sleep.

YOSHIMURA: Nor do I have a place where I can relax and sleep.

TAMIKO (*Sarcastically*): What about that splendid second home in Takasago?

YOSHIMURA (*Appears not to hear her sarcasm*): With all the shit that's going on, it's like she's some other person. (*Without strength.*) If I could've held on for two more days, I wouldn't have ended up all exposed like this. . . . Yesterday and today, for two straight days, the market went sky high. This time, especially now, I realize destiny's finally abandoned me.

TAMIKO (*Unimpressed*): She won't let you get near her at Takasago? Is she so cold-hearted? (*Spoken as though thinking aloud.*)

YOSHIMURA: That's not the case, but please don't talk about her now. Here recently, my head's been swirling with all sorts of problems, and everything's happened all at once. Got wrapped up in a major failure, a lost cause, so I gave up on her. So for the time being I thought I'd slip in here. You planned to be here, too, didn't you? (*Speaks affectionately.*)

TAMIKO (*With a disgusted expression*): I'm planning to head back to Tokyo tonight. You're going to stash yourself here for the time being? . . . Uh, that's strange. I don't get it. Yesterday didn't I lay everything out with you and decide that I was going to take the opportunity to follow my own path? They took away all the clothes you'd had made for me, so I, too, am now stripped naked. And for me to be around is just to be in the way, definitely an annoyance for you, so, as I said yesterday, please limit it to this and pay no more attention to me. . . . Because I wouldn't even have dreamed of seeing you here today.

YOSHIMURA: What you were saying yesterday was just in desperation. To leave me at your age can't be a good thing. As you were saying not too long ago, if we're mismatched, even that's OK. Continuing the mismatched marriage for life is, bottom line, much better for you.

TAMIKO (*Swiping at a horsefly or mosquito*): I've had enough of your fake kindness. You shut me up in this kind of place while you were doing your own thing in Tokyo, but from now on things won't go as you want. The woman in Takasago and your Tokyo friends don't think much of you, so why've you tailed after me all the way here? (*Speaking scornfully.*) . . . You're totally spineless, you know.

YOSHIMURA (*In a commanding tone*): This is my house. What's the matter with me coming to my own house?

TAMIKO: What! This is your house? That sort of loose talk won't work with me.

YOSHIMURA (*Laughs cheerlessly*): Oh, right. Neither one of us has a house. . . . (*Suddenly his tired eyes brighten.*) But you're still listed in my family registry. For sure we're still nominally husband and wife.

TAMIKO (*Suddenly feeling weird*): So what? Are you going to make me your property for good on some legal pretext? So whenever you want, you just crawl under the law even so far as to take someone else's things, and then you go on with your bullying under the pretext of law. You're blocked in on all sides, so you've seized me as a last resort to see if you can squeeze any more money out of me. (*Using a deliberately joking tone.*)

YOSHIMURA: It's as you imagine. Whether I cut off your hands or slice off your ears, if your body parts can bring in money, that's what I want. . . . I'm dead serious. . . . I wanted to drink with Midono, and I've come to Ōiso to get a solid night's sleep. I didn't expect to run into you. Even with our ill-starred marriage, we can't split completely. I groundlessly suspected that you were somewhere in Tokyo, taking off those wet clothes, wiping off your smudged face, and applying makeup, but in fact, when we parted yesterday, you came here as is. It's totally unexpected. (*Stares at her as though surprised.*)

TAMIKO (*Glaring at him*): I came here only because I wanted a place where I could sleep without any worries. . . . I was on the verge of getting some long-awaited, uninterrupted sleep, so I'm pretty pissed that you awakened me just as I was nodding off. (*As though talking to herself, she closes her eyes and lays down her head.*)

YOSHIMURA: If you're sleepy, go ahead and make yourself comfortable and go to sleep. I can't keep my eyes open any longer either. . . . We'll get to the important stuff after sleeping.

(YOSHIMURA *lies down and closes his eyes but opens them slightly two or three times in fits and starts, then closes them again, assured that she is still there.* TAMIKO, *too, opens her eyes slightly two or three times, then closes them again, checking whether he is there. Finally, both fall into a sound sleep, breathing evenly.* MIDONO *returns. Looking at one, then the other, and seeing how obliviously they are sleeping, he gives a disgusted look and walks between them into the house.*).

ACT II

Same house. TAMIKO*'s former powder room. Seedy and without furniture, like the room in act I. Tatami mats have been pulled up, and the floorboard underneath has been turned over.* MIDONO *lifts his dust-covered body from under the floor, wipes the dust from his face with the palm of his hand, and lets out a big sigh.* YOSHIMURA *enters, reading the telegram.*

YOSHIMURA: What the hell're you doing under the floor? Woke up just now to all this racket and came to check it out.

MIDONO: I'm getting something I lost.

YOSHIMURA: Something you lost? What? (*Peers down.*)

MIDONO (*Flustered*): A silver coin, but it's so dark, I can't make anything out. . . . It's only one ten *sen* coin. Doesn't really matter.

(MIDONO *climbs out and tries to replace the floorboard.* YOSHIMURA *stops him.*)

YOSHIMURA: You dropped money down there? Be serious. This was Tamiko's powder room, and she wouldn't ever let me set foot in here. No doubt there are secrets lurking about. (*Suddenly shows* MIDONO *the telegram.*) Look at this. Just found it stuck to my foot. You must know about this telegram.

MIDONO: Yep. I received it.

YOSHIMURA: And you must know this Umeura guy?

MIDONO: I don't.

YOSHIMURA: Come on, you really don't know him? . . . The reason I had you come here over the summer was to keep an eye out for guys like Umeura. Look, if Tamiko bribed you and you're keeping a straight face about it, you're betraying me. (*Gives him an intimidating look.*)

MIDONO: Absolutely not!

YOSHIMURA (*As if thinking out loud*): But I've found something promising. Put this telegram back where it fell. Also, keep an eye on her and don't let her go back to Tokyo tonight. . . . Even this telegram might be turned into something that makes money.

MIDONO (*Disgruntled*): Keeping an eye on your wife isn't exactly why you got me here to this country cottage. If you're going to give me such a disagreeable job, I'll be outta here and back to Tokyo this very night.

YOSHIMURA (*Restraining his anger*): I'm scraping bottom here, and even you are thinking of leaving me in the lurch. Even though I've had you, a good-for-nothing guy, all this time and fed you and let you do what you want, not so much as a peep of gratitude.

MIDONO (*Unmoved*): I'm not mercenary like the people around you. But you, always into some big deal, for you to suddenly stoop so low, it's really outrageous. (*His voice getting stronger.*) Things like making me monitor your wife, trying to turn that telegram into money, trying to finesse the landlord out of the moving fee—even taking into account your business failures, you're just, at bottom, mean-spirited. . . . Is that the true character of the owner of the Yoshimura store?

YOSHIMURA: You want to think that, go right ahead. I've lost out on a big deal, so I'm into winning some small ones.

MIDONO (*Calming down*): You still have confidence you can win something? You wife has emotionally split from you, so she's got to be watched? I'm . . . (*He hesitates, looking at* YOSHIMURA*'s face.*)

YOSHIMURA: Whether over money or a house, I've also broken off relations recently with a number of people, one person at a time, but being insulted even by the likes of you, well, that just makes it perfect, tops it all off. Insulted even by the freeloading Midono Shōichi. (*As if ridiculing himself.*)

(MIDONO *again tries to replace the floorboard.* YOSHIMURA *looks around the room like a ravenous dog sniffing out food, shrivels up his nose, and looks under the floor. He lets loose with a sneering laugh, as if something's occurred to him.*)

YOSHIMURA: You said you dropped a ten *sen* silver coin, right? . . . (*Eagerly.*) OK, I'll get in there and find it. How about you look, too? Let's hurry while Tamiko's still asleep.

MIDONO: Not worth it. You'll get your clothes dirty.

YOSHIMURA: We might come across something. There may be a vein of gold ore down there someplace. I have this recollection. . . .

(YOSHIMURA *energetically rips up the floorboard.* MIDONO, *making no effort to help, looks on feeling ill at ease.*)

YOSHIMURA: Here recently when Tamiko was cleaning up, she was overly concerned about this room. And she was really touchy about me coming in. Knowing that woman, I wouldn't put it past her to maybe dig a hole down there and squirrel away money. The way she was talking before was a little weird, like she had money in secret. No way a penniless person like her could take on such a confident tone. That's it, got it figured. (*Looks back at* MIDONO.) Give me a hand here. Because if I'm right, we'll dig it up right away. Get over to the rice store nearby and maybe borrow a shovel or a hoe or something.

MIDONO: Let's cut this craziness. (*Regards* YOSHIMURA *uneasily.*)

YOSHIMURA: What's so crazy? (*Getting more and more into it.*) If not for that, the bitch would never have deliberately made the trip today, all the way here to Ōiso.

(YOSHIMURA *disappears under the floor.*)

YOSHIMURA (*From under the floor*): Strange that you were down here before. Weren't you also trying to sniff something out while we were sleeping? Pretty sly.

(*Worried,* MIDONO *unconsciously peers underneath the floor.*)

YOSHIMURA: Something's here! (*Elated.*) Something's for sure buried here. For sure.... Hurry up and get the shovel. Can't dig it up with my bare hands.

MIDONO: Something's really been buried down there? Amazing. When it comes to your greed, there's no matching your sense of smell. Is it putting off the scent of money?

YOSHIMURA: Scent of money, whatever, it's like super smelly. . . . Hey, Midono, stop talking shit. Hurry up and get a shovel and a candle.

(YOSHIMURA *partially emerges, the upper half of his body quite dirty; he breathes with difficulty.*)

MIDONO: If it's true something's there, wouldn't it be better to ask the missus first?

YOSHIMURA (*Wipes the sweat off his forehead with a dirty hand and gives him a threatening look*): That's for only after I've seen what the hell it is. I won't forgive you if you let the cat out of the bag.... Because I've gotten to the point where I can't trust you, don't even take one step away from here. I'll look in the kitchen myself and bring something to use. You keep an eye out here.

(YOSHIMURA *issues the order and leaves. Once he is out of sight,* MIDONO *hurriedly climbs under the floor.* TAMIKO *enters languidly, looking as if she's still half asleep.*)

TAMIKO: Wonder why the floorboards are turned up? (*Talking to herself.*)

(MIDONO *emerges, his upper body dirty.*)

TAMIKO (*Laughing loudly*): What the hell're you doing?

MIDONO (*Not hiding anything*): The boss says he found money, and we're about to dig it up.

TAMIKO: Money? Yoshimura's hiding money away in a place like this? Really? He's hidden money from both me and his creditors before, so maybe he's buried it in such a place as a hedge against falling on hard times. . . . Really incredible. But that's how His Greediness thinks.

MIDONO: That's not it. (*Lowers his voice.*) Didn't you say you had in secret something like tens of thousands of yen? Didn't you hide that money here?

TAMIKO (*Laughs*): When would anyone have put money under the floor? You're out of your head, too.

MIDONO: Maybe you're right. A man like your husband would be hardly likely to do something so stupid. (*Looks around, feeling at a loss.*) But Missus, when you arrived here a while ago, and I, just by chance, peeked into this room, the tatami mats were turned over and the floorboards pulled up.

TAMIKO: Something weird has got hold of you today, same as Yoshimura. This room had a really bad roof leak, so the tatami was turned up some time ago.

MIDONO: Oh.

TAMIKO: You're dizzy with greed, too. (*Anxiously.*) Oh my! You wouldn't tell Yoshimura what we were talking about earlier. I thought you were on my side.

MIDONO: I'm absolutely not saying anything. (*Looks under the floor.*) But something's for sure buried down there.

TAMIKO: You're not saying Yoshimura secretly buried money, are you? . . . So, what is it? Look like money?

(YOSHIMURA *returns with a rusty hoe. Seeing* TAMIKO, *his facial expression says, "Oh, shit!"*)

YOSHIMURA (*Commanding tone*): You give a hand too. . . . We'll talk later. After we dig the treasure up.

(YOSHIMURA *climbs under the floor and digs with the hoe.* MIDONO *helps. Filled with curiosity,* TAMIKO *looks on.*)

YOSHIMURA: OK, we're getting it. (*Quite animated.*) . . . A pot! It's a pot!

MIDONO: It's a pot. A dirty pot. Doesn't look like any money's in there.

YOSHIMURA: Well, wait till you look inside. . . . Here, I'm pulling it out.

(YOSHIMURA *climbs out holding a small, dark-colored pot. The three surround it and gaze at it.*)

YOSHIMURA: Take a look at the secret unmasked.

(*With a side-glance at* TAMIKO, YOSHIMURA *removes the lid. All three together stare into the pot.* MIDONO *laughs. The expression on his face despondent,* YOSHIMURA *keeps his eyes fixed on the pot.* TAMIKO *is seized with blank amazement.*)

MIDONO: Not even one pebble inside.

TAMIKO: Why would this be buried here?

MIDONO: Might be some kind of talisman?

TAMIKO: Well, it's good there's nothing weird inside.

(YOSHIMURA, *bereft of hope, says nothing. He throws the pot to the floor. It rolls around, unbroken.*)

TAMIKO: This was the unmasked secret?

(YOSHIMURA *remains silent.*)

TAMIKO: Did you think there would be some of those small-sized, oval-shaped Edo gold coins or something like that inside? . . . Big man brings a hoe, and you two together take great pains for this? . . . Your braggart face, hasn't it become just like the features of this muddy piece of work? My ears and nose, even defiled as they've been, might be worth something. But you, when your body dissipates, it won't amount to one red cent. (*Laughs.*) More important, you and Midono should really get all the dust off your clothes and wash up. So you don't look so much the worse for wear. (*Makes a funny gesture.*) If people see you, what'll they think?

YOSHIMURA (*Crestfallen, his words lacking strength*): Are you going back to Tokyo alone tonight?

TAMIKO (*Pulling herself together*): Well, nothing else is keeping me here.

YOSHIMURA: Are you going because of the telegram from Umeura?

TAMIKO: Won't work to threaten me with Umeura's name. (YOSHIMURA *points to the telegram, but she remains unperturbed.*) If you think you can use that as a way to threaten me, then better guard it closely and take it to him instead. He just might pay something to take it off your hands.

YOSHIMURA (*Putting on a show of strength*): I'm your husband, see! You're legally my wife and I'm your husband.

TAMIKO (*Not giving in*): You would stand behind the law and talk big to me like that? No matter how much you would try to wield authority over me, you're just a mummified person who used to be called Yoshimura Torazō. You're a ghost. When your stuff was seized from the truck because of your debt, you showed signs of life, but since then, wherever and however you've been lurking about, the life's just drained out of you. Digging under the floor with a rusty hoe, you look like a bag of bones. You look like a ghost tenaciously grasping at money. You might well listen carefully to Mr. Midono or somebody.

YOSHIMURA (*Putting on a show of strength*): Winning or losing is the luck of the draw. You don't understand the heart of a man like me.

TAMIKO: OK then, don't sniff around in this cramped, dirty space underneath the floor, but try finding a big gold mine somewhere. Do that, and even beautiful women will flock around and come on to you. Still and all, as a mummy, you really have lost the ability to catch the scent of money.

YOSHIMURA (*A sneer on his lips, in a weak voice*): Real brilliant, talking like a sage about things anybody knows. How about if I let you in on the bond between husband and wife? Think that you, with that face and shriveled-up body, can tempt other men? You're not what you used to be. You're just an empty husk left over after I sucked the lifeblood out of you. (*Suddenly pulls* MIDONO *by the hand, points at* TAMIKO*'s face, and speaks in a wavering voice.*) Take a close look and tell me about this. Be objective now. . . . Would a man be tempted by this face? Would a man's heart be attracted by this lusterless, leathery skin? Speak up, no holding back. Even if you desert me and walk out right now, I won't object. Give a real answer to what I've asked—to someone I've had a long relationship with. Let's have your unadulterated critique right here in front of me and Tamiko.

(MIDONO *looks away and remains silent.*)

TAMIKO (*Covering her ears with both hands*): OK, try not to regale us with trivial stuff. (*Pauses.*) Since I'm going to leave here, please don't come looking for me. (*Starts to leave but hesitates, as though somehow reluctant to leave.*)

YOSHIMURA (*Imperiously*): Midono, as I asked you before, keep an eye on Tamiko.

MIDONO (*Lifts his head and speaks calmly*): Rather than that, I'd like to excuse myself from the role of caretaker. I'll be returning to Tokyo. Wouldn't it be better for the two of you to live here together? . . . Even if creditors repossess your Tokyo house and even if there'll be no moving fee from here, you won't have to leave here for the time being. I bought lots of food yesterday. If you stay here for the time being, no need to worry about dying from starvation. . . . And the food the missus ordered has already come, so there's enough for the two of you to eat and have a good time. Everything's in the kitchen. I'm also giving back the soft recliner chair you left for me, so you can relax there with peace of mind. . . . (*As if speaking to himself.*) I don't need a moving truck or anything like that. I'll just leave with a bag in my hand.

TAMIKO: Mr. Midono, are you really going? Even though I've begged you to stay?

YOSHIMURA: It'll be sad if you run out on me.

MIDONO: In Tokyo, I might look for and dig up a pot that's not empty. . . . Many thanks for everything.

(MIDONO *says his piece and takes his leave without regrets. Stunned,* YOSHIMURA *and* TAMIKO *watch him in silence.*)

ACT III

Evening the same day. YOSHIMURA *and* TAMIKO *are sitting opposite each other in chairs on the veranda. In the room behind them is a low dining table with the remains of a meal just finished.*

YOSHIMURA: The insects' cries have calmed down, haven't they?

TAMIKO: Your noticing strong and weak insect cries is a bit odd, isn't it?

YOSHIMURA: Maybe so. . . . The moon is bright tonight. Sitting here like this just now, I feel like we're marooned on an island. (*Lazily.*) Pigging out on an empty stomach has worn me out again and made me sleepy. You look worn out, too. You really have to go back tonight, no matter what? We've eaten together and had wine together, so no regrets here. . . . If you're really going home tonight, I'll see you off at the station. It'll be the last time. Probably won't ever see you again.

TAMIKO (*Anxiously*): So, what'll you do now?

YOSHIMURA: What I said earlier.

TAMIKO: So until you settle on a goal, you'll be all alone here? Too bad. Would've been better if Midono had stayed for you. . . .

YOSHIMURA: That jerk, he's been taking you and me for fools. He sees us as scum. I can still see plain as day that look in his eye when he left and turned back to look at us.

TAMIKO: You think he took me for a fool, too? (*Heaving a sigh.*) . . . . The guy's a cocky sort, isn't he, with a face like a pickpocket's.

YOSHIMURA: When I had money, I wasn't arrogant. If only I'd known how arrogant I could've been with the power of money, I would've been so to my heart's content. Now, look, with a guy like Midono, even if you fall on your knees in front of him, imploring him, he wouldn't hear a word you say.

TAMIKO: You poor thing. (*Looks at his face as though feeling sorry for him.*) When I covered my ears, what did Midono say to you?

YOSHIMURA: Nothing really different. But he's also contemptuous of you. It's because he was aware that you'd lost both the power of money to buy him and the youthfulness to entice a man.

TAMIKO (*Losing control of herself*): That's a lie! A lie! The SOB used to come on to me all the time. What's more, he was well aware I had money.

YOSHIMURA: You say Midono came on to you? No bullshit.

TAMIKO: It's not bullshit. The reason he really wanted this recliner is because I always used it. Even more than this chair itself, he yearned for my scent. You didn't know that?

YOSHIMURA (*Gives a forced laugh*): Hard to believe but, if that's the case, whatever.

TAMIKO: You've got a bad habit of constantly circulating groundless suspicions (*Becoming irritated.*) Midono definitely knows that I've got money. He definitely knows that I've got about 20,000 yen.

YOSHIMURA (*Suddenly reinvigorated with surprise and delight*): You have 20,000 yen? Really?

TAMIKO (*She holds her tongue, as if suddenly catching herself*): That doesn't mean the cash is close at hand. I've entrusted it to someone who's putting it where it'll draw good interest.

YOSHIMURA: I see. You may not have the cash at hand, but you must have a certificate or something.

TAMIKO: I'd forgotten that I'd put away the deposit certificate in the bookshelf in my room. Good nobody ripped it off. (*Speaking almost disinterestedly.*)

YOSHIMURA (*With a fixed stare*): Do you have the certificate with you now? How about showing it to me? . . . You were approaching the pros and cons of the interest as a woman. . . .

TAMIKO: Are you going to be happy for me that I kept the money secret?

YOSHIMURA (*Laughs*): Of course.

TAMIKO: . . . (*As though thinking aloud.*) I'm not thinking about making tons of money or being extravagant or boastful, just about living on that money quietly, in the country. (*Looks intently at her husband.*) Both of us are fading physically and we're getting older. . . .

YOSHIMURA (*Losing patience*): Who did you entrust the whole amount to?

TAMIKO (*Casually*): To Mr. Sawai.

YOSHIMURA: Sawai? (*Shakes his whole body.*)

TAMIKO: Didn't you used to say he was the smartest of the sales guys in the store, that he was trustworthy?

YOSHIMURA: However it might've been before, now he's an enemy. He's more or less a member of the gang that did me in.

TAMIKO: I don't know anything about that.

YOSHIMURA: . . . So, you've always been in cahoots with Sawai to steal my property. Didn't you realize at some point that if Sawai failed, I'd succeed, and if I failed, he'd succeed? That destiny has not shone on me and him equally? (*He speaks agitatedly but suddenly swallows his anger.*) However, you totally believed me before when I said Sawai was smart and trustworthy, so maybe it makes sense you'd trust him. . . . Anyway, can you let me see that deposit certificate?

TAMIKO: I've carelessly blurted everything out, so I have no choice. (*Reluctantly, she produces the certificate from the folds of her sash.*) If you're not careful with this, I'll be in trouble. It's important. . . . Here (*Quietly hands it over.*).

YOSHIMURA (*Snatches it away and scrutinizes it with obvious delight*): Anyway, with this, we won't end up starving.

TAMIKO (*Incredulously*): So, you won't blow up at me for entrusting the money in secret to Mr. Sawai?

YOSHIMURA (*Paying her no heed, he speaks as though thinking aloud*): Tomorrow morning I'll have to go to Sawai's place to get as much money as I can squeeze out of him. (*Carefully puts the certificate into his pocket.*) Let me have another glass of wine.

TAMIKO: Amazing. With not so much as a by-your-leave, you would take what is mine?

YOSHIMURA: Even though this was yours, Sawai is not the sort who'd calmly hand it over. Let me handle this. . . . If I could've gotten hold of this even ten days earlier, I wouldn't have fallen into such wretched circumstances. But now it's just fruitless bellyaching, and I'm going to stop yelling at you.

TAMIKO: Then I'm always to be by your side, just merely subsisting like this? (*Adds a brief follow-up.*) I guess there's no other way.

(*Calling out "Mr. Midono,"* ISHIKAWA *enters.*)

TAMIKO (*Seeing him, she speaks in a cheery voice*): Mr. Ishikawa, welcome!

ISHIKAWA (*Approaches and greets* YOSHIMURA): Is Mr. Midono here?

TAMIKO: Midono suddenly decided to return to Tokyo. He probably won't be returning here. (*Moves away from her soft chair.*) Please, do sit down.

ISHIKAWA: No, no, I'm fine here. (*Sits down on the veranda.*) When I saw Mr. Midono earlier in the day, he didn't talk as though he were going to go home so soon. It's odd.

TAMIKO: He's a whimsical guy, you know. I mean, although you befriended him and, thanks to you, he was happy with his opportunity for study, it's quite rude, isn't it, that he didn't say a proper good-bye.

YOSHIMURA (*As if suddenly hitting on something*): That's right, it's perfect that Mr. Ishikawa is doing us the favor of a visit. I'll bring the pot and let's have him take a look. (*Leaves his chair and goes inside.*)

ISHIKAWA: Pot? Is it a pot with some kind of history?

TAMIKO: It's a filthy, worthless pot. Yoshimura seems on edge or something, probably because his business has taken a bad turn. He's thinking of the pot he dug up as if it's a pot of gold and would bring him good fortune in business. So, Mr. Ishikawa, if you would please shore up his confidence by taking a look at the pot and saying something to make him happy. It may turn out to be a really stupid memory, however.

ISHIKAWA: Uh, well . . . I can't give any kind of expert assessment of antiques. But isn't it strange to dig up something like that?

TAMIKO (*Abruptly*): What time is it now?

ISHIKAWA: It just struck seven o'clock.

TAMIKO: It's still quite early, isn't it? I thought the evening was already well under way.

ISHIKAWA: Will you be staying here tonight?

TAMIKO: Well, it wasn't in the plans, but Midono went home, so now there's no caretaker. . . .

(YOSHIMURA *enters carrying the dirty pot.* ISHIKAWA *pays more attention to* YOSHIMURA*'s awkward manner than to the pot.* TAMIKO *also is paying concerned attention only to her husband's manner.*)

YOSHIMURA: This is it. Please take a look and give your assessment. I'd say it's not just an ordinary pot.

ISHIKAWA: Let me have a look.

(*Takes the dirty pot in hand and looks at it, turning it on its side and upside down and tapping on it with his fingertips. From left and right,* YOSHIMURA *and* TAMIKO *look on, as though observing an expert at work.*)

ISHIKAWA: It's from a fairly old period, isn't it. And the shape, too, is interesting.

YOSHIMURA (*Delighted*): It must be something quite valuable. Me, I'm without refinement, totally ignorant, but the shape is interesting. This dent here is good. What was it used for?

TAMIKO (*Also paying close attention*): What was it used for? (*Takes the pot and tries to tap on it as* ISHIKAWA *had done.*) It makes a good sound. Midono's an idiot. An uneducated guy like that looks at this kind of thing, he's got no clue as to its value.

YOSHIMURA: What was it used for? I wonder if maybe it wasn't used for human bones.

TAMIKO: Surely not! . . . Surely something precious was inside.

YOSHIMURA: Something more precious. . . . OK, then, maybe someone's ancestors or descendants put even some of those small-sized, oval-shaped Edo gold coins in there to fall back on if they fell on hard times.

TAMIKO: Strange that there was nothing inside.

YOSHIMURA: Somebody probably took the contents. It's really too bad.

ISHIKAWA (*In deep thought*): Something may have been sealed inside and buried to inflict harm to people, to cast a spell. In ancient Western fairy tales, you find the devil sealed in pots.

YOSHIMURA (*Understanding for the first time*): Right, that's it! Now I understand. Demon or devil, no doubt it was sealed up in here to prevent him from taking revenge on some person. (*Takes the pot and heaves it into the garden.*) After we dug this up and took the lid off, Midono ran out on us. Me and you, we're both wilted, like the wind's got knocked out of our sails.

TAMIKO: Well, I inadvertently showed you something it would've been better if I hadn't. I don't feel now as I did when I came here today.

ISHIKAWA: You've done a regrettable thing. If you didn't like that pot, it would've been better if I could have it and take it away.

YOSHIMURA: Whether the pot looks good or is interesting, please put a stop to this bad karma. (*As he speaks, his eyes take on a look of regret; he scrutinizes the damaged pot and thinks aloud.*) Just looking at it, it has some elegance—would have been better if I'd left the lid on and tried to foist it off on somebody.

TAMIKO: Instead of a pot with bad karma, Mr. Ishikawa, why don't you take this recliner, if you don't have any objection? Since Midono is no longer here, this chair is no longer needed.

ISHIKAWA (*Delighted*): If I could have that, it would be better than anything. Is it all right?

TAMIKO: If I can hand over to you what remains of my life at Ōiso, I'll feel refreshed, like starting over. Besides this, I don't have anything of my own.

YOSHIMURA (*Forces a laugh*): So you'd give the things Midono wanted to Mr. Ishikawa? That's OK with you? You had all kinds of things made for you, and this chair is something you've liked for a long time.

TAMIKO: I no longer have anything now. . . . Mr. Ishikawa, please take this chair right away. . . . It's no longer mine. Because now it's yours. (*Stands up from the recliner and looks down at the clothes she is wearing.*) Except for these, I'm penniless.

YOSHIMURA: Without that recliner chair, there's no place for you to sleep here tonight. You planning to return to Tokyo tonight, after all?

TAMIKO: Either way.

YOSHIMURA: You feel like spending the night, here together with me?

TAMIKO: But I have no money. I have no choice.

YOSHIMURA: So you think if I go back to Tokyo, it's OK for you to go with me?

TAMIKO: I've got no choice. I'm penniless, so there's no other way, is there, than to entrust what's survived—myself—to you?

(ISHIKAWA *remains, uncomfortably looking out at the garden.*)

TAMIKO: Mr. Ishikawa, you must think we're a strange couple.

ISHIKAWA: Not at all, I'm the one who has disturbed you. (*Abruptly stands up.*) I have some urgent writing that I have to finish by tonight, so I should say good-bye.

YOSHIMURA: How industrious you are to be working so late.

TAMIKO: Then, for the recliner, we'll get someone to deliver it later. I'm very happy to have a person like you use it. (*She ends with a flirtatious tone.*)

ISHIKAWA: Receiving it is quite something, so if you don't need it, let me pay an appropriate amount to take it. . . . At any rate, till next time. . . . (*Leaves.*)

YOSHIMURA (*Facing* TAMIKO, *sarcastically*): You'll have him sniff your smell that's embedded in the chair?

TAMIKO: Whatever, that's the way it is. . . . That chair just may be the final resting place of that tuberculosis patient.

YOSHIMURA: You made a lot of picky requests when you had me make that chair, but there's no way you could've thought it'd be used as a deathbed for someone. . . . (*Changes his tone.*) We were interrupted with that disturbance, but isn't Umeura waiting for you to come tonight? It's OK for you to look at that telegram and just toss it aside? (*Speaks as if grilling her.*)

TAMIKO: Mr. Umeura also is expecting my money. I'm broke, wearing clothes soaked with rain, a sickly face—things have come to this. So why would he welcome me?

YOSHIMURA: Then you'll no longer approach the likes of Umeura, but you'll stick with me through thick and thin? You're fickle, can't rely on what you say.

TAMIKO: . . . I've counted for a long time on something I've kept close to me, and now I've carelessly handed over to you something as dear as my life.

YOSHIMURA: I see. Your life is something you've had in your breast pocket and nurtured over a long time. (*Takes the certificate of deposit out and gazes intently at it.*)

TAMIKO: Even though I've handed over things as dear as my very life, instead from you I get no feeling of being given anything more valuable than money. It's discouraging. I'd rather tear up that certificate of deposit right in front of you.

YOSHIMURA (*Quickly puts the certificate of deposit back into his pocket*): Think I'd let you tear this up?

TAMIKO: I won't tear it up. (*Smiles.*) But still, I was just thinking, if it were torn up, wouldn't things you can't buy with money come our way?

YOSHIMURA: What utter foolishness.

TAMIKO: It's really true. (*Suddenly, in a tone of intimacy.*) Whether we stay here or go home, it's up to you. I'm going to comb my hair and wash my face. (*Puts her hand to her hair.*) It's full of dust and must look a sight. (*Murmuring.*)

YOSHIMURA: Sounds good. I'll wash my face too. That character Midono, leaving like that, where's he gotten to by now?

CURTAIN

Murayama Tomoyoshi, *A Nero in Skirts,* directed by Murayama Tomoyoshi, May 1927.

A NERO IN SKIRTS

MURAYAMA TOMOYOSHI

TRANSLATED BY YUKO MATSUKAWA

A *Nero in Skirts* (*Sukāto o haita Nero*), "a puppet play in ten scenes" by Murayama Tomoyoshi (1901–1977), was published in the journal *Engeki shinchō* in May 1927 and was first staged in May 1928 by the Kokoroza (Soul Theater), a short-lived, politically progressive troupe that staged both new kabuki and *shingeki* plays. Murayama directed the production himself. Although allegedly written for puppets, Murayama employed actors for the premiere.

Murayama used various historical and fictional accounts as sources for his text, which underscores his view of the lasciviousness of Catherine the Great (1729–1796) of Russia, whose outrageous conduct he contrasts with that of her common soldiers, who feel solidarity with their supposed enemies.

The subject of Catherine's private life seems to have been a popular subject in the interwar period and afterward, particularly in the United States. The director Joseph von Sternberg directed *The Scarlet Empress* (1934), a lavish film starring Marlene Dietrich that was one of her early American successes, and Mae West wrote and performed in the satirical play *Catherine Was Great*, first produced in New York in 1944 by the legendary Michael Todd. Neither stressed the political and social concerns that Murayama had. In 2008, a highly popular Russian musical yet again took up the subject of Catherine's lurid life.

The Puppets

CATHERINE II's Skirt from Days Gone By
CATHERINE II's Present-Day Skirt
CATHERINE II's Skirt from the Future
CATHERINE II
MADAME DE PROTASOW, head lady-in-waiting
MADAME DE MELLIN, colonel of the Simbirsk regiment
LANSKOI, flag bearer of the Simbirsk regiment, later captain
OFFICER
OLD MAN
SOLDIER ON DUTY
CHAMBERLAIN
EXECUTIONER
Plus many Russian and Turkish soldiers, imperial guardsmen, courtiers, lady's maids, execution officers, executioners, priests, horses, coachmen, and so on.

Time: From early autumn to midwinter, 1788.
Place:

Scene 1. Catherine II's bedroom in her palace at Czarskoe-Selo
Scene 2. The Russian army's encampment in front of the Turkish fortress at Kinburn
Scene 3. The cemetery behind the Russian army's encampment
Scene 4. The same as in scene 2
Scene 5. On the Neva River, St. Petersburg
Scene 6. A secret room in the Hermitage
Scene 7. Catherine II's drawing room in the Winter Palace
Scene 8. A prison cell
Scene 9. The scaffold
Scene 10. The slope in front of the Turkish fortress at Kinburn

N.B.:

- Compared with the size of the puppets, the stage props should be proportionately very large.
- This play owes much to the five or six short stories about Catherine II written by Masoch.[1]

1. Because Murayama writes about his indebtedness to Leopold von Sacher-Masoch, in this translation of Murayama's play, the spelling of names and places is that used in an English translation of Leopold von Sacher-Masoch, *Venus and Adonis and Other Tales of the Court of Catherine II* (New York: privately printed, 1929).

- Because all the character traits and movements of, as well as the lines spoken by, the characters are puppet-like, unless the director takes pains to direct them very carefully, this play should not be performed by humans.

SCENE 1

After a quaint, elegant, nostalgic polonaise plays for a while, the curtain quietly rises. The luxurious bedroom of CATHERINE II *in her palace at Czarskoe-Selo. The chandelier's candlelight dims as the day dawns. The bedroom is behind the heavy purple velvet curtain in the center of the stage. The polonaise continues.* CATHERINE II*'s Skirt from Days Gone By abruptly appears and starts singing a song. It is a small skirt with whalebone hoops and decorated with ivy and moss.*

The Song of the Skirt from Days Gone By

My mistress was born in Germany,
And came to Russia at fifteen.
She started studying the Russia language then
But because she was willful from the time she was born,
She studied in midwinter in the middle of the night
Wearing only a nightgown and not even socks,
So her small lungs were filled with blood
And it was a close call—she almost died.
Now whether it was better for her to have died then
Is not for a mere skirt like me to understand.
In any case, she quickly recovered
And fulfilled her role as
The link between France and Russia.
Grand Duke Peter, who became her husband, was
A pockmarked good-for-nothing creature
Who loved military parades, military uniforms, and gold buttons
And nothing else—that was it.
My mistress, barely sixteen,
Promptly despised this beast.
Living in the midst of selfishness, power, and dissolution,
An existence diametrically opposed to a life lived humanly,
No one would be surprised if my mistress rotted
But the extent of her rotting was extraordinary.
Well, do listen to how it went.
First of all, my mistress

Fell into horrific sexual depravity.
She pursued men avidly if they were strong and beautiful,
Soldiers or officers,
Or diplomats or artists—
They all made lots of bothersome work for me.
Gourmands need not only delicious things to eat
But also different dishes to eat daily.
Sorikow, Mirowitsch,
And Potemkin, who lasted for quite a while, were the first
Of a long list of official lovers who will be remembered throughout history
A list so long that headless me cannot remember them all.
The Present-Day Skirt and the Skirt from the Future
Will also suffer because of this.
Now, after eighteen years of marriage,
Queen Elizabeth died so
Peter was made czar.
My mistress, who hated her husband so,
Used Gregory Orlow, a favorite of hers
Who was luckily the commander of the Imperial Guard
To suddenly stage a revolt to take the throne
And take Peter's life while doing so.
In this way did the famous reign of Catherine
Emerge onto the world's stage.
Now my mistress, who was a famed beauty
Can't beat aging—she's sixty this year.
That beauteous figure people swooned over
Can now be mistaken for a barrel of Dutch herring
And even emits strange odors.
(*A cock crows.*)
Oh dear, it's almost morning.
That barrel of herring will wake and
Appear from behind that curtain
So why don't you take a good long look at her yourself?
(*To stage right.*)
Oh, Present-Day Skirt!
I bid you all adieu.
(*Exits stage left. The cock crows again. It is light outside the window. From stage right appears the Present-Day Skirt. It is decorated with gems that dazzle the eye—it is a large, stately skirt.*)

The Song of the Present-Day Skirt

Well, you are such a chatterbox, Skirt from Days Gone By.
But then again, sixty years is a long time
And it must have been quite eventful.
Compared with that, I have it easy
Since what is present is what you are
Going to see on stage.
So my chattering is unnecessary.
(*The morning sun shines on the scarlet woolen cloth on the floor.*)
Oh dear, the sun is shining into the room. Let me leave before I'm yelled at from behind the curtain.
(*Toward stage right.*)
Oh Skirt from the Future!
After the ten scenes in this play,
I leave everything else up to you.
(*Runs behind the center curtain. The Skirt from the Future appears from stage right. It is an insanely decorated, obviously garish skirt.*)

The Song of the Skirt from the Future (*in a hushed voice*)

If I tell you too much about the future
The laws of nature will be messed up.
Suffice it to say that that old woman
Becomes insane because of her hysteria,
And though her Turkish conquest finally ends,
She starts to plan an incredible Indian conquest
But drops dead suddenly of a stroke.
(*From behind the curtain we hear a yawn.*)
Oh dear, she wakes—I mustn't be found.
I invite you to stay, sit back, and watch.
(*Exits stage right.*)

CATHERINE II (*Shouts from behind the curtain*): Pro—ta—so—w—

MADAME DE PROTASOW: Yeeess, Your Majesty. (*Runs in from stage left. Thirty years old and a beauty in the Rubens style, she stands outside the curtain.*) Are you awake?

CATHERINE II: Yes, I'm awake. Help me get up.

MADAME DE PROTASOW: Yes, Your Majesty. (*Lifts the curtain and makes her way through.*)

CATHERINE II: Up-si-daisy. (*Eventually, she runs outside the curtain. Her voluminous body is encapsulated in a white nightgown trimmed with the highest-quality Flemish lace. Her face is ravaged by her dissolute way of life, but since she had been, after all, a great beauty, she looks far younger than her sixty years. She looks, at the most, forty. Only her eyes are as beautiful and seductive and dignified as in the olden days. Her hair is as white as snow. But in any case, there's no denying that she is a fat and flabby old woman. She goes straight to the full-length mirror and poses in front of it coyly.*) Hmmm. (*She seems satisfied.*)

MADAME DE PROTASOW: You are indeed beautiful, Your Majesty. You are particularly bright and shining this morning.

CATHERINE II: Yes, this morning I think I do look especially brilliant. Look at the color in these cheeks. They're like jewels. The glow comes from deep inside. Those of the lower class and weaklings don't have this glow, you know. Well, maybe the queen of the Amazons had it.

MADAME DE PROTASOW: But aren't those Amazons a myth?

CATHERINE II: Don't be stupid. Scholars turn everything they find inconvenient into myths. There's nothing strange about women rising up against male despotism in order to build a nation—I'd say it is the natural thing to do. And it's what I'm trying to do all by myself. Well, in my army, I have a commander like Madame de Mellin, but I just put an old-fashioned refined young lady in a green velvet coat trimmed with gold braid and gave her a saber to keep by her side, and also an ivory walking stick with a gold head to hold. But I'm different. I'm Alexander reincarnated. Just like Nero, I see my whims through to the end.

MADAME DE PROTASOW: Would you like to get dressed now?

CATHERINE II (*Not listening*): So what I want are not friends but slaves. And though you won't understand this, the people don't want to be my friends but my slaves. And this is why Russia can flourish. St. Petersburg is built on the dead bodies of serfs, you know. We built it by sinking the columns for this city in the swamp, along with serf carcasses.

MADAME DE PROTASOW: Yes, Your Majesty. Slaves, Your Majesty. Only slaves surround you, Your Majesty. They are toys. They are your playthings. They are pet dogs. If you are bored with them, they are things to be tossed aside. And everyone is happy about this from the bottom of their hearts.

CATHERINE II: Now, we can't generalize and say that, can we? Our lives depend on the lives of those serfs. Building a detached palace, say, or going to war—these things we can't do if the serfs aren't around. Just because they are smelly and dirty doesn't mean we can get rid of them arbitrarily. The slaves I can get rid of easily when I'm bored with them are the ones like you. Now kneel! Kiss the soles of my feet! (*She commands imperiously.* MADAME DE PROTASOW *obeys.*) Yes, now I will get dressed. (*She puts her arm around* MADAME DE PROTASOW*'s shoulders in a familiar way, and they exit through the central curtain.*)

MADAME DE MELLIN (*Enters hurriedly from stage right. She is a lithe and youthful beauty. She stops and stands in front of the curtain wearing exactly the dashing outfit *that* CATHERINE *described a few moments ago. She clicks together her shiny black patent leather boots and speaks*): I, commander of the Simbirsk regiment Madame de Mellin, have come to say farewell before going off to the Turkish expedition!

CATHERINE II (*From behind the curtain*): Oh, my dear brave Amazon. Wait a moment for me. (*To* MADAME DE PROTASOW.) Powder!—more, more, lots more!—Now the skirt!—(*To* MADAME DE MELLIN.) Are you off immediately?

MADAME DE MELLIN: Yes, Your Majesty, directly after I take leave of you!

CATHERINE II (*From behind the curtain*): And where do you propose to catch up with Potemkin?

MADAME DE MELLIN: I intend to catch up with the commander at Novgorod, Your Majesty.

CATHERINE II (*From behind the curtain*): And are you taking your whole regiment?—(*To* MADAME DE PROTASOW.) No, not these shoes! I want those, with the lily decorations!

MADAME DE MELLIN: Yes, Your Majesty. They are waiting in front of the gates.

CATHERINE II (*Sticks out her made-up face from between the curtains. Her makeup is unseemly and thick for a woman her age, with a thick layer of lipstick on her lips, dark-colored rouge on her cheeks, and three beauty spots drawn on her face. She sticks out her neck and speaks in a hushed voice*): That good-looking Lanskoi, he's the flag bearer of your regiment, isn't he?

MADAME DE MELLIN: Yes, Your Majesty.

CATHERINE II: Is he going too?

MADAME DE MELLIN: Yes, he is.

CATHERINE II: Now, now, I dropped the ball on that one, didn't I? I suppose it's too late now. Though the boy's face is a little long, he has a good mouth on him. A good mouth. That mouth and that chin combined. That mouth's like someone pinched it a little; it's pursed just so (*As she says this she brings her right hand from behind the curtain to gesture this*), and that chin, don't you think it looks a little cocky? But it curves up like this, doesn't it? And then his torso, from his chest to his hips, looks (*As she says this, her left hand also emerges*) like this.

MADAME DE PROTASOW (*From behind the curtain*): Your Majesty, please don't stick your body out so much. Please wait just a little more, and we'll be done.

CATHERINE II: (*Returns both hands to behind the curtain*): Call that boy over here, won't you?

MADAME DE MELLIN: Do you mean Lanskoi, Your Majesty? I will go immediately. (*She leaves.*)

CATHERINE II (*Her head goes back behind the curtain. Soon she finishes dressing, however, and appears on stage with* MADAME DE PROTASOW *wearing the Present-Day Skirt*): I saw that boy at the spring military parade. The Simbirsk regiment was lined up on the left wing. As I was reviewing the troops, my horse suddenly reared. I thought "uh-oh" and pulled on the reins, and then there was right in front of my nose, a cute face blushing deeply, looking straight at me. That was that boy. I intended to call for him right after I got back, but it slipped my mind for some reason. The poor thing—still just the regimental flag bearer.

MADAME DE MELLIN (*Returns, whispering something to* LANSKOI. LANSKOI *is a vibrant beautiful young officer. He has a little moustache and carries the regimental flag in a bag*): I've brought Lanskoi to you, Your Majesty.

(LANSKOI *is in a daze and simply bows deeply.*)

CATHERINE II: Yes, yes, it was you, it was you. You're a lovely boy. Come closer, now. (LANSKOI *nervously approaches.* CATHERINE *places her hand on his chin and brings his face closer to her.*) Stay still. Don't move. Hmm. Yes, yes. I'm Catherine.

LANSKOI (*Stuttering*): Your Majesty, you—how—beautiful—you—are.

CATHERINE II: Good, good. You know, I've had my eye on you for a while. You are a pretty fine soldier.

LANSKOI (*Prompted by* MADAME DE MELLIN *as he goes along*): I am—simply—Your Majesty's—slave. –Your Majesty's toy.

CATHERINE II: Hmm. Hmm.

LANSKOI: Your—play—thing. Your—pet—dog—

CATHERINE II (*In great spirits*): Do I really seem beautiful to you?

LANSKOI (*Poked by* MADAME DE MELLIN): Yes, of course, Your Majesty, you are. You are so very beautiful. You are truly, truly, truly, beautiful.

CATHERINE II (*To* MADAME DE MELLIN): Good, good. This man seems to be a man with ample capabilities. Let us make him captain. (LANSKOI *is so surprised he almost drops his flag.* MADAME DE MELLIN *is unperturbed and replies, "Yes, Your Majesty," and bows.*) And I'll write to Potemkin myself, so Madame de Mellin, you take it and deliver it to him.

MADAME DE MELLIN: Yes, Your Majesty.

CATHERINE II (*Starts writing the letter using the small desk that* MADAME DE PROTASOW *brings*): Madame de Mellin, this is to say that your regiment shall be in reserve till the very end—(*At that moment, outside the military band suddenly starts to play. Everyone is startled, and the music sounds like it is moving farther away.*)

MADAME DE MELLIN (*Upset, runs to the window*): Oh no, my regiment is leaving! (LANSKOI *hears this and runs off like a rabbit.*)

CATHERINE II: What? They're leaving? Without their commanding officer and their flag bearer?

MADAME DE MELLIN (*Shouts from the window*): Stop! Halt! Stop, I tell you! Please halt! (*But the military band moves farther and farther away, so she is about to run off.*)

CATHERINE II (*Dismayed*): Wait, Mellin! I said, "Wait"! The letter, I haven't finished the letter yet! (MADAME DE MELLIN *hesitates a moment but then is about to sprint off.*)

CATHERINE II (*Overturns the desk as she runs after her*): Wait! Mellin! Wait! You fool!!!

CURTAIN

SCENE 2

The curtain rises as the sounds of cannons, rifles, yelling, shouts of "hurrah," and so on indicate confusion and disorder. The encampment of the Russian army in the front of the Turkish fortress at Kinburn.

Stage right, in the background, there can be seen half of the fortress and the hill it is built on. Stage left is a cross section of a Russian tent that is torn and broken. Inside, there is only dirty straw strewn on the floor. There are no blankets. There are misshapen buckets and pots hanging. The Russian troops attacked the fortress but were rebuffed, and so the SOLDIERS *have just returned, dejectedly.*

Grimy, unshaven SOLDIERS *wearing rags walk past, from stage right to stage left. Seven or eight of them enter this tent, bury themselves in the straw, and close their eyes. They don't have the energy to speak. In addition, they all are half crazed. After the other* SOLDIERS *return to their tents, the strains of a polonaise can be heard emanating from a place not far away.*

SOLDIER 1 (*Suddenly laughing in a loud voice*): Ahahahahahahahaha.

(*Beat. The delirious ramblings of the* SOLDIERS *can be heard from inside the lanternless tent.*)

SOLDIER 2 (*Crying in a low voice*): It hurts. It hurts. Oh, it hurts.

SOLDIER 3 (*In a crushed voice*): Hurrah! Charge!

SOLDIER 4 (*Mumbling*): They got it good over there, they do, and vodka drips from their whiskers all the time. Forever and ever it drips from their whiskers. Beef. Pork. Beef. Pork. My, my, it's a very fancy mansion they have there. Dance, Walinka, Walinka, Walinka. And you, cute Maria Demitrievna. May I trouble you to please fetch me that porcelain pipe? Yes, yes, of course. Do you mean this one? What a magnificent pipe it is. Oh, now if you say such things, I get shy, Maria Demitrievna. Let me tell you about this pipe—. Oh, my dear bishop. Why are you crying? Your child died of cholera? Oh, I'm so sorry to hear that. Well, my dear man, if that is the case—

SOLDIER 5 (*Sings out of tune*):

Mr. Potemkin and his wooden palace.
Here, Maria, there, Katya.
Having banquets daily, regardless of day or night.
Here, here, Soldiers, come closer now,
With this here war
I really want to obtain
The Grand Ribbon of the Order of St. George. (*Two or three* SOLDIERS *add their voices and sing together.*)
Even though I may be Catherine's lover
I need to see active duty

Or else I won't get that decoration.
So that's why I started this war
And even though the Turkish soldiers might be strong
This is a war that must be won.

OFFICER 1 (*Hearing the singing, runs into the tent*): Hey! Who's singing? Didn't I tell you that anyone singing that song is to be shot to death? Who was it now? Hey, (*Kicks someone*) get up! It was you, wasn't it? (*He grabs* SOLDIER 5 *by the collar and drags him out of the straw.*) You others I'll forgive just this once. If I hear you singing that song again, I'll shoot you all to death, every last one of you. (*Using the whip he had tucked into his belt, he starts thrashing it around. The* SOLDIERS *suddenly come to their senses and start crying.*) Walk! Go outside! You're to be shot dead! (*He exits the tent as he beats the crying* SOLDIER *in front of him.*)

SOLDIER 2: It hurts. It hurts. Oh, it hurts.

SOLDIER 4 (*Starts to cry*): Oh the general is too cruel. There's nothing much good even after death, I bet.

SOLDIER 1: Ahahahaha.

SOLDIER 3: Commander! They got me.

SOLDIER 4: Oooh, the horror, the horror. You there, some sympathy for me, please.
(*From afar, the sound of a rifle shot. Two, three* SOLDIERS, *astonished, sit up.*)

SOLDIER 2: Aahh.

SOLDIER 6: Shot to death!

SOLDIER 4: Oh my God. (*He crosses himself.*)
(*Beat. Strains of the polonaise again.*)

SOLDIER 7: I'm starving. (*Hearing this, they all realize that they are about to die of hunger and start moaning "I'm starving" in desolate voices.*)

SOLDIER 4: They have stuff at Commander Potemkin's place. Beef. Pork. Beef. Pork. They have everything there. And vodka drips from their whiskers all the time. Forever and ever, it drips from their whiskers.

FADE TO BLACK

SCENE 3

A moonlit night in the cemetery behind the encampment. Crude crosses are stuck in the snowy ground; some have fallen.

LANSKOI *sits on a rock and is in a daze. Occasional cannon sounds. In the darkness, someone suddenly yells.*

LANSKOI (*Shouts*): Who's there? (*No answer.*) Who's there? If you don't answer, I'll shoot you dead!

OLD MAN (*Crying as he emerges from a hole toward the rear of the stage*): I beg yer pardon, beg yer pardon. I'm to blame, I am. I did wrong.

LANSKOI: You, what were you doing? What's that you're carrying?

OLD MAN: Ahh, beg yer pardon, sir, beg pardon.

LANSKOI (*Wrests it from the* OLD MAN): Huh? This is a uniform. You were stripping things from dead bodies, weren't you?

OLD MAN: It's my fault, sir, I did wrong.

LANSKOI (*After a while, suddenly laughs*): Ahahahaha, this is probably better, actually, to be rid of such filthy clothes and be buried stark naked in the snow. But you there, why did you yell?

OLD MAN: Oh, my God, I saw such a frightful thing—

LANSKOI: What did you see?

OLD MAN: Behold, over there, over there. Can you hear that moaning?

LANSKOI: I can't hear a thing. But what are those pale blue things?

OLD MAN: Dead bodies, sir, carcasses. But they're not yet dead.

LANSKOI: Not dead yet? (*He jumps into the hole. After a while, he climbs out of it.*) They're all dead, already. But did you drag them there?

OLD MAN: Oh, they died, did they? Until a few moments ago they were alive, I tell ya. They were moaning and twitching as they crawled.

LANSKOI: I see. Yesterday when they dumped thirty-five men who died of illness into that hole all at once, they also threw in some who weren't dead yet. So the ones who were alive probably crawled part of the way out and then gave up the ghost.

OLD MAN: I'm sure yer right. It's horrible, sir.

LANSKOI: What's so horrible? You were the one who was stripping the bodies of their belongings. How can you say such balderdash when you yourself are like the devil?

OLD MAN (*Shouts*): The devil, the devil I am, yessiree. But who's the worse devil: me, who strips dead bodies, or you and yer kind who kill people? Yer lot suddenly showed up in our village and started a war. Yer cannonballs made a mess of our fields and crops. And burned our houses and barns. How can we live if we don't take clothes from them who don't need 'em? I'm an honest farmer, not like you and yer shameful business. Who made us into devils? It was you and yer kind, that's who.

LANSKOI (*In a small voice*): Not I—not I—

OLD MAN: So, take a good look—this is what yer lot made me into. And watch—I'm about to go strip that dead man's body. (*He hides in the hole.*)

FADE TO BLACK

SCENE 4

Same as scene 2.

SOLDIER 4: They have stuff at Commander Potemkin's place. Beef. Pork. Beef. Pork. They have everything there. And vodka drips from their whiskers all the time. Forever and ever, it drips from their whiskers—

SOLDIER ON DUTY (*Carries everyone's rations and slips into the tent*): Hey, it's dinnertime, wake up, wake up. (*Everyone crowds around him.*) Hey, I have something important to tell you. Someone stand watch at the entrance. (*To* SOLDIER 7.) Would you be the lookout?

SOLDIER 7: All right. (*Goes to the entrance.*) It's starting to snow.

SOLDIER ON DUTY: Listen up, everyone. We've talked it over with the other regiments and at last we decided to send a messenger to St. Petersburg.

SOLDIER 4: Lord, please protect our poor messenger.

SOLDIER 2: Who's the messenger?

SOLDIER ON DUTY: Lanskoi. That ladies' man Captain Lanskoi.

SOLDIER 3: Good! If it's Captain Lanskoi, that's good! He's the czarina's favorite, so if he says bad things about Potemkin, she'll listen to him. We're like insects to her, but we can still at least make a request.

SOLDIER 4: Our czarina doesn't know what dire straits we're in. So if he tells her how it really is—the truth, I mean—she'll be surprised and shed big tears and say, oh my poor little children, forgive me, I didn't know.

SOLDIER ON DUTY: That's right. That's bound to be right. And we asked Lanskoi to tell her everything. How Potemkin built a magnificent palace and invited twenty foreign beauties there so that they could party with lavish banquets and host balls. All while we're almost dead of hunger because we have no rations. And that many of us are sick and we're dying like flies. While our commander is frolicking, every day more soldiers die, and so we can't even take this one fortress at Kinburn.

(*At that moment, outside the tent,* CAPTAIN LANSKOI *arrives, dressed as a peasant, with an escort of ten* SOLDIERS.)

LANSKOI (*In a small voice*): Now, return before you're found out. On my life I swear to see this mission through, so don't worry. Just wait for me.

SOLDIER 8: Oh, Captain Lanskoi. Thank you, thank you. (*Kisses his hem and cries. The* SOLDIERS *inside the tent also tumble outside in tears to see off* LANSKOI. *Strains of a polonaise.*)

CURTAIN

SCENE 5

St. Petersburg. On the Neva River. In the background we can see the Winter Palace. The river is frozen solid, and on it is a layer of snow. There is a mountain of snow almost fifty feet high. The slope is as smooth as glass, so one could slide down on a sled and play. On either side of the sledding track, fir trees stand in the snow in two tidy rows. There are wooden steps on the backside of the mountain so that one can climb to the top. The curtain rises amid happy cheers, playful shouts, and the jingle of sleigh bells.

Courtiers in warm clothing are sledding and making lots of noise. The imperial guards are in charge of dragging the sleds up the mountain of ice and pushing them down again.

The moment the curtain rises, CATHERINE II, *along with* MADAME DE PROTASOW, *sleds down the hill.*

MADAME DE PROTASOW (*Getting off the sled*): Ahh, that was scary!

CATHERINE II (*Handing over the sled reins to a guard*): Now once more!

MADAME DE PROTASOW: Let's stop now, Your Majesty. This is clearly not good for one's health. It feels like one leaves one's heart behind while one's body whooshes down the hill. It must be bad for one's health. Everything in front of one's eyes passes by so quickly, this must not be good for the eyes either. The eyes can't focus.

CATHERINE II: Then why don't you throw away your heart and eyes and hurry up and come with me?!

(*At this moment,* MADAME DE MELLIN, *wearing women's clothing, appears, riding in a sleigh pulled by a pair of horses.*)

CATHERINE II (*Shouts*): Ah, my dear brave Amazon. (*Running toward her.*) I'm glad you were able to come. So this means your leg injury has healed?

MADAME DE MELLIN (*Gets off the sleigh and bows deeply*): Yes, Your Majesty. It's healed completely.

CATHERINE II: Show me.

MADAME DE MELLIN: Yes, Your Majesty. (*Lifts her skirt a bit, lowers her stockings, and shows the scar on her ankle.*)

CATHERINE II (*Squats and touches it*): Hmm, the scar after a bullet passes through you is a strange shape, isn't it? Well, at least it wasn't your face or your chest. So now that you're well, are you going back to the battlefield?

MADAME DE MELLIN: Oh, not a chance! I don't think I'll forget that place till the day I die—that's why I keep twitching nervously.

CATHERINE II: Well, well. You're a miserable thing now, aren't you? But that's fine—I thought as much from the very beginning. You look dashing in uniform, but I like you even more when you're wearing women's clothes. So make sure you don't ever mouth off courageously again. (*To* MADAME DE PROTASOW.) Let's go.

(*The two arrive at the top of the ice mountain and slide down with great speed. When they are halfway down the hill,* LANSKOI *appears stage left, wearing peasant's clothes. At that moment, the sled overturns, and* CATHERINE II *and* MADAME DE PROTASOW *are thrown out onto the ice. As everyone grows pale and runs toward them,* CATHERINE II, *unperturbed, gets up by herself and helps* MADAME DE PROTASOW, *who feels as though she is about to die, board the sled again, and then they finish sledding down the rest of the mountain.*)

MADAME DE MELLIN (*Runs over to her*): Are you all right? I was so surprised my heart is still beating so fast!

CATHERINE II: I saw that boy. Suddenly, I saw that boy's face. And I was startled so that my steering went awry, and so we fell over.

MADAME DE MELLIN: Who is "that boy"?

CATHERINE II: You know, the one who used to be the flag bearer for your regiment. Lan—Lan—

MADAME DE MELLIN: Oh, Lanskoi.

CATHERINE II: Yes, Lanskoi.

MADAME DE MELLIN: Where?

CATHERINE II (*Looking around her*): I saw him somewhere. That boy had such a pale face.

LANSKOI (*Pushing past people and then kneeling*): Your Majesty.

CATHERINE II: It was you, after all. Why are you dressed that way? When did you return from the battlefield?

LANSKOI: I have a secret and important request to make of you.

CATHERINE II (*Taking his chin in her hand and drawing him near*): Well, well . . . but before I listen to your request, you'll have to listen to me first. (*Her mouth nears his ear.*) Come to the back gate of the Hermitage at eleven this tonight. (*To* MADAME DE PROTASOW.) Let's go home.

MADAME DE PROTASOW (*Limping*): I'm not feigning anything, I really fell down. Ah, this is the last straw. Whatever you say, I'm never going to go sledding with Your Majesty again. (*The two climb into a sleigh drawn by two horses and leave.*)

MADAME DE MELLIN (*Nearing* LANSKOI, *who is still kneeling, dumbstruck*): Lanskoi, you are a lucky man. I have no idea why you escaped the battlefield wearing such clothes but come to the Hermitage tonight without fail. The czarina has taken a fancy to you. (LANSKOI *grows pale.*) Now, now, there's nothing to be afraid of. Just do exactly as the czarina says. If you do, she'll grant you your so-called important request just like that.

CURTAIN

SCENE 6

CATHERINE II*'s secret trysting place, a hidden room in the Hermitage. The walls are covered with oil paintings of myths. The furniture is covered in ruby-red cloth, and the candlelight is dim.* CATHERINE *is wearing only a thin pink negligee and is leaning over the long sofa in front of the stove, trying to build up a fire. After a while, from a door, stage left, comes the sound of footsteps.*

LADY'S MAID (*Outside the door*): Now, open the door, and please enter. Happiness awaits you inside. (*The door opens and* LANSKOI, *wearing the formal uniform of an army captain enters nervously, like a child.*)

CATHERINE II (*Without looking back at him*): It's cold here. Or maybe I am dressed too lightly.

LANSKOI (*His voice shaking*): Let me—let me fan the flames—Your Majesty. (*He kneels at her feet and fans the flames with all his might.*)

CATHERINE II (*After watching for a while his face made red by the reflection of the flames, she puts her hand on his shoulder*): Lanskoi, ever since you went away to the battlefield, all I could think of was you. I hope you were thinking of me.

LANSKOI: Yes, yes, Your Majesty. I also—thought of you all the time—yes.

CATHERINE II: I'm a lonely woman, a woman who hungers for love.

LANSKOI: Of course you couldn't be, Your Majesty. You have all sorts of—power.

CATHERINE II: Even if I have all that power, can I order someone to love me?

LANSKOI: Ye—Yes, you can. That is—I'm certain that—you can.

CATHERINE II: You know what it means to love me, don't you?

LANSKOI: Ye—Yes, certainly—I still remember. It means—to become a slave—a toy—a plaything—a pet dog.

CATHERINE II: Yes. But that isn't all. There's more. You'll learn soon. Put your face here. (*She brings his face close onto her lap and cradles it with both hands.*)

LANSKOI: Your Majesty—I actually—as a representative of the troops of the Turkish expedition—have a serious request—

CATHERINE II: Shhh. Be quiet. I'm not thinking of such things right now.

LANSKOI: But Your Majesty, many lives—

CATHERINE II (*Covers his mouth*): I said, Be quiet. Potemkin wanted to go to war, so I let him. It's Potemkin's war, so he should fight it any way he wants. It has nothing to do with me. Never speak of it again to me. And remember, Potemkin is your senior. What did you just say? That to love me is to become a slave, right? So keep quiet and go over there and lie down. (*Points to a canopied bed at the back of the room.* LANSKOI *stands up listlessly, goes over to the bed, and falls over.* CATHERINE *covers him with herself.*)

CURTAIN

SCENE 7

CATHERINE II*'s drawing room in the Winter Palace. Outside, it is snowing heavily.* CATHERINE *wears a yellow lounging outfit with lots of lace and toasts her feet by the stove as she reads a letter from Voltaire.*

MADAME DE PROTASOW *enters.*

MADAME DE PROTASOW: Your Majesty, do hurry up and release him. It's been about a month already.

CATHERINE II (*Continues to read the letter*): Shhh! Oh, Voltaire! My, my, Voltaire, you. Ahahahahaha.

MADAME DE PROTASOW: Your Majesty! Aren't you thinking of poor Lanskoi? Let him out of prison quickly, I say.

CATHERINE II: Didn't you hear me say "Shhh!"? Ooooh, Voltaire, you old man. (*Suddenly she stops laughing.*) You, bring me that document on the desk there. I forgot to sign it.

MADAME DE PROTASOW (*Looks at the document in her hands and is shocked*): This is Lanskoi's death warrant.

CATHERINE II: Yes, it is. Now bring me a pen and ink.

MADAME DE PROTASOW: You're really going to sign this, Your Majesty?

CATHERINE II: Yes, indeed. Tomorrow morning, I'm having that head chopped right off. Hurry and bring the pen and ink. Have you forgotten? You're my slave!

MADAME DE PROTASOW: Yes, Your Majesty. (*Gives her the pen and ink.*)

CATHERINE II (*Signs. Claps her hands to summon a chamberlain*): Deliver this to Neglujew. This should be executed at seven o'clock sharp tomorrow morning. Tell him I'll come and watch too.

SERVANT: Yes, Your Majesty. (*Takes the document and leaves.*)

CATHERINE II: Now, I'll be done with this one, too. One needs to destroy one's favorite toys before one gets bored with them.

CURTAIN

SCENE 8

LANSKOI*'s prison cell. Moonlight streams in from a small high window. The one wooden bed has straw strewn over it.* LANSKOI *lies on top of it.*

From the stone corridor come footsteps, and light from a lantern shines into the cell. Someone opens the iron door and enters. It is MADAME DE PROTASOW. LANSKOI *is startled and sits up. His face is pale and drawn but beautifully shaven.*

MADAME DE PROTASOW (*In a small voice*): It is I, it is I, Madame de Protasow: You poor thing.

LANSKOI (*Kneeling*): Your servant.

MADAME DE PROTASOW (*Notices* LANSKOI*'s face is beautifully shaven and is surprised*): Well, your face—why do you take such care with it?

LANSKOI: The czarina commanded me to do so. The czarina comes here secretly every night—

MADAME DE PROTASOW: What? The czarina comes here every night?

LANSKOI: Yes, she comes every night, and if my face is not cleanly shaven, she gets annoyed.

MADAME DE PROTASOW: The czarina, every night. I had no idea.

LANSKOI: Every night at around midnight, she comes from behind this stone wall.

MADAME DE PROTASOW: Midnight? That's not too far off. We can't waste time. But what a czarina! To have a secret even here. I'm always with her, but she's never said anything to me about this. I thought I knew all her secrets—what a frightening person she is. She may be listening to us from somewhere, even now. But Lanskoi, you are an unfortunate fellow. You are going to be executed.

LANSKOI (*Surprised*): Really?

MADAME DE PROTASOW: Yes.

LANSKOI: That can't possibly be true. No. The czarina told me that if I stayed here for a month, she'd let me out right away. She asked me to put up with being in prison because I am a deserter, and the army needs to keep up appearances.

MADAME DE PROTASOW: You are going to be executed tomorrow morning at seven.

LANSKOI: That's a lie! A lie! That can't be true. I won't believe it. I can't possibly believe such rubbish.

MADAME DE PROTASOW: Today the czarina signed your death warrant. I saw her sign it with my own eyes.

LANSKOI: That's a lie! A lie! The czarina really loves me.

MADAME DE PROTASOW: The czarina may well love you. But you are going to be beheaded tomorrow morning at seven. I thought I'd help you escape—that's why I came. So quickly, follow me. The czarina may come at any minute. Hurry. (*Goes toward the door.*)

LANSKOI (*Takes two, three steps in her direction but then falls on his knees, half crying*): The czarina loves me. You don't understand.

MADAME DE PROTASOW (*Takes* LANSKOI*'s hand and tries to pull him out the door*): Quickly!

LANSKOI (*Still kneeling, he moves toward the door but then takes his hand away from hers and starts crying*): You—I've never been loved by a woman like the czarina.

(*At that moment, the stone wall stage left makes a sound and starts to move.* MADAME DE PROTASOW *is amazed; she goes out the door, shuts it, and runs away.* LANSKOI *remains in the same position. The stone wall opens, and* CATHERINE II *appears, wearing a pure-white fur coat over her night clothes, holding a candle.* LANSKOI *doesn't move.* CATHERINE *is surprised. She puts down the candle and runs to him and holds him up.*)

CATHERINE II (*Holding his upper body on her lap*): Lanskoi! Lanskoi! My dear, dear Lanskoi. What's the matter with you?

LANSKOI (*In a small voice*): Catherine!

CATHERINE II: Ohh. (*She embraces him and smothers his face with kisses.*) No, no, you shouldn't sleep here. You'll catch cold. And besides, tomorrow morning, you have a big mission to accomplish.

LANSKOI: Tomorrow morning.

CATHERINE II: Yes, tomorrow morning. You'll have to do some playacting for me. I'll tell you all about it, so let's go sit on the bed. (*She leads him to the bed and sits him down and kneels by his feet.*) You're a brave soldier, so you have to act naturally. In the ruse tomorrow, you'll climb the scaffold and will almost be executed.

LANSKOI (*Jumping up*): The scaffold?

CATHERINE II: Don't be shocked. It's just playacting. The moment you are about to be executed in front of all those people, I'm going to arrive and pardon you. The ministers and the people all are saying that you justly should be executed because you're a deserter, and they won't listen to anything else. If you aren't sentenced to die, then the war with Turkey, which is not going well anyway, will have lots of deserters, and we'll lose. That's what they're saying. But if I pardon you at the last moment, they'll be satisfied. So tomorrow, do this and act naturally for me—you can do it, right? If you can't, you may really have to be executed.

LANSKOI: I believe in you, Your Majesty. That's because I love you with all my heart.

CATHERINE II: Sweet, sweet Lanskoi! After tonight you'll be free from this awful prison cell. And then I'll build you a beautiful little house. I'll have lots of trees planted in the garden, and I'll give you a splendid sleigh. So tomorrow, go to the scaffold calmly. It would be unsightly for my lover to be shaking, my dear sweet Lanskoi, my sweet!—(*She climbs on top of* LANSKOI. *The candle falls and is extinguished.*)

LANSKOI (*Joyfully*): Catherine!

CURTAIN

SCENE 9

The execution grounds. The fallen snow glitters as the sun rises. In the center is the scaffold; around it are SOLDIERS. *Around them are countless spectators. Among the rows of* SOLDIERS *are aristocratic women in their beautiful sleighs, adjusting their opera glasses. The priest,* EXECUTIONER, *and others are strolling around. Eventually, with the sound of a monotonous drumbeat preceding him,* LANSKOI, *with his hands tied behind his back, is led out. He seems unperturbed and looks happy. Underneath the beheading stand, he kisses the cross a priest offers to him. The* EXECUTIONER *reads* CATHERINE*'s decree.*

EXECUTIONER: Simbirsk regiment infantry captain Semyon Mikhailowitsch Lanskoi. For deserting the army attacking Kinburn fortress, you are to be beheaded. Signed, Catherine.

(*Finally* LANSKOI *stands on the scaffold. He looks stage right, but there is not even the sound of* CATHERINE*'s sleigh. People try to blindfold him, but he doesn't let them. He kneels in front of the block where he is to lay his neck. And he looks stage right again. The* EXECUTIONER *picks up his ax. At that moment,* CATHERINE *arrives in her splendid sleigh, bells jingling merrily. The sleigh stops stage right, near the scaffold.* CATHERINE, *swathed in furs, looks straight into* LANSKOI*'s face. The* EXECUTIONER *swings up his ax.* CATHERINE *smirks. The* EXECUTIONER *shouts as he starts to swing his ax down.*)

LANSKOI (*At that moment, everything becomes clear in his mind, and he shouts as he tries to jump up*): Aargh! Shi—

(*The ax falls, and* LANSKOI*'s head, with bright red blood spewing from it, rolls to* CATHERINE*'s feet. She laughs radiantly.*)

CURTAIN

SCENE 10

The slope in front of the fortress at Kinburn. Nighttime. Snowstorm. Several dozen RUSSIAN SOLDIERS *are crawling from stage left through the snowstorm.*

SOLDIER A: Can you move?

SOLDIER B: The fortress—are we near the fortress yet?

SOLDIER C: It's right in front of us—right in front of us.

SOLDIER D: Can't move.

SOLDIER E: Ahh.

SOLDIER F: Soon—we can die.

SOLDIER G: Soon—we can die.

SOLDIER H: Don't—don't give up.

(*From stage right,* TURKISH SOLDIERS *appear, crawling in the same way.*)

TURKISH SOLDIER A: The pain.

TURKISH SOLDIER B: The pain.

TURKISH SOLDIER C: Let's hurry—hurry up—and get shot.

(*The* SOLDIERS *of the two armies meet in the center of the stage.*)

RUSSIAN SOLDIER A: Who's there?

TURKISH SOLDIER A: Who's there?

RUSSIAN SOLDIER B: The enemy!

TURKISH SOLDIER B: The enemy!

(*Both groups of* SOLDIERS *try to muster their strength to stand and fight, but they can't stand.*)

RUSSIAN SOLDIER B: Wait. Is there anyone who can speak Russian?

TURKISH SOLDIER B: Yeah.

RUSSIAN SOLDIER B: Why did you leave the fortress?

TURKISH SOLDIER B: No food. We haven't eaten anything for five days. There are only twenty-eight of us left.

RUSSIAN SOLDIER B: We don't have food, either. And there are only fifty-six of us. We can't even stand.

TURKISH SOLDIER B: Neither can we.

RUSSIAN SOLDIER B: So, are we supposed to fight?

TURKISH SOLDIER B: What else can we do?

RUSSIAN SOLDIER B (*Shouts*): We can make peace.

TURKISH SOLDIER B (*Surprised*): Oh.

RUSSIAN SOLDIER B: Our commander is our enemy. Our czarina beheaded our messenger. And no one in St. Petersburg said that that was wrong. Everyone in Russia is the enemy of us fifty-six.

TURKISH SOLDIER B: Oh, it's the same with us. Other than us twenty-eight, everyone in Turkey is our enemy. So we killed our commander and our officers, then we came out to be killed.

SEVERAL RUSSIAN SOLDIERS (*Simultaneously*): We also killed ours and came here. We chopped off their heads and came. We torched their wooden mansion and came here.

TURKISH SOLDIER B: So we should make peace.

RUSSIAN SOLDIER B: And we ought to die here together as friends.

TURKISH SOLDIER B: Right, let's die together, holding on to one another.

RUSSIAN SOLDIERS (*Each saying this*): Let's die together. Let's hold on to one another —together—

(*After this, silence. The snowstorm worsens.*)

CURTAIN

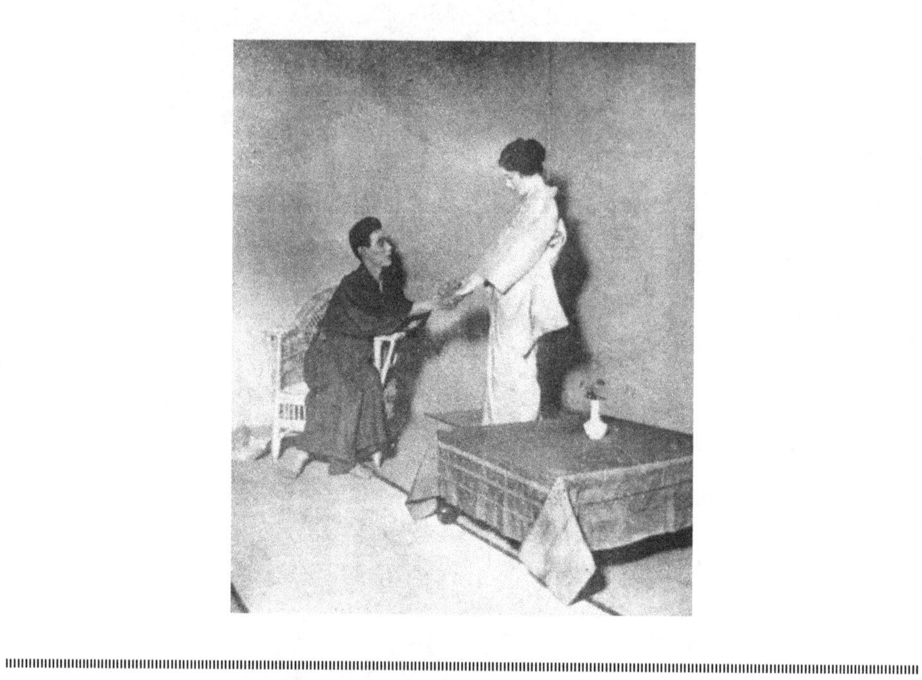

Kishida Kunio, *Paper Balloon*, Aoi tori, 1926.
(Courtesy of The Tsubouchi Memorial Theatre Museum Waseda University)

PAPER BALLOON

KISHIDA KUNIO

TRANSLATED BY RICHARD McKINNON

Paper Balloon (*Kamifūsen*) is a one-act play by Kishida Kunio (1890–1954), first published in 1925 in the journal *Literary Chronicle* (*Bungei shunjū*). The play was first produced in 1926, by the Aoi tori (Blue Bird) troupe. Since then, it has been staged several times and is generally considered the most representative of Kishida's short plays.

Like others composed in the same style, Kishida's dialogue in *Paper Balloon* is poetic and spare, composed with a sense of fantasy that may remind American readers of the playful spirit of Thornton Wilder's play *Our Town* (1938). The play has only two characters, the Husband and the Wife, and their interplay continues until the end, when the tone becomes more somber. The paper balloon seems to symbolize the whole fantasy played out during the touching dialogue between the two.

Characters

HUSBAND

WIFE

Time: A bright Sunday afternoon.

Place: The sitting room facing the garden.

HUSBAND (*Reading a newspaper on the veranda as he sits in a rattan chair*): "The modern village of Mejiro, recently acclaimed as a Los Angeles in miniature by Mr. Turner, Managing Director of the Fuller Building Supplies Company, U.S.A., has today become an elegant and beautiful residential area."

WIFE (*Sitting on a cushion near the veranda as she knits*): What is that about?

HUSBAND (*Reading on*): "The area, which covers 40,000 *tsubo*, is ideally situated: Streets are laid out systematically. A sewage system, running water, electric heat—the most hygienic facilities are provided. Tennis courts have been installed. There are many pretty little bungalow-type houses. There are houses that are built in the impressive style of Frank Lloyd Wright. There are even houses built in the graceful, cottage-style Japanese architecture. This residential area is set in cheerful surroundings. Situated on high ground from where one can view Mount Fuji, it is heavily covered with trees." (*Tosses the newspaper aside.*) Look, how about a walk?

WIFE: Never mind. Why don't you go ahead and go over to the Kawakamis.

HUSBAND: I really don't have to go.

WIFE: The mood has to strike me just right or I can't get interested.

HUSBAND: For a walk, you mean?

WIFE: A walk or anything else. (*Pause.*)

HUSBAND: "A walk or anything else." But do you have anything else to do?

WIFE: No, isn't that all right?

HUSBAND: Sure.

WIFE: Why don't you go visit the Kawakamis without worrying about me?

HUSBAND: I don't feel like it any more.

WIFE: Oh, go on.

HUSBAND: No, I'm not going. I want to stay with you. Don't you understand?

WIFE: Sorry, I understand all too perfectly. (*Pause.*)

HUSBAND: Ho, hum. So this is the way I spend my occasional Sundays off.

WIFE: I guess so.

HUSBAND (*Picks up the paper again but isn't really interested in reading*): I think it would be fun if some newspaper offered a prize for the best answer to the question of what to do in situations like this.

WIFE: I'll send in an answer.

HUSBAND (*Still looking at the paper, showing little interest*): What will you say?

WIFE: What's the question?

HUSBAND: The question? Well, the question will say, "How would you spend your Sundays when you have been married a year?"

WIFE: That's too vague.

HUSBAND: What's vague about it? All right, how would you put it?

WIFE: How to keep the wife from getting bored on Sundays?

HUSBAND: And how not to inconvenience the husband at the same time?

WIFE: All right.

HUSBAND: Do you have a good idea?

WIFE: Why, I sure do. As soon as the wife gets up in the morning, she will take a bath, put on her makeup, get dressed, and then say, "I'm off to visit a friend of mine for a while."

HUSBAND: What happens then?

WIFE: Then her husband is sure to look displeased.

HUSBAND: There's nothing certain about that.

WIFE: I am talking about you.

HUSBAND: When did I look displeased?

WIFE: Don't you?

HUSBAND: Well, let's let that go. What do you do then?

WIFE: He looks displeased, you see. Then this is what I would say: I'm not really very anxious to go, but it would be awkward if they found out later that I had stayed home doing nothing. You see, every time I see her she keeps asking me to come over to her place. "If it's a Sunday, my husband will be at home. Why don't you and I go see a play together," she says. Since you're going to be home anyway, I thought I might as well go today. But of course if you have other plans, I would say and gently sound you out. Very indirectly, you understand.

HUSBAND: Yes, very indirectly. No. I wouldn't mind, but what would I do about lunch, with you gone.

WIFE: I prepared your lunch already.

HUSBAND: What about supper?

WIFE: I'll stop at the Azumaya's on my way out and ask them to deliver a big bowl of rice with chicken and egg on top.

HUSBAND: Oh, not that again. I suppose you're going to be late.

WIFE: Well, I can't be sure. But when ten o'clock comes around, will you get out the bedding and go to bed?

HUSBAND: Do you have any money?

WIFE: As a matter of fact, I'm completely out.

HUSBAND: Well, you'd better take this, then.

WIFE: Thank you.

HUSBAND: It's getting chilly at night. Take your muffler along.

WIFE: Yes, I will.

HUSBAND: Now then. I guess I'll leisurely read a book. Say, would you get the fire started for my bath before you go? Now if I have any visitors, I suppose we still have some cookies left from the last time. I'll skip shaving today. Ho, hum. What a relaxing Sunday.

(WIFE *silently looks down.*)

HUSBAND: What's the matter?

WIFE: You're no good.

HUSBAND: Why?

WIFE: Because.

HUSBAND (*Tossing the paper aside*): All right. Then what would you do in such a case if you were the husband?

WIFE: In what case?

HUSBAND: Would you stop her?

WIFE: I'd certainly try to stop her somehow!

HUSBAND: What would you say to her?

WIFE: I'd say something like, "If you really don't have to go, how about my taking you to the theater?"

HUSBAND: I see. What if he suggested that?

WIFE: She ought to go.

HUSBAND: Fine, if she will. But if she didn't want to go, then what? Or even if she did, if the circumstances made it impossible, like today, for instance.

WIFE: Why couldn't we substitute the movies for the theater?

HUSBAND: Movies? Why that's not something a husband and wife go together to see.

WIFE: Why not?

HUSBAND: Ask anyone.

WIFE: That's what's wrong with you. I'm different from other girls.

HUSBAND: Sure you're different. That's all the more reason why it would be unwise.

WIFE: What are you talking about?

HUSBAND: Well, it seems better not to have stopped her if she had wanted to go out.

WIFE: I guess you're right. So why don't you go, to the Kawakamis or wherever else.

HUSBAND: My, you're persistent, aren't you? What was it that you said this morning? When I told you that I was going over to visit Kawakami you said, "You keep mentioning Mr. Kawakami's name as if you didn't see him every day at your office. Why do you long for him so much? Is there any reason why you can't stay at home on a Sunday, at least?" What's the point of my being here?

WIFE: What if I did say so?

HUSBAND: Nothing. The question is what is the point of your being here.

WIFE (*Somewhat peevishly*): Well, is something wrong with my being here?

HUSBAND: But there are ways and ways of being here. I read the newspaper, and you start knitting. I heave a sigh, and you heave a sigh. I yawn, and then you yawn. I . . .

WIFE: That's why I suggested that we go out somewhere, and then you hedge about this way and that . . .

HUSBAND: Yes, yes. I understand. But surely we didn't get married just so we could go somewhere on Sundays. We ought to be able to get on more cheerfully even if we stayed home.

WIFE: That's because you don't talk.

HUSBAND: Talk? What is there to talk about?

WIFE: Talk is not being; it is an act of doing.

HUSBAND: What on earth! Philosophizing? All right, so let's say that talk is an act of doing. But what about you? You say nothing yourself.

WIFE: That's because you tell me to shut up.

HUSBAND: That's because you talk when I'm doing something.

WIFE: That's not true. You say that even after we are in bed.

HUSBAND: But I'm sorry.

WIFE (*Softly*): Actually I am quite content to be at your side saying nothing. If you'd only pay a little more attention to me, I could wish for no one better.

HUSBAND (*Looking triumphant*): What's for supper?

WIFE (*Spiritedly*): Nothing definite. It all depends on your grade.

HUSBAND (*Not quite equal to her mood*): You are still just a high school girl, aren't you?

WIFE: Meaning what? I've always felt that going to the theater or eating out is fine for Sundays if one has that much leeway. But that's still only secondary in importance. Surely there are any number of things that one can enjoy as a family. Take our garden, for example. Why, it's a disgrace. If you'd lend me a hand, I could so easily have a decent bed of flowers. Just imagine the cosmos in full bloom. It would look beautiful even from the street.

HUSBAND: That's what I mean about your being a high school girl.

WIFE: In that case you're a grade school boy.

HUSBAND (*Laughing*): Is there really something of a school boy in me, now?

WIFE: Sure there is.

HUSBAND: Look, let's go for a walk.

WIFE: It's too late now.

HUSBAND: Oh, just around the neighborhood.

WIFE: Where? Inokashira Park?

HUSBAND: Or even Tamagawa.

WIFE: Let's wait until there is more time. To make it real fun, we ought to make an occasion of it and have lunch out somewhere.

HUSBAND: How much money do you have?

WIFE: Oh, let's not talk about that today.

HUSBAND (*Counting on his fingers*): Sixteen, seventeen, eighteen, nineteen.

WIFE: We really ought to have everything ready in the morning, and plan to be off as soon as we are through breakfast.

HUSBAND: Yes, with plans all laid out the night before.

WIFE: That's right. To have a definite idea as to where we are going.

HUSBAND: It would be fun, wouldn't it, to take a day trip to Kamakura?

WIFE: I have some places I'd like to go.

HUSBAND: Let's see now. There is an eight-something train leaving Tokyo station in the morning.

WIFE: Second class, mind you.

HUSBAND: Naturally. What we ought to do is to get there early and occupy the two seats near the window facing each other. I would put my walking stick and your parasol up on the luggage shelf like this. . . .

WIFE: No, I would rather carry mine.

HUSBAND: I see. Those coming in after us would see us and try to sit as near to us as possible, saying to themselves, "Oh, boy, look at them at it."

WIFE: Oh, silly!

HUSBAND: The train starts to move.

WIFE: Would you open the window?

HUSBAND: Smoke will come in. See that over there. That's the ruins of the Hama Detached Place.

WIFE: My, is that so?

HUSBAND: Shinagawa, Shinagawa! All passengers taking the Yamate line must transfer.

WIFE: Already? I want to buy some caramels.

HUSBAND: OK. Hey, bring me some caramels.

WIFE: Would you like some?

HUSBAND: I guess so. We just passed Omori Station. We should be able to see the company president's home pretty soon.

WIFE: Is that the one? My, what a skimpy house!

HUSBAND: We'll skip Kamata and Kawasaki, and here we are in Yokohama. Well, we have no business here either. Hodogaya, Tozuka, and we are in Ofuna at last.

WIFE: I want to buy some sandwiches.

HUSBAND: OK. Hey, bring me some sandwiches.

WIFE: Would you like some?

HUSBAND: I guess so.

WIFE: Wait, now. Don't be so greedy. Leave some for me.

HUSBAND: Now, get ready to leave. Put your clogs back on. . . .

WIFE: I never had them off, for goodness' sake!

HUSBAND: I suppose the first place to go is the Hachiman Shrine. Do you know about this shrine?

WIFE: Of course I do. I'd rather go to the seashore, though. How about you?

HUSBAND: That would be all right, too. Let me see. . . .

WIFE: Why not get a cab.

HUSBAND: That's an idea. Hey, taxi! Now you go first.

WIFE: That's very kind of you.

HUSBAND: Well, I guess I'll light up a cigarette.

WIFE: But first tell the driver where to go.

HUSBAND: What's the matter with saying, "To the seashore."

WIFE: That sounds a bit strange. "Driver, to the Beach Hotel."

HUSBAND: Won't the Beach Hotel be closed?

WIFE: You know it isn't.

HUSBAND: All right. To the Beach Hotel. Toot, toot!

WIFE: What's all that for. We're already there.

HUSBAND: Goodness, already? Would you take us to a room with a good view?

WIFE: The dining room would do.

HUSBAND: Of course. So, why don't you order something.

WIFE: How about you?

HUSBAND: Anything would do.

WIFE: Two glasses of fruit juice. Be sure they are good and cold.

HUSBAND: Waitress, we are going for a little stroll. There's still some time before noon. We'll be back by twelve, so have something good ready for us.

WIFE: That's the spirit.

HUSBAND: Oh, one more thing. Are there any good rooms available, rooms with a *salle de bain*? We intend to stay here for a while.

WIFE: *Salle de bain*? Oh, you mean a bathroom.

HUSBAND: Sh! Oh, fine. We'll take that. No, we don't have to look at it first. Oh, by the way, doesn't your hotel have airplane service?

WIFE: Please!

HUSBAND: No? Oh, well, it can't be helped. Let's walk. Now for my walking stick.

WIFE: Are you sure you didn't leave it in the train again?

HUSBAND: I handed it to the bellhop. Ah, there it is!

WIFE: Which way shall we go?

HUSBAND: That island over there is Enoshima.

WIFE: What a lovely view!

HUSBAND: Watch your step. You'll fall. Let me hold your hand.

WIFE: People would look at us.

HUSBAND: That's too bad for them. Tired? Well, let's sit down and rest a bit, or if you'd rather, we might go bathing.

WIFE: I think I will.

HUSBAND: Go ahead. Hmm. You look very trim in a bathing suit. Don't go too far out.

WIFE: Don't worry.

HUSBAND: Wait, wait. Stand right there. I'll take a picture of you. Ready? Hey, this is wonderful. (*Becoming more and more excited.*) I've never seen you so pretty! Just look at that figure! What a marvelous complexion! Stay right where you are. Did you have your hair that long? And your bosom, so round and soft! Why, you're smiling. Look this way. Heavens, were these your eyes, and those lips? (*He shouts, forgetting everything.*)

WIFE (*Raising her head for the first time as if about to take him to task*): Please!

(*Long silence.*)

HUSBAND: Come over here.

(WIFE *just smiles.*)

HUSBAND (*Extending his hands*): Come over here.

WIFE: No.

HUSBAND: Oh, come on now. Come over here, I say.

(WIFE *rises and takes her husband's hands, swinging them.*)

WIFE: There's no middle ground in you, is there?

HUSBAND: How do you mean? (*He tries to draw his wife to him.*)

WIFE: Let me go!

HUSBAND (*Holding his wife's hands*): Won't there be a time when you will be tired of me, tired of holding hands with me like this?

WIFE: How about you?

HUSBAND: The fact is I am beginning to like this very much, this holding hands, and when I think of being left alone without you, I get so worried I don't know what to do. This, too, is a fact.

WIFE: Which one represents the truth?

HUSBAND: Both. (*Pause.*) That's why I feel that something is wrong. But I can't help it. (*Pause.*) So you sit and knit by me in silence. Are you really satisfied with that? I see no reason why you should be. Maybe in my absence there are times when you sit and brood all by yourself in the corner of a room somewhere. Away from home, I often picture you in my mind sitting there looking lonely. Don't you get sick and tired leading the kind of life we do, in which all we think about is how spend my less-than-hundred-yen paycheck in as grand a manner possible? Maybe you are resigned to the situation, feeling that nothing gained by talking this way. But I know that you have your ideals, and I'd like to know what you think about it at this point. Aren't you wondering what will become of us as we go on living like this? Am I wrong? Or are you dreaming again the dream that you had as a young girl?

WIFE: You are being foolish. (*She tries to smile, but she begins to cry.*)

HUSBAND: People are all fools. They don't know about themselves. Oh, let's cut out this kind of talk.

WIFE: I haven't cried like this for a long time.

HUSBAND: I go out visiting on a Sunday, leaving you all alone. You're unhappy about it. It's to be expected. Of course you'd like a change once in a while. Why should I make a fuss about movies! Let's plan to go after supper, huh?

(WIFE *nods.*)

HUSBAND: Fine. You want to go take a quick bath?

WIFE (*Wiping her tears away*): No, I'll skip it today.

HUSBAND: Why?

WIFE: Why don't you? You haven't had one in three days.

HUSBAND: Well, I've got a touch of cold. Oh, I think I'll skip it today. Let me see; it's 3:30 now, I think I'll go out for a while before supper instead.

WIFE (*Sitting down on her cushion again, resentfully*): Where are you going?

HUSBAND: Oh, I'll be back in no time.

(WIFE *stares at her husband, starts to say something, but then suddenly looks down.*)

WIFE: All right.

HUSBAND (*Sheepishly*): I'm not going to Kawakami's.

WIFE (*Embarrassed*): It doesn't matter at all.

HUSBAND (*Kneeling down beside his wife*): I suppose you think I'm going out to play billiards.

WIFE (*Looking the other way*): Don't mind me. Run along.

HUSBAND: Are you angry?

(WIFE *begins crying again.*)

HUSBAND (*At a loss*): What's the matter, anyway?

WIFE: I'm sorry. It was my mistake.

HUSBAND What do you mean, "mistake"? We are going to the movies afterward, don't you see?

WIFE (*Heaving a sigh*): I understand.

HUSBAND: You understand what?

WIFE: I might as well face up to it.

HUSBAND: To what?

WIFE: I'm sorry.

HUSBAND: Look, something's wrong with you.

WIFE: It's funny, you know. Other wives say they can relax and enjoy things when their husbands are out of the house. But it seemed so odd to me.

HUSBAND: Sure it's odd.

WIFE: But, it's no longer odd to me now.

HUSBAND: What?

WIFE: Men, I guess, are after all made to leave home in the morning and return in the evening.

(HUSBAND *smiles sardonically.*)

WIFE: I wonder why men make such a fuss over the fact that they are staying home, as if they were doing you a favor. Women, I suppose, just can stand for that.

HUSBAND: I'm not making a fuss about it.

WIFE: Anyway, if you have somewhere to go, go, run along. It makes me feel a whole lot better.

(HUSBAND *sits down in his chair again and starts reading the paper.*)

WIFE: I'm afraid to face Sundays.

HUSBAND: So am I.

(*Pause.*)

WIFE: You are spoiling me too much. (*She takes up her knitting.*)

HUSBAND: No, I can't say I am.

WIFE: But you are, really.

HUSBAND: Complicated, isn't it?

WIFE: See how they do it in other families.

HUSBAND: I know how they do it.

WIFE: Follow suit.

HUSBAND: I can't.

WIFE: Women are given to taking advantage of situations, you know?

HUSBAND: I know that.

WIFE: Well, just so long as you do.

(*Long pause.*)

HUSBAND: Actually, I think we are getting along better than many.

WIFE: Just a little more effort, I guess.

HUSBAND: You mean money?

WIFE: Oh, no.

(*Long silence.*)

HUSBAND: How about getting a dog?

WIFE: Won't a bird be better?

(*Long silence.* HUSBAND *yawns.* WIFE *yawns.*)

(*Pause.*)

HUSBAND: Would you like me to tell you a story?

WIFE: Yes, do.

HUSBAND: Long, long ago there was a boy and girl. The boy, as soon as he finished school, went to work in an office. The girl was still in high school. Every morning the two saw each other at a suburban bus stop. In time they greeted each other. When the boy got there first, he waited for the girl to come. When the girl arrived first, she . . .

WIFE (*Taking it away from him*): Went on ahead.

HUSBAND (*Matter of factly*): There were times like that.

(*At this point, the voice of a little girl is heard crying out: "Oh, dear!" A big paper balloon rolls into the garden.*)

(HUSBAND, *tossing the newspaper aside, steps off the veranda into the garden and picks up the balloon.*)

WIFE (*To herself*): Chieko-chan at home today?

(HUSBAND *quietly starts tossing the balloon.*)

WIFE: Don't do that. (*In a loud voice.*) Chieko-chan, come over here. I'll toss the balloon with you.

(HUSBAND *continues to toss the balloon eagerly.* WIFE *rises, brings her clogs around from the front entrance, and then comes out into the garden.*)

WIFE: No, no, don't hit it so hard. (*She calls to the little girl, who apparently is on the other side of the fence.*) I am ready to play with you now. (*As she says this, she manages to snatch the balloon away from her husband.*) Chieko-chan, come around from the front.

HUSBAND (*Chasing his wife, impatiently*): Now, let me have a turn. Look here, I tell you. . . .

CURTAIN

Murayama Tomoyoshi, cover design of *Prott*, January 1932, in which *Fascist Doll* was first published.

FASCIST DOLL

KUBO SAKAE
TRANSLATED BY YUKO MATSUKAWA

Fascist Doll (*Fuashito nigyō*) by Kubo Sakae (1900–1958) was first presented in 1931 as a Living Newspaper (a theatrical form that originated in Russia and presents factual information on current events). It was a joint production of the New Tsukiji Theater (Shin Tsukiji gekidan), one of the companies formed after Osanai Kaoru's death and the subsequent breakup of his company, and the Left Theater (Sayoku gekijō), which by this time was well known for performances of left-wing plays by Murayama Tomoyoshi and others. Because Kubo's one-character play is short, the program contained other works as well. The occasion for these performances was to honor the formation of the Japan Proletarian Cultural Federation (Nihon puroretaria bunka renmei), which was active until 1934, when all such organizations were prohibited by the Japanese government.

This early work by Kubo reveals the sort of mordant humor and social consciousness found in his later, full-length plays, among which is his masterpiece, *Land of Volcanic Ash* (*Kazanbaichi*, 1937/1938). Murayama himself directed the production of *Fascist Doll.*

In the center of the stage, a DOLL VENDOR *with a few dolls displayed in his nighttime street stall.*

DOLL VENDOR (*To the audience*): Step right up, step right up, folks. Here we have automated spring mechanism celluloid dolls that are all the rage right now. Ranging from those dolls you know and love and have purchased over the years to the cutting-edge popular versions so new that their patents are still pending, we have a wide array and you can buy any of them for only ten *sen*. Now folks, the factory shifts just ended, so the trains are crammed and crowded. And I don't mean to be disrespectful, but after a hard day's work for a mere pittance, to be shoved and squeezed in the train so that you're hanging on by a strap, it's only human nature to blow your top as soon as you open your front door and to want to belt your wife in the face a couple of times. So why not let five or six packed trains go by, and why not, though our shop is small, take a look at our advertised merchandise and see if anything catches your fancy? If something does, you can buy it and take it home as a present. So don't stop by one of those dangerous spots like commie meetings. Go home: you'll be able to stretch out your arms and legs on a nearly empty train so that your good woman and the little ones will be overjoyed to see you—your home will be safe and sound and your family happy to boot. I know that some folks with no foresight will think, huh, these are just a night vendor's wares and will ridicule me from the start. But our goods are not at all like those of other street stalls. All over the world—well, I'd like to say that, but Russia's in bad shape. Even the other day, in that country, a top-notch doll maker got materials from France and made a rare and spectacular kind of doll called the industrial party doll, but once the authorities, who have no eye for such things, got hold of this, they said, if you sell this, our social order will be disrupted, and so they confiscated the doll—such a sad story. So except that country, but far and wide in the countries of Europe and America, these dolls are flying off the shelves like they've grown wings. These dolls are special merchandise, unique and already tested abroad, as it were. (*To one part of the audience.*) Hello, hello, the older gentleman there in the short workman's coat, how about you buy one? This model is old but it's the social democratic doll everyone knows, made of Dutch yellow celluloid and is an especially fine, well-made item. (*Saying this, he lifts a doll.*) You have to try it—put some paper money in front of this doll and see. It uses a miraculous and mysterious spring mechanism that takes advantage of the latest scientific advances, so as soon as it sees the money, this doll extends its hands and bows repeatedly as if it were alive—if I may say so myself. Eh? What? This won't be popular in your social circles? Eh? What? I should sell it to some bourgeois fat cat? Oh, be like that. Hey, you over there—you have only enough money for one train ticket in that work apron pocket of yours, right? Customers who can't make up their minds about making a mere ten-*sen* purchase just take up valuable space, so I ask you not to stand in front of the merchandise. (*Looking toward another section of the audience.*) Hello, buddy, you in the work uniform over there, how about this one? It's a bright red energetic celluloid doll, the kind that's popular right now. It's called the left-wing social democratic doll—don't you like it? What? Huh? Your pal Tora from next door bought one? So what? If you buy one, then the two of you will match. Huh? What? When Tora scrubbed it with a rag, the red paint came off and what was underneath was as predicted, bright yellow? Oh, thanks a lot for letting the cat out of the bag. Huh? What? When you tried and showed the doll some paper money, it stretched out its hands and bowed? Hmmm, OK. That's great. Yup, the customers tonight are a class apart. Since you all have good discerning eyes, I guess I have no choice but to switch my plans and bring out the special stuff. (*He picks up another doll.*) OK, hold on to your hats. This one is called the fascist doll, and if you want to hear its origins, well, the Mussolini Company of Italy started to sell this doll for the first time in 1920, and it shocked the whole world, that's how splendid and notorious this doll is. It was right after the red commie dolls made of steel sold by the Bolshevik Company were banned in Italy, and those who bought those dolls and those who sold them got yelled at severely by the authorities, so this fascist doll spread over the whole country in a flash. To tell the truth, the doll wasn't that well received by the workers, but those middling farmers and the bourgeoisie—those brave folks who hated anything red—eagerly coveted this doll. The fascist doll, otherwise known as the prop of monopoly capitalism, is made of celluloid, but what celluloid it is! I'm not exaggerating: it's strong and durable, see, just like this (*Places the doll on the ground and steps on it.*) You can step on it and kick it, but it won't break. What? Step on it with more force? That's not good. Why? Because it's made of celluloid, so it's not like that red commie doll that was made out of steel. (*Picks the doll up carefully.*) So because this doll sells so well, doll makers wanting to follow Italy's example are increasing daily and monthly in places like Hungary, Poland, and Spain. So at long last, this doll is making itself well known in the middle of Europe, even in Germany's Weimar Republic. In countries all around the world, workers are becoming smarter and smarter, so no one wants to buy the social democratic doll any more. So up until now, those who made those yellow celluloid dolls are changing their tune, and most of the clever ones are now exclusively selling this fascist doll using threatening means. Of course a very few of our colleagues are—well, no, we can't say very few but those idiots who can't see past their noses—have shifted to become red commie doll makers, even though they shouldn't do that. I should cut the small talk, but suffice it to say that because of the trends abroad, Japanese in the same business are now eyeing the fascist doll. And so my distributor decided to get ahead of the competition and submitted a patent application before anyone else did. While we wait for the patent to be authorized, for publicity's sake we're slashing prices, so even though I'd like to ask fifty *sen*, I'm asking forty *sen*, thirty *sen*, twenty *sen*, fifteen *sen*, how about a rock bottom price of ten *sen*? Step right up, step right up, folks, buy your hearts out. Huh? What? With such a poor spiel, you're not likely to buy the doll, even though you wanted to at first? Huh? You have no clue as to why the fascist doll became popular even in Germany? Gotcha. I look like I'm clueless about what I'm doing? Not likely. The latest news is that for the purposes of expanding fascist doll sales, Germany's dictatorship's publicity value is 100 percent. You can't even begin to know how much more interesting it is than some red propaganda speech. In that country, Germany—I know you know this already—until the spring of last year, the social democratic dolls manufactured by the Hermann Müller Company, which were so much better than the Japanese social democratic dolls, dominated their market. But this company fell on hard times, and so on one hand they reduced wages and reduced unemployment insurance while on the other hand they made gigantic cruisers and crushed May Day that the commies supported and dissolved that frightful society called the something or other Fighters' League. After all the service they provided with amazing versatility for the financial bourgeoisie, at that point this was no longer simply a social democratic doll. It somehow quickly transmogrified into a fascist doll. Where this doll differs from the Japanese version is not only that this celluloid is very hard and the finish is stupendous, but also, unlike the Japanese version, what makes this doll a keeper is that when you show it small amounts of money, it won't give you a cheap bow. But finally, the Hermann Müller Company created a big hole in its financial holdings and had to sell itself to the Brüning Alliance Company. This company is even more of a fascist doll distributor. That's because just behind it lurks the dark horse of this field, the Hitler Company. So the Brüning Alliance Company is finally putting all its skills together—now that the world economy is so bad, you really can't talk about sluggardly bourgeois democratic parliamentary government. So what if they're called high-handed and despotic—they have to concentrate all their forces and get stuff done lickety-split or else who's going to maintain global security, or German security, for that matter? Eh? What? You're saying that's all security only for the bourgeoisie?—Hey, no heckling here. The Brüning Alliance Company has been promulgating countless "emergency orders" from July of last year to this past October seventh. What? High-handed? How could this possibly be high-handed? This here is written ostentatiously in article 48 of the Weimar Constitution. Ignoramuses won't know this, but the current republic was founded after the kaiser and his whiskers faded away from the international limelight in 1918. Then those German bourgeois folks went around saying that the Weimar Republic's Constitution was the most liberal constitution in the world, and you know what? That's true. So they're doing exactly what that most free constitution dictates, so no one can complain. Ergo, what allows the German president, in times of emergency, to take any military, fiscal, or administrative measures he wants without going through the parliament is article 48. What? You're absolutely opposed to dictatorships? Oh, shut up and listen quietly. So to make it through this unprecedented depression, the whole country has to come together and bear the suffering. Hey, hey, buddy, you over there, don't toss your cigarette butt just anywhere. Our products are made of celluloid, you know. Just like in Japan, in Germany, there's a flood of out-of-work folks. At the end of the year before last, there were two point one million unemployed. At the end of last year, there were three point eight million. At the beginning of this year, there were four point eight million, and this summer there were five million unemployed. At this rate, who knows how far it'll go, but the reason why we have such staggering multitudes of unemployed workers—argh, be quiet, be quiet—it's because those shortsighted commies are taking advantage of the people's dissatisfaction and are preaching incredible nonsense and putting the country in disarray and making the workers play hooky from work. Because they don't work, the national productivity of Germany is decreasing. Because productivity is decreasing, depression happens, and because we're in a depression, people are losing their jobs—argh, shut up, shut up. This is the important part. So, the great thing about this fascist doll that we're advertising right now is its facade of ultranationalism. Japan wants to preserve ultranationalist thought just as much as any country around the world. What? The reason why fascism is nationalist and exclusionist is because it's preparing for a war of aggression? Errh, wait, wait a second, wait I tell you. These "emergency orders" that bypass a pesky parliament, on one hand, reduce the taxes on companies and securities so that the current big shot financial bourgeoisie of the world have an easier time of it so that they can work toward rebuilding the economy, but on the other hand, the orders ask the people to bear with it, since the World War I was a while ago, and so relief allowances to disabled soldiers and families of those soldiers who were killed in action are being reduced as much as possible, and the salaries of petty bureaucrats and lower-ranking military men are also being cut, so the plan is to sacrifice the little fish in order to let the big fish live. So this is how it goes: in this capitalist world, all sorts of trendy items like the social democratic doll and the fascist doll keep appearing and serving as props, but like it says in the instructions that come with the red commie doll, fantasies no longer come true. What? You don't think that a celluloid doll like this can be a prop? I'm not kidding, I already did the experiment before your very eyes and showed you how sturdy this is and how it won't break even when you step on it. Are you calling me a liar? I'll show you again. Look, see? Just like this, just like this. Harder, harder. (*Uses too much force, and the doll cracks and disintegrates underfoot.*) Oh boy, I did a terrible thing. I wasted a precious piece of merchandise. (*Picks up the doll remorsefully.*) Oh great. All those customers I gathered are now scattered. (*Making his voice even louder.*) Step right up, step right up, gather 'round everyone, and take a look at the famous automated, spring mechanism, fascist doll. Since we're promoting this item while we wait for its patent to be approved, we're slashing prices, so it's only ten *sen*. They're marked down, folks, and they're selling like hotcakes. Tonight we started out with a hundred of these dolls, but we only have ten of them left. It's getting late, so out of a sense of sacrificial social service, even though we want the popular price to be ten *sen*, I'll give it to you for eight *sen*, six *sen*, five *sen*, four *sen*, oh, let me slash the price even further and ask for just one *sen*, just one bronze one-*sen* piece. Oh shit, no one's buying even at this price? Won't someone buy one? Buy one?

(*As the* VENDOR*'s voice grows hoarse because he's still yelling, the stage grows dark.*)

CURTAIN

Enchi Fumiko, *Restless Night in Late Spring*, directed by Matsunami Kyōsuke, Seinen gekijō, November 2004. (Photograph by Kurahara Teruhito)

RESTLESS NIGHT IN LATE SPRING

ENCHI FUMIKO

TRANSLATED BY AYAKO KANO

R*estless Night in Late Spring* (*Banshun sōya*) is a one-act play by Enchi Fumiko (1905–1986), published in the September 1928 issue of the magazine *Women's Arts* (*Nyonin geijutsu*) and produced in December of the same year at the Tsukiji Little Theater. As the translator Ayako Kano points out, this was a remarkable accomplishment for such a young woman during this period.

The conflict in the play is between the attitudes of two women painters concerning their differing commitment to art and politics, thus mirroring in successful dramatic terms one of the important conflicts in Japanese intellectual life at the time.

Enchi wrote a number of plays into the 1930s and then fell silent during the war. Then in the postwar period, she became famous for her series of novels and stories about various aspects of feminine psychology. She also produced a much-admired translation into modern Japanese of the eleventh-century classic *The Tale of Genji*.

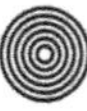

No bird soars too high
If he soars with his own wings.

WILLIAM BLAKE

Characters

YUZURU, a middle-aged man
EMI SHIZUKO, a woman around age twenty, the maid
KAYOKO, a woman of twenty-five or twenty-six, YUZURU's younger sister
SHINOZAKI MITSUKO, a woman of twenty-four or twenty-five, KAYOKO's friend

Time: Present (1928).
Place: Tokyo.

The second floor of a shabby rental house. Beyond the corridor upstage, the distant lights of the town at night are visible through the tops of a few trees in the yard. (However, when the curtain is raised, the shōji *screens are closed, and thus the distant view is invisible.) To the left at the back of the corridor is the top of a staircase. There are two connected rooms. The room on the left is about eight mats large; the room on the right is smaller. The larger room is the younger sister's room and also her studio. A jumble of frames for Japanese-style painting, brushes, paper, and paint dishes are on one side. A large vase on a tall pedestal holds purple wisteria and yellow Japanese roses past their peak. These scatter sensual colors that do not match the atmosphere of this impoverished room. They are protectively surrounded by a small old folding screen. Nearby stands a frame with a silk canvas painting of these flowers, about three-quarters finished.*

The lights are off in this room. Subdued light from the adjoining room comes in through the open fusuma *screen door, and one can perceive dim shapes. The adjoining room is the older brother's sickroom, and except for his futon, there is hardly any decoration or furniture.*

It is a night in late spring, with a barely warm wind from the south blowing wildly. Just past nine o'clock at night.

When the curtain opens, YUZURU *is on his bed.*

For quite a while, only the ominous sound of the wind.

Suddenly YUZURU *starts to cough, like someone suffering from asthma. While coughing, he turns over on his stomach and tries to pour water from a kettle by his pillow into a glass. Finding the kettle empty, he clicks his tongue in frustration and claps his hands. Pause. No answer. After a while, he struggles to his feet holding the kettle. He is a middle-aged man, with a pale face and a skinny frame. He exits to the hallway and walks to the top of the stairs.*

YUZURU (*Croaking like an old man*): Miss Emi, Miss Emi.

(*The voice of a young woman answers from downstairs.*)

YUZURU: Could you please get me some water in this kettle—yes, it's all gone.

SHIZUKO (*From halfway up the ladder*): Why didn't you just call me—you shouldn't have gotten up. You'll get worse again.

YUZURU (*Laughs sadly*): No big deal.

SHIZUKO: I'll bring it right away. You should get yourself back to bed. (*Goes down the steps.*)

(YUZURU, *nervously fidgeting, returns to the room, then looks in his sister's room. He keeps his hands in his pockets as if too lazy to take them out. Stands comparing the flowers in the vase and his sister's painting.*)

SHIZUKO (*Comes upstairs with the water. She is around twenty years old, chubby and girlish*): Oh no! You're still standing there? It's bad for you. Really. What if you get sick again like night before last?

YUZURU (*Stumbles back to his bed. Drinks a swig of water*): It's all right. As long as I get the injection, it won't be so bad.

SHIZUKO (*Closes the screen door to the adjacent room*): Is that so? It looked like you were in a lot of pain. I'd never seen such a thing; I was scared. —Does this sort of thing happen all the time, then?

YUZURU: Well, it gets this bad only five, six times a year.

SHIZUKO: Gosh. That many times?

YUZURU: It happens just as I'm beginning to relax. So I can't let my guard down. —For a while it looked like I was going to die, didn't it?

SHIZUKO: Yes, it really did. But I was a bit relieved when I saw how calm your sister was.

YUZURU: It's like being tortured. (*Pause.*) For almost ten years, this disease has bullied me and the people around me.

SHIZUKO: Is there no way to get yourself cured completely?

YUZURU (*Jokingly*): Short of getting myself killed, no.

SHIZUKO: Oh no. Don't say that!

(*Downstairs, the clock strikes ten.*)

YUZURU: It's ten already?

SHIZUKO: Yes, but that clock's running fast. (*Pause.*) She's late, isn't she?

YUZURU: Who? Kayoko?

SHIZUKO: She said she'd be home by nine.

YUZURU: That's not likely once she's left the house. It's the art school's anniversary party tonight, isn't it? That's got to be some party. She won't be back till eleven.

SHIZUKO: You think so?

(*A slight pause.*)

SHIZUKO: Speaking of which, have you heard the rumor about Miss Shinozaki Mitsuko?

YUZURU (*With eyes shining*): That Miss Shinozaki who comes to visit Kayoko?

SHIZUKO: Yes, you know everyone at school is talking about her.

YUZURU: Really. (*Pause.*) That she's getting married?

SHIZUKO: That's what they say.

YUZURU: Is that right.

SHIZUKO: And the groom is a leftist scholar of economics, they say. Rumor has it that Miss Shinozaki herself is getting pretty red these days.

YUZURU: Is that so. That's news to me. Did Kayoko tell you?

SHIZUKO: No, I heard it from other people. She's so pretty, you know, she's already broken lots of hearts, and now she's getting married—some say the art school's popularity's sure to crash, like she was some kind of actress. (*Amused laugh.*)

YUZURU (*Laughs along listlessly*): Indeed, that might happen.

(*A bell rings downstairs.*)

SHIZUKO: She's home. (*Runs off.*)

(*A long pause. Footsteps coming up the stairs.* KAYOKO *sticks her head in while standing in the hallway. She is twenty-five or twenty-six, a woman with a dark complexion and an intelligent look.*)

KAYOKO: I'm home.

YUZURU: You're early.

KAYOKO: I know. I brought Mitsuko. How are you feeling?

YUZURU: I'm all right, I guess.

KAYOKO: Good. I'll be next door, call me if you need me. (*Closes the* shōji *screen.*) Come in, come in, don't just stand there.

MITSUKO (*Offstage*): It's all right. (*Laughs.*)

KAYOKO: Don't be silly. (*Comes into her room and turns on the light.*) Ugh, so humid! (*Opens the* shōji *screen.*)

MITSUKO (*She is twenty-four or twenty-five and beautiful*): It really is humid tonight, isn't it.

KAYOKO: Looks like it's going to rain.

MITSUKO: What a nuisance, I didn't bring an umbrella. (*Looks at the flowers.*) How pretty. Those are gorgeous flowers.

KAYOKO: They're going to scatter any second—so fragile.

MITSUKO: I like how you've put the screen around it. You should paint that, too.

KAYOKO: You must be kidding. (*Laughing, goes toward the stairs.*) Miss Emi, some tea, please.

MITSUKO: It's OK, Kayoko; I'm in a hurry tonight.

KAYOKO: Oh, don't worry. You can stay here if it gets too late.

MITSUKO: No, I can't do that. I've another place to go after this.

KAYOKO: After this? (*A slight pause.*) Oh, I remember, you said before that you had something to tell me. All right, I'm listening.

MITSUKO: OK, I'll tell you. (*Pause.*) Don't be shocked.

KAYOKO: I won't be shocked. (*Instinctively.*) Are you getting married?

MITSUKO (*Pause*): Yes.

KAYOKO: Really?

MITSUKO: You knew?

KAYOKO: Of course I knew. It's been on the grapevine for quite some time.

(SHIZUKO *comes upstairs with tea and sweets.*)

KAYOKO: Thank you, you can put it down there.

(SHIZUKO *leaves.* KAYOKO *pours tea silently.*)

KAYOKO: There you go.

MITSUKO: Thank you.

(*Pause.* YUZURU *listens in on their conversation from the next room.*)

MITSUKO: Kayoko, weren't you angry at me? That I kept it a secret from you?

KAYOKO: Of course not. (*Pause.*) So the person in question, it's that Mr. Shimizu they're talking about?

MITSUKO: That's right. Who told you?

KAYOKO: Who? All kinds of people have been telling me about him. But I thought it was pointless to ask you something like that directly, so I kept quiet.

MITSUKO: I wish everyone were like you and left me alone (*Pause.*) You know, these past few months, so many awful things have happened, I could hardly bear it by myself. I thought of asking you for advice, just you. But in the end, it comes down to my own attitude, you know? And I'd only cause you trouble if I told you, so I didn't on purpose.

KAYOKO: That's fine. I really think one must solve one's own problems. If you rely on someone else's advice, you'll only regret it later. (*Pause.*) But I'm glad for you, that it's been resolved. I heard that your family was objecting, or something like that.

MITSUKO: It was a big fight. (*Laughs bitterly.*) They disowned me, you know.

KAYOKO: Really. —That was brave of you.

MITSUKO: They just would not agree to it. (*Slight pause.*) But don't ask me any more right now, OK? I'll tell you all about it some time.

KAYOKO (*Nods*): You'll stay in town after you're married, won't you?

MITSUKO: No, that's just it. Shimizu will be going to Kyushu soon. He's been lecturing in all kinds of places, but now they're asking him to go to Fukuoka. There'll be a lot of things to research, so he's really excited about going. That's one reason the marriage question came up so soon.

KAYOKO: I see. But if you go along, it'll be pretty hard for you to keep on painting, won't it?

MITSUKO (*Silent. Then*): I made up my mind. I'm going to stop painting.

KAYOKO (*Surprised*): My, but that's . . . Really?

MITSUKO: Yes.

KAYOKO: But that would mean wasting everything you've achieved until now. . . . I don't understand.

MITSUKO: I knew you'd be against it. But I don't want us to part having told you some kind of lie, so I'll tell you everything today. I've kept it hidden from Professor Mizuki and you as much as I could, but for quite some time now, from the time I fell in love with Shimizu, my philosophy has changed completely. (KAYOKO *says nothing.*) I feel bad for the professor, but I've lost all interest in this kind of painting (*Points to the frame*) or in any kind of conventional art that doesn't connect with modern science. I submitted a piece to the imperial art exhibit last year, but that was just by sheer inertia; even when the acceptance notice came, I didn't feel elated like the first time, and in any case, I just felt disgusted looking at the faces of those fancy ladies and gentlemen, staring vacantly at my painting. That's when it started really sinking in that my painting's of no use whatsoever, except to satisfy my own vanity and the spiritual vanity of the bourgeoisie. And I started thinking that I can't keep messing around with this kind of stuff any longer. Hiding behind the name of art and ignoring the injustice of society in which people live—such egoism disgusts me. Our era is not one where we can wallow in such superficial narcissism. I think it's inevitable that an ordinary artist like me, born in this era, would turn into an ordinary Marxist girl. When I go to Kyushu, I shall use my body and my mind to help Shimizu as much as I can. And I want to start by fundamentally transforming myself to adapt to the proletariat way of life.

KAYOKO (*As if talking to herself*): Can one actually transform one's life so fundamentally?

MITSUKO: At least I can, right now. In fact, I believe right now that I've managed to cut myself off from everything in my past. From now on, I'm no longer the daughter of a country landowner or the last painter in the line of the Shijō school. I'm determined to throw away all those things and devote my whole life to vital and honest work as Shimizu's wife. Right now must be a turning point for my own life. (*A slight pause.*) But Shimizu's the one who will guide me in a good direction from here.

KAYOKO: In that case, you've sold your whole past to Mr. Shimizu.

MITSUKO: I suppose you could say that. But I believe in him. (*Passionately.*) I'm so grateful he woke me out of my empty dream and led me to this place where I am now. As long as I'm with him, no matter what difficulties we may have, I'll never regret it.

KAYOKO: I have no reason to dismiss something you trust so much. But I myself would never think of what we've been doing until now as just an empty dream. Holding a paint brush isn't messing around; it's not vanity, it's honest labor. It's reality, nothing more, nothing less. If the viewer treats my painting as a mere trifle, that's not my problem. My own feeling when I am trying to paint is always serious, almost unbearably so. (*Falls silent, then after a pause.*) I can't help but be serious, in every sense of the word.

MITSUKO (*Smiling cheerfully*): I understand that. I went through that period, too. But I could never lose myself in such insignificant feelings now.

KAYOKO: Insignificant?!

MITSUKO: Well, if insignificant is a bad word, you could call it too leisurely or too quiet. In any case, for myself right now, I just can't think that a life like this, stuck in my room, facing a canvas, cutting off contact with the outside world, is truly real. If I have the time to make washed-out conventional art, to give a bit of refreshment to the bloated guts of the bourgeoisie, it would mean much more for humanity to lend my hand to awakening the blind masses that are starving in the streets. (*Pause.*) My own hands have been smeared with paint for so long. I mean to purify them by baptism in soil.

KAYOKO (*Becomes agitated by* MITSUKO*'s words but gradually controls herself. She is silent for a while*): You and I are quite far apart in how our personalities have developed, aren't we. I guess we weren't meant to keep walking hand in hand through life. (*Pause.*) If I told you what I thought, we'd just end up arguing for no good reason, so I won't say anything right now. Just one thing—your decision right now may or may not be the result of a passing infatuation. That's something only time will tell. But in any case, you're willing to draw a clear line in your life. I really envy that. (*Pause.*) A person who can decide "what ought to be" and can act on that is lucky indeed.

MITSUKO (*Laughs lightly*): Lucky or unlucky, it doesn't matter. I was propelled by an inevitable force.

KAYOKO: And I, on the other hand . . . (*Begins but stops.*)

(*Another long pause.*)

MITSUKO: Since I've already upset you tonight, I want to go ahead and talk about you, too. Will you hear me out?

KAYOKO (*Nods.*)

MITSUKO: I'm worried about your art.

KAYOKO (*Tries to say something.*)

MITSUKO: Don't worry, even as a believer in "what ought to be," I'm not going to tell you to leave the studio or anything like that. But I want to advise you, since this is a good opportunity, about your artistic style. You say you want to make a career as a painter in the Japanese tradition—but right now you're conforming too much to the conservative style of Professor Mizuki's school, don't you think? Good art must reflect its age in every sense of the word. We worked so hard to master this artistic style, but no matter how you look at it, it's just a remnant of the Edo era. It's completely unsuited to our contemporary way of life. It's too simplistic and too conventional, even for expressing what I know you have in yourself right now. . . . Don't you think so?

KAYOKO: I know all that. (*Pause.*) But there are no easy solutions to this problem. (*Pause.*) It's because I've struggled twice, three times as much as you to get where I am today, in material terms and in terms of talent.

MITSUKO (*Pressing further*): But you can't believe that if you stay here in comfort you'd be able to produce art of the first order, right? You don't believe, as our teacher does, that our style of painting is the best?

KAYOKO (*Pause*): Mitsuko, I beg you, leave me alone. I'm thinking about all that myself too, you know.

MITSUKO: Of course, I don't want to force this kind of speech on you, but it doesn't look like we'll have another chance to sit down like this and discuss art. . . . I just wanted to tell you, as a favor before I cut myself off from conventional art and disappear into the whirlwind of the class struggle. (*Pause.*) I don't want to think of you as someone who'd be content with the title "painter accepted into the imperial exhibition" and wouldn't try to improve herself artistically. Kayoko, I beg of you, please lead a healthy and honest life, at least in the art world, OK? Please?

KAYOKO (*Suddenly sarcastically*): Thank you. But in any case, I doubt my way of life could be as healthy as yours. (*Pause.*) Mitsuko, you're lucky. (*Gazes at her.*)

MITSUKO: Don't be silly. (*Starts to laugh but, struck by the gravity of the other's facial expression, turns serious.*) Why?

KAYOKO (*Does not answer but looks down.*)

(YUZURU *has been listening intently to the conversation in the next room but now suddenly starts to cough.*)

MITSUKO (*Looking up*): Your brother is still sick?

(KAYOKO *nods.* YUZURU *stops coughing.*)

KAYOKO: Mitsuko, you said a moment ago that my life was too quiet and filled with leisure. But from my perspective, you're the one who's leisurely, much more so than I. You have the leisure to be altruistic. (*Hesitant pause.*) Far from messing around with a paintbrush, I clutch it desperately; that's the kind of human being I am. Other than painting pictures, I have no way of making a living, no source of self-respect. (*Pause.*) That's probably also the real reason I'm stuck in one place and can't move easily. I'm a human being who's not allowed to keep looking ahead and moving forward. (MITSUKO *is silent.*) I understand everything you're saying. But to me, you seem a bit cruel. (*Laughs casually.*)

MITSUKO (*Thinks a little*): I'm sorry. I think I've forced my ideas on you. But I couldn't help telling you. Please don't take it the wrong way.

KAYOKO: I know, I know, I understand. (*Laughs bitterly. A slightly awkward pause.*) When are you leaving?

MITSUKO: At the beginning of next month.

KAYOKO: That's pretty soon, then.

MITSUKO: Yes, that's why— (*Begins to say more but looks at the clock.*) Oh, it's half past ten already. I have to go. (*Stands.*)

KAYOKO: Where are you going now?

MITSUKO: Well, you know, it's that big fight over at M University. Professor Sawa being fired because of his political beliefs and our protesting his termination? There's a rally tonight at the youth center, and Shimizu went there to give a speech. I meant to go there after this—I'll stop by again. Sorry to stay so long. Take good care of your brother, OK?

KAYOKO: Thanks. (*The two go downstairs.*)

(YUZURU *gets up and goes toward the veranda. A long pause.* KAYOKO *goes up the stairs again.* YUZURU *hurries back into his bed. Noticing that* YUZURU *seems to have been awake,* KAYOKO *stands quietly by the veranda. She is about to talk to him but stops. Another long pause.*)

SHIZUKO (*Enters. Clears away the cups, laughing*): Is it true, then, that Miss Shinozaki is going to get married?

KAYOKO (*Standing on the veranda, sullenly*): It seems that way.

SHIZUKO: So it was true, then. The rumors kept flying, so I was wondering.

KAYOKO: It's none of your business. Just hurry up and clean that away.

SHIZUKO (*Taking note of the other's mood*): Certainly. (*Hurriedly collects the teacups and tries to stand up and leave. Her sleeve is caught on a branch in the flower vase. The vase tips over, and water splashes on the canvas.*) Oh!

KAYOKO (*Agitated, face distorted, runs over*): Don't just stand there, hurry up and get a rag!

(SHIZUKO *runs downstairs.*)

KAYOKO (*Puts the vase back and tries to gather up the flowers. The petals of the wisteria and Japanese rose scatter. Looks back at the painting*): Oh! What a mess. (*With a sponge, she gently wipes off the water. The damage is irreversible. Upset, she stands brooding.*)

(*A downpour of rain begins and gradually grows louder.*)

SHIZUKO (*Comes upstairs with cleaning rag. Tries to wipe the floor, then notices*): Oh! Did something happen to the painting? (*Peering at it.*) Oh no, a big mess—what am I going to do? I'm so clumsy. (*Close to tears.*)

KAYOKO (*Spitting it out*): There's nothing we can do. Just hurry and wipe up the floor.

SHIZUKO: Yes, of course. (*Cleans.*)

KAYOKO (*Has come out to the veranda with the flowers in her hand and has been glancing back at the painting but, suddenly upset, shakes the flower branches with full force. All the remaining petals scatter.*)

SHIZUKO (*A bit taken aback, looks on silently*): Oh, I'm really sorry. You worked so hard on that painting, and now—can't it be fixed? (KAYOKO *is silent.*)

SHIZUKO: What am I going to do? And this was a commissioned painting, wasn't it?

(KAYOKO *is silent.*)

SHIZUKO (*Pleading*): If it's just the flowers, I think I can buy them again somewhere—what do you think?

(KAYOKO *silently comes into the room, puts her hands on the frame, and tries to rip out the silk canvas.*)

SHIZUKO (*Shocked*): What are you doing?

KAYOKO (*Calmly*): I'm pulling it out. This painting can't be saved.

SHIZUKO: But you could try again tomorrow to fix it—and then you could—

KAYOKO (*Not answering, keeps trying to rip without success.*)

(SHIZUKO *finally starts to cry.*)

YUZURU (*In a severe tone, from the next room*): Kayoko!

KAYOKO: —

YUZURU: Kayoko, what are you doing?!

KAYOKO: —

YUZURU: Why don't you answer? (*Rises and comes over.*)

(KAYOKO *roughly flings down the frame, throws herself over it, and begins to cry.*)

YUZURU: Fool! Look at you. What do you think you're doing?

(KAYOKO *cries even harder.*)

YUZURU (*Looks at his crying sister with hatred in his eyes. Slight pause*): Stop it. That's enough. You've made your point already.

KAYOKO: —

(SHIZUKO *has stopped crying and is looking at* YUZURU *questioningly.*)

YUZURU: You don't need to do all that. I know well enough what you're thinking. (*Continuing to cough, laughs coolly.*) I may be an invalid who's half dead, but my nerves are as sharp as anyone's.

KAYOKO: You've got me wrong.

YUZURU: If you think I got you wrong, I got you wrong. But I think I understand you all too well.

KAYOKO (*Annoyed*): You understand nothing. You— (*Hesitates slightly but then resolutely.*) you're the one who's picking on me because you heard Mitsuko's getting married.

YUZURU: Stop that nonsense. I know exactly what you're thinking. I know that *you're* upset because Mitsuko's running off to get hitched.

KAYOKO (*Laughs a little hysterically*): You say that, but it's you, you who's suddenly lonely because you lost Mitsuko. I feel sorry for you.

YUZURU (*Pale*): Fool! Try saying that again!

KAYOKO: You think I'm blind?

(YUZURU, *furious, stares at his sister's face. Suddenly the door bell rings.* SHIZUKO, *relieved at the opportunity, runs downstairs.* YUZURU, *finally controlling himself, is about to withdraw to his room without saying anything.*)

KAYOKO: Wait.

(YUZURU *does not answer but slams shut the* fusuma *door.*)

SHIZUKO (*From downstairs*): It's Miss Shinozaki again.

KAYOKO (*Doubtfully*): Miss Shinozaki?

(MITSUKO *comes hurriedly upstairs. Her clothes are wet from the rain.*)

KAYOKO: My goodness, what happened?

MITSUKO (*Extremely agitated*): I'm sorry. I'm a mess.

KAYOKO: What happened? You're sopping wet. No umbrella?

MITSUKO: No time for that—they've arrested Shimizu.

KAYOKO: But why?

MITSUKO: After I left here, I immediately went to the youth center. It was still early, but they told me the rally was canceled. Things felt kind of tense, so I asked some students from M University who were still there. And they told me that Shimizu had been taken into custody! I was so shocked. They say he mentioned something incendiary during his speech, so some right-wing activist types jumped up on the stage and punched him. And then, of course, Shimizu's friends and students from M University jumped into the fray. —In the end, the police came and took everyone away. They say Shimizu was hurt. But by the time I got there, it was all over. I was so mad!

KAYOKO: Well, then, it was Mr. Shimizu who was the victim of violence, wasn't he. And besides—

MITSUKO: No, no. With someone like Shimizu, the authorities are always hostile. Besides, who knows what kind of connection they've got to those gangs that came to the rally tonight? (*Pause.*) It can't be helped. Something like this was going to happen, and it won't be the last time, either.

KAYOKO (*Has recovered from her own excitement and calmed down again*): So what are you going to do tonight? Are you going to go to the police?

MITSUKO: Yes. It may be a lost cause, but I'll go there tonight.

KAYOKO: By yourself?

MITSUKO: No, I phoned various places trying to find Shimizu's friends, but most of them couldn't be reached. Finally I found someone who's willing to come right away—I'm really sorry to trouble you, but since your house is on the way, I told him I'd meet him here. I'm sorry—it's so late.

KAYOKO: I don't care about that. But it must be hard on you. You must be worried.

MITSUKO: It happens to him all the time, they say, but it's the first for me. (*Laughs a bit.*) But I'm ready for it. Since I'm going to be his wife, I can expect worse, much worse, much more hardship for me to endure. . . .

(KAYOKO *looks at* MITSUKO*'s excited face rather coolly.*)

MITSUKO (*As if swearing to herself*): No matter what may come, I will not be defeated. Because we are led by proper reason and inevitable passion. —Deep in our hearts lies a rapture that no one else can see. (*Suddenly collapses.*)

KAYOKO (*Shocked*): Mitsuko, what's wrong? Mitsuko! (MITSUKO *does not respond.*) Did she faint? Miss Emi, Miss Emi?

SHIZUKO (*Comes upstairs*): Oh dear! What happened? Did she faint?

KAYOKO: I think so, but in any case . . . (*Tries to lay* MITSUKO *down.*)

(MITSUKO *moans faintly and tries to rouse herself.*)

KAYOKO: Are you all right, Mitsuko?

MITSUKO: Th-thank you. It's nothing. Just a bit . . .

KAYOKO (*To* SHIZUKO): There's wine in my brother's room. Bring it please.

(SHIZUKO *goes and brings wine in a cup. Not moving,* YUZURU *lies fully covered under his blanket.*)

KAYOKO: Drink some of this.

MITSUKO: OK. (*Drinks.*) Thank you. I was just a bit dizzy. (*Stands up unsteadily.*) I'm all right now.

KAYOKO: Take it easy. Shall I make a bed for you?

MITSUKO: No, it's all right. I'm fine now.

KAYOKO: But you can't go like that to the police tonight.

MITSUKO: Nonsense—I have to go.

(*The bell rings again.*)

MITSUKO: There he is. Good-bye then. I'll come again to thank you.

KAYOKO: But Mitsuko. . . .

MITSUKO: No, no, it's all right. I'm not that fragile. (*Runs downstairs.*)

(KAYOKO *and* SHIZUKO *follow downstairs. The wind and rain are even worse. The stage turns dark. In the darkness, only the noise of the storm continues. The clock strikes two in the morning.*)

(KAYOKO, *in nightclothes, comes upstairs with a lamp in her hand. She opens the sliding door to her brother's room and peeks in but then closes the door. She turns over the frame, which had been standing wrong side up, and stands gazing at the painting. A long pause.*)

YUZURU: Is it you, Kayoko?

KAYOKO (*Surprised*): You're awake?

YUZURU (*Vaguely*): Mm. (*Pause.*) Quite a storm.

KAYOKO: The lights went out.

YUZURU: Yes.

KAYOKO: I was afraid the roof might leak, so I came to look. (*Using that as an excuse, looks around the hallway.*)

(YUZURU *tries to call to her but hesitates. A long pause.*)

KAYOKO (*Suddenly enters her brother's room*): Please forgive me, brother.

YUZURU: What?

KAYOKO: What I said before. I was wrong.

YUZURU: No need to apologize. You told the truth. But since you know me so well, I was upset that you'd go and expose feelings I was hoping to keep hidden forever. It's me who's being selfish. I should ask *you* to forgive me.

KAYOKO: No, it's me who's wrong. I got excited over nothing. I feel bad about what I did to you and Miss Emi.

YUZURU (*Pause*): Kayoko, I'm a coward. And I'm certainly not a good brother to you. But I just don't feel like showing my suffering to others. I don't even want anyone touching it with a finger. I want to put a seal on my own suffering, shut it up inside my own breast, and bear it by myself alone. It's a selfish request, but if you feel sorry for an invalid like myself, don't touch what is painful to me, now or ever. Since you know me so well, I can tell you this much. Is that all right? I'm begging you. (*Pleading.*)

KAYOKO: I know. Say no more, brother. I'll never do anything so foolish again. (*Pause.*) But you might misunderstand me because of what's happened—that's what scares me the most. You believe me, don't you? (*Takes her brother's hand.*)

YUZURU: Thank you, Kayoko. I feel so sorry for what I've done to you. I've become such an invalid, restricting your freedom in every way—you have no idea how bad that makes me feel. And yet instead of feeling grateful to you, I always end up abusing you. The more I pity you, the more my feelings become bent and twisted, and I end up lashing out at you. My illness has consumed not just my body but also my soul. It's making me rot from the inside. (*Sobs.*)

KAYOKO: Brother, let's bear each other's burdens and go on. We're used to working away from the limelight, aren't we? (*Pause.*) You know, I've been lying awake and thinking about this, and I've finally come to accept that Mitsuko and I are not going to be walking on the same path.

YUZURU: I won't say anything about myself. But as for you—and you know I'm thinking about this seriously—you should probably get married sooner or later, don't you think? I'm against your staying single like this forever.

KAYOKO: No, but that's impossible. I have no intention of getting married. (YUZURU *tries to say something.*) No, don't think it's because of you—of my having to support you. Just think of me as someone who can't easily find a good companion as Mitsuko did. (*Pause.*) Actually, when I heard that Mitsuko was finally getting married, I felt lonely and frustrated, like being plunged to the bottom of an abyss. Someone beautiful and smart like Mitsuko staying single and devoting herself to art—that had been such a source of strength and comfort to me. But then she surprised us all by finding that lover (*Pause*) and she left. She even turned her back on the conventional art we'd treasured until now. I felt like the two most important principles in my life were suddenly toppled over with her marriage —And then when I thought of your feelings about her, I was just so frustrated and flustered and couldn't help being so ridiculously upset like that.

YUZURU: And I, I was resentful because I thought the way you made Mitsuko talk about all that while I was lying next door was some kind of ruse. (*Laughs bitterly.*) It's jealousy. I know your feelings all too well, yet I just can't help myself from thinking like that. What an idiot I am.

KAYOKO: I'm no different. (*Pause.*) But now my thoughts are totally calm. Words like leisure and quiet—when she made fun of them earlier, I totally rejected them, but now I feel like they're living inside me in a different way. If she has chosen her path, I have my own path as well. I can affirm that clearly and gladly now. (*Pause.*) You missed seeing her expression when she came back here a while ago, the second time, right? (YUZURU *nods.*) Till now, I'd always envied her and never once felt sorry for her. But tonight, I pitied her somehow. In her excited eyes I caught a glimpse of the proud martyr. And all at once, every one of her gestures started looking like a stage actor's tricks, and I felt the urge to ridicule her passion. (YUZURU *is silent.*) I don't know about her future, but her current passion for becoming a communist doesn't strike me as very healthy. I can't see it as anything more than a bourgeois girl playing with fire out of boredom. When you think about it, she talks of renouncing the past, but I wonder how well she understands it. And that's exactly why she can throw away the past so easily, or talk of being reborn. When I thought about it like that, I started appreciating my own stubborn personality.

YUZURU: It may be dogmatic, but that's one way of thinking about it. In any case, it's good to trust yourself. There's nothing sadder and more pitiful than losing trust in oneself.

KAYOKO: I'm ashamed I was taken in by Mitsuko's spectacular and flamboyant passion, and I was tempted for a moment to deny my own path. She has the right to keep dreaming of the future. And I'll keep shouldering a past I cannot shake off, in my life and in my art. Who can blame me? I have principles, too. (*Pause.*) The more the storms rage on the outside, the deeper the tranquillity I'll maintain on the inside. A pure art transcending the past, present, and future might be born from such quiet detachment, don't you think?

YUZURU: Someone said, "Humans are inept executors of the will of others." It's fine to pursue one's passions. It's also fine to remain quiet. In either case, you should try to grow without losing sight of yourself (*Pause.*) Life has many paths. No reason why there should be only one way to live.

(*The light of the candle is extinguished by the wind.*)

KAYOKO: Oh, it went out. (*Strikes a match and lights the candle.*) We've been talking too long. Let's go to sleep. (*Stands up.*)

YUZURU (*Laughs*): The wind seems to have died down a little.

KAYOKO: The rain's letting up, too. (*Pause.*) I wonder what's happened to Mitsuko?

YUZURU: Who knows? (*Pause. As if to change the subject.*) Tomorrow will be sunny for sure.

KAYOKO: True. This storm might bring a change.

YUZURU: Spring should be over soon. All the gloomy rain and wind, day after day. I can't wait to see the refreshing sunshine of early summer.

KAYOKO: For sure. The beginning of summer's also the best season for your health, isn't it. Well, good night then.

YUZURU: Can you sleep? Do you want some of my Calmotin? (*Picks up the medicine by his pillow.*)

KAYOKO (*Takes it*): Thanks. Good night then.

YUZURU: Good night.

(KAYOKO *goes downstairs. Darkness as before. The sound of rain.*)

CURTAIN

JAPANESE WOMEN PLAYWRIGHTS

From Meiji to the Present

YOSHIE INOUE

At the end of the twentieth century, several women playwrights appeared who dazzled the public. Although they were thought to be the first in Japanese theater, women playwrights actually have been active since the Meiji period. Very few of them, however, have been included in most drama and/or literary histories. No doubt this is because drama histories are mostly about theater movements rather than individual dramatists and because these women were part of a literary history that still is monopolized by men. Next, then, is a brief history of Japanese women playwrights and their work from the Meiji period to the present.

THE APPEARANCE OF WOMEN PLAYWRIGHTS

Beginning in the Meiji period (1868–1912), in addition to kabuki, the new drama (*shingeki*) began to be performed, and so there was a great demand for playwrights. Women playwrights were first noticed in the first decade of the twentieth century, about ten years after their male counterparts. In 1910, Matsui Sumako (1886–1919), one of the first trained professional actresses in Japan (since the kabuki performers were male), made a sensational debut, and a year later, performances by the actresses' troupe at the Imperial Theater (Teigeki joyūgeki) were begun. At the same time, Hiratsuka Raichō (1886–1971) and other graduates of Japan Women's University (Nihon joshi daigaku) founded the journal *Bluestocking* (*Seitō*, 1911–1916), a creative forum for graduates of women's schools to write novels, poetry, and plays.

OKADA YACHIYO AND HASEGAWA SHIGURE

The first two women playwrights in the twentieth century were Okada Yachiyo and Hasegawa Shigure.[1] Okada Yachiyo (1883–1962), the younger sister of the theater director Osanai Kaoru and the wife of the famous Western-style painter Okada Saburōsuke, started writing novels in her teens, which were published under the name Osanai Yachiyo. Her first play, *Wasteland* (*Yomogiu*), was published in 1905 in the literary journal *Morning Star* (*Myōjō*). Her last play was *A Dressing Table* (*Kyōdai*), published in 1949 in the journal *Kabuki*. In all, she wrote thirty-six plays, many of which were first performed by *shinpa* or kabuki troupes. *The Boxwood Comb* (*Tsuge no kushi*, 1912), *The Thirteenth Night* (*Jūsanya*, 1922), and *The Repentance of Jirokichi* (*Jirokichi zange*, 1926) are set in the Meiji era and focus on issues concerning women. Yachiyo also worked in children's theater and wrote reviews of contemporary theater, kabuki, *shinpa*, and *shingeki*, as well as women's theater, a valuable source for theater historians of this period. After World War II, she founded a study group to nurture up-and-coming women playwrights.

The first play that Hasegawa Shigure (1879–1941) wrote, *Tidal Soundings* (*Kaichōon*), had a fortunate start because Tsubouchi Shōyō recommended it to Ii Yōhō and Kitamura Rokurō, two important *shinpa* actors, who performed it in 1908. After this auspicious debut, Shigure wrote a number of plays for kabuki and *shinpa*, such as *Kaōmaru*, *Chastity* (*Misao*), *The Tale of the Bamboo Cutter* (*Taketori monogatari*), and a dance play, *Eshima and Ikushima*. Some of her plays are still performed. Most are lyrical, historical dramas with strong elements of fantasy, but she also wrote plays like her realist drama on a contemporary theme, *One Afternoon* (*Aruhi no gogo*), published in *Bluestocking* in 1912, about women who live in farming villages. With the emergence of actresses like Matsui Sumako, as well as the literary movement led by the contributors to *Bluestocking*, women playwrights were now encouraged to write these kinds of plays. Shigure and Yachiyo also were the editors of *Women's Arts* (*Nyonin geijutsu*, 1928–1933), for women writers.

Many of the plays about love and marriage that were written by women in this period were influenced by Maurice Maeterlinck's dramas and Sigmund Freud's dream theories, but not Henrik Ibsen's *A Doll's House* (first performed in Japan in 1911, starring Matsui Sumako as Nora), which strongly influenced women's liberation and the emergence of the "new woman." The reason was that Japanese women playwrights believed that they first had to express their need for free will in discussions of love and marriage.

1. Translations of Okada Yachiyo's *The Boxwood Comb* and Hasegawa Shigure's *Rain of Ice* (*Itōri no ame*) are in M. Cody Poulton, *A Beggar's Art: Scripting Modernity in Japanese Drama, 1900–1930* (Honolulu: University of Hawai'i Press, 2010), 47–66, 191–205.

FROM THE ART THEATER TO THE TSUKIJI LITTLE THEATER AND FROM *BLUESTOCKING* TO *WOMEN'S ARTS*

After Shimamura Hōgetsu founded the Art Theater (Geijutsuza, 1913–1919) and traveled with his troupe all over Japan, contemporary theater, which until that time had been limited to performances in major urban areas, now began to spread to the provinces. New small theater groups that would have been unimaginable a few years earlier now began to crop up and their audiences grew, in part because after the Russo-Japanese War (1904/1905), the number of well-to-do and very rich people increased. These families sent their children to middle schools, high schools, and (their daughters) girls' schools, where they learned about the theater. Some even began writing and performing plays. In general, as the theatergoing population expanded, it became possible for women, who had had only a marginal role in the theater, to move to a more central position as modern playwrights.

The founding of the Tsukiji Little Theater (Tsukiji shōgekijō) in 1924 marked the end of the so-called age of Taishō drama, during which time many well-known women writers—such as Yosano Akiko, Tamura Toshiko, Nogami Yaeko, Yanagihara Byakuren, Kamichika Ichiko, Nakajō Yuriko, Okamoto Kanoko, and Shiraki Shizu—also wrote one-act plays. Few of their works, however, are still performed.

In classical theater, the first play, *Chrysanthemum* (*Kiku*) by Kimura Tomiko (1890–1944), the wife of the playwright Kimura Kinka (himself the cousin of two kabuki actors, Ichikawa Ennosuke II and Ichikawa Chūsha), was performed by Nakamura Utaemon V. Tomiko went on to write plays for kabuki, as well as dance plays, most of which were performed. Although not as famous as Tomiko, another *Bluestocking* member, Hirotsu Chiyo, wrote historical plays.

ŌMURA KAYOKO, OKADA TEIKO, TANAKA SUMIE, UEDA FUMIKO, AND OZAKI MIDORI

Among the women who wrote for *Bluestocking*, the most famous after Yachiyo and Shigure was Ōmura Kayoko (1883–1953), who was in the first graduating class of Japan Women's University. She studied playwriting under the new kabuki playwright Okamoto Kidō (1872–1939), who edited *Stage* (*Butai*, founded in 1930) and nurtured many male playwrights, such as Nukata Rokufuku, Hōjō Hideji, and Nakano Minoru, as well as a number of female playwrights. Among Ōmura's plays are *The Tale of the Purple Lotus* (*Shirentan*, first performed at the Yūraku Theater in 1913) and *A Daughter of the Thread Merchant of Honchō* (*Honchō itoya no musume*, Imperial Theater, 1927). Because of Ōmura's connection to Kidō, her plays were quickly produced. Most of them are historical and were performed by kabuki and female troupes.

Another important early female playwright, Okada Teiko (1902–1990), also was a student of Kidō. Her first play was published in the January 1929 issue of the journal *Reform* (*Kaizō*), helped by the influence of her father, a politician who served in the Lower House of the Diet. Okada also published plays in Shigure's *Women's Arts*, as well as in Kidō's *Stage*. Her *Masako and Her Career* (*Masako to sono shokugyō*, 1930, first performed at the Tsukiji Theater in 1933), questions what real independence for women might mean. Plays like *Rice Planting* (*Taue*, Tsukiji Theater, 1932) and *The Class Reunion* (*Kurasukai*, Tsukiji Theater, 1937) were performed as *shingeki* plays. Before World War II ended, Okada returned to her hometown of Matsuyama and stopped writing for the theater.

Tanaka Sumie (1908–2000) also was a playwright who got her start in Kidō's *Stage*. Unlike Ōmura and Okada, she was able to participate in the playwriting workshops run by Kishida Kunio (1890–1954) and Kikuchi Kan (1888–1948). In her one-act plays, like *A Shimmering* (*Kagerō*, 1934), *Akiko's Face* (*Akiko no kao*, 1936), and *The Bereaved Family* (*Izokutachi*, 1937), Tanaka depicts life in middle-class families, based on her own experience. Her first work, a multi-act play, *Spring, Autumn* (*Haru, aki*, Literary Theater, 1939), was directed by her husband, the playwright Tanaka Chikao. Other plays are *A Wicked Woman and Eyes and Wall* (*Akujo to me to kabe*, 1948), *Gratia, Lady Hosokawa* (*Garashia, Hosokawa fujin*, 1959), and *The White Peacock* (*Shirokujaku*, 1967), which she wrote for the actress Mizutani Yaeko. Both before and after the war, Tanaka wrote radio and film scripts to eke out a living, and after the war she also wrote for television.

The careers of Ueda Fumiko (1905–1986) and Ozaki Midori (1896–1971) were different from those of the preceding three playwrights. Ueda Fumiko—better known by her pen name, Enchi Fumiko—is famous as the writer of novels such as *The Waiting Years* (*Onnazaka*, 1957). In her younger years, inspired by Osanai Kaoru, Enchi began to write plays, which were published in the journals *Drama and Criticism* (*Geki to hyōron*) and *Women's Arts*. Her play *Restless Night in Late Spring* (*Banshun sōya*), a translation of which is included in this volume, was first performed at the Tsukiji Little Theater in 1928. The incident about Osanai Kaoru's dying at a banquet hosted by the Ueda family (Enchi's father, Ueda Mannen, was a famous scholar of Japanese literature) after her play's final performance is well known. Enchi also wrote plays and commentaries about ongoing revolutionary movements, an indication of the appeal of the leftist theater to young people at that time. Finally, however, the Depression forced her to move from drama to fiction.

Ozaki Midori is now the focus of much research in women's studies, as her innovative works, many of which were published in *Women's Arts*, describe modern Shōwa sensibilities. But perhaps because Ozaki did not have an influential father, as did Okada Teiko and Ueda Fumiko, few of her plays were performed during her lifetime. Nonetheless, the critic Hanada Kiyoteru (1909–1974) was greatly impressed with her plays *Apple Pie Afternoon* (*Appuru pai no gogo*, 1930), *Wandering in the World of the Seventh Sense* (*Dainanakankai hōkō*, 1931), and *Miss Cricket* (*Kōrogi-jo*, 1932). The inclusion of *Wandering in the World of the Seventh Sense* in the series Discovering Contemporary Literature (Gendai bungaku no hakken), published by Gakugei shorin in 1969, revived interest in Ozaki's work. In 1998, the film *Wandering in the World of the Seventh Sense—Searching for Ozaki Midori*, directed by Hamano Sachi, was released, and in the same year her collected works were published. Even now, her plays retain their originality.

POST-WORLD WAR II WOMEN PLAYWRIGHTS

YAMADA TOKIKO, TERASHIMA AKIKO, MAYAMA MIHO, MIZUKI YŌKO, AKIMOTO MATSUYO, AND ARIYOSHI SAWAKO

Yamada Tokiko (b. 1923) is a playwright from the Labor Union Theater movement, which started shortly after Japan's defeat in World War II. Yamada's play *A Good Match* (*Ryōen*, 1947) was performed by the theater group of the Dai-ichi Seimei Insurance Company. Subsequently, many organizations performed her plays, which dealt with such subjects as women's independence and marriage. The theater company Mingei staged the first production of *Records of the Women's Dormitories* (*Joshiryōki*) in 1948. Yamada is one of the few playwrights active during the short period after the war when many people thought that revolution in Japan was imminent.

Terashima Akiko (1926–2010) promoted writers for radio and television and became a member of the Shinkyō Theater in 1948, after having studied at the Tōhō Theater Workshop (Tōhō engeki kenkyūkai). She wrote for both the Shinkyō Theater and the Tokyo Art Theater (Tokyo geijutsuza) but later turned to writing scripts for radio and television programs and films.

Mayama Miho (1922–2006), the daughter of kabuki playwright Mayama Seika (1878–1948), was first affiliated with the Zenshin Theater and the Shinkyo Theater troupes. Although she composed only a few plays, in order to work toward her goal of popularizing *shingeki*, she founded a theater company, the Shinseisaku Theater, in which she remained active, writing and directing plays and overseeing the company. Accordingly, she is regarded as a forerunner of the women playwrights of the 1980s and later.

Mizuki Yōko (1910–2003), slightly older than those women playwrights writing after World War II, became known soon after graduating from Kikuchi Kan's Playwriting Study Group. At first, Mizuki wrote plays like *A Woman's Life* (*Onna no issho*, 1950), which deals with the problems of working women regarding marriage, pregnancy, and the care of aging parents. She also described workers' anxieties caused by the mechanization of labor and similar subjects. Later, Mizuki turned to writing scripts for films directed by Imai Tadashi, including *Till We Meet Again* (*Mata au hi made*) and *The Tower of Red Star Lilies* (*Himeyuri no tō*), and for Naruse Mikiyo's film version of Hayashi Fumiko's novel *Floating Cloud* (*Ukigumo*).

Okada Yachiyo, too, was an important figure in this period, establishing a new organization for women playwrights in 1948. The organization's newsletter, *Acanthus*, sought to strengthen the ties among women playwrights, by running playwriting workshops and nurturing young writers, many of whose works were collected in *Selected Plays by Contemporary Women Playwrights* (*Gendai joryū gikyoku senshū,* privately published in 1954). Later, Himawarisha published four more volumes. The playwrights in this organization differed from the women playwrights mentioned previously because they were well-to-do housewives who had been writing since before the war. They, and Okada, also wrote radio dramas and scripts for the commercial theater, which became an increasingly important outlet for writers at this time.

Akimoto Matsuyo (1911–2001), who said she attended only one of Okada's meetings, got her start in playwriting after participating in a playwriting workshop run by the important *shingeki* playwright Miyoshi Jūrō (1902–1958). Akimoto quickly wrote several plays—including *Ceremonial Clothes* (*Reifuku*), which is included in this book—depicting postwar Japan and the problems faced by a traditionally patriarchal family. But Akimoto felt undervalued as a playwright and often bemoaned her fate as a radio and television scriptwriter who received no praise from the public. Nonetheless, her play *Kaison the Priest of Hitachi* (*Hitachibō Kaison*, 1964)[2] was highly regarded by the important critic and occasional screen writer Hanada Kiyoteru and was first performed by the Engeki Theater in 1967. Since that time, many of her plays have been performed.

Ariyoshi Sawako (1931–1984), who, like Akimoto, explored women's lives, was thrust into the spotlight early in her career. Although she is more famous as a novelist than as a playwright, she also wrote many plays for Kikuta Kazuo's Art Theater, as well as for other *shinpa* and *shingeki* companies. When she was a student, Ariyoshi's essay "On Actors" (Haiyūron) won a prize in the contest by the journal *Theater World* (*Engekikai*). After that, she continued to write plays, which were performed at a steady pace: examples are *The Damask Drum* (*Aya no tsuzumi*, a dance play), *The Empress Kōmyō* (*Kōmyō kōgō*, first performed by the Literary Theater in 1962), *Precious Flower* (*Kōka*, Art Theater, 1963), *Arita River* (*Aritagawa*, Art Theater, 1965), *A Time of Distrust* (*Fushin no toki*, Art Theater, 1969), and *Moss Pink* (*Shibazakura*, 1970). In particular, the plays *The Doctor's Wife* (*Hanaoka seishū no tsuma*, 1966) and *My Sleeves Not Moist from American Rain*: *The Death of a Courtesan* (*Furuamerika ni sode wa nurasaji—Kiyū no shi*, 1962) have often been performed by *shingeki*'s Sugimura Haruko and kabuki's Bandō Tamasaburō.

Mukōda Kuniko (1929–1981) and Hashida Sugako (b. 1925) were television scriptwriters when television was becoming a dominant force in the entertainment industry. These two writers raised the status of those who wrote for radio and television, and because of them, the names of scriptwriters began to be listed in the credits. Mukōda began as an editor but started to write for television in the 1960s, producing more than a thousand scripts, including those for such well-known television drama series as *The Seven Grandchildren* (*Shichinin no mago*, TBS, 1964), *It's Time* (*Jikan desu yo*, TBS, 1971), *Daikon*

2. Translated in David G. Goodman, ed., *Japanese Drama and Culture in the 1960s: The Return of the Gods* (Armonk, N.Y.: Sharpe, 1988), 121–75.

Blossoms (*Daikon no hana*, TBS, 1974–1977), and *Like the God Ashura* (*Ashura no gotoku*, NHK, 1979). Mukōda's works, which feature nuanced depictions of the subtle changes in women's emotional responses, as well as portray women characters who tolerate men's weaknesses, are still very popular among male viewers.

Hashida Sugako started writing scripts for the Shōchiku Film Company and then wrote scripts for such television series as *Gazing at Love and Death* (*Ai to shi o mitsumete*, TBS, 1964). The television series that catapulted her to fame was *Oshin* (NHK, 1983), a story about one woman's life as she progresses from rags to riches. Broadcast all over Asia, *Oshin* became one of Japan's most famous television series. Hashida's works were based on the moral values of the past and emphasized human relations.[3]

WOMEN PLAYWRIGHTS SINCE THE 1980S

The most recent playwright to use realistic forms of expression is Kawasaki Teruyo (b. 1946). *Praying for a Good Catch* (*Shioe mōsō*, 1978), which was based on memories of her family home in Kagoshima, received the special drama prize from the Agency for Cultural Affairs and was first performed in 1981 at the Literary Theater. Since then, she has written a series of plays about women and the problems they face in their domestic lives. These include *Nagura* (*Group Eight*, 1987), *Harbor Breeze* (*Minato no kaze*, 1993), and *A Strong Wind in Autumn* (*Nowake tatsu*, Literary Theater, 1995).

Tsutsumi Harue (b. 1950), who set many of her plays in the Meiji period, received the Yomiuri Literary Prize (Drama Division) for both *Another Story of Rokumeikan* (*Rokumeikan ibun*), which received official recognition for her dramatic work from the Agency for Cultural Affairs in 1987, and *Kanadehon Hamlet* (first performed in 1992).[4] The latter work has been revived several times and was performed in New York and London in 1997 and 2001, respectively.

Among the playwrights who sought new forms of expression are Ichidō Rei (b. 1957), Kisaragi Koharu (1956–2000), Kishida Rio (1949–2003), Nagai Ai (b. 1951), Watanabe Eriko (b. 1955), Tanno Kumiko (b. 1960), Yū Miri (b. 1968),[5] Takaizumi Atsuko (b. 1958), Iijima Sanae (b. 1963),[6] and Hitsujiya Shirotama (b. 1967). Like their

3. Yoshie Inoue discusses film, television, and radio drama in greater detail in *Dorama kaidoku* (Tokyo: Shakai hyōronsha, 2009).
4. "*Kanadehon Hamlet*: A Play by Tsutsumi Harue," intro. Faubion Bowers, trans. Faubion Bowers, David W. Griffith, and Hori Mariko, *Asian Theatre Journal* 15, no. 2 (1998): 181–229. A translation by Mari Boyd of Tsutsumi Harue's *Destination Japan* (*Saishū mokutekichi wa Nippon*) is in *Half a Century of Japanese Theater*, ed. Japan Playwrights Association (Tokyo: Kinokuniya shoten, 2008), 10:198–228.
5. A translation by Yuasa Masako of Yū Miri's *Festival for the Fish* (*Uo no matsuri*) is in *Half a Century of Japanese Theater*, ed. Japan Playwrights Association (Tokyo: Kinokuniya shoten, 2000), 2:121–61.
6. A translation by Sue Herbert of Iijima Sanae and Suzuki Yumi's *Rhythm Method* (*Hōōchō no hininhō*) is in *Half a Century of Japanese Theater*, 2:294–366.

male counterparts in the 1980s, these women playwrights also created their own companies to perform their work.

The most remarkable of these women playwrights may be Ichidō Rei, because no woman with this name exists. Instead, it is a name used for all six members of the women-only theater group Blue Bird (Aoi tori, founded in 1974). They write, direct, and perform all their plays together. *Before the Curtain with Beautiful Clouds* (*Utsukushii kumo no aru maku no mae*) was their first play; their collaboration continued until 1993. The name of the playwright itself is a pun on the phrase "Take a bow, everyone."[7]

Unlike the others, Kisaragi Koharu was not focused solely on theater work but also appeared on television and worked as a musician. She said that she formed a theater company and wrote plays with the same casualness that others might display when trying to organize a party. In 1976, she founded the student theater company Kiki, which had an immediate success with its first performance, *A Table with Romeo and Ophelia* (*Romeo to Ophelia no aru shokutaku*). Kisaragi's style was different from that of earlier movements, and since she died at an early age, her legacy is still evolving.[8]

The plays that probably will be regarded the most highly by future generations are those by Kishida Rio and Nagai Ai, as they are on the same level as those of today's popular male playwrights—for example, Noda Hideki, Hirata Oriza, and Sakate Yōji. Indeed, Kishida Rio's plays about women and the emperor system—*Thread Hell* (*Ito jigoku*, 1984)[9] and *Permanent Home, Temporary Lodging* (*Tsui no sumika, kari no yado*, 1988)—and Nagai Ai's socially incisive plays since the 1990s—*Time's Storeroom* (*Toki no monooki*);[10] *The Murderous Malice of Language* (*Ranuki no satsui*); her Chekhovian *The Three Hagi Sisters* (*Hagi-ke no san shimai*);[11] *New Light and Darkness* (*Shin meian*), a rereading of Natsume Sōseki's novel; *Elder Brother Returns* (*Ani kaeru*), her take on Kikuchi Kan's *Father Returns*, which is translated in this volume; and *Men Who Want to Sing* (*Utawasetai otokotachi*)—seem to me to be superior to those by the male playwrights of the same generation. That the male playwrights still receive precedence is a sign of the lasting influence of patriarchy.

---

7. A translation by David G. Goodman of Ichidō Rei's *Miss Toyoko's Departure* (*Aoi mi wo tabeta*) is in *Half a Century of Japanese Theater*, ed. Japan Playwrights Association (Tokyo: Kinokuniya shoten, 2001), 3:102–28.
8. "*MORAL*: A Play by Kisaragi Koharu," intro. Colleen Lanki, trans. Tsuneda Keiko and Colleen Lanki, *Asian Theatre Journal* 21, no. 4 (2004): 119–76.
9. A translation by Carol Fisher Sorgenfrei and Tonooka Nami of Kishida Rio's *Thread Hell* is in *Half a Century of Japanese Theater*, ed. Japan Playwrights Association (Tokyo: Kinokuniya shoten, 2002), 4:174–221.
10. A translation by David H. Shapiro of Nagai Ai's *Time's Storeroom* is in *Half a Century of Japanese Theater*, ed. Japan Playwrights Association (Tokyo: Kinokuniya shoten, 1999), 1:180–257.
11. "*The Three Hagi Sisters*: A Modern Japanese Play by Nagai Ai," trans. and intro. Loren Edelson, *Asian Theatre Journal* 21, no. 1 (2004): 1–98.

PART III

WARTIME AND POSTWAR DRAMA

The war years brought many constraints to the theater world. Not only were the left-wing theater companies closed down by the government, but even Kishida Kunio and his colleagues in charge of the Literary Theater (Bungakuza), which continued its attempt to stage plays of literary merit, either foreign or Japanese, sometimes ran afoul of the authorities.

The influence of the Japanese wartime government was not merely restrictive. The Cabinet Information Office also tried to develop what it termed a new "national drama": "The morality of the emerging new Japan was to be a national morality and this emphasis must be made clear in its drama. A national drama could not devote itself to pursuing artistic ends; it had to help to realize the goals set by the state."[1]

Kabuki troupes were sent on overseas tours,[2] while *shinpa* and *shingeki* troupes were urged to produce wholesome and uplifting plays in tune with the necessary national "spiritual mobilization." An important leader of this movement was Iizuka Tomoichirō (1894–1983), who began his literary career as a kabuki scholar, with the aim of encouraging traveling groups within Japan. These "mobile theater" *shingeki* companies did in fact succeed in visiting many small towns and villages, where live modern theater was itself a new

---

1. Brian Powell, *Japan's Modern Theatre: A Century of Continuity and Change* (London: Japan Library, 2002), 118. His chapter "Theatre Mobilized" provides the most comprehensive treatment of this period in English.
2. James R. Brandon offers extensive research on the activities of wartime kabuki troupes, as well as valuable information on some aspects of *shingeki*, in *Kabuki's Forgotten War, 1931–1945* (Honolulu: University of Hawai'i Press, 2009).

phenomenon. Directives called for plays with small casts, minimal scenery, and scripts that were easy to understand, preferably in one act. Ironically, this activity may have helped lay the groundwork for the success of the left-leaning Rōen (the abbreviation for Kinrōsha engeki kyōgikai)[3] in promoting touring theaters in the early postwar period. Even though all these activities from 1940 to 1945 surely involved compromises, they did help employ those involved in the theater, as well as providing at least some hope of a brighter future.

With the end of World War II in 1945, the practitioners of theater—like those in so many cultural, intellectual, political, and artistic areas important to Japan's early postwar life—quickly began to seek out fresh values. For most of the theater community, the earlier period of official silence lasted for five years. On the surface, this may seem like a relatively short time, but the change in psychic distance between 1940, when most of the theaters were shut down, and the autumn of 1945 was vast indeed.

As it turned out, in many ways the issues that had faced the *shingeki*, *shinpa*, and other troupes and their playwrights in the 1930s had not greatly changed. The craft of acting still had to be brought to a satisfying level; problems funding theatrical troupes remained; and larger audiences had to be attracted to the theater. Between 1945 and 1960, all these concerns were addressed, many successfully.

On the whole, the practitioners of the modern theater still looked leftward politically. But this seemingly lockstep attitude eventually softened, less because of a weakening commitment to social and political causes than because of an increasing impetus toward more explicit artistic standards, often driven by audiences' expectations, which helped direct their energy away from purely political concerns.

Some of this new energy can be sensed in the writings of Hijikata Yoshi, one of Osanai Kaoru's most important colleagues. Hijikata left Japan for the Soviet Union in 1933, and when he returned to Japan in 1941, he was immediately put in prison, where he remained during the war years. In an article he wrote in 1945, he stressed both the importance of developing a new enthusiasm and the need for carefully reflecting on the dark history of the war years. Like so many of his colleagues, Hijikata was determined to use every strategy to avoid returning to those attitudes so prevalent in the period often referred to as the "dark valley" in which so many practitioners of the theater found themselves in the 1930s.

Because the Occupation and early postwar period was a time of new possibilities for the theater, many of the prominent prewar practitioners—whether playwrights, actors, or directors—now sought to fulfill in new ways their careers begun in the prewar years. And perhaps unwittingly, they brought their older habits and aspirations with them, however much they wished for a clean start. It was, generally speaking, not until the first postwar generation of writers and directors came of age that the paradigms began to shift altogether.

---

3. The model for Rōen goes back to the German Volksbühe (People's Theater movement), founded in the 1890s to make subscription tickets available at reduced prices.

HIJIKATA YOSHI

MY TWO MOTIVES FOR ADVOCATING WHAT I CALL THE "NEW JAPAN FREE THEATER ASSOCIATION"

I would like to explain quite clearly my "personal plan," which has given birth to a fanciful, and as yet not inaugurated, vision of a theatrical troupe.

I recently set forth my plan in a recent issue of the *Tōmai shinbun*. Here I will explain my motives for advocating such a plan.

Now it goes without saying that the "theater" that was Japan has been crushed, yet the "troupe" that constitutes Japanese society and those Japanese who make up the "directors" and "performers" have not all been done away with. Unlike before, they have not been driven away by other theaters. Yet in the wake of all this destruction, they now face a new epoch in which a free and fresh "theater" can begin again.

And so this "Japanese theater troupe" and these "Japanese directors and performers," willing or not, now must volunteer for this reconstruction. And in the midst of this "theater troupe" that is Japan, the tiny world of the Japanese theater itself and those who participate in that theater can equally look forward with happiness to their encounter with this momentous period in which we now live. . . .

As we face this great revolution, I believe that I and my colleagues, and indeed all those who make up the world of the theater in Japan, will surely, to some degree or other, come to celebrate this new frame of mind and the position we can then put forth. Some among my friends, when they think of this new Japan now released to freedom, will carry on their work in the theater with the thought that the future awaits them; they are filled with happiness and are surely trembling with excitement. Yet others, who suddenly find themselves in a world too bright for them, will feel the dream is too dazzling, thinking that at some point or other, we will all surely awake to find ourselves back in the same dark valley as before.

Other friends, who would clear away altogether those roots grown in our place of exile, forget the nature of the enthusiasm and ambition necessary for creativity in the theater, while others, aware that they themselves are somehow fellow conspirators with those criminals who brought this war about, wish in some fashion to hurry so as to somehow try to patch things over. And there are not a few, I am convinced, who, holding that same point of view, have become aware of this situation in terms of their own consciences and so vacillate between whether or not to restore the old ways of doing things all over again.

And there must be others among my friends who, in this period when a theater for the new Japan can now be created, have a correct and clear cognizance of the situation and who possess enthusiasm and conviction, hoping to plunge on ahead, yet who at the same time still remain filled with cheerless thoughts, finding themselves still bound by those chains of duty and their debt to the dark days of that past that formed their destiny.

FROM HIJIKATA YOSHI, "SHIN NIHON JIYŪ ENGEKI KYŌKAI" (NEW JAPAN FREE THEATER ASSOCIATION), IN *NASU NO YOBANASHI* (*EVENING TALKS IN NASU*) (TOKYO: KAPPA SHOBŌ, 1947), 49–51.

SENDA KOREYA

Since before the war, the task that the *shingeki* movement has pursued concerned the establishment in Japan of the kind of drama known in the West since the Renaissance—what in Japan we would term "modern drama." At the least, it can be said that such drama has followed a path that emphasizes such themes as the emancipation of mankind and ideas of democracy. It was just for such reasons that the movement found itself so terribly oppressed before and during the war. We are now heirs to this tradition of *shingeki*, and as we progress forward, I believe that we should be able to accommodate ourselves to our contemporary society in fine fashion.

Five years have now passed since the war has ended. It seems that once again, at a time when signs of a reaction can be observed that may allow us to attempt to recover from the confusions of this postwar period, we must now tread the path established by the traditions of our movement in the prewar period and make straight the distortions brought about by our unlucky history. We must, I believe, while always adopting a forward-looking stance, seek in our theater to deepen our fundamental knowledge and our theoretical understanding.

Nevertheless, because our *shingeki* is a form of theater, it must also serve to entertain its audiences. Indeed, perhaps the most obvious distortion in our movement has been the fact that so much of our theater has not been entertaining enough. Perhaps the weakest point in our movement so far is the fact that we have failed to create the tradition of an art of the playwright or of the performer capable of truly entertaining an audience. In fact, we have thoughtlessly denied or and thoughtlessly copied the methods employed by our popular theater, kabuki, and the rest. So in such a situation, surely nothing new and fresh can be brought to life. No doubt it is very important that we study the arts of the past, but what we must now try to create is a more "modern" kind of pleasure, a pleasure that thrives on the liberation of humanity, a pleasure that is truly democratic.

FROM SENDA KOREYA, "SHINGEKI WA TANOSHIMU MONO" (*SHINGEKI* IS TO BE ENJOYED), IN *SENDA KOREYA ENGEKI-RONSHŪ* (*COLLECTED ESSAYS ON THE THEATER BY SENDA KOREYA*) (TOKYO: MIRAISHA 1980), 2:13–14.

Senda Koreya (1904–1994), himself intermittently under arrest and unable to remain active during the war years, used his time to write a still-valued book on the training of actors and laid his plans to establish a new theater company, the Actors' Theater (Haiyūza), which, by its very name, revealed Senda's deepening consciousness that the performance aspects of theater, whatever the politics involved, were crucial to its success.

In an essay he wrote in 1950, Senda stated that he came to realize that the success of the theater rested in a variety of spheres; that despite the importance to him of social activism, the audiences, whatever their prior interest in political and social enlightenment, justifiably sought pleasure and entertainment in any theatrical event. For Senda, this understanding seemed to develop not from any abstract adherence to a set of ideals or principles but from his own experience.

Senda made plans to begin his new company in 1944, and his first public performances at the Actors' Theater were held in 1946, setting a new model for the activities of a progressive *shingeki* theater troupe. Senda's school for training actors, the Haiyūza Training Institute, was perhaps the most influential organization for training actors in the whole history of *shingeki*.

In some ways like Osanai before him, Senda was convinced that the theater was one way to provide the kind of "entertainment" he felt his audiences wished and deserved, so he set out to produce many of the world's classics at the Actors' Theater. Accordingly, audiences in the early postwar years saw productions of such plays as Pierre de Beaumarchais's *The Marriage of Figaro* and works by William Shakespeare and Albert Camus, among others. After the mid-1950s, Senda became more and more interested in Bertolt Brecht and staged a number of his plays.

Unlike Osanai, however, Senda placed in his repertory several plays by established Japanese playwrights, such as Tanaka Chikao, who joined the troupe in 1961, and encouraged important new postwar authors and playwrights, such as Abe Kōbō.

By the 1950s, three theater repertory companies dominated the field, each favoring particular playwrights. The Literary Theater continued to present plays without any strong ideological coloring, staging many of Mishima Yukio's plays until 1963, when, because of a dispute, he left the company. As noted, Senda's Actors' Theater produced a mixture of classics and avant-garde experiments, notably those of Tanaka Chikao and Abe Kōbō. The Mingei troupe (People's Art Theater) was founded in 1950 by a group that included the distinguished actor Takizawa Osamu, who became famous for his performances in Arthur Miller's *Death of a Salesman*. The Mingei troupe emphasized plays of social significance and often performed Kinoshita Junji's plays. Taken together, these companies provided three sites where the whole spectrum of theatrical and dramatic possibilities could find a home.

Although these productions were usually staged in Tokyo, the development of the labor union–related organization commonly referred to as Rōen offered inexpensive tickets to its members. Under Rōen's sponsorship, productions of modern theater now toured the country, often performing in provincial cities where little live modern theater had been seen. The purpose of touring these productions was to provide opportunities for ordinary workers to participate in their country's culture. Even though the motivations for such activities was at least partially political, the ticket buyers soon came to comprise a preponderance of white-collar workers, eager after the deprivations of the war years to experience European high culture. This sustained interest in relatively nonpolitical drama helped broaden the public's taste and lessen to a certain extent the public perception of *shingeki* as an exclusively leftist phenomenon. This need to attract larger audiences thus branched off in some unexpected directions. Indeed, among the most admired productions during this period were Japanese productions of two American plays: Arthur Miller's *Death of a Salesman* and Tennessee Williams's *A Streetcar Named Desire.*

Given the fact that so many of the theater practitioners in 1945 were veterans from prewar days, it should not be surprising that the postwar theater productions began with Anton Chekhov. In 1945, as a kind of ceremonial gesture, a group of major theater figures came together to create a new joint production of *The Cherry Orchard*. The postwar theater thus began by returning to its Western roots. The increasing exposure of postwar audiences to the best of Western theater of all periods—from Shakespeare and Molière to Sartre and Brecht—brought new sources of inspiration to Japanese playwrights active during the period. With this came a new consciousness among Japanese directors and playwrights of important ways in which Western classical theater continued to influence contemporary theater in Europe and the United States. Senda himself went so far as to call Shakespeare the father of modern world drama, more important to Japanese playwrights than even Zeami or Chikamatsu.

From this consciousness grew a new challenge. A number of early postwar dramatists now began to feel a need to devise strategies capable of integrating at least some elements from the Japanese past, either historical or artistic or both, into what was a predominantly realistic Western-style frame employed in early postwar Japanese drama. The long national theatrical genius for presentational theater, partly buried for half a century or more, now, at least tentatively, began to reassert itself. The first step in these attempts required acknowledging just how difficult it would be to bridge this gap. In 1963, Kinoshita Junji, himself actively involved in such experiments, wrote persuasively about those challenges.

Most of the playwrights represented in part III of this anthology sought, through one means or another, to at least partially transcend or bypass such a purely realistic dramaturgy. But the tensions that these attempts provoked were not fully resolved until some of the next generation's playwrights began writing. Part IV shows that the work of the avant-garde and its use of presentational dramaturgy could lead to still more possibilities and to create openings where certain elements from the classical theater could enter again, often fractured or transformed, thereby creating a new and striking dramaturgical mix. Nevertheless, the years between 1945 and 1965 marked a high point in the quality of dramas largely inspired by Western models, and the work of the best playwrights of the period represents the development of a mature and responsible Japanese theater.

SEEKING A TOTALITY

Of all the plays included in part III, the closest to the model of the well-made play is *A Woman's Life* (*Onna no isshō*), by the dramatist Morimoto Kaoru (1912–1946). Morimoto began his playwriting career as a disciple of Kishida Kunio and wrote a number of promising plays in the prewar period. He officially joined the staff of the Literary Theater in 1941, where his energy and resourcefulness helped steer the company through difficult times with the censors. His most important work, *A Woman's Life*, remains his most lasting contribution.

Written and staged in 1945, just before the end of the war, this long play examines the life of a woman who has suffered through the endless political and social vicissitudes of the twentieth century. When the war ended, Morimoto rewrote the play, removing the required patriotic emphasis that appeared from time to time in the original script and replacing those sections with new passages expressing an enthusiasm for the new freedoms of the emerging postwar culture.[4] Already ill with tuberculosis, Morimoto died a year later, but this play, in various guises and adaptations, went on to become one of the most popular and beloved plays of the entire postwar period. The text is fully in the realistic mode and concentrates on the emotional life and search for spiritual integrity by its heroine, Kei, a character who provided a defining role for the popular actress Sugimura Haruko.

THE PAST IN THE PRESENT

Kinoshita Junji (1914–2006) was another playwright who, as the postwar era continued, searched for an expanded dramaturgy. While many of his plays, such as his drama concerning the Richard Sorge spy case, *A Japanese Named Otto* (*Otto to oyoberu Nihonjin*, 1962), are basically realistic, others sometimes mix naturalistic scenes with more poetic interludes. Kinoshita also wrote a number of experimental plays, in which he attempted to mine material from Japanese history and folklore. In his dialogue, he uses a mixture of the poetic and realistic in order to bridge the gap between historical modes of theatrical expression and present-day speech.

Of those experiments, still the most famous and beloved is Kinoshita's one-act play *Twilight Crane* (*Yūzuru*, 1949), in which he re-creates material from a folktale while maintaining in the text the kind of social awareness that had long played an important part in his own personal convictions.

Kinoshita continued to write realistic plays of social concern, but the problems of integrating the classical theater's language and dramaturgy continued to preoccupy him until the end of his life. In that regard, the language and dramaturgy of his lengthy play *Requiem on the Great Meridian* (*Shigosen no matsuri*), first staged in 1977 and frequently

4. For some telling details on the history of the play, see Guohe Zheng, "Reflections *of* and *on* the Times: Morimoto Kaoru's *A Woman's Life*," in *Modern Japanese Theatre and Performance*, ed. David Jortner, Keiko I. McDonald, and Kevin J. Wetmore Jr. (Lanham, Md.: Lexington Books, 2006), 189–203.

KINOSHITA JUNJI

Generally speaking, all the speeches in old European plays—for example, original Shakespeare—are written logically. As we stated earlier, even if you were to analyze the text with the *shingeki* realism that we are considering now, the meaning would all hang together. Admittedly, expressions are in poetic form, and there are plenty of exaggerated expressions that one does not find in so-called realistic plays, but these can be seen as artistic exaggerations of genuine feelings. Providing, then, that you have the skills to express them on a large scale, you can imbue it all with realism.

Thus when the modern theater movement arose—on account of the nineteenth-century theater management and the star system that grew to accompany it—in order to restore a theater that had grown distant from real lives, it was only natural that its repertory contain Shakespeare plays, written long ago, alongside modern plays. Shakespeare and Molière wrote realistic plays that even we Japanese can see are not meaningless nonsense.

In Japan, however, *shingeki* cannot incorporate kabuki into its repertory in the same way. It is very hard to follow logically even the seven- and five-syllable metered speeches of Mokuami, who wrote from the end of the Tokugawa period into the Meiji period and whose work is said to be realistic kabuki. . . .

. . . These logical speeches [in Shakespeare and elsewhere] are written in verse form, so intonation is added when they are recited. I suppose they are declaimed, really. This intonation is also logical, and thus as the actor emphasizes one place and weakens another, his personal character comes into relief. When he imparts this personality to the audience, what person does he do so as? It is essentially his own understanding, thought processes, and sentiments that the actor is expressing. With most kabuki speeches . . . it is impossible to say where, logically, emphasis should be applied. . . . There are, therefore, very many elements in kabuki that are quite unrelated to the realism of *shingeki*.

I seem to have declared that it is only the actors who are responsible, but because of the way that historically the art of the Japanese *shingeki* actor is cut off from classical theater, I think that this sort of thing is inevitable. . . . Playwrights, on contrast, should be able to learn methodologically, thinking of the Western tradition as a tradition that they themselves should absorb. In other words, I believe that it should be possible for playwrights, unlike actors, to tune into a world tradition without distinguishing between the Japanese tradition, the European, and so on.

FROM KINOSHITA JUNJI, "ON *SHINGEKI*," IN *REQUIEM ON THE GREAT MERIDIAN* (TOKYO: NAN'UN-DO, 2000), 267-68, 270-71.

revived, was the result of his thinking through this problem. Based on incidents from the great medieval classic *The Tales of the Heike* (*Heike monogatari*), Kinoshita's attempt to reintroduce the Japanese language on the stage, using elements of Buddhist-inspired chant and other devices, here reached its peak.

A HEIGHTENED REALISM

Akimoto Matsuyo (1911–2001) began her career as a playwright after the war and relatively late in her life, but with the production of her second play, *Mourning Clothes* (*Reifuku*), in 1949, she began a distinguished career in the theater, with her plays staged by such important directors as Senda Koreya and Ninagawa Yukio. As Morimoto Kaoru does in *A Woman's Life*, Akimoto concentrates on interpersonal family relationships. In the play, although societal pressures do help tailor individual motivations, the edge in her dialogue moves the larger thrust of the drama in the direction of what David Goodman identified as its deep theme, "death and the inability to mourn it," on both a personal and a national level.[5] In some of her later plays, notably *Kaison, the Priest of Hitachi* (*Hitachi Kaison*, 1964), the dialogue moves even further away from prior realistic models, using a shamaness to introduce a kind of dark poetry that Akimoto employs to present her critical vision of the empty spiritual values that she found in Japan's postwar culture.

A SURREAL BLURRING OF REALITY

Abe Kōbō (1924–1993) is better known in the West as a novelist than as a playwright, but throughout his career he wrote a number of plays paralleling in style and ambition the themes and concerns found in his often surrealistic novels. Eventually, in order to carry out and refine his theatrical vision still further, Abe founded his own theater company, the Abe Kōbō Studio, in 1973. Even his early plays, such as *The Uniform* (*Seifuku*), written in 1949, already reveal an ambition to break through the received model of the naturalistic play. Political and philosophical issues are presented with irony and a certain ideological bent; indeed, at that time, Abe was still a member of the Japan Communist Party, which was legalized after World War II. Brought up partially in Manchuria, Abe had the ability to observe, and critique, Japanese society using a personal intellectual and ideological framework developed outside the culture. This technique certainly can be seen in the point of view, both sardonic and sharp, that he constructs in his often puzzling and gnomic texts, here represented by his short drama *The Man Who Turned into a Stick* (*Bō ni natta otoko*).

---

5. David G. Goodman, "The Quest for Salvation in Japan's Modern History: Four Plays by Akimoto Matsuyo," in *Modern Japanese Theatre and Performance*, ed. Jortner, McDonald, and Wetmore, 51–63.

STRATEGIES OF TRANSCENDENCE

Tanaka Chikao (1905–1995), like Morimoto Kaoru, got his start with Kishida Kunio and the Literary Theater, first as a director and then as a promising playwright. In 1951, he joined Senda Koreya's Actors' Theater, and in the early postwar period, he wrote a number of lyrical plays, often colored by his deepening attraction to the Catholic faith. No doubt, the most famous of these works is *The Head of Mary* (*Maria no kubi*, 1959), which chronicles in poetic fashion the psychic and spiritual life in Nagasaki after the atomic bomb. His play *The Plover* (*Chidori*, 1960) explores some of the same concerns, played out in a lyrical and sometimes dreamlike setting.

Tanaka's long attachment to French literature found its apogee in his long one-act play *Education* (*Kyōiku*, 1953), which actually is set in France. Few Japanese playwrights, with the exception of Mishima Yukio, have attempted to write entire plays involving only foreign characters. The establishment of this alternative space, plus his skillful use of a highly poetic and lyrical stage language, allowed Tanaka to portray the urgent need for humankind to grapple with the sometimes ambiguous realities of religious sensibility. In that regard, the play is both ambitious and surprisingly successful.

Each of these playwrights managed, therefore, to expand the parameters of dramaturgy in order to find some means of moving away from the received Western model of the realistic play. In this regard, we should mention one of the most prolific playwrights—and in so many genres—Mishima Yukio (1925–1970), and his efforts to move *shingeki* dramaturgy away from a representational toward a presentational style.

Like Abe, Mishima is better known in the West as a novelist, but his playwriting, always much admired in Japan, continued for nearly his entire career. Both Abe and Mishima were younger than the other playwrights cited in this part of the anthology, and their careers as playwrights started at the beginning of the postwar period when they were still developing their skills and talents for the stage.

Many of Mishima's popular plays were written for *shingeki* troupes, including perhaps his most popular work for Japanese audiences, *Rokumeikan* (1962), a sort of Meiji melodrama written for the famous and beloved Sugimura Haruko, who also performed the leading role in Morimoto Kaoru's *A Woman's Life*, as noted earlier. Both were staged at the Literary Theater. In subsequent productions, the leading role was performed as well by the revered *shinpa* actress Mizutani Yaeko. Yet even in these relatively realistic plays, Mishima uses a highly poetic, even unnatural, dialogue that sometimes seems to collide with his otherwise realistic dramaturgy. Like Kinoshita Junji, Mishima also experimented with introducing certain elements of classical theater into the dramaturgy of *shingeki*, notably in his series of modern nō plays. Mishima's writing for the kabuki theater is discussed in part VI.

In sum, it seems clear, at least in hindsight, that even during the period covered in part III, dramatists often sought to incorporate some elements of the past—historically, linguistically, or theatrically. In addition, I believe, these tentative experiments were conducted well within the framework of the possibilities available in current world theater dramaturgy at the time. In this regard, many of these early postwar writers were unwittingly echoing the initial efforts made several generations earlier by Osanai Kaoru, whose final project, unrealized because of his untimely death, was to be a staging with modern actors of a Chikamatsu play from the eighteenth century.

The next generation of playwrights deconstructed and reworked these earlier models. Even though many more senior or commercially inclined dramatists continued to create variations on the well-made play, the avant-garde writers— Betsuyaku Minoru, Kara Jūrō, Shimizu Kunio, and the others—produced something startlingly, and excitingly, different.

J. THOMAS RIMER

Morimoto Kaoru, *A Woman's Life*, directed by Inui Ichirō, Bungakuza, June 1964.

A WOMAN'S LIFE

MORIMOTO KAORU
TRANSLATED BY GUOHE ZHENG

A *Woman's Life* (*Onna no isshō*), a long play in five acts and seven scenes, which Morimoto Kaoru (1912–1946) finished in 1945, has a complex history. The first performances were staged in April of that year by the Literary Theater (Bungakuza) and directed by the playwright Kubota Mantarō. The play was to have been staged at the Tsukiji Little Theater (Tsukiji shōgekijō), but because the building had been destroyed by the Allied bombings of Tokyo, another site was selected. The war ended only months later. According to Guohe Zheng, in early 1946, while ill with tuberculosis, Morimoto rewrote the first and last acts, among other changes, in order "to make the play compatible with the postwar political atmosphere."

The role of Kei was performed by Sugimura Haruko (1909–1997), one of the leading actresses of her time, and she was so popular that she was chosen for the role again in numerous revivals of the play. Spanning, as the play does, almost a half century, from the 1920s through the early postwar period, the role of Kei provides several opportunities for the actress playing it to show various facets of the character.

Because each act takes place at a different point in the narrative, we are able to include one act here, as it is relatively self-contained.

Characters

KEI, the estranged wife of TSUTSUMI SHINTARŌ, now the pillar of the Tsutsumi Trading Company
SHINTARŌ, the elder son of the Tsutsumi family, now separated from KEI
CHIIE, the daughter of KEI and SHINTARŌ
EIJI, SHINTARŌ's brother and the object of KEI's secret love before her marriage to SHINTARŌ
SHŌSUKE, the uncle of EJI and SHINTARŌ on their deceased mother's side and a consultant for the Tsutsumi Trading Company
FUMI, the younger daughter of the Tsutsumi family

ACT 4

A midautumn afternoon in 1928.

The setting sun of a late autumn afternoon is shining on the bushes in the garden. CHIE, *now twenty-two years old, sits on the veranda staring absentmindedly at the garden.* EIJI, *forty-three years old, enters. He searches inside a briefcase in the corner of the room.*

EIJI: Chie-chan, what are you looking at?

CHIE: Nothing.

EIJI: You seem to be staring into the air.

CHIE: Really? Sometimes I find myself doing that. I don't feel like doing anything, or thinking about anything.

EIJI: The atmosphere in this house is somehow depressing. The autumn weather doesn't seem to be the only reason for this chilly feeling. I feel like I've fallen to the bottom of a pond. The water in some ponds can be too muddy for you to see the bottom. The water here, however, is clear, but still I can't see the bottom. I wonder when the house became like this.

CHIE: I don't know. But it's been like this ever since I began to remember things.

EIJI: It wasn't like this before. Your late grandpa and grandma both liked festival parties, and the whole house was always filled with laughter. Your father liked painting and was always trying to grab someone in the house to be his model. Aunt Fumi wanted to study in Europe after she graduated from music school. Neither your father nor Aunt Fumi has turned out to be any more than a mediocre artist. In any case, the house wasn't like this before.

CHIE: Wow! Really!? It's hard for me even to imagine that this house was like that once upon a time.

EIJI: But times have changed. At that time, my biggest dream was to go to China and become a bandit.

CHIE: Well, Uncle Eiji, you did go to China, didn't you? That means that you're the only one in the house who realized the dream of your younger days.

EIJI: Well, I'm not sure you can say that I've realized the dream of my younger days.— Does your father still paint these days?

CHIE: Sometimes. . . . When his old habit occasionally reasserts itself, he paints things like potatoes or carrots. But I don't think he paints because he wants to. It seems to me that he does it only because he doesn't have the urge to quit a habit from the past.

EIJI: He paints potatoes or carrots? I see. . . . There are indeed all sorts of ways of living life in this world, aren't there?

CHIE: Uncle Eiji, where do you live in China?

EIJI: Well, I've lived in different places. At first I was in Beijing. In recent years, I've been in Shanghai. I also lived in Canton and Wuchang for a long time.

CHIE: What kind of jobs did you do when you moved around from place to place?

EIJI: Well, I've done all kinds of jobs. I was once an engineer at a cement company. I also worked as a kind of a coolie. China is really an extraordinary country. But I'll tell you about that some other time. —Have your father and mother been separated for a long time?

CHIE: Uncle Eiji, you don't talk much about yourself, asking only about our family.

EIJI: That's not true. But people grow tired of talking about their own affairs because they know too much about them. So they naturally are curious about other people's lives. I've come back to my own home after a long absence only to find that the master and the mistress of the house are separated. I really don't know where I should stay and settle down. . . .

CHIE: Well, even though I've been living in this house since I was born, I still have never had a sense of being settled.

EIJI: Whom do you like better, your father or your mother?

CHIE: I don't know. When I'm with Mother, I feel sorry for Father; when I'm with Father, I feel sorry for Mother.

EIJI: Does your father walk to work at the Yokohama International Institute every day from his apartment?

(KEI, *forty years old now, enters. In contrast to the active and ambitious impression she gave in act 3, she appears to be calm but somehow inapproachable.*)

KEI (*Reading a newspaper while coming in*): "The Chinese Government Bans Imports of Japanese Goods . . ." "China Trade at a Halt . . ." All Japanese doing business with China will soon be bankrupt, I'm afraid, one after another.

EIJI: Well, the Chinese foreign minister, Wang Zhengting,[1] takes the Tanaka cabinet's military intervention in Shandong[2] to be a sign of Japan's territorial ambition in China. So more than likely, the situation will stay this way for some time to come.

KEI: Is that so? But in the Jinan incident,[3] Japanese properties were vandalized, Japanese nationals were attacked. So doing business was totally out of the question. So why is it that they still think Japan has territorial ambitions in China? The Chinese government has ordered the Chinese Trading Association to register all the goods imported from Japan, even goods under completed contracts. I also heard that transportation by Japanese vessels has been banned. The Nisshin Steamship Transportation's ships are running empty on the Yangtze River.

(CHIE, *who was silently listening, stands up and is about to leave.*)

KEI: Chie-chan, where are you going?

CHIE (*Without looking back*): Nowhere in particular. I'm not interested in talking about China. (*Goes out.*)

KEI: . . .That child has gotten thinner recently. . . . Or is it just me?

EIJI: Older Sister, you and Chie-chan are like the sun and the moon. Wherever you are, Chie-chan is not; wherever she is, you are not.

KEI: It's really hard to raise a child. Some parents have five or even six children and take them all to walk on the street as if that were the most natural thing in the world. Every time I see that, I can't help but be amazed. I wonder how they can look so casual, with so many children.

---

1. Wang Zhengting (1882–1961) was China's foreign minister from 1927 to 1928 and the Chinese ambassador to the United States in 1936. He studied in Japan in 1905 and joined Sun Yat-sen's revolutionary United League (Tongmeng Hui) in Tokyo the following year. Later, he studied in the United States and in 1910 earned a master's degree in literature from Yale.
2. Known in Japan as Santō shuppei, the intervention refers to the three occasions in 1927 and 1928 when, to protect Japanese residents and Japanese interests in China, Prime Minister Tanaka Giichi (1927–1929) sent troops to China's Shandong Province (Santō in Japanese). These interventions led to Japan's further imperialist ambitions in China as well as the anti-Japanese movement among the Chinese.
3. The Jinan incident took place during the second of Japan's three military interventions in Shandong Province. Known in China as the Jinan can'an (Jinan massacre), it resulted from an armed conflict between the Japanese troops and the Chinese Kuomintang army in Jinan, the capital of Shandong Province, in 1928 during the Kuomintang's Northern Expedition against the northern warlords in an attempt to unify China. In 1927, the Shandong warlord Zhang Zongchang allied with Japan to resist the push of Kuomintang forces into northern China. In April 1928, the Kuomintang army arrived in Jinan and engaged in heavy fighting with Zhang's and the Japanese armies. On May 3 of that year, during negotiations to withdraw Japanese forces, the Japanese started firing again on Chinese civilians. They also captured the Chinese diplomats sent to negotiate, including the Kuomintang official Cai Gongshi, who later was disfigured and tortured to death. Fighting resumed between the Chinese and Japanese troops, and not until March 1929 when a cease-fire was arranged did the Japanese agree to pull out of Jinan. More than three thousand Chinese civilians were killed during this conflict. According to some Japanese sources, the Chinese also committed acts of violence and vandalism against the Japanese.

EIJI: Well, if you take it too seriously, there'll be no end to your difficulties. But if you take it easy, things will take care of themselves and life will go on. Just look at me. My Chinese can hardly get me around without difficulty in China, but I married a Chinese woman and have four daughters with her. I never felt it particularly hard to raise children. But perhaps that's because I've been too busy with my work outside to worry about things at home. For that reason, when I do come home occasionally, we all cherish those precious times together.

KEI: Well, my case is the opposite of yours. The busier I find myself with company work, the further away Chie-chan gets from me. Since the two of us have been living apart, I occasionally have tried to get closer to her when I do find time, but unfortunately things never go the way I intend.

EIJI: But that child seems to understand your circumstances and feelings quite well.

KEI: Exactly. She knows me better than I even know myself. But still she can't stand it. She can't bear the way I look at things, but she tries hard not to betray her feelings about me. It's hard to see her trying so hard.

EIJI: If you care so much about Chie-chan, why don't you get back together with my brother?

KEI: It wasn't I who wanted to separate. After all, this is his house. If I had wanted to separate, I would have been the one who had moved out. Besides, he doesn't want me to move out of this house, either—the fact is that the trading company would be in trouble without me.

EIJI: Is my brother happy with his life now, I wonder?

KEI: Yes, being the person he is, he seems very happy. He had wanted to become a language teacher since he was young, and his job now appears to be fulfilling to him. The International Institute is a school for Indians and Chinese living in Japan. Besides language, he also is teaching Japanese history there.

EIJI: How is he managing his meals?

KEI: He signed a contract with a nearby restaurant and has his breakfast and dinner delivered every day. Once a week, I go and clean his apartment and bring back his laundry.

EIJI: Well, that's a rather elaborate arrangement for living separately. So, you also give him money to help him cover his expenses?

KEI: He's doing his best. Whenever he has difficulties, I have no trouble helping him out.

EIJI: How do *you* feel about this? Are *you* satisfied with this way of living?

KEI: Well, satisfied or not . . . I've never thought of it that way . . . I've tried my best, and this is the way things have turned out. That's all. It's fine with me.

EIJI: . . .

(SHŌSUKE, *fifty-two, comes in.*)

SHŌSUKE: Hello.

KEI: Hello, Uncle Shōsuke. Welcome.

EIJI: Are you on your way home, Uncle Shōsuke?

SHŌSUKE: Yes. Oh, I'm tired. I get tired very easily these days. I don't know whether it's my age or it's because the wind in the floating world is getting rougher.

EIJI: I think it's because you've been working too hard to make money. The time might have come for you to retire.

SHŌSUKE: Yes, I would love to retire now. But I haven't found someone to take over yet.

EIJI (*Laughing*): How about me?

SHŌSUKE: If you would be willing to take my place, I wouldn't have any complaints.

EIJI (*Getting somewhat disconcerted*): Oh, we'd better forget about that. Nobody knows when I'd abandon the company and disappear again. Hahahahaha. —By the way, Uncle Shōsuke, you've remained stubbornly single all your life. Have you ever had any second thoughts about it?

SHŌSUKE: Nope. Not really. —But I've been really surprised that my small Jersey Company has also been plagued by labor unrest just like everywhere else.

KEI: My goodness . . .

SHŌSUKE: The world is going to the dogs: the strikes at the City Tram, the labor dispute in the mining industry, banks being robbed. It's like the pandemonium at the end of the Edo period. Where on earth is Japan heading, I wonder?

EIJI: Well, it's heading where it's supposed to.

SHŌSUKE: What do you mean, "where it's supposed to?"

EIJI: Well, I wish I knew.

SHŌSUKE: Come on. Don't talk as if you know it all. It's irritating to me these days to hear that kind of talk.

KEI: Really. If things keep going the way they are now, soon our Tsutsumi Trading Company will also go to "where it's supposed to."

SHŌSUKE: I suppose. Chiang Kai-shek has finally come back to power after driving out the communists, with Japanese support. But if things keep going this way, the Nationalist Party will soon collapse after all, in spite of its success in overcoming all its earlier difficulties.

KEI: And in spite of its close relationship with Japan, established by Sun Yat-sen.[4]

SHŌSUKE: The United States is behind Wang Zhengting. As soon as Wang took office as the Chinese foreign minister, the Americans began to talk to Prime Minister Tanaka in an intimidating manner. The Americans have not been popular among the Chinese so far. But now they are trying to curry favor with them and encourage

4. Sun Yat-sen (1866–1925) lived in Japan for six years, during which time, particularly between 1897 and 1907, he secured considerable Japanese political and financial support for the Chinese republican cause. In Japan in 1897, he began his lifelong friendship with Miyazaki Tōten (1871–1922), a Japanese pan-Asianist. Miyazaki adopted the Japanese alias Nakayama (Zhongshan in Chinese), by which he is commonly known in China. Through Miyazaki, Sun met the eminent politicians Ōkuma Shigenobu (1838–1922) and Inukai Tsuyoshi (1855–1932), the latter giving him living quarters and funds.

anti-Japanese feelings by giving up some of the U.S.'s special interests in China, those no longer valuable, politically and economically, as in their returning Weihaiwei.[5]

KEI: I don't quite understand what you're talking about. But who on earth is running Chinese politics, anyway?

EIJI: Well, no matter who is in office, as long as it's oligarchic politics, as we've seen up to this day, it will be business as usual. The only ones who stand to lose are the ordinary people, who are exploited every time something happens.

SHŌSUKE: One thing bad about China is that it always tries to use the power of one foreign country to hold back that of another. It has been like that since the Sino-Japanese War and the Russo-Japanese War. The United States, Great Britain, Russia. It's so disgusting.

EIJI: That's right. China must be returned to the hands of the Chinese. All foreign countries involved with China must take their hands off China. Chiang Kai-shek committed a huge blunder in chasing true revolutionaries like Chen Youren[6] and Borodin[7] into Soviet Russia.

KEI: I don't agree with you, I'm afraid. China can't maintain its independence unless it joins hands with the country most deeply involved with it. —And that country is none other than Japan. (*About to leave.*)

SHŌSUKE: If you are going to make tea, I don't need any.

KEI: No, I should at least get some tea for you. (*Exits.*)

EIJI (*Watching her leave*): If I remember correctly, she should be three years younger than I . . . But she looks older than her age.

SHŌSUKE: Neither you nor I can even hope to do what she has accomplished in her work. To be prematurely aged for her, I should say, is like a soldier's medal of honor for bravery.

EIJI: Maybe you're right. But isn't she going a little too far?

---

5. Morimoto is mistaken here. Weihaiwei (today called Weihai), a port city in China's Shandong Province, was leased to Britain in 1898. Then in 1930, after extended negotiations, Britain returned it to China.

6. Chen Youren is the Chinese name of Eugene Chen (1875–1944). Born in Trinidad, he studied law in England and became acquainted with Sun Yat-sen while practicing law in London. Returning to China after the 1911 Revolution, he became the editor in chief of the English-language newspaper the *Peking Gazette* and, later, the *People's Tribune* in Shanghai. In 1919, he was a delegate to the Paris Peace Conference, where he clearly articulated China's demands, to protect its interests against the world's imperial powers. He later became Sun Yat-sen's secretary until the latter's death in 1925. Although Chen never learned to speak Chinese, this legendary patriotic statesman served several times as China's foreign minister.

7. Mikhail Borodin (1884–1951) was a Soviet Comintern agent. He joined the Bolshevik faction of the Russian Social Democratic Labor Party in 1903. After the October Revolution, he returned to his motherland, Russia, after years of exile in the United States. From 1919 to 1922, he worked as a Comintern agent in Mexico, the United States, and the United Kingdom. From 1923 to 1927, he was the representative of the Comintern and the Soviet Union to China's National Party government. In 1928, when Chiang Kai-Shek purged the Communists and tried to arrest him, he returned to the Soviet Union. In 1949, he was accused of being an enemy of the Soviet Union and was sent to a work camp in Siberia, where he died two years later.

SHŌSUKE: Well, that woman was put in a position where she had no choice but to do what she has done. It's extremely unfair to her to make her do the work when she is needed and then blame *her* for the effect that the work had on her.

EIJI: But she used to be an idealistic dreamer, a sensible girl. I can't help but feel that I'm looking at an entirely different person now.

SHŌSUKE: All of us, when we're young, are idealistic dreamers and full of sensibility. But we get old, our sensibilities dry up and we become completely pragmatic and worldly. What's remarkable about this woman is that she, of her own will, abandoned her dreams and emotions. Moreover, she has never indicated even once how she felt about her decision. That's truly remarkable.

EIJI: I'm amazed, Uncle Shōsuke. You've never believed that the world has anything that's beautiful, pleasant, or happy, but you don't seem to hold back in praising her.

SHŌSUKE: You may say what you want. It's the first time in many years that you've seen again the woman you were once in love with. Did you expect a quieter, more romantic meeting than this? Or do you take pleasure in seeing the woman, who once abandoned you, abandoned by her husband? Whichever is the case, you are wrong, misguided, and pitiful.

EIJI: Well, neither is the case. I'm already more than forty years old and not a person so romantic as to be obsessed forever with my youthful dreams. Still, when I look at the way she is now, I simply can't help but feel disappointed.

SHŌSUKE: If you knew who turned her into such a disappointing person, you would probably not feel that way any more.

EIJI: Is there . . . such a person? Who is it, then?

SHŌSUKE: It was your mother and *I* myself.

EIJI: My mother and . . . ? But why did you do that?

SHŌSUKE: When I suggested to your mother that she should let Shintarō take over the family business, she was convinced that Shintarō simply couldn't do the job by himself. And so she wanted this woman to marry Shintarō and help him with the business. In your mother's mind, she was giving this woman a special favor. But she didn't consider how the girl felt about the matter and simply made her do it out of her egoistic love for her own child. Soon afterward, I found out that the marriage was not the girl's wish. I didn't say anything about it because she herself never said anything.

EIJI: I see . . . Is that what happened?

SHŌSUKE: . . . That woman never revealed a trace of it, of course. She just worked quietly from that day to this. I'm fully aware that as a human being, the woman has her share of shortcomings. But she's perhaps not aware of them because she has devoted her entire self, body and soul, to the battle of her life. These shortcomings are merely the by-product of that battle.

EIJI: I see . . . I knew *nothing* about *any* of this.

(KEI *brings in the tea.*)

KEI: Here's some tea. It's not very high quality, though.

SHŌSUKE: Oh, that's fine.

EIJI: Thanks.

(EIJI *silently stares into* KEI*'s face.*)

KEI: Is there something on my face?

EIJI: Oh, no . . . Hahaha . . .

(EIJI *turns his face away from* KEI.)

KEI: Uncle Shōsuke, could I speak to Eiji alone for a moment?

SHŌSUKE: Right now?

KEI: Yes.

SHŌSUKE: That's sort of a rude request. I'll excuse myself, then.

KEI: I'm sorry if I'm chasing you away.

SHŌSUKE: No problem. I'll go upstairs to get some sun. When you finish, just yell. (*Exits.*)

EIJI: What is it, Older Sister? We're together every day. Why do you, all of a sudden . . . ?

KEI: Eiji, I meant to ask you what business brought you back to Japan this time, but I haven't been able to.

EIJI: Well, no business. As I told you earlier, I just want to take it easy and relax for a while.

KEI: How can you afford to leave your wife and four children alone in China and come all the way to Japan to relax by yourself?

EIJI: Faraway as it may be, Japan is a place I will come back to sooner or later. I can't spend all my time with my wife and children. —They also like to have some time by themselves around the house, without me nagging at them.

KEI: Right now, China is a place where no one knows when or where war will break out. Can your wife and children afford to have you away at such a time?

EIJI: Well, this sounds like an interrogation. Is that what you want to talk to me about?

KEI (*Ignoring him*): Where did you go last night?

EIJI: I don't have to tell you that. I'm not a child and have to ask you for permission for what I do.

KEI: No, you *must* tell me. As the wife of the heir of the Tsutsumi family, I have to know what my husband's relatives are doing. If my husband were home, he would have asked you the same question. So please tell me.

EIJI: Well, in that case, I'll simply refuse to answer your question.

KEI: So you don't want us to know what you've been doing in China. And you don't want the world to know about the business that brought you back from China this time. Is that right?

EIJI: I'll let you figure it out. At any rate, I don't see why I need to discuss with you what I do.

KEI: . . . I see . . . I have no choice then. —There are some visitors at the gate who want to see you. (*Taking out two business cards and throwing them down on the table.*) Please go and meet them yourself.

EIJI (*Startled and suddenly looking around for a split second*): Older Sister, did you tell them that I'm here?

KEI: Before I came back to this room, I asked myself whether I should have told them otherwise. But listening to what you have just said, I'm convinced I did the right thing.

EIJI: Damn it! Do you think you understand politics? (*Standing up and trying to go down to the garden. Two men slowly pace across it.* EIJI *returns to the living room.*) Older Sister, just a moment ago, Uncle Shōsuke told me something about you that I didn't know before. For a second, it really shocked me. I was genuinely touched by the bittersweet story, but only for a second. So, you . . . you can sell even me, no one else but me, Eiji?!

KEI: Please go where you were planning to and think about this. As for whether I have sold you, that's a matter that you can talk about with your friends. As far as I'm concerned, I don't remember ever being your friend.

EIJI: Hahaha. You got the better of me there. You're right. You certainly aren't a friend of mine. Rather, you're more like my enemy.

KEI: Please give me your . . . wife's contact information. I'll make sure that you won't have to worry about her and your children while you're gone. I'll take care of them.

EIJI: Thank you for your kindness, but I'm afraid your offer is declined. Even if I accepted it, my family would not—they would rather starve to death. Moreover, their anger may cause them to turn on you. —But it's strange indeed: You and I, as I remember, once talked about China in this same room a long, long time ago. It was a rambling and dreamlike talk about China, but it brought us close to each other. To you, China was the place where your father was buried; to me, it was the place where my father found his way to success. Today, though, as we're talking about China again in this room, you and I have become enemies. Time has passed, and people also have changed. It's strange indeed. (*The two figures are seen pacing in the garden again.*) Well, those people seem to be in a hurry. I'd better go. Take care. (*Exits.*)

(KEI *sits there motionless as a statue. Moments later, she suddenly stands up and tries to run after* EIJI, *when* CHIE *appears from the hallway.*)

CHIE: Mother!

KEI: . . . (*Coming back and sitting down.*)

CHIE: Who are those people who took Uncle Eiji away?

KEI: What is it? If you want to talk to me, please sit down there and don't get in my way.

CHIE: Mother, what did Uncle Eiji do to deserve to be taken away by those people?

KEI: I don't know what your uncle did or what he plans to do in the future. I don't need to know any longer.

CHIE: Mother, couldn't you do something for Uncle Eiji? Couldn't you think of a more gentle way to treat him, instead of throwing him out of the house like that?

KEI: You wouldn't understand even if I told you.

CHIE: No, I already know. Since he came back, Uncle Eiji has never talked about himself. I thought there must be some reason for it. And I assumed all along that you also knew why.

KEI: If I had known, I wouldn't have waited until today.

CHIE: Mother, in doing what you did, don't you feel bad? Isn't Uncle Eiji Father's brother by the same mother? Isn't he a relative you haven't seen for years? You tied him up with your own hand, Mother. Doesn't doing this bother you?

KEI: There're things in life that we must do, no matter how painful or how difficult they are. Your uncle also knows that.

CHIE: No, I can't understand it. Aunt Fumi and Aunt Fusako used to visit us all the time. But now neither of them comes any more. Father moved out to an apartment and has never come back to this house again. Other relatives don't drop in either, even when they pass by. Day in and day out, there are only the two of us. Just when I was *so* happy that Uncle Eiji unexpectedly returned, you did this to him. I don't understand you, Mother.

KEI: I never expected, either, that I would end up parting in this way from your uncle, whom I hadn't seen for twenty years. But there's nothing that I can do about it. Your grandma once told me: "We all have our own dreams about life. Sometimes, though, we have to give up those dreams. And family is more important than your own self." —But I've just realized today that there's actually something else that is even more important than family, let alone one's own self.

CHIE: But we're all human beings, alive and with blood flowing in our bodies, aren't we? Mother, have you ever found yourself folding your own arms across your chest when you wake up suddenly at night? Have you never, not even once, experienced the irrepressible happiness of life when you see flowers blooming by the road? Mother, you . . .

KEI (*Suddenly slapping* CHIE*'s face.*)

CHIE (*Stunned, staring at* KEI*'s face for a moment.*)

(SHŌSUKE *comes in. Seeing what is going on, he is at a loss as to what to say.*)

SHŌSUKE: What's going on?

(CHIE *suddenly stands up and is about to run away.*)

SHŌSUKE: Hey, where are you going?

CHIE: To Father's place. I'll live with Father from now on.

(CHIE *exits.*)

SHŌSUKE: Chie! Stop, Chie! . . . Well, she's gone.

KEI: . . . That's fine. It's probably better for her, too, as I was saying to myself. So I'm really left by myself. But that somehow makes me feel relieved. Uncle Shōsuke, you'll finally leave me, too, this time, won't you? Please, go ahead. I won't be surprised if you do.

SHŌSUKE: But I'll never leave you. Even if all the people in the world leave you, I'll stay with you.

KEI: Is that so? Well, whatever you want. —They told me that Eiji scattered flyers at the speech rally in the public auditorium. He believes that Japan should take its hands off China. But what's going to happen if we do? To expect a nation of such weakness to remain independent on its own is like expecting a baby to be able to run. Chie doesn't know what she's talking about, and I don't believe that I've done anything wrong. —Even so, I was stunned to hear Chie questioning me like that. What would pass as noble if it's done by other people appears disgusting and offensive if it's done by me. Obnoxious, self-righteous, coldhearted, and inhuman. . . . I've gradually come to realize how I look in people's eyes, but there's nothing I can do about it. It's only to be expected that people should run away from me. I've come to find myself repugnant.

SHŌSUKE: What are you talking about? What should *I* do if you talk like that? Thanks to you, I came to believe in what people call humanity. Now isn't it ridiculous that even *you* can't believe in *yourself*? Kei-san, don't give up. To me, you are a . . . (SHŌSUKE *puts a hand on* KEI*'s shoulder. . . . Then he suddenly takes his hand off. Walking to the veranda, he remains standing there.*)

(*The twilight sky turns darker.*)

CURTAIN

Abe Kōbō, *The Man Who Turned into a Stick*, directed by Abe Kōbō, Kinokuniya, November 1969.

THE MAN WHO TURNED INTO A STICK

ABE KŌBŌ

TRANSLATED BY DONALD KEENE

The Man Who Turned into a Stick (*Bō ni natta otoko*) was first presented in a production staged at the Kinokuniya Hall in 1967. Later, after Abe Kōbō (1924–1993) formed his own theater company, the Abe Kōbō Studio, he restaged the play and combined it with two other short plays he had written, *The Cliff of Time* (*Toki no gake*, 1964) and *The Suitcase* (*Hako otoko*, 1969). He then combined the three into a loose trilogy, in which they all were given new subtitles. In this new scheme, *The Suitcase* represents *Birth*, *The Cliff of Time* is subtitled *Process*, and *The Man Who Turned into a Stick* becomes *Death*.[1] All are evocative puzzles and parables that require an actively involved audience to interpret.

A hot, sticky Sunday afternoon in June. A main thoroughfare with the Terminal Department Store in the background. Crowds of people passing back and forth. (It is best not to attempt to represent this realistically.) A young man and a young woman sit on the sidewalk curb at stage center front about three yards apart. They

---

1. All three plays were translated by Donald Keene and published in *The Man Who Turned into a Stick: Three Related Plays* (Tokyo: University of Tokyo Press, 1975). Abe's play *Friends* (*Tomodachi*, 1967), also translated by Keene, has been published in several editions, and his translations of additional plays can be found in *Three Plays by Kōbō Abe* (New York: Columbia University Press, 1993), which also includes pertinent background material. For more about the Abe Kōbō Studio, founded in 1973, see Nancy K. Shields, *Fake Fish: The Theater of Kobo Abe* (New York: Weatherhill, 1996).

are hippies. They stare vacantly ahead, completely indifferent to their surroundings, with withdrawn expressions. (If desired they can be shown sniffing glue.) All of a sudden a stick comes hurtling down from the sky. A very ordinary stick, about four feet long. (It can be manipulated, perhaps in the manner of Grand Guignol, by the actor playing the part of the man before he turned into a stick.) The stick rolls over and over, first striking against the edge of the sidewalk, then bouncing back with a clatter, and finally coming to rest horizontally in the gutter near the curbstone, less than a yard from the two hippies. Reflex action makes them look at where the stick has fallen, then upward, frowning, to see where it came from. But, considering the danger to which they have been exposed, their reactions are somewhat lacking in urgency. MAN FROM HELL *enters from stage left, and* WOMAN FROM HELL *from stage right. Both are spotlighted.*

Characters

MAN FROM HELL, a supervisor
WOMAN FROM HELL, recently appointed to the Earth Duty Squad
THE MAN WHO TURNED INTO A STICK
HIPPIE BOY
HIPPIE GIRL
VOICE FROM HELL

HIPPIE BOY (*Still looking up*): God-damned dangerous.

MAN FROM HELL: In the twilight a white crescent moon, a fruit knife peeling the skin of fate.

WOMAN FROM HELL: Today, once again, a man has changed his shape and become a stick.

HIPPIE BOY (*Turns his gaze back to the stick and picks it up*): Just a couple of feet closer and it would have finished me.

HIPPIE GIRL (*Looks at the stick and touches it*): Which do you suppose is the accident—when something hits you or when it misses?

HIPPIE BOY: How should I know? (*Bangs the stick on tile pavement, making a rhythm.*)

MAN FROM HELL: The moon, the color of dirty chromium plate, looks down and the streets are swirling.

WOMAN FROM HELL: Today, once again, a man turned into a stick and vanished.

HIPPIE GIRL: Hey, what's that rhythm you're tapping?

HIPPIE BOY: Try and guess.

HIPPIE GIRL (*Glancing up*): Look I'm sure that kid was the culprit.

HIPPIE BOY (*Intrigued, looks up.*)

HIPPIE GIRL: Isn't he cute? I'll bet he's still in grade school. He must've been playing on the roof.

HIPPIE BOY (*Looks into the distance, as before*): Damned brats. I hate them all.

HIPPIE GIRL: Ohh—it's dangerous, the way he's leaning over the edge.... I'm sure he's ashamed now he threw it.... He seems to be trying to say something, but I can't hear him.

HIPPIE BOY: He's probably disappointed nobody got hurt, so now he's cursing us instead.

STICK (*To himself*): No, that's not so. He's calling me. The child saw me fall.

HIPPIE GIRL (*Abruptly changing the subject*): I know what it is, that rhythm. This is the song, isn't it? (*She hums some tune or other.*)

HIPPIE BOY: Hmmm.

HIPPIE GIRL: Was I wrong?

HIPPIE BOY: It's always been my principle to respect other people's tastes.

HIPPIE GIRL (*Unfazed by this, she waggles her body to the rhythm and goes on humming.*) (*In the meantime,* THE MAN WHO TURNED INTO A STICK *is coordinating the movements of his body with those of the stick in* HIPPIE BOY*'s hand, all the while keeping his eyes fastened on a point somewhere in the sky.*)

MAN FROM HELL (*Walks slowly toward stage center*):

The moon is forgotten
In a sky the color of cement,
And the stick lies forgotten
Down in the gutter.

WOMAN FROM HELL (*Also walks in the same deliberate fashion toward stage center*):

The stick lies forgotten in the gutter,
The streets from above form a whirlpool.
A boy is searching for his vanished father.

(MAN *and* WOMAN FROM HELL *meet at stage center, several feet behind* HIPPIE BOY *and* GIRL, *just as they finish this recitation.*)

MAN FROM HELL (*In extremely matter-of-fact tones*): You know, it wouldn't surprise me if this time we happened to have arrived exactly where we intended.

WOMAN FROM HELL (*Opens a large notebook*): The time is precisely twenty-two minutes and ten seconds before—

MAN FROM HELL (*Looks at his wristwatch*): On the button ...

WOMAN FROM HELL (*Suddenly notices the stick in* HIPPIE BOY*'s hand*): I wonder, could that be the stick?

MAN FROM HELL (*Rather perplexed*): If it is, we've got a most peculiar obstacle in our path.... (*Walks up to* HIPPIE BOY *and addresses him from behind, over his shoulder.*) Say, pal, where did you get that stick?

HIPPIE BOY (*Throws him a sharp glance but does not answer.*)

WOMAN FROM HELL: Lying in the gutter, wasn't it?

HIPPIE GIRL: It fell from the roof. We had a hairbreadth escape.

WOMAN FROM HELL (*Delighted to have her theory confirmed*): I knew it! (*To* MAN FROM HELL.) Sir, it was this stick, as I suspected.

MAN FROM HELL (*To* HIPPIE BOY): Sorry to bother you, but would you mind handing me that stick?

WOMAN FROM HELL: I'm sure you don't need it especially.

HIPPIE BOY: I don't know about that. . . .

MAN FROM HELL: We're making a survey. A little investigation.

HIPPIE GIRL: You from the police?

WOMAN FROM HELL: No, not exactly . . .

MAN FROM HELL (*Interrupting*): But you're not too far off . . .

HIPPIE BOY: Liars! You're the ones who threw the stick at us. And now you're trying to suppress the evidence. You think I'm going to play your game? Fat chance! (*Beating out a rhythm with the stick, he starts to hum the melody* HIPPIE GIRL *was singing.*)

MAN FROM HELL (*In mollifying tones*): If you really suspect us, I'd be glad to go with you to the police station.

HIPPIE BOY: Don't try to wheedle your way around me.

HIPPIE GIRL (*Looks up*): You know, I think it was that kid we saw a while ago. . . . He's not there anymore.

HIPPIE BOY: You shut up.

WOMAN FROM HELL (*Animatedly*): That's right, there was a child watching everything, wasn't there? From the railing up there on the roof. . . . And didn't you hear him calling his father? In a frightened, numb little voice . . .

HIPPIE GIRL (*Trying not to annoy* HIPPIE BOY): How could I possibly hear him? The average noise level in this part of town is supposed to be over 120 decibels, on an average. (*Shaking her body to a go-go rhythm.*)

WOMAN FROM HELL (*To* MAN FROM HELL): Sir, shall I verify the circumstances at the scene?

MAN FROM HELL: Yes, I suppose so. (*Hesitates a second.*) . . . But don't waste too much time over it.

(WOMAN FROM HELL *hurries off to stage left.*)

STICK (*To himself. His voice is filled with anguish*): There's no need for it. . . . I can hear everything. . . . In the grimy little office behind the staircase marked "For store employees only" . . . my son, scared to death, surrounded by scabby-looking, mean security guards . . .

MAN FROM HELL (*To* HIPPIE BOY): It's kind of hard to explain, but the fact is, we have been entrusted, for the time being, with the custodianship of that stick. . . . I wish you'd try somehow to understand.

HIPPIE BOY: I don't understand nothing.

HIPPIE GIRL (*With a wise look*): This is the age of the generation gap. We're alienated.

STICK (*To himself. In tones of unshakable grief*): The child is lodging a complaint. . . . He says I turned into a stick and dropped from the roof. . . .

MAN FROM HELL (*To* HIPPIE BOY): Well, let me ask you a simple question. What do you intend to use the stick for? I'm sure you haven't any particular aim in mind.

HIPPIE BOY: I'm not interested in aims.

HIPPIE GIRL: That's right. Aims are out of date.

MAN FROM HELL: Exactly. Aims don't amount to a hill of beans. So why can't you let me have it? It isn't doing you any good. All it is, is a stick of wood. But as far as we're concerned, it is a valuable item of evidence relating to a certain person....

HIPPIE GIRL (*Dreamily*): But one should have a few. People don't have enough...

MAN FROM HELL: Enough what?

HIPPIE GIRL: Aims!

MAN FROM HELL: You're making too much of nothing. It's bad for your health to want something that doesn't really exist. The uncertainty you feel at the thought you haven't got any aims, your mental anguish at the thought you have lost track of whatever aims you once had—they're a lot better proof that you are there, in that particular spot, than any aim I can think of. That's true, isn't it?

HIPPIE GIRL (*To* HIPPIE BOY): How about a kiss, huh?

HIPPIE BOY (*Gives her a cold sidelong glance*): I don't feel like it.

HIPPIE GIRL: You don't have to put on such airs with me.

HIPPIE BOY: I don't want to.

HIPPIE GIRL: Come on!

HIPPIE BOY: I told you, lay on the euphoria.

HIPPIE GIRL: Then, scratch my back.

HIPPIE BOY: Your back?

(HIPPIE GIRL *bends over in* HIPPIE BOY*'s direction and lifts the back of her collar.* HIPPIE BOY, *with an air of great reluctance, thrusts the stick down into her collar and moves the stick around inside her dress, scratching her back.*)

HIPPIE GIRL: More to the left.... That's right, there....

HIPPIE BOY (*Pulls out the stick and hands it to* HIPPIE GIRL): Now you scratch me. (*Bends over toward* HIPPIE GIRL.)

HIPPIE GIRL: You don't mean it from the heart.... (*All the same, she immediately gives way and thrusts the stick down the back of* HIPPIE BOY*'s collar.*) Is this the place?

HIPPIE BOY: Yes, there. And everywhere else.

HIPPIE GIRL: Everywhere?

HIPPIE BOY (*Twisting his body and emitting strange noises*): Uhhh... uhhh... uhhh.... It feels like I haven't had a bath in quite some time....

HIPPIE GIRL (*Throwing down the stick*): You egoist!

(MAN FROM HELL *nimbly jumps between the two of them and attempts to grab the stick. But* HIPPIE BOY *brushes his hand away and picks up the stack again.*)

MAN FROM HELL: Look, my friend. I'm willing to make a deal with you. How much will you charge for letting me have this stick?

HIPPIE GIRL (*Instantly full of life*): One dollar.

MAN FROM HELL: A dollar? For a stick of wood like this?

HIPPIE BOY: Forget it. Not even for two dollars.

HIPPIE GIRL (*To* HIPPIE BOY *in a low voice, reproachfully*): You can find any number of sticks just like this one, if you really want it.

MAN FROM HELL: A dollar will keep you in cigarettes for a while.

HIPPIE BOY: Me and this stick, we understand each other. . . . Don't know why . . . (*Strikes a pose, holding the end of the stick in his hand.*)

HIPPIE GIRL (*With scorn in her voice*): You look alike. A remarkable resemblance.

HIPPIE BOY (*Staring at the stick*): So we look alike, do we? Me and this stick? (*Reflects a while, then suddenly turns to* HIPPIE GIRL.) You got any brothers and sisters?

HIPPIE GIRL: A younger sister.

HIPPIE BOY: What was her name for you? (HIPPIE GIRL *hesitates.*) You must have been known as something. A nickname, maybe.

HIPPIE GIRL: You mean, the way she called me.

HIPPIE BOY: Precisely.

HIPPIE GIRL: Gaa-gaa.

HIPPIE BOY: Gaa-gaa?

HIPPIE GIRL: No, that's what my brother called me. My sister was different. She called me Mosquito.

HIPPIE BOY: What does Gaa-gaa mean?

HIPPIE GIRL: Mosquito—that's what my sister called me.

HIPPIE BOY: I'm asking what Gaa-gaa is.

HIPPIE GIRL: You don't know what Gaa-gaa is?

HIPPIE BOY: Has it got something to do with mosquitoes?

HIPPIE GIRL: Yes, but it's very complicated to explain.

MAN FROM HELL: Excuse me, but would you . . .

HIPPIE BOY: Yesterday there was a funeral at that haberdashery across the street.

HIPPIE GIRL (*Looking around at the crowd*): But it had nothing to do with any of these people, had it?

HIPPIE BOY: But what about Gaa-gaa and Mosquito?

MAN FROM HELL: Wasn't it Gar-gar rather than Gaa-gaa?

HIPPIE GIRL: She died.

MAN FROM HELL: Who died?

HIPPIE GIRL: My sister.

MAN FROM HELL: What happened to her?

HIPPIE BOY: She became a corpse, naturally.

MAN FROM HELL: Of course. That's not surprising.

HIPPIE GIRL: That's why I don't understand anything anymore. Everything is wrapped in riddles.

HIPPIE BOY: What, for instance?

HIPPIE GIRL: Was it Gaa-gaa or Gar-gar?

HIPPIE BOY: You're just plain stupid.

MAN FROM HELL: By the way, in reference to that stick—she says you look like it. Let's suppose for the moment you do look like the stick—the meaning is not what you think it is.

HIPPIE GIRL: Tomorrow people will be calling tomorrow today.

MAN FROM HELL: To begin with, your conceptual framework with respect to the stick is basically—

HIPPIE BOY: I see. Once a human hand grabs something, there's no telling what it can do.

HIPPIE GIRL: I missed grabbing it. It's too awful to think that the day after tomorrow will always be tomorrow, even hundreds of years from now.

(WOMAN FROM HELL *returns, walking quickly.*)

WOMAN FROM HELL (*She stops at some distance from the others*): Sir. . . .

MAN FROM HELL (*Goes up to* WOMAN): Well, what happened?

WOMAN FROM HELL: We've got to hurry . . .

MAN FROM HELL (*Turns toward* HIPPIES): This crazy bunch—I offered them a dollar for the stick, but they refuse to part with it.

WOMAN FROM HELL: The child is coming.

MAN FROM HELL: What for?

WOMAN FROM HELL: Just as I got into the department store, I heard them making an announcement about a lost child. The child was apparently raising quite a rumpus. He claimed he saw his father turn into a stick and fall off the roof. But nobody seemed to believe him.

MAN FROM HELL: Of course not.

WOMAN FROM HELL: Then the child gave the matron the slip and ran out of the store, looking for his father.

(MAN *and* WOMAN FROM HELL *look uneasily off to stage left.*)

STICK (*Talking brokenly to himself*): The child saw it. I know he did. I was leaning against the railing at the time, the one that runs between the air ducts and the staircase, on a lower level. I was looking down at the crowds below, with nothing particular on my mind. A whirlpool. . . . Look—it's just like one big whirlpool . . .

(*Actual noises of city traffic gradually swell in volume, sounding something like a monster howling into a tunnel. Suddenly* HIPPIE BOY *lets the stick drop in alarm.*)

HIPPIE GIRL: What happened?

STICK (*Continuing his monologue*): I stood there, feeling dizzy, as if the noises of the city were a waterfall roaring over me, clutching tightly to the railing, when my boy called me. He was pestering me for a dime so he could look through the telescope for three minutes. . . . And that second my body sailed out into midair. . . . I had not the least intention of running away from the child or anything like that. . . . But I turned into a stick. . . . Why did it happen? Why should such a thing have happened to me?

HIPPIE GIRL: What's the matter, anyway?

HIPPIE BOY (*Stares at the stick lying at his feet with a bewildered expression*): It twitched, like a dying fish . . .

HIPPIE GIRL: It couldn't have . . . You're imagining things.

WOMAN FROM HELL (*Stands on tiptoes and stares off into the distance at stage left*): Look! Sir, look! Do you see that child? The little boy with the short neck, prowling around, looking with his big glasses over the ground?

MAN FROM HELL: He seems to be gradually coming closer.

STICK (*To himself*): I can hear the child's footsteps . . . bouncing like a little rubber ball, the sound threading its way through the rumblings of the earth shaking under the weight of a million people . . .

HIPPIE GIRL (*Steals a glance in the direction of the* MAN *and* WOMAN FROM HELL): Somehow those guys give me the creeps. . . . Why don't you make some sort of deal with him?

(HIPPIE BOY, *who has kept his eyes glued on the stick at his feet, snaps out of his daze and stands up.* GIRL *also stands.*)

HIPPIE BOY (*With irritation*): I can't figure it out, but I don't like it. That stick looks too much like me.

HIPPIE GIRL (*Her expression is consoling*): It doesn't really look all that much like you. Just a little.

HIPPIE BOY (*Calls to* MAN FROM HELL, *who has just that moment turned toward him, as if anticipating something*): Five dollars. What do you say? (*He keeps his foot on the stick.*)

MAN FROM HELL: Five dollars?

STICK (*To himself*): He doesn't have to stand on me. . . . I'm soaked from lying in the gutter. . . . I'll be lucky if I don't catch a cold.

HIPPIE BOY: I'm not going to force you. If you don't want it.

WOMAN FROM HELL (*Nervously glancing off to stage left*): Sir, he's almost here.

(THE MAN WHO TURNED INTO A STICK *shows a subtle, complex reaction, a mixture of hope and rejection.*)

HIPPIE BOY: I'm selling it because I don't want to sell it. That's a contradiction of circumstances. Do you follow me?

HIPPIE GIRL: That's right. He's selling it because he doesn't want to. Can you understand that?

MAN FROM HELL (*Annoyed*): All right, I guess . . . (*He pulls some folding money from his pocket and selects a five-dollar bill.*) Here you are. . . . But I'll tell you one thing, my friend, you may imagine you've struck a clever bargain, but one of these days you'll find out. It wasn't just a stick you sold, but yourself.

(*But* HIPPIE BOY, *without waiting for* MAN *to finish his words, snatches away the five-dollar bill and quickly exits to stage right.* HIPPIE GIRL *follows after him, smiling innocently. She waves her hand.*)

HIPPIE GIRL: It's the generation gap. (*She exits with these words.*)

(MAN *and* WOMAN FROM HELL, *leaping into action, rush to the gutter where the stick is lying. Just then the sun suddenly goes behind a cloud, and the street noises gradually fade. At the very end, for just a second, a burst of riveting is heard from a construction site somewhere off in the distance.*)

MAN FROM HELL (*Gingerly picks up the dirty stick with his fingertips. With his other hand he takes the newspaper that can be seen protruding from his pocket, spreads it open, and uses it to wipe the stick*): Well, that was a close one . . .

WOMAN FROM HELL: Earth duty isn't easy, is it?

MAN FROM HELL: It was a good experience on your first day of on-the-job training.

WOMAN FROM HELL: I was on tenterhooks, I can tell you.

(THE MAN WHO TURNED INTO A STICK *suddenly exhibits a strong reaction to something.* MAN *and* WOMAN FROM HELL *alertly respond to his reaction.*)

WOMAN FROM HELL: There's the child!

(MAN FROM HELL, *greatly alarmed, at once hides the stick behind his back. On a sudden thought, he pushes the stick under his jacket and finally down into his trousers. He stands ramrod stiff for several seconds. Then, all at once, the excitement melts from the face of* THE MAN WHO TURNED INTO A STICK. MAN *and* WOMAN FROM HELL, *relieved, also relax their postures.*)

STICK (*To himself*): It doesn't matter . . . There was nothing I could have done anyway, was there?

MAN FROM HELL (*Pulling out the stick*): Wow! That was a close shave . . .

WOMAN FROM HELL: But you know, I kind of feel sorry for him.

MAN FROM HELL: Sympathy has no place in our profession. Well, let's get cracking. (*Holds out the stick.*) That crazy interruption has certainly played havoc with our schedule.

WOMAN FROM HELL (*Accepts the stick and holds it in both hands, aloft to make a ceremonial offering*): I didn't realize how light it was.

MAN FROM HELL: It couldn't be better for a first tryout. Now, make your report, in exactly the order your learned . . .

WOMAN FROM HELL: Yes, sir. (*Examines the stick from every angle, with the earnestness of a young intern.*) The first thing I notice is that a distinction may be observed between the top and bottom of this stick. The top is fairly deeply encrusted with dirt and grease from human hands. Note, on the other hand, how rubbed and scraped the bottom is. . . . I interpret this as meaning that the stick has not always been lying in a ditch, without performing any useful function, but that during its lifetime it was employed by people for some particular purpose.

STICK (*To himself. Angrily*): That's obvious, isn't it? It's true of everybody.

WOMAN FROM HELL: But it seems to have suffered rather harsh treatment. The poor thing has scars all over it . . .

MAN FROM HELL (*Laughs*): Excellent, but what do you mean by calling it a poor thing? I'm afraid you've been somewhat infected by human ideas.

WOMAN FROM HELL: Infected by human ideas?

MAN FROM HELL: We in hell have a different approach. To our way of thinking, this stick, which has put up with every kind of abuse until its whole body is covered with scars, never running away and never being discarded, should be called a capable and faithful stick.

WOMAN FROM HELL: Still, it's only a stick. Even a monkey can make a stick do what he wants. A human being with the same qualities would be simpleminded.

MAN FROM HELL (*Emphatically*): That's precisely what I meant when I said it was capable and faithful. A stick can lead a blind man, and it can also train a dog. As a lever it can move heavy objects, and it can be used to thrash an enemy. In short, the stick is the root and source of all tools.

WOMAN FROM HELL: But with the same stick, you can beat me, and I can beat you back.

MAN FROM HELL: Isn't that what faithfulness means? A stick remains a stick, no matter how it is used. You might almost say that the etymology of the word faithful is a stick.

WOMAN FROM HELL (*Unconvinced*): But what you're saying is too miserable.

MAN FROM HELL: All it boils down to is, a living stick has turned into a dead stick—right? Sentimentality is forbidden to Earth Duty personnel. Well, continue with your analysis. (WOMAN *remains silent.*) What's the matter now? I want the main points of your report!

WOMAN FROM HELL (*Pulling herself together*): Yes, sir. Next I will telephone headquarters and inform them of the exact time and place of the disappearance of the person in question, and verify the certification number. Then I decide the punishment and register the variety and the disposition.

MAN FROM HELL: And what decision have you made on the punishment? (WOMAN *does not reply.*) Surely there can be no doubt in your mind. A simple case like this . . .

WOMAN FROM HELL: You know, I rather enjoy wandering around the specimen room, but I just don't seem to recall any specimens of a stick. (*Shakes her head dubiously.*)

MAN FROM HELL: There aren't any, of course.

WOMAN FROM HELL (*Relieved*): So it is a special case, isn't it?

MAN FROM HELL: Now calm yourself, and just think . . . I realize this is your first taste of on-the-job training, but it's disturbing to hear anything quite so wide off the mark. . . . The fact that something isn't in the specimen room doesn't necessarily mean it's so rare. On the contrary . . .

WOMAN FROM HELL (*Catching on at last*): You mean, it's because sticks are so common!

MAN FROM HELL: Exactly. During the last twenty or thirty years the percentage of sticks has steadily gone up. Why, I understand that in extreme cases, 98.4 percent of all those who die in a given month turn into sticks.

WOMAN FROM HELL: Yes, I remember now. . . . Probably it'll be all right if I leave the stick as it was during its lifetime, without any special punishment.

MAN FROM HELL: Now you're on the right track!

WOMAN FROM HELL: The only thing I have to do is verify the certification number. It won't be necessary to register the punishment.

MAN FROM HELL: Do you remember what it says in our textbook? "They who came up for judgment, but were not judged, have turned into sticks and filled the earth. The Master has departed and the earth has become a grave of rotten sticks. . . ." That's why the shortage of help in hell has never become especially acute.

WOMAN FROM HELL (*Takes out a walkie-talkie*): Shall I call headquarters?

MAN FROM HELL (*Takes the walkie-talkie from her*): I'll show you how it's done, just the first time. (*Switches it on.*) Hello, headquarters? This is MC training squad on earth duty.

VOICE FROM HELL: Roger. Headquarters here.

MAN FROM HELL: Request verification of a certification number. MC 621 . . . I repeat, MC 621 . . .

VOICE FROM HELL: MC 621. Roger.

MAN FROM HELL: The time was twenty-two minutes ten seconds before the hour. . . . The place was Ward B, 32 stroke 4 on the grid. Stick full from the roof of Terminal Department Store. . . .

VOICE FROM HELL: Roger. Go ahead.

MAN FROM HELL: No punishment. Registration unnecessary. Over.

VOICE FROM HELL: Roger. Registration unnecessary.

MAN FROM HELL: Request information on next assignment.

VOICE FROM HELL: Six minutes twenty-four seconds from now, in Ward B, 32 stroke 8 on the grid. Over.

WOMAN FROM HELL (*Opens her notebook and jots down a memo*): That would make it somewhere behind the station . . .

MAN FROM HELL: Roger. Thirty-two stroke eight.

VOICE FROM HELL: Good luck on your mission. Over.

MAN FROM HELL: Roger. Thanks a lot. (*Suddenly changing his tone.*) I'm sorry to bother you, but if my wife comes over, would you mind telling her I forgot to leave the key to my locker?

VOICE FROM HELL (*With a click of the tongue*): You're hopeless. Well, this is the last time. Over.

MAN FROM HELL (*Laughs*): Roger. So long. (*Turns off walkie-talkie.*) That, in general, is how to do it.

WOMAN FROM HELL: Thank you. I think I understand now.

MAN FROM HELL: What's the matter? You look kind of down in the mouth. (*Returns walkie-talkie to* WOMAN.)

WOMAN FROM HELL (*Barely manages a smile*): It's nothing, really . . .

MAN FROM HELL: Well, shall we say good-bye to our stick somewhere around here?

WOMAN FROM HELL: You mean you're going to throw it away, just like that?

MAN FROM HELL: Of course. That's the regulation. (*Looks around, discovers a hole in the gutter, and stands the stick in it.*) If I leave it standing this way, it'll attract attention and somebody is sure to pick it up before long. (*Takes a step back and examines it again.*) It's a handy size, and as sticks go, it's a pretty good specimen. It could be used for the handle of a placard . . .

(WOMAN *suddenly takes hold of the stick and pulls it from the hole.*)

MAN FROM HELL: What do you think you're doing?

WOMAN FROM HELL: It's too cruel!

MAN FROM HELL: Cruel? (*He is too dumbfounded to continue.*)

WOMAN FROM HELL: We should give it to the child. Don't you think that's the least we can do? As long as we're going to get rid of it anyway . . .

MAN FROM HELL: Don't talk nonsense. A stick is nothing more than a stick, no matter who has it.

WOMAN FROM HELL: But it's something special to that child.

MAN FROM HELL: Why?

WOMAN FROM HELL: At least it ought to serve as a kind of mirror. He can examine himself and make sure he won't become a stick like his father.

MAN FROM HELL (*Bursts out laughing*): Examine himself! Why should anyone who's satisfied with himself do that?

WOMAN FROM HELL: Was this stick satisfied with himself?

MAN FROM HELL: Don't you see, it was precisely because he was so satisfied that he turned into a stick.

WOMAN FROM HELL (*Stares at the stick. A short pause*): Just supposing this stick could hear what we have been saying . . .

STICK (*To himself. Weakly*): Of course I can hear. Every last word.

MAN FROM HELL: I have no specific information myself, since it's quite outside my own specialty, but scholars in the field have advanced the theory that they can in fact hear what we are saying.

WOMAN FROM HELL: How do you suppose he feels to hear us talk this way?

MAN FROM HELL: Exactly as a stick would feel, naturally. Assuming, of course, that sticks have feelings . . .

WOMAN FROM HELL: Satisfied?

MAN FROM HELL (*With emphasis*): There's no room for arguments. A stick is a stick. That simple fact takes precedence over problems of logic. Come now, put the stick back where it was. Our next assignment is waiting for us.

(WOMAN FROM HELL, *with a compassionate expression, gently returns the stick to the hole in the gutter.* THE MAN WHO TURNED INTO A STICK *up until this point has been registering various shades of reaction to the conversation of* MAN *and* WOMAN, *but from now on his emotions are petrified into any immobile state between fury and despair.*)

STICK (*To himself*): Satisfied . . .

WOMAN FROM HELL: But why must we go through the motions of whipping a dead man this way?

MAN FROM HELL: We are not particularly concerned with the dead. Our job is to record their lives accurately. (*Lowering his voice.*) To tell the truth, it is extremely dubious whether or not we in fact exist.

WOMAN FROM HELL: What do you mean by that?

MAN FROM HELL: There is a theory that we are no more than the dreams that people have when they are on the point of death.

WOMAN FROM HELL: If those are dreams, they are horrible nightmares.

MAN FROM HELL: That's right.

WOMAN FROM HELL: Then there's no likelihood that they're satisfied. To have nightmares even though you're satisfied; that's a terrible contradiction, isn't it?

MAN FROM HELL: Perhaps it might be described as the moment of doubt that follows satisfaction. In any case, what's done is done . . . (*In tones meant to cheer* WOMAN.) We'll have to hurry. We have exactly three minutes. If we're late, there'll be all hell to pay later on . . . (*Starts walking, leading the way.*) Don't worry. You'll get used to it before you know it. I was the same way myself. Sometimes you get confused by the false fronts people put on. But once you realize that a stick was a stick, even while it was alive . . .

WOMAN FROM HELL (*Still turns to look back at the stick, but somewhat more cheerful now*): Is the next person going to be a stick too?

MAN FROM HELL: Mmm. It would be nice if we got something more unusual this time.

WOMAN FROM HELL: What do you suppose those kids who tried to keep us from getting the stick will turn into?

MAN FROM HELL: Those hippies?

WOMAN FROM HELL: They didn't seem much like sticks, did they?

MAN FROM HELL: If they don't turn into sticks, maybe they'll become rubber hoses.

(MAN *and* WOMAN FROM HELL *exit to stage right.*)

STICK (*To himself*): Satisfied? Me? Stupid fools. Would a satisfied man run away from his own child and jump off a roof?

(*In another section of the stage,* MAN *and* WOMAN FROM HELL *reappear as silhouettes.*)

MAN FROM HELL: The sky is the color of a swamp, cloudy with disinfectant. On the cold, wet ground another man has changed into a stick.

WOMAN FROM HELL: He has been verified but not registered. He is shut up inside the shape of a stick. He is not unlucky, so he must be happy.

STICK (*To himself*): I've never once felt satisfied. But wonder what it would be better to turn into, rather than a stick. The one thing somebody in the world is sure to pick up is a stick.

MAN FROM HELL: He has been verified but not registered. The man's been shut up inside the shape of a stick. He can't so much as budge anymore, and that's a problem.

WOMAN FROM HELL: Supposing he begins to itch somewhere. What'll he do? How will he fare?

MAN FROM HELL: I'm afraid a stick would probably lack the talent needed to scratch his own back.

WOMAN FROM HELL: But anyway, you mustn't mind, you're not the only one of your kind.

MAN FROM HELL (*Steps forward and points his finger around the audience*): Look—there! A whole forest of sticks around you. All those innocent people, each one determined to turn into a stick slightly different from everybody else, but nobody once thinking of turning into anything besides a stick... All those sticks. You may never be judged, but at least you don't have to worry about being punished. (*Abruptly changes his tone and leans farther out toward the audience.*) You know. I wouldn't want you to think I'm saying these things just to annoy you. Surely, you don't suppose I would be capable of such rudeness... Heaven forbid... (*Forces a smile.*) It's just the simple truth, the truth as I see it....

WOMAN FROM HELL (*Goes up to* THE MAN WHO TURNED INTO A STICK *and speaks in pleading, rather jerky phrases*): Yes, that's right. You're not alone. You've lots of friends... men who turned into sticks.

CURTAIN

Akimoto Matsuyo, *Ceremonial Clothes*, directed by Okakura Shirō, Haiyūza, August 1949. (Courtesy of Haiyūza)

CEREMONIAL CLOTHES

AKIMOTO MATSUYO

TRANSLATED BY GANSHI MURATA

Ceremonial Clothes (*Reifuku*), by Akimoto Matsuyo (1911–2001), was published in the June 1949 issue of the theater magazine *Playwriting* (*Gekisaku*) and, in August of the same year, was first performed by the part of Senda Koreya's Actors' Theater (Haiyūza) company that produced the work of new playwrights.

David Goodman described the play as dealing with "the inadequacy of prescribed forms . . . for coming to terms with the loss of a parent." But, he continued, "on a metaphysical level, the play reflects the difficulties Japanese society encountered during the immediate postwar period coming to terms with the death of the quasi-familial order set out in the Imperial Rescript on Education."[1] That is, in Akimoto's dark vision, there now seems little to hold the family, or the nation, together.

Akimoto's later plays often deal with religious themes and the search to find rituals capable of controlling human suffering. In that regard, perhaps her most striking success is *Kaison the Priest of Hitachi* (*Hitachibō Kaison*, 1967).[2]

Ganshi Murata's colleagues and students at Macalester College collaborated with him on the translation.

1. David G. Goodman, "The Quest for Salvation in Japan's Modern History: Four Plays by Akimoto Matsuyo," in *Modern Japanese Theater and Performance*, ed. David Jortner, Keiko I. McDonald, and Kevin J. Wetmore Jr. (Lanham, Md.: Lexington Books, 2006), 56–57.
2. Translated in David G. Goodman, ed., *The Return of the Gods: Japanese Drama and Culture in the 1960s*, photo reprint ed. (Ithaca, N.Y.: East Asia Program, Cornell University, 2003).

Place: In a country town somewhere in Japan.
Time: Early spring, the dawn of one day and the following day, 1948.

Characters

ICHIZŌ
KEIKO, his younger sister
TOKUJI, his younger brother
YASUKO, his younger sister
IKU, his grandmother
FUMIE, his former wife
SHIGEMASA, his uncle
MASATARŌ, KEIKO's husband
DR. KAJIMA
ICHIZŌ'S BOSS
TOWN OFFICIALS 1, 2, 3
NURSE
FUNERAL HELPERS
FUNERAL GUESTS

SCENE 1

The large guest room of ICHIZŌ*'s house. Stage left are* fusuma, *sliding paper doors. Stage right are* shōji, *paper partitions leading to the other rooms. Upstage is a veranda overlooking a Japanese garden. The outside shutters are closed. Toward stage left of the room are a bed, a small table and chair, and a screen. In the center of the room are a sofa and a desk. The entrance to the house appears to be stage right of the veranda. It is just before dawn, and in the room a bright lamp is lit. Outside, heavy rain is falling. The body of* ICHIZŌ*'s mother, Nobu, is lying on the bed. A* NURSE *is quietly removing oxygen equipment.* ICHIZŌ*'s sisters,* KEIKO *(thirty-four) and* YASUKO *(twenty-three), are sobbing by the bed. Off to one side,* ICHIZŌ *(forty) and* DR. KAJIMA *are standing quietly, lost in thought. Uncle* SHIGEMASA *(sixty-five), Nobu's brother-in-law, is leaning against the* fusuma, *staring at the ceiling, and* MASATARŌ *(forty),* KEIKO*'s husband, is sitting with his head bowed in sorrow. A long pause.* DR. KAJIMA *bows respectfully to the corpse and walks slowly to the sofa.* ICHIZŌ *also bows to the corpse and moves to the sofa. They exchange bows and remain in silence.*

DR. KAJIMA: It was just 4:35.

ICHIZŌ (*Bows.*)

DR. KAJIMA: Please accept my deep sympathy. . . . Please accept my deep sympathy. . . . I did my best, but . . .

ICHIZŌ: . . . Thank you for your . . .

DR. KAJIMA: . . . No, no . . .

ICHIZŌ: It, it was so sudden. . . . I, I just . . . (*Swallows a sob.*)

DR. KAJIMA: I know.

ICHIZŌ: If only I'd noticed earlier. . . . It was all my fault.

DR. KAJIMA: No, don't say that. It's not true.

ICHIZŌ: . . .

DR. KAJIMA: Anyone would feel the same.

ICHIZŌ: Would they?

DR. KAJIMA (*Sitting down on sofa*): Well, my work is finished, but as a friend, if there is anything I can do. . . .

ICHIZŌ: Thank you, maybe later, but for the moment.

(*A cock crows in the distance, and they both notice it distractedly.*)

DR. KAJIMA: She was sixty, wasn't she?

ICHIZŌ: Sixty-one, actually.

DR. KAJIMA: Too soon, wasn't it?

ICHIZŌ: Ummm. . . . She lived longer than my father.

DR. KAJIMA: Ummm.

ICHIZŌ: She was so healthy.

DR. KAJIMA (*Nodding, but doubtfully*): Yes.

ICHIZŌ: Nobody . . . could have imagined this.

DR. KAJIMA: That's very true.

ICHIZŌ: It was the first time she'd ever seen a doctor . . . the first and the last time. (*His head drops.*)

DR. KAJIMA: . . .

ICHIZŌ: All her life she kept working. She never once complained. She never seemed to rest, even in bed. (*Wipes his tears.*)

DR. KAJIMA: . . .

(*The* NURSE *comes up to* KAJIMA *and whispers something to him.* KAJIMA *nods and goes toward the bed.*)

KEIKO (*To* KAJIMA): Thank you so much for everything, Doctor.

DR. KAJIMA: I'm really very sorry. (*Bows to* YASUKO, MASATARŌ, SHIGEMASA, *and the others.*)

NURSE (*Drawing the screen around the bed*): Will somebody help us?

KEIKO (*Nods.*)

SHIGEMASA: I will. I'm old enough.

(KAJIMA, SHIGEMASA, KEIKO, *and the* NURSE *go behind the screen.* YASUKO *and* MASATARŌ *go toward the sofa.*)

ICHIZŌ: After I was promoted to department head at the town hall, I promised to take her to a hot spring, but we never had a chance. (*Wipes his eyes with his handkerchief.*)

YASUKO: Ichizō. (*Sobbing.*)

ICHIZŌ: If only she'd lived . . . another ten years.

YASUKO: Ichizō, don't.

MASATARŌ: Ichizō, Older Brother, please, don't.

ICHIZŌ: Even though I was here with her, look what happened. It was my fault. (*Wipes a tear.*) I thought it was just a cold. She was so strong and determined. She wouldn't stop working. Then it turned into pneumonia. It took only a couple of days. When I told you, it was too late. I was too late, too careless. (*Cries.*)

MASATARŌ: Don't say that. Don't blame yourself. (*Holds back his tears and quietly leaves by the veranda.*)

YASUKO: Ichizō, I still can't believe it.

ICHIZŌ: Hmm, I know, me neither.

YASUKO: She's really dead.

ICHIZŌ: It's happened.

YASUKO (*Clings to* ICHIZŌ *and cries.*)

(*Pause. The sound of falling rain. A cock crows in the distance.*)

ICHIZŌ: We gave her such a hard time.

YASUKO (*Crying, nods.*)

ICHIZŌ: She was a wonderful mother. . . . A mother like that. (*His voice is choked.*)

YASUKO: Please don't. It only makes it worse.

ICHIZŌ: Well, anyway, the least we can do is pray that she's gone to a better place.

YASUKO: Yes.

ICHIZŌ: They say we shouldn't feel sad for those who have died . . . it's not good for their spirits.

YASUKO: Yes, that's true. . . .

ICHIZŌ: It's in the hands of fate. . . . We all have our trials.

YASUKO: Yes. . . . But, somehow I feel we should have been able to avoid this one.

ICHIZŌ: You're not alone. I feel that, too.

YASUKO: I could see this coming six months ago. Each time I saw her.

ICHIZŌ: Hmm . . . I could sense something as long as three years ago. (*Becoming more agitated.*) Actually, I was sure of it. I knew in my heart that sooner or later, this day would come. I knew it was coming. And here it is.

YASUKO: . . . (*Moving away from* ICHIZŌ.)

ICHIZŌ: I knew this would happen . . . at least I knew.

YASUKO: Then . . . why . . . ? But it's a bit late to say . . . (*Cries.*)

ICHIZŌ: Yes, it's too late. But I really feel it's all our faults. We can't blame ourselves enough.

YASUKO: . . .

ICHIZŌ: She really had a hard time. There was never a moment when she wasn't worrying about something. . . . She worried about us right up to the moment she died. But look at us: you Yasuko, Tokuji, wherever he is, and me, did we ever truly try to make things easy for her, to make her happy? Think about it.

YASUKO: . . . (*Stops crying.*)

ICHIZŌ (*Starts pacing up and down the room*): . . . Just think of what she said before she died. Remember her life, full of sincerity, love, and sacrifice. The least we can do in return is learn how we should live our lives. If we can't do that, there isn't much hope for us.

YASUKO: . . .

MASATARŌ (*Comes back quietly and sits on the sofa.*)

ICHIZŌ: Anyway, we weren't good children. . . . I mean, look at Tokuji. He isn't even here yet. Where was he when his mother was dying? Maybe he didn't even know she was sick. He doesn't care about her at all. What would people think if they knew that? And you, too, Yasuko. You always say you are busy working, so I haven't mentioned it, but you're not even married yet. At least I took care of my duties as a son. I did as much as I could. I was the only one out of four of us. I wonder what Mother. . . . I can't let this go. (*Walks around, getting more irritated.*) Yasuko, don't you have any idea where Tokuji might be?

YASUKO (*Shakes her head.*)

MASATARŌ (*Hesitatingly*): Well . . . you know . . . We did send telegrams to as many places as we could think of . . .

ICHIZŌ: And he hasn't turned up! It's always like this. . . . Yasuko could at least have been in contact with Tokuji. He didn't get in touch with you, so you didn't bother with him. Your cheap "independence" really infuriates me.

DR. KAJIMA (*Puts his head around the screen*): Ichizō, excuse me . . .

ICHIZŌ (*Goes behind the screen.*)

SHIGEMASA (*He passes* ICHIZŌ *coming out; his eyes are red and wet*): Ah, ah, she's very beautiful. . . . Her toenails are shining like seashells . . . (*Stares at the ceiling.*) . . . Ah, it's raining . . . "Rain at dawn" . . . hmmm . . . "A person passes on as it rains." (*He takes out a notebook and writes the poem in it.*)

(*Pause. The sound of rain.*)

DR. KAJIMA (*Coming from behind the screen with* ICHIZŌ): I'll go now. Would somebody come by later and pick up the certificate? I'll prepare it for you.

ICHIZŌ: Thank you.

DR. KAJIMA: You aren't well, Ichizō. So don't try to do too much. Should I make up your usual prescription?

ICHIZŌ: Yes. . . . Please.

DR. KAJIMA: Well. Good-bye. (*Bows to* MASATARŌ, YASUKO, *and the others. Leaves by the veranda. The* NURSE *and* ICHIZŌ *go out with him.*)

(*Short pause. The sound of rain.*)

KEIKO (*Coming slowly from behind the screen*): Is that . . . the sound of rain? Ah, it's been raining. . . . It's cold.

SHIGEMASA: Look, I'm just writing a haiku. (*Writes and crosses out in the notebook.*)

KEIKO: Yes, maybe I'll write one, too. What about you, Yasuko?

YASUKO: What?

SHIGEMASA: "Rain at dawn the oxygen tank . . . pom pom pom" . . . hmmm.

KEIKO: Do you know where my coat is, dear? It's cold.

MASATARŌ: Uh? Yes. (*Goes off to the right.*)

ICHIZŌ (*Comes in restlessly and sits at the desk*): Er, Uncle Shigemasa, could you send some telegrams? I'll write them now. . . . To the town hall, relatives, and others. (*Looks over his shoulder.*) On your way back, drop into Dr. Kajima's office and pick up the death certificate. Take it straight to the town hall, because we need permission for burial. Then go to the undertaker's and make arrangements for the funeral. . . . Ah, yes, what about the temple? . . . Before or after? . . . Before, of course.

SHIGEMASA: Hmm, well . . . maybe . . . (*His mind is on something else.*)

ICHIZŌ: Did you hear what I said?

SHIGEMASA: Eh? Yes, yes . . .

MASATARŌ (*Coming back in*): Keiko, I can't find your coat, honey.

KEIKO: What? . . . Are you blind? (*Goes off to the right.*)

ICHIZŌ: Masatarō, can you do your best to find Tokuji? I don't want this to look bad to others.

MASATARŌ: Do you have any ideas . . . ?

ICHIZŌ: That's why I'm asking you! Go out and look for him, please! Damn. . . . There must be some way!

MASATARŌ: OK . . . I'll go and look for him.

ICHIZŌ: Well go. (*Starts writing at the desk.*)

KEIKO (*Coming back with her coat around her shoulders*): Oh . . . are you going out? Now?

MASATARŌ: . . . To look for Tokuji . . .

KEIKO: Can you find him, dear? . . . I know you, the first thing you'll do is go to a bar. . . . You want a drink now, don't you?

MASATARŌ: No, of course I don't . . . Anyway, I can't just hang around here. (*Leaves.*)

ICHIZŌ: Which relatives should I contact? Eh, Uncle Shigemasa?

SHIGEMASA: Don't, don't talk to me just now . . . (*He's writing in his book.*)

KEIKO: You'd better let them all know, or there'll be trouble later.

ICHIZŌ: Then they'll all come.

KEIKO: Yes, of course, I suppose so.

ICHIZŌ: It's going to be quite a job . . . futons, food. . . . Should I hire someone to help out? What about a hibachi and teacups? We don't have enough here, do we?

KEIKO: Of course not.

ICHIZŌ: The wake is tonight, so we'll need drinks and food, too . . . so, so . . . provide rice and saké, quick. I don't want it to look shabby, Keiko.

KEIKO: Do I have to do it?

ICHIZŌ: It's a woman's job. Besides, you are the oldest sister. And another thing . . . Yasuko, you go to the bank; then there must be something else . . . Everybody think about it, make notes so we don't argue later. . . . Uncle, what are you writing over there?. . . . Are you listening to any of this?

SHIGEMASA: Eh? I'm sorry . . .

ICHIZŌ: You . . . you're always like this.

SHIGEMASA: What? I . . . I'm still thinking about her.

ICHIZŌ: That's your business but this is urgent! Aghhh! I'm the only one who cares about any of this! I have to think of everything . . . (*He tears up some paper and throws it on the floor.*) You're all useless!

KEIKO: Why don't you calm down? Someone from the town hall or the neighborhood will come by later and take care of things.

SHIGEMASA: Anyway, sit down and let's talk about all this. It'll be morning soon. . . .

ICHIZŌ: What? That's just typical of you . . . maybe you don't care, but I do! . . . Besides I'm the head of this house. . . . I do things my way! . . . So, Uncle, take these to the post office, drop into Dr. Kajima's on the way back, then the town hall, then deal with the undertaker. Ah, don't forget your seal and the ration card for the rice.

SHIGEMASA: Yes, yes. (*Leaves to the right.*)

ICHIZŌ: And Keiko, you go to the bank.

KEIKO: It isn't light yet!

ICHIZŌ: I know . . . I mean after it gets light.

IKU (*Grandmother, eighty-five, crawls in from the next room*): Ichizō, it's light. Can I have my breakfast. . . . Please.

ICHIZŌ: Granma . . . just wait a moment. You shouldn't be in here.

IKU: Ichizō, listen . . . Nobu doesn't care about old people. She's the worst daughter ever. . . . She never gives me food; my clothes are in rags. (*She tears a piece off her sleeve.*) Look at this!

ICHIZŌ: Have some respect. Nobu just died. Look.

IKU: Don't lie. Nobu didn't die. She'll live a thousand years!

ICHIZŌ: Grandma, that's a good girl, go back in there.

(*Takes hold of* IKU *and leaves.*)

ICHIZŌ: Whatever you do, don't let her out of there. Put her to bed. . . . Aghhhh. What a crowd! I'm (*Kicks the chair.*) I'm going mad here.

KEIKO: It's not good for you Ichizō. It's bad for your heart.

ICHIZŌ: What? . . . How can you be so trivial? It's your . . .

(*The sound of the front door banging open and closed is heard. After a short pause,* TOKUJI, ICHIZŌ*'s brother, about twenty-seven, comes in, wearing a bright suit and flat cap.*)

TOKUJI (*He mouths a greeting*): Hi.

ICHIZŌ: Hello. (*Takes off his cap.*)

Hey . . . you . . .

TOKUJI: On the way here. . . . I just met Dr. Kajima.

ICHIZŌ: . . . (*He nods toward the screen.*)

TOKUJI: . . . Hmmm.

ICHIZŌ: About 4:35.

TOKUJI: . . . (*He goes behind the screen.*)

(*Pause.*)

(*The sound of falling rain and a cock crowing nearby are heard.*)

KEIKO: Well . . . It's morning. . . . Should I open the shutters?

ICHIZŌ: Hmmm, could you?

KEIKO (*She opens the shutters and breathes deeply*): Ahhh, it's really morning. Will this rain ever stop? . . . I need a nap. (*Goes off to the right.*)

TOKUJI (*Coming from behind the screen, grabs a pair of scissors from the desk, and goes back to the screen.*)

ICHIZŌ: What are you doing, Tokuji?

TOKUJI: . . . I want a lock of her hair. (*Goes behind the screen.*)

ICHIZŌ (*Sighs. Then wanders around the room.*)

TOKUJI (*Holding a lock of hair on a piece of paper, comes dejectedly from behind the screen.*)

ICHIZŌ: Tokuji, where were you?

TOKUJI: . . .

ICHIZŌ: We were looking all over for you.

TOKUJI: I didn't know . . . that she's almost completely white . . . (*He stops himself from crying.*)

ICHIZŌ: . . .

TOKUJI: I . . . I meant to come. I do care . . .

ICHIZŌ: How could we get in touch with you?

TOKUJI: The other day, I came as far as the corner. . . . Just a little while ago.

ICHIZŌ: You came here only to ask for something.

TOKUJI: That time, I thought maybe she'd be walking outside. I stood on the street. (*Sobs.*) But then I changed my mind.

ICHIZŌ: It's too late now.

TOKUJI: . . .

ICHIZŌ: I can't say she died peacefully. . . . I'm not talking about the pain or fever from her illness. . . . I'm sure you know what I mean.

TOKUJI: . . .

ICHIZŌ: I wanted you to hear what she had to say. . . . She was really worried about you . . . as she would be . . . She said again and again we should help each other and try to get along together. That's what she said.

TOKUJI (*Whispering*): I see.

ICHIZŌ: But . . . nevertheless, the fact that you weren't here when she was dying is . . .

TOKUJI: OK, OK, I didn't . . .

ICHIZŌ: You weren't here because that's how you are.

TOKUJI: . . .

ICHIZŌ: You ought to think about that. I've told you about this many times, but even so . . .

TOKUJI: OK, it's enough. I know, I know.

ICHIZŌ: Well, all right then. (*Paces around the room.*) You opened that stall in the market and had Mother there from eight in the morning until ten at night. . . . Without a single day off, in rain and snow. . . . And you were always changing what you sold. First clothes, then flowers, shoes, china, pictures of film stars . . . I don't know what else. Mother didn't know anything about business. She was exhausted from trying to remember what she was supposed to be selling. Worst of all, I heard you often messed things up, bringing a truck full of plants to your shoe shop . . . that kind of stupidity, eh? . . . Not only that, but I heard you used to shout at her when stuff was stolen from the shop, until she had terrible headaches.

TOKUJI: No, no. That was . . .

ICHIZŌ: There's more. She had to sit the whole day in the market, in the filthy air, while you took advantage of her and went off dancing, skating, and playing mahjong. Then at night you'd get drunk and throw up on her, rolling around the street, waking everybody up, starting fights with people.

TOKUJI: Wait, wait . . . I didn't mean to . . .

ICHIZŌ: Stop making excuses. . . . Your sordid life wore her out, mentally and physically. That's why she got ill. I can't think of any other reason.

TOKUJI: You're saying I . . .

ICHIZŌ: What have you done since you left the army? You pretend you are suave and exceptional. But all you did was make her suffer.

TOKUJI: I . . . (*Starts crying.*)

ICHIZŌ (*A little more kindly*): You've never taken any notice of Mother since you were a child. You were always misbehaving just to annoy her, always complaining and being sarcastic. Those are all your bad points. . . . Even I can't like you, so think what Mother. . . .

TOKUJI: I was always taking advantage of her, always being selfish. I'd ask for the impossible and get her to try and give it to me. I just wanted to be treated like a spoiled child. . . . But in the end, I did that because of the way I am; it turned out badly. I thought, behind it all, she understood me, so anything I did would be OK between me and her.

ICHIZŌ: I can't accept that mentality. Love should be more ethical and natural.

TOKUJI: Ichizō, that's enough preaching. . . . Besides, whatever you say, you'll never understand how I felt because you always got special treatment.

ICHIZŌ: Eh? What are you talking about?

TOKUJI: I mean, there's a world that the favorite son can never imagine.

ICHIZŌ: Oh, I know, you think she thought more of me. But our mother had a lot of love and was very fair. Equal love is lost if the one receiving it is twisted. Who is to blame? Some people are loved a lot, and some are loved less, depending on their character and nature.

TOKUJI: I knew that was what you'd say. . . . "Nature," "character." . . . You got special treatment because of the house and the family. There's that stupid custom to care for the first son above all else. I wanted to rescue her from that. . . . But she was always flattering you, hanging on your every word. She was always on edge and looking up to you. . . . A mother's love is sometimes . . . vicious.

ICHIZŌ: Vicious? What are you talking about? Watch your mouth.

TOKUJI: You made me say that. You must have known what she was feeling, and inside, you were really pleased about it. You were always flaunting your cheap superiority with your "character" and "nature," weren't you?

ICHIZŌ: Aren't you ashamed of yourself? . . . To be jealous of your own brother? . . . Keep to the point! All I'm trying to say is you should think carefully about our mother's death and, more than that, about your responsibility.

TOKUJI: Don't make me the only villain in this case. You weren't always so concerned about our parents. There were times when you thought she was just a burden. Do you want to hear more?

ICHIZŌ: What? What did I do?

TOKUJI (*Walking around the room*): She told me what kind of tyrant you were in the house. While you were out at parties and hot springs, you didn't even give her ten yen spending money, but you used her just like a servant. You were very stylish, changing your shirt every day, but you didn't even let her buy herself a pair of *tabi* socks. She hated having to show you the bills. There was always a big uproar; you'd complain for an hour and finally throw some money at her, like you were being charitable or something.

ICHIZŌ: Nonsense!

TOKUJI: She used to say she liked Tokuji more than that mean, cruel, moaning Ichizō. She'd rather work in my stall than for you.

ICHIZŌ: At least I didn't make her cry because I had problems with a prostitute. It was snowing heavily that night, and Mother was worried about you. I couldn't stop her, and in tears, she went to the town with an umbrella. She humiliated herself by going to every brothel in town to find you. The sight of her that night . . . I . . .

TOKUJI: If you want to get rough, OK! You blamed Mother for your divorce from Fumie, but the fact is, Fumie just didn't like you. But you bitched at Mother and bullied her, didn't you? And in the end, you got hysterical and ran around on the tatami in your shoes. You swore at her and told her to get out.

ICHIZŌ: Shut up! So what? (*His body shaking with anger.*) Even if there were a couple of ugly scenes, it was a private thing between a mother and her son. It's just a fact of life. Mother and I understood each other. Fumie and Mother didn't get along at all, so I decided to divorce her. Mother tried to stop me, but . . . underneath, I think she was relieved. I accepted her with my whole heart and forgave her. . . . That's how close we were.

TOKUJI: Well, fine. But you can't say you didn't notice Mother's illness if your relationship was so "close." She hadn't been well for quite a while, and in fact, I secretly paid for her to go to see Dr. Kajima.

ICHIZŌ: Eh?

TOKUJI: She'd been weak for a long time. She needed rest but was too scared to tell you about it. Do you know why?

ICHIZŌ: . . .

TOKUJI: She was worried sick about what your reaction would be if she ever mentioned it.

ICHIZŌ: That's not true! It's a lie!

TOKUJI: What have I got to lie about? Dr. Kajima can tell you it's true.

ICHIZŌ: But . . . Why didn't she . . . Why? . . . Tell me!

TOKUJI: You'd better ask yourself that.

ICHIZŌ: . . .

TOKUJI: I don't know exactly myself, but I do know why she was so uneasy about your feelings. . . . You made her that way.

ICHIZŌ (*Grabs* TOKUJI *by the collar*): You're a liar!

TOKUJI (*Casually pushes away* ICHIZŌ*'s hand*): Fool . . .

YASUKO (*Rushes in from the next room*): Stop this, both of you!

TOKUJI: Yasuko knows about all this, too.

ICHIZŌ: Is that true, Yasuko?

YASUKO: Yes.

ICHIZŌ: Why didn't you tell me?

YASUKO: Because . . . Mother told me not to tell you. . . . She said that if she became of no use to you, you'd have nothing to do with her . . .

ICHIZŌ: But, but that's stupid. . . .

YASUKO: She kept her sickness a secret so she wouldn't bother you.

ICHIZŌ: That, that can't be true. . . . It's impossible.

TOKUJI: I wonder why she was so scared of you? . . . I can't stand to think of it.

YASUKO: Me neither, I was so upset to see . . . (*Starts crying.*)

ICHIZŌ (*Sits on a chair and closes his eyes in pain.*)

TOKUJI: So in the end, she was just a weak, powerless Japanese woman. It made me angry and very sorry. . . . In fact, I hated it.

YASUKO: What was . . . the point of her life, anyway?

ICHIZŌ (*Groans with his eyes closed.*)

TOKUJI: Exactly.

ICHIZŌ: . . . So I knew absolutely nothing?

TOKUJI (*Gently*): It seems that way. . . . The fact is, you were just making her submit to you.

ICHIZŌ (*With his head in his hands*): Uhm. . . . But no . . .

TOKUJI: Ichizō, don't be so hard on yourself.

YASUKO: Come on, let's forget all this.

ICHIZŌ (*Groans.*)

TOKUJI: I said too much. . . . But it's true, and sometimes the truth hurts.

ICHIZŌ (*His eyes wide in shock*): Then . . . what . . . what was I supposed to be? Who the hell was I?

TOKUJI: Eh? What's wrong, all of a sudden?

ICHIZŌ: This is a question of my identity. It's between Mother and me.

TOKUJI: But that's all finished now, isn't it? Let's not drag it up again. I'm tired of it.

ICHIZŌ: So who was the one obeying? Was it me, or was it Mother? Who was scared of whom? That's what I've been asking myself. And who do you think comes to mind?

TOKUJI: How the hell should I know?

ICHIZŌ: You just said Mother was a weak and powerless person, didn't you?

YASUKO: Ichizō, calm down, please. It's not good for you.

ICHIZŌ: Yasuko, keep quiet. . . . What comes to mind is my mother, who was with us until just yesterday. With her peaceful eyes, her graceful movements, and her slow, thoughtful speech. . . . (*He paces nervously around the room.*) Cool and collected. . . . She did everything just so . . . She never worried about what I thought. She was the strong one. . . . I was scared of her.

TOKUJI: Hum . . . Hum, you're joking! . . . That doesn't fit. . . . But . . .

ICHIZŌ: Hmm . . . You just said I was mean and a tyrant. But can't you see that actually, I was being smothered by her. So sometimes I had to fight back. . . . That was my resistance. Damn! Do you think it helped? It made it even worse. She didn't show any concern, no matter how mad I got. In a fight I always gave in first. . . . She was always all right, because she had such a strong will.

TOKUJI: Are you all right, Ichizō?

ICHIZŌ: "Ichizō, you're changed these days, you're so lazy." She would stare at me. I would freeze, then run off to the office, holding my bag! "Is that good enough, Ichizō? Why don't you do it properly, Ichizō? You're always the same, Ichizō." I worked really hard, put on a determined face. . . . "Come on, Ichizō, harder!" She would order me and I would obey.

TOKUJI: Wait a minute . . .

ICHIZŌ: No! . . . I would complain, but not her. Not even once. I would be exhausted, but she never showed a sign of it. She always walked ahead of me. . . . Just one small step. . . . Sometimes she'd look back at me . . . disappointed in me. . . . It drove me crazy. I hated her. . . . But even so, I could never catch up to her.

TOKUJI: She was just pushing you on, even at her age. . . . You should be grateful.

ICHIZŌ: Hmm . . . Then one day, I realized we were always pushing on harder and harder, out of breath. We were always competing. But both of us hated to lose. . . . We were both obsessed. . . . Then she got older, more tired, and her body wore out. But she kept on at the same pace. Because she couldn't stand to show me any weakness. That was what she was like.

TOKUJI: Oh, that's enough, Ichizō.

YASUKO: Really, Ichizō, enough. You're scaring me.

ICHIZŌ: She didn't tell me . . . even when she got sick. . . . She pretended everything was all right . . . to me anyway.

TOKUJI: Well, don't get so worked up about it. I mean, it can't be helped. It was different when she was alive, but now . . .

ICHIZŌ: No, she hasn't changed, she's just the same now as she was before . . . That's finally becoming clear to me. . . . Of course she was kind to me. She never took her eyes off me. Like she was holding my reins all the time. She looked after me like a prize stallion. . . . She was always in some corner, keeping an eye on me. . . . Those eyes . . . And I went along with it. Because she was stronger than I was. . . . (*He sways.*) It's like I was tied with invisible wires. . . . Those wires cut into me deeper and deeper every year.

YASUKO: Ichizō, what's the matter . . . ?

ICHIZŌ: She held the ends of the wires. . . . Yes, now I see it, it was her . . . (*He stumbles excitedly around the room.*) That's how she tamed me, little by little. . . . A well-trained, obedient pet, with a collar and leash around my neck . . . You (*He stares at* YASUKO *and* TOKUJI) were hanging on that leash, and so were Keiko, Uncle Shigemasa, Grandmother, and Mother herself. Everybody in the family. No, even this house, too. (*He looks up at the ceiling.*) Yes, this . . . this house, yes, I'm a pet and this is my kennel . . . forty years . . . Working like a dog, kowtowing to my bosses, pushing away my friends, and being hard on the people below me. . . . And what's my reward? This miserable life. . . . I'm old, I'm sick, and on top of that . . . (*He grabs his chest in pain.*) This . . . Aghh, agh, I can't breathe . . .

TOKUJI: What, what's wrong . . . ? (*Grabs* ICHIZŌ.) What's the matter, Ichizō?

YASUKO (*Clinging to* ICHIZŌ): Hold on, Ichizō, calm down. Somebody get a glass of water. Uncle Shigemasa!

SHIGEMASA (*Rushes in from the next room with a glass of water*): I knew this would happen. Here, Ichizō, water, take it. (*He tries to make* ICHIZŌ *drink.*)

ICHIZŌ (*Slaps the glass away*): I don't need it. Get away from me! All of you. Get out! Leave me alone! (*Falls on the sofa.*)

SHIGEMASA: Well, this is it, then?

TOKUJI: Ichizō, are you all right?

ICHIZŌ (*Groans.*)

SHIGEMASA: Leave him. (*Takes* TOKUJI *by the arm and leads him away from the sofa.*) It's an attack . . . but you two . . . He's your brother. You've got to take care of him.

TOKUJI: I know. . . . It's not like I enjoyed telling him that, it hurt me.

SHIGEMASA: Did it? . . . Maybe this is the modern way . . . I don't know. . . .
TOKUJI: What are you talking about? . . . Uncle Shigemasa, just keep out of this.
SHIGEMASA: Yes, . . . Yasuko, I'll leave Ichizō to you. (*He leaves.*)
YASUKO (*Covers* ICHIZŌ *with a blanket and wipes his forehead.*)
ICHIZŌ (*Groans.*)
TOKUJI (*Beckons to* YASUKO): Yasuko . . .
YASUKO: . . .
TOKUJI: Can you come here a minute?
YASUKO: What?
TOKUJI: Don't be angry with me.
YASUKO: You should apologize to Mother and to Ichizō. Mother's body isn't cold yet. . . . You should be ashamed of yourself. (*Cries.*)
TOKUJI: Does this happen to him very often? . . . Or is he just being hysterical?
KEIKO (*Comes in from the next room and looks at* ICHIZŌ): He looks like he's asleep. . . . Let's be quiet.
YASUKO: He's sick.
TOKUJI: I said too much. . . . Silence can be a virtue sometimes.
KEIKO: Hmm. Tearing Mother to pieces like that was very virtuous, wasn't it?
YASUKO: Is this how a family should behave at a time like this, eh, Tokuji?
TOKUJI: Well, it's a long hard road.
YASUKO: So let's try to go together. We don't have to tear each other to pieces. . . . Let's talk like friends.
TOKUJI: Right! "Friends"!
YASUKO: Let's try from now on. We should be able to be friends.
TOKUJI: You're renting a room because you couldn't stand living here with Ichizō.
YASUKO: . . .
KEIKO: Family and also friends. . . . Hmmm, it's idealistic . . . but I like it.
TOKUJI: But Ichizō's becoming more and more difficult to get along with.
YASUKO: It's not his fault, it's because of his health. We haven't cared about him enough.
KEIKO: You know what Ichizō's sickness is? . . . It's called neurosis. . . . I read about it in a magazine the other day.
TOKUJI: Well, I hope you read about the cure, too. You could say something to him.
KEIKO: They said about 45 percent of modern people are neurotic.
YASUKO: How do you cure it?
KEIKO: Well, . . . perhaps in Ichizō's case, a wife would be the best thing. . . . Don't you think?
TOKUJI: Typical.
KEIKO: No, really, I'm serious. He won't be cured by treatment from a quack like Kajima. . . . Actually, I've really been thinking about this. Remember Fumie? Bringing her back would be the best idea. What do you think, Tokuji?
TOKUJI: Yes, she wasn't that bad.

KEIKO: She's living quite close by.

TOKUJI: Really? How's she doing?

KEIKO: Not so good.

TOKUJI: Eh?

KEIKO: She didn't get along with Mother. But now Mother's gone. Maybe Fumie's got another chance.

TOKUJI (*Screwing up his face*): Hmmm, maybe so, but I can't be quite as blunt as you. What do you mean . . . chance? Mother's only been dead two hours? . . . I'm going to wash my face. (*Leaves to the right.*)

KEIKO (*Awkwardly*): Underneath, Tokuji is really very sincere. Crying that much. . . . I can't cry like that now.

YASUKO: . . .

KEIKO: Yasuko, what's on your mind?

YASUKO: Eh? . . . Hmmm.

KEIKO: Come and see us some time; we'll all be lonelier from now on.

YASUKO: Yes, I will.

KEIKO: You've completely lost touch with us. You shouldn't avoid us that much.

YASUKO: No, It's Just that I've been busy working, but I'll come by some time soon.

KEIKO: Please do. . . . By the way . . . (*Stares at* YASUKO.)

YASUKO: Eh? What?

KEIKO: Well . . . since we last we saw you, you've really grown up.

YASUKO (*Blushing*): What are you talking about?

KEIKO: It's true.

YASUKO: . . .

KEIKO: People grow up so quickly.

YASUKO: . . .

KEIKO: You were still a baby when father died.

YASUKO: . . . I didn't know what was happening then. . . . I was lucky. Not like this time.

KEIKO: That's true. . . . It's probably a bigger shock to you than to anybody else.

YASUKO (*Sobbing*): It's like she suddenly just abandoned me. . . .

KEIKO: It was so sudden . . . and you were mother's favorite, which makes it harder on you. . . .

YASUKO: . . .

KEIKO: You were the youngest and she was devoted to you. . . . You must be completely shattered by this.

YASUKO: It seems like God's judgment.

KEIKO: No, but . . . Mother was worrying only about you up to the moment she died. . . . Never about me . . .

YASUKO: That's because she was so sure of you.

KEIKO: Do you think so?

YASUKO: That moment was the only time I ever felt that maybe I should have gotten married.... She was so worried and full of regret.... Wasn't she? (*Wipes a tear from her eye.*)

KEIKO: Well, It's too late now.

YASUKO: But I don't feel that now.

KEIKO: It would have been nice if you had gotten married.

YASUKO: It was just a momentary feeling.

Even so...

...

KEIKO: Why did you refuse that earlier time?

YASUKO: Oh, I... I wasn't talking about that... but...

KEIKO: I'd like to know... because I don't understand you. After you two were introduced, you both said "yes," and you both looked very happy.

YASUKO: I don't want to talk about it.

KEIKO: But that's not fair.... Because since then, I've always felt awkward with his family.... You're so selfish.

YASUKO: I... I'm sorry.

KEIKO: Is it true that you told him you'd marry him only if he'd take Mother too?

YASUKO: ...

KEIKO: I heard that a long time afterward from someone in his family.... I was shocked.

YASUKO: ...

KEIKO: These days nobody would accept a wife along with her mother.... Are you stupid? Everybody knows that....

YASUKO: I know...

KEIKO: And saying that you didn't want to leave Mother.... You're not a school kid anymore, are you?

YASUKO: ...

KEIKO: "A woman leaves her parents' house and gets on with her life"..., even the kids in the missionary school know that.

YASUKO: Keiko... you couldn't possibly understand.

KEIKO: Oh?... Try me.

YASUKO: Did you ever really, truly think about Mother?

KEIKO (*Coolly*): Certainly.

YASUKO: Then you should understand what I'm going to say.... Neither you nor Ichizō really knew Mother's grief. She used to sit on the edge of the veranda and stare into the garden with her eyes full of tears.... I asked her what was the matter. She told me she didn't know why she was sad; she couldn't explain it without crying. She said she felt herself only when she was crying alone. She said maybe women were born to be old and sad. (*Sobs.*) ... When I thought about her life of sixty years, I hated father. It was said he was a combination of grandmother and Ichizō. Cold, stubborn, and obstinate. And he didn't treat mother like a human being.... Yes, that's right, a few days after they got married, he introduced her to some guests as the woman he'd acquired as a maid!

KEIKO: I heard that story, too.

YASUKO: And his mother slept all day and stayed up all night, keeping her awake.

KEIKO (*Shaking her head bitterly*): That's terrible.

YASUKO: Then father would shout at our mother, blaming her for keeping grandmother awake.

KEIKO: Men!

YASUKO: He told her she could only say "yes"; she could forget any other words. He told her he'd beat her.... And he didn't only say it, he did it.

KEIKO: Is that so?

YASUKO: He was a beast.... That's what her life was like, misery and hard work, and all she got in return was white hair and a bent back. I couldn't allow myself to get married for my own happiness and leave Mother to that life. I don't know how you and Ichizō could get married so easily.... I don't understand.

KEIKO: Oh, don't you?

YASUKO: No, I don't. When I think of what it did to Mother, the idea of marriage makes me sick.

KEIKO: ... Aren't you ... a bit neurotic?

YASUKO: What, what are you talking about?

KEIKO: Up to a point, even I can understand what you mean. You're still young and naive, but it looks like you were influenced a lot by Mother's pessimism.

YASUKO: Oh! Pessimism ... ?

KEIKO: A kind of dislike of people ... Yes, Mother definitely had that, always seeing the worst side.

YASUKO: If she did, then that was because ...

KEIKO: Yes, because she wasn't a happy woman..... I sympathize with her, but if that gave you a marriage phobia.... Hopeless, I say.

YASUKO: Don't be so rude.

KEIKO: Look, the fact you get so upset shows you aren't aware of it. Your engagements ... Mother always wrecked them in the end. No parent wants to let their children go, some stronger than others, but in Mother's case, it must have been a relief for her to talk to you. But her hatred of other people was contagious.... Even if it wasn't intentional ... but then again, maybe it was a little bit intentional.

YASUKO: But for what reason?

KEIKO: ... Mother was a woman.... And a woman's burden had to be borne silently. ... It became a collection of her bitter memories as a woman. She told the stories and you listened. She may have spoken quietly, but she was passionate.... Finally you took on her emotions ... they became your experiences, not hers. She wanted you to hate what she hated.... A woman's suppressed emotions are ...

YASUKO: Please stop, Keiko. (*Starts crying.*)

KEIKO: Don't get angry when I'm telling you the truth. . . . I tried to help you. . . . So I . . .
YASUKO: Shut up! (*Cries.*)
KEIKO: Stop crying all the time.
ICHIZŌ (*Groans and turns over.*)
YASUKO: You, too, you're her daughter, too. How can you talk like that . . . ?
KEIKO: We're both her daughters, but Mother saw us differently.
YASUKO: Oh? How were we different?
KEIKO: Well, what can I say . . . ?
YASUKO: If it's true . . . I shouldn't say this, but . . . maybe it was your fault. . . .
KEIKO: Really?
YASUKO: Mother said . . . Keiko was . . . (*Stops herself.*)
KEIKO: . . . "Not an admirable daughter" . . . Was that it?
YASUKO: . . .
KEIKO: I know that. I accept it. If I was a son, I'd be a mutt, but maybe I'm just a bitch.
YASUKO: Don't talk like that! . . . It's because you think like that, that Mother's love . . .
KEIKO: She was cool to me ever since I was born. She never showed me any affection. . . . She felt a kind of spite toward me. It was always a confrontation with her.
YASUKO: Why . . . What happened? There must have been something.
KEIKO: No. . . . You still don't understand? . . . No, I suppose not. There's no such thing as "mother's love"—Every mother is different.
YASUKO: The same old story. . . . You're such a cheat. You know what you did that broke her heart? Why she never trusted you afterward?
KEIKO: What do you mean?
YASUKO: What do I mean? . . . Back when you didn't do what she wanted, you ran away with Masatarō instead . . .
KEIKO: What? That?
YASUKO: Yes. . . . That drove her crazy. Think about it—That's why she cooled toward you.
KEIKO: What? That's what she told you?
YASUKO: . . .
KEIKO: That bitch. . . . She forced me to marry him.
YASUKO: Oh, Keiko, don't lie!
KEIKO: I'll tell you the whole thing, and you decide who was lying, me or Mother. . . . It was right after father died, and we were very short of money. Ichizō was still at school; we had nothing . . . but we had to do something to get by. . . . Around that time, Masatarō came to our house once. He was a friend of Ichizō's. . . . Really, just an acquaintance from school. He was from a wealthy family, and he seemed like he'd be easy to fool. Mother called me into the garden and said I should seduce him into going to Tokyo for a week. . . .
YASUKO: Oh. Keiko . . .
KEIKO: The look in her eyes . . . the way she stared at me . . . at that time she wasn't like . . . it wasn't like a mother and a daughter, we were two women, and . . .

YASUKO: No, no, stop it; I don't want to hear this. (*Cries.*)

ICHIZŌ (*Wakes up groggily*): . . . Is that . . . Is that true?

KEIKO: Agh! . . . Don't scare me like that!

ICHIZŌ (*Depressed*): Tell me, Keiko.

KEIKO: No, no more. You shouldn't get worked up again.

ICHIZŌ: Whatever you say, it won't surprise me anymore. . . . I'd rather drag the whole thing out into the light.

KEIKO: No, no . . . (*Tries to leave to the right.*)

MASATARŌ (*Enters very drunk*): I've searched . . . I've searched all over Japan . . . under bushes, below floors, but the enemy is nowhere to be found.

KEIKO: Look, he's drunk again.

MASATARŌ: What about her funeral, the funeral . . . We've got to do it quickly and in good taste. . . . We're living in the age of atomic bombs now . . . I'm an atomic BOMB! (*Marches toward the screen.*)

ICHIZŌ: What the hell are you doing? (*Grabs* MASATARŌ *by the scruff of the neck and pulls him back.*) Control yourself!

MASATARŌ: What? Let go of me!

ICHIZŌ: Keiko, get him out of here.

KEIKO: No, It's too late now.

MASATARŌ: No, no . . . Everything's shit!

ICHIZŌ: Tokuji, Tokuji. . . . Give us a hand here.

TOKUJI (*Comes in sleepily from the next room*): What's all the noise?

ICHIZŌ: Get him out of here and put him to bed.

MASATARŌ: What? You won't catch me again. . . . You cheats!

TOKUJI (*Holding* MASATARŌ): He's drunk again. Normally he wouldn't have the nerve to say anything. . . . What happened?

MASATARŌ: Who, who's that? . . . Oh, Tokuji . . . I'm too choked up to speak (*Sobs.*) . . . She's dead. . . . She was a wonderful mother. . . . She had Keiko buy two tickets to Tokyo.

TOKUJI: All right, come on stupid, come over here.

MASATARŌ: You won't catch me with the same trick twice. I . . .

TOKUJI: Come on! (*Takes him to the next room.*)

ICHIZŌ: . . . How shameful.

KEIKO: He talks like that when he gets drunk.

ICHIZŌ: Shameful! You were too weak. Why didn't you say "no" in the beginning, stupid?

KEIKO: Yes, I was stupid . . . (*Gradually getting more emotional*) to run away for the sake of you and Mother. He was like a wallet that somebody had dropped on the street, and she told me to pick it up . . . So . . . Why am I shameful? (*Bursts into tears.*)

YASUKO: Keiko . . . (*Clings to* KEIKO.) I'm sure, in her heart, she regretted lt. She was sorry for you and blamed herself. . . . Yes, she must have.

KEIKO: But she never . . . even up to her last moment, she never said anything to me . . . I thought that maybe, possibly, in the end, but when I looked into her eyes . . . she turned away. Her face didn't show anything.

YASUKO: That's because she felt so guilty.

KEIKO: No, it wasn't like that. She didn't look at me because she hated me to the very end.

YASUKO: No, she didn't.

KEIKO: Yes, she did.

ICHIZŌ: Oh, stop it, stop it. . . . None of it matters. . . . You've all torn her to pieces. . . . And I . . . (*Cries.*) . . . I can't . . . How could you do this to me?

SHIGEMASA (*Comes in from the next room*): Ahhh, we're all guilty, we're all sinful. . . .

TOKUJI (*Following him in*): Stop, Uncle. . . . They're all crazy enough as it is.

SHIGEMASA: No, I don't mean that. . . . We should tell everything. That's the only way we'll be redeemed.

TOKUJI: I'm not sure this is such good idea.

SHIGEMASA: I can't pretend to be the only innocent one here. . . . Let me confess, too.

ICHIZŌ: What? . . . There's more?

TOKUJI: After hearing everybody else's stories, Uncle Shigemasa has gone mad, too!

SHIGEMASA: It's difficult to say in front of you, but . . . Nobu and I were lovers. . . . No, no, don't misunderstand me. It was after your father, I mean my brother, died. . . . We were both very serious. I swear to God. (*Bows low with both hands on the floor.*)

ICHIZŌ: . . .

KEIKO: . . .

TOKUJI: . . .

YASUKO: . . .

SHIGEMASA: Now . . . That's a great weight off my chest. Ahhh. (*Looks up shyly.*)

ICHIZŌ (*Wearily*): But, why . . . with a fool like you . . . ?

KEIKO: I can't believe it.

TOKUJI: I knew about it. . . . Maybe it wasn't such a bad thing, Ichizō.

ICHIZŌ: Wh, what? It's unforgivable. . . . It's a disgrace! Get out. You made me sick. . . . Get out!

SHIGEMASA: I'm sorry. . . . But will you at least accept that I was sincere?

ICHIZŌ: Sincere? . . . You dirty old man!

SHIGEMASA: Umm . . . Your mother was a lonely woman in her final years. I helped her; we comforted each other. . . . She often used to say that, quite honestly, children were of no use. Every child was like a monster, all different monsters. She said you were all like a big noisy, annoying load on her back. She wondered when she'd be able to throw off that load and stretch, to take a deep breath like a real human being. . . . I could understand that.

ICHIZŌ (*Depressed*): All right. . . . Just shut up.

KEIKO: Well, Mother . . . she was still a woman.

SHIGEMASA: Hmm . . . She had a dream to build a small hut on a quiet beach, or at the foot of a hill, and to live on her own . . . on her own, she said . . . that hurt me a little though . . . umm . . .

KEIKO (*Laughs*): . . . That sounds nice.

SHIGEMASA: So you've all been talking about her. Some of the things you said were true, but others we'll never know if they are true or not.

ICHIZŌ: Shut up. Just keep quiet.

YASUKO (*Crying*): I don't know . . . I don't understand.

TOKUJI: Whoever started these confessions is to blame. You should all go back to the beginning again.

ICHIZŌ: And you should all apologize. Go on, do it.

KEIKO: To whom? We are the ones who were hurt.

SHIGEMASA: If we all confess and forgive each other, that will take care of it; that will be a good ending.

YASUKO: We only felt sad for her . . . for five minutes after she died!

ICHIZŌ: . . . Well, we're not sad anymore. Even if we wanted to be, who is there to be sad for? . . . For her, we children gave her neither hope nor strength. And for us, her memory gives us neither joy nor happiness. (*Sobs.*) The bonds that held us together have fallen to pieces. From now on, each of us can go off in whatever direction he likes, and I . . . I'm going off now. (*Stands up unsteadily.*) I think I'll become a monk.

SHIGEMASA: Ichizō, Ichizō . . . What about the funeral?

ICHIZŌ: I'll leave that to you. You be the chief mourner, and you bury her.

SHIGEMASA: That's terrible; it's not like you.

ICHIZŌ: No, no more. I've had enough. I don't want to even see your faces anymore. I'm not going to have anything to do with the funeral or with you.

TOKUJI: Me neither. I'll hold my own funeral for Mother, alone.

KEIKO: Oh . . . Yasuko, which funeral are you going to go to?

YASUKO: Neither of them. . . . I'll do it by myself. (*Cries.*)

ICHIZŌ: That's all right. That sounds just like you anyway.

SHIGEMASA (*Starts crying*): Nobu . . . She's still having a hard time . . . even now that she's dead.

ICHIZŌ: Well, that's that. I'm going off somewhere far away, on my own. Ah, this is my house . . . (*Looking toward the screen.*) Mother . . . Who were we, you and me? . . . What was our forty years together all about? Who are you, anyway? . . . What kind of a person are you? (*Walks unsteadily toward the screen.*) Who was she? . . . I don't know, I can't see it. . . . Tell me please, Mother. (*Looks behind the screen.*) Mother, . . . Mother, . . . Agh, agh. (*Suddenly jumps back, shaking.*) She, she moved! She opened her eyes! . . . She's alive. Alive! (*Almost falls over.*)

(KEIKO *and* YASUKO *scream and cling to* ICHIZŌ.)

TOKUJI (*Rushes behind the screen but quickly comes out, pale and shivering*): . . . Stu, stupid . . . Stupid . . . She's . . . She's not alive.

SHIGEMASA (*Clings to* TOKUJI): Tokuji . . . Tokuji . . .

TOKUJI: You, you're all stupid . . . She's not alive . . . Don't scare me.

ICHIZŌ: Those, those eyes . . . looked at me . . . stared at me . . . (*Starts to feel a sharp pain in his chest.*) How, how dare she curse . . . me! . . . Agh, agh . . . I . . . I can't breathe . . . (*Falls over.*)

TOKUJI: Water. Water. . . . Bring him some water.

YASUKO: Ichizō, . . . Somebody, get water

SHIGEMASA (*Upset, runs off to the right.*)

TOKUJI: Ichizō, it . . . it's all right . . . (*Holds* ICHIZŌ *up.*) You're all right. . . . You made a mistake. . . . Look, get a grip on yourself.

ICHIZŌ (*Groans with his eyes closed.*)

KEIKO (*Still clinging to* ICHIZŌ): . . . Again, Tokuji, once again . . . Go and have another look . . . I'm scared.

TOKUJI: No. No, don't be stupid. No. . . . (*Shivers.*) Everybody just calm down. . . .
(*They all fall silent. There's a noise from behind the screen. They all freeze. Silence. Men's whispering voices can be heard from the entrance.* SHIGEMASA *comes in with three town hall* OFFICIALS. *The* OFFICIALS *sit on the right.*)

ICHIZŌ (*Opens his eyes slightly*): . . .

SHIGEMASA: They're from the town hall.

OFFICIAL 1: We got your notice . . . It was so sudden . . . We're very sorry . . . (*The three* OFFICIALS *bow.*)

ICHIZŌ: Oh . . . Thank you for your concern. . . .

OFFICIAL 1: It must have been a terrible shock to you . . . .

ICHIZŌ: . . .

OFFICIAL 1: We'd like to help if we can . . . I'm sure we'll be of no use, but if there's anything we can do. . . .

ICHIZŌ: It's very kind of you . . . We don't really know what we should do . . . So if it's not too much trouble. . . .
(*Everybody bows. Lights fade to black.*)

SCENE 2

The following day. All the furniture has been removed from the room and replaced by some hibachi and cushions on the floor. To stage left hang black and white funeral curtains, behind which the funeral ceremony has begun. Incense is being burned, and a priest can be heard chanting prayers. Mourners come and go through the garden to offer condolences by burning incense. FUNERAL HELPERS *dressed in black are busy coming and going along the veranda. Pause.*

ICHIZŌ (*Dressed in black, enters from the left followed by* OFFICIAL 1.)

OFFICIAL 1: . . . You must be tired. . . . It all takes so long. . . . (*Offers a cigarette.*)

ICHIZŌ: Yes . . . but maybe I'm just a little tense . . . Where is my boss, the general manager?

OFFICIAL 1: He'll be here soon.

ICHIZŌ: I'm very grateful to you for all the trouble you've taken.

OFFICIAL 1: No, no, not at all. . . . By the way, when the hearse leaves, could you sit in the front car and hold the family memorial plaque . . . ? It should be you, the chief mourner and an assistant mourner side by side. . . . Normally, your wife would be the assistant . . . but in your case, maybe your sister.

ICHIZŌ: Oh . . . yes.

OFFICIAL 1: This is such an old family . . . such a grand funeral . . . and you have such wide connections. . . . The funeral flowers are lined up almost down to the main street. . . .

ICHIZŌ: Yes . . . Mother would have been pleased.

OFFICIAL 2 (*From the veranda*): Excuse me.

OFFICIAL 1: Ah . . . Yes. (*Leaves with* OFFICIAL 2.)

ICHIZŌ (*Slowly smokes cigarette*): . . .

(FUMIE, *thirty-two,* ICHIZŌ'*s former wife, dressed in a black kimono, enters from the right carrying condolence telegrams on a tray. She sees* ICHIZŌ *and hesitates.*)

FUMIE: Well . . . What should I . . . ?

ICHIZŌ: Uh?

FUMIE: . . . do with these telegrams?

ICHIZŌ (*In a restrained voice*): So you're still here? . . . I thought I told you to go as soon as you could.

FUMIE: . . . I'm sorry . . . But you looked so busy that I . . .

ICHIZŌ: It's so humiliating . . . you here in front of everybody . . . Think about my position.

FUMIE: . . . I'm sorry.

ICHIZŌ: Why didn't you leave yesterday? . . . That Kajima . . . He's the one who insisted that you come and pay your respects . . . for my mother's sake. I said it would be OK, just to save his face . . . But there are so many people here today. Please, just leave.

FUMIE (*Sobbing*): I'm sorry . . . I'll go.

(DR. KAJIMA *passes on the veranda.*)

DR. KAJIMA: Ah, Ichizō . . . (*Gives a quick bow.*) I've just been offering my condolences.

ICHIZŌ: Thank you.

DR. KAJIMA: I wanted to come earlier, but I've been so busy.

ICHIZŌ: Don't worry about it. Thank you for coming.

DR. KAJIMA: This must be difficult for you. Don't strain yourself. (*Takes* ICHIZŌ'*s pulse.*) . . . How do you feel?

ICHIZŌ: Not especially . . .

DR. KAJIMA: Well, take care of yourself. I have some more calls to make, so if you would excuse me now. . . . (*Bows to* FUMIE *and is about to leave.*)

ICHIZŌ: Er, look . . . Dr. Kajima?

DR. KAJIMA: Uh?

ICHIZŌ (*Indicates* FUMIE *with his eyes*): . . . Er, today, there're so many guests here. Take her with you, won't you?

DR. KAJIMA: But Ichizō, be a little more flexible, please, think of the situation. She just wants to pay her last respects.

FUMIE: I'm sorry, I didn't want to cause trouble.

DR. KAJIMA: No, no. (*To* ICHIZŌ.) I've met your wife often and had long talks with her at the factory. I'm the medical officer there.

FUMIE: Yes. Dr. Kajima always told me about you. I hear you were promoted to section chief, dear . . . Congratulations.

ICHIZŌ: Yes, yes . . . well.

DR. KAJIMA: As a friend, I'm concerned about you, Ichizō. I don't want to be too forward, but I think you two should talk together a little, especially in view of the present situation.

ICHIZŌ (*Looks disgusted.*)

DR. KAJIMA: Anyway . . . (*Looks at his watch.*) it's late, I must excuse myself.

FUMIE: Thank you so much for your kindness. (*Tries to see him off.*)

DR. KAJIMA: No, please, it's all right. (*Leaves.*)

ICHIZŌ (*Disgusted*): . . .

FUMIE: I, I . . . don't know what to say. (*Looks apprehensively at* ICHIZŌ.) It's like a dream, seeing you again now . . . and your mother no longer with us.

ICHIZŌ: That Kajima and his infernal meddling . . . to do such a thing to me! . . . God damn it!

FUMIE (*Dejectedly*): I'll go. It was wrong of me to try to see you, after all the trouble we had. Please forgive me . . . and take care of yourself.

ICHIZŌ: Oh, it's all right . . . now go home.

FUMIE: Yes . . . now that I've seen you're all right and I've paid my last respects to your mother, I'm satisfied. (*Looks around the room nostalgically.*) Everything looks just the same as when I was here . . . so full of memories.

ICHIZŌ (*Angry*): Only if you visit. . . . Everybody looks at this house and sees such a perfect family. Damn! What do outsiders know?

FUMIE: It's been so long since I was last here. Your mother was a great person. Not many people have such character; very few could be like her. You must be very sad. Yes? . . . (*Turns away.*) But you must be strong. Your whole future lies ahead of you; you're in the prime of your life. I wish you every success (*Moved to tears.*) and I'll pray for you.

ICHIZŌ: Yes, OK.

FUMIE: If only you'd try and understand my feelings, that would be enough for me. (*Hesitates slightly.*) Yes, I know I betrayed both you and your mother when I ran away from this house. But now I feel that finally I'm beginning to understand human nature and the world around me.

ICHIZŌ: Yes, I feel the same way, and I can't stand this anymore. I've got to do something about it, especially now with my mother gone.

FUMIE: I understand how you must be suffering and how it feels to worry all alone. . . .

ICHIZŌ: I've always been alone . . . nobody was ever truly honest with me, nobody showed me real affection. No, in fact, I never knew anything at all; I don't know what kind of life I've been leading. What the hell does it all add up to? (*Paces around the room.*) Have you any idea how much I suffered, stuck between you two? A battle between a bride and a mother-in-law? An endless quarrel, even when I was at work at the town hall, I got headaches thinking of the atmosphere in this house. She despised you, and you did nothing but oppose her. I was torn to pieces between the two of you. But then, on top of that, you were both against me, trampling on me together. You'd call me weak, stupid, and stubborn. I was so miserable; I don't know how I stood it. I'll never let such a thing happen again.

FUMIE: I'm so sorry I caused you such suffering, I'm sorry. How can I apologize, how . . . ? It was all my fault. How can I apologize . . . to her, too.

ICHIZŌ: Uh? . . .

FUMIE: I was such a bad wife, a terrible daughter-in-law.

ICHIZŌ: But part of the fault was Mother's, I mean, the family's, something fundamental. . . .

FUMIE: No, I was so young and inexperienced. I didn't know anything about the outside world.

ICHIZŌ: Wait a minute . . . At that time, didn't you say that my family was . . . feudalistic or something; it wasn't human, that you were being suffocated? You said you needed more freedom or else your soul would be crushed, so your only solution was to abandon me . . . ?

FUMIE: Please don't talk about it anymore.

ICHIZŌ: Why not?

FUMIE: It's so humiliating . . . don't.

ICHIZŌ: Eh? . . . I think there's a misunderstanding here.

FUMIE: Really? Do you?

ICHIZŌ (*More gently*): Yes. . . . You think I'm angry with you, don't you? But no, no . . . The fact is what you said was true. You don't need to feel ashamed. Lately . . . just very recently . . . I came to understand that.

FUMIE: Well . . . then . . . aren't you angry with me?

ICHIZŌ: Uh? Yes . . . (*A little stricter.*) Of course, it was terrible at the time. I was put in a very embarrassing position. Do you think it was easy for me to deal with it?

FUMIE: I'm sorry, I'm so sorry. (*Cries.*)

ICHIZŌ: . . . So embarrassing . . . all this crying. . . . Somebody is coming. . . . Shh!

(OFFICIAL 1 *passes along the veranda, casting a slight sideways glance at* FUMIE. ICHIZŌ *closes the* shōji.)

FUMIE: You hate me now and always will. . . .

ICHIZŌ: No . . . Even then I didn't hate you. . . .

FUMIE: I'm sorry . . . I don't know what to say. . . .

ICHIZŌ: Well, it's all in the past now . . . But Fumie, . . . there's something I want to . . . ask you (*Hesitates.*) . . . I don't know how to say it.

FUMIE: Please just ask me, it's only you and me

ICHIZŌ: . . . Well, I mean . . . I respect your judgment and your strength in leaving. That's what I wanted to tell you.

FUMIE (*Disappointed*): Ah . . . that's all you wanted to talk about?

ICHIZŌ: Yes, but don't be so modest.

FUMIE: I'm not being modest.

ICHIZŌ: I understand now, people have to move forward. You did it three years ago. I guess you were able to see a new life that wasn't possible in this house. That's why you were able to leave here so confidently, so proudly, like it was the natural thing to do.

FUMIE: Don't be so cynical . . . It sounds very mean.

ICHIZŌ: No, not at all . . . Really, I respect you. No, more than that, I have faith in you. I want you to use your strength to help me.

FUMIE: . . .

ICHIZŌ: Last night when you appeared at the door, I felt like I saw a beam of light, actually, as though it was a sign from God! I had an incredible premonition.

FUMIE: Me too. It was like . . .

ICHIZŌ: You felt it, didn't you? I'm not the same person I was before. . . . You will help me, won't you?

FUMIE: Yes, yes. (*Her eyes fill with tears.*) I'll do anything . . . People, you and me, we all lead lonely lives, don't we?

ICHIZŌ (*Moved to tears*): Yes, we do . . . So I beg you, Fumie, please show me the place, take me to where you ran away to . . . the place where you found a free life . . . There, there, let's go as soon as the funeral is finished!

FUMIE: . . . (*Looking at* ICHIZŌ.) What are you dreaming of at your age? What's wrong with you, have you gone mad?

ICHIZŌ: I'm really going to do it!

FUMIE: Your mother's death must have affected you very much . . . but even so . . .

ICHIZŌ: What's the matter? . . . You're upset . . . Why?

FUMIE: Because you're being cruel to me, awful. . . . You shouldn't say that. . . . (*Cries.*) You're teasing me. . . .

ICHIZŌ: What do you mean, "teasing you"?

FUMIE: . . . Just the thought of that experience makes me shudder . . . but you want me to go through it all again . . . No, I won't do it.

ICHIZŌ: . . . But Fumie, . . . I've made up my mind. I want to crush this old and trifling house, destroy it and start a new, brighter life. If I don't, I'll be lost. Free my soul! I want to make a fresh start.

FUMIE: Oh . . . You don't have to repeat exactly what I said at that time. (*Bursts into tears.*)

ICHIZŌ: . . . What's wrong, Fumie?

FUMIE (*Sobbing*): . . . After I left here, I thought I'd be able to go step by step and build a new life. . . . But no matter where I went, even in Tokyo, it was the same. Every day working like a dog but getting hardly any money, living from hand to mouth . . . always afraid of losing my job and being kicked out of my apartment . . . Everybody seemed to hate me; I was so miserable. Every night I cried myself to sleep.

ICHIZŌ: But . . . but there must have been something good about it . . . some kind of satisfaction . . . ?

FUMIE: No, not at all. At first I thought so, too. That's why I was always moving around . . . I was stupid, wasn't I? . . . And finally I found myself back in the next town. . . . Strange, it seems I was always being drawn back toward this place, this house

ICHIZŌ: But why?

FUMIE: Because even this was better than those other places.

ICHIZŌ: . . .

FUMIE: Also, I used to often think of your mother. . . . You know, last night, when I visited your mother's body . . . she opened her eyes and stared at me . . . it was like she was saying, "Fumie, I knew you'd come back. . . ."

ICHIZŌ (*Shocked*): . . . Wh, what a lot of nonsense . . . It, it's stupid, stupid. . . .

FUMIE: I know it's not possible . . . but somehow, it seemed to me . . . It seemed her eyes moved. . . .

ICHIZŌ: Stop it! Cut it out!

FUMIE: And . . . so I felt I had to apologize to her. I was so scared . . . I told her, "Mother, it was all my fault. I'm sorry I never listened to you, obeyed you. I was too proud." And then she closed her eyes, like she was telling me it was all right.

ICHIZŌ (*Getting irritated*): What a stupid . . . so childish! I've never heard anything like it.

FUMIE: No? . . . When I first saw her last night, I naturally bowed in respect. She seemed so dignified, her white hair, her thin, tired face. . . .

ICHIZŌ: . . .

FUMIE: I'm sure she's still watching us from somewhere. Don't you feel it?

ICHIZŌ (*Shivering*): No! . . . Never . . . Her life is over. Now my life is going to begin. She's gone, forever. . . .

FUMIE: But we shouldn't forget her, should we? Either of us.

ICHIZŌ: Either of us? You and me?

FUMIE: Yes, everything you've achieved was with her help, wasn't it? You owe it all to her. She made you what you are. She knew what had to be done, and she did it. If we do what she did, we two can be happy again. Yes, that's it. Let's do it.

ICHIZŌ: You haven't heard anything I've said, have you? Get out! (*Stamps his feet.*) I said, go. . . .

FUMIE (*Laughing*): . . . You're like a spoiled child . . . You call me childish, but you're the one who's a child. . . . That's always been one of your best qualities. I remember it well. (*Laughs.*)

ICHIZŌ (*Irritated*): Don't bring that up now; it's not the time. Just don't talk about it, I won't allow it.

FUMIE: OK, I won't. (*Laughs.*)

ICHIZŌ: Don't laugh! It's not funny . . . I have to think of what to do . . . what should I . . . I . . . do . . . Yes, think, think! (*Walks around the room.*)

FUMIE (*Worried*): Ichizō, aren't you finished thinking . . . ?

ICHIZŌ: Shut up! . . . I don't want to get stuck here . . . What should I do first?

FUMIE: What are you brooding about? Remember how well off you are, your position and this good life . . . I don't know what to do with you.

ICHIZŌ: I can't stand it. I can't bear it anymore . . . no more. (*His eyes fill with tears of regret.*) One more step and I feel my back will break. I just can't hold it all up any longer. It's too painful.

FUMIE: Well . . . I'll help you, OK? You just said you don't hate me, which made me so grateful that I cried . . . You know, I knew that you'd say that to me, because I know that you're not capable of hating another person. So, I'll help you. I'll dedicate all my love and sincerity to you.

ICHIZŌ: . . . Wait a minute, I don't quite understand what you're talking about . . . What is it you're going to do? What have you decided?

FUMIE: Well, I'll . . . be just like your mother. I'll devote myself to you. If I follow her example, I'm sure that one day, I'll be as strong as she was.

ICHIZŌ: No, no . . . that's not what I want to hear! . . . Don't do that . . .

FUMIE: You don't feel comfortable with me, do you? Listen, I'll never leave you again . . . Please, just trust me.

ICHIZŌ: It's not a question of trust . . . No, no, I said no . . . I'm, I'm too confused now . . . let's talk about it some other time . . .

FUMIE: All this has upset you, hasn't it? But you know, you must pull yourself together, or else what will happen to this house?

ICHIZŌ: . . . Fumie, you . . . sound just like my mother used to. No, don't imitate her . . . No . . .

FUMIE (*Smiling*): I'm sorry . . . I didn't mean to . . . but maybe it's just natural . . . Anyway, from now on, I'll try to help you work harder. It will give me a reason to live, and maybe it will be a way to make it up to your mother.

ICHIZŌ: What are you. . . . Get rid of that idea right now. . . . No, Fumie, no . . .

FUMIE (*Sobbing*): You don't trust me . . . That's my fault, isn't it? But made up my mind. I've decided.

ICHIZŌ: Who gave you the right to make such a decision? Who do you think you are? Well, I'm not accepting your one-sided decision, so just forget it!

FUMIE (*Laughs*): You're very strange today.

ICHIZŌ: You're the one who's strange.

FUMIE: Oh, don't be so rude. Anyway, I've decided, and it's the right decision, I feel it in my bones.

ICHIZŌ: In your bones? . . . Oh (*Staggers.*) . . . Do whatever you want . . . You're a monster; devour me if you want to . . .

OFFICIAL 1 (*Running in*): Did you call . . . ?

ICHIZŌ: Agh! Mind your own business.

OFFICIAL 1: . . .

IKU (*Coming in from the next room*): Ichizō, Ichizō, everybody is so well dressed . . . except me. (*Tears her sleeve.*) . . . Look, look at these rags. Ichizō, listen, please let me wear Nobu's black kimono. It was mine originally, anyway. She took it and never gave it back to me. (*Cries.*)

FUMIE: Oh, poor Iku. (*Laughing.*) Come on, Grandma, I'll dress you in it. (*To* ICHIZŌ.) All right? . . . Look, Grandma, he said it was all right. (*Takes* IKU *into the next room.*)

OFFICIAL 1: . . . Wasn't that lady your . . . ?

ICHIZŌ: The wires. That's . . . (*Looks in great pain*) . . . the wires, again the getting tighter. . . . I, I'm suffocating. Agh! Water. . . . Wire!

OFFICIAL 1 (*Gripping* ICHIZŌ): Are you all right? Pull yourself together.

ICHIZŌ (*Groans.*)

OFFICIAL 1: Look, I'll go and get somebody.

ICHIZŌ: No, no . . . just leave me alone . . . please . . .

OFFICIAL 1: You must be exhausted.

ICHIZŌ: Yes . . . have you ever . . . been trapped before?

OFFICIAL 1: Er . . . no.

ICHIZŌ: Oh . . . then you can't understand . . . just how tired I am . . .

OFFICIAL 1: Ah . . .

ICHIZŌ: I'd like to sleep . . . just for a little while . . .

OFFICIAL 1: Please, hold on for just a little longer.

ICHIZŌ (*Sits powerless*): . . . You know, a man . . . is a worthless . . . in fact . . .

OFFICIAL 1: . . .

OFFICIAL 2 (*Stumbles into the room*): . . . The general manager is here. Please . . . (*Leaves.*)

OFFICIAL 1: What will you do? Are you all right?

ICHIZŌ: Yes . . . (*Walks unsteadily along the veranda to the right with* OFFICIAL 1.)

(*The sound of the priest chanting prayers can be heard. People are coming and going to burn incense and offer condolences.* ICHIZŌ *passes along the veranda to the left, accompanying his* BOSS *and others.* FUNERAL HELPERS *are preparing cushions in the guest room. Pause.* ICHIZŌ, *his* BOSS, *and the* OFFICIALS *come into the guest room, followed by* TOKUJI, KEIKO, MASATARŌ, YASUKO, *and* SHIGEMASA, *all dressed in black.*)

ICHIZŌ: . . . Please . . . have a seat.

BOSS: Thank you.

ICHIZŌ: I must apologize for all this mess.

BOSS: No, not at all.

ICHIZŌ: I'd like to thank you all very much for taking the trouble to come all this way to express your condolences, especially you, sir. Mother would have been so grateful. Thank you very much. (*They all bow.*)

BOSS: May I offer my very sincere regrets . . . I can imagine how you must all be feeling now. (*They all bow.*)

ICHIZŌ: It really was very thoughtful of you to take the time to come and pay your respects. Thank you again. (*They all bow.*)

BOSS: If it's not too rude . . . how old was your mother?

ICHIZŌ: She was sixty-one.

BOSS: Sixty-one? That's most unfortunate. What was the cause of her death?

ICHIZŌ: She died of acute pneumonia.

BOSS: Hmm. acute pneumonia? Most unfortunate.

ICHIZŌ: We did everything we could, but . . . she had a full life. . . .

BOSS: Yes, I'm sure she did . . . You mustn't be too upset. . . .

ICHIZŌ: Well, thank you. . . .

BOSS: Pneumonia can be quite painful.

ICHIZŌ: Yes . . . quite . . . but finally, she died peacefully . . . almost as if she had just fallen asleep. . . .

BOSS: Hmm, I see . . .

ICHIZŌ: It was as though she'd decided she'd done everything she had to and so . . .

BOSS: I'm sure she led a full and most satisfying life.

ICHIZŌ: Yes, yes . . . she had no regrets . . . we had all grown up. . . .

BOSS: Yes, of course.

ICHIZŌ: At least . . . we completed that obligation to our parents, I believe.

BOSS: And most successfully.

ICHIZŌ: We couldn't have asked more of her.

BOSS: Yes, I see.

ICHIZŌ: There can be nothing worse than to lose one's parents, even if they lived to be one hundred.

BOSS: Very true.

ICHIZŌ: In that sense, I'm envious of you. Your parents are both so well. You're very lucky.

BOSS: No, no . . . I've often felt envious of you because of your fine brothers and sisters.

ICHIZŌ: Oh no, not at all . . . none of us has amounted to very much.

BOSS: Two sons and two daughters, perfect. . . . Your mother was blessed with her children, wasn't she?

ICHIZŌ: Ha, umm . . .

BOSS: Is this . . . your younger brother?

ICHIZŌ: Yes, this is my brother, Tokuji.

TOKUJI: Nice to meet you. (*Bows.*)

BOSS: Nice to meet you, too . . . and what do you do?

TOKUJI: Well . . . now . . . ah.

ICHIZŌ: He . . . he was discharged just last year and now he's very active in . . . in the commercial field. Such an ambitious man, so full of character and spirit . . . Ha, ha . . . he leaves me lost for words. . . .

BOSS: He must be a great inspiration to you.

ICHIZŌ: Well, I'd rather just believe in his abilities. His character and way of doing things are really quite different from mine. Myself, I take satisfaction in small successes. . . . But he's a modern young man, so of course he has his faults. However, I'm sure he has a bright future ahead of him. An unknown quantity is a beautiful thing, isn't it?

BOSS: Ah, it's fortunate to be young. . . . Good luck with all your hard work.

TOKUJI (*Bows*): . . .

ICHIZŌ: And . . . this is my younger sister, Keiko.

KEIKO (*Bows.*)

ICHIZŌ: After our father passed away, she was a great help to my mother. She may not look like it, but she's been taking great care of her brothers.

BOSS: I see . . .

ICHIZŌ: As the older brother, I've only had to put up with minor difficulties, but I imagine Keiko, as a woman (*Tears well up in his eyes*), has had a much harder time. . . . Ah, to be a daughter is a hard thing, isn't it? How can I even repay a tenth of her kindness? . . . But I should try . . . Ah, and this is Keiko's husband, Masatarō, a close friend of mine. He and I were in the same law department at university and graduated together.

BOSS: Oh, really?

MASATARŌ (*Bows.*)

BOSS: Nice to meet you . . . And what field are you in now?

MASATARŌ: Well, ah . . .

ICHIZŌ: He's so well educated, but he underestimates himself; he doesn't force himself. In fact, I really feel I should do more. It's my duty as a friend to push him harder. At one time, we were both so full of enthusiasm, discussing everything. (*His eyes fill with tears.*) . . . We were so full of life.

KEIKO (*In a small voice*): Ichizō . . .

ICHIZŌ: Oh, and this is our youngest sister, Yasuko.

YASUKO (*Bows.*)

ICHIZŌ: She's very well established in the field of . . . er . . . English typewriting. She tries her hardest not to bother us . . . it's amazing that even a girl so young can have such a clear path to her life. On the other hand, she is such a serious girl that I really feel I should make her happy as soon as possible. . . . Now, this is our uncle, Shigemasa. He's like a father to us. He's a very cheerful old soul and something of a poet. Occasionally he judges haiku and *tanka* competitions.

SHIGEMASA: How do you do? (*Bows.*)

BOSS: How do you do? . . . This really is such a close family. I can see how you must all support each other.

ICHIZŌ: Er . . . maybe, yes. indeed, I am lucky in that way.

BOSS: I presume it must all come from your mother. I can see what a clever mother she was.

ICHIZŌ: Oh, no . . .

BOSS: I hear she was very brave.

ICHIZŌ: Yes . . . no . . . an affectionate mother. Yes, affectionate.

BOSS: Ah, I see.

ICHIZŌ: When I think of all she did for us . . . it's beyond description. It's bigger . . . deeper . . . there was no obligation, no motive . . . only Mother could know why; we children cannot begin to imagine it. I sometimes think, "Yes, this is Mother," but then there is . . . also another mother beside her, and another, and another . . . it's like that. It was really something . . . I am not sure you would say a clever mother . . . I'd rather say an affectionate mother. She must have been affectionate if she wasn't clever, mustn't she? . . . Yes, if I say that, I can look back on it with a certain amount of satisfaction . . . yes . . . Otherwise, I . . . I wouldn't be able to stand it (*Sobbing*) . . . Maybe that's it . . .

BOSS: Yes, absolutely, I agree with you.

ICHIZŌ: . . .

(IKU *appears, dressed in the black kimono, followed by* FUMIE.)

IKU: Ichizō, look, look at this beautiful kimono. Isn't the cloth so smooth? I finally got my kimono back from Nobu. Fumie helped me put it on; she is such a good wife for you . . . eh, Fumie?

FUMIE: Grandma, don't be rude to our guests. . . . Come on, won't you greet them?

IKU: . . . I'm very glad that you came here. . . .

ICHIZŌ: Ha, ha . . . this is my grandmother. She's such an innocent, simple person. She seems to be reliving her childhood. . . .

FUMIE: Please excuse Grandmother. Please forgive us . . . (*Bows.*)

BOSS: Is this . . . your wife?

ICHIZŌ: . . . Er, yes.

BOSS: I heard that you'd had to leave here, because of illness . . . ?

ICHIZŌ: Yes . . . she was sick . . . for about three years . . . but now she feels she's able to come back . . . She's so determined . . . she . . .

BOSS: Well, that's good news. She does look healthy, doesn't she?

ICHIZŌ: . . . Yes, she's as well as can be expected.

BOSS (*To* FUMIE): I'm always indebted to your husband for his hard work and support.

FUMIE: Please excuse me for not having introduced myself before. I've often heard about you from my husband.

BOSS: It's very nice to meet you.

FUMIE: It's nice to meet you, too.

BOSS: Now, if you don't mind, I must excuse myself. Please take care of yourself and, again, please accept my sympathies. (*Bows to all.*)

(ICHIZŌ *stands up first and leads his* BOSS *out to the right. Everybody follows them. Pause.* MASATARŌ *and* SHIGEMASA *come back together. They sit by a hibachi and smoke quietly.*)

MASATARŌ: . . . Uncle?

SHIGEMASA: Hmm?

MASATARŌ: . . . It's a fine day . . . isn't it?

SHIGEMASA: . . . Ah, yes.

MASATARŌ: It's like . . . what can I say . . . ?

SHIGEMASA: Hmm?

MASATARŌ: It's like a New Year's Day, isn't it?

SHIGEMASA: Mmm . . . a New Year's Day . . . well, yes and no, that's not quite it.

MASATARŌ: You know, I used to be a bit of a poet when I was a student.

SHIGEMASA: Oh, really?

MASATARŌ: I think I'd like to . . . take it up again.

SHIGEMASA: Yes . . . you should.

MASATARŌ: . . .

SHIGEMASA: . . .

(TOKUJI *and* KEIKO *come back in, followed by* YASUKO.)

KEIKO: That Kajima, he's quite a doctor, isn't he?

TOKUJI: Uh? . . . ah, yes.

KEIKO: Fumie couldn't have hoped for a better outcome.

TOKUJI: No . . . (*He and* KEIKO *sit by another hibachi.*) Keiko, does this suit look all right on me?

KEIKO: . . . Not too bad. No one would know you'd rented it.

TOKUJI: Maybe I should have a new suit made.

KEIKO: Yes, do it . . . this is a good chance. You'll need it for your wedding someday, won't you?

TOKUJI: . . . "Ambitious, young businessman" . . .

KEIKO: Yes, that's what you look like, actually.

TOKUJI: Thank you.

KEIKO (*Takes out a compact and rearranges her hair*): . . . You behaved much better today.

TOKUJI: . . . I didn't have a choice.

KEIKO: . . . Well, you should keep it up.

TOKUJI: Hmm . . . Yasuko, come over here and sit by the heater. . . .

YASUKO: No, thanks. I'm not so cold.

TOKUJI (*To* KEIKO): You know, Ichizō deserves some credit after all. He's done a good job as an elder brother. He had his own way of doing it, but that wasn't necessarily wrong.

KEIKO (*Adjusting her hair*): No, of course not.

TOKUJI: I feel a bit foolish now to have been tearful when I heard his speech.

KEIKO: . . .

TOKUJI: You know, these formal ceremonies once in a while are a good thing. Perhaps we should have them more often.

YASUKO: You mean, you need a formal ceremony before you can speak honestly?

TOKUJI: No, not exactly . . . I just thought it's not a bad thing.

YASUKO (*Her eyes fill with tears*): It's stupid . . . absurd.

TOKUJI: Mmmm, maybe . . . but what you were talking about before, that friendship . . . I feel that now for Ichizō. When you see people who are always complaining suddenly change and start being more sensible and generous. . . . I just can't hate him anymore.

YASUKO: God! Wearing these rented ceremonial clothes! . . . We look so stupid . . . like clowns.

TOKUJI: But think about it. Whoever invented these clothes was very smart. They put everybody on the same level, you see?

YASUKO: Great. You've just escaped from your army uniform, and now you're keen on ceremonial clothes? I don't believe it . . .

TOKUJI: Well, that's straight to the point . . .

KEIKO: Come on you two. (*Puts away her compact.*) I thought you were both friends? Can't you get on just for today?

YASUKO: I'm going to change out of these clothes. . . . I can't stand this.

KEIKO: Yasuko, that's not a good idea. Wait a bit longer. You'll look out of place.

TOKUJI: It's true. You, the most serious of us all, would look the least serious.

YASUKO: . . .

TOKUJI: Why are you bothered by these clothes? Be honest! Don't you feel like wearing them?

YASUKO: No, that's not true.

(ICHIZŌ *comes back in, followed by* FUMIE.)

ICHIZŌ: Ah, good, good . . . at last, those people are gone. Finally, there's just us left . . . What a relief. It went fine. You all did very well. Thank you. You saved me . . . I really appreciate it. If only you were always like that. (*With tears in his eyes.*) Anyway, it's all right, everything went OK. It's like we've passed through a gate. The outside world is so solid; it's like a wall, and we couldn't pass through it without finding a gate. And that's not easy. . . . You can climb up the wall, but if you don't pay attention, you'll fall . . . and there's nothing you can do about it.

TOKUJI: Ichizō . . . You've had a hard time today. You've almost had your back broken by it all.

ICHIZŌ: Hmm . . . worse than that . . . I've had my backbone ripped completely out of me . . . there are no bones left to break. I'm like a snail, crawling from this gate to the next . . . but I've got no choice now . . . I've done it for forty years, and I'll carry on . . . I don't care anymore.

TOKUJI (*Gently*): Ichizō, stop it, please . . . We've all followed your instructions today, haven't we?

ICHIZŌ: Yes, that's true . . . I imagine you pitied me . . . but actually, I pity you. I led you through that gate today, but after this, how will you pass through the other gates. . . . You'll be driven into that wall. . . . When I think of it . . . but no, you're young, you all have a future in front of you. You won't do what I did. Even if you are driven into the wall, you won't fall. . . . Once I tried to make a new start, but what other kind of person could I become? I know you know, but don't tell me now. . . . Oh, I'm so tired . . . exhausted. I had to take care of everything today, so . . .

TOKUJI: Ichizō, sit down here. Please, have a rest . . .

ICHIZŌ (*Sits down but then immediately stands up again, agitated*): I don't want to rest . . . I want to see it through completely to the end. It's my mother's funeral. We tore her to pieces, and then we held a ceremony for her. But it's a ceremony for all of us, too. (*Wanders around, looking sad.*) Yesterday, we were at each other's throats, but today the ceremony's brought us together. That's the point of her death. This is what we get out of it. . . . By the way, I've called a photographer, and he'll be here very soon. I thought we should have a memorial photograph taken on this occasion. . . . Let's have a picture of ourselves . . . something to remember it by. It's good to look back at old photos sometimes.

TOKUJI: Er . . . I'm not so sure . . . let's not.

ICHIZŌ: Why not? We'll probably never have the chance again, such a fine day. And we're all dressed in our ceremonial clothes. . . . It will look like we're all close, reconciled. . . . To tell the truth, I've been waiting for something like this for a long time. . . . It took mother's funeral for it to happen, but today is better than yesterday. Why don't we have a picture taken, a happy picture, just for me? Let's do it. But let me sit in the center. I'm the hero of the day.

TOKUJI: . . . No, I don't want to . . . no.

ICHIZŌ: Why not? What's wrong with you?

TOKUJI: Something's wrong (*Stands up*) . . . Ichizō, are you all right? . . . You look strange . . . your face . . .

ICHIZŌ: Ha, ha . . . What are you saying? I feel fine (*Struggling for breath*) . . . honestly, I'm all right . . .

YASUKO: But Ichizō, you're so pale. (*Almost crying.*) Please, sit down. . . .

TOKUJI: Shall we call Dr. Kajima?

ICHIZŌ: No, don't. He's worthless. . . . (*Goes out to the veranda unsteadily.*) Listen, somebody line up the chairs in the garden, please? We're going to have a memorial picture taken.

(FUNERAL HELPERS *enter and carry chairs into the garden.*)

ICHIZŌ: Make sure to put the best chair in the center for me.

TOKUJI (*Pulling* ICHIZŌ *back*): Ichizō, that's not important now. You should lie down . . . please.

ICHIZŌ: Leave me alone . . . OK? . . . I . . .

TOKUJI: Ichizō, this is ridiculous. Calm down, please . . .

ICHIZŌ (*Pleads, breathlessly*): . . . It's not ridiculous . . . how dare you say that? . . . You're my brother. Don't criticize me, not now . . . leave me alone . . . I'm . . . Don't make a fool of me. . . . Don't be so hard on me. . . . Let's not start all that again . . . no, no more . . . enough . . . I'm so ashamed . . . (*Grabs his chest in pain.*) I . . . I can't . . . breathe . . . Agh. agh . . .

TOKUJI (*Grabs* ICHIZŌ): What's the matter? Hold on . . . Hey! Somebody, quick, call the doctor . . . Bring some water, quick . . .

(SHIGEMASA, MASATARŌ, *and the* FUNERAL HELPERS *run off to the right in confusion.*)

TOKUJI: Ichizō, I'll do whatever you want me to do, don't worry . . . just take it easy.

ICHIZŌ: Uh . . . sorry . . . it's OK just like this . . . but I . . . I feel bad. There's a pain . . . right here. (*Holds his chest.*) I can't breathe . . . What happened to the photographer . . . quick . . . or else I . . . (*Collapses.*)

TOKUJI: Oh, Ichizō . . . (*Holds* ICHIZŌ*'s head.*) What . . . What's the matter . . . ?

YASUKO: Ichizō! (*Clings to him.*)

FUMIE: Darling, what's happened . . . ?

KEIKO: Ichizō . . . he's dying . . . (*Holds on to him.*)

TOKUJI: Ichizō . . . (*Crying.*) Ichizō, don't . . . Hold on a little longer . . . Ichizō . . .

(ICHIZŌ *doesn't move.* FUMIE *and the others still call his name.* IKU *sits alone in a corner with her back to the audience.*)

CURTAIN

Kinoshita Junji, *Twilight Crane*, directed by Okakura Shirō, Budō-no-kai, October 1950.

TWILIGHT CRANE

KINOSHITA JUNJI

TRANSLATED BY BRIAN POWELL

Twilight Crane (*Yūzuru*) is a one-act play by Kinoshita Junji (1914–2006), written in a "literary" folk-art style.[1] The play was published in the January 1949 issue of the journal *Women's Review* (*Fujin kōron*) and first staged in April of the same year by the Grapes Society (Budō no kai), a small company founded in 1947 by the actress Yamamoto Yasue (1902–1993) and several of her colleagues. Yamamoto, by then one of the most famous performers in the Japanese theater world, began her career with the Tsukiji Little Theater and was at this time one of Kinoshita's favorite actresses.

The play, in the words of Brian Powell, soon became "a phenomenon in Japanese theater," appealing to a variety of audiences. During his career, Kinoshita wrote a number of experimental plays using folk stories, which he infused with multiple layers of meaning, ranging from folktale to political allegory, with *Twilight Crane* the most frequently performed of the series. Indeed, Yamamoto Yasue remained an admired icon in the postwar years through her many performances as Tsū, the mysterious and beautiful crane wife of her unwitting peasant husband, Yohyō.

With its flexible and poetic text, the play has been staged many times by *shingeki* companies, nō troupes, and, in 1962, as a very successful opera, with a

1. More about *Twilight Crane* can be found in Brian Powell, *Japan's Modern Theatre: A Century of Continuity and Change* (London: Japan Library, 2002). In addition, see Carol Fisher Sorgenfrei, "A Fabulous Fake: Folklore and the Search for National Identity in Kinoshita Junji's *Twilight Crane*," in *Rising from the Flames: The Rebirth of Theater in Occupied Japan, 1945–1952*, ed. Samuel L. Leiter (Lanham, Md.: Lexington Books, 2009), 317–34.

score by the highly respected Japanese composer Ikuma Dan (1924–2001), well known in the West for several film scores.

Characters

YOHYŌ

TSŪ

SŌDO

UNZU

CHILDREN

Snow all around. In the middle of it one small, solitary shack, open on one side. Behind it an expanse of deep red evening sky. In the distance the sound of CHILDREN *singing*:

Let's make a coat for grandpa to wear,
Let's make a coat for grandma to wear,
Lah-lala lah, lah lah lah,
Lah-lala, lah-lala, lah lah lah.

The house has two rooms. One (to the right) is closed off by shōji. *In the center of the other, visible to the audience, is a square open hearth.* YOHYŌ *is fast asleep beside it. The singing stops and the* CHILDREN *come running on.*

CHILDREN (*In unison, as if they were still singing*):
Come out and sing us a song, please do.
Come out and play some games, please do.
Come out and sing us a song.

YOHYŌ (*Waking up*): What's all this?

CHILDREN:
Come out and play some games. Sing us a song, please do.

YOHYŌ: Are you calling Tsū? She's not in.

CHILDREN: She's not in? Really not in? That's no good. Where's she gone?

YOHYŌ: Where? I don't know.

CHILDREN: Where's she gone? When's she coming back? Tell us, tell us, tell us!

YOHYŌ: You're getting on my nerves! (*Stands up.*)

CHILDREN (*Running away*): Ah! Look out! Yohyō's cross. Yohyō! Yohyō! Silly Yohyō!

YOHYŌ: Hey! Don't run away. Don't run away. I'll play with you.

CHILDREN: What'll we play?

YOHYŌ: Well, what shall we play?

CHILDREN: Knocking over Sticks.

YOHYŌ: OK. Knocking over Sticks.

CHILDREN: Singing.

YOHYŌ: OK. Singing.

CHILDREN: Snowball Fight.

YOHYŌ: OK. Snowball Fight. (*As he speaks, he moves into the* CHILDREN*'s group.*)

CHILDREN: Bird in the Cage.

YOHYŌ: OK. Bird in the Cage.

CHILDREN (*Chanting*): Stag, Stag, How Many Horns.

YOHYŌ: OK. Stag, Stag, How Many Horns. Right, I'm coming. I'm coming.

CHILDREN: Stag, Stag, How Many Horns. (*They run off repeating this.*)

YOHYŌ (*Starting to go after them. To himself*): Hang on! It'll be awful for Tsū to come back and find the soup cold. I must look after her—she's precious. (*Goes back into the house and hangs the pot over the fire.*)

(TSŪ *glides swiftly in from the back of the house.*)

TSŪ: Yohyō, really, you are not . . . ?

YOHYŌ: Where were you?

TSŪ: I just slipped out . . . you are not supposed to do that . . .

YOHYŌ: Well, I thought it would be awful for you to come back and find the soup cold. So I put it over the fire.

TSŪ: Oh, thank you so much. I will start preparing the rest of the meal for you.

YOHYŌ: All right. So I'm going out to play. It's Knocking over Sticks.

TSŪ: Really—Knocking over Sticks?

YOHYŌ: And then, Snowball Fight. And then, singing songs.

TSŪ: And then . . . Bird in the Cage. And then, Stag, Stag, How Many Horns?

YOHYŌ: Yes, yes. Stag, Stag, How Many Horns. You come too.

TSŪ: I would like to. But I have the meal to prepare . . .

YOHYŌ: Leave it! Come. (*Takes her hand and pulls her.*)

TSŪ: No.

YOHYŌ: Come on. Why not? We'll both of us play.

TSŪ: No, no. No, I say. (*Laughing, she allows herself to be pulled off.*)

(*The* CHILDREN*'s singing is heard in the distance.* SŌDO *and* UNZU *appear.*)

SŌDO: Her? Is she Yohyō's wife?

UNZU: She is too. He's a lucky bugger, suddenly getting a fine wife like that. Nowadays he spends a lot of his time taking naps by the fire.

SŌDO: He used to be such a hard worker—bloody idiot! And now he's got a fine woman like that—in a place like this! Why?

UNZU: Nobody knows when she came or where she came from. She just came . . . But thanks to her, Yohyō doesn't have to do anything now—and he's made a lot of money.

SŌDO: You weren't having me on, were you? When you told me about that cloth.

UNZU: No, it's true. Take it to the town and you can always get ten gold pieces for it.

SŌDO (*Ponders*): And you say she weaves it?

UNZU: Yes she does. But there is one thing. Before she goes into the room where the loom is, she tells Yohyō not to look at her while she's weaving. So Yohyō accepts what she says, doesn't peep into the room, and goes to bed. Then the next morning, there it is—all woven, so he says. It's beautiful cloth.

SŌDO: Crane Feather Weave—that's what you called it, wasn't it?

UNZU: That's what they call it in the town. They say it's so rare you'd have to go to India to find anything like it.

SŌDO: And you're the middleman. I bet you're raking it in.

UNZU: Well—not all that much.

SŌDO: Don't come that with me. But . . . if that's real Feather Weave, we're not talking about just fifty or a hundred gold pieces.

UNZU: Go on! D'you mean it? What is Crane Feather Weave anyway?

SŌDO: It's cloth woven from a thousand feathers taken from a *living* crane.

UNZU (*Puzzled*): But where would Yohyō's wife be collecting all those crane feathers?

SŌDO: Hmm. This is the weaving room, I suppose . . . (*Without thinking, he goes up into the house and peers into the closed-off room through a chink in the* shōji.) Yes, there's a loom there. . . . Ah! (*Cries out in astonishment.*)

UNZU: What is it? What is it?

SŌDO: Take a look. Crane feathers. . . . Well. That seems to . . .

UNZU: So the cloth could be the genuine article.

(*Pause.* TSŪ *has returned and glides in from the back.*)

UNZU (*Startled*): Ah!

SŌDO (*Thrown off guard*): I'm sorry—we shouldn't have come up into the house while you were out . . .

TSŪ: . . . (*Pause. Watches the two of them suspiciously, with her head inclined to one side like a bird.*)

UNZU: Oh . . . ah . . we've met—I'm Unzu from the other village—I'm much obliged to your husband for that cloth. . . .

TSŪ: . . . (*Remains silent.*)

SŌDO: Yes, well, what happened was . . . I heard about the cloth from him. (*Indicates* UNZU.) . . . I'm Sōdo—from the same village—what I want to know is—pardon me asking—is it genuine Crane Feather Weave?

TSŪ: . . . (*Remains silent. Stays watching them suspiciously; then suddenly, as if she had heard some sound, she wheels round and disappears into the back.*)

SŌDO: . . . ?

UNZU: . . . ?

SŌDO: What do you . . .

UNZU: What was that? We spoke to her and . . .

SŌDO: She didn't seem to understand a single word. . . . Everything about her's just like a bird.

UNZU: You're right. Just like a bird.

(*Pause. The dusk gradually deepens. Only the flames in the hearth flicker red.*)

SŌDO (*Looking at the crane feathers*): You know . . . there are stories about cranes and snakes . . . how they sometimes take human shape and become men's wives.

UNZU: What the . . .

SŌDO: Come to think of it . . . Ninji from the village had a story like that yesterday . . . he was passing by that lake in the mountains, in the early evening, four or five days ago, and there was a woman standing at the water's edge, he said . . . he thought there was something strange about her, so he kept watching without letting her see him. He saw her glide into the water, and then—she turned into a crane. . . .

UNZU: Eh?

SŌDO: The crane played around in the water for a while. Then it changed back into a woman and glided away.

UNZU: Ah! (*Runs out of the house.*)

SŌDO: Hey! What're you doing, screaming like that . . . (*Instinctively he leaves the house, too.*)

UNZU: So . . . so . . . his wife . . . is . . . a crane?

SŌDO: Shut up you idiot! You don't know that! Don't be such a fool as to even mention it . . .

UNZU: What am I going to do? I've cheated Yohyō, made a lot of money out of him . . .

SŌDO: Don't worry about it. If that's genuine Crane Feather Weave, we can take it to the capital and make ourselves a thousand gold pieces.

UNZU: What did you say? A *thousand*?

SŌDO: And from what you say, Yohyō's got quite greedy recently. If we talk about money, he'll listen all right.

UNZU: I suppose so. . . .

SŌDO: So, we've got to get him thinking like us—and he's got to get a steady supply of cloth from his wife.

UNZU: Well . . . yes . . . I suppose so . . .

SŌDO: Look, he's back.

YOHYŌ (*Returns, tired and happy*): Got it.

"Let's make a coat for grandpa to wear"

What's next? Ah . . .

"Lah-lala, lah-lala, lah lah lah"

That's right, isn't it? . . . Oh, I completely forgot to put the rice on for Tsū.

SŌDO: Heh, Yohyō.

YOHYŌ: What is it?

SŌDO: Forgotten me? Sōdo, from the other village. Unzu—you do the talking.

YOHYŌ: Ah, Unzu. Is there more money for us to make?

UNZU: Bring me some more of that cloth and you can have as much as you like.

YOHYŌ: No, there's no more cloth.

SŌDO: Why's that?

YOHYŌ: Tsū said there'd be no more after the last lot.

UNZU: You can't have that—not when I'm going to make more money for you.

YOHYŌ: I know, I know . . . but . . . she's very dear to me.

SŌDO: She may be—but you can pile up the money if you get a steady supply of cloth from her.

YOHYŌ: All right, all right, but she's always a lot thinner after she's been weaving.

SŌDO: Thinner, did you say? . . . Let me ask you a question. It's about Tsū moving in with you as your bride. When was that? Anything special about the way it happened?

YOHYŌ (*Takes a moment to absorb the question*): When was it now? One evening . . . I was about to go to bed . . . she came in and offered to be my wife. (*Chuckles happily at the memory.*)

SŌDO: Mmm . . . I don't suppose . . . you've ever had anything to do with a crane, have you?

YOHYŌ: A crane? Oh, a crane—yes, some time ago . . . I was working in the fields, when a crane came down on the path. It had an arrow in it and was in a lot of pain. So I pulled the arrow out.

SŌDO: Did you now? . . . Hmm . . . (*To* UNZU.) It's looking like the genuine article more and more.

UNZU (*Trembles*): . . .

SŌDO: And if it is, it's big money. . . . (*To* YOHYŌ.) You know that cloth . . . well, the cloth . . . Unzu—you do the talking.

UNZU: Uh . . . how shall I put it . . . if you take that cloth to the *capital* and sell it, you could get a thou . . .

SŌDO (*Breaking in*): Idiot! Look here, Yohyō, we could make you hundreds of gold pieces next time. Why not get her to weave again?

YOHYŌ: Did you say "hundreds"?

SŌDO: Yes, hundreds. (*To* UNZU.) We could, couldn't we?

UNZU: Yes, yes. Hundreds.

YOHYŌ: Really? Hundreds of gold pieces?

SŌDO: So talk to your wife a bit more . . . (*Notices* TSŪ, *who has been watching them from inside the house.*) Come over here. I'll spell it all out for you. (*Drags* YOHYŌ *into the shadows.*)

(UNZU *follows them.* TSŪ *comes out of the house and watches them go. A shadow of sadness passes over her face. The* CHILDREN *come running on.*)

CHILDREN (*In turn*): She's back! (*To* TSŪ.) Come on, let's play. Why were you out? Let's sing songs. Bird in the Cage. Hide and Seek. Songs. Ring-o-Ring-o-Ring. (*Form a circle round her.*) Come on.

TSŪ: It's dark already. Enough for today.

CHILDREN: No, no. Let's play. Songs.

TSŪ (*Vacantly*): Songs?

CHILDREN: Hide and Seek.
TSŪ: Hide and Seek?
CHILDREN: Ring-o-Ring-o-Ring.
TSŪ: Ring-o-Ring-o-Ring?
CHILDREN: Bird in the Cage.
TSŪ: Bird in the Cage?
CHILDREN: Yes, Bird in the Cage. (*They surround her and begin dancing round.*)
Bird in the Cage.
Bird in the Cage.
When, oh when, will you fly away?
In the night, before the dawn,
Slip, slip, slip, you slipped away.
Who's behind you? Guess.
Who's behind you? Guess.
Who's behind you? Guess.
What's the matter? You're supposed to cover your eyes. Why don't you? Aren't you going to crouch down?
TSŪ (*Stays standing, lost in thought*): Eh? . . . Oh. (*Crouches down and covers her eyes.*)
(*The* CHILDREN *dance round her singing. All around becomes suddenly dark. Only* TSŪ *is left, picked out in a pool of light.*)
TSŪ: Yohyō, my precious Yohyō. What has happened to you? Little by little you are changing. You are starting to inhabit a different world from mine. You are starting to be like those terrible men who shot the arrow into me, men whose language I do not understand. What has happened to you? And what can I do about it? Tell me, what can I do? . . . You were the one who saved my life. You pulled the arrow out because you took pity on me—you were not looking for any reward. I was so happy about that. That is why I came to your home. Then I wove that cloth for you, and you were so delighted—like a child. So I endured the pain, and wove more and more for you. And then you exchanged it for "money." I see nothing wrong in this—if you like "money" so much. Now you have plenty of this "money" you like, so I want us to live quietly and happily together in this little house, just the two of us. You are different from other men. You belong to my world. I thought we could live here forever, in the middle of this great plain, quietly creating a world just for the two of us, plowing the fields and playing with the children . . . but somehow you are moving away from me. You are steadily getting farther and farther away from me. What am I to do? Really, what am I to do?
(*The singing has stopped. The lights come up. The* CHILDREN *have gone.* TSŪ *suddenly looks to the side and hurries into the house as if she were being pursued. Pause.* SŌDO, UNZU, *and* YOHYŌ *appear.*)
SŌDO: So you know what you've got to do. If she refuses to do any more weaving, you threaten her—say you'll leave her.

YOHYŌ (*Contentedly*): That cloth's beautiful, isn't it? And it's because Tsū wove it.

SŌDO: Sure, it *is* beautiful, so next time we're going to sell it for two or three times as much money as we got for it before. Get it? We are going to sell it for two or three times what we sold it for before. Tell your wife that.

YOHYŌ (*Repeating*): We're going to sell it for two or three times what we got for it before. How did I do?

SŌDO: Fine. For hundreds of gold pieces.

YOHYŌ: For hundreds of gold pieces. Right?

SŌDO: Good. So get her to weave straightaway. Yes, Unzu?

UNZU: Yes. Get her to weave straightaway—tonight.

YOHYŌ: But Tsū said she wouldn't weave any more.

SŌDO: Don't be an idiot. If you sell it for a high price and make a big profit, she's bound to be pleased as well.

UNZU: Yes, yes. She's bound to be pleased as well.

YOHYŌ: Mmmm . . .

SŌDO: There's something else—listen to this—we're going to take you sightseeing in the capital. Unzu will tell you what a great place the capital is.

UNZU: Yes, yes. It's a great place.

YOHYŌ: I suppose the capital must be a great place.

SŌDO: Of course it is. So have you got it? You're going to make a lot of money and you're having a sightseeing tour of the capital thrown in. Like I've just said, we'll show you masses of interesting things in the capital. Are you with me? Or perhaps you don't want to go to the capital.

YOHYŌ: No, I *do* want to go.

UNZU: You want money too, don't you?

YOHYŌ: Mm. I do want money.

SŌDO (*Noticing* TSŪ *in the house*): Right. In you go. You know what you've got to do—make her weave straightaway. If she won't, say you're leaving her.

YOHYŌ: . . . mmmm . . .

SŌDO (*Pushing* YOHYŌ *into the house*): It'll be all right. You're great. (*To* UNZU.) We'll get out of sight and watch what happens.

(*The two of them hide again.*)

TSŪ (*As soon as the two have disappeared, rushes toward* YOHYŌ): Yohyō, come into the house, quickly. You are so wet—you will catch a cold. Supper is all ready. You put the soup on the fire for me, so it is nice and hot. Come on, start eating. Come closer to the fire.

YOHYŌ: . . . all right . . .

TSŪ: Please, do eat.

YOHYŌ: All right. (*Eats.*)

TSŪ: What is the matter? . . . Why are you so low? . . . You really should not do such things—staying out so late, in the cold . . . Please do not go away anymore. Please do not talk to any strangers. Please.

YOHYŌ: All right. . . .

TSŪ: Promise me, will you? Whatever you tell me to do, I will do. Whatever it is, I will do it for you. And you have the "money" you like so much. . . .

YOHYŌ: Yes, I've got money. Lots of it. It's in this bag here.

TSŪ: There you are. So from now on, let us live happily together, just the two of us.

YOHYŌ: Yes. I do love you.

TSŪ: And I really love you too. So, please, please stay as you are now, for ever.

YOHYŌ: Yes, I love you, I really do.

(*Pause.*)

TSŪ: Have another helping. . . . What is the matter? . . . Are you not going to eat any more? . . .

YOHYŌ: Mmmm . . . look, Tsū . . .

TSŪ: Mm?

YOHYŌ: You've done lots of good things in your life, haven't you? You went to the capital quite often. . . .

TSŪ: Well, not really, just in the sky—(*Pulls herself up short.*) What is it? Are you not going to have any more food?

YOHYŌ: Mmmm. . . . (*Hesitating.*) look, Tsū . . .

TSŪ: Yes?

YOHYŌ: I want . . . no, I can't say it.

TSŪ: What is it? What is the matter?

YOHYŌ: I want . . . it's no good, I can't say it.

TSŪ: Why? What is it you cannot say? . . . Shall I try and guess?

YOHYŌ: Yes, yes.

TSŪ: Well now . . . you want me to make some of those cakes again. . . .

YOHYŌ: No, it's not that.

TSŪ: Wrong? So . . . you want me to sing you a song. Is that it?

YOHYŌ: No. Of course I like your singing. But not today.

TSŪ: Wrong again? So . . . you want me to tell you about the capital again. . . . Yes? I have guessed it.

YOHYŌ: Well, half right, and half wrong.

TSŪ: Really? Half right, and half wrong? . . . So what is it? Tell me.

YOHYŌ: You won't get angry?

TSŪ: Me be angry? About something to do with you? . . . What is it? Tell me, tell me.

YOHYŌ (*Hesitates*): I . . . I want to go to the capital.

TSŪ: Eh?

YOHYŌ: I'm going to the capital and I'm going to make piles of money. . . . So . . . I want some more of that cloth . . .

TSŪ (*Startled*): The cloth? You cannot . . .

YOHYŌ (*Flustered*): No, no, I don't, I don't need it.

TSŪ (*As if to herself*): I told you . . . there was to be no more . . . of the cloth . . . and you promised me so faithfully . . .

YOHYŌ: Yes, you did say that. So I don't need it. I don't need it.... (*Tries desperately to stop himself bursting into tears, like a child who has been scolded.*)

TSŪ (*Suddenly realizing*): Ah, those men. Those men that were here just now. It was them was it? Yes, that must be it. They are gradually drawing you away from me.

YOHYŌ: What's the matter?... Don't get angry....

TSŪ:...

YOHYŌ: Tsū...

TSŪ (*Blankly*): Money... money... why do you want it so much?

YOHYŌ: Well, if I've got money, I'll buy everything I want—all the good things there are.

TSŪ: You will "buy." What does "buy" mean? What do you mean by "good things"? What do you need apart from me? No, no, you must not want anything apart from me. You must not want to "buy" things. What you must do is be affectionate to me—and only me. You and I must live together, just the two of us, for ever and ever.

YOHYŌ: Of course—I like being with you. I really do love you.

TSŪ: Yes, you do! You do. (*Hugs* YOHYŌ.)... Please stay as you are, like this, for ever. Do not go away from me. Please do not go away from me.

YOHYŌ: Don't be silly. Who could part from someone like you? Silly, silly.

TSŪ: ... When I am being held tightly by you, like this... I remember how it used to be ... the whole vast sky around me, without a care in the world, with nothing to worry about... I feel now like I did then.... this is what makes me happy now—as long as I am with you, I am happy.... Stay with me for ever.... Please do not go to any far-off places, will you. (*Pause. Suddenly thrusts him away from her.*) You are still thinking about the capital, are you not? You are still thinking about your "money."

YOHYŌ: Tsū, look...

TSŪ: Yes, you are. You are, aren't you. As I thought... (*Suddenly agitated.*) No, no, you mustn't go to the capital. You will never come back. You will never come back to me.

YOHYŌ: Of course I'll come back. I will come back. I'll go to the capital, I'll make a big profit on the cloth and—oh, yes, you're coming to the capital with me.

(*Pause.*)

TSŪ: Do you want to go to the capital that much?... Do you want this "money" so much?

YOHYŌ: Look, everybody wants money.

TSŪ: You want it so, so much? You want to go so much? You like money so much more than you like me? And the capital as well? Do you?

YOHYŌ: What do you think you're... you talk to me like that and I shall stop loving you.

TSŪ: What did you say? You'll stop loving me?

YOHYŌ: I don't love you. I don't. I don't love you, Tsū. You get on my nerves.

TSŪ: Really...

YOHYŌ: WEAVE THE CLOTH! I'm going to the capital. I'm going to make money.

TSŪ: That's too much, too much. What are you saying?

YOHYŌ: Weave the cloth! If you don't... I'll leave you.

TSŪ: What did you say? You'll leave me? Yohyō, what happened to you?

YOHYŌ: . . . (*Stubbornly remains silent.*)

TSŪ: Yohyō, Yohyō. (*Grabs his shoulders and shakes him.*) Do you mean it? Yohyō. Were you serious?

YOHYŌ: . . . I will leave you. So weave the cloth.

TSŪ: Ah . . .

YOHYŌ: Weave the cloth. Weave it now! We're going to sell it for two or three times what we got for it before. For hundreds of gold pieces.

TSŪ (*Suddenly very alarmed and flustered*): Eh? Eh? What did you just say? I heard "Weave the cloth now." Then what did you say?

YOHYŌ: I said, for hundreds of gold pieces. We're going to sell the cloth for two or three times as much money as we got before.

TSŪ: . . . (*She tilts her head to one side like a bird and watches* YOHYŌ *suspiciously.*)

YOHYŌ: Listen to me. This time the money we get will be two or three times . . .

TSŪ (*Screams*): I don't understand any more. I don't understand anything you are saying. It's the same as with those other men. I can see the mouth moving. I can hear the voice. But what is being said . . . Ah, Yohyō, you've started talking the language that these men used—the language of a different world—that I cannot understand. . . . What am I to do? What am I to do?

YOHYŌ: Tsū, what's the matter? Tsū . . .

TSŪ: "What's the matter?" "Tsū." You did say that, didn't you? You did say "What's the matter?" just then?

YOHYŌ: . . . (*Taken aback, he just gazes at* TSŪ'*s face.*)

TSŪ: I heard right, didn't I? You did say that? Eh? . . . Ah, you are gradually getting farther and farther away from me. You are getting smaller . . . Ah, what am I to do? What? (*Out toward where* SŌHO *and* UNZU *might be.*) Don't go on doing this. Don't! Stop drawing Yohyō away from me. (*Comes out of the house.*) Where are you? I beg you, I beg you. Don't draw my Yohyō away from me. (*Turns this way and that.*) Please, please, I beg you, I beg you. . . . Aren't you there? . . . Are you hiding? Come out! . . . Cowards! . . . Louts! . . . Louts, that's what you are. . . . Oh, how I hate you! I hate you. . . . You're taking my Yohyō. . . . Come out of there! Come out!. . . . No, no, I'm sorry. . . . I shouldn't talk like that. . . . Please, please, I beg you. I beg you, please. (*Her strength gradually fails, and she sinks down in the snow.*)

YOHYŌ (*Comes out to her, fearfully*): What's the matter? Tsū . . . (*Puts his arms around her.*)

TSŪ (*Coming to*): Ah, Yohyō.

YOHYŌ: Come, Tsū, let's go into the house. It's cold, in the snow . . . (*Almost carries her to the fireside.*)

(*For a few moments the two of them warm themselves at the fire, in silence.*)

TSŪ: You are so keen to go? You want to go to the capital that much?

YOHYŌ: Look, Tsū . . .

(*Pause.*)

YOHYŌ: The capital's beautiful. And just about now, the cherry trees must be in bloom.

(*Pause.*)

YOHYŌ: And then there are the oxen, lots of them. Pulling carriages with people riding in them. You've often told me about all this.

(*Pause.*)

YOHYŌ (*Yawns*): Oh, I'm tired. (*He stretches out and goes to sleep.*)

(TSŪ *realizes he has gone to sleep and puts something over him. She stares at his sleeping face, immobile. Then she suddenly rises and fetches a cloth bag from the corner of the room. She empties the contents over the palm of her hand. The bag contains gold coins and they spill out over the floor. She stares at them. All around suddenly becomes dark; only* TSŪ *and the gold coins remain, in a pool of light.*)

TSŪ: This is what it is all about. . . . Money . . . money . . . I just wanted you to have beautiful cloth to look at . . . and I was so happy when you showed how pleased you were. . . . That was the only reason I wore myself down weaving it for you. . . . and now . . . I do not have any other way of keeping you with me . . . weave the cloth to get the money . . . if I do not do it . . . if I don't do this, you will not stay by my side, will you . . . but . . . but . . . perhaps I have to accept it. . . . if getting more and more of this money gives you so much pleasure . . . if going to the capital is so important to you . . . and if you will not go away and leave me, provided I let you do all these things . . . well, one more time, I will weave just one more length of cloth for you. . . . And then . . . and then you must be content. Because if I weave more, I might not survive. . . . So you take the cloth, go to the capital . . . make lots of money and come home. . . . Yes, come home. You must come back. You must, must come back to me. Then finally we shall be together, the two of us, and we can live together for ever, for ever. . . . Please let it be like that.

(*The lights come up.*)

TSŪ (*Shaking* YOHYŌ *awake*): Yohyō, Yohyō.

YOHYŌ: Mmm? Ah . . . (*Mumbling.*)

TSŪ: Listen. The cloth. I will weave it for you.

YOHYŌ: Eh? What was that?

TSŪ: I will weave the cloth for you.

YOHYŌ: The cloth? Ah—you'll weave it for me?

TSŪ: Yes, I will weave it. One piece only.

YOHYŌ: You really will?

TSŪ: Yes, really. I will really weave it for you. So you can go to the capital with it.

YOHYŌ: I can go to the capital? Really?

TSŪ: Yes. So you will come back with lots of the money you like so much. And after that . . . and after that . . .

YOHYŌ: Oh—you're going to weave it? I can go to the capital? Oh . . . yes, I'll come back with piles of money. Piles and piles of money.

TSŪ: . . . (*Staring at how pleased* YOHYŌ *is*): So—just one thing—the promise you always make. You know you must never peep at me while I am weaving. You know that, don't you? You absolutely must not.

YOHYŌ: No, no, I won't. Ah, you're actually going to weave the cloth for me?

TSŪ: Listen to me. I'm begging you. You must keep the promise, you must. Don't look in at me. . . . If you do, everything is over between us.

YOHYŌ: Yes, yes, I won't look. Heh—I'm going to the capital. I'm going to make two or three times the money I made last time.

TSŪ: . . . Don't . . . don't look . . . (*Goes into the other room where the loom is.*)

(*The sound of a loom is heard.* SŌDO *leaps out of the shadows.* UNZU *follows.*)

SŌDO: We've done it! She's started weaving—at last!

UNZU: All right but, watching her from the shadows, I began to feel very sorry for her.

SŌDO: You're a bloody idiot. We're on the brink of making a lot of money—it's not the time to start feeling sorry for people. . . . (*Bounds up into the house and goes to peep into the weaving room.*)

YOHYŌ: Hey—you can't do that. You're not to look.

UNZU: Sōdo, you know you're not supposed to look while she's weaving.

SŌDO: Shut up, both of you. If I don't see her weaving, how do I know whether it's genuine crane feather weave or not?

YOHYŌ: No, no, you can't. She'll be angry with you. Stop!

UNZU: Sōdo, stop!

SŌDO: Let go of me. Let go! (*Looks into the room.*) Ah . . . ah . . .

UNZU: What is it?

SŌDO: Ah . . . have a look. It's a crane. A crane. A crane is sitting at the loom and weaving.

UNZU: What? A crane? (*Looks in.*) Ah . . . ah . . . it *is* a crane. The woman's not in there. It's a crane. It's holding a few of its own feathers in its beak and moving forward and backward over the loom . . . I've never . . .

SŌDO: Well there you are, Unzu. Looks as though we've got it right.

UNZU: I suppose it does.

YOHYŌ: What is it? What's going on?

SŌDO: That's what you're in love with—in there. Right, Unzu, we should have the cloth by tomorrow morning. We can go home and wait.

UNZU: I suppose we can. . . .

YOHYŌ: Heh, you two—what's in there? . . . Isn't it Tsū?

UNZU (*Being hustled off by* SŌDO): It's a crane. There's a crane in there.

(SŌDO *drags* UNZU *off.*)

YOHYŌ: A crane? Can't be . . . can there? In the room? . . . I want to have a look. . . . No, I mustn't, I mustn't. Tsū will be angry with me. . . . But what's a crane doing in there? Oh, I do want to have a look. . . . Would it be wrong to have a look? Tsū, tell me. Tsū, I'm going to have a quick peep. . . . No, I mustn't, I mustn't. Tsū said I must not look.

Tsū, Tsū. Why don't you answer? Tsū, Tsū. . . . What can have happened? What's happened? Tsū . . . no answer . . . I want to have a look . . . I want to look . . . Tsū, I'm going to have a little look. . . . (*Finally he looks in.*) Eh? There's just a crane in there . . . no sign of Tsū. . . . Eh? . . . What's happened? . . . Tsū . . . Tsū . . . She's not there. . . . What am I to do? . . . She's not there. She's gone. Tsū . . . Tsū . . . Tsū . . . (*He goes out of the house and disappears offstage, searching for her frantically.*)

(*Afterward only the sound of the loom is heard. Blackout. Above the sound of the loom a poem is read aloud.*)

Yohyō, Yohyō, where do you go?
Over the dark, snowy plain, hither and thither,
Searching for Tsū.
Tsū . . . Tsū . . . Tsū

Your voice is cracked and hoarse,
Soon the rays of the morning sun play on the snow,
Afternoon arrives and it is the same:
Tsū . . . Tsū . . . Tsū
Now in the evening, behind the house,
Today as yesterday the whole sky is a deep, deep red.

(*The lights come up. The sound of the loom continues.* SŌDO *and* UNZU *come on supporting* YOHYŌ, *who is in a bad way.*)

UNZU: Yohyō, are you all right? Pull yourself together.

SŌDO: I didn't believe it—there you were, lying in the snow—why did you go so far?

UNZU: You'd have frozen to death if we hadn't brought you back.

YOHYŌ: Tsū . . . Tsū . . .

UNZU: He's come round. Hey, Yohyō.

SŌDO: Yohyō, pull yourself together.

YOHYŌ: Tsū . . . Tsū . . .

(*Pause.*)

SŌDO: Is she ever going to stop weaving?

UNZU: You're right. She usually weaves it all in one night. But this time it's taking a night and a day.

SŌDO: Hmm. Perhaps I'll take another look.

(*The sound of the loom stops abruptly.*)

UNZU: It's stopped.

SŌDO: She's coming out!

(*The two of them panic and jump down from the house. They hide in the shadows.* TSŪ *emerges carrying two lengths of cloth. She looks emaciated.*)

TSŪ: Yohyō . . . Yohyō . . . (*She shakes* YOHYŌ *awake.*)

YOHYŌ (*Almost calling, as before*): Tsū . . . Tsū . . .

TSŪ: Yohyō.

YOHYŌ: Tsū . . . (*Realizes.*) Ah—Tsū. (*Embraces her tightly as he breaks into tears.*) Tsū, where did you go? You weren't here and I . . .

TSŪ: I am sorry. I took so long, didn't I? I have woven the cloth. Look . . . here you are . . . the cloth.

YOHYŌ: The cloth? Oh, you've woven the cloth. . . .

TSŪ: . . . (*Stares at the delighted* YOHYŌ.)

YOHYŌ: This is great. It's beautiful. Oh, there're two pieces, aren't there?

TSŪ: Yes, two pieces. That's why it took me until now. So you take the cloth and go off on your trip to the capital.

YOHYŌ: Yes, I'm going to the capital. You're coming with me, aren't you?

TSŪ: . . . (*Weeps.*)

YOHYŌ: Yes—you're coming with me and we'll go all round sightseeing.

TSŪ: Yohyō . . . you looked, didn't you?

YOHYŌ: I want to get to the capital quickly. Tsū, you've woven it so well.

TSŪ: I begged you so hard . . . and you promised so faithfully . . . why, why did you look?

YOHYŌ: What is it? Why are you crying?

TSŪ: I wanted to be with you for ever—for ever. . . . One of those two pieces is for you . . . keep it back and treasure it. I put my whole heart into the weaving so that you could have it.

YOHYŌ: Really, this is superbly woven.

TSŪ (*Grasping him by the shoulders*): Keep it back and treasure it. Take great, great care of it.

YOHYŌ (*Like a child*): Yes, I will take great, great care of it as you tell me to. I always listen to what you say to me. (*Pleading.*) Let's go to the capital together.

TSŪ (*Shaking her head*): I shall be . . . (*Smiles and stands up—suddenly she is white all over.*) Look how thin I have become. I used every single feather I could. What's left is just enough to let me fly. . . . (*She laughs quietly.*)

YOHYŌ (*Suddenly sensing something*): Tsū. (*Tries to embrace her, but his arms enclose only empty space.*)

TSŪ: Yohyō . . . take care of yourself . . . take good care of yourself always, always . . .

(*In the distance the* CHILDREN*'s singing is heard.*)

Let's make a coat for grandpa to wear,
Let's make a coat for grandma to wear,
Lah-lala lah, lah lah lah,
Lah-lala, lah-lala, lah lah lah.

TSŪ: I have to say good-bye to the children too. . . . How many times have I sung that song with them? . . . Yohyō, don't forget me, will you. We only had a short time together, but I will not forget how your pure love was all around me, or all the days when we played and sang songs with the children. I will never, never forget. Wherever I go, I will never . . .

YOHYŌ: Heh, Tsū . . .

TSŪ: Good-bye . . . good-bye . . .

YOHYŌ: Tsū, wait, wait I say. I'm coming too. Tsū, Tsū.

TSŪ: No, you cannot, you cannot. And I cannot stay in this human form any longer. I have to return to the sky, where I came from, alone. . . . Good-bye . . . take care . . . good-bye—it really *is* good-bye . . . (*Disappears.*)

YOHYŌ: Tsū, Tsū, where have you gone? Tsū. (*Confused, he comes out of the house.*)

(SŌDO *and* UNZU *leap out and hold him back.*)

UNZU (*Out of breath, to* SŌDO): Heh . . .

SŌDO (*Out of breath*): She's disappeared.

(YOHYŌ *is in a state of stupor in* UNZU'*s arms. The* CHILDREN *come running on.*)

CHILDREN (*In unison, as if they were singing*):

Come out and sing us a song, please do.

Come out and play some games, please do.

Come out and sing us a song.

(*Total silence.*)

ONE CHILD (*Suddenly points up to the sky*): A crane! A crane! Look, there's a crane flying up there.

SŌDO: A crane?

UNZU (*Scared*): Ah . . .

CHILDREN: A crane. A crane. A crane. (*Repeating this, they run off following the crane.*)

UNZU: Yohyō, look, a crane.

SŌDO: It looks as though it's having to struggle to stay in the air.

(*Pause.*)

SŌDO (*To no one in particular*): We've got two pieces of cloth. That's great. (*He tries to take the cloth that* YOHYŌ *is holding, but* YOHYŌ *clutches it to himself.*)

UNZU (*Absorbed in watching the crane fly away, still with his arms round* YOHYŌ): It's gradually getting smaller. . . .

YOHYŌ: Tsū . . . Tsū . . . (*Takes one or two unsteady steps as if following the crane. Then stands stock still, clutching the cloth tightly.*)

(SŌDO *also seems to be drawn in that direction, and the three of them have their gaze fixed on a point in the distant sky. From offstage the sound of the* CHILDREN *singing drifts faintly in.*)

CURTAIN

Tanaka Chikao, *Education*, directed by Tanaka Chikao, Haiyūza, December 1954. (Courtesy of Haiyūza)

EDUCATION

TANAKA CHIKAO

TRANSLATED BY J. THOMAS RIMER

Education (*Kyōiku*), a one-act play written in 1953 by Tanaka Chikao (1905–1995), is the first of his mature plays and indicates his deep interest in portraying his characters' spiritual lives. This continuing commitment can perhaps be best seen in his play *The Head of Mary* (*Maria no kubi*, 1959), set in Nagasaki, which examines Japan's spiritual situation in the early postwar years, with special reference to the atomic bombing of Nagasaki, where Tanaka himself was brought up as a child.[1]

Education was originally written as an exercise piece for young actors working at the Actors' Theater (Haiyūza), an important theatrical company established at the end of World War II in Tokyo by Senda Koreya (1904–1994), one of the leading actors and directors of postwar Japan. As with the later *The Head of Mary*, Tanaka seeks, in *Education*, to establish the dramatic and linguistic strategies needed to create an ambience in which the tensions of shifting spiritual states can be manifested on stage. The play is set in France, and in an important sense, the text represents a dramatized version of the anguished insights articulated in Charles Baudelaire's poem "Lethe" (Le léthé) recited by the heroine, Nellie, during the play. The stage language that Tanaka uses is elevated and somewhat abstract, altogether different from the kind of dialogue written by the Marxist-leaning Japanese dramatists of the prewar period. Jean Giraudoux and Henry de Montherlant come to mind as models. Perhaps this is

---

I want to acknowledge the advice and aid of Mrs. Sachiko Howard, whose help with translating this often difficult text was invaluable.

1. Translated in David G. Goodman, ed., *After Apocalypse: Four Japanese Plays of Hiroshima and Nagasaki* (Ithaca, N.Y.: East Asia Program, Cornell University, 1994).

not surprising, as Tanaka worked for a number of years with the dramatist Kishida Kunio (1890–1954), who himself, as noted earlier, studied with the director Jacques Copeau in Paris just after the end of World War I. Tanaka joined Kishida's company, the Literary Theater (Bungakuza), which was founded in 1937.

Characters

ROUALT
HELENE
NELLIE
PIERRE

A small country house near a wood. The house still retains some of its quality as an old farm house, but it has been refined and modernized in some of its details. There is a kitchen attached to the living room. The fireplace has been lit, but there is electric light for the kitchen table, so that whatever the gloom the years have added to the sobriety of the spot, there are bright areas as well. From the decor, the art works placed about, and the taste revealed by the furniture, the owners of the house are certainly women. There is a certain atmosphere suggesting powder and rouge yet something a bit childish as well, and a sense of purity.

To the right or left, there is a door leading to a side entrance, and a staircase to the second floor. On the wall, or perhaps on a pillar, a shrine has been installed. A statue of Mary is enshrined there and two candles in their holders.

It is late afternoon. A clear sky. The sound of a bugle can be faintly heard.

ROUALT *(sixty years old) lies on the sofa, drinking brandy. He has the bleary eyes of one who likes to drink, and his face is weather beaten through long years of wind and rain, the countenance of an old warrior.*

Sitting across from him is his wife, HELENE *(forty-five years old). She is short of stature and attractive, with a round face. She sits nervously on the edge of a chair, twisting and untwisting a handkerchief she is pulling at as she stares out at a spot in space. She wears a dark dress, trimmed in lace; there is something artless and full of charm about her, and the glossy pearls she wears around her neck make her a somehow touching figure.*

NELLIE, *their daughter (twenty-five years old), is wearing a pullover sweater and pants that appear to be tight and too short, the sort referred to as "toreador pants." She wears no stockings. All her clothes are a shade of faded blue somehow reminiscent of the color of clothing that prisoners might wear. She has a sharp gaze and is thin lipped. She holds a book of poetry in her hand, and just as though her parents were not there in the room, she looks beyond them as she moves back and forth. She appears to be reading something out loud, but her words cannot be clearly heard.*

The silence seems to continue on for a certain time Then ROUALT, *with some confidence, begins to hum occasionally and with a somewhat detached air; he seems amused. As usual, he has apparently shown no sense of concern.* HELENE *slowly wipes the top of the table with her handkerchief. Then she rises.*

HELENE (*Without looking at* NELLIE): I'd like to go to my own room now if you don't mind.

ROUALT: Of course. Go ahead. Right ahead. (*He had been on the verge of saying that he was waiting for this himself. She starts to leave.*) Ah. The money! The money. (*He points with his chin toward the top of the table.*)

HELENE: Nellie. Afterward, will you . . .

ROUALT: How would you like to try making a somewhat longer sound every once in a while? It doesn't actually matter to me what you may want to say. Every time I hear you speak, your voice is beautiful. The older you get, the more charming your voice becomes. Something like moistened snow. Ha, ha . . . (HELENE *is no longer there. Before she disappears, she kneels before a small shrine on the wall.*) Helene . . . (*There is no response. He turns the bottle upside down in order to catch the last drops. With a certain discontent.*) Well, you knew I was coming, didn't you? And the maid must have been sent out to buy something, right?

NELLIE (*Going on with the same movements as before*): Yes, I sent her. (*There is a certain coldness in the tone of her voice.*) And as always, after four or five drinks, you look as though you're ready to turn in.

ROUALT: Well then. If that's the case, then I would be just as happy to leave. (*With a certain emphasis.*) But today . . . today is a little different.

NELLIE (*Repeating*): . . . a little different? What do you mean by that? (*Raising her voice.*)

Je veux dormer! dormer plutôt que vivre!

Dan un sommeil aussi doux que la mort . . .[2]

ROUALT: What is it that you're reading so intently?

NELLIE: A kind of story.

Sur ton beau corps poli comme le cuivre . . .[3]

ROUALT: Your hips are still too thin. Are you planning to go through your life a barren woman? Or is it that you haven't found a man you can love? Huh? Well such are the times we live in; if two people don't work together, they can't find a way to make a living. Certainly, a girl like you, brought up in luxury, would need a lot of money, right?

---

2. I want to sleep! Not live, but sleep!
In drowsiness sweet as death itself . . .
All the translations of the quoted lines from the poem "Le Léthé" are from Charles Baudelaire, *Les Fleurs de Mal: The Complete Text of The Flowers of Evil*, trans. Richard Howard (Boston: Godine, 1982).

3. The gleaming copper of your skin . . .

NELLIE:

Pour engloutir mes snaglots apaisés
Rien ne me vaut l'abîme de ta clouche;
L'oubli puissant habite sur ta bouche . . .[4]

ROUALT: It might be all right for you to become a doctor. But how about getting a pharmacy license? That might really be good. Or finding a little café somewhere, and opening up shop? . . .

NELLIE: Where could I get the money to do that? I certainly can't ask you for any more help than I've been getting. That's why I'm working at the hospital.

ROUALT: I know, I know. Anyway, I know you hate me. Why doesn't that maid come back? Shit!

NELLIE:

L'oubli puissant habite sur ta bouche,
Et le Léthé coule dans tes baisers . . .[5]

ROUALT (*Holding his glass, he totters to his feet*): I'm asking you now. Isn't she back? And don't be so snobbish. Talk to me.

NELLIE (*All the more expressionless*): The wine seller in the village is pretty far away. (*Reciting.*) *Je veux dormir! dormer plutôt que vivre!*

ROUALT (*Suddenly striking his glass*): Do you really hate me as much as all that? You hate your own father. . . . And if I weren't your real father . . . if I really weren't, you know, you might think that I was just some pitiful case. So you wouldn't hate me then. Isn't that right . . . ? But more than hating me, you just simply disregard me altogether. You ignore me. A human being. So please. Please, really . . . Please feel sorry for me, have just that much feeling for me. I can't bear your cold eyes staring at me. No, more than cold. Those eyes are selfish, the most selfish in the whole world. So please stop. Stop this, I ask you. Have some feeling, some feeling for me. (*Kneeling, he weeps forlornly.*) For me, who is so lonely. You seem so absolute, so unconditional. It is so frightening . . . terrifying . . . frightening . . .

HELENE: Nellie, shall you and I go out now?

ROUALT: Helene, I won't make any more trouble. It's just that I'm getting drunk. Actually, I'm just pretending that I'm drunk, you know. Just to see if I could get some sympathy. I'm showing my true colors. . . .Ha, ha. (*He rises.*) I'm letting you see my real motives, you know . . .

HELENE: If you don't leave now, then I suppose we'll just have to go away ourselves.

---

4. For nothing silence my sobs
Like the abyss that is your bed;
Oblivion occupies your mouth . . .

5. Oblivion occupies your mouth.
And Lethe runs between your lips . . .

ROUALT (*Taking up his carefree attitude again, he returns to the sofa*): Come on now. You have to forgive me if, even for a moment, I'm attempting to show myself as the head of the house. And you know, I'm not all that thick headed a fellow. I get to make just one visit a month. So if I want to make my stay last five minutes or ten minutes more, you don't have to be so mean to me. So then, just a little . . . I'd like to drink just a little more. And then, today, well, there is one thing more . . . you see, there's a reason this time. Nellie, those shards of glass on the floor can wait. Come over and sit down in front of me.

HELENE (*Shuddering*): No. Remember that when you finished your business here, you promised to leave. That's the agreement. I do feel sorry for you. Yes. But whatever your reasons may be, I'm afraid to stay any longer under the same roof with you. So I must ask you to respect the proprieties as far as we are concerned. (*She starts to walk.*) So then, Nellie. Come on, and tuck that money away. (NELLIE *does not move.*) Nellie?

ROUALT (*Standing up quietly, he picks up his hat and umbrella, which are near the sofa, pulling along a trunk with one hand. He speaks in a facetious manner as he starts to move*): So, dear Helene. Thank you for all you have done for me, and for so long . . . Today, I . . . feel on top of things . . . ha, ha . . . (*He begins to leave.*)

NELLIE (*In spite of herself*): No, wait.

HELENE (*Without turning to look*): Nellie! (NELLIE *runs up to take his umbrella and hat from him.*) Nellie! (NELLIE *pushes her father roughly down where he was sitting before.* ROUALT, *confused, mutters but obeys her.* HELENE, *elated for the first time, leaves, the sound of her footsteps echoing loudly. The bell hanging inside the door rings as she leaves.*)

ROUALT (*Moved*): Nellie! (*He goes to take her two hands in his.*)

NELLIE: Don't touch me. But tell me instead what that "reason" is you mentioned.

ROUALT: Is it a mercurochrome stain? Tobacco? Look at those fingers, all stained yellow.

NELLIE (*Turning to him*): What is that "reason"?

ROUALT: Would you like to know? (*He drinks straight from the bottle.*) Hey, she's late, isn't she? (*He makes a point of trying to change the subject.*)

NELLIE: What is it?

ROUALT: Mama . . . don't you want to bring her back?

NELLIE: That's just her way. In thirty more minutes, she'll turn up as if nothing had happened.

ROUALT: Is that so? . . . Listen, Nellie, how would you fancy the two of us taking a trip together? (*Quietly.*) Just the two of us.

NELLIE (*Gloomily*): I would like to. And as far away as possible . . . to a place where there is a wide river.

ROUALT: A river? What about the ocean?

NELLIE: The ocean?

ROUALT (*Rising abruptly, he leans over beside her*): Yes. Let's go to my island. It's a sulfur island, covered with rocks, but right next to it there is a beautiful green island, with palm trees and covered with jungle. It's an island you could live on. And there are charming natives there. And there's still a hut left there. In the old days . . . I lived before . . .

NELLIE: Gamia . . . Was that her name?

ROUALT: Ah, that black Gamia? (*Suddenly.*) Oh . . . what did you just say?

NELLIE (*Suddenly rising, as she moves away*): And what happened to Paula? Paula?

ROUALT: Paula? How do you know about these women?

NELLIE: Why? Aren't you taking Paula along?

ROUALT: Because this time I'd be the one who would get killed.

NELLIE: Ah . . . so she ran away, then. Serves you right!

ROUALT: Shit! What is that maid doing?

NELLIE: So that's why you want to take me along instead. You've figured it all out, I see.

ROUALT: I'm not forcing you. Like any good parent, I am simply saying that this might give you a pleasant diversion. You seem to be satisfied with the fact that in your world, you have to look over your shoulder all the time. And this tiny little house is your nest.

NELLIE: So then . . . what would happen if I said I really would like to go?

ROUALT: Huh . . . ? Well . . . what kind of . . .

NELLIE: But I do want to go somewhere. A place where there are no people at all. I want to sleep . . . I want to go alone . . . (*Suddenly calling out.*) Why, why did mother have me born as a girl?

ROUALT: Well, that's just how it was. And remember, you will be loved by someone or other.

NELLIE: To be loved. What does that mean? Isn't that just why all women are doomed to be unhappy? First Mama. Then Jeanne. Then that black girl! . . . then, finally, Paula. The one who escaped.

ROUALT (*Fiercely*): That was different. Now certainly in the case of your mother. To live in a snug, unconventional household and without any constraints . . .

NELLIE: Snug? Hmm. In order to take care of Jeanne. In order to confine her and suffocate Gambia. And this was the same house in which you buried me and my mother, stifled us in the proprieties. Even though we were alive. That's the sort of house it was. And you thought I didn't know a thing about it. The odor of the black girl, like cheap whiskey, still comes drifting in out of the kitchen. (*She spits.*)

ROUALT: Who told you all this?

NELLIE: I made my own personal investigations. And if I had thought to find a detective agency, there are lots of them.

ROUALT: A hint from your mother?

NELLIE: Is that what you think? Anyway, I carried through my plan.

ROUALT: So if you followed me around so much, why were you interested in me? Ah, I bet you must have thought I had some money hidden away somewhere. And did you wonder whether there was an illegitimate child of mine somewhere as well? (*Scornfully.*) So then. You are that kind of woman, are you . . .

NELLIE: No, Papa, that's not right.

ROUALT: If not, then why?

NELLIE: I just wanted to know who you were as a man. That's all.

ROUALT: And so, did you figure things out? What kind of person I am? (NELLIE *does not respond.*) If you really want to dig out who I was before, so long ago, then you'll have to bring out into the open your Mama's . . . (*Looking at her sharply.*) . . . yes . . .

NELLIE: What about Mama? What are you talking about?

ROUALT: No, no, never mind about all that now. As far as the idea of any illegitimate child of mine, if that were the case, do you think that I would have come to *this* house? Now listen, Nellie, I've had to bear this shame, this shame as a man, and I've had to swallow the scorn and the defiance of you and your mother. Every time I come by once a month to bring your living expenses. And just why do you think that I am doing that?

NELLIE: Your duty as a husband and as a parent, I suppose. And even if that weren't the case, your duty would be to save as much money as possible, so as not to have the cost of an agent to bring it here, I guess.

ROUALT: What a shrew you are!

NELLIE: In any case, I'm sure it wasn't for love.

ROUALT (*Angry*): If not for love, then what do you think it was for?

NELLIE: Listen, this isn't your mine in the mountains, you know.

ROUALT: Now listen, if this were my mountain, I'd be the one in charge of some hundreds of rowdy men. Now listen, I'm a busy man. Do you think that to get this business taken care of, I would just brazenly come around here because it gives me some sort of pleasure? If there's one thing I would like to take a poke at, it's that frozen-looking face of yours. There's only one thing to say. After today, I'm going back to my island. And I don't intend coming back.

NELLIE: That's because Paula ran away from you, isn't it?

ROUALT: Well, sure, why not. Anyway, this is the last time I will see you. I haven't told anybody this, but I've decided to carry this old skeleton of mine back there. In all that twenty-five years since you first came bawling into this world, I've been hiding something in the depths, the very depths of my heart. Just one word.

NELLIE: I don't think there's just one word that can explain all that.

ROUALT: What? Yes, yes, there is.

NELLIE: Don't frighten me like that. Please hurry and explain what you are talking about. And you can be just as melodramatic about it as you like. (*She adopts a contemptuous attitude.*)

ROUALT (*Struggling with his feelings of malice*): A woman like you.... You're the perfect substitute for your mother. All right then, I'll go ahead and say what I have to say. And then we'll see if I have any love left for you or not. Nellie, you are not my daughter. (NELLIE *stands up rigidly.*) So then. Are you surprised? Well... (*He walks about with a sense of elation.*) Well, aren't you at least embarrassed about this? Why don't you say something?

NELLIE: I see... well... I somehow feel relieved. I feel happy. And I can't find a thing to say.

ROUALT: If you want to find the right words, you might try listening to your mother. Listen to that chaste and proper wife of mine. (*He goes back to where he was standing before and lights his pipe.*) The fact that you were born early, after only eight months, yes, you might just ask her about that.

NELLIE (*She suddenly runs up to him, puts her hands around his neck, and tries to strangle him*): You mean you can still talk like that? Can you? And I... my Papa, my Papa... however much...

ROUALT: Hey... stop that! (*With the happiness a father might feel.*) It tickles!

NELLIE: And however much, however much...

ROUALT: Well... stop it now... it tickles!

NELLIE: However much love I feel... .I feel... (*Exhausted, she falls into his lap.*) Please forgive me... Papa... please forgive me.

ROUALT: I did think you just went a little crazy. After all, you're just a young girl. That's just all it is... (*Hugging her, he pulls her up.*)

NELLIE: Don't touch me! No! No!

ROUALT: I really didn't think that my confession would have such an effect on you. (*He pulls her down beside him, turns the brandy bottle upside down, and examines it.*) Now in the first place, I didn't want your hysterics to take over. But I did decide to try to give you a good shock, though. At first, that is. I knew that at some point, though, I would really want to confide in you, and without telling your mother. Anyway, that's how I came to feel. And why is that? Because it's not a nice thing if your real father isn't someone like me.... (*He makes a contrary gesture.*) Yes, yes, it must be twenty-five years ago by now.... As far as I am concerned, if I thought that the connection with your mother meant that your sense of hatred for me was only a matter of course, then you wouldn't really weigh on my mind, one way or the other. So Nellie, if I now tell you the whole truth, it's really for your sake. Because I want you to know that your father was a better scholar than I ever was, a splendid, quite a brilliant, person.

NELLIE: You don't... you don't have to put yourself down like that.

ROUALT: Well, that's how I feel about things. At mining school we were the best of friends. We really got along so well. I guess you could say that I made it through by instinct. But François was the real student. We worked together, and with remarkable results. We found some wonderful stone specimens. It was our job to walk through the mountains, so we both turned black from the sun together. And his eyes were so full of goodness. Yes, his eyes were just like yours. (*He rises.*) Well, I'm going to look around here myself. (*He moves toward the kitchen.*) Yes, just look around. (*Looking for something in the cupboard.*) You're right, there is an unusual odor.... Makes me feel a bit nostalgic. Probably Gamia. Yes, your eyes are just like his.... His eyes were like a lake, clear, I guess you would say. A kind of fresh look, that seemed to go on endlessly. If it was a lake, then the lake had its master. Something mystical about it. ...Yes, that's right. The water looked as cool as a desert at night. That's the reality of it. (*He searches for a bottle of wine and takes a glass from the cupboard.*) This is the kind of water I drink. I'll guess I'll settle for this wine. And since his eyes were like that, many women fell for him, you know. (NELLIE *turns away.*) It was really surprising. Everyone came running to him, it seemed. One glimpse was enough. And can you imagine how envious I was about that? Sometimes I wanted to go and kill him, for sure!... That François! (*He goes back where he was before.*) And he drank a lot. And he always paid up, you know, even though he was hard up. Everybody loved him. Even when he was completely broke. Even to the point where the women paid for him.

NELLIE: Those women. They were fools.

ROUALT: And me? When I came around, not a single woman would pay any attention to me. Can you understand what my feelings were like? So all I did was to drink and drink. Just imagine, then, when an innocent young girl turned up. And now comes the real story.... (NELLIE, *suddenly resuming her frigid attitude, seems to hum to herself, perhaps a jazz tune, but she cannot seem to reveal openly her interest in what is of the greatest concern to her.*) Now those women we'd been hanging around with were really for hire. The ones who collected at the bar were prostitutes, really. But *this* young woman really did seem like some sort of goddess to us. (NELLIE *smiles wanly.*) Things really seemed to be going downhill for her, but somehow she maintained, under some pretext or other, that she was the daughter of some good family, that girl. Do you remember that old country house? Your grandmother's house? At the foot of the hill, covered with grapevines.

NELLIE: I don't remember.

ROUALT: The first time I met her... yeah, I seemed to drink in her very soul. I thought that in that girl, there was some kind of inner, uncanny light.... And yes, I saw her as the light of my destiny. Well as far as I am concerned, what an unhappy light it turned out to be.

NELLIE: So this becomes a house full of grubs and worms, where your destiny crumbled and your entrails rotted.

ROUALT: Do you mean that as a joke? You see, because of the shame I felt, and my age, I had lost all my self-confidence... what could I flatter myself about? So I took all the money I'd saved up until then, and I bought her presents to make her happy. My heart was beating so fast, I can tell you, when I went to see her. With that thirty-five-year-old mug of mine. And one of the things I brought her was that pearl necklace.

NELLIE: Ah! (*Almost imperceptibly, she writhes in pain and puts her head in her lap.*)

ROUALT: But remember, Nellie, I was all full of myself, thinking she was mine and that the contest was actually already over. That was really stupid of me. (*Laughing.*) Ah, that dammed François! Real love—now listen, Nellie—real love comes at the moment when a man and a woman, when they even glance at each other, seem to have feelings that spring from both of them at the same time. Then afterward, of course, all sorts of useless things get added in, but that's just the way things are. Stupid as I was, I did understand that much. So I just gave up. But for the sake of our friendship, I had to congratulate him. But then something unexpected can happen. Fate can be a pretty fierce thing, you know. The winner suddenly vanished from the earth. (NELLIE *raises her head.*) Pneumonia, you know. It was all over in a couple of days. But in his lover's belly there was a baby, been there for two months. And that was you. But no point in gossiping about all that. Anyway, I knew all about it. And so I openly exchanged wedding rings. With your mother. (*He turns his own ring around and around.*)

NELLIE: And when Mama agreed to do this, was she the one who asked you? Or did you . . .

ROUALT: Well, of course it was she who asked me. . . . She didn't have the courage to give birth to a child with no father . . . and she was afraid of what people might say and for the family name. . . . And so swallowing her pride, right in front of me, she bowed her head to me, me, worse than if I'd been a perfect stranger, a man she didn't love . . . even though I did have some money, I was fifteen years older than she was, and a homely fellow at that. So perhaps you know now why your mother hates me . . .

NELLIE: So you mean that, even though you knew that she didn't love you, you just gathered up your courage and nonchalantly went ahead and married her. What a shameless thing to do!

ROUALT: If this is how you are going to take this, then I guess I mustn't protest. After all, you can say that I took advantage of your mother's unhappiness in order to move the situation along. Now just be quiet, wait a minute. Just try to take into account all the things I've told you. But of course, if you naively believe everything that I told you, then my calculations will have gone astray (*He gives her a comical look.*)

NELLIE: Oh, I understand. I'm supposed to sanction your "philosophy of life," or whatever.

ROUALT: Exactly. So, let's continue. . . . What you really want to say is that however foolish or however good natured people may be, they still may harbor some ulterior motives. So when a tray is passed around, they might be tempted to snatch something away for themselves. Isn't that right?

NELLIE: Yes, I suppose that's so. That's just the way things are.

ROUALT: But you see . . . (*He looks at her quickly, with real pain.*) You see, what the human soul really wants is to join with others, with sincerity, submissively. The heart, in all its truth. But to say so doesn't mean that this is all just some simple instinct or some haphazard response. . . . I can't really explain this very well, but please try to think about what I'm saying in these general terms.

NELLIE: Hmm . . . and for all that . . . (*She holds back a derisive laugh.*)

ROUALT: And when this happens, you see, your sense of self, your ego, does not come into play; when you can just trust everything to your heart, then all the selfishness and meanness can disappear. That's what I believe. That feeling that I have of myself, that I am somehow vulgar or worthless . . . well, even if I can't quite blame it on the will of God, still, there *is* something above and beyond my offensive self. Perhaps it's fate, but there *is* something for which I must show reverence. Does that make any sense to you?

NELLIE (*Finally laughing*): Yes, I can follow at least that much. And even if you didn't speak in such an exaggerated and roundabout way, I still can understand how you could fall in love. But you can really say this in a couple of words. So why are you giving yourself such a hard time in trying to explain it?

ROUALT (*Meekly*): Is that so . . . yes, I suppose so. I guess it is my fault . . . (*Suddenly.*) No. No, that's not right. You don't really understand. And your mother doesn't understand, either. To talk about a man and a woman sleeping together, well, that comes at the very end of things. Nellie, so you know what sleeping together really involves? Legs and arms entwined together, so that your very bones seem to squeak. . . .

NELLIE (*Rising*): Stop. Be quiet. That's quite enough. There's nothing exceptional about this.

ROUALT: Well, you are a fledgling doctor yourself, so you surely must know each part of the human body in more detail than I do. But adding one piece after another still doesn't make up a living body. A living body has eyes that see, ears that hear, and at the same time there is real red blood running through, pulsing without cease, giving birth to a voice that rises from the heart . . . all becomes one, working in harmony. Have you ever dissected a body? Never, right? (*Suddenly, he gives a high laugh, in a bantering fashion.*)

NELLIE: Please stop this. It's stupid. So stupid.

ROUALT: So then . . . the bodies together become like scalpels, wounding each other, and as their blood splashes about in sympathy, both bodies are forced open without mercy. Their very blood courses together, resounding, reverberating. You don't know about this, do you? Well, I told you so! (*Again, he laughs drily.*)

NELLIE: That's a fate you describe for yourself. And why do you laugh like that? Because that's what you want. (*Irritated.*) Love, love as prostitution. You reveal your tastes. Prostitution, isn't it? What stupid nonsense.

ROUALT: Are you saying that love is no more than some kind of stupid prostitution? That's not true. It seems there are some good things in that book you're always quoting. Yes, just like it says, that goddess, that goddess who appeals to me so much, she just went right ahead and slept with that friend of mine. Legs and arms all tangled together, just like I said.

NELLIE: Why do you force me to listen to all this?

ROUALT: If you're in love, anyone will behave like this. Even a prostitute.

NELLIE: Ha!

ROUALT: But you know, I'm not like that. My way of loving, well, not to brag, but it's altogether different. (*Humbly.*) I never gave myself to your mother. Myself, that is.

NELLIE: It this true? Is what you are saying true? (*Suddenly, she is suddenly filled with a strange joy, which soon vanishes.*) That's a lie. It's Mama who never gave herself to you. What a lie . . .

ROUALT (*Sincerely*): Did your mother ever give birth to a child of mine?

NELLIE (*Walking around as she begins to think*): So then . . . well, you must have hated my mother. You wanted revenge. Yes . . . that must be . . .

ROUALT: Revenge? What on earth for? Was there any other man who adored your mother as much as I did? Why, on our wedding night, I put your mother to bed, and in a gentle voice, such a gentle voice, I said to her, "Sleep well." And the next word I said was, "Good-bye," when I left the room. I swear to you. I never touched a hair on her head.

NELLIE (*With cruelty*): Well, you just said that when people fall in love, they all behave like this. So why not with my mother?

ROUALT: Why not? . . . You know I'm sorry for you because you don't yet know that you yourself are a woman. Because that's what it means to be a woman . . . that's a woman's real nature.

NELLIE: What? And just where is that true nature you are rattling on about? I don't understand what this is all about, but when you speak like this, you seem to be obsessed with the need to show the depths of some transgression of yours.

ROUALT: No, no, that's not true. The depth of transgression, the height of benevolence, the range of blessings, I don't really understand that sort of thing. But I do know that at that moment, your mother was in the midst of a dream. Her soul was flickering, as in a cool spring breeze . . . yes, I could see it myself. I really could.

NELLIE: A dream? What dream?

ROUALT: Yes. A dream. She was the kind of person who could have such dreams. Well, after all, women are like that, with dreams. After I said good-bye that night, just as I was about to leave the room . . . (*In a perplexed manner*) all of a sudden I was assaulted by two fragile arms, hugging me around the neck. Light and soft as a spring breeze, and with an unsteady sigh, her long breaths made my cheeks hot! (NELLIE *walks about in an irritated manner.*) And just then, a woman's voice, more beautiful than any I've ever heard . . . in a voice that seemed to be whispering my fate . . . (*In a voice emptied of all emotion.*) She said, "François . . . suckle my breast . . . please François . . ."

NELLIE: François? François!

ROUALT: That was the name of your mother's lover.

NELLIE: If it had been me, I would have killed her on the spot. My mother.

ROUALT: You can't kill a woman who is having a dream. Why is that? . . . because at that time, a woman is at her most deeply beautiful. So I put your mother back in bed to sleep. Just as though . . . as though it had been François. I said nothing. And I left. And somehow or other, I was overflowing with happiness. Ah, the echoes of the organ . . . all wrapped in her bridal address, adorned with white, with reflections of red, green, and yellow falling from the stained glass, a pale angel with a faint blush of the red of her blood! The spirit of a white rose, blooming in that somber room. That there could have been such a blessed day in the midst of my squalid life! And yet such a pitiful day!

NELLIE (*Bitterly*): So then, I see. You made the most of your sentimental feelings. You just put them first. You made use of the natural course of events, and your money, to acquire her as your wife. Well, you wanted to move in the proper social circles. And you thought to augment your strong points. That's about right, isn't it?

ROUALT (*Somehow delighted*): So . . . you see then, that's how I escaped from her bed. I ran to a tavern to have a drink. And I drank, and I drank. I lost any sense of who I was, I collapsed, and I found myself awake in the bed of another woman. That's what happened. So that's how, in the first place, I first became intimate with Jeanne.

NELLIE: I bet there was hell to pay!

ROUALT: Ah, no flattery please. And you are surprisingly mean.

NELLIE: And then?

ROUALT: And then? If you want to know what happened to me after that, then why not consult a detective? Everything is just as you know it. Once a month, I come back from the island, unless the waves are just too rough, in order to do my duty in terms of financial support. That's why I appear before you both. It's a very ordinary tale, this.

NELLIE: Ordinary? Certainly not. Don't leave the story half finished. Mama is your living sacrifice. You go on the way you do because carrying out your revenge gives you pleasure, bit by bit.

ROUALT: Whatever the circumstances, you'll just go on saying what you want. A pallid, weak-kneed child like you, what can you understand of this?

NELLIE: I'm twenty-five. And at twenty-five, I might as well be thirty. You'd better remember that.

ROUALT: Well now, as for your uncompleted finished revenge, why do you think that I've just gone on, year after year, well, until this year anyway, when I've become an old man of sixty? Why didn't I just give up? Just why is that? "The man of the house goes to his work at the mine and can return to his home only once a month." What's the point of an excuse like that for your mother? It doesn't make any sense. And actually . . . the truth is . . .

NELLIE: The truth . . . well, what about that?

ROUALT: Even if you are betrayed by a woman, you know, well, if you've fallen for her, then you can't forget her. A man has to shoulder the consequences of his original intention. Is that a kind of feeling that you can understand? Can you grasp the kind of suffering that a man goes through, and the fact that he can offer no resistance to those unceasing lashes from that whip . . . can that mean anything to you?

NELLIE: So for you, it's fate, then . . . but no, that's nothing more than an evil attachment. And a revolting, devilish tenacity.

ROUALT: Now, is that so? An evil tenacity, is it? Well, whatever. So that I could love your mother, I've embraced Jeanne, Gamia, and Paula. I just had to do it. And while I was doing this, I was seeking through them the only woman that I really wanted to hold close. And those others, whose names I don't even remember . . .

NELLIE (*Unable to bear this any longer*): No, no more . . .

ROUALT (*Grasping her hands firmly*): But you see. (*She struggles to free herself, but he will not release her but pulls her up, forcing her to listen to the end.*) And yet you see, as the number of women increased; then surprisingly, Mama's very existence seemed to move further and further away from me. What is the real meaning, the deep significance, of this? What if, just what if, even if I did actually embrace her body, it was to be only a shadow of her that I could touch? . . . Nellie, could you somehow call *this* my revenge? My tenacity? That evil attachment? (NELLIE *twists herself as though in pain.*) So if you would call this my revenge (*He loosens her hands*), then it becomes a revenge against me.

NELLIE: Revenge? By whom? For what?

ROUALT: For my loneliness . . . my loneliness. (NELLIE *grins at him.*) So, then, you think that's funny? Yes, of course, it's ridiculous. . . . (*He, too, gives out a weak laugh.*) Well, I guess I don't understand any of this myself. In fact . . . just now, all that rattling on about nature, or fate; that was really a foolish way to lecture you. But in the end, you know, I seem to be the kind of man whose character can't really let him speak of the word "love." And I think it's because, in the end, the only person I can apparently love is myself. And that gives me the creeps. Really. So now I'm really going to leave. I'm really going home, this time. (*He rises.*) Please forgive me for all the deceptions I've forced on you, for so long, posing as your father. But you know, it was a rather interesting role to play. So it doesn't matter whether you hate me for it or not. I don't suppose I'll ever lay eyes on you again in this life. I'm going to pack up and go to the harbor tonight. The ship sets sail tomorrow. And listen, I don't need you to worry about me. A second Gamia will appear. And while making rotgut wine, she will take care of me on the island. It sounds good to me. Yes, it certainly does. Hey . . . (*Leaning forward, he rises behind her, then puts both hands on her shoulders, speaking in a gentle voice.*) You feel like a real daughter to me now. And I've changed your diapers two or three times, you know.

NELLIE: Oh, just stop this!

ROUALT: Well then. . . . Starting next month, a notary public, instead of me, will come out here and give you your monthly payments. At least as long as I'm alive. . . . He promised me he would let me know how you are doing. And if I do kick the bucket, maybe from drinking too much, if I die, then all the proceeds of my mine, all of them, should come to you. And all the bonds as well. So you'll have absolutely no problems with your living expenses. But as for the island, well, I want you to let that second Gamia have it. Can you do this for me? (*He takes his hat, umbrella, and trunk as he leaves.*) And finally, as for Mama, you must look after her in my stead. And as for me, that lewd old man who drinks too much, please let her know what I said. Because Mama, you see (*He hesitates*) . . . I really respect her . . . she gives me a reason for living . . . the light of life continues to shine out from her. . . . Well, then, good-bye. (*He starts to leave.*)

NELLIE (*Screaming out*): Papa! (*He stops. She wrings her hands.*)

ROUALT: Did you say something?

NELLIE: No. It was nothing. I was just thinking how to say good-bye and farewell.

ROUALT: Well, how about a farewell kiss perhaps? As a dutiful child?

NELLIE (*Hugging him fiercely, she speaks rapidly*): No. No this is all wrong. I really am your child. You just made up all those things you told me, because you are leaving. It's just your little play you've put together. It's so, isn't it so? Just say it's a lie. A lie. (*Letting out a sound like a groan, she suddenly pulls away.*)

ROUALT (*Indifferent*): Either way you take it is fine, as far as I'm concerned. Whether you're my real daughter or not. Either way. Whichever, it won't change my own sense of loneliness. And by the way, who taught you to kiss like that? I'm sure you wish you could strangle me to death. Or, is that really so different from wanting to fall for me, I wonder? Ha . . .

NELLIE (*Rubbing her lip*): You smell of wine, of nicotine.

ROUALT: Ha. You're just like Gamia, you are. Now there's fire, you know. Be careful! (*He begins to sing.*) *Auprès de ma blonde* won't work for you, with your frizzy hair, *qu'il fait bon dormir* . . . (*Still singing, he leaves.*)

(*The bell tinkles at the door.* NELLIE, *startled, starts to go forward. Then she stops, lights a cigarette, turns on the radio, and sits down on the sofa. There are tears in her eyes, and she seems lost in thought. Softly, she puts one hand to her lips. Then she grabs the money left on the table and puts it in her pocket. She gulps down the wine that is left. Putting one hand behind her head, she stretches out her legs on the sofa. There is something rough in her movements. She watches the smoke rise from her cigarette. The bell sounds again. She stays where she is, just raising her head a little.*

Carrying a briefcase, PIERRE *[age forty-eight] now peers in. There is a trace of timidity in his eyes, but there is something tenacious about him, and he is relaxed in a way typical of a scholar. He does not look particularly impressive; he has casually loosened his necktie on his light brown shirt and so has something of the look of a sportsman, with a kind of artless common good manners. He has come by bicycle, and he wipes his forehead.*)

PIERRE: It is all right to come in?

NELLIE (*Rising*): Ah, I thought it was Mama . . . (*She turns off the radio.*)

PIERRE (*Coming in*): The front door was shut. A guest?

NELLIE: Yes, there was. And my mother's not here. (*More formally.*) Well, welcome, in any case. (*She shakes hands.*) Please excuse me, I just suddenly decided to take the day off. And no urgent patients for you?

PIERRE: If so, I'll soon find out. I asked Francis to take over for me, and I just left. Also riding a bicycle, you know, there was some old guy, who seemed to be drunk. He sort of lunged at me. He had an umbrella in one hand, and he held a trunk in the other. He seemed to be in a good mood, just singing away.

NELLIE (*On her guard*): Oh . . . and what song was he singing?

PIERRE: The sort of song I wouldn't like someone like you to hear, some military song, you know. (*He takes a package wrapped in paper from his briefcase.*) And what happened to you?

NELLIE: What? No, no, nothing. (*She laughs politely.*)

PIERRE: Were you having a drink at the end of a long day? The rims of your eyes are all red. Like you've been crying. But you seem sort of chilly, just as though a rainstorm had just passed.

NELLIE: You don't paint a very attractive picture of me. . . . There was a fight with Mama. Strange, you know. Excuse me just a moment. . . . (*She goes in front of the mirror.*).

PIERRE: A quarrel, with that good-tempered mother of yours?

NELLIE: She's not always so good natured, Mama. She's really quite a nervous person. That's why we don't get along. That's why we always fight.

PIERRE: If it were me, I would treat her with respect. She's beautiful, like some precious treasure.

NELLIE: Is that so. (*Painfully.*) She has the kind of face that men like.

PIERRE: She's like a dark angel. And creatures like these seem to be vanishing from this world we live in. Today, you know, I bought a plate to give her. It's eighteenth century. (*He unwraps the antique plate and puts it on the table.*) That's what they said, anyway . . .

NELLIE: My goodness. Quite a gift, Doctor.

PIERRE (*Taking a bar of chocolate from his pocket*): This is something to eat. I heard recently that your mother is fond of pottery.

NELLIE: Now I'm in trouble.

PIERRE: No you're not. That shelf looks kind of sad and empty, so this will line up very nicely. (*Stepping away, he looks at the painting on the wall.*) Do you like Marie Laurencin's paintings?

NELLIE: Yes I do. So I suppose you'll up and buy one for us. Have you and Mama had a good talk? She's really rather reticent, you know.

PIERRE: Do you? I don't really think so. She's really quite affectionate, don't you agree? And she's has such a graceful dignity about her.

NELLIE: Really? I wonder. Men really like that kind of woman, I suppose.

PIERRE: I really can't understand the feelings of a husband who can allow someone like that to remain alone. I really don't. Or is it because he's too possessive? (*Lightly.*) So, the one who came here. That was your father, was it?

NELLIE: Yes. And that's why I took the day off.

PIERRE: Just when I came in, you know, it seemed to me there was a smell of tobacco. Not the kind people smoke around here. A sort of beast-like, male smell.

NELLIE: There are all sorts of smells that stagnate in this house. (*She takes the chocolate out of its wrapper.*) Thanks so much for this.... And you didn't chatter on a little too much with Mama... about me?

PIERRE: We didn't go on and on. But just a little...

NELLIE: About what?

PIERRE: So you go skiing?

NELLIE: About something like that? And you, Doctor?

PIERRE: Well, not when you get to my age, I'm forty-eight, you know. (*He takes the plate in his hand.*) Look at this. They say it came from the Netherlands. Eighteenth century. A piece like this is really beautiful, don't you think. There's something serene about it.

NELLIE: Really? Eighteenth century?

PIERRE: Is it the Virgin Mary? . . . or perhaps it's Venus. But from the clothing, it couldn't be Venus.

NELLIE: You don't sound really convinced. You're easy prey for those antique dealers, Doctor. (*She gets up, takes the wine from the kitchen table, turns on the switch to heat the coffeepot, and so forth.*)

PIERRE: It's not impossible for some heathen goddess to become a saint. (*He takes the plate in his hand and puts it on the shelf.*) I bought this because I thought that she would enjoy having it. I looked around for an hour and a half, but I never thought I would find a bargain like this. For my sake, you know, you should hold it in your hands, admire it.

NELLIE: Sorry if I seemed rude. But let me ask you, why do you bring a present every time you come?

PIERRE: It's kind of my expression of gratitude. Since you are so nice to me.

NELLIE: Hm...

PIERRE: Nice, and gentle. That's your real nature, you know. Of course, people say exactly the opposite.

NELLIE: Is that so... you're moving right in on me, aren't you? But I'm not particularly taken with you, you know.

PIERRE: Well, be that as it may . . . (*Suddenly he sees a fragment of a cup on the floor.*) Look, isn't that a piece of glass? (*He picks it up and comes close to her.*) And forget about the coffee. (*Extending both his arms.*) So this is a chance to make some rapid progress, don't you see. (*Annoyed,* NELLIE *laughs awkwardly, then faces the kitchen table.*) Now I'm not saying you have to jump into my arms! Now then . . . (NELLIE *stiffens and, without looking at him, wrings her hands.*) I'm not going to hurt you. It's just my way of paying my compliments to you.

NELLIE: Compliments?

PIERRE: Of course. That's perfectly reasonable.... No, wait, that's not quite true. We are parting from each other. This is my final greeting.

NELLIE (*Fearfully*): So then, are you, too, going far away?

PIERRE: Well, there's no one in the office to hold me back. But this is the best way I can say it.... And in the end, as for making any difference.... Hey, now what is it? Why are you making that face? I'm really sorry. Don't make too much of this. It's true, I'm exaggerating a little. I'm not saying that it's a question of any physical distance. It's a kind of psychological parting of the ways. To put it bluntly, it's breaking off our friendship. Me. With you. (*He laughs.*)

NELLIE: Breaking off?

PIERRE: So that's the reason for this official parting.

NELLIE: I really don't understand.

PIERRE: Yes... there's a kind of nice echo to that sound, "breaking off."

NELLIE: I really don't understand, because you are the one who began to come here.

PIERRE: Since we started to meet each other outside the hospital... no, sorry, I mean since we've started to have these conversations...

NELLIE: Well, today is only the third occasion. But whether there or here, I don't remember your ever complaining.

PIERRE: Of course, you're right.

NELLIE: Even so, why this talk of a parting of the ways?... And what do you mean by "psychological"... I simply don't understand what the reason for all this is...

PIERRE: Well, yes, I suppose I can see what you mean. (*He walks about.*) Now I understand. It's all right. You can just keep silent and go on living here as you are. Really, there's nothing more for you to do than that.... And then, even if I disappear from your sight forever, you probably won't even notice. And as for me, of course, there is no reason for me to ask you to pay attention to me. But by the way, I do have just a couple of tips for the road, as it were, for you to hear. For practical use. From me, as a fellow companion. It seems that as far as you are concerned, our relationship *is* merely practical, like handing out directions. So how can I make our parting seem somehow more meaningful? When there seems to be no reason for that...

NELLIE: But why, if we're never going to see each other again... ah, but you are really must be talking about something different.

PIERRE: Now remember: I told you that, far apart or close together, I won't disappear completely. In any case, at the hospital, we'll simply be doctor and assistant. And if you felt like studying a little more, you could earn quite a reputation in the surgery, you know. And to the extent of my meager abilities, I could help you with all that.

NELLIE: I would be the only young woman with any ambitions like that.

PIERRE: Remember, wielding a scalpel isn't something you've already learned as a well-brought up young lady.

NELLIE: But I've always wanted to try something that no one else would try.

PIERRE: Sure. And that's one really good thing about you . . . (*Gently, he hugs her; his hair brushing against her cheek; they stand quietly still. A bugle sounds. In their emotion, they do not move. A moment of silence.*) Well, don't just stand there dangling your arms.

NELLIE (*With a certain coolness; still, she is not angry*): What do you think I should do, then?

PIERRE: You *are* troublesome. (*He is happy to speak.*) You see, I have to talk to you like a kid. Even though you're twenty-five years old. So, do it this way (*Putting both her hands on his shoulders.*) Now, that's right. (*He hugs her again.*) It may be better if you don't think of me as a man.

NELLIE: Actually, I never gave it a thought. (*She quickly drops her arms.*)

PIERRE: How dare you say that! (*Filled with tender love as he takes in the smell of her hair.*) Because you didn't know any way to think about it . . . ah!

NELLIE: What is it?

PIERRE: The smell. The smell of your hair.

NELLIE: Um . . .

PIERRE: If we really are to part, then you must allow me to keep at least the scent of your hair with me. . . . There was some poet who wrote about the smell of hay. Rémy de Gourmont, was it? Wonder why he said that? And you know, you don't have one white hair yet. Wait. Ah, yes. A single silver one.

NELLIE: Doctor, when you say you want to go away, what exactly do you mean? Can't you really explain your feelings to me? (*She takes the silver thread and looks at it.*)

PIERRE: Well . . . later perhaps. I think you'll just figure it out all by yourself. So, thanks very much then. And excuse me. (*He lightly hugs her shoulders and returns to the sofa.*)

NELLIE: And you won't give me a kiss?

PIERRE (*Looking to say something, he looks at her upturned face but then, adopting a moralistic stance*): No. No, I won't do it.

NELLIE: Sorry. At a moment like this, I just thought it might be the proper thing to say.

PIERRE: On an occasion like this? Well, your good intentions are quite enough. Is it that you're trying to say? Because you've let yourself become twenty-five years old without ever having let a man at you? I think it's appropriate that I provide a little primer for you.

NELLIE: And what about your wife? Is she good at this? (*She takes the things no longer needed off the table.*)

PIERRE: Well, I certainly appreciate your showing respect for my wife! I thank you on her behalf! And by the same token, I must treat you honorably as well. So we'll dispense with the idea of a kiss. Still, I do intend to take on the role, more or less, of educating you. Now perhaps this may seem bothersome for you. Ah, and don't put in any milk, please.

NELLIE: Why do you speak of bothering me? On the contrary, I know that you'll always explain everything to me very politely, at least at the hospital or at school. (*She puts the coffee pot and mugs on the table and faces him.*)

PIERRE: That's not the kind of education I'm talking about. And don't pretend that you don't know what I mean. (NELLIE *looks him full in the face and, more brightly, wrinkles her eyebrows as she pours the coffee.*) So then . . . concerning the male sex. Just what is a man? I'm going to educate you about the male's true nature. Remember, I've lived on this earth twice as long as you. You can't go so far as to say I'm an old-timer, but in terms of the world we live in, I have had some valuable experiences. And remember, I'm a doctor. And in the surgery. I'm precise in my investigation of the truth, just as I am when I do an autopsy. I have to know everything about how a human being functions. From both a physiological and a psychological point of view. In the end, I have to know about everything, even pathology, everything.

NELLIE: Um . . . but when you talk about the human body, you mean just the physical body itself, don't you?

PIERRE: Well, there are various ways to describe all that.

NELLIE: Medicine is the art of taking all those separate things you mention and then connecting them all together, isn't it? (*With irony.*) All those scattered parts—an eye as an eye, an ear as an ear, even a heart as a heart—don't constitute a living body in and of themselves. In fact, most people think they can live separately like that, only with their brains. And even somebody who really thinks about all this still may not come to realize that our roots have become somehow separated from the earth. That we are really unsettled. We walk around with a cheerful face, even though there seem to be so many different kinds of people inside us. We're strange creatures, I guess. But be that as it may, since we have to go on living, just as we are, perhaps it's not the fault of our animal nature but of the society around us. I really don't understand. But you know, when we can manage to forget all about those separate parts of ourselves and we can connect them, then when there is a kind of harmony of the whole, then a human being can truly become the real thing. That's what Papa . . . Papa said.

PIERRE: Your Papa! That mining engineer! So he saw through all the gloom that's affected us since the beginning of this century. Well, what benevolence on his part! A real philosopher! No question about it. Walking around in his mountains, he could let all vulgar considerations of life just slide away. He must be a fine fellow. And your mother, being the kind of lady she is . . . Yes, I would really like to meet him.

NELLIE: Why?

PIERRE: So as to know you all the better. In order to truly say good-bye to you and to truly forget you, I want to investigate your real nature as thoroughly as possible. Does this sound all too professional?

NELLIE: My true nature, then. Well, just as you please.

PIERRE: Which one do you resemble the most? Your mother? Or your father . . . ?

NELLIE: Oh, my father. But you know, Doctor, you caught a glimpse of my father, quite by chance . . . or at least I think so.

PIERRE: What? I did? When was that . . .

NELLIE: The old drunk, singing the military song . . .

PIERRE: Military? Ah, you mean . . . just now, that one . . . really!

NELLIE: Weren't you surprised? There's nothing to be done about it; he's a heavy drinker.

PIERRE: Well then, you have to respect him as your father. But when you speak about him in a general way, what is the actual situation with him? After all, he only comes home to see you and your mother once a month.

NELLIE: That's the situation. Nothing to be done about it.

PIERRE (*After remaining quiet for a moment*): You love him, don't you.

NELLIE: Yes, yes I do.

PIERRE (*Just a bit disappointed*): Is that so, then. . . . But when you were growing up, you were left to take care of yourself, weren't you? That is why a proper education is absolutely essential. The kind of education that only a real father can give you.

NELLIE: "Education, education," that's all you talk about. But I've never been able to acquire it. There was nothing I could take in from my surroundings. Papa probably was right. His morals may not be the best, but there's no necessary connection there.

PIERRE (*Reddening*): I'm sorry. I said something stupid.

NELLIE: I'm quite inexperienced, you know. I've just had myself. Myself. So at this point, there's nothing I can do. And I don't know how I might be affected now.

PIERRE: Well, I didn't know you loved your father as much as that. (*Thinking again.*) Well, purity is a good thing . . . but Nellie, happiness for a woman comes from getting married, being in charge of a family . . .

NELLIE: That doesn't sound like something a real teacher would say. It's just an ordinary idea that anyone would come up with . . .

PIERRE: What difference does that make? It may be a very ordinary thought, but it's absolute. It's the real truth. Yes it is. And the situation for you is just the same. Wouldn't you like to have a life like that? Or if you don't like that idea, then perhaps something more brilliant, some more unreliable way of getting through this world. That could give you a sense of purpose. Becoming a successful doctor or not is, of course, an altogether different matter. I'm talking about you as a woman. That's what I'm keeping my eye on.

NELLIE: Whether you have your eyes on me or not, you've managed to hit the mark. Most women are like that, whoever they may be.

PIERRE: So you think so? When talent is involved, there's no loss in receiving an education. I have a wife of my own, and even though I myself don't have any outstanding talents, I'm not unreliable, I am an amiable man . . . (*She steals a glance at him but does not laugh.*) It's true, you know. And yet as a man like that, if I can lay the foundations properly for you, one way or another, then when you face such a battle, you won't stumble and let the right person escape from right under your nose. But if you never try, then you'll never allow yourself to be carried away.

NELLIE: I've never found myself wavering like that, not in the way you say.

PIERRE: That's because it looks unbecoming. And the beginning of misfortune. First of all, Nellie, you are a disciple of a cool and rational science.

NELLIE: That's because evidently my nature is too is cool and rational.

PIERRE: What do you mean?

NELLIE (*Laughing*): Well, everyone tells me that it's so. And if I listen to what the head of the hospital tells me, it must be true, because he teases me about it.

PIERRE: The head of the hospital is just a vulgar person. Yes. And in this case he's putting his responsibility off on others. That's because there's a kind of cold war going on. He doesn't really grasp the passions that flow so deeply in the others; he can't see through them. And surprisingly, you understand less than any of the others, isn't that so? You yourself don't seem to realize that you possess such powerful passions yourself.

NELLIE: Even if I did know that, what's to be done about it? Absolutely nothing.

PIERRE: So you pretend not to notice and just get by, don't you.

NELLIE: There's no room for any scenario I know that's right for a woman full of passion like that.

PIERRE: You're making every effort to get the better of me. I see we are in a cold war, too.

NELLIE: Whatever else, you do seem to want to assign this passionate nature to me. Doctor. But there's no reason we have to go to war.

PIERRE: All right. I know I'm the one who started this. But I'm not the one who's loading up now with live shot.

NELLIE: If I thought I were bound to accept your challenge, by showing you the proof that I had blood flowing in my veins, then I suppose you would have thought that things were going well for you, I suppose . . . as for me, fortunately, I am not shrewd enough to have wanted to let you hear any noises made by an unloaded gun. I'm sorry. Doctor, I'm just a woman, after all, full of common sense and with a strong penchant for prudence. Just an ordinary person. That's what I'm like inside. So, Doctor, I think that you greatly overvalue me. Now as for the head of the hospital, he's an interesting person.

PIERRE: Well you seem to get along with him, which means that you're smart. But a dull-witted person like me, I don't stand a chance.

NELLIE: Are you suggesting you want to take a chance with me? (*With a sweet smile.*)

PIERRE: That phrase you use isn't really very conciliatory . . .

NELLIE: But you, you see . . .

PIERRE: And what do you mean, specifically, by that phrase you just used?

NELLIE: Ah? (*Now she understands.*) Well, won't you drink something?

PIERRE (*Shaking his head*): Let's just stop the warfare now. (*He drinks the coffee. Silence. The western sun shines in from the window and fills the room with light and shadows. A group of small birds are chirping as they return to their nest. Suddenly the room is noisy.*

NELLIE *lights a cigarette.* PIERRE *picks up* NELLIE'*s book.*) Ah, Baudelaire, I see. (*He riffles through the pages.*) So, it is all right for me to stay on like this?

NELLIE: Of course. Why do you ask?

PIERRE: Do you find it interesting to talk to me? Or not? (*She smiles faintly.*) I wonder if you are making efforts to make me your partner. After all, I am your teacher. (NELLIE *says nothing.*) You aren't annoyed? After all, I've visited you three times in two weeks. (*She remains silent.*) And I hope that I haven't hurt you in any way, up until now. (*She shakes her head.*) I value you so much. I don't think you can have any notion of how grateful I am to you. And you know what I'm like. Every day. I put on a serious face, don't I? Properly, as a doctor at the hospital should. But on a day like this, with just the two of us here, I become so talkative. Perhaps too much. And in fact, I'm somehow tired of my own self-centeredness. That's thanks to you as well. And it's so rare for me to find myself chattering along happily, like some Pierrot.

NELLIE: So, you can't be this way with your wife?

PIERRE: No, and that's why, I really need to thank you so profoundly.

NELLIE (*Stubbornly*): So you can't talk to your wife this way.

PIERRE: No I can't. I'm the one who seems assigned to listen to her complaints. (*Silence.*) Apparently any couple seems fated to become that way. Now, of course, I want you to know that she really does look after my needs.

NELLIE (*Quietly*): That puzzle you've posed. About our parting, I seem to be able to unravel it now, somehow or other . . .

PIERRE: And so?

NELLIE: There are those who pursue what is absolute, pure. What is unsullied, what is beautiful. Yet, you know, it seems to me, that those very qualities can be found in a happiness of the most ordinary kind, in things that are close at hand. And you, too, Doctor, perhaps you have followed this kind of wandering path yourself.

PIERRE: I, too?

NELLIE: A man, you see, when he pursues a woman, he sometimes seeks . . . well, something that is no more than a phantom. And the sooner he knows this, the better.

PIERRE: While a woman, on the other hand, pursues only the substance of things, I suppose.

NELLIE: And that is because a woman seeks only reality itself.

PIERRE: While, for a man . . .

NELLIE: No, a man sets out thinking to create that reality. The truth has some objective existence out there, but it can't simply be revealed at one's convenience. By now you have come to some understanding of that. (PIERRE *does not respond. She continues gently.*) Men are covetous, you know. Really greedy.

PIERRE: Nellie! Go ahead, reproach me. Go ahead and whip me. Yes . . . (*As he says this, he throws himself down and kneels. Coming close to* NELLIE, *he grasps her knees and buries his head there.* NELLIE *softly strokes his hair. Then she gently pushes him back with her fingers.* PIERRE *remains as he was.*) Listen to those little birds, singing away.

... (*He lifts his head.*) Listen, Nellie. Somehow or other, there is something missing in you. You are somehow unfulfilled. What is it that is missing? I can't quite understand what it is. And it's the very same thing that attracts me to you.

NELLIE (*Smiling*): I don't understand.

PIERRE: I want to see some sign in you of something brighter, something more vivid, some sign that you are reaching out to the future, for some kind of happiness. That's what I would like to see in you. And that's the kind of person you must somehow become. Because that is the kind of character you're blessed with.

NELLIE (*Speaking in a mysterious fashion*): Actually, when it comes to me, I'm greedy as well, Doctor. (*She holds* PIERRE*'s head between her hands and looks at him steadily.*) I have a hunger for a kind of happiness that no one can understand, not even me myself.

PIERRE (*Rising*): Well, that's just fine then. Nellie, in the future I don't know what kind of happiness you may try to seek for yourself, whatever it may be, but well, when that time comes, please take that plate with the virgin, smash it, and throw it away. Although I guess that when you do become the mistress of your happiness, you probably won't have time to worry about things like that, I'm sure. (*Going back to where he was before.*) And for the opposite, when you find yourself in a period of bad luck, it would be good if that plate could be a useful means for you to think about the past. Because at that time, you were still young. And you indeed did have one man, so that, for a brief time at least, you could act on those feelings, grasping that happiness with your own two hands. The plate is not meant to serve as a memory of that man. It is to help you remember yourself. It may seem to you that somehow I am anticipating some sort of misfortune for you. I wonder. But in the end, it's best that you forget all about me.

NELLIE (*After a silence*): Doctor, you *are* a lonely person, aren't you?

PIERRE: I won't put it quite so starkly as that. But I do enjoy the role of the sad Pierrot. And I believe I can understand why. Some doctors might want to turn to religion. As for me, this Pierrot I play is a dangerous character, prone to temptations of self-rapture. If a woman tells me "you are covetous" or "you are lonely," I can simply feel elated, even me, who has had so much experience.

NELLIE: Why do you think that's the case?

PIERRE: Why? "You are a lonely person, aren't you? So it will be good if I come and comfort you, then."

NELLIE: Ah . . . (*I see.*) . . .

PIERRE: Um . . .well, don't you think I'm right?

NELLIE: Doctor, I didn't mean in that sense . . .

PIERRE: Yes, it's true, you are like that. Perhaps I misunderstand, but I think that you feel that at my age, I should know better. But it's not a question of age. Because psychologically speaking, people feel young until they die. So please, Nellie, won't you let me teach you something worth knowing? Because when a man tempts a willing woman, the situation for the man is different. We can act without so many words, without any indiscriminate flirting. There's no point going on about it. The most skillful way to handle that situation is to . . . well . . . somehow for the man to put on a piteous expression, an appearance of being oppressed. It won't do to seem sentimental. And the man needs to show some coolness, a bit of reserve. Take someone like me. Spellbound, a woman looks at me. She will think, "I would do anything for him." And so a love is born. That's what happens.

NELLIE: Ah . . . as easy as that.

PIERRE: As easy as that. That's exactly how it is. That's how things get started, for a woman. And particularly when an intelligent woman sees that man for the first time.

NELLIE: Is that so? It appears you've had a lot of practice at this.

PIERRE: Remember, I'm an experienced man of the world. This world.

NELLIE: Um . . . and so you've come to think that I'll somehow get entangled that way, too.

PIERRE: I've been giving it my best, but no luck so far, I guess. At least it seems that way.

NELLIE: So then, Doctor, you must be setting out to seduce me. In a number of the meanings of that word.

PIERRE: So that's what it comes to, is it? (*Laughing.*) Well, let's make good use of my position as your teacher. Still, I'm just playing my role of Pierrot. And today you've played your part of Columbine in a brilliant way, so very cool, so detached. Yet in the end, hasn't something happened today, after all? I'm the one who had to suffer a beating just now. And I was very happy about it. But in fact, things may be better this way. So come after me boldly, with resolution. Boldly.

NELLIE: I'm sorry. I seem to be somehow all stirred up today.

PIERRE: You are a little different from the Nellie I've been used to. Actually, you sound a little annoyed.

NELLIE: Well, maybe so. But Doctor . . . in the end, you are invulnerable.

PIERRE: What? Invulnerable?

NELLIE: Well yes, the empty bullet simply recoiled back on itself, didn't it . . .

PIERRE: Ah yes. Yes, I see. But you know, I am honestly trying to put myself in your place. Just as you said a moment ago, I'm your self-styled teacher. And my deepest desire for you, you know, is that you will give your hand, without blemish, to a young man who is suitably gallant. Someone who will really suit you, who will know your worth, a young man who can bring you happiness. (NELLIE *says nothing.*) Someone who will make your life worth living, someone who will allow you to demonstrate your true value . . . those eyes of yours, as though brilliantly polished, when they sparkle so beautifully: they show first and foremost the human being you have become. More than anything, they are the best sign of the human being you have become. . . . How I would like to see you at just such a moment. I'm not the one to make this happen, and of course that happy state is not only limited to the relations between men and women. And perhaps I interfere too much. But while I have this ardent wish, at the same time, because of your gentleness, I have come to realize that perhaps I too must have good feelings, too. Still, nothing can be guaranteed. As for you, of course, you may not feel about it this way at all. These may just be an expression of my own willful feelings. So when you said that I'm a lonely fellow, your words actually gave me a shock.

NELLIE: Even you, Doctor.

PIERRE: It's not a question of "even me." If it comes to that. This is a new discovery. That's why this is an education, don't you see?

NELLIE (*Protesting*): But listen, Doctor. What's wrong with simply pointing out that you feel lonely?

PIERRE: I'm telling you, I'm not complaining. I feel an immense sense of gratitude. To you, Nellie. For your kindness, your friendship.

NELLIE: But I've been trying to tell you.... I'm not that kind of person.

PIERRE: Why do you speak so earnestly like that?

NELLIE (*As if to herself*): There are different kinds of lonely faces...

PIERRE: Eh?

NELLIE: And that face—what did you say before? How guileless it was? Yes, the way that face looks, its appearance. And what lies beneath that appearance.

PIERRE: What do you mean when you say "beneath"?...

NELLIE: If the man is, well (*Teasingly*), young, fresh and unspoiled, a bit melancholy, and, on top of that, his face is manly, she will give him the comfort he seeks. But what if he had an air of discernment, was prey to no foolish dreams, and had only a withered face and sagging cheeks?

PIERRE: "You will catch cold—why don't you go home at once." What a defeat.... And I think it's about time for me to leave myself. (*He finishes the cold coffee left in the cup and pulls his necktie out of his pocket.*)

NELLIE: Ah, but I wasn't talking about you. Perhaps I *am* doing battle with you.... And you're not playing fair.

PIERRE: No, no, it's all right. I meant to come all prepared. But I see I'm inclined to wishful thinking after all. (*The bell rings.*)

NELLIE (*Rising*): Ah, it must be the maid. She's really late this time. (NELLIE *exits.*)

PIERRE (*Also rising, he walks to the decorative shelf*): "No foolish dreams, and only a withered..." was that it?

NELLIE'S VOICE: You're a little late. Papa already left . . . is that all you got? The butcher is closed today? Nothing to be done about that, I suppose. Well then, I know it's pretty far, but go to Old Man Emile's... you know, don't you, the place just beyond the church. Some eggs, and then . . . ah yes, how about borrowing Dr. Pierre's bicycle?... (*She sticks her head out.*) Would that be all right, Doctor? Your bicycle, just for a bit... ?

PIERRE: Well, those patients are waiting for me, you know... appendicitis, and a cesarean section, or worldwide influenza...

NELLIE (*Laughing as she withdraws her head*): Hurry up and come back quickly, then. The doctor has to go home quite soon. (*He shrugs his shoulders.*) And don't fool around with that delivery boy.

YOUNG MAID'S VOICE: Yes, I know. Eggs, and some carrots . . .

NELLIE: Simpleton!

MAID: Oh, oh . . . (*Her voice recedes.*)

NELLIE (*Reenters, with a bottle of wine and several cans of food*): Well, what can you do. She's just a child. . . . (*She puts the wine bottle on the table.*)

PIERRE: Are you going to drink something?

NELLIE: I suppose so. And you too. (*She takes the cans away, pulls the cork, and brings glasses.*)

PIERRE (*During this time, he has been looking slowly around the room and has picked something up in his hand to look at, something he finds quite unusual*): Let me take a good look around this room. It's the last time I'll see it. If this house had a trellis of roses outside, how exactly a house for a mistress it might be, hidden away like this.

NELLIE (*Without reserve*): You are right. Because a mistress did live here before. A woman of mixed blood, black and white.

PIERRE: Eh? Black and . . . (*He can't fathom this. Rather timidly.*) Are you cross with me?

NELLIE (*Pouring the wine*): Please.

PIERRE (*Returning to his seat*): I suppose a situation like that isn't so unusual, after all. It is really quiet here, and the earth has a fragrant smell, just as it should. . . . But Nellie, why do you adopt such rebellious posture? Just look at your clothes.

NELLIE: Me? Rebellious? What a tiresome idea. Perhaps this outfit doesn't suit you, but I'm just trying to dress up.

PIERRE: Well, in fact, you do look good. And I know it's not by accident.

NELLIE: Father likes this style.

PIERRE: So you dress up this way for your father? In a way, you look a bit boyish. Or perhaps like a mother who works in a factory, possibly with a couple of kids.

NELLIE: Ah, now that makes me feel good!

PIERRE: Why's that?

NELLIE: Because I want children.

PIERRE: And the father?

NELLIE: Why do you talk about that?

PIERRE: You mean, without a husband?

NELLIE: You see, I once seriously considered the possibility of artificial insemination.

PIERRE: But who would . . .

NELLIE: I . . . well, what about it? You've never met anyone who said a thing like that to you?

PIERRE: Well . . .

NELLIE: "Well . . ." Is that all you can say? I've searched around and read up on the whole thing. In fact, I've been to see a gynecologist. And the rate of success is pretty good.

You probably know all about this. It's not just one person involved, you know. You make a mixture from two or three men. And there's no contact between the ones giving and the one receiving. So there's no possibility of any personal identification, who is who, and so forth. . . . Let me gather my courage and tell you plainly. My idea was to add Papa to the mixture. (*She drinks.*)

PIERRE: Your father . . . well now, that's quite an idea. . . . Actually there's something rather sweet and sentimental about that. . . . It would make him happy, wouldn't it? Your papa, a philosopher, a drunkard . . .

NELLIE: No, this is not a question of pleasing my father. It is for me . . . for my own sake.

PIERRE: And, for the offspring . . . ?

NELLIE: It's so I can love the child.

PIERRE (*Looking at her intently*): So that's how it is. Yes, well, I guess I understand.

NELLIE: As I said to you before, I'm a woman with common sense. I'm not so different from any other ordinary woman. And I'm not that strong-minded at all.

PIERRE: I'm sure you're right. I did figure out that much about you.

NELLIE: That's my true nature, you know. Surprisingly, it's just like that.

PIERRE: It's a little old-fashioned to talk about any "true nature" these days, you know. (*Drinking.*) This is pretty strong, you know.

NELLIE: It's 87 percent. If you bring a match nearby, you'll start a fire. Sometimes I'm really tired when I come back from the laboratory. I drink this, then go right to sleep.

PIERRE: Out like a light.

NELLIE: Like a light.

PIERRE: You don't have any virginal dreams? Leaving out, of course, the question of artificial insemination . . .

NELLIE: You're right. I don't.

PIERRE: You know, the last couple of weeks, there have been lots of nights when I couldn't sleep at all. Because I was thinking about you. Apparently just when you were happily snoring away.

NELLIE: Not that happily. I can tell you it was boring. (*Quietly she begins to hum a song, the one that had been on the radio earlier.*)

PIERRE (*After a silence*): You know, I have a sense that I'm making quite a poor showing here. Now it doesn't matter if my efforts turn out to be fruitless, but still, I can't help wondering why. Maybe it's selfish on my part, but I really would like you to understand. . . . Do I have to explain all of this explicitly, in my own words?

NELLIE: Mother's late too. (*She sighs, hoping he will hear.*)

PIERRE: What does it really mean to be in love with someone? . . . I've thought about it during these past two weeks. I've tried to examine my own feelings. As a man who has a wife of his own, I've thought about it, just as I should, quite naturally. . . . I've tried to analyze things. The question is, as you put it so well a moment ago, what is the nature of purity? For it must exist. Is there no way, somehow or other, to get at the essence of the thing? There's something, well, unsettled about matters of this nature. Maybe it's all just some sort of illusion in the end.

NELLIE: I have no idea. What I was talking about before . . .

PIERRE: If you could only somehow get at this purity, extract it, then we human beings could stop wounding each other, I think.

NELLIE: Rather than putting human beings in a test tube and boiling them with an alcohol lamp, it would be quicker to have a good talk with your wife. Wouldn't that be a good thing?

PIERRE: If I tried this with my wife, she would hold her stomach and laugh. (*It has become quite dark by now.*) So then, Nellie . . . don't you . . . really . . . don't you have any consciousness of me as a man? (*She does not reply.*) You don't, do you. (*She nods in agreement.*)

PIERRE: Well, how about it then? . . . Have you ever found yourself in an atmosphere when you could feel as though you had somehow been embraced? (*She says nothing.*) Even as an illusion?

NELLIE: No.

PIERRE: I know that you feel no passion for me, but I wonder if have you ever felt anything like real passion? (*She does not reply.*) When people use the word "passion," most everyone seems to think that this means something strong, something fierce. But that's not necessarily true. Because, it can be something internal, introspective, you see . . .

NELLIE: Well of course, it doesn't necessarily mean something overwrought. . . .

PIERRE: That's right. And it can be something that can be very easy to miss. Something vague, indistinct but, in fact, something very powerful . . . and that's why at first, before you come to take in what you are feeling, there somehow comes a sudden sense of softness, as though your body were being stroked, very gently. (NELLIE *twists herself around in distaste. The twilight thickens, and the sound of evening bells from the church can be heard.*) There's something yearning, something nostalgic, a feeling that penetrates deep into you. . . . (NELLIE *unconsciously puts a cigarette to her lips and holds up a match.* PIERRE *leans forward and looks straight at* NELLIE.) Please say something, Nellie. Please say something to put me at my ease. Please. Just one word. (NELLIE *slowly strikes the match and brings it close to her glass. The flame lights everything sharply, and during the instant it continues to burn, lights up the room.*) Anything will do. But just speak. Tell me that smoke has just begun coming out of the chimney . . . or that the grape seeds are so tiny.

NELLIE: Doctor.

PIERRE: What is it?

NELLIE: Doctor, you seem quite content. Just by yourself.

PIERRE (*Nodding*): You mean, without any connection to you.

NELLIE: Yes.

PIERRE: Ah!

NELLIE: I can't really stop you if you are enjoying this. But even if you ask me to say something, I still can't find anything to say.

PIERRE (*Muttering to himself*): Don't worry about it. As long as you can say even that much. Thank you. (*He presses his hands to his cheeks.*)

NELLIE: It's quite an honor to me, you know, to have been chosen as a student to receive your education in love. And I thank you for this. But now, Doctor (*She speaks in a prosaic manner*), there is one thing that I would like to have you explain to me.

PIERRE: And what's that?

NELLIE: I feel so bored, so weary. Nothing seems to interest me. And so I would like to do something about it. Something. It's embarrassing to say this in front of you, but I really can't devote myself wholeheartedly to the work at the clinic. Under these circumstances, what should I do?

PIERRE: That's the sort of thing you should ask your father about. Ask your papa. I have no idea, myself. (*He speaks in a rough tone, somehow filled with self-scorn.*)

NELLIE: Why don't you become my father and answer as he would?

PIERRE: As your father?

NELLIE: Yes, that's right. (*She stares straight at him.*)

PIERRE: Well, that puts me in a spot. What's the prescription, the medicine for that? As a parent, that is. (*The bell rings.* NELLIE *gets up to see who it is, then quickly returns.*)

NELLIE: It's Mother. (HELENE *comes in.* NELLIE *pushes the switch and the electric light comes on.*) How far did you go?

HELENE: As far as the church. (*She places her head veil over her shoulders.*)

NELLIE: Is that so? Excuse me just a moment. (*She goes upstairs.*)

PIERRE (*Becoming formal*): I hope I'm not intruding. (*He has already finished tying his necktie.*)

HELENE: No, no, not at all. (*She seems somehow embarrassed.*)

PIERRE (*Sitting down again of his own accord*): It must have been delightful to go walking in the woods at twilight, I'm sure.

HELENE: Yes. The sheep crowd together as they come home, and the songs of the small birds fall like a shower. And already one or two stars, sparkling. . . . All of this makes me think of my dead mother, who lived in the country. . . . I . . . really . . . love these forests . . . so much . . .

PIERRE: Yes, I see. You can breathe the clean, fresh air, and your beautiful complexion becomes ever more fresh and transparent. (HELENE *says nothing but fumbles with her necklace.*) And that beauty of yours, you somehow store it up, waiting for that visit from your husband once a month, is that not so.

HELENE: Of course.

PIERRE: And when I think how strong his feelings must be, when he comes one a month to devour that beauty in one day, it brings a sense of happiness, even to me.

HELENE: Yes, it's a blessing for me. I do believe so.

PIERRE: A flawless couple, altogether. And so different from the others around here, who simply confront each other, day after day.

HELENE: Still . . .

PIERRE: Yes?

HELENE: One thing which concerns me is my daughter . . . she will never open up her heart to her father . . .

PIERRE: Ah, is that so? Well, I . . .

HELENE: Yes. You see, I think she's so self-willed because she's been brought up in the way she has. . . . It's really as though she had never had a father around at all.

PIERRE: Be that as it may, she's at a marriageable age now. A time when girls are liable to behave in capricious ways. She probably feels seems sulky about him, feels fretful, and so forth. Don't you think so?

HELENE: So . . . is that how you see it? That she's cynical about him?

PIERRE: I wouldn't worry about it. There's no way that feelings between parents and children can be examined in any logical fashion. Their feelings are likely to be somewhat the opposite of how they appear on the surface. . . . (*A pause.*) At this point, perhaps I might ask how, as a mother, you contemplate Nellie's future. She can certainly exert her energies as a doctor, and that, of course, would be a good thing in and of itself. . . . (HELENE *says nothing.*) But actually, she has reached the marrying age. And in that sense . . .

HELENE: As for that, well, you might want to ask her about the situation directly. I believe that would be best. (*She smiles faintly.*)

PIERRE: But if it comes to that, then as a mother you would, I suppose, be thinking about leaving your daughter and living alone by yourself. Isn't that true?

HELENE: Of course. (*With a delicate smile.*) Of course. But do you think that this child can do that? Go away from me to live alone?

PIERRE: Why not? After all, if she marries, she will have her own resources then.

HELENE: But, Doctor, that child, that child and I have been together for twenty-five years. Twenty-five years, just the two of us. We have never been separated from each other, even for a day . . .

PIERRE: But suppose that your husband . . . should he decide to return here and stay permanently . . .

HELENE: Are you thinking of her father? Outside of me, she feels no affection for anyone. However you try to explain it, the bond of blood is thick between us. Thick . . .

PIERRE: Still . . . (*As he thinks.*) Ah, I see then. . . . Well, if that's so, then I guess there is no room for people on the sidelines like me to attempt any unnecessary interference.

HELENE: What is it that you are trying to say to me?

PIERRE: Well, it's just that as far as I can see, rather than her trying to become a doctor, perhaps trying to live her life as an ordinary young woman would, in the end . . .

(NELLIE *comes back down the stairs. She has changed into a yellow skirt and a silk blouse. She has let down her hair, which hangs freely.*)

NELLIE: What are you two talking about in secret here?

PIERRE (*Rising*): Nellie, you look as beautiful as a princess now. Don't you think so, Helene?

NELLIE: Well, it has gotten a bit chilly. Certainly for the princess part, anyway.

PIERRE (*To* HELENE): When it comes to a question of your daughter's happiness, I'll be glad to be of help in any way that I can. Please don't forget what I've said. So then, Nellie, I'll see you tomorrow.

NELLIE: Yes, at the hospital. Ah—what about the bicycle?

PIERRE: There's only one road from here that leads to the church. I'll certainly meet the maid on the way. So good-bye then. (*As he leaves, to* NELLIE.) If you're feeling bored, Nellie, you might try skiing. If nothing else, it can give you a sense of purpose, some resolve, a feeling of movement. (*Mother and daughter go to see him off.*)

NELLIE: Movement, is it? Still, I wonder what the purpose might be. Best regards to your wife.

PIERRE'S VOICE: Good-bye, then. And my best to your father. Good-bye, and see you tomorrow. (*The bell rings. Mumbling to herself, "I'm so tired, and that doctor certainly overstayed his welcome,"* NELLIE *returns and throws herself on the sofa.* HELENE *looks down at her, as if to say something, then begins to clear various things from the table.*)

NELLIE (*Somehow troubled*): Just leave things the way they are. The maid can clean up, you know.

HELENE: Of course, you're right. . . . Did Papa and the doctor see each other here? (*There is something timid about her question.*)

NELLIE: No.

HELENE: So your father left soon after, I suppose.

NELLIE (*Shutting her eyes*): Why did you go to the church?

HELENE: To pray.

NELLIE: And for what? To pray for what?

HELENE: For you, dear Nellie.

NELLIE: You are always saying that you do things for me, Mama.

HELENE: What do you mean by that?

NELLIE: Nothing.

HELENE (*Beginning to walk about*): There is no other place for me to go. . . . My, the doctor is such a kind, intelligent man, don't you think?

NELLIE: Really?

HELENE: He seems so solid. He must be a great blessing to his wife.

NELLIE: Well yes, I wonder about that.

HELENE: You know that he's very concerned about you. He went out of his way to say so. (*She starts to go toward her room.*)

NELLIE: He's an affected mamby-pamby. Papa is much more a man than he.

HELENE: What? Your father?

NELLIE: I said that the doctor is an affected nincompoop. Mama, have you ever prayed for Papa? Prayed for him as a drunkard, besotted with women, all old and rotten? Have you?

HELENE (*Horrified*): Nellie!

NELLIE: Well, I admit I haven't. But who made him the way he is? You did, Mama . . . and so did I.

HELENE: Your father said something to you, didn't he, while I was gone. . . . Now I understand fully that at the bottom of your heart, you don't truly love me. And please don't become so angry. I would never, never do an evil thing to you . . .

NELLIE: Well, my father certainly never would. Or, rather than saying that he never would . . .

HELENE: Nellie, I have gone on living because of you. Your being here is what kept me alive. If this were not so, why would I have gone on, so shamelessly, somehow content with this useless, narrow life that I have led for so long?

NELLIE: That's a lie. (*She rises.*) Which man was it that you chose for the seed that gave birth to me? Which one? . . . I want you to explain this to me, and clearly.

HELENE: Oh!

NELLIE: Papa told me everything. Even now, you still think back on that first love of yours. It's to that lover that you offer your prayers. The love that you feel for this man (*Speaking hatefully*) makes you look so much younger, so much more beautiful than I am. That's exactly how it is. And all while Papa was on his rocky island or camping out on top of that frozen mountain, my father was whittling away his very flesh and bones. Papa was your victim. You used him as a living sacrifice. I feel so sorry for Papa! Oh, whatever happened, Papa still loved you. He tried to love you so much. And in order for you to remain satisfied with your revenge, he hurried to you once a month, from the island, from the mountaintop, from wherever. Ah! It's horrible. Now, what about that string of pearls around your neck? On that day, that very day, why do you just flaunt them and put on airs all the more? Why, why is that? Isn't it just to make Papa feel ashamed? I feel so sorry for him. He has to bear up under everything, until the end. Until he dies. Loving you all the while. I'm so sorry for him. (*She leans against the stove as she weeps. Shortly before this,* HELENE, *as the cruel silence now continues, sits down to listen quietly.*)

HELENE: Until the end . . . until he dies . . .

NELLIE: Yes, that's right. Father won't come here again. He's leaving tomorrow for the island. You won't see him again. Now I feel all the more that I would like to apologize to him.

HELENE: I see. So that's the situation. Now I understand. . . . This is so like him, that's just the kind of clever little performance he'd like to foist off on you.

NELLIE: Clever little performance . . .

HELENE: Exactly. In fact, brilliant is the word. He wants you to think that you are the daughter of some other man. He wants to appropriate for himself all your love and affection. And what's more, at the same time, you know, he wants to destroy the affection that you and I feel for each other. What an ugly scheme. I can see right through it. He has cleverly pulled you to him, and he's managed to fool you completely. Because even though you look like an adult, you are really still a child. You don't really understand this man who is your father.

NELLIE: That's not so. I do know him. I know who he is. I know him better than you.

HELENE: Don't get up. Just sit down there. . . . Now it is my turn to speak very frankly to you. Wouldn't you like to hear what I have to say? (NELLIE *sits on the sofa.*) Your father's true nature—no, let me say any man's true nature—can be found in the story of those circumstances. Let me explain this to you. For the sake of your own education. Are you ready? Compared with men, we women are virtuous, rather like a bunch of sheep, beautiful, just the way the Lord Jesus said we were. And as for Papa's ideas for this cock-and-bull story, well, it's really not so hard to see through the whole thing. He told you, didn't he, that you are not his child? (NELLIE *nods.*) I see . . . and that besides him, there was perhaps another. Isn't that right? A friend of your father's . . .

NELLIE: Someone he was close to.

HELENE: Yes. Someone he was close to. I thought it would be something like that. Yes, and that at the time . . . there was a group of young men and that he would come with his friend to have a good time with me. And that they came to our family house, which had fallen into ruin and virtually disappeared. Isn't that about it?

NELLIE: And that you deeply loved this friend of his. At one glance. François . . . François . . .

HELENE: Exactly. Well, that part is true.

NELLIE (*Angry*): So it *is* true then?

HELENE: Yes, but there is no reason your father should have felt betrayed. After all, I wasn't yet formally engaged to him.

NELLIE: You mean that he bore a grudge or something like that? That's completely wrong. In fact, it was just the opposite. Unfortunately, I think it is you, Mama, who didn't understand.

HELENE: The other way around? I certainly wouldn't say that. It's really you who don't understand your father. In his heart, he conceals a hard, a frightening, core. There was very little I could do with my meager strength. I could only retract, timidly, no more than a lifeless clod of earth.

NELLIE: He must have become that way because of your love for that young man.

HELENE: Yes. I did love him. So you may be right. But think about it this way: if two people truly love each other, what harm does that do to anyone? And if such a love is not wrong in and of itself, then the very act of living itself cannot be a bad thing.

NELLIE: Then, why didn't you just go ahead and marry him? That man.

HELENE: Ah! To think that my own daughter would look at me with such fierce eyes. And charge me in such cold words. This is a bitter thing for me, Nellie. You are hard on me. I really understand now that you do not love me. (*She dabs her eyes with her handkerchief.*)

NELLIE: If you really loved him deeply, you would have married him. As a matter of course.

HELENE: But he no longer remained in this world. Don't you know that he died and left me behind? (*She weeps.*)

NELLIE: Ah yes, pneumonia. In a period of two days.

HELENE: No. That's not true.

NELLIE: What? Why, Papa . . .

HELENE: Nellie! (*She stares fixedly at her, speaking in a muffled voice.*) In a valley in the mountains . . . he fell . . . and it may well be that he was pushed . . .

NELLIE (*Controlling herself after almost bursting out in panic, she throws herself on the sofa. Her shoulders are shaking. In the midst of her shock, she interrupts*): Did Papa . . . Papa . . .

HELENE: There is absolutely no proof. The dead do not speak. . . . Your father said that there was no time for anyone to help him. . . . Papa did everything he could to comfort me, and so I finished by marrying him.

NELLIE: I see. (*She rises.*) And yes, perhaps, within a period of ten days. Without your even wearing mourning clothes for the one you loved.

HELENE: You may have some memory of my family home. A rusted iron gate, a porch half fallen in ruin, a garden gone to seed, where weeds might grow. . . . In the end, remember, your father had quite a lot of money.

NELLIE: So, then, you are telling me that you sacrificed yourself for the good of the family. That's an excuse that so many women use.

HELENE: Now don't excite yourself. At least listen to me until the end. As far as I was concerned, I wanted to forget everything. I wanted to become the best, the very finest wife to him that I could be . . .

NELLIE: Now just a moment. Had you . . . had you already been with Papa?

HELENE: What? What are you saying?

NELLIE: Well, in other words, Father explained to me that you were already pregnant with me. He said that's what you told him.

HELENE: What are you trying to saying to me? Your father really did a good job of pulling the wool over your eyes, I see. I warned you about that a moment ago.

NELLIE (*Shaking her head*): What is all this . . .

HELENE: It is the mother who knows the father of her child. Isn't that so? I did not betray him. I promised myself to become the best wife I possibly could to him, until the time I entered my bridal bed. I'll swear an oath to you.

NELLIE: What good is an oath like that? It's just for your own peace of mind.

HELENE: You can berate me just as much as you please. Perhaps I only deserve it.

NELLIE: That's enough. Nothing changes the fact that you loved that other man. More than my father.

HELENE (*Mysteriously*): The one who brought that about—the one who made me unable to forget that man . . . was you, Nellie.

NELLIE: How can you say that? (*She rises, distancing herself from her mother.*) How could I have had anything to do with this? I wasn't even born. Please stop these baseless accusations. (*She sits in front of the kitchen table.*)

HELENE (*Rising, she goes to pray to the Virgin Mary in an indescribable sense of joy, then, slowly*): Ah, the sounds of the organ. . . . My white wedding dress. . . . I looked up in reverence at the sight of the blessed Virgin Mary, hugging the infant Jesus, and I felt a powerful sense of grace. And then, that evening, on my bridal bed, an angel appeared, you see, splitting my body, cutting me open. And then my very soul rose up, higher and higher.

NELLIE: A knife! A scalpel! (*While listening to her mother's monologue, she goes to the silver tray, and before she knows it, takes up a knife that is lying there but then, at the sound of her own words, taken aback, drops it again. The sound of sharp metal.*)

HELENE: Ah, how painful it is . . . how painful. . . . Then the blood from my whole body burst forth like flowers from the wound . . . and the blood that I lost flowed together with his blood, brought back together again . . . such was my dream!

NELLIE: Fresh blood! From him!

HELENE: Yes. . . . Please, grant me this, Nellie. And I didn't like to talk this way about your father, whom you love so much. But you are the one who made me do it. I have never, never betrayed your father. Please believe me. (*She returns to her former place.*)

NELLIE: But then, in the end, whose daughter am I? The angel's? Whose?

HELENE (*Happy, with a delicate smile of victory*): The dark angel's!

NELLIE (*As if mumbling to herself*): It's a dream . . . a dream . . . it can only be a dream. . . .

HELENE: And from the next day onward, your father, just as you might expect, began coming home only one day a month. "Just seven or eight minutes at a time." Your father turned me into a widow. Because he knew that I would remain a perfectly chaste woman. And so, Nellie, I have lived my life with only you for my companion. And I have gone on living. And I still see the results of my dream, even now. I live that dream through you. What else can I do?

NELLIE (*With compassion*): I won't interfere. Not anymore. So please, Mama, continue with your dream. And in that dream, even if Father should kill someone, I will go on believing that Papa is my real father. And if that is my dream, then you, Mama, you cannot interfere with me.

HELENE: I see. (*Quietly, she takes off her necklace, and holding it with both hands near her breast, she speaks as if to the pearls.*) If you, Nellie, will not embrace me, then it is I who will try to embrace you. (NELLIE, *abruptly rises, and picking up her book of poems from the table, moves away. During the following speech, she reverts to the movements and appearance she had at the beginning of the play.*) So, Nellie, I have discharged all those duties I assumed until today. . . . I'd like to be excused now, to go to my room.

. . . (*She rises.*). So Papa won't be coming back again, then? . . . and so, my dear, what do you think about that? (*She rubs her hands together, making with a noise.*) What? You think he will certainly come back? And why is that? . . . (*Smiling faintly.*) Ah yes, I see now. Because Papa, you see. . . . He likes to see you peeking at my tiny nipples . . . all open, from the base of my white neck. . . . Oh, what a pleasure it is! So then now, surely, with that nonchalant face of his, he can come home.

(*Her two voices blend in a state of rapture, as though toying with a selfless sense of gladness and delight. And yet it is a sweet voice, permitted only to a lonely woman, a honeyed voice filled with both shame and romantic longing.* NELLIE, *like a god looking down from a great distance, manages with considerable effort to disregard her mother's disgraceful performance and, somehow or other, manages to loose herself in her book. Then as her speech nears its end,* HELENE *throws open the door and then vanishes, as though sucked through the space. Somehow relieved,* NELLIE *leans her back against the door and takes a breath. Soon, she thrusts one hand into her pocket and begins to move about as before. Suddenly she remembers, puts in her hand and finds in the trousers she wore before she changed, the bunch of bills. She knocks on her mother's door, then opens it. Light floods out from within the bedroom. And at the same time,* HELENE *can be heard singing a lullaby. She is evidently buried away in a rocking chair, all her energy used up, mindlessly singing her song. The voice shows no sign of the pride and romantic longing heard before. It is a voice grown old, a plaintive voice.*)

HELENE: *Dormez . . . dormez . . .*

NELLIE: Mother . . . what . . .

HELENE: *Sonnez les matines . . . sonnez les matines . . . ding . . . ding . . . dong . . .*

NELLIE: Mama. The money he left. I'll throw it away. I'll wake you up for dinner.

(*She closes the door.* HELENE*'s song can still be faintly heard.* NELLIE *continues to walk around. She raises her voice while reading.*)

NELLIE:

Je sucerai, pour noyer ma rancœur,
Le népenthès et la bonnie ciguë
Au bouts charmants de cette gorge aiguë
Qui n'a jamais emprisonné de cœur.[6]

HELENE'S VOICE: *Sonnez les matines, sonnez les matines, . . . ding ding dong . . .*

NELLIE (*Lifting her head as she reads aloud*):

A mon destin, désormais mon délice,
J'ai obérai comme un prédestiné;

---

6. I'll suck enough to drown my spite
Hemlock is sweet, nepenthe kind
At those entrancing pointed breasts
Which have never confined a heart.

Martyr docile, innocent condamné,
Dont la ferveur attise le supplice.[7]

(*She suddenly pauses.*) *Obérai* . . . no, no, I won't obey . . . (*She begins to walk, then stops again.*) The crime . . . the crime of being born a woman. . . . (*She covers her face with both hands. She allows the book of poetry to fall to the floor. Abruptly, she throws herself into a chair and buries her head in its back. As though in prayer, she puts her two hands together and touches her forehead. Presently, the sound of her whispering voice can be heard.*)

A purpose . . . a purpose . . . I am so tired of sleeping, sleeping on like this. Please give me a purpose. A purpose . . .

(*Her strangled voice, fruitlessly expressing the depths of her very nature, seems to continue endlessly on, mixed with* HELENE*'s lullaby, blending in turn with the melancholy sound of the bell. Yet now, there can be heard in her a desperate struggle not to give in.*)

NELLIE: I am so weary of this . . . I pray you to give me a purpose. . . . Yet if I do not sleep . . . if I do not sleep, I cannot become as one, whole. I am so weary of this . . . a purpose . . . a purpose . . . (*As though she would throw herself into some austere penance,* NELLIE*'s forehead seems somehow about to be pierced.*)

CURTAIN

---

7. My destiny is my desire
Which I obey as if foredoomed:
Innocent martyr, eager prey
Whose fervor hones his agony . . .

PART IV

THE 1960S AND UNDERGROUND THEATER

As we saw in part III, *shingeki* emerged from the ashes of defeat in 1945 with a renewed sense of mission. It soon achieved unprecedented legitimacy with the establishment of major companies (Literary Theater [Bungakuza], Actors' Theater [Haiyūza], and People's Theater [Gekidan mingei]) and a production system (Rōen) that ensured stable ticket sales for audiences across the nation. But then political events began to overtake the influence that Japan's prewar generation of theater artists had achieved. Now, in the postwar era, *shingeki*—which had defined itself as a voice of resistance to traditional theatrical practices and the status quo—became an orthodoxy closely aligned with the Japan Communist Party (JCP) and a 1930s Russian-style socialist realism. But after Joseph Stalin's death in 1953, revelations of the gulags began to undermine its leftist loyalties. Abe Kōbō, for one, was expelled from the JCP when he criticized the Soviet Union's invasion of Hungary in 1956.

As the Japanese emerged from the deprivations of the immediate postwar years, the 1960s marked a watershed, not only in politics and society, but also in culture. The country experienced unprecedented prosperity and economic power that lasted until the 1990s. Although the new generation, which came of age in the 1960s, enjoyed a degree of freedom their parents never had, they also had to confront the legacy of Japan's imperialist aggression in Asia. Especially in the context of its relationship with the United States, as the war in Vietnam grew more intense, this relationship became even more contentious. The major figures in 1960s Japanese theater—people like Terayama Shūji, Shimizu Kunio, and Kara Jūrō—were born in the late 1930s and early 1940s.

Some—like Abe Kōbō, Betsuyaku Minoru, Ōta Shōgo, and Saitō Ren—were born in Japan's former colonies on the Asian mainland. All had vivid memories of the devastation and defeat wrought by the war, and like Germany's postwar generation, there was a sense that the country had still not come to terms with this experience.

The decade of the 1960s was bookended by two dramatic events that symbolized the political tensions that postwar democracy and economic reconstruction had left unresolved in Japan: popular resistance to the renewal of the United States–Japan Mutual Security Treaty in 1960 and the shocking suicide of the writer Mishima Yukio in 1970. On both the left and the right, playwrights like Abe and Mishima were distancing themselves from *shingeki*'s political and artistic orthodoxy. The publication in 1960 of Mishima's short story "Patriotism" (Yūkoku) signaled the emergence of an increasingly rightist message in his writing throughout this decade. In 1963, Mishima broke with the Literary Theater, for which he had written several plays, over ideological differences. Likewise, Abe found *shingeki* a poor vessel for his absurdist vision, and as both a playwright and a director, he attempted to create a more radical and experimental theater. Resistance to the treaty's renewal in 1960 galvanized opposition across political and generational lines, but when the treaty was forcibly renewed by the Kishi government, despite massive demonstrations (330,000 turned out in front of the national Diet on June 18, 1960), this temporary alliance crumbled. Japanese culture finally realized that the old leftist politics had failed to effect the necessary changes.

Avant-garde theater was a showcase for the Japanese counterculture of the 1960s. The decade was distinguished by a search for new ideas and forms to express them, along with a considerable crossover in the arts. Theater practitioners teamed up with graphic designers like Yokoo Tadanori, photographers like Hosoe Eikō, and critics like Shibusawa Tatsuhiko to create a distinctive look that was cocky and erotic, a syncretistic and often a tongue-in-cheek montage of references to recent Japanese history and cultural shibboleths. Some of these people were not only playwrights but actors, photographers, and screen and stage directors, too. Moreover, contemporary culture, like politics, could be found in public—in the streets, parks, and precincts of shrines or temples—and not only indoors.

The avant-garde theater that emerged in 1960s Japan has been called alternatively *angura* (underground), the "little theater movement," or simply "post-*shingeki* theater." The following chronology shows how this movement evolved in tandem with other developments, culminating in the late 1960s in a veritable cultural revolution:

1960 The United States–Japan Mutual Security Treaty is renewed. The first Japanese version of Samuel Beckett's *Waiting for Godot* and plays by Terayama Shūji are produced, including Terayama's radio play *Adult Hunting* and *Blood Sleeps Standing Up*, as well as a stage play directed by Asari Keita, who later, with the Four Seasons Theater (Gekidan shiki), directed Japanese productions of such Broadway plays as *Cats* and *The Lion King*.

1961	Hijikata Tatsumi coins the term *ankoku butō* (the dance of utter darkness) to describe his style of choreography. (In 1959, he directed himself and Ohno Kazuo in the sensational *Forbidden Colors*, based on Mishima Yukio's homoerotic novel of the same name.)
1962	Suzuki Tadashi and Betsuyaku Minoru first produce Betsuyaku's *The Elephant* at the Free Stage (in 1966, the name is changed to Waseda Little Theater).
1963	Kara Jūrō's Situation Theater (Jōkyō gekijō) debuts with Jean-Paul Sartre's *The Respectful Prostitute*. The Free Stage produces Sartre's *The Flies*.
1964	The "bullet train" (*shinkansen*) opens between Tokyo and Osaka, and the 1964 Summer Olympics are held in Tokyo. During this decade, Tokyo becomes the largest city in the world, with more than 10 million people.
1966	Satoh Makoto, Kushida Kazuyoshi, Yoshida Hideko, and Saitō Ren found the Freedom Theater (Jiyū gekijō), a precursor to the Theater Center 68/71 and the Black Tent Theater (Kuro tento). The Freedom Theater's first production is a pair of plays by Satoh—*Ismene* and *The Subway*—directed by Kanze Hideo.
1967	Terayama Shūji's Tenjō sajiki (an independent Japanese theater troupe) debuts with *The Hunchback of Aomori*. Kara Jūrō's Situation Theater begins performing in its trademark red tent at various locations, like the Hanazono Shrine in Shinjuku (Tokyo).
1968	Students demonstrate on more than a hundred Japanese college campuses. Hijikata Tatsumi performs *Hijikata and the Japanese: Revolt of the Flesh*. Ōta Shōgo establishes the Theater of Transformation (Tenkei gekijō).
1969	Ninagawa Yukio and Shimizu Kunio establish the Modern Man's Theater (Gendaijin gekijō). Betsuyaku leaves the Waseda Little Theater to become an independent playwright. Tenjō sajiki makes its first overseas tour. Kara, Terayama, and members of their companies are arrested after a fight.

A SYNTHESIS OF THE WESTERN AVANT-GARDE AND JAPANESE TRADITIONS

Just as *shingeki* had been a reaction against traditional Japanese theater, the theater of the 1960s rejected the European-inspired naturalistic theater that *shingeki* emulated. Whereas *shingeki* stood for reason, realism, and "universal" (typically Western) values, *angura* was an experimental and anarchic attempt to revive certain discredited traditions and discover what was uniquely "Japanese." Even so, Japanese artists and intellectuals of this generation did not turn their back on European trends. Western, especially French, intellectual movements such as Dada, surrealism, and existentialism had an immediate (yet not uncritical) impact. The works of Walter Benjamin, Georges Bataille, Herbert Marcuse, and Michel Foucault were translated into Japanese earlier than in most English-speaking countries, and their ideas were hotly debated. Hijikata Tatsumi and Shibusawa

Tatsuhiko frequently cited the works of Comte de Lautréamont and the Marquis de Sade as inspirations for their work. Any revival of Japanese traditions initially may have seemed like a betrayal of *shingeki* ideals and a capitulation to what David Goodman calls "the murky mythologies of militarist ultranationalism" of prewar Japan.[1] Indeed, this seems to have been the culmination of Mishima's reaffirmation of the imperial mystique as a counterdiscourse to the materialist consumerism of postwar Japanese democracy. But increasingly, Japanese intellectuals and artists of the 1960s sought a synthesis of the Western avant-garde and new left ideology in a critical reappraisal of traditional beliefs, folkways, and popular culture, linked to a quest for identity in a world in which conventional ideals, both native and foreign, had lost their credibility. To some degree, Western modernist ideas of the primitive (such as the contemporary Japanese interest in the work of anthropologists like Claude Lévi-Strauss and Marcel Mauss) were used for a new nativism that resonated with the very different kind of ethnology of Yanagita Kunio and Orikuchi Shinobu. A rediscovery, even an "invention" of tradition, as well as a certain reverse Orientalism, characterized this revival.[2] The critic Tsuno Kaitarō wrote that "our hope is that by harnessing the energy of the Japanese popular imagination we can at once transcend the enervating clichés of modern drama and revolutionize what it means to be Japanese."[3]

The year 1960 marked the first production in Japan of Samuel Beckett's *Waiting for Godot*. The realism and rationalism that had dominated modern theater in both Japan and the West in the first half of the twentieth century no longer seemed able to explain or give artistic form to the shattering events the world had experienced in the 1930s and 1940s. The absurdist theater provided for playwrights like Abe Kōbō and Betsuyaku Minoru an aesthetic frame to address horrors like Hiroshima or the atrocities of the Japanese imperial army.

THE NEW PHYSICALITY

Ever since Osanai Kaoru's rejection of kabuki in the 1920s, modern theater in Japan had divorced itself from traditional Japanese performance, but increasingly in the 1960s, certain artists sought inspiration in such premodern theaters as nō and kabuki. The major contribution of the traditional theater to avant-garde performances in the 1960s was a foregrounding of the actor's body as an essential part of the theatrical experience. Once again, the pendulum swung, away from a reverence for the text toward a stress on live performance. This tendency mirrored, and to some extent even anticipated, the rise of

1. David G. Goodman, introduction to *The Return of the Gods: Japanese Drama and Culture of the 1960s*, ed. David G. Goodman, photo reprint ed. (Ithaca, N.Y.: East Asia Program, Cornell University Press, 2003), 9.
2. See, for example, Uchino Tadashi, *Crucible Bodies: Postwar Japanese Performance from Brecht to the New Millennium* (Salt Lake City: Seagull Books, 2009), 85.
3. Quoted in Goodman, introduction to *Return of the Gods*, 16.

BETSUYAKU MINORU

In those days, reconciling literature and theater was an issue for me, and one of the theater magazines like *Shingeki* had a survey asking people, "Do you consider yourself a writer of dramas, or scripts?" That sort of thing. If you circled "drama," then you wrote literature; if you circled "script," then you considered the text as no more than a blueprint for performance. I circled "script," but the fact was that such a matter was taken very seriously then. All playwrights were extremely aware of it, making comments like "this is very literary" or "this part is very direct theatrically." It was a time then when we could really think afresh about such things.

I'm not sure to what extent we have gone beyond such debates now, but then we all felt compelled to create drama that was theatrically immediate. This, of course, meant our getting rid of theater's narrative qualities. So rather than create extremely fictional, illusionist conditions, it was a time when we put immense effort into creating a connection with the audience, a sense of novelty, having actors pop out from among the spectators, and so on. This made no great difference in the end: popping out from the audience failed to make a real connection between the actors and the audience. I just went along with this trend, scarcely aware of it at the time. My tack was to get on board with what had come before in the traditional theater, ride it out, and see where it took me. But even so, when overly literary elements crept into my work, I unconsciously made notes of them.

FROM BETSUYAKU MINORU, CONVERSATION WITH SAKATE YŌJI, "SEKAI TO KŌSHIN SURU" (TO COMMUNICATE WITH THE WORLD), *KOKUBUNGAKU: KAISHAKU TO KYŌZAI NO KENKYŪ* 52, NO. 8 (2007): 9-10.

performance studies in the West by scholars like Richard Schechner. The restitution of physicality as a cardinal feature of the theatrical experience is one of the greatest legacies of modern performance, and in many respects the Japanese avant-garde was a global trendsetter. A disenchantment with old ideologies, both foreign and native, made many in the Japanese theater at this time turn to the body as the one site that seemed both pure and immediate for the exploration of identity. Even playwrights who were not also performers, like Betsuyaku, felt it essential to write scripts that infused a sense of immediacy and raw theatricality into the performance of their work.

Front and center to the new theatrical style was a carnality that had not existed in Japanese art theater since kabuki. Initially, many of the new theater companies were amateurish, seeking novelty for the sake of experimentation, but gradually an interest in

KARA JŪRŌ

Where can we find a way of acting [*gei*] we can revere? I'd go for a restrained style, like the boulevardier who, when told, "You're on!" goes from telling a dirty joke backstage straight into his role without missing a beat. One can't become the flesh and blood of other beings just by getting a glimpse into what they are. All you can express that way is a pale imitation of yourself. Acting that flourishes by feeding off the blood of others can be no better than academic. The art we want to offer the world can be bought only with our own blood shed in real life. Thus, acting will always remain something vulgar. That's reality for you. So radical actor training doesn't create some kind of monopolistic system with dynasties of actors [like kabuki], nor is it like the Stanislavsky method, in which amateurs learn how to be "artistes," as if they were being spewed out on a conveyor belt. By acting alone, a radical actor may be vulgar in real life but becomes ultimately a legendary figure. As vulgarity overcomes reverence, the privileged body of the actor must overcome the ordinary body. In that moment, artistic expression makes the raid, the invasion on the city, something real. So long as an actor cannot see or grasp this truth, the theatrical spirit will remain irreconcilably stymied by a dualism that has always existed between politics and art.

FROM KARA JŪRŌ, *TOKKENTEKI NIKUTAIRON (THEORY OF THE PRIVILEGED BODY)* (1970; REPR., TOKYO: HAKUSUISHA, 1997), 17–18.

physical training as an essential part of an actor's education grew. Undoubtedly, modern Japanese theater's greatest legacy to the world is *butō*, the dance form created by artists like Hijikata Tatsumi and Ohno Kazuo in the late 1950s and early 1960s. Both artists had studied modern Western dance, particularly the expressionist German *Neue Tanz*, but increasingly they sought a form more congenial to the Japanese physique. Hijikata later termed his dance style "Tōhoku kabuki," after his native region; he felt that *butō* epitomized the physique, postures, gestures, and habitual actions of the Japanese, people shaped by an agrarian life spent cultivating rice. Many artists fell under Hijikata's spell in the 1960s. One of Kara Jūrō's lead actors, Maro Akaji, trained with him and in 1972 founded the still active dance troupe, Great Camel Battleship (Dai rakudakan). Like Hijikata, Kara wanted to return theater to the carnivalesque, risqué roots of early kabuki, in which the actor was an outcast gypsy, a "riverbed beggar" (*kawaramono*) thumbing his nose at the status quo. If *shingeki* was governed by reason and a preoccupation with psychological portrayal of character, *angura* regarded the body as a site to express whatever language had repressed: the unconscious, the erotic, the instinctive, the immediate, the violent, the natural.

Implicit in Kara's notion of the "privileged body" was a duality in which the actor was both social pariah and a medium through which the audience's dreams and desires could be manifested. That is, the performer became a kind of shaman whose metamorphoses and epiphanies created on stage, for all to see, something mythic, ambivalently divine, or demonic, an ambiguous site for nostalgia, longing, transcendence, and even derision.

A restoration of the erotic, carnivalesque spirit of early kabuki was one of the chief achievements of 1960s theater, especially in the work of such artists as Hijikata and Kara. At the same time, certain traditional theater artists teamed up with *angura* companies to create new works. Kanze Hisao and his brother Hideo collaborated with avant-garde directors like Suzuki Tadashi and Satoh Makoto; their ideas and techniques were instrumental in the injection of a new physicality, as well as discipline, into contemporary performance.

Nō's influence on the Japanese avant-garde has been profound. Director Suzuki Tadashi became interested in the possibilities of the classical theater in 1972 after he saw

SUZUKI TADASHI

Because the theater, in either Europe or Japan, has kept up with the times and has come to use non-animal energy in every facet of its activities, one of the resulting evils is that the faculties of the human body and physical sensibility have been overspecialized to the point of separation. Just as civilization has specialized the job of the eyes and created the microscope, modernization has "dismembered" our physical faculties from our essential selves.

What I am striving to do is restore the wholeness of the human body in the theatrical context, not simply by going back to such traditional theatrical forms as nō and kabuki, but by employing their unique virtues, to create something transcending current practice in the modern theater.

We need to bring together the physical functions once "dismembered," to regain the perceptive and expressive abilities and powers of the human body. In doing so, we can maintain culture within civilization.

In my method of training actors, I place special emphasis on the feet, because I believe that consciousness of the body's communication with the ground leads to a great awareness of all the physical junctions of the body.

FROM TADASHI SUZUKI, "CULTURE IS THE BODY!" TRANS. KAZUKO MATSUOKA, *PERFORMING ARTS JOURNAL* 8, NO. 2 (1984): 28–34.

Kanze Hisao perform on a stage in Paris. His productions starring Kanze Hisao and Shiraishi Kayoko in *The Trojan Women* (1974) and *The Bacchae* (1979) defined the Suzuki style: a compelling synthesis of the traditional theater's physical presence with *angura*'s experimentalism. During the 1970s, Suzuki developed what has become his trademark style of intense lower-body and voice training, aimed at restoring to performance the "animal energy" he felt that humanity had lost through the overwhelming technologization of modern life.

In his search for a more natural environment in which to create and perform his theater, in 1976 Suzuki moved the Waseda Little Theater to Toga, a mountain village in Toyama Prefecture, where he has hosted an international theater festival every August since 1982. He changed his company's name to SCOT (Suzuki Company of Toga) in 1985. Next to *butō*, the "Suzuki method" of actor's training has become modern Japanese theater's most successful export. Actors from around the world have trained with Suzuki and the American director Ann Bogart in workshops for Suzuki exercises.

Like Suzuki, the playwright and director Ōta Shōgo found in nō's deliberate pace and stylized gestures an inspiration for his own intense performance style. Although Ōta founded his Theater of Transformation in 1968, his first work to garner major critical attention was *The Tale of Komachi Told by the Wind* (*Komachi fūden*, 1976), a work inspired by a cycle of nō plays about the Heian poet and beauty Ono no Komachi and performed on a traditional nō stage. In contrast to the speed, noise, and garrulousness of modern life, Ōta wished to restore the sense of silence, tranquillity, and deliberation to theater that he had discovered in nō. Ōta was perhaps the most radical of the playwrights whose works are presented in this anthology. To a degree greater than that of any of his contemporaries—except perhaps for the dancers of *butō*, in paring down the elements of performance—he eschewed spoken dialogue altogether in a series of works, here represented by *The Earth Station* (1985).

ALTERNATIVE PERFORMANCE SPACES

The fundamental elements of the theatrical experience—the text, the identity of the actor, the use of performance space, and the relationship between actors and audience—all came under intense scrutiny during the 1960s. To some degree, the matter of where to perform was a practical and economic consideration: few could afford to rent anything more than the "little theaters" (often no more than studios or rooms over cafés and restaurants) that gave one name to this movement, and many were alienated from the *shingeki* system, which would have given them access to larger theaters. But it soon became evident that this lack of conventional performance space provided opportunities foreclosed to a theater of realism, with its proscenium arch and "fourth wall," which separated audiences from the actions and actors on stage. For Kara and Satoh, performance in a tent provided a womb-like intimacy between actor and audience that emulated the

TERAYAMA SHŪJI

Theatres have become entertainment-industry spaces rather than dramatic spaces, and the history of theatre has degenerated from the history of drama into the history of the entertainment industry. I have come to realize that to make drama independent of "theatre" facilities, we must discard the idea of "theatres" as aspects of inner reality. Our theme as theatre people ought to be to organize the power of the imagination in order to transform all places into theatres. The most important thing in dragging "drama" outside "theatre buildings" is removing the borderline between fiction and reality. Drama must be at the same level as history, where fiction and reality are often ambiguous. . . . Revolutions do not have drama. This is because as long as the revolution itself remains a social crisis, it is a dramatization of history.

FROM TERAYAMA SHŪJI, "THE LABYRINTH AND THE DEAD SEA: MY THEATER," IN *UNSPEAKABLE ACTS: THE AVANT-GARDE THEATRE OF TERAYAMA SHŪJI AND POSTWAR JAPAN*, BY CAROL FISHER SORGENFREI (HONOLULU: UNIVERSITY OF HAWAI'I PRESS, 2005), 287–88.

experience of the circus sideshow or early kabuki. At the same time, it afforded a mobility and freedom for theater artists, enabling them to bring their performances to people in various locales. Both Kara and Satoh took their work on tour throughout Japan and, later, Asia, and Suzuki's move to Toyama to create a more natural environment for the theater was partly inspired by Jerzy Grotowski's Poor Theater.

Along with Bertolt Brecht, Antonin Artaud was undoubtedly the most influential radical theorist for Japanese theater during this time. His greatest proponent was Terayama Shūji, a man of protean talents who first won critical acclaim as a poet of classical *tanka* while he was still in high school. Like Hijikata, Terayama was a native of Aomori Prefecture in the far north of Japan, and his sensibilities were forged by the poverty and unique folkways of this region. In the early 1960s, Terayama wrote plays for radio and the stage, increasingly experimenting with other media such as photography and film. His Tenjō sajiki troupe, a reference to the Japanese title of Marcel Carné's classic film *Les enfants du paradis* (*Children of the Peanut Gallery*, 1945), was a company founded in 1967 devoted to the practical applications of Artaud's Theater of Cruelty. With his Tenjō sajiki troupe, he could test the relationship between actor and audience and the limits of theatrical experience. Along with Ōta and other playwrights, Terayama experimented with language, its distortion, and even its eradication in performance. His later works (often written in collaboration with Kishida Rio) became less text based and more attempts to design novel and disturbing events, like "happenings," intended to break down the boundaries between reality and fiction, actor and observer, while involving the audience in the performance. In the creation of his so-called city theater, Terayama, like Kara, used public spaces like parks and city streets to demonstrate his theory that theater, art, and culture at large should "infect" citizens, passing from one person to the next. Even though Terayama never articulated a coherent political stance (and in this respect, he resembled Kara as well), he believed that theater was a place to stage a revolution that was simultaneously cognitive, artistic, and social.

POST-*SHINGEKI* DRAMATURGY

In their exploration of topics such as war, sexuality, violence, and the irrational, the plays of this period are challenging, morally, intellectually, and artistically. Betsuyaku noted how, with its emphasis on the performative, the new dramaturgy also pointed toward a rejection of conventional narrative. *Angura* drama tends to be nonlinear and illogical, mixing dream and reality. Metamorphosis and multiple role-playing are dominant tropes in such plays. Their shifting and complex temporal and spatial structure frequently draws on myth and archetypes to present multifaceted and unstable characters who sometimes appear as godlike heroes and antiheroes who transcend their times. The plays are richly allusive, like collages, drawing inspiration from history or contemporary news, culture both high and low, and sources both foreign and homegrown. There is a preoccupation with memory (both public and personal) and its loss, as well as a desire for a transcendent eschatology to make sense of the world, yet at the same time a deep ambivalence toward narratives of spiritual redemption or political revolution.

THE LEGACY OF THE 1960S

Many critics have noted that the political and cultural revolution promised in the 1960s was never realized. The United States–Japan Security Treaty was renewed again in 1970, with scarcely an echo of the protest that had accompanied it a decade before. To a great extent, the energy and fervor of post-*shingeki* theater faded as the Japanese public in the 1970s and beyond became increasingly complacent, disengaged from political action. Few new playwrights or directors were able to distinguish themselves artistically or ideologically from the generation of the 1960s. Tsuka Kōhei, a *zainichi* (Japanese-born) Korean, was one of the few playwrights of significance to emerge from the 1970s.

Nonetheless, the radical experiments of the 1960s had an impact on nearly every kind of theater produced in Japan in the past fifty years. It is safe now to say that the influence of *angura* on modern Japanese theater has been as great as, if not greater than, that of *shingeki*. Much of the best work from this generation was created in the 1970s and 1980s, and most of these artists are still active. To date, having written more than a hundred dramas and sketches for numerous theater companies—including *shingeki* troupes like that of the Literary Theater—in addition to fiction and essays, Betsuyaku Minoru is perhaps Japan's most prolific and highly respected playwright. Shimizu Kunio continued to write and direct for both the stage and radio into the new millennium. Kara Jūrō still writes and performs in his plays, touring in his red tent. Satoh Makoto now mostly directs the work of others and has particularly distinguished himself as a major interpreter of opera. Suzuki Tadashi and Ninagawa Yukio are world famous, frequently touring and directing abroad.

A few of these figures have passed on but still exert a profound effect on a younger generation of artists: Terayama Shūji died in 1983, but many artists, like Ryūzanji Show (his romanization of his name) and J. A. Seazer carry on his tradition, and Terayama's plays are frequently revived; Ōta Shōgo succumbed to cancer in 2007; Hijikata Tatsumi died in 1986, as did Kazuo Ohno in 2010, but former students like Maro Akaji and Tanaka Min, and Amagatu Ushio's Paris-based group Sankai juku, have ensured that *butō* would become a global phenomenon.

Last, but not least, we should mention the work of Inoue Hisashi, another prolific playwright and novelist who became established in the 1960s. Unlike the others mentioned here, Inoue firmly planted himself in the mainstream of Japanese theater, creating for large audiences accessible entertainments that still express the leftist sentiments and Brechtian theatrics that were features of postwar *shingeki* in its heyday. Like Satoh and Saitō Ren, Inoue distinguished himself in the creation of musical theater. With a strong narrative thread and well-rounded characters like those in much of *shingeki* drama, Inoue's *Living with Father*, included in part IV, nonetheless demonstrates certain thematic and stylistic concerns in common with much avant-garde theater of this time: an interest in the psychological trauma of war and a blurring of the boundaries between the living and the dead.

M. CODY POULTON

Betsuyaku Minoru, *The Little Match Girl*, directed by Suzuki Tadashi,
Waseda shōgekijō, November 1966.

THE LITTLE MATCH GIRL

BETSUYAKU MINORU
TRANSLATED BY ROBERT N. LAWSON

One of Japan's greatest postwar playwrights, Betsuyaku Minoru was born in 1937 in Manchuria. During the war, his father died and Betsuyaku experienced severe deprivation. In 1946, he was repatriated with his mother and siblings to Japan. He entered Waseda University in 1958 to study journalism but became increasingly involved with the university's theater movement, which, since Tsubouchi Shōyō's time, has been a center for theater studies in Japan. In 1961, together with Suzuki Tadashi, Betsuyaku established the Free Stage (Jiyū butai), a precursor to the Waseda Little Theater. At the same time, he got caught up in the political demonstrations against the renewal of the United States–Japan Security Treaty. Although he dropped out of university to engage in leftist political action, he soon became disenchanted with the Marxist rhetoric. Like Abe Kōbō's increasingly absurdist plays, Betsuyaku's first major work, *The Elephant* (*Zō*, 1962), a play in the style of Samuel Beckett and Eugène Ionesco, marked a turning point in postwar Japanese drama away from conventional realist storytelling methods. Both the Free Stage and the Waseda Little Theater produced many of Betsuyaku's best plays in the 1960s, including the one featured here, *The Little Match Girl* (*Matchi-uri no shōjo*, 1966). Since 1969, when he left the Waseda Little Theater, Betsuyaku has worked mainly as a freelance dramatist, writing plays for other companies, including major *shingeki* troupes like those from the Literary Theater (Bungakuza) and the Theater Circle (Gekidan en). His drama is distinctive for its spare stage, frequently occupied by only a single telephone pole, like Beckett's bare tree in *Waiting for Godot*, and nameless characters identified only by their gender or social function: Man, Woman,

Doctor, and so on. His language—sparse, prosaic, and colloquial, sometimes dark, often funny—masks the absurdity of his characters' thoughts and actions.

The Little Match Girl, which won the Kishida Kunio Award, is Betsuyaku's most representative play. Drawing on the Hans Christian Andersen fairy tale (Betsuyaku frequently bases works on fairy tales and even writes literature for children), the playwright places a middle-aged couple in the company of a young woman who claims to be their daughter, dredging up memories of hard times and a tragic loss in the immediate postwar years. As in so much of his work, Betsuyaku's feckless protagonists are at the mercy of their uncertain memories and socioeconomic forces over which they have no control.

Characters

WOMAN
HER YOUNGER BROTHER
MIDDLE-AGED MAN
HIS WIFE

At center stage, there is an old-fashioned table with three chairs, a little to stage left a small serving table with one chair. This may be called an old-fashioned play, so it should open on an old-fashioned, slightly melancholy note. The theater gradually goes dark, without its being noticed. From out of nowhere, a song from long ago, on a scratchy record, faintly comes to be heard. Then, unexpectedly as right in the next seat, a WOMAN'S VOICE, *hoarse and low, can be heard whispering.*

WOMAN'S VOICE: It was the last night of the year, New Year's Eve, and it was very cold. It had already become dark, and snow was falling. A poor little girl was trudging wearily along the dark, deserted street. She had no hat, nor even any shoes. Until a little while before she had been wearing her dead mother's wooden shoes, but they were too big for her, and, trying to dodge two carriages that came rushing by, she had lost both of them. Her little feet were purple and swollen as she put one in front of the other on the stiffly frozen snow. Her apron pocket was filled with matches, and she was holding one bunch in her hand. She had been trying to sell them, but no one had bought a single match from her that whole day. No one had given her so much as a single penny.

(*From stage right, a* MIDDLE-AGED MAN *and his* WIFE *appear, carrying evening tea things. They begin to place them on the table, meticulously. In this household the way of doing such things is governed by strict rule, it seems. The* WIFE *sometimes makes a mistake, but her husband then carefully corrects it. Various things—taken from a tray, from the folds of their kimonos, from their pockets—are carefully positioned. A teapot, cups, spoons, a sugar bowl, a milk glass, kitchen jars of jam, butter cookies, various spices, nuts, shriveled small fruits, miniature plants and animal figurines, and other small things are all arranged closely together. As this is going on, the two mumble to each other.*)

MAN: Setting a table is an art, you know. If you arrange everything just right, even a dried lemon will show to advantage.

WIFE: The people across the street place the powdered spinach next to the deodorizer.

MAN: Hum, what kind of pretentiousness is that?

WIFE: Right . . . just what I said to them. "Isn't that pretentious?" But listen to what they answered. "In this house we have our own way of doing things."

MAN: Their own way, huh? Well, fine. But, even so, there should be some principle . . . such procedures should be according to rule.

WIFE: That's right. Just what I told them. There should be some principle. . . .

MAN: Hey, what's that?

WIFE: Garlic.

MAN: Garlic is for morning. I never heard of garlic for evening tea.

WIFE: But we saw the sunset a little while ago. Don't you always say, "Garlic for sunset"?

MAN: Garlic for sunrise. Onion for sunset.

WIFE: Was that it? Well, then, onions.

MAN: But let's not bother with them.

WIFE: Why?

MAN: They smell.

WIFE: Of course they smell. But is there anything that doesn't? You can't name a thing that doesn't have some drawback. Ginseng may not smell, but it has worms.

MAN: Yes, but those worms are good for neuralgia, you know.

WIFE: I like to eat onions. Then I don't feel the cold. One works for one night. Two for two nights. So three will work for three nights.

MAN: Roasted crickets are good if you are sensitive to cold. I keep telling you that. One cricket for one night.

WIFE: But there aren't any crickets now. What season do you think this is? There's snow outside.

MAN: All right, then, do this. First, heat some sesame oil. Then, after letting it cool, lick salt as you drink it. Lick and drink. Lick and drink. Three times. It works immediately.

WIFE: Isn't that what you do when you haven't had a bowel movement?

MAN: No, then it's soybean oil. In that case you lick and drink four times. You don't remember anything at all, do you?

WIFE: Say . . . over there . . . isn't that cheese?

MAN: Hmm, it seems to be. It wasn't there last night. Well . . . where should we put it? In the old days, we used to put the cheese next to the dried dates, but. . . .

WIFE (*Picking it up*): I wonder when we got this. It's pretty stale, isn't it?

MAN: Yes, getting hard. Didn't there used to be something called hard cheese? Cheese that had become hard. . . . (*Thinking.*)

WIFE: Look, teeth marks. You took a bite and then left it, didn't you?

MAN: Ridiculous! Let me see. I'd never do an ill-mannered thing like that. Those are your teeth marks.

WIFE: My teeth aren't that sharp.

MAN: I don't know about that . . . but it could have been the cat.

WIFE: Well . . . maybe. In the old days we had a cat. Could it have been Pesu?

MAN: Pesu was the dog. Kuro was the parrot, Tobi was the goat, and the horse was Taro, so the cat . . . could it have been Pesu after all?

WIFE: The cat was Pesu. Kuro was the parrot, Tobi the goat, the horse was Taro, the dog . . . the dog . . . I wonder if the dog was Pesu. . . .

(*A* WOMAN *appears stage left.*)

WOMAN (*Quietly*): Good evening.

MAN: Huh?

WOMAN: Good evening.

WIFE: Good evening.

WOMAN: Are you having evening tea?

MAN: Well, after a fashion. . . .

WIFE: We never miss having tea in this house, from long ago.

WOMAN: It was that way in my family, too, long ago.

MAN: Ah, well, since you have taken the trouble to come, won't you please join us?

WOMAN: Yes, thank you.

WIFE: Please do. Not just for evening tea, but any time you have tea it's nice to have company. In the old days we frequently entertained.

MAN: Please sit down.

(*The three of them sit down. The* MAN *pours them tea.*)

MAN: Now then, before tea in your home, I mean before evening tea, do you say a prayer?

WOMAN: Ah . . . I don't really remember.

MAN: Well then, let's skip that. Actually, saying a prayer before evening tea is not proper. You might even say it is a breach of etiquette. Do you know why?

WOMAN: No.

MAN: Because it's not to God's liking. It says so in the Bible. (*To his* WIFE.) Do you remember?

WIFE: No.

MAN: She forgets everything. Because of her age. Sugar? How many?

WOMAN: Yes . . . well, if it's all right, I'll serve myself.

MAN: Of course. Please do. That's the best way. People should be completely free.

WIFE: In this house we always have guests who visit at night join us for evening tea. Now, after so many years, you are the victim.

MAN: How many years has it been? But you are late in coming . . . which way did you come from?

WOMAN: I came from City Hall.

WIFE: Ah, City Hall! That gloomy building? Don't you agree that it's gloomy?

WOMAN: Yes, it's gloomy.

WIFE: Gloomy!

MAN: Would you like a sweet?

WOMAN: Thank you.

MAN: We have rich things, too, if you'd prefer. By the way, speaking of City Hall, how is that fellow?

WIFE: What fellow?

MAN: That guy who sits there on the second floor and spits out the window.

WIFE: Oh, he died. Quite a while ago.

MAN: Is he finally dead? He was a problem for everybody. As many as thirteen times a day. People avoided passing that place.

WIFE: Well, no one avoids passing there these days. His son is sitting there now, and that young man is very courteous. But did you come directly from City Hall to our house?

WOMAN: Yes.

MAN: Directly here? That is to say, intending to come to our house?

WOMAN: That's right, directly here.

WIFE: Is that so? (*A little perplexed.*) Well then . . . ah . . . how nice of you to come.

MAN: Yes. You are certainly welcome. We've had very few visitors lately.

WIFE: But what did they say about us at City Hall?

WOMAN: Nothing in particular.

MAN: That we are good citizens?

WOMAN: Yes.

WIFE: Exemplary?

WOMAN: Yes.

MAN: And harmless?

WOMAN: Yes.

WIFE: Well, that's certainly true. We are the best, most exemplary, citizens.

MAN: Last year the mayor went out on the balcony and gave a speech. Then, at the end, he said, "In our city we are pleased to have 362 citizens who are not only good, and exemplary, but also harmless." Those last two are us . . . really.

WIFE: The city tax isn't much, but we pay it right on time. And we don't put out much trash. And we don't drink much water.

MAN: Our ideas are moderate, too. We are both, relatively speaking, Progressive Conservatives. Those Reform Party people are so vulgar. Neither of us can tolerate that. One of those guys, you know, will yawn without putting his hand to his mouth. Really! In the old days that would have been unthinkable.

WOMAN (*With feeling*): It is really . . . nice and warm here.

WIFE: Yes, isn't it? And refined, too. We aren't rich, but we try not to be unnecessarily frugal.

MAN: Now, to put it briefly, you've been sent here from City Hall.

WOMAN: No, I wouldn't say that exactly.

WIFE: Perhaps we should say, "dispatched."

WOMAN: No, that's not it. I heard about this place at City Hall. Something that made me want to visit you . . . so I came.

MAN: I see. I understand. You say that you heard something about us at City Hall. That made you want to visit us. And so, here you are— visiting us. That's certainly logical.

WIFE (*In admiration*): That makes sense. In short, since you wanted to visit us, you visited us. That's different from saying that you didn't want to visit us but visited us anyway.

MAN: It's a goodwill visit, isn't it?

WOMAN: I just had to meet you.

WIFE: My, what a sweet thing to say. Another cup of tea? (*Offering tea.*)

WOMAN: Thank you.

MAN: In that case, whatever questions you have, or whatever requests, please just tell us. It is our established policy never to disappoint anyone who has come so far. Why are we so healthy in spite of growing old? Why are we so cheerful? So full of humor? Why, though we aren't rich, are we not unnecessarily frugal? How can we be both progressive and conservative at the same time? Why are we such good citizens? Why, to sum it all up, are we us?

WIFE: Go ahead and ask your questions. He will certainly answer them well, whatever they are about, I'm sure.

WOMAN: Thank you. But for right now it's enough just to be allowed to sit here this way.

MAN: Don't you have at least one of these "questions"? There are usually three questions for every person.

WIFE: And three for me, too.

MAN: And you know the answers already anyway, right?

WOMAN: Really, I . . . just to be sitting here . . . and you have even served me a warm cup of tea. . . .

WIFE: Ah, of course. This lady is interested in the domestic environment . . . our home's unique domestic environment.

MAN: I see. I understand. This so-called family atmosphere takes some doing. Now, the first thing you can't do without for that homey feel is a cat. Second, a fireplace, or something of the kind. Things like whiskey or home-brewed saké, like detective stories or fairy tales, knitting needles and wool yarn, or torn socks and gloves, and, to top it off, some reading glasses . . . right? We used to have a cat, too, but he seems to have disappeared recently. . . .

WIFE: If you'd given us a little notice that you were coming, we could have borrowed one from the neighbor. . . .

WOMAN: Please, never mind about that. I'm happy just to be here, in a warm place, with such kind people, quietly drinking tea. It's very cold outside. It's snowing. No one is out there.

MAN: I can well believe that. It's supposed to snow tonight. Did you walk all the way?

WOMAN: Yes, all the way. . . .

WIFE: Poor thing. You must be hungry. Please help yourself to whatever you'd like.

MAN: We always like to help those less fortunate as much as we can. That's our way. . . .

WOMAN'S VOICE (*From no particular direction*): The little girl was hungry now. She was shaking from the cold as she walked. The snow came drifting down on the back of her neck, to fall among the beautiful curls of her long golden hair. But from every window the light was shining, and there was the strong and savory smell of a goose roasting. That was as it should be, the little girl was thinking. It was, after all, New Year's Eve. There was a small space between two houses. She drew her body into that corner and crouched down there, pulling her little feet under her. Even so, she could not escape the cold. . . .

WIFE (*In a small voice*): Dear, I think that this lady has something she'd like to say to us.

MAN: Is that so? Well then, please don't hesitate. For that matter . . . well . . . if you'd prefer, I could leave. I know that, as they say, women feel more comfortable talking to one another. . . . (*Beginning to stand.*)

WOMAN: No, please. Don't go. This is fine. Really. Just this, just sitting here quietly like this is fine. I'm perfectly happy this way.

WIFE: Well, if you say so. But you went to a lot of trouble to come here, and we'll feel bad if we don't do anything for you.

MAN: Right. We wouldn't want you to think we were so insensitive.

WOMAN: No, really, I wouldn't think anything like that. . . .

WIFE: Ah, well, isn't there something you'd like to eat? If there is, I'd be happy to fix it for you.

WOMAN: Thank you, but not just now.

MAN: Well, just as she says . . . that's fine. She has just arrived, dear, and probably doesn't feel like asking questions or giving orders yet. That's what it is. It's better just to leave her alone. You know what they say about excessive kindness . . . now what is it they say? . . .

WIFE: Maybe you're right. (*To the* WOMAN.) Just make yourself comfortable. We're not in any hurry.

WOMAN: Thank you.

MAN: But, please don't hesitate . . .

WOMAN: Yes . . . well. . . .

WIFE: As if it were your own home. . . .

WOMAN: Yes. (*The* MAN *starts to say something, and then stops. There is an awkward silence.*)

MAN (*Suddenly thinking of something to say*): Outside . . . was it snowing?

WOMAN (*Nods.*)

WIFE (*Eagerly pursuing the thought*): Powdered . . . snow?

WOMAN: Yes. . . . (*Nods.*)

(*Silence.*)

MAN (*Again thinking*): You're tired . . . aren't you?

WOMAN: No.

MAN (*To his* WIFE): But she must be tired. Why don't you ask her to lie down for a little while? . . .

WIFE: That's a good idea. Why not do that?

WOMAN: No, this is just fine.

MAN: But. . . .

WOMAN: Really. . . .

WIFE: Well, whatever you think . . .

(*There is another awkward silence.*)

MAN: Say, I've got an idea. Why don't you sing her a song?

WIFE: A song? I can't sing . . . not me!

MAN: "Not me?" Did you hear that? She's just being shy or too modest. I shouldn't brag about my own wife, but her singing is something to hear. Come on, sing something for her?

WIFE: I can't do that.

MAN: Of course you can. She'd like to hear it, too. Right? Wouldn't you like to hear her sing something?

WOMAN: Yes . . . but. . . .

MAN: See! Don't be so shy. Go ahead and sing. After all, she has taken the trouble to come. (*To the* WOMAN.) She's not much good at anything else . . . just singing. But she's not bad at it. She's rather good.

WIFE: I don't have a good voice any more . . . at my age.

MAN: At your age? . . . Listen to that. Just yesterday she was saying that she could still sing pretty well in spite of her age, because she has always taken care of her voice. . . .

WIFE: But I just meant . . . for in the family. . . .

MAN: In the family, outside the family, what's the difference? Go ahead and sing. Try that song . . . "The snow is. . . . (*Trying to remember.*) The snow is. . . . (*Thinking.*) The snow is getting deeper . . . no keeps getting deeper. . . ."

WOMAN (*Quietly*): I was selling matches . . .

WIFE: What?

WOMAN: I was selling matches.

WIFE: My, did you hear that, dear?

MAN: What's that?

WIFE: She's selling matches.

MAN: Matches? Ah, I see! Yes . . . I understand . . . finally. About buying matches. Well, it would have been better to have said so sooner, but . . . you went to City Hall to examine the city directory to find the household most in need of matches . . . and that was us. That's what it is! Fine. I can understand that. And we'll buy them. Buy them all. I don't know if you've got a truckload . . . maybe two . . . but we'll buy them all. Here and now. I promise.

WIFE: But we just bought matches. Far too many. Of course, since she took the trouble to come, we should buy some. Yes, let's buy some. But we can't use many.

WOMAN: No, that's not it. I was selling matches a long time ago.

MAN: Ah, a long time ago. . . .

WIFE: Then what are you selling now? If it's something useful around the house, we'll buy some. You've gone to so much trouble.

MAN: That's right. Even if it's a little expensive . . .

WOMAN: Nothing in particular right now . . .

MAN: Nothing? . . .

WOMAN: That's right.

WIFE (*A little disappointed*): Oh . . . well . . .

MAN: Ah . . . I see. You were telling us a story about something you remember from when you were small. . . .

WOMAN: Yes, that's it.

WIFE: About selling matches? . . .

WOMAN: Yes.

MAN: How old were you?

WOMAN: I was seven. . . .

WIFE: It was terrible, wasn't it?

MAN: And you can't help remembering. . . .

WOMAN: Well, really, until just recently, I didn't understand it.

MAN: You didn't understand? . . .

WOMAN: It was twenty years ago.

WIFE: You don't say. . . .

MAN: And you had forgotten about it?

WOMAN: I didn't understand. Until just recently, I didn't understand at all. I was married and had two children. One, a boy, is four years old. The other, a girl, is barely two. So far as the girl is concerned, everything is fine, but a four-year-old boy requires a lot of attention.

WIFE: Isn't that the truth!

MAN: A boy of four can take care of himself.

WIFE: Nonsense!

WOMAN: People say that two children are too many at my age. But I don't feel that way.

MAN: You're right. Two is normal.

WIFE: They say you haven't really done your duty till you've had three.

MAN: Well, where are those children?

WOMAN: Don't worry about that.

MAN: Ah. . . .

WIFE: Are they healthy?

WOMAN: Yes, quite healthy . . .

MAN: That's good.

WIFE: That's the important thing . . . for children to be healthy.

WOMAN: Then I read in a book. . . .

WIFE: In a book? . . . My . . .

MAN: A child-care book?

WOMAN: No . . . fiction. . . .

MAN: Ah, that's good. When a woman gets married and has children, she usually quits reading books. Especially fiction.

WIFE: What was it about?

WOMAN: Various things.

MAN: Various things, indeed. Those writers of fiction write about all kinds of things, don't they?

WOMAN: Among other things, about a match girl. At first I didn't understand it. I read it again. Then I had a strange feeling.

MAN: Strange?

WOMAN: Yes. After that I read it many times, over and over . . .

WIFE: About how many times?

WOMAN: Five . . . or more. . . .

MAN: Then? . . .

WOMAN: Then I saw it. I was amazed. It was about me.

WIFE: About you? . . .

WOMAN: Yes.

MAN: It was written about you?

WOMAN: That's right. I hadn't understood.

WIFE: About selling matches? . . .

MAN: . . . About the little match girl? . . .

WOMAN: Yes. It was about me. I was the little match girl.

WIFE: My goodness . . . that one? . . .

MAN: But. . . .

WOMAN: After that I remembered many things. Many things gradually became clear. . . .

MAN'S VOICE (*Low, in a murmur*): People were starving then. Every night was dark and gloomy. The town was built on swampland, sprawling and stinking. Here and there shops had been set up, like sores that had burst open. Small animals were killed in the shadows, and secretly eaten. People walked furtively, like forgotten criminals, and now and then, unexpectedly, something would scurry by in the darkness. That child was selling matches at the street corner. When a match was struck, she would lift her shabby skirt for display until the match went out. People made anxious by the small crimes they had committed, people who could not even commit such crimes, night after night, in their trembling fingers, would strike those matches. Directed at the infinite darkness hidden by that skirt, how many times that small light had burned, until it had burned out.... Those two thin legs held a darkness as profound as that of the depths of the sea, darker than all the darkness of that city floating on a swampland gathered together. As she stood there above that darkness, the little girl smiled aimlessly, or seemed empty and sad.

WIFE: Isn't there someone at the door?

MAN: Nonsense! In this cold? Aren't you cold?

WOMAN: No.

MAN: But then, how about that? Seeing yourself revealed in a story gives you a strange feeling, doesn't it?

WOMAN: Yes, very strange. After that I thought about it for a long time. I had suffered greatly. But there is still one thing I can't understand.

WIFE: One thing?...

MAN: What?

WOMAN: Why did I do a thing like that?

MAN: A thing like that?

WOMAN: Yes.

WIFE: Selling matches?

WOMAN: Yes.

WIFE: Well....

MAN: Wasn't it because you were poor? I don't mean to be rude, but....

WOMAN: Still, to do that kind of thing....

WIFE: You shouldn't be ashamed of that. Everyone did such things then. Those who didn't, didn't survive. Children stole things. After I had worked so hard to make hotcakes for his birthday, they stole them. It was like that then.

MAN: You should forget the things from that time. Everyone has forgotten. I've forgotten, too.

WOMAN: But I want you to think back, to recall those memories.

WIFE: Well, even if you try, there are some things you can't forget. But what good does it do to remember?

MAN: I had to do such things, too. Just as you did, I tried to sell things as a peddler. It's not that important. It's nothing to be ashamed of. Really.

WOMAN: But how could I ever have thought of doing such a thing? I was only seven years old. Could a child of seven think of that kind of thing?

WIFE: That kind of thing?...

WOMAN: That kind of... of... terrible thing...

MAN: ... what kind of?...

WOMAN: I was selling matches.

MAN: Yes, selling matches . . . you were selling matches . . .

WOMAN: . . . and while they were burning. . . .

MAN: . . . impossible. . . .

WOMAN: No, it's not.

MAN: I can't believe it. . . .

WOMAN: But that's the way it was. It was me. I was the little match girl. . . .

WIFE: Ah . . . you were the one. . . .

WOMAN: Yes, do you remember? That time? . . . That place? . . . (*A pause.*)

MAN: But, well, all kinds of things happened then.

WIFE: That's true. All kinds of things. It was very different from now. No one knew what to do. It wasn't your fault.

MAN: It's nothing to worry about. That was all over long ago. An old story. My philosophy is to forget it. Forget everything. Without exception! Everything. If you don't . . . well, anyway . . . let life go on.

WOMAN: But I can't forget it.

WIFE: Why?

WOMAN: Because I have remembered.

MAN: I see. Yes, there is such a time in life. Just be patient a while. You'll soon forget. But, let's stop talking about it. Say . . . I'll make you forget in three minutes. Do you know the story of the kind weasel?

(*The* WOMAN *does not answer.*)

MAN: How about fixing us another cup of tea, dear. . . .

WIFE: Fine, let me do that. It has gotten quite cold. (*Taking the pot, she leaves.*)

WOMAN: Are Mother's feet all right now?

MAN: Mother . . . ah, you mean my wife? No, they still aren't good, particularly when it gets cold. But I'm surprised that you know so much. Things like my wife's trouble with her feet.

WOMAN: I don't mind forgetting that story, either.

MAN: Please do. Just forget it. It happened twenty years ago.

WOMAN: But I would still like to know one thing.

MAN: What?

WOMAN: I'm sure that someone must have taught me to.

MAN: To what?

WOMAN: To do such a thing. . . .

MAN: Ah well, that's probably true. No doubt.

WOMAN: Was it you?

MAN: What?

WOMAN: Were you the one who taught me to?

MAN: Me?

WOMAN: Yes.

MAN: Me?

WOMAN: Yes.

MAN: Me? . . .

WOMAN: Yes.

MAN: . . . Why would I have?

WOMAN: Don't you remember?

MAN: What?

WOMAN: Don't you remember me?

MAN: Remember you?

WOMAN: I'm your daughter.

MAN: You? . . .

WOMAN: Yes.

MAN: Impossible.

WOMAN: There's no doubt about it. I've made inquiries. That's what they told me at City Hall, too. It's the truth.

MAN: It can't be. It's not possible. I don't have a daughter. We did have a daughter . . . but she died. She is dead.

WOMAN: I don't blame you for making me do that kind of thing. I don't bear a grudge. But I would just like to know. That's all. Why was I doing that? If someone taught me to, who was it? I . . . if I thought of something like that all by myself, when I was just seven years old . . . I can't believe that . . . that would be frightening. Absolutely frightening! I'd just like to know why it bothers me so much that I can't sleep at night.

MAN: But it wasn't me. My daughter is dead. She was run over by a streetcar. I saw it . . . my daughter . . . right in front of my eyes . . . run over and killed. I'm not lying to you. My daughter is dead.

WOMAN: Father. . . .

MAN: Stop it. Please stop it. Your story is wrong. You have things confused somehow. That's it. A misunderstanding. Such things often happen. But a mistake is still a mistake. (*The* WIFE *appears, carrying a pot of tea.*)

WIFE: What's going on, dear?

MAN: Well . . . a little surprise . . . she has just claimed that she is our daughter.

WIFE: Oh, my! Really?

WOMAN: It's true.

MAN: Don't be ridiculous! Our daughter is dead. Our daughter was run over by a streetcar and killed.

WIFE: That's true. But if she were living she would be just about this girl's age.

WOMAN: I am living. It is true!

MAN: But I saw it happen. I . . . with these eyes . . . right in front of me . . . very close.

WOMAN: I checked on that at City Hall, too.

WIFE: At City Hall?

MAN: Still. . . .

WIFE: But, dear, who can say for sure that she isn't our daughter?

MAN: I can!

WIFE: Why?

MAN: Because I saw it . . . I . . .

WIFE: I saw it, too. But we need to remember the circumstances. Our daughter behaved a bit strangely. She often ran out in the middle of the night. The first time, she was just three years old. A fire alarm sounded in the middle of the night, and, when I looked, she wasn't there. We ran out after her, frantic. The bridge over the river outside the village was down. That child, drenched to the skin, was being held in the arms of a volunteer fireman. A bonfire was burning . . . I didn't know what to do. . . .

MAN: It happened a number of times. She died after we moved to town, so she was perhaps seven.

WIFE: She was seven.

MAN: I didn't know what happened. My wife shook me awake. It was in the middle of the night and it was raining. That child, still in her nightgown, went running out in the street where the streetcar line was, running in the deserted street. I ran after her. I called to her . . . again and again. Then, just as we turned the corner, there came the streetcar.

WIFE: That's right. It was raining that night . . . I remember.

WOMAN: Don't you remember me?

WIFE (*Staring at her intently, then in a low voice*): It's her.

MAN: You're wrong.

WIFE: But that kind of thing might be possible.

WOMAN: It's me.

WIFE: Please, stand up for a minute.

(*The* WOMAN *stands, rather awkwardly. She walks a little.*)

MAN: Just who in the world are you?

WOMAN: The daughter of the two of you.

WIFE (*To the* MAN): She looks like her.

WOMAN: There's no mistake. The man in charge of family records examined many thick record books. That's how I found out. He said that my father and mother lived here.

WIFE: What do you think?

MAN: I don't believe it.

WIFE: But let's talk about it a little. Then we can see.

MAN: What?

WIFE: Oh, all sorts of things. But even if, let's say, she isn't actually our child, wouldn't that still be all right? She's had such a hard time.

MAN: I understand that . . . but. . . .

WOMAN: I . . . I don't blame you, Father . . . for that . . .

MAN: Blame? . . . Me? . . .

WOMAN: I can forget even that, now.

MAN: You're wrong. It's all a mistake.

WIFE: That's all right. Let's just sit down. We'll sit and talk.

MAN: Yes, let's sit down. Standing won't get us anywhere. And since you went to the trouble to fix hot tea. . . .

WIFE: Right. Let's have our tea. After that, we'll have a long overdue parent-child conversation.

(*The three of them sit down and begin to drink their tea, in a somewhat pleasant mood.*)

MAN: Well, I don't deny that there's a resemblance. And, if she had lived, she'd have been just about your age. . . .

WIFE: She did live. I can't help feeling so.

MAN: Now, dear, don't say such things so lightly, even joking, because she is quite serious. . . .

WOMAN: What's best is to see that father and mother are well.

WIFE: My, how often have I thought I would like to hear that!

MAN: But, dear, I keep telling you, it is all a mistake.

WOMAN: Ah . . . I . . . it is difficult for me to say this, but . . . ah . . . my younger brother is still waiting outside.

WIFE: Younger brother?

WOMAN: Yes.

MAN: You have a brother?

WOMAN: Yes. We agreed that, if I found out that you really were our father and mother, I'd call him.

WIFE: But we had only the one daughter.

MAN: She was an only child. Of course, I always wanted a son, very much, but . . . We never had one.

WIFE: Your real brother? . . .

WOMAN: Yes, he is. So . . . your real son.

WIFE: That would seem to follow, but . . . but we really didn't . . . have a son. . . .

WOMAN: It's cold outside, and, if it's all right, I wonder if you could call him in? . . . (*Standing and moving off stage left.*)

MAN: But . . . just a minute. . . .

(*The* WOMAN *reappears, bringing in her* BROTHER. *She guides him to the small serving table.*)

WOMAN: See, this is your mother.

BROTHER: Good evening, Mother.

WOMAN: And this is your father.

BROTHER: Good evening, Father.

WOMAN: Please sit down. (*Seats him beside the small table.*)

BROTHER: Yes. (*Sits.*)

WOMAN: You were probably cold, weren't you?

BROTHER: No, not at all. . . .

WOMAN: My brother has remarkable self-control. He has sometimes stood in the snow all night long. And he'd never even sneeze. Have some tea.

BROTHER: Yes. (*Taking a large cup, saucer, and spoon from a bag he is holding.*)

(*The* WIFE, *holding the teapot, pours tea into his cup. While handing him the sugar she observes him closely.*)

WOMAN: He likes tea very much. Two spoons of sugar. Always. Then he drinks slowly. I taught him that. They say it's best for the body, and for the heart, to drink slowly.

(*The* BROTHER *drinks the tea.*)

WOMAN: Aren't you hungry?

BROTHER: No.

WOMAN: But take something. Since you haven't had anything since yesterday.

WIFE: My, since yesterday?

WOMAN: Yes, my brother's self-control is very strong. He has sometimes gone for over three days without eating. But he never says a word about it.

WIFE: Three days? . . . But that's not good for his health. Even Gandhi went only two days at the most. Well, there's not much, but please eat all you want.

WOMAN (*Passing the plate of cookies*): Please take one.

BROTHER: Thank you. (*Bows politely, takes one, and eats slowly.*)

WOMAN: Chew it well. The better we chew our food, the better it is for us.

BROTHER: Yes.

WIFE: You are a good sister. And your brother is very polite.

MAN: He's very sensible. That's an excellent quality.

WOMAN: When you are ready, tell father and mother your story.

BROTHER: All right. But it's not necessary.

WOMAN: Why?

BROTHER: I can tell them later.

WOMAN: My brother is very reserved. Shy. Bashful and uncommunicative besides.

WIFE: But that's good. Not to talk too much is excellent in a man.

MAN: Yes, that's true. Real gentlemen usually don't talk much. Still, to say that it is excellent not to talk misses the point. Speaking from my long experience, I would say that you should talk when it is time to talk. To be more precise, then, it is excellent in a man not to talk when it isn't time to talk.

WOMAN: Mother, won't you tell my brother something about when he was little?

WIFE: But, you know, you're confused about that. We never had a son.

MAN: We never had a son. We had a daughter. And she died. So there are no children. None. . . .

WOMAN: We can't get Father to believe us. . . .

WIFE: But . . . really. . . .

BROTHER: Mother. . . .

WIFE: Me?

BROTHER: A long time ago, you suffered from a bad case of asthma. I remember that very well. I used to rub your back. You'd be short of breath, and your face would get red. To see you bent over suffering like that was terrible. When I rubbed your back, that seemed to help, though, and you would go to sleep. . . .

WIFE: My, I wonder if that could be true. . . .

MAN: Did you ever have asthma?

WIFE: No.

MAN: Then this story doesn't fit, does it?

WIFE: But when a person catches a cold they cough a little.

WOMAN: That must be it . . . that mother had a cold, and that's what he's remembering. He has a very good memory. Would you like another one? (*Offering him the plate of cookies.*)

BROTHER: No, that's fine.

WOMAN: You needn't hold back. This is our home.

BROTHER: All right, then. Thank you. (*Takes one.*)

MAN: Now . . . please listen carefully. I want this quite clear.

WOMAN: He remembers everything . . . many things about Father and Mother in far greater detail than I can.

MAN: That's all very well, but . . . now listen! We did not have a son! I want to make that very clear. Did not have! That's the truth! We had a daughter. We had a cat. But no son. There . . . never . . . was . . . one. Do you understand? All right. Now, saying that doesn't mean that I want to put the two of you out. So please, just relax. Eat as much as you like. Drink as much as you like. I just want to make this one point. It may seem a mean thing to say, but I think it's important to be sure that it's clear. About this . . . this house. It is our home! You . . . are our guests.

WIFE: Dear, don't be so. . . .

MAN: I know. Yes, I know. Please don't misunderstand me. And if we agree on that one point, then we might welcome you as if you were a real daughter and a real son. Wouldn't you say that we have welcomed you almost as we might have a real son and daughter?

BROTHER: And Father suffered from neuralgia. Whenever it got cold, he had a pain in his hips. When that happened, he got irritable. Mother, and Sister, you both knew that. So, whenever he had an attack, you'd go out and leave me home alone with him. His sickness was the cause, of course, but he sometimes hit me and kicked me. At first I would yell, "It hurts! It hurts!" and cry. But I soon stopped that. Because, no matter how much I cried, he still kept on. I just learned to endure it. But, from that time on, my arm bends like this. (*Moves his left arm with a jerk.*)

MAN: I never had anything like neuralgia. . . .

WOMAN: His endurance is remarkable. No matter what happens, he never cries. Here, have another. (*Offering him the cookies.*)

BROTHER: Thank you. (*Taking one.*)

WOMAN: He's just naturally mistreated by everyone. He's hit and he's kicked. But he bears it patiently. He keeps quiet; he crouches down, he rolls up on the ground in a ball. But he doesn't cry.

MAN: I have never once used violence against another person. . . .

WOMAN: But, Father, he doesn't hold it against you. I have taught him that that isn't good. It wasn't your fault. You were sick.

MAN: I had no son.

BROTHER: Father, I don't hold it against you. It was because you were sick. That's what made you do it. Sometimes my arm hurts. When it gets cold . . . just like with your neuralgia . . . there's a sharp pain, right here. But I put up with it. I accept it. Sister said, "Please endure it." So I do. I endure it.

WOMAN: His body is covered with bruises. It's terrible. But he doesn't complain. He puts up with it. Show Father and Mother . . . so they can see just how much you've endured.

BROTHER: Yes, Sister. (*Begins to unbutton his clothing.*)

WIFE: Stop! Please, stop. Don't do that! I understand. I believe you. You probably are our son.

(*The* BROTHER, *uncovering his upper body, stands up.*)

MAN (*Standing, solemnly*): I see. You're the one. You were born. I wanted it. I always wanted a son. So you were born. Evidently that's what it is. They say that if you want something badly enough you'll get it, don't they? That was you. And I never knew it at all . . . it's unbelievable. I'm really surprised that you were born. (*Pause.*) This one . . . kept quiet about it, and I never knew it. That's clear. And you . . . you are my daughter. It's no mistake. I thought that you were dead, but you were alive. The little girl I was chasing that evening was someone else. You say that's so, so it must be. It was a dark evening. To me it was just a fluttering white thing dancing in the wind. That wasn't you. You went flying the other way, running somewhere else. And you never came back. That must be what happened. So you are my daughter and son. My real daughter and son. I remember everything. So, then . . . what do you want? What now? . . . Since I am your father, what do you want me to do for you? To look at you with affection? To speak to you in a tender, caring voice? Or do you want money? What is it? . . .

WOMAN: Father?

MAN: What?

WOMAN (*Quietly*): And Mother. We don't want you to misunderstand either. We didn't come here to trick you, or to beg for anything. We really are your son and daughter . . . that's all. . . .

MAN: Really? And I never knew. (*To his* WIFE.) Please ask these people to leave. We must go to bed now. We old people become sleepy earlier than you young people do.

WOMAN: Father.

MAN: Get out.

BROTHER: Not so loud. Please. The children have just fallen asleep.

MAN: Children?

WOMAN: My children. The two-year-old and four-year-old I told you about. I had them come in. It was presumptuous of me, I know. But I couldn't leave them out there in the cold. They were already almost frozen. They couldn't even cry. I felt so sorry for them. . . .

WIFE: Please leave.

WOMAN: Mother . . . don't be so cruel. . . .

WIFE: Please go. I beg you. just go. I can't stand it. I'll give you money. It's so disagreeable. This is our house.

BROTHER: That's all right with me, Mother, but please think about the children. They're sleeping now, but they're very hungry. My sister has nothing to feed them. We kept telling them, as we came, "When we see Father and Mother, we'll ask them for something for you to eat." We barely got them to walk here. My sister is exhausted. Extremely exhausted. We walked for a long time.

WOMAN: But we are finally able to meet you, Mother. We walked a long way. It was very cold. Snow was falling. . . . (*Gradually laying down her head and seeming to fall asleep.*) Just for one look at Father and Mother . . . that's all we were thinking. . . .

WOMAN'S VOICE: To warm her freezing hands the little girl struck the match she was holding. The tiny stick flickered for a moment, enveloping the area in bright light. The ice and snow glittered a purple color. But, then, the match went out. The little girl remained there, crouching all alone on the cold stone pavement, with the wind blowing, freezing.

(*The* WOMAN*'s head is on her crossed arms on the table.*)

WIFE: What happened to her? What's your sister doing?

MAN: She's sleeping.

BROTHER: Sleeping. Sometimes she sleeps. Then, sometimes, she wakes up.

WIFE: My, I wonder if she is crying . . . look. . . .

BROTHER: Yes, she's crying. She cries in her sleep. She's very unhappy.

MAN: Will you please wake her up, and leave? Look, I don't say that out of meanness. If you hadn't come with a strange trick like this, if you had come without saying anything, you would have received a warm welcome. Really. But now listen to me. Are you listening?

BROTHER: Yes.

MAN: Please leave.

BROTHER: But my sister is very tired.

MAN: Are you her real brother?

BROTHER: Yes, I really am. . . .

WIFE: Since when have you thought that?

BROTHER: What?

WIFE: How long ago did you become aware that she was your sister?

BROTHER: That was quite a while ago . . . quite a while. . . .

WIFE: Please try to remember clearly. It's very important.

BROTHER: But even when I first became aware of it, she was already my sister. . . .

MAN: Already at the time you became aware of it? . . . Well, that's not a very reasonable story.

WIFE: There had to be something before that.

BROTHER: There were many things. Many things. Then I suddenly realized . . . she was my sister.

MAN: It sounds like a miracle . . .

(*Pause. The* BROTHER *gets up stealthily, takes a cookie from the table, goes back, sits down, and eats it.*)

MAN (*Lost in thought. To his* WIFE): Can you remember back to that time? We were sitting somewhere on a sunny hill . . . the sky was blue, white clouds were floating lightly by, there was not a breath of wind . . . perhaps dandelions were blooming. . . .

WIFE (*Prompted to reflection*): There was that, too, wasn't there?

MAN (*In the same mood*): And then . . . some large thing was dead . . alongside the road . . . what was it? . . .

WIFE (*In the same mood*): A cow . . . it was a large, gray-colored cow . . . just like a cloud. . . .

MAN: Ah, was it a cow? That thing . . . just like a cloud. . . .

WIFE: How about it, dear?

MAN: About what?

WIFE: These people . . . should we keep them overnight? . . .

MAN: Well, I was thinking that, too. We'll let them stay.

WIFE: I feel sorry for them.

MAN: Right, and people like that, no matter how they seem, they are unfortunate.

WIFE: Let's be kind to them.

MAN: Let's do that. Because there's nothing wrong in that.

WIFE: You two. It'll be all right for you to stay here tonight. We'll let you stay.

MAN: Make yourself at home. These other things . . . well, let's talk about them later. . . .

WIFE: Do you understand?

BROTHER: Yes, but that isn't necessary. Don't worry about us. Just leave us alone.

WIFE: Tell your sister, too, to put her mind at ease.

BROTHER: She already knows.

MAN: She already knows.

BROTHER: She told me that a while ago . . . that Mother had asked us to stay.

WIFE: Mother?

BROTHER: Yes.

WIFE: Meaning me?

BROTHER: That's right.

WIFE: So . . . then that's all right.

BROTHER: Is it all right if I take one more?

WIFE: Yes.

(*He eats a cookie.*)

MAN'S VOICE: Good evening.

MAN: Good evening.

MAN'S VOICE: I'm a city fire marshal. Is anything missing in your home? Is anything lost? Has anything disappeared?

MAN: Has anything?

WIFE: No.

MAN: It seems not.

MAN'S VOICE: So everything is in order?

MAN: I can't say that absolutely. You see, this is a very poor household.

MAN'S VOICE: How about your fire?

WIFE: It's all right. We haven't gone to bed yet.

MAN'S VOICE: Not yet? But you're not going to stay up all night, are you?

MAN: We'll check it before going to bed.

MAN'S VOICE: Did you notice?

MAN: What?

MAN'S VOICE: Can you hear the breathing of someone sleeping? Two small ones. . . .

WIFE: Children. There are children.

MAN'S VOICE: Be careful, please. Tonight is especially cold. Be careful that they don't freeze to death while they sleep. The city authorities are drawing special attention to that danger.

(*There is the striking of wooden clappers, which gradually fades. Then, "Watch your fire," is heard from afar. The* WOMAN *raises her head, as if still half asleep.*)

WOMAN: Father, while I was asleep, how many cookies did he eat?

MAN: Well, one, wasn't it?

WIFE: It was one, definitely. . . .

WOMAN: No, it was two. He ate two. I had counted them. I don't appreciate your letting him do that. Don't you remember, Father, how many times I asked you not to? He knows no limits. If you let him do it, he'll eat far too many. I have only eaten one so far. That's true, isn't it, Mother?

WIFE: Yes, but since there are plenty, don't feel that you have to restrain yourself. . . .

WOMAN: No, I don't mean it that way. I told him about it, but no matter how often I tell him, he doesn't seem to understand. It's the same with Father. I've asked you so often!

MAN: But I didn't. . . .

WOMAN: No, I had spoken to you earlier. But it's not your fault. (*To her* BROTHER.) You're the one. Mother, I hate to trouble you, but would you put these away?

WIFE: Yes, but there are plenty.

WOMAN: It will become a habit. Now apologize to Father and Mother.

MAN: Well, that's all right. Your brother was probably hungry.

WOMAN: Everyone is. Everyone is hungry. But people exercise self-control. You . . . you're the only one . . . doing such greedy things. . . . Well, apologize.
(*She gives him a jab with her fingers.*)

WIFE: Please, don't do that! Really, please stop. It's all right. In this house it doesn't matter at all.

WOMAN: Mother, don't interfere. This is our affair. I raised this child. Apologize. Why don't you apologize? Don't you feel ashamed? What did I always say to you?

MAN: Well, I understand your point very well. It's commendable. It's very commendable. However. . . .

WOMAN: Apologize!

MAN: Listen . . . will you? Here's another way of looking at it. What you say is sound, but don't tell me that if he gets hungry, it's his own fault? Really. Shouldn't you think again?

WOMAN: Please stay out of it. I'm the one who raised him. I taught him better.

MAN: Yes, I can understand how difficult that must have been.

WOMAN: No, you can't understand. You don't know how much I have done for him. From the age of seven. I have done things I'm ashamed to admit in front of other people in order to raise him. (*To her* BROTHER.) Why can't you understand? Why don't you listen to me? Why don't you do what I tell you?

WIFE: He seems to obey you quite well.

MAN: That's certainly true. Your brother is very courteous.

WOMAN (*Becoming more agitated*): I'm a despised woman. It's because I became that kind of woman that you won't listen to me, isn't it?
(*She twists her* BROTHER*'s arm. He stands up slowly and then slowly crouches down on the floor.*)

WOMAN: What did I do that was so shameful? What do you say I did? And if I did, who did I do it for? Just who did I have to do that kind of thing for? Tell me! Please tell me! Compared to what you have done, what does what I have done amount to? Which is worse? Tell me, which is worse? Tell us. Come on, out with it!

MAN (*To the* BROTHER): You'd better apologize. Please. Apologize. You shouldn't disobey your sister. You know that she's suffered many hardships to raise you. You understand that, don't you? And that she loves you. It's not good not to obey her instructions. That's bad.

WOMAN: Father! Please be quiet for a while! He doesn't understand yet. What I did . . . and who I did it for. And how miserable I have felt about doing it . . . to this very day. (*To her* BROTHER.) Listen! What did I keep telling you? Did I say you could sink so low just because you're hungry? Did I teach you to be so rude in front of Father and Mother? Now apologize! Say "pardon me" to Father and Mother. I say apologize! Can't you see how ashamed I feel because of what you did? Then, apologize. Apologize! Apologize! Apologize! (*While saying this, she bangs his head, with a thumping sound, on the floor.*)

WIFE: Please stop that! It's all right. Really, he doesn't have to. Don't be so harsh.

WOMAN: Please stay out of it! (*Increasingly violent.*) Whose cookie did you eat? Because of you, who won't have any?

WIFE: There are plenty. Plenty. We can't possibly eat them all.

WOMAN: Whose was it? Who won't get any? Please tell us!

MAN: Stop it. I'll go get them immediately. We have plenty (*Grabbing her arm to stop her.*)

WOMAN: Let go of me, please!

MAN (*Becoming angry*): Stop! What in the world is this all about? What are you doing?

WOMAN (*Startled, suddenly becoming humble, bowing her head to the* MAN): I beg you. I'll make him apologize. I'll make him apologize immediately Please forgive him. He didn't mean anything. He'll apologize right now. He's usually more obedient. He's usually a well-behaved child.

MAN (*A little bewildered*): But that's all right. Because we're not really concerned about it.

WOMAN: I'll have him apologize, though, because I don't feel right about it. And, please, forgive him. He's already sorry about it, too, in his heart. He is apologizing. He's crying. It's just that he can't say anything.

WIFE: You....

WOMAN: Please forgive me, Mother. I was wrong. I was a bad woman. I did such a shameful thing....

WIFE: That's not the point. It's all right.

WOMAN: No, it's not all right. But please don't say that my brother is bad. He's feeling sorry. Forgive him. He's basically a gentle, courteous human being. He's usually very self-controlled. Please forgive him. I'll make him apologize. Right now. He was hungry That's all it is. We can't blame him for that. Please don't blame him for that. I'll make him apologize. I apologize, too.

MAN (*Approaching her tenderly and trying to lift her to her feet*): That's all right. Let's stop all this. I understand.

WOMAN (*Brushing him away*): No, please forgive me. Don't touch me! You must forgive me. I'm a bad woman. Please forgive me. (*Crawling away from him as she says this.*)

MAN: What are you doing? (*Again extending his hand.*)

WOMAN (*Retreating in the direction of the* WIFE): Forgive me, Mother. I did a bad thing. Please forgive me. At least give me your forgiveness.

WIFE: What's wrong?

MAN: What in the world is it?...

WOMAN: Forgive me, Father. (*Again retreating from the* MAN.) Forgive me, Father. Forgive me, please. Matches. Please don't strike the matches....

(*She bends down on the floor covering her head, and remains motionless. The* MAN *and his* WIFE *stand dazed. The* BROTHER *rises slowly. They stand quietly for a moment. The* WIFE *is about to kneel down next to the* WOMAN.)

BROTHER (*Quietly*): Please don't touch her. She's a woman who can't sink any further. That's why she doesn't want to be touched. (*He goes to her, hugging her and lifting her to his knee. The* MAN *and* WIFE *stand bewildered.*)

WOMAN (*As from afar*): Matches . . . don't strike the matches.

BROTHER (*Murmuring*): Father bought matches. Father bought matches. Father bought matches; every night . . . every night . . . for my sister . . . night after night for my sister. . . .

MAN: No. . . . (*To his* WIFE.) I didn't do that. I never did such a thing.

BROTHER: But I don't blame you. Whatever you did, I can't blame you. Because my sister said, "Don't blame him. Don't blame him. . . ."

WOMAN'S VOICE (*Low and hoarse*): Then the little girl struck the rest of the matches all at once, in a great hurry. In doing this, she hoped that she would be able to hold firmly to her mother. The matches were burning very brightly, lighting up the whole area, so that it became brighter than daylight. There was never a time when her mother looked larger, or more beautiful. She took the little girl in her arms, wrapped her in light and joy, and went climbing high, high up. There was no more cold, hunger, or fear. The two of them were called up to heaven.

MAN'S VOICE (*Stealthily*): Did you notice?

MAN: What?

MAN'S VOICE: You can't hear the children breathing in their sleep any more.

(*There is the striking of wooden clappers, which gradually fades. Then, "Watch your fire" is heard from afar. The* MAN *and his* WIFE *sit silently at the table, solemnly beginning "morning tea."* . . .)

WOMAN'S VOICE (*A little more clearly*): It was a cold morning. The little girl, with red cheeks, and with even a smile playing on her lips, was dead. The New Year's morning sun illuminated that little body. One hand held a bunch of matches, almost entirely burned up. People said, "She must have tried to warm herself. . . ." It was true. This child had been very cold.

CURTAIN

Kara Jūrō, *Two Women,* directed by Ishibashi Renji, Dai nana byōtō, November 1979.

TWO WOMEN

KARA JŪRŌ
TRANSLATED BY JOHN K. GILLESPIE

Born in 1940, Kara Jūrō was active in the student theater at Meiji University. He joined the Youth Art Theater (Seinen geijutsuza) after his graduation in 1962 but soon became disenchanted with conventional *shingeki*. After a brief stint working for an Asakusa burlesque house, Kara established the Situation Theater (Jōkyō gekijō), inspired by Jean-Paul Sartre's existentialism, in 1963. By the late 1960s, as an actor, director, and playwright, Kara had moved his theater into red tent that was pitched in public places like the Hanazono Shrine in Shinjuku, Tokyo. Together with his wife, the Korean *zainichi* (Japanese-born) Ri Reisen, and Maro Akaji (who later established the *butō* company Great Camel Battleship [Dairakudakan]), Kara attempted to create the erotic, intimate, and carnivalesque spirit of Izumo no Okuni's early kabuki theater. Indeed, he regarded himself and his company as the offspring of Okuni's "riverbed beggars" (*kawara kojiki*), countercultural rebels, yet belonging to a venerable native tradition of performance untainted by European notions of theatrical and social propriety. With a new company called the Kara Group (Kara-gumi), he continued to write plays and perform in his signature red tent. Absurd, surrealistic, outrageous, and often hilarious, Kara's plays defy easy summary. Many of the characters in his best plays—such as *John Silver: The Beggar of Love* (*Jon Shirubā: Ai no kojiki*, 1970), *A Tale of Two Cities* (*Nito monogatari*, 1972), and *Matasaburō of the Wind: Kara Version* (*Kara-ban kaze no Matasaburō*, 1974)—are engaged in a quixotic quest to recover their personal histories, a quest often overshadowed by darker episodes in Japan's wartime and imperial history. The search for roots in utopian dreams that quickly becomes apocalyptic presents a confrontation with, and even transcendence over, the past. The play here, *Two Woman* (*Futari no onna*, 1978), is a fine example of Kara's bricolage dramaturgy. As Mishima Yukio did before him, Kara has transformed the classic nō drama *Lady Aoi* (*Aoi no ue*), itself based on an episode from *The Tale of Genji*, into a contemporary work that explores the nature of madness, love, and jealousy. Kara's version, however, even more radically undermines the idea of a fixed personal identity that has been one of the linchpins of modern selfhood.

Characters

WOMAN / PATIENT 1
AOI / PATIENT 2
ROKUJŌ / PATIENT 3 / THE MADMAN
KŌICHI / MOTHER
KOREMITSU / JIRŌ, little brother of AOI
NURSE / PARKING LOT ATTENDANT
OLD MAN / REAL ESTATE MAN
YOUTH

Note: The roles of the WOMAN, AOI, and ROKUJŌ are to be played by the same actress.

PROLOGUE

A sandy beach. Rosy music. Pat Boone's 1950s hit song "Love Letters in the Sand." A man loiters about.

My beloved Aoi, how are you? I'm here at Izu; the wind has just died down. It's just the right time to write you a secret love letter in the sand. If my thoughts get through to you, please put on Pat Boone's "Love Letters in the Sand," which we once listened to together, and read this my sweet letter to you. It's so full of sweet talk I'd be embarrassed if someone else read it. And, if the wind blows and destroys my love letter in the sand, I'll take it as a sign that the wind is a mailman delivering my love to you far away. Aoi, a gem so fine it wouldn't chafe even mounted in the eye. I've really got the hots for you. If I could, I'd have the mailman carry me on the wind to your arms. And then I'd corner you in the kitchen and really ravish you. So, Aoi, understand how I feel; I am hoping you won't be taking on dumb men. By the time the Fuji Circuit Grand Prix that you like so much begins, I'll be back for sure. Count on it. The hospital at Izu is depressing, so on my lunch break I always head to the beach, try to forget the world of the sick, and think only about you. Don't two-time me. Koremitsu at the hospital, who, as you know, has been my friend since our intern days, was saying that he would like to see you again—now that you are engaged—the next time he is in Tokyo. But he has a weakness for women, so be careful, OK? Aoi, my Aoi, let's definitely go to the Fuji Circuit Grand Prix. I can just see your face, listening to the roar of those huge engines, wearing your straw hat with the red sash. Until then, for a while, we'll be apart. Finally, I should share a perverse confidence with you. Aoi, listen carefully. The fact is that today while on my rounds at the Izu Hospital I met a married woman, someone I didn't know, who called me "Darling," as if she were my wife.

SCENE 1. THE HOSPITAL ROOM

The patients' lounge—a flimsy affair partitioned by curtains and about as sturdy as a castle made of sand. Beyond a window with iron bars, the sea breeze is blowing. Splendid sunlight. PATIENTS 1 *and* 2, *a man and a woman (or two men), are playing house. The two bow repeatedly, then one of them sets about making preparations for supper going through the hand motions of slicing radishes. The other says, "Mother is it ready yet?" Then* PATIENT 3 *(the* MADMAN*)—probably an ex-student gone wrong—crawls around on the partition wall. There is also an* OLD MAN *in a chair in the middle of the room, munching on a pear. He drops a bite of the pear onto the floor and looks intently at something. There is a* WOMAN, *down on all fours, looking at the same thing. It is unclear what they are looking at.*

CRAWLING MADMAN: Ladies and gentlemen who've gathered here. We must possess the resolve always to pay for our mistakes with respect to our own counterrevolutionary natures. For one counterrevolutionary action, we'll cut off a finger; for the second, cut off another; then another and, again, another. For ten such acts, we'll chop off all ten fingers. The reason we have to be worried is having only ten fingers when we notice eleven counterrevolutionary acts. The problem is where to find one more finger!

OLD MAN (*Pointing to the* MADMAN*'s feet*): Don't step there.

MADMAN (*Pointing to the* OLD MAN*'s finger*): It's not that kind of finger. "My own unseen eleventh finger! That's what I'm looking for." Pull that finger back. In paying for your mistakes, you are definitely not to borrow another person's finger.

OLD MAN: You SOB, I thought I told you don't step there!

MADMAN: All you people, what's that you say?

OLD MAN: You're stepping on the performers!

(MADMAN *jumps aside.*)

OLD MAN (*Gets down on all fours*): Are they all right?

WOMAN: Barely. (*Shows him something she shields with her hand.*)

OLD MAN: Good job.

WOMAN: Not bad.

OLD MAN: That much?

WOMAN: Yes.

OLD MAN: You want to try getting in that much?

WOMAN: Don't you think it'll work out?

OLD MAN: Yes, you can do it. Certainly, you can.

WOMAN: They won't treat me mean?

OLD MAN: You think anyone would treat you mean? They'll be your fans. You'll have fans. Look, they're all black, right? If you were to become one of them, don't you know you'd become the star overnight?

WOMAN: But I want to start at the bottom.

OLD MAN: I'm not so sure that's a good idea.

WOMAN: I have to start at the bottom, or I'll never improve.

OLD MAN: That may be so, but it's a group of circus ants. With your body, no matter how much experience you get at the bottom, you'd be like the Alps to those characters, no? (WOMAN *cries.*)

OLD MAN: It does no good to cry.

WOMAN: Say, Mister.

OLD MAN: Don't bat your eyes at me.

WOMAN: What about Gulliver?

OLD MAN: Gulliver?

WOMAN: Right. How was it Gulliver became good friends with the Lilliputians?

OLD MAN: They tied him up.

WOMAN: You mean, S and M?

OLD MAN: No, no sexual passion to it.

WOMAN: What about appetite?

OLD MAN: Well, he must have been hungry, also. (*Drops a bite of pear for the ants.*)

WOMAN: I'm hungry too.

OLD MAN: Want a mouthful of this?

WOMAN: No.

OLD MAN: OK.

WOMAN: I . . .

OLD MAN: There! Go on! (*To the ants.*) Suck the sweet juice, show us the way out. (*Whereupon he squashes one, and the juice spills over.*)

WOMAN: Once when I was peeping through a microscope, I dozed off. I believe it was in the science laboratory in fourth grade. When we looked at the bees swarming on flower petals, at some point I was drowsy and got lost in the bees' world and found myself in the bee fortress. They were waiting for the queen to be born any minute and getting terribly bloodthirsty; when the newborn queen came, they decided two females was one too many, and they chased me all over the place. When I woke up from the dream, I went home, and even sipping my soup at dinner, I couldn't forget that blood-tingling, flesh-crawling bees' world. It even made my soup taste bad.

OLD MAN: That sort of thing was a good dream?

WOMAN: I don't know whether it was a good or a bad dream unless I dream it some more.

OLD MAN: In that case, you don't have time to be awake.

WOMAN: That's right. I really hoped I could dream it one more time. But it never came back. Not in junior high or high school either. Zilch. So, then, that was it. I thought, from now on, I'd waste my life on men and money. I'd try to become an ordinary woman. But . . .

(OLD MAN *looks at her inquiringly.*)

(WOMAN *trembles.*)

OLD MAN: Hey . . .

WOMAN: Yes?

OLD MAN: You all right?

WOMAN: Ari, you know, an ant! Ari, aari!

OLD MAN: Ali? Mohammed Ali has retired, you know.

WOMAN: Ant. I had become an ant.

OLD MAN: An ant?

WOMAN: Ah, right.

OLD MAN: Weren't you a bee?

WOMAN: That's why I can get in without being tied up, can't I? Can't I start at the bottom in the ant circus, even without acting sexy?

OLD MAN: If the ants say it's OK.

WOMAN: But they all said we were ants and to say good morning when you meet one. In the evening, good evening.

(OLD MAN *pauses.*)

WOMAN: They all called that hole the secret exit. Sitting with knees drawn up for two days and two nights and nibbling on cookies, they swore they would wait, like ants in the ground. I have nothing in the way of a political creed, but I can become an ant. I was enticed by their idea of organizing ourselves like an army of ants, and at some point I got mixed in with them. But what with the bugs crawling on the back of your neck, and their not giving me anything decent to eat, I started to see things differently: I thought being taken on by the waiters in a cabaret boiler room would be a hell of a lot more fun than this. But I didn't so much as breathe a word about it. I'd had enough of this whole strategy. From the beginning I planned to make a run for it, if anything happened.

MADMAN (*Abruptly*): Back when the proletarian vanguard stormed the Bastille, what was the Marquis de Sade doing!?

(WOMAN *walks aimlessly toward the window.*)

MADMAN: Nay, what did they do to de Sade! Mindful of the women he sadistically abused with fart-filled bonbons, they went around setting fire to pages of his voluminous manuscripts.

WOMAN (*Looking at her feet*): Hey, the ants are crawling over here.

MADMAN: Nevertheless, that's the reason Justine burned with passion they never dreamed about! Furiously burning like a cathouse sucking on eleven penises! Like a monster pussy sucking in a penis that will be cut off in atonement! (*Unzips his trousers and sets fire to his pubic hair.*)

(*He falls over in a burst of flame. Silence.*)

WOMAN: Say there.

OLD MAN: What is it?

WOMAN: Is there sand on my back?

OLD MAN: None.

WOMAN: It's full of it.

OLD MAN: Full of it?

WOMAN: Look, when I straighten my back, it makes a sifting noise.

(OLD MAN *pauses.*)

WOMAN: Even then, when I was lying buried in sand, everybody trampled on me. When things got tough, I got scared, and I was grabbed by the police unit that rushed in, so I screamed out that I didn't do anything, that they lured me here, that if anything better comes along I'd quit right away—I blurted out such awful stuff. While I was saying I shouldn't have come and how stupid I was, stuffing my mouth with sand and feeling some remorse, just then a lump of earth toppled over on me, and I really was about to become an ant buried in the ground. And so nobody said a word of criticism to me. First one left and then another until no one was there—that's when he came up. Even while being chased by the cops, he came up and asked me to keep a pass with identity papers and an attached key. And then he piled sand on me and said he'd come again for sure, and he left.

OLD MAN: Well, did he come again?

WOMAN: No.

OLD MAN: He was caught, wasn't he?

WOMAN: Perhaps so.

OLD MAN: Well, then, nothing left but to go home, was there?

WOMAN: But I was there another two days.

OLD MAN: How come?

WOMAN: It really felt good.

(OLD MAN *pauses.*)

WOMAN: I'd suddenly sit up in the dark, grab sand, and pour it lightly on my bare nipples. I felt like a really bad woman, and then I'd squeeze it between my thighs. And when I'd squeeze them tightly together, almost as if to bind them, I felt as if I was giving birth to an outrageous sand monster. Forgive me. Does this sort of talk bother you?

OLD MAN: I'm no longer young and. . . .

WOMAN: You no doubt think this is some lunatic confession, don't you?

OLD MAN: "Here now, here now, dance of the rabbit."

WOMAN: "Taratta, ratta, ratta, ratta, ratta, ratta." (*Jumps about, kicks wall, and sits down.*) (*Such actions occur abruptly, symptomatic of schizophrenia.* WOMAN *laughs lightly.*)

OLD MAN (*Approaching her from the rear*): Boo!

WOMAN: You don't scare me, you don't scare me.

OLD MAN: Oh, I'm worn out.

WOMAN: Say . . .

OLD MAN: Huh?

WOMAN: You see, I . . .

OLD MAN: Yes, you. . . .

WOMAN: I, I'm not me.

OLD MAN: Hm.

WOMAN: Really!

OLD MAN: Really?

WOMAN: Since that time, I've had his pass and key, and I figured out where he works from his identity papers and paid a visit. To Ochanomizu. The autumn sky was very, very high. While looking down at that ditch of a river, I thought about a lot of things. That this is momentary. And that because it is, I'd just take care of this, then quickly get back home. But a woman who swears such a thing in her heart is, on the other hand, also one who sticks to a dreadful plan. And, when I was allowed into the office, before I knew it, I somehow . . .

OLD MAN: Before you knew it, what?

WOMAN: It went beyond a brief relationship.

OLD MAN: You got on well with him?

WOMAN: No, not all that well, but before I knew it I'd become his wife . . .

OLD MAN: That is to say. . . .

WOMAN: That is to say?

OLD MAN: Just like that, he got you in bed, didn't he.

WOMAN: Not so! He didn't get me in bed. I only looked like his wife.

OLD MAN: But a man who wouldn't do it to you is not a man.

WOMAN: That's right. But, there in his office, nothing at all really happened. Even while I was politely allowed in as his wife, he never showed up. I couldn't meet him the next day either. So when I went again after several days, this time he used the old "not-at-home" excuse. Then, on the lunch break, when I once slipped in to pilfer the pass and key I'd left behind, this time I was called a thief. . . . So then I idled about for two or three days when I noticed I was standing in front of that hole that had caved in along with their Operation Ant. I thought I'd return the items I'd been entrusted with right to the hole, or, rather, I'd bury them there. At that point, I was caught by the police, who were reinspecting the scene of the crime. I was asked what this pass was. Of course, he was also contacted. . . . That's enough.

OLD MAN: Why is that?

WOMAN: I don't want to talk about it.

OLD MAN: Did you want him to say you were his wife?

WOMAN: No.

OLD MAN: But did you want him to say you had some relationship with him?

WOMAN: Yes.

OLD MAN: And?

WOMAN: He said I was troublesome.

OLD MAN: That was his reaction?

WOMAN: From his office they even put out a report of the theft to the police, and no matter what I said I didn't get across to them anymore.

OLD MAN: I see.

WOMAN: Then after several days of life in the detention house—I couldn't take it, so I swallowed the cigarettes they'd given me.

(OLD MAN *pauses.*)

WOMAN: When I did, I ran a temperature, and they sent me to a hospital.

OLD MAN: You were brought here, right?

WOMAN: No. I put in to come here myself.

OLD MAN: Why?

WOMAN: You can hear the rolling of the sea....

OLD MAN: But that's the only good thing...

WOMAN: In addition, when I look at a line of ants, like this, I feel as if I can go anywhere, even to my old science room... and also when I talk about all sorts of things like this, sand monsters come out in swarms from inside my panties and (*Sings.*) hey, ta ta ta, ta ta ta....

OLD MAN: One more time.

WOMAN: What?

OLD MAN: Sing that last part again.

WOMAN (*Sings*): Hey, ta ta ta, ta ta ta.

OLD MAN: Thank you.

WOMAN: Not at all, don't mention it.

OLD MAN: I really thank you. I was wondering what I'd do without that nonsense refrain. Your confession is too consistent. There is nothing I can say about it. The only thing I can do is cheer up crazy kids. (*Stands up and grasps her shoulders.*) I really thank you. The last part got a little strange. But go ahead, put yourself into it. You can do it. You can do it. You can do it here just as much as you like!

(*A clanging sound. The door has been opened. The* NURSE*'s voice can be heard from the door.*)

NURSE: Soon we'll be leaving, won't we? I heard so from Dr. Koremitsu, that you have a beautiful fiancée waiting for you in Tokyo?

(*Everyone looks in the direction of the voice.* PATIENTS 1 *and* 2, *who are playing house, and* PATIENT 3, *the* MADMAN *who appears to be a student, start to speak all at once.*)

PATIENT 1: Say, have you met his fiancée?

PATIENT 2: Well, Daddy, you probably won't like her.

PATIENT 1: Whether I like her or not, I'm his father, you know.

PATIENT 2: But, Daddy, you always say so and. . . .

PATIENT 3: What the hell is medical treatment to a doctor, anyway! What the hell is care to a patient!

NURSE: Please be quiet.

PATIENT 1: Mother, she says to be quiet.

PATIENT 2: Am I not being quiet?

(PATIENT 3 *crawls along the wall.* KŌICHI *stands behind the* NURSE *for some time.* KOREMITSU *also stands behind the* NURSE *for some time.*)

NURSE (*To* KŌICHI *and* KOREMITSU): This is about normal for the abnormal.

KOREMITSU: I wonder if what you mean isn't that rather than the abnormality of normality we face every day, this is somehow more nakedly open?

NURSE: Certainly it's more nakedly open, but is this "openness" a step forward? It's like fevers babies get that protect them in their own way. It's also a step backward.

KOREMITSU: In that case, they're still not ready to go out into the world?

NURSE: In stages, they could.

KOREMITSU: If only we could know the number of stages.

NURSE: I won't try to stop you from doing whatever you choose.

KOREMITSU (*To* KŌICHI): This nurse here, she's a bit critical of what I'm doing.

KŌICHI: You mean in this ward lounge?

KOREMITSU: Well, for the time being it is a lounge, but I'm thinking about widening this wall more. In other words, when the patients get up in the morning, their enclosure will be bigger. A meter at a time so it's not noticed, till finally it becomes as big as a gym, and then we'll tear that wall down. In other words, with nothing at all to partition them off, the place will be a really spacious beach!

NURSE: Who would be able to control such a large space?

KOREMITSU: Control. . . .

NURSE: Look, even if you can control it, it doesn't mean a thing at all to the patients. You are thinking that space is freedom, but inside these people, it's too spacious, and they're not free. If you don't take that into consideration—

KOREMITSU: But who can say Adam and Eve weren't crazy?

NURSE: Instead of that sort of thing, I'd worry about how to pay the plasterer who is going to widen the wall a meter at a time.

KOREMITSU: Do that, and you'll douse my ideal, won't you? (*Touches her rear.*)

NURSE: Stop that, not here! (*Sweeps his hand away.*) Shall we go?

(*Starts to leave.*)

WOMAN (*Taking a step forward*): Oh! . . . Darling . . .

NURSE: Darling?

WOMAN (*Pointing at* KŌICHI): Darling . . .

KŌICHI: Me? (*Pointing to himself.*)

WOMAN: Don't you remember me?

KOREMITSU: Tell her you do.

KŌICHI: Y-yes.

WOMAN: I am. . . .

KŌICHI: Do you need something?

WOMAN: No, it's all right. (*Tries to withdraw.*)

KŌICHI: You are (*Looks at the* NURSE*'s clipboard.*) Ms. Rokujō, aren't you?

(WOMAN *says nothing.*)

KŌICHI: Do you need something from me?

WOMAN: If I could have you dispose of the sand that's accumulated on my back (*With her back to him*), I think you will understand.

(KŌICHI *is puzzled.*)

WOMAN: Or else when I show it like this (*Lifts up her hair*), I think I look like somebody . . .

(*She is about to turn around, but the* NURSE *steps between her and* KŌICHI.)

NURSE: Doctor, there's no end to this.

(WOMAN *drops her hair strand by strand.*)

OLD MAN (*To the* WOMAN): Do it, like that, like his wife!

WOMAN: Right.

OLD MAN: One more time.

WOMAN: Darling!

KŌICHI: What do you want with me?

WOMAN: How many times have I called you "Darling"? It's three times. Three times. Please take note, Kōichi. The third of these three times surely clinches the truth.

NURSE: How stupid. Let's go.

KŌICHI: Yes.

WOMAN: Wait. A little longer. Just a tiny bit.

OLD MAN: Be crazy!

WOMAN (*Sings*): Ta, ta, ta . . . , ta, ta, ta. . . .

(PATIENTS *laugh.*)

NURSE: Don't laugh without reason.

WOMAN (*Approaching* KŌICHI): I'm leaving here tonight!

KŌICHI: How?

WOMAN: The ants.

KŌICHI: The ants?

WOMAN: Yes, I'll join the ant circus, and from their small house I'll come into your world. Look (*Takes out a tree leaf.*), I've even received a letter to this effect from the circus director. He's asking me to please come soon and be the star of the company

KŌICHI: This is a leaf off a tree.

WOMAN: No. It's a pass to the company. A pass.

NURSE: Let's go. It's a classic insane declaration.

WOMAN: I'm not insane! You're a devil!

NURSE: Cut that out now!

KŌICHI: Right, no need to get tough.

WOMAN: Right, it's not good to get tough.

NURSE (*To* KOREMITSU): Why aren't you saying anything at such a moment as this?

KOREMITSU: The money for the plasterer. . . .

KŌICHI: So that's how it is. Well, it would be good if the director comes for you soon.

WOMAN: He won't come for me.

KŌICHI: Oh? He won't?

WOMAN: I have to go. See, the ant circus will ride a boat made of pear peelings. It will go down a stream, and day and night it will splash right along. When the moon shines, it will look like a blue magic lantern to the crabs lurking on the river bottom. That's why, to overtake it, you have to fly along in a sonic dune buggy at two hundred kilometers per hour, racing along, kicking sand, cutting the wind. And then, tonight, I want you to park my dune buggy right beneath this window.

(*Holds out a key.*)

KŌICHI: Isn't this an apartment key?

WOMAN: Do people who live in apartments have sonic dune buggies?!

KŌICHI: Well, I'll take care of it for now.

(*Takes key.*)

WOMAN: I'm counting on you.

KŌICHI: But unless you can slip away like an ant from a small hole in this room, you won't see any dune buggy.

WOMAN: But didn't we once live like ants?

(KŌICHI *is silent.*)

WOMAN: Well.

KOREMITSU: Yeah.

NURSE: It's time.

(*Opens door and leaves. Strained silence.*)

WOMAN (*To the* OLD MAN): Say.

OLD MAN: What?

WOMAN: I made them think I'm crazy, didn't I?

SCENE 2. THE CORRIDOR

The cloth at the front of the room falls with a rustle. It becomes a cloth corridor. KŌICHI *and* KOREMITSU *walk in.*

KOREMITSU: What a blockhead you are.

KŌICHI: I'm a blockhead?

KOREMITSU: You're a blockhead. I wonder how a blockhead like you could become a doctor. You took the key, but what do you expect to come of it?

KŌICHI: Now it doesn't mean I've taken her virginity.

KOREMITSU: It amounts to the same sort of thing.

KŌICHI: I took her key. How much value does a promise sworn to me in a patient's delusion really have? Is it something that she'll forget completely after several delusions? Or will she remember her promise, even if she forgets the delusions?

KOREMITSU: You won't know unless you penetrate that woman's brain. If she begins to feel resentment toward you, it may be a sign of recovery, and if tomorrow she completely forgets about it, she's a normal patient. And besides—

KŌICHI: And besides? . . .

KOREMITSU: Provided deep down she feels resentment toward you while her face shows she's completely forgotten; well, this means she leaves the hospital!

KŌICHI: But that deep down feeling you don't understand. How do you propose to penetrate it?

KOREMITSU: While I'm talking about you with her.

KŌICHI: You'd use me as a tool?

KOREMITSU: Right you are. As far as that woman is concerned, you are the black jack. What matters to her is where that one-eyed jack is looking. . . . Anyway, what are you going to do about the dune buggy?

KŌICHI: I don't need that old thing.

KOREMITSU: But from now on, wherever you go, won't you see the dune buggy that goes with that key?

KŌICHI: If she could just slip out of here like an ant. (*Darkness.*)

SCENE 3. THE RACETRACK

The Pat Boone song.

VOICE: Darling. (KŌICHI *is silent.*)

VOICE: Darling! (*Louder and stronger.*)

(*Suddenly, the sounds of race cars starting up one after another.*)

AOI: What are you thinking about?

KŌICHI: I was just thinking about the letter I sent you.

AOI: Look, there! It's Kurosawa. Kurosawa's about to start. There, the yellow Porsche. He had a one-year suspension; this is his first start in a long time. He looks like a gentleman, but that man, once he's in his car, there's no telling what he'll do. (*She is in pain from morning sickness.*)

KŌICHI: Of all the dumb things. You are hurting from morning sickness because you look at Death when you're pregnant.

AOI: That's so. But it doesn't hurt. Not at all.

KŌICHI: Looks like it's threatening to rain.

AOI: If it doesn't, it'll surely be a wicked, nasty race.

KŌICHI: Did you get over your nausea?

AOI: Argh.

KŌICHI: What luck. We come all the way out to the track, and your morning sickness is awful.

AOI: I don't like being a woman.

KŌICHI: Why?

AOI: The design of our bodies is a real pain.

KŌICHI: God made it. It can't be helped.

AOI: Listen, put your hand on my back.

KŌICHI: Like this?

AOI: It would be nice to have some grapefruit.

KŌICHI: I'm having Jirō go get some right now. Are you all right? Shall . . . should we go to the toilet?

AOI: I'm fine, fine. If we go to the toilet, someone will take these good seats you went to such trouble for.

KŌICHI: Jirō's slow, isn't he?

AOI: Would you get my handkerchief from my handbag, darling, my handkerchief?

KŌICHI: We should have listened to your mother. But we couldn't wait until the ceremony she told us to stay conservative, inconspicuous, not to attract attention, to be newlyweds with a clean slate; but if somebody sees you suffering like this, there'll be no hiding what we did before the marriage then. Aoi, are you all right?

AOI: Kōichi, put on that song, that song.

(KŌICHI *switches on the Pat Boone song. Sound of a race car passing by.*)

KŌICHI: Isn't it growing a little cold?

AOI: A bit.

KŌICHI: Shall we go back to the car?

AOI: I'll stay here. But what about the grapefruit?

KŌICHI: I'll go see.

AOI: Please don't go.

KŌICHI: But after it starts to rain, it'll be too late to go and see.

(JIRŌ *arrives.*)

JIRŌ: Hey, Sis.

AOI: You're late, you bum. What about the grapefruit?

JIRŌ: Here you are.

AOI: What took you so long?

JIRŌ: Late or not, the parking lot was packed, junk-heap jalopies getting in the way, and cars coming in one after another clogging things up. I could only barely get through to the car, slipping between other cars. It took some doing. Here's the key.

AOI: This is not our key.

JIRŌ: Oh, this one's your key.

AOI: Look, whose key is it?

JIRŌ: I met up with my buddies over there, and I'm going to their place for just a little while. You two go home together.

AOI: Hold it.

JIRŌ: See you later.

AOI: Jirō. (*Chases after him.*)

(*Sounds of race cars zipping by. An announcer's voice. This noise changes to the sound of waves.* KŌICHI *squats down and scoops up a handful of gravel. As he does so, the words of his love letter suddenly flow from his mouth: "My beloved Aoi, how are you?—" The* WOMAN *approaches him.*)

WOMAN: Doctor. Aren't you the doctor?

KŌICHI (*Vacantly*): Eh?

WOMAN: It's me. It's me. Rokujō.

KŌICHI: Rokujō?

WOMAN: Yes. With my hair dyed like this, you might have forgotten me, but look, here I am, the Rokujō you ran into at the hospital in Izu.

(KŌICHI *is speechless.*)

WOMAN: You needn't be so surprised.

KŌICHI: But...

WOMAN: Yes, I left the hospital one month ago. The one you were just with, is she the one you're going to marry?

KŌICHI: Yes. You said your name was Miss Rokujō?

WOMAN: Your face says you still don't believe me.

KŌICHI: The actual fact is I am surprised. I remember clearly what you spoke to me about....

WOMAN: Oh, you do. When we were at the place by the sea, I spoke of absurd things. It may have been quite annoying to you. But now that I'm back in normal society, please forget all that.

KŌICHI: Have you often been to the racetrack?

WOMAN: No, it's my first time. Right now I'm doing cosmetic sales in this town, and by chance, I saw a poster on a telephone pole about some star named Kurosawa who, I thought, really looked like a person I'd met somewhere, so I brought my car right here. Then I unexpectedly bump into you, and we talk about old times. I wish it were that simple, but things are a lot more complicated. Actually, there was some trouble over at the parking lot, and I chased someone as far as here.... Doctor, do you have the key?

KŌICHI: Key?

WOMAN: The one who was here a little while ago, he's your brother-in-law, right?

KŌICHI: Yes.

WOMAN: Didn't he hand you a key?

KŌICHI: What about it?

WOMAN: It's my key.

KŌICHI: What did you say?

WOMAN: There was a mix-up in the parking lot. When I went to get a parking coupon, your brother-in-law deliberately moved my car, see, squeezed it to the back so he could get his car out easily. That's OK, but he even took my key.

(JIRŌ *comes running in.*)

JIRŌ: Kōichi, my sister over there! . . .

(ROKUJŌ *recognizes* JIRŌ. *Seeing* ROKUJŌ, JIRŌ *jumps and tries to flee.*)

KŌICHI (*Grabs him*): What's happened to Aoi?

JIRŌ (*Struggles to get away*): Go see for yourself.

(ROKUJŌ *stands directly in* JIRŌ*'s way and slaps him on the face.*)

JIRŌ (*Falls over*): What the hell are you doing? You slut!

ROKUJŌ: You little bastard, you think you can take me for a fool!

JIRŌ: Who the hell is this character? (*To* KŌICHI.) Don't tell me you know her.

KŌICHI: If you have the key, give it back right now!

PARKING LOT ATTENDANT: Uh, we have to close up now . . .

WOMAN: I don't have my key . . .

JIRŌ: You want the key, it's right here. (*Produces it.*)

ROKUJŌ (*To* KŌICHI): This is the one.

(ROKUJŌ *tries to take it.*)

JIRŌ (*Draws back*): First, decide which you want—my sister or this.

(KŌICHI *says nothing.*)

JIRŌ: She's collapsed with morning sickness!

KŌICHI: Anyway, just give it back.

JIRŌ: So that's how it is. (*Throws key.*)

(ROKUJŌ *picks it up.*)

JIRŌ: Is that how it's going to be?

KŌICHI: What do you mean?

JIRŌ: You and her!

(JIRŌ *leaves.*)

(KŌICHI *starts to go look for* AOI.)

ROKUJŌ: Doctor.

KŌICHI (*Stops briefly*): That was inexcusable. I apologize for him.

WOMAN: You don't have to apologize. I don't like you apologizing to me.

KŌICHI: Well, take care.

WOMAN: Doctor, I'm no longer angry. Please convey this to your wife and her brother. That I'm not offended. That's right. (*Opens her bag.*) This is what I'm selling now. Please give it to your wife to show there's no hard feelings.

KŌICHI: Thank you. Well, take care.

WOMAN: Also, I'm planning a business trip to Tokyo soon. I have a favor to ask you. If there is someone you know in real estate, I'd like to have them look into an apartment for me.

KŌICHI: I can at least ask about it. . . .

WOMAN: Yes, that's all I want. Please. I'll be calling you. I'm sorry to lay this on you all at once.

KŌICHI: Well, then. (*Leaves.*)

WOMAN (*To self*): Oh, and Doctor, how wonderful it wasn't you that got burned to death just before the pit stop.

(*The* PARKING LOT ATTENDANT *runs in from the* hanamichi.)

PARKING LOT ATTENDANT: We have to close up now . . .

ROKUJŌ: Oh. (*Heads toward* hanamichi.)

PARKING LOT ATTENDANT: Is that your car?

(ROKUJŌ *suddenly falls down.*)

PARKING LOT ATTENDANT: Madam! (*Runs to help her.*)

ROKUJŌ: Say it once more.

PARKING LOT ATTENDANT: Huh?

ROKUJŌ: Madam.

PARKING LOT ATTENDANT: What's happened to you?

ROKUJŌ: Nothing really.

PARKING LOT ATTENDANT: Do you feel bad?

ROKUJŌ: A bit nauseous. . . .

PARKING LOT ATTENDANT: That's not good. (*Leans over.*)

ROKUJŌ (*Places his hand on her stomach*): It's like something being stirred up in there. . . .

PARKING LOT ATTENDANT: Oh, that's not good. (*Pulls his hand away.*)

ROKUJŌ: What's wrong?

PARKING LOT ATTENDANT: My hands are unworthy of touching a woman's body. They take a tremendous beating in the parking lot. In the olden days, I'd be like a groom for horses. Please, madam, don't take hold of such hands as these.

ROKUJŌ: You . . .

PARKING LOT ATTENDANT: Yes.

ROKUJŌ: You have a sweetheart?

PARKING LOT ATTENDANT: No. . . .

ROKUJŌ: But you must have at least one?

PARKING LOT ATTENDANT: It's no use.

ROKUJŌ: Why not?

PARKING LOT ATTENDANT: Not someone like me.

ROKUJŌ: Why's that?

PARKING LOT ATTENDANT: I'm lacking something.

ROKUJŌ: You're not lacking anything.

PARKING LOT ATTENDANT: No, I've already given up. It's always a holiday here.

ROKUJŌ: Holiday?

PARKING LOT ATTENDANT: It's a long, long Sunday, madam, so I'm accustomed to seeing everything that way. And you're telling me to be attached to someone?

ROKUJŌ: Are you weeping?

PARKING LOT ATTENDANT: Does it look like I am?

ROKUJŌ: That, or it could be something else.

PARKING LOT ATTENDANT: That's because you're looking at my shadow.

ROKUJŌ: Your shadow?

PARKING LOT ATTENDANT: Look, it's wavering there, isn't it? (*Sways his body.*) But a shadow'll just get blown away by a big storm someday. Then I can tell you who I am, if you want.

SCENE 4. THE ROOM

While the conclusion of the previous scene is taking place on the hanamichi, *the stage is changing into* AOI*'s house.* AOI*'s* MOTHER *and* KŌICHI *are in front of the sliding doors. The two are playing cat's cradle. Their shadows fall against the sliding doors.*

MOTHER: Why didn't you come earlier?

KŌICHI: I just didn't know there was a call for me at the hospital. How is Aoi?

MOTHER: The rain that day must have cast an evil spell on her. The fever won't go down.

KŌICHI: I'm sorry I didn't take better care of her. Even though I was with her, I noticed hardly any change. If only it were a simple cold.

MOTHER (*Referring to cat's cradle*): Oh, there, you've got to do it like this.

KŌICHI: But isn't it like this? (*Their game may continue if it takes time for* AOI *to enter.*)

(*Sounds of sliding doors opening.*)

AOI: Mother, who's there?

MOTHER: It's Kōichi.

AOI: The "cosmetics" you gave me recently was pomade, not cosmetics.

KŌICHI: But I asked for cosmetics, and that's what I bought.

AOI: My face got all chapped from being in bed so long, and when I put some of the stuff on a while ago it got sticky and stuck to the pillow. I was just now cleaning it off with a tissue. That's why I'm so annoyed, see, the things men buy! Where did you pick that stuff up?

(KŌICHI *says nothing. The telephone rings.*)

MOTHER (*Answers*): Yes, this is Miyamoto. Kōichi? Just a minute, please.

KŌICHI: Thanks. (*Takes telephone.*) Hello. . . . Hello. . . .

AOI: Who is it from?

KŌICHI: . . . Hello? (*Hangs up.*)

AOI: What a strange call. Mother, would you throw out the stuff in this wastebasket? It still smells.

MOTHER: I'lı go change your ice pack.

AOI: Yes.

(*The* MOTHER *opens the sliding doors and goes out.*)

AOI: Hey, come here, come a little closer.

KŌICHI: How long have you had a fever?

AOI: Since I left you. Also, my stomach sometimes cramps up.

KŌICHI: Your fever doesn't seem terribly bad, but I'm concerned about your stomach.

AOI: Tell me, where did you go?

KŌICHI: Huh?

AOI: After that, you saw my brother, didn't you?

KŌICHI: Yeah.

AOI: I called your place all night long.

KŌICHI: I just met up with an old friend.

AOI: Tell me, do you still smell it?

KŌICHI: What?

AOI: Put your face a little closer. Doesn't that pomade smell?

KŌICHI: No.

AOI: Perhaps you met her?

KŌICHI: What are you trying to say?

AOI: At times like this, my intuition is clear. You went to return the key, didn't you?

(KŌICHI *says nothing.*)

AOI: I heard it from my brother. That you did everything but beat it out of him, and then he finally handed it over to her.

(*The telephone rings.*)

KŌICHI (*Answering*): Yes?

WOMAN'S VOICE: Uh, Doctor? It's me. Excuse me for calling you in such a place.

KŌICHI: What is this?

AOI: Who's it from? Who's it from?

WOMAN'S VOICE: Finally today I found a room. This is with your help. Thank you. And one more thing. Tomorrow if possible I'd like to celebrate in that room my new life in Tokyo. Do you think you could come by?

KŌICHI: Just now I'm terribly wrapped up with something...

WOMAN'S VOICE: Wait, I also want you to return my key.

KŌICHI: Your key? Haven't I returned it?

WOMAN'S VOICE: I don't have it yet. Look, it's the key I once gave you in Izu. Heh, heh, heh, if I can't have it back, I won't be able to ride in the vehicle of my dreams. I'm sorry. That's a joke, just a joke.

KŌICHI: Enough's enough, please. (*Hangs up telephone.*)

AOI: What is she saying to give back?

KŌICHI: A key.

AOI: Not this key, is it?

KŌICHI: How did you get that?

AOI: When you came back from Izu. I found it stuck in a corner of your suitcase. I didn't think it was the key to your room, but I thought I'd try it once to find out.

KŌICHI: Throw it away, Aoi, throw that thing away.

AOI: This is that woman's room key, isn't it?

KŌICHI: That's stupid.

AOI: Since when, since when have you taken up with that crazy woman?!

KŌICHI: What do you mean? Give it here. I'll throw it away for you!

AOI: No. This is my key! You think you can take it away? Just try. Look, here and here. (*Laughs in a strangely husky voice.*) Ha ha ha ha, the key you love is here. You can tell by the scent of pomade on it. Let's turn out the lights, shall we? While you grope about catching the scent of my pomade, you can crawl slowly over here. Listen, darling, darling, darling, darling—why do you make me call you as many as four times? Please come closer.

KŌICHI: Aoi, pull yourself together, Aoi.

AOI: What are you going to do?

KŌICHI: Aoi.

AOI: No. Because my body's still clean and unsullied, ha ha ha, ha ha (*Gradually her voice turns into* ROKUJŌ*'s*), I say no. What're you doing, climbing up on top of me? Isn't your sweetheart waiting for you somewhere? You don't need to be concerned with a woman like me. It's better if you move on quickly. I say no. Don't touch my breasts. I won't have it. I won't. Do you hear me? I'm going to leave here. I'll be leaving this hospital, and when I do, then I'll let you. What do you think you're doing? You're hurting my stomach. Where's my director.

KŌICHI: Aoi, it's me. Do you understand? Aoi!

(*Ambulance siren in the distance slowly takes over the slightly feverish dynamic between these two.* AOI*'s hollow laughter.*)

AOI: I won't give you the key. Absolutely not! You think I'd go back to that kind of hospital?!

KŌICHI: Aoi.

SCENE 5. ON THE *HANAMICHI*

The PARKING LOT ATTENDANT *and the* OLD MAN *are drunk, stumbling about and hanging on one another.*

PARKING LOT ATTENDANT: Are we going to get there soon?

OLD MAN: No, not yet, not yet.

PARKING LOT ATTENDANT: Do you really have a house?

OLD MAN: Do I look like I don't have a house?

PARKING LOT ATTENDANT: That's not what I meant. Just that before, when I picked up a person who'd fallen over drunk like this, he started to look for his former house, and when we got near the Edo River, he said to cross it. . . .

OLD MAN: Well, did you?

PARKING LOT ATTENDANT: No way. We couldn't really swim across, so we take an old boat, and when we're about halfway, he thrusts his hands into the water and calls out the name of his dead son.

(OLD MAN *vomits.*)

PARKING LOT ATTENDANT: Are you all right?

OLD MAN: . . . Then, what happened then?

PARKING LOT ATTENDANT: Morning came.

OLD MAN: What are you?

PARKING LOT ATTENDANT: Huh?

OLD MAN: I said, what are you?

PARKING LOT ATTENDANT: Let me see.

OLD MAN: What the hell are you!?

PARKING LOT ATTENDANT: I'm me.

OLD MAN: You lie.

PARKING LOT ATTENDANT: You say I lie, but I'm just being myself.

OLD MAN: But not everyone acts like you.

PARKING LOT ATTENDANT: Is that so?

OLD MAN: They run around frantically just looking out for number one. Are you doing this to drunks!? (*Makes a sign with his finger to indicate a pickpocket.*)

(PARKING LOT ATTENDANT *looks at a dim light in a room in front of them.*)

OLD MAN: What are you looking at?

PARKING LOT ATTENDANT: The little. . . .

OLD MAN: You mean the little happiness of home?

PARKING LOT ATTENDANT: No.

OLD MAN: Then, what, what, what?

PARKING LOT ATTENDANT: The little flickering flames of the will-o'-the-wisp.

OLD MAN: Hmm.

PARKING LOT ATTENDANT: Kind of hazy, like they're taking shelter in each one of those apartments over there. Sometimes they're beyond the discotheque and other times in the big appliance stores in Akihabara. I'm sorry, you're not the one who's drunk, it's me.

OLD MAN: Even you can. . . .

PARKING LOT ATTENDANT: Even I can what?

OLD MAN: Even you can be happy someday.

PARKING LOT ATTENDANT: It won't work. Not for me.

OLD MAN: But you're young.

PARKING LOT ATTENDANT: No, I'm dead.

OLD MAN: Dead?

PARKING LOT ATTENDANT: Look. . . . (*Puts the palm of his hand on the* OLD MAN.)

OLD MAN (*Withdrawing*): You're young. Still so young, aren't you?

(*Exits.*)

(*Silence.*)

PARKING LOT ATTENDANT (*Lends his shoulder to an imaginary person*): Well, old fellow, let's go.

SCENE 6. THE ROOM

The echoing sound of an ambulance leaving.

WOMAN'S VOICE: Doctor, Doctor.

(*Sound of ambulance farther away.*)

WOMAN: Doctor!!!

KŌICHI: What?

WOMAN: What happened to you?

KŌICHI: Was I having a bad dream?

WOMAN: Yes. You looked really terrible. I didn't intend to wake you up.

KŌICHI (*Gets up*): Didn't an ambulance just go by?

WOMAN: There's an emergency hospital right behind here.

KŌICHI: I see.

WOMAN: I wanted to invite your wife too. Will you give her my regards?

KŌICHI: Yes. May I have some more wine?

WOMAN: Sure. Well, how is she now?

KŌICHI: Well, women during pregnancy on occasion will experience some confusion.

WOMAN: Confusion?

KŌICHI: She speaks with your, with your voice.

WOMAN: Don't say such a frightening thing to me!

KŌICHI: I've seen that sort of spirit medium before, but it never occurred to me that she was capable of such a stunt.

WOMAN: Does she really sound exactly like me?

KŌICHI: Not like you, it is you.

WOMAN: Is it acceptable for a scientist to say such things?

KŌICHI: It was the same thing with that other spirit medium. I couldn't forget the younger female factory worker who had worked together with me when I was eighteen. So I asked the spirit woman to enter the spirit world and call her back. But you know what became of her? She got separated from herself. In other words, at the moment she entered into the spirit world, she began to look for her real self that had possessed that girl, using the voice of that female factory worker.

WOMAN: But I haven't been looking for your wife or anything like that.

KŌICHI: No, but you are always there in the palm of her hand.

(WOMAN *pauses.*)

KŌICHI: Do you remember the key you gave me in Izu?

WOMAN: Let's stop talking about that.

KŌICHI: You did give me the key, and it's the one that's in Aoi's hand right now.

WOMAN: Really?

KŌICHI: That's why, you know, when she closes her fingers around it, she can change into you and also speak with your voice.

WOMAN: I have no intention of being an apparition of a living person, and for that matter, I've got no reason to possess her.

KŌICHI: The cosmetics you gave me, wasn't it some pomade?

WOMAN: I wouldn't call it cosmetics, my goodness, Doctor. Didn't I say pomade?

KŌICHI: You said pomade?

WOMAN: That's right.

(KŌICHI *says nothing.*)

WOMAN: Why are you looking at me like that?

KŌICHI: It's that smell.

WOMAN: Huh?

KŌICHI: You have on the same stuff now too, don't you?

WOMAN: Yes, the same stuff.

KŌICHI: You still have a lot of it?

WOMAN: Huh?

KŌICHI: Don't you have ten or twelve dozen in the closet?

WOMAN: What are you getting at?

KŌICHI: This is half used already, but I'll return this jar to you. And the key, too, that you left with me at the hospital in Izu. A little while ago, I snatched it from her hand while she was sleeping. I want to return all this to you.

WOMAN: You didn't come to congratulate me, did you?

KŌICHI: Here, I've set everything here.

WOMAN (*Places her hand on his*): And then . . .

KŌICHI: And then?

WOMAN: What about the dune buggy?

(KŌICHI *pauses.*)

WOMAN: Didn't you promise? That if I could sneak out like an ant, you'd have the dune buggy waiting for me?

KŌICHI: You've even got me aboard that invisible vehicle?

(WOMAN *laughs lightly.*)

KŌICHI: Why would you do that?

WOMAN: What do you mean?

KŌICHI: Why did you say such things back then? I've been thinking about it ever since. And why is it you remember only those kinds of things?

WOMAN: Because you were my you.

KŌICHI: Do you think you could speak clearly?

WOMAN: Don't you think everything is clear?

KŌICHI: Is this what you mean by being clear? You weren't crazy. You were faking it. You found your way into the field of mental rehabilitation, and finished your training just for fun. And even now, you would "insert" me into your laughable experience.

WOMAN (*Grasps his hands*): That's not so.

KŌICHI: OK, just try and tell me in what way you were crazy!

WOMAN: In all sorts of ways.

KŌICHI: What the hell's that mean?

WOMAN: I . . . I'm . . .

KŌICHI: What's this climbing all over me!

WOMAN: I can't say it well, but I was thinking only of you. It was a one-way passage. Whether my one-way ticket made me brood like that over you, I can't tell, but at some point everything about the time when I met you somehow or other came into focus for me. And I wanted to know more, to taste more. I had no intention of becoming your wife, but from the time I was told I resemble your wife, it was a greater honor than being in your wife's place. These thoughts will surely not amount to real-life happiness. They're just something really very tiny, like peeking through a microscope, like a brass key and sand and ants being hemmed in together. But from long before, ever since I was a child, I wanted to go back there and was hoping someone would take me.

KŌICHI: It's not that I don't understand what you're saying . . .

WOMAN: Please understand.

KŌICHI: But it doesn't have to be me.

WOMAN: If not, why did you entrust the key to me?

KŌICHI: The key is. . . .

WOMAN: To me, small as an ant?

(*Sound of knocking on the door.*)

MAN: Excuse me. Miss Rokujō. Miss Rokujō.

WOMAN: She's not here.

MAN: You say not, but she's here, isn't she?

(*He opens the door.*)

MAN: Is there a Mr. Kōichi here?

(WOMAN *does not answer.*)

MAN: How about it, he's here, isn't he?

KŌICHI: Who is this?

WOMAN: It's the real estate man.

KŌICHI: What do you mean, coming here so late?

MAN: I'm sorry she badgered me into directing her here at all costs.

KŌICHI: Who did?

MAN: She said her name was Aoi.

KŌICHI: What are you saying? Aoi's supposed to be in the hospital.

MAN: She was in the hospital? No wonder she was so pale and very much in pain, but she implored me to bring her here.

KŌICHI: Well, where is she?

MAN: She's there.

KŌICHI: There?

MAN: There, there. My god! She's been eavesdropping on the two of you. . . .

KŌICHI: Aoi. . . .

(*Rushes out of the room.*)

WOMAN: Say.

MAN: Yes.

WOMAN: How is it outside?

MAN: It's very. . . .

WOMAN: The wind is whistling?

MAN: Not only the wind.

WOMAN: What else?

MAN: Something.

WOMAN: What something?

MAN: It's really awful.

WOMAN: Then, for a sick person . . .

MAN: Right, it's rough.

(KŌICHI *returns, slumps to the floor.*)

WOMAN: Did you look in the direction of the pedestrian overpass?

KŌICHI: No.

WOMAN: She must be there. (*Goes out.*)

(KŌICHI *and the* REAL ESTATE MAN *remain.*)

MAN: I'm sorry. Perhaps I shouldn't have accompanied her.

KŌICHI: How did she know?

MAN: Huh?

KŌICHI: How did she know about this place?

MAN: May I have a piece of cake?

KŌICHI: Maybe. . . .

MAN: May I have a piece of cake?

KŌICHI: The wind is. . . .

MAN: Well. . . . (*Nibbles on cake.*)

KŌICHI: . . . blowing from this apartment toward the hospital, isn't it?

MAN: Yes.

KŌICHI: Then the fragrance of the pomade may well have wafted that far and. . . .

MAN: No, the fact is she received a phone call.

KŌICHI: A phone call?

MAN: Yes. That said you were here.

KŌICHI: Who from?

MAN: I don't know. She said that's why she ran over dressed like she was, and she showed me her bare feet stuck with glass.

VOICE: Darling.

KŌICHI: What?

(*Stage grows dark.*)

AOI: Darling, I'm here.

(KŌICHI *looks up and sees* AOI *kneeling on one of the ceiling crossbeams. Startled, he is speechless.*)

AOI: I've been here all along.

KŌICHI: What are you doing there?

AOI: So you were at her place.

KŌICHI: Come down.

AOI: Don't come near me. I'm about to bear your child. I don't want anything to do with a father who'd fool around with that sort of woman. I'm saying don't come near me! A while ago, when I woke up in bed, my key was gone. I knew what had happened. But while I was dozing off again, the phone rang. It was a strange call, someone like me was calling me. Even her face I could vaguely see. And a feeling came over me like I could forgive everything. Because being attracted to a person like me means, after all, that you won't forget me.

KŌICHI: Just a minute.

AOI: Kōichi, you're the one who will be my husband. Both in the past and now I've decided it would be that way, and that's why I've been intimate with you. And so from now on, too, you are the one who must be my eternal husband. Listen closely, Kōichi. I will remove from your eyes forever that woman Rokujō. Forever! When I do, you and I will be alone, and until that time comes, you are not to approach me. Kōichi, she is going to disappear just like that from in front of us.

(*She stands up. The lower half of her body is covered with blood.*)

KŌICHI: Aoi! Come down from there!

AOI: Darling, listen well to my voice. Do you know who I am? Look, this key, the key she left there, I picked it up. Now, the key is in my hand again—the wind will be blowing from here to there. Then you will surely smell this very pomade. Well, come on, turn out the lights all over Tokyo, and grope your way over here. (AOI*'s voice.*) I am Rokujō, your wife, ha, ha, ha, ha, ha.

(*She leaps down from the lintel with her full weight and stops with a jerk in midair. She is hanging by her neck; the key slips out of her hand and falls to the floor. Music.*)

SCENE 7. A SANDY BEACH

The sound of waves from afar. This is the beach by KOREMITSU*'s hospital in Izu.*

KOREMITSU: Well, what will you be doing from now on?
(KŌICHI *says nothing.*)

KOREMITSU: Any idea? Don't you plan to be at the hospital in Tokyo?
(KŌICHI *still says nothing.*)

KOREMITSU: You should take a trip somewhere. Stay for even half a year at such a remote hospital and you have to long for the craziness of the city again.

KŌICHI: No, I'm not going on a trip.

KOREMITSU: Well, what are you going to do?

KŌICHI: Would you admit me here to room number six?

KOREMITSU: What?

KŌICHI: I want to get to the bottom of what that woman was thinking in that room.

KOREMITSU: You're carrying this game too far.

KŌICHI: C'mon. Just get me into that room.

KOREMITSU: What can you learn in a place like that?

KŌICHI: Things about me reflected in that woman's eyes, things about Aoi, who has died. . . . When I think about it now, she didn't say the pomade was pomade. She simply handed it to me, but there's no doubt she even had in mind that Aoi would mistake it for something to put on her face.

KOREMITSU: Do you hate Rokujō that much?

KŌICHI: When I think of Aoi, crushed as she was like a ripe tomato, you can't imagine how much. . . . (*Utters a groan.*)

KOREMITSU: It simply won't do for me to put you in that room.

KŌICHI: Why, why not?

KOREMITSU: I'm telling you, being in that room with your frame of mind, you won't learn a thing about Rokujō!

KŌICHI: You're wrong, you're wrong! What I'd learn is how Rokujō recovered her health so quickly!

KOREMITSU: If I could answer that question, I would not be this kind of doctor!

KŌICHI: You're the one who stirred her up so she'd be obsessed with me.

KOREMITSU: Hey, hey, do you know what you're saying?

KŌICHI: Before, why didn't you take charge of the key I got from her? You just let me have it! You took me, your friend, as a guinea pig and used me so that that woman would completely recover!

KOREMITSU: You say that, and you're a doctor in the mental ward?

KŌICHI: I am a patient. That's why I'm telling you to just get me in room number six.

KOREMITSU: But look, there's no place here to put the likes of you, a seriously ill person!

KŌICHI: There's room number six, room number six.

KOREMITSU: Right now it's filled with less seriously ill patients.

(*The* NURSE *approaches.*)

NURSE: Doctor, there's someone who says he wants to meet someone.

KOREMITSU: Meet with a patient?

NURSE: No, with you. It's about the patient in room number eight.

KOREMITSU: Ah, that one who wants to pay for his mistakes with his ten fingers?

(*The man comes out. It is the* PARKING LOT ATTENDANT.)

KOREMITSU: Yes?

(*The* PARKING LOT ATTENDANT *lowers his head has something wrapped with a large cloth in his hand. Somehow he resembles the patient who had set fire to his pubic hair.*)

KOREMITSU: What's on your mind?

PARKING LOT ATTENDANT: This. (*Holds out the cloth bundle.*)

KOREMITSU: What is that?

PARKING LOT ATTENDANT: It's underwear.

KOREMITSU: You want to deliver it?

PARKING LOT ATTENDANT: Directly, if possible.

KOREMITSU: I wonder if we could manage that.

PARKING LOT ATTENDANT: Doctor.

KOREMITSU: Yes.

PARKING LOT ATTENDANT: Concerning my older brother, I believe I have given you letters for some time. . . .

KOREMITSU: Right. I took a look at them.

PARKING LOT ATTENDANT: If he wants to grovel against the walls, he can do that in my apartment too. If he wants to set fire to his "eleventh finger," I could even buy him a substitute from an adult toy store.

KOREMITSU: Hmmm. . . .

PARKING LOT ATTENDANT: Recently I caught the students playing mah-jong and made them confess. My older brother was only caught in the dorm toilet by a med student whose part-time job was hunting up patients. Don't you think a job like that is odd, if crying all alone in the restroom means you're crazy?

KOREMITSU: However, he can't in fact take care of himself, can he?

PARKING LOT ATTENDANT: I'm thinking I'll give him a ride on the ferry.

KOREMITSU: On the ferry?

PARKING LOT ATTENDANT: The ferry that crosses the big river. It's a river big as an ocean where once several hundred fingers were washed ashore from a neighboring country. Even with swollen, rotting fingers and the corpses and garbage drifting about in the river, if he just gives himself over to the trip, he'll free himself of the walls where he cringes and buries his voice. I thought he'd understand that. Doctor, my older brother is a fragile man, like a virgin. Did you see his white fingers? Did you hear his cramped, bird-like voice? Those things are stains of the city that fly away when he clings to a rusty deck and gulps down the river wind. Otherwise, how shall the blood-curdling, flesh-tingling juvenile classics make our hearts boil?

(*In the distance, the siren sounds, ending lunchtime.*)

KOREMITSU: Well, anyway (*To the* NURSE), look after the underwear for him.

NURSE: Yes. (*Tries to take it.*)

PARKING LOT ATTENDANT: No. You people won't deliver it. You'll only wonder if there isn't something in them and even take out the rubber from the briefs—you would cut open even a tube of toothpaste with a knife—and in the end you'd deliver a discarded husk.

NURSE: Don't be rude.

KOREMITSU: Let's go.

PARKING LOT ATTENDANT: Doctor. (*Grabs him.*)

KOREMITSU: What? Why are you putting a hand on me?

PARKING LOT ATTENDANT: Please look closely at my face. My older brother looks like me, doesn't he? I'm the younger brother. When we were kids and I'd force my hand into the milk bottle and look at my hand and cry at how weird it looked, my brother would look at me and laugh. But now that hand has become my brother's face. Why? Doctor, why did my wrist look so weird then? And why does my brother act so strange now? It's because he is on the other side. On the inside of the glass bottle—behind the iron bars! And while we're here wasting time, that other side is gradually moving farther and farther away from us.

KOREMITSU: Hey, take it easy.

(KOREMUTSU *pushes the* PARKING LOT ATTENDANT *away.*)

PARKING LOT ATTENDANT: If you don't believe me, throw me into the hospital for just as long as my brother has been here. And (*Grasps a handful of sand*) I give my word to you on these smoothly crumbling playing cards of sand that even while acting like my older brother, if you put your ear to my breast, you can hear the gong of the ferry crossing the river!

(*Music.* KOREMITSU *and the* NURSE *exit. The* PARKING LOT ATTENDANT *stands in silhouette. The sand spills from his hand. Sound of waves. Lights upon* KŌICHI. *He is writing in the sand a love letter he once wrote.*)

KŌICHI: My darling Aoi, how are you? I'm here at Izu; the wind has just died down. It's just the right time to continue my love letter to you that I once wrote in the sand. If my thoughts reach heaven, please put on Pat Boone's "Love Letters in the Sand," which we once listened to together, and read this my sweet letter to you.

(*Sound of frothy waves. A woman—it is* ROKUJŌ *herself—peeks out from behind the silhouette of the* PARKING LOT ATTENDANT. *It's as though she has emerged from his shadow.*)

WOMAN: Doctor.

KŌICHI: So it's you, isn't it, the one standing there.

WOMAN: I heard from Dr.. Koremitsu that you were at the beach. . . . I won't stay long. I'll be going soon.

KŌICHI: And you'll call to me again from behind?

WOMAN: No, I probably won't be calling you again.

KŌICHI: Are you going away somewhere?

WOMAN: Yes. To a place where you'll be out of reach even if I tried to call you.

KŌICHI: Good-bye.

WOMAN: You even went to room number six, didn't you? Dr.. Koremitsu told me. And also that you really have it in for me.

KŌICHI: Let's forget it. Haven't I said good-bye? I beg of you, won't you leave me alone? I'm just now writing a letter.

WOMAN: Yes, I know. I read it.

KŌICHI: I wasn't writing it to you. I . . .

WOMAN: It's for Aoi, isn't it?

KŌICHI: That's right. I have to choose the right moment when the wind calms and write quickly.

WOMAN: But now, with waves washing up, look, it's completely disappeared, hasn't it?

KŌICHI: Then I'll write it any number of times. Any number of times.

WOMAN: No, it's one time only for love letters written in the sand. High tide will be coming on.

KŌICHI: Now, you've made me forget what I was writing.

WOMAN: Doctor, look, I know I've been a big nuisance to you, but I've come here because it occurred to me that there was at least one thing I had to give back before we part.

KŌICHI: The tide is rising. Look there, the waves are as far as where I was sitting a while ago.

WOMAN: Yes, now the love letter you wrote in the sand, you can no longer see it.

KŌICHI: The wind has gotten stronger, hasn't it?

WOMAN: Doctor, no need to write love letters to heaven anymore. I'm the one who had your pass and key, who was looking down that day at that ditch of a river and was mistaken for your wife when I went to your office. I'm right here.

KŌICHI: You're Rokujō.

WOMAN: Listen to my voice, close your eyes and listen to my voice, because the thing I must give back to you is this very voice. My voice that didn't answer when you called to me in that shrine of a sand hole I was in. If you had heard it then, we might have gotten by without taking this sort of roundabout route. But I knew that, unless worked twice as hard at it, the memory of that ant that you've forgotten and forsaken would never cut its way into your heart.

KŌICHI: All that is . . .

WOMAN: Don't talk. Just be silent and look over there. My tongue is the waves in the sea. It has completely licked away the love letter you gave me. Now then, try closing your eyes slowly. It's like there's a big lens above our heads, and sunshine is pouring through, like we're in a big laboratory That's right. That's the spirit. We'll be getting smaller and smaller now, we'll enter the world of the microscope.

KŌICHI (*Intending to kill her*): You, you're Rokujō, Rokujō from room number six! (*Grabs her by the neck, and pushes her down.*)

WOMAN (*Turning the tables and getting on top of him*): No, there's no room number six here. No Rokujō here. We have to go slowly back home, like this.

(*Throws a handful of sand. The two writhe about in the sand, and as though dragged into it, they disappear like ants going back into the sand.*)

CURTAIN

Terayama Shūji, *Poison Boy*, directed by Terayama Shūji, Tenjō sajiki, 1978. (Courtesy of Terayama World)

POISON BOY

TERAYAMA SHŪJI

TRANSLATED BY CAROL FISHER SORGENFREI

Poet, playwright, director for stage and screen, photographer, essayist, and novelist, Terayama Shūji (1935–1983) exemplified the experimentalism and edgy imagination of Japanese culture in the 1960s and 1970s. Born and raised in Aomori Prefecture in Japan's north by a domineering mother (his father died in the war), Terayama was already a published poet of classical *tanka* and haiku in his teens before distinguishing himself as a writer for radio, stage, television, and screen. Chronic liver illness prevented him from graduating from Waseda University and eventually killed him after a brief, yet brilliant, life. His first stage play, *Blood Is Standing Asleep* (*Chi wa tatta mama nemutte iru*), staged by Asari Keita in 1960, signaled a fascination with sex and rebellion that runs throughout his work. The same year, his radio play *Adult Hunting* (*Otonagari*; it was made into the film *Emperor Tomato Ketchup* [1970]), about a children's revolt against society, created a sensation similar to Orson Welles's radio adaptation of *War of the Worlds* (1938), since many listeners initially seemed unaware it was fiction. Terayama came into his own as a playwright and director in 1967 when he established his troupe, Tenjō sajiki, named after the Japanese title of Marcel Carné's classic film *Les enfants du paradis* (1945). French writers like Comte de Lautréamont, Georges Bataille, and, above all, Antonin Artaud were powerful influences on his concept of theater as a countercultural weapon. As Terayama's drama evolved, it became less lyrical and text based and increasingly shocking and metatheatrical, breaking theatrical convention, audience expectations, good taste, and sometimes even the law. His reputation traveled worldwide after tours in Europe and the United States beginning in the late 1960s.

Representative plays include *The Hunchback of Aomori* (*Aomori-ken no semushi otoko*, 1967), *La Marie-Vison* (*Kegawa no marī*, 1967), *The Dog God* (*Inugami*, 1969), *Heretics* (*Jashūmon*, 1971), and *Lemmings* (*Remingu*, 1979). Like his thirty-hour-long street-theater epic *Knock* (*Nokku*, 1974), the play featured here, *Poison Boy* (*Shintokumaru*, 1978), was co-written with Kishida Rio. Based on a medieval tale (the source for the nō play *The Blind, Stumbling Monk* [*Yoroboshi*] and possibly even inspired by Euripides's *Hippolytus*), Terayama's play portrays the incestuous love of a mother for her son, a perennial theme in his work. Evoking the myths, folkways, and superstitions of his native Aomori, *Poison Boy* also marks a return for Terayama to more conventional forms of dramatic narrative after more radical experiments like *Knock* and *Heretics*, with their encounter of audience and actor.

Kishida Rio (1946–2003), who is responsible for parts of *Poison Boy*, was part of Terayama's company from 1974 to 1977, when she began working on her own theater projects. It is not clear who wrote which sections of the final script. She collaborated with Terayama on other works and, with his approval, began to write plays about women's issues and formed her own company. Later, she developed an interest in politics and wrote and staged works critical of Japan's colonial policies in prewar Korea. She worked with such notable directors as Suzuki Tadashi, and her interest in international cooperative projects resulted in several projects undertaken with Singapore's Ong Keng Sen, including a version of *King Lear* involving actors from many traditional Asian genres speaking their own languages and using Japanese subtitles.

A musical extravaganza based on a chanted Buddhist tale (*Sekkyō-bushi*).
First performed in June 1978 at Kinokuniya Hall, Shinjuku, Tokyo.

Characters

STEPMOTHER / TEACHER
NARRATOR / FEMALE STUDENT
FATHER
SHINTOKU
SENSAKU, SHINTOKU's stepbrother
SIDESHOW BARKER
YANAGITA KUNIO / MALE STUDENT 1 / STAGEHAND
MALE STUDENT 2 / STAGEHAND
LEADER OF THE SIDESHOW TROUPE, on crutches / MALE STUDENT 3 / STAGEHAND

BABY-KILLING WOMAN 1 (DEMON / GODDESS KISHIMO)
BABY-KILLING WOMAN 2 (KISHIMO)
SIDESHOW PERFORMER: AIR PUMP SELF-INFLATING MAN / DWARF BOY
ISSUN-BOSHI (THE ONE-INCH BOY) / BIG-HEADED LUCKY GUARDIAN DWARF
FEMALE SUMO WRESTLER / KISHIMO
MALE MIDDLE SCHOOL STUDENT
KISHIMO / SIDESHOW GO-BOARD GIRL
OBI GIRL / PHANTOM MOTHER 1
DWARF GIRL / PHANTOM MOTHER 2.
LONG-NECKED FEMALE MONSTER IN SIDESHOW / PHANTOM MOTHER 3
PHANTOM MOTHER 4
PHANTOM MOTHER 5
PHANTOM MOTHER 6
STAGEHAND 1
STAGEHAND 2
STAGEHAND 3
STAGEHAND 4
PROSTITUTE
[In addition, not listed in the script are *a* BEGGAR, *a BIWA* CHANTER, and *a* STUDENT DRESSED IN TAISHŌ STYLE.]

1. THE MERCIFUL CUCKOO

A KUROGO, *beating wooden clappers, is walking around through the audience seats, the dressing room, the stage, and so on. Near the wings, another* KUROGO *is setting up a roadside Buddhist altar. The stage is veiled in dusk. After he is done, one* KUROGO *makes a sound like a cuckoo, singing out "horo-horo." Then the other does the same, as if he is responding to the call. As the second, the third, and more cuckoos join in, darkness falls. All of a sudden, the sound of a temple bell is heard from somewhere. As if this were a signal, the* KUROGOS *disappear, and the theater is plunged into pitch darkness.*

When the altar candle is lighted, a BEGGAR *is seen, cradling a* biwa *in his or her arms as though it were his or her child. He or she is playing the* biwa.[1]

(*Song.*)
I gaze afar—what flutters by?
Look! A butterfly,
My mother's ghost

1. An audio recording made in 1978 has a female *biwa* singer, but the text does not specify who sings.

Appears upon my palm.
A hundred times I write her name,
Till hand and tomb become the same.
(*On the temporary stage in the middle of the audience, a* FEMALE STUDENT *with her back turned is bouncing a ball. A blindfolded* MALE STUDENT *in a navy blue kimono with a splashed pattern passes by and, without taking off the blindfold, talks to the* FEMALE STUDENT.)

MALE STUDENT: Well, excuse my abrupt question. . .
(FEMALE STUDENT, *without turning, keeps bouncing the ball.*)

MALE STUDENT: Are there any railroad tracks around here?
(FEMALE STUDENT *keeps bouncing the ball.*)

MALE STUDENT: I heard a whistle several days ago, and I've looked all over, but no matter where I go, I can't find the tracks. (*Without being asked.*) I wonder if the train I'm supposed to take has already left, or if it hasn't yet arrived. . . . Hey, you. Am I lost?
(FEMALE STUDENT *keeps bouncing the ball.*)

MALE STUDENT: I have to hurry; my body is being eaten away by leprosy. I wanted to see my biological mother at least once before I die, so I found a nurse who is supposed to know her whereabouts, but last year on New Year's Eve, the nurse took her three-year-old child and ran away from her husband. All I wanted was to see her face at least once, so I asked them to show me her photograph, and to my surprise, I saw that my mother had no face.
(FEMALE STUDENT, *bouncing the ball, turns around. We see that she, too, has no face. Like pelting rain, the* CHORUS *sings.*)
(*Song.*)
Weeping and longing for Mother, no longer devout,
When suddenly, a temple bell rang out:
"Go-wong! Go-wong!"
It seemed to shout. No time to cry.
A dream or reality? Was it meant to be?
The present world means nothing to me.
The Me of the past, my tragic plight.
The midmonth moon was full that night
When Mother died,
When Mother died.
(*With each stanza, a light is lit in the sideshow tent. A signboard can be seen, on which is written such things as "Rare Species and Deformed Specimens," "Tokyo Freak Show," "Issun-bōshi—The One-Inch Boy," "The Two-Faced Midget," "The Go-Board Girl," "The Man with an Upside-down Head on His Neck," "Fukusuke, the Balloon-Headed Dwarf: He's the Guardian of Good Fortune," and so on.*

A faceless BARKER *checks customers' shoes at the door. The faceless* LEADER OF THE TROUP, *who is on crutches, pulls the curtain of this one-penny sideshow to reveal the faceless* SNAKE GIRL. *A few faceless* CUSTOMERS *are gathering under the signboard. As though blown into hell by a violent wind, the* MALE STUDENT *stands there, speaking involuntarily.*)

MALE STUDENT: Ah, there's that train whistle again. . . . I want to see the train that I'm going to take!

(*So saying, he takes off his blindfold. Suddenly, a black curtain falls, closing the eyelids of the stage. Blackout.*)

2. THE SNAKE GIRL

NARRATOR: These are the seven flowers of autumn: Bush clover, Japanese pampas grass, creeping vine, yellow maiden-flower, boneset, balloon flower, and one other that I can't recall.

After the evening sun sinks behind the forest of Mount Seto and everything is shrouded in darkness, the sideshow performers who, again today, have had no customers, start putting things away. Issun-Bōshi, the one-inch boy who has two faces, is folding a banner.

It has been many years since the sounds of laughter and applause from inside the show tent spilled out into the precincts of the shrine behind the military base. Now, though the autumn wind blows through the tent, it blows in no customers. Once in a while, neighboring village children run into the tent without paying admission, playing hide and seek, turning over straw mats that are strewn about, or unrolling hanging ones. Long ago, a little girl burst into tears and begged for help, and the crippled shoe-check man who used to drag himself along the ground was so charmed by her that they married. Weeds have popped up among the shadows, growing so tall that their tops have become red. Daily life for the show people is the same as always, except for occasional rumors like the one about the electrician who ran off in the dead of night carrying a bundle wrapped in arabesque-patterned cloth. "Ah, autumn again," says the troupe leader, "I fear there may be no more lotus flowers." Still, if you listen carefully. . . . (*Then, as traditional* jinta *circus music gets louder, the* VOICE OF THE MALE BARKER *is heard from somewhere, like an auditory hallucination.*)

BARKER: Come one, come all! See our sideshow exhibits—These are the real things—don't settle for fakes!

Just the other day, a lovely, glowing baby girl popped out of her mother's belly, but her whole body is covered in scales. She has a human face and a snake's body. That's right, just take a peek. Come on in, you can pay later, just come on in and take a gander. She's devouring a live rooster right now.

I don't know whether or not she likes them or if she just eats chickens because she's sick, but she eats one every day. Would I lie to you? I'm not making this up. She's a real, honest-to-goodness Snake Girl. I wonder what terrible sins her mother committed to have such karma. Hey, you can pay later, please come on in and take a look.

Be careful, it's dangerous to get too close to her. Sometimes when she sees a young man, a handsome fellow, her sexual instincts are aroused, since she's beginning to grow up.

(*A woman shrieks "Kyaaah!" and roaring laughter is heard.*)

BARKER: Yes, now you know, she bites. Hey, hey, look. The lights in the tent are turned off. The Snake Girl will jump out and crawl slowly all over the stage, from one end to the other, using her snake's lower body.

Look carefully and you'll see which part of her snake belly she uses. In the dark, her lovely scales glimmer, looking so pure. . . . When she slowly raises her snake body to stand tall and erect, making eerie sounds like rain drizzling, please clap your hands. Now!

(*And phantom applause—soon, a gust of wind blows, drowning out the applause. Then silence returns.*)

(*During the preceding,* SHINTOKU *and his* FATHER *enter, push aside the door made of straw mats hanging at the entrance of the dressing room, and peep inside. They seem to be discussing something.* FATHER *lights a pipe with a small metal bowl and smokes, but soon he gives it to* SHINTOKU *so he also can smoke.* SHINTOKU, *although he is still a middle-school student, does not flinch, and deeply inhales. Then* ISSUN-BŌSHI, THE ONE-INCH BOY, *dragging a woman's red obi, comes out of the straw-mat door.* FATHER *and* SON *can't help looking at it, then hide themselves in the shadows. The obi seems to stretch on forever.*)

(*Song.*)

The length of an obi measures quite well
The escape route for wives
Trapped in kimono-shop hell.

(*After* ISSUN-BŌSHI *runs away,* SHINTOKU *and* FATHER *boldly push open the straw-mat door. Then, they see that the dressing room is completely empty and nobody is there. A bright light illuminates only a set of Girls' Day dolls displayed on a five-tiered stand.*)

NARRATOR: Driven into a corner by poverty, the troupe started to sell its young women in order to eke out a living.

The Dog Woman, whose show had been popular in Tokyo, no longer got down on all fours but stood up straight, and the Snake Girl removed her scales. They did up their hair and gleefully left the tent with nary a backward glance, hiding fringed pink *nadeshiko* flowers in a set of facing mirrors.

To disguise the sale as an act of pious charity, they used a catchphrase. It was "We donate mothers to families who lack them," but the only buyers were a carpenter from Rice-Selling Town whose wife had deserted him, and a drunken, childless rickshaw driver. However, there had once been a widowed policeman and also a widowed teacher who had each come with their children to buy a second wife.

"What do you think, Shintoku, about that woman with her hair done up in an old-fashioned chignon?"

". . ."

"I like her. Her face is a little thin, but she has a finely chiseled nose. She is much more beautiful than your dead mother."

"Dad, that's a snake woman."

Father laughs and doesn't listen to him, and says, "What fool takes a sideshow trick seriously?" and he chooses as his second wife a woman who looks sexy even when she sleeps.

(SHINTOKU, *unable to bear it any longer, takes a black cloth out of his pocket and covers his eyes with it, like a blindfold. In a flash, everything in the sideshow tent is once again gaudily colored.*)

(*Quiet melody, with alternating voices.*)

(*Song.*)

Layered kimono Upon her breast
Firmly placed One hand is pressed Spiritual strength Upon that breast
Tinged with blue It gleams: Grotesque!
Namu Amida Butsu Longing for Stepmother's raven hair,
So glossy, black The boy's beguiled, but should beware!
For as the Mother sleeps,
Her snakelike spirit writhes
And from her body slowly creeps.

(STEPMOTHER *arises, as if abruptly wakened from a dream. Looking around, she loosens her chignon, the hairstyle she kept while she was sleeping, and takes out the fringed pink* nadeshiko *flower that she had hidden in her black hair.*)

Nadeshiko flower, called Fringed Pink:
Of autumn's seven, the forgotten link.
It burns upon a woman's skin
And leaves a scar like deepest sin.

(STEPMOTHER *starts to walk calmly, having* FATHER *carry the fringed pink* nadeshiko *and a package bundled up with cloth that was beside her pillow.* FATHER *follows her happily. A gust of wind blows, and* SHINTOKU *crouches down, with his face covered.*)

3. THE LONG-HORNED BEETLE: CRIMES AT A NATIONALIZED ELEMENTARY SCHOOL

A KUROGO *erects a blackboard and writes "morals" on it with a piece of white chalk. Other* KUROGOS *bring in school desks. Four* STUDENTS, *including* SHINTOKU, *come in and take seats, each in his own way. Before we realize it, the temporary stage in the center of the audience has turned into a classroom.*

STUDENT 1: Kidnapped by a wild goose.

STUDENT 2: Who was?

STUDENT 1: My dad.

STUDENT 3 (*Smoking a cigarette serenely*): Liar. He just died.

STUDENT 1: He flew off to heaven. Kidnapped by a wild goose.

STUDENT 3: He was a carpenter who fell off a roof. How dumb can you get?

STUDENT 2 (*Laughs*): "There once was a teacher who planned to make all the orphans lift up their hands."

STUDENT 3: "Among forty-nine

STUDENT 2: "Only one boy did pine"—Hey, raise your hand!

(STUDENT 1 *raises his hand.*)

STUDENT 2: "On the way home from school, his classmates all said:

STUDENT 3: 'You'll never have friends since your father is dead.' "

STUDENT 1: "He's in heaven, I know it, I know it, I do!"

ALL: "With rocks for his mattress, as stupid as you!"

(SHINTOKU, *alone without joining in the chorus, keeps a bottle on his knee, as if it were something important. He covers the top with his hand so the inside cannot be seen. From somewhere far away, a* BOY SOPRANO *is heard, singing, "Wild geese in the sky / In lines they do fly."*)

STUDENT 2: Talk.

STUDENT 3: What about?

STUDENT 2: Who cares?

STUDENT 1: The first evening star just came out!

STUDENT 2: Erased, erased, I erased the evening star. No more evening star.

STUDENT 3: You can't just decide to erase it.

STUDENT 1: We'd get lost on our way home.

STUDENT 2: Yeah, well, my eraser can erase your way home, too. I've bought an eraser that can erase anything.

STUDENT 1: Huh?

STUDENT 2: I've bought an eraser that can erase anything.

STUDENT 3 (*Stubbing out his cigarette*): Let me see it!

STUDENT 2: No, if I show you, you'll steal it.

STUDENT 3: No, I won't. I just want a peek.

STUDENT 2 (*Shaking his head*): You think I don't know what's on your mind? You're gonna rub me out; then you get to be the teacher's pet.

STUDENT 1: She's really swell, that hot new teacher, ain't she!

STUDENT 2: You're practically drooling.

SHINTOKU (*All of a sudden, as if vomiting it out*): I hate her!

STUDENT 2: . . .

SHINTOKU: Teachers like her, they disgust me!

(*Without being noticed, a* FEMALE TEACHER *comes in and stands right behind* SHINTOKU. *Hearing* SHINTOKU*'s abuse, her beautiful eyebrows bristle up, and a whip in her hand starts to tremble slightly due to her anger.*)

TEACHER (*Trying to keep her composure*): Somebody was smoking secretly again, wasn't he?

ALL THREE (*Banging down their desktops at the same time*): Not me, ma'am.

(FEMALE TEACHER, *holding her hands behind her back, circles* the STUDENTS. *She happens to see the bottle on* SHINTOKU*'s lap.*)

TEACHER: What's this?

SHINTOKU (*Hides it quickly.*)

TEACHER: Show me! What's inside?

SHINTOKU (*Stubbornly keeps his lips tightly shut.*)

TEACHER: So, then I must assume it's a bottle for cigarette butts, right? (*Takes it in a violent manner.*) Give it to me. (*She takes hold of it and discovers an insect inside.*) Oh, it's a bug, and it's shining like black velvet or enamel. Those long feelers look like a pair of scissors.

STUDENT 2: Teacher, ma'am, it's a long-horned beetle.

TEACHER: A long-horned beetle?

STUDENTS 1, 2, and 3 (*Imitating the sound of a long-horned beetle*): Kicchi, kicchi, gii gii gii.

STUDENT 3: It bites off a woman's hair and eats it.

TEACHER (*Touches her hair involuntarily*): What a horrible bug! (*Suddenly she starts to speak in a coaxing voice.*) Shintoku, why are you keeping a bug like this?

SHINTOKU (*Without answering, he grabs the long-horned beetle and puts it back in the bottle and covers it with his hand*): . . .

STUDENT 1: Ma'am, Shintoku said that he was planning to have the bug eat all of his mother's hair! (*Bursts into laughter.*)

ALL: Kicchi, kicchi, gii gii gii.

STUDENT 3: His mother will become bald!

(STUDENTS *burst into laughter again.*)

TEACHER: Why would you do such a thing?

SHINTOKU: Because she's my stepmother.

TEACHER: Lots of stepmothers are nice. And from what I've heard, your mother is very religious, isn't she?

SHINTOKU: She panders to Buddha to make up for bullying her child.

TEACHER: You know that's a terrible thing to say, don't you?

SHINTOKU (*Strongly, as if challenging her*): Teacher, ma'am!

TEACHER: . . .

SHINTOKU: My stepmother looks just like you.

TEACHER: . . .

SHINTOKU: I think that maybe you're really my stepmother, my fake mother. My real mother had short hair that was always warm, like grass in the summer sun. But both you and my stepmother have long, coal-black hair like the feathers of a wet raven.

TEACHER (*Without noticing, her way of talking gradually begins to sound like the* STEPMOTHER*'s*): Now, I understand your real motive, Mr. Shintoku. You plan to drive your new mother away, although she's finally settled comfortably in your home, isn't that right? Not only that, you're trying to make your mother and your stepbrother Sensaku lose all their hair until they go bald. That's your plan, isn't it? First a divorce, then TB, and after that, freak shows in a fifty-cent sideshow tent, snakes, ill will, ropes, handrails, crippled babies, newspaper articles, and cherry-blossom viewing. Now, pay attention, Class. See how I punish a boy who fails to follow instructions. Let this be a warning. Look carefully. (*Caustically.*) Shintoku, drop your trousers and let us see your bare buttocks!

(*Lifts the whip.* STUDENTS, *all together, start to shake their bodies and make sounds of long-horned beetles.*)

ALL: Kicchi, kicchi, gii gii gii.
Kicchi, kicchi, gii gii gii.

(SHINTOKU *pulls down his pants halfway. Action freezes when the* TEACHER, *with furrowed brow, lifts the whip.*)

(*In the distance, a* BOY SOPRANO *can be heard singing an elementary-school song, but transposed into a higher key.*)

(*Song.*)

Oh cherry tree, Oh cherry tree
That grows beside the schoolhouse door
My son it was Who planted thee
My son who died In long past war

Oh cherry tree, Oh cherry tree
That once our family's grave did grace,
My son it was Who planted thee,
Dug up and carried To this place.

Oh cherry tree, Oh cherry tree
Once shorter than a twelve-year-old
My son it was Who planted thee
Two stories tall You've grown tenfold!

Kicchi, kicchi, gii gii gii.
Kicchi, kicchi, gii gii gii.

SHINTOKU (*Suddenly, all alone, he comes out of the tableau vivant*): Now! If I race back home really fast, I can get there before she does. Then I'll be able to see if it's really true that Stepmother is disguised as my teacher. Fly away, you long-horned beetle! (*He runs off at full speed, as fast as a thrown stone!*)

4. THE TRANSFORMATION OF KISHIMO, THE MERCIFUL GODDESS WHO DEVOURS HER OWN CHILDREN: A PORTRAIT OF HELL

(*Slowly, chanted narrative accompanied by the* biwa.)
The shortcut home from school:
Jump the railroad track,
Zip through the alley in back
Of the geisha house,
Turn right at the tobacco shack.
At the second telegraph pole, I halt
And do a mental somersault again today:
Her kimono's dyed with letters of red,
Hair's twisted round combs behind her head
Like the Mother I recall
After her bath when I was small.

NARRATOR: Muttering, "It can't be . . ." Shintoku stops, then follows her for few steps but realizes that it was a mistake—she's not his birth mother—and he rushes into his own house.

(*The sound of the wooden clappers, and a thirty-watt bulb lights up. Seated around a low dining table are* SHINTOKU*'s* FATHER, STEPMOTHER, *and* SENSAKU, *who is the* STEPMOTHER*'s child from a former marriage. Koto music is heard, overlapping with the continuous announcements on "Missing Persons."* SHINTOKU, *his school bag on his shoulders, hurries in and opens the sliding door, which makes the sound "gara gara." He is astonished to see* STEPMOTHER *sitting there.*)

SHINTOKU: Oh no! How could that bitch be back already?

NARRATOR: He is so surprised that he almost stops breathing. He thought he'd get home before his stepmother, who had been disguised as his schoolteacher today, but she must have taken a shortcut and arrived home early enough to be waiting for him with the dinner already prepared.

STEPMOTHER: Shintoku, you're so late coming home.

NARRATOR: She says.

STEPMOTHER: Now, let's have dinner. Go on, be quick and wash your hands and feet.

(*A gust of wind makes the hanging lightbulb swing, and it seems to be about to go out. A short musical performance describes the family. All four people face front, each carrying a rice bowl and chopsticks.*)

SENSAKU: Father, please give me the Mother card of the family of Mr. Ieo Mamoru, the Home Protector.

FATHER: I don't have it. Mother, please give me the child of Mr. Money-Tree Kaneno Narukichi.

STEPMOTHER: Someone has taken one of my cards. Sensaku, please give me the pet dog of the Nation Protector Kunio Mamoru family.

SENSAKU: I don't have it. Father, please give me the Mother of the Home Protector Ieo Mamoru Family.

FATHER: I don't have it. I already told you that I don't have it. Mother, please give me the Mother of the Money-Tree Kaneno Narukichi family.

SHINTOKU: My turn never comes. Even though I have four matching cards.

FATHER: Mother, please give me the Mother of the Money-Tree Kaneno Narukichi family.

SHINTOKU: I've got that one.

STEPMOTHER: Well, I don't, and it's my turn. Sensaku, please give me the child of the Nation Protector Kunio Mamoru Family.

SENSAKU: Someone's taken one of my cards. But no matter how long we play, if we can't get any Mother cards, we'll never finish the "Family Reunion" game.

STEPMOTHER: That means . . .

SENSAKU: Someone's been hoarding them all.

FATHER: All four of the same cards.

SENSAKU: What's more, they're all Mother cards,

STEPMOTHER: Hoarded in sweaty palms,

(*The* CHORUS*'s song seems to flow from this line.*)

(*Song.*)

Hoarded in sweaty palms
The Mother cards all look the same.
In the Family Reunion Game

Shall I toss them in the flowing stream?
Or late at night, when others dream,
Bury the cards in a vacant lot?
Coming or going, ready or not,
Straight across town, to some other place.
Leaving or coming, I crave your face.

A temple novice, a year times three,
Or selling rice, five years for me?
What should I do?
Where should I be?

My devilish Stepmother's
Fresh-washed hair
On her bare neck again: I must beware.

Hateful   Hateful
Treated like dirt, I hurt
Until one day, I become a puppet of clay.

Even puppets of clay
Will surely transform to human form
After searching the city for a trace of your face.

5. THE MYSTERIOUS DR. YANAGITA KUNIO

SHINTOKU, *slipping out alone, stares at the long-horned beetle in the bottle, shining in the dark. After one clap of the wooden clappers, the lights on the house upstage go off, and out of the blue, a* DEMOBILIZED SOLDIER *appears, standing in front of* SHINTOKU.

SHINTOKU: Oh, it's you, dear old Dr. Yanagita.

YANAGITA: I'm glad you remember me. Indeed, I'm the very same Yanagita Kunio.

SHINTOKU: You're dressed very strangely today, aren't you?

YANAGITA (*Taking off false whiskers*): These long, raggedy whiskers are fake. Yesterday, I wore this pair of pince-nez glasses. I change my appearance every day.

SHINTOKU: The day before yesterday, I saw a picture of you in *Boys' Club* magazine. If I remember correctly, you wore a black mask.

YANAGITA: Right. And when we last met, I was an air-pump man in a derby hat. Before that, I was a projectionist at the Station-Front Cinema, and before that I ran the Rising Sun Lunch-Box Shop and supplied lunches to the military academy. And before that I was an astronomer who observed the scattering—from almost two miles up in the air—of flyers promoting a new department store. I have been hanging around you for a long time. It's just that you didn't notice.

SHINTOKU: So, you're not a lightbulb salesman today, are you?

YANAGITA: I decided not to do that anymore. Lightbulbs simply light themselves, but they don't light up a house. On top of that, the more light a bulb casts in the space below where it hangs, the darker the space surrounding it. In the dark, a dwarf will always turn over a tatami mat and start plowing the rice field. Good harvests or bad harvests, they're all due to that demon electricity.

SHINTOKU (*Overwhelmed by the magician-like movements of his hands*): . . .

YANAGITA: So, starting today, I've decided to change my policy and sell this instead. (*And he takes out something like a round, black piece of cardboard.*)

SHINTOKU: What is it?

YANAGITA: A hole.

SHINTOKU (*Surprised*): A hole?

YANAGITA: Yes, a hole.

(*The mysterious* THEME SONG OF THE HOLE *begins to engulf the night.*)

YANAGITA (*Perhaps he sings*):

This single thing,
If you stick it firmly on the wall,
You can dive right through, then fall
Into the other side.
You can exit anywhere, worldwide
With nothing but this!
Like rubber, it can expand or shrink,
As fast as a wink. Take it anywhere—Just think!
Fold it small,
And it's a peephole through the wall.
Spread it wide upon the floor,
And voila! A brand new trap door.

SHINTOKU: It's unbelievable! To think that you can carry around a hole.

YANAGITA: Just watch this trick:

Put it on the ground,
Then lickety-split,
You slide right down into the hole you've found.

SHINTOKU: Dear old sir! (*Boldly.*) Could you please let me buy this hole?

YANAGITA:

I can lend it for free,
But sell it? That can't be.
It's being invented,
It's not yet perfected.
For instance,
What about the lid?
Listen, kid: I still don't have a solution.

SHINTOKU:

So, it's possible
To let me borrow it, right?

YANAGITA: But only for a day.

SHINTOKU: Thank you, Gramps! (*He takes the hole in his hands and puts it on the ground.*)

SHINTOKU:

Can I really go down to the underworld?
How deep is the hole?
Is there a ladder?
What if, as soon as I step into it,
I fall down, tumbling head over heels?
That's what I'm afraid of.

(*Looks inside.*)
Wow, it's pitch-dark.
It's as though the sky is underground,
And in it, the galaxy is shining.
(*He looks up.*)
(YANAGITA KUNIO *is no longer there.*)
Oh! He's disappeared!
(*Looking around.*)
Well, now's as good a time as any.
(*He dives into the hole. Halfway down.*) Oh!!
(SHINTOKU *cries out. Everything goes black. It is not clear whether his head got stuck or if he fell down head over heels; it is like a great nebula, a black hole in the galaxy. The* THEME SONG OF THE HOLE *emanates from the underworld, overwhelming the stage.*)

6. OSHIRA-GAMI (THE GUARDIAN GOD OF FARMERS) IN HELL

In the dark, a sound like digging in the ground. And an echo like water dripping in a limestone cave. After a while, the voices of people in hell calling one another flow in seductively, as if a mandala is being woven by lotus threads. The sounds become a chorus, as though many Buddhist pilgrims are singing hymns of praise at the thirty-three temples sacred to Kannon [Avalokitesvara], the goddess of mercy, as they trace gold-dust words in the dark blue mire of the ground. The sounds spread out.

1: The Lotus Sutra is chanted over and over
2: Birds chirp
3: Chorus

Dead Mother's	Grace	Profound
In the darkness	Buddha's face	Is found
Known?	Or not?	
After I found it		
Purple	Clouds surround it	
Mother's paradise		
In the next life	I wait	To banish hate
From my mind	Looking back, I always find	
Mother's black hair		
If I look back,	Despair. The world falling into ruin	
Falling	Don't look back, beware!	

Purple *tabi*, purple footwear.

(SHINTOKU *wanders about, almost like a sleepwalker. In fact, he is hauled by a string held by a* KUROGO, *who is actually* YANAGITA KUNIO *in disguise.*

As if turning hell into a freak show, a large two-wheeled hand-drawn cart [such as a son would use to abandon his aged mother in the mountains] and a two-wheeled vehicle [meant to carry an unwanted, abandoned child] roll by. None of the passersby has a face, but since SHINTOKU *has his eyes closed, he does not notice. Appearing from behind, several* MOTHERS *or* KISHIMO *slowly gather.*

The winter wind howls, making a sound like a flute as it blows through bamboo fences. One MOTHER *transforms into a prostitute, beckoning to* SHINTOKU. *Another* MOTHER, *carrying a stone Buddhist statue [of Jizō] on her back as if it were her baby, asks for salvation. Yet another* MOTHER, *in pilgrim's garb, is ringing a bell. And another, wearing* monpe *[baggy work pants gathered at the ankles] and an air-raid hood, keeps calling* SHINTOKU*'s name. They all gradually surround* SHINTOKU *and form a circle by holding one another's hands.* SHINTOKU, *covering his eyes, crouches. He protectively holds the blue bottle with the long-horned beetle inside on his lap.*)

NARRATOR:

Natural mother
Foster mother
Godmother
Stepmother

Bird in the cage
Bird in the cage
Mother in the cage,
When will you come out?
Before dawn, when it's dark throughout
Shintoku-maru
Plays the flute. Here's a clue:
Guess who's standing right behind you?

(*A flaming red slip, the long, crepe undergarment of a kimono, decorated with an irregular design of fading letters here and there, like the text of a sutra; but this* MOTHER *has not tucked up the hem, but rather, she lifts the edges higher so that her bare white ankles peek out from the damp, red lining, as she beckons* SHINTOKU.)

(SHINTOKU *feels that the person who stands right behind him may be his real mother, but he cannot turn around. Before one notices, a* WOMAN *dressed in mourning enters and joins the hand-holding circle; she stands right behind* SHINTOKU. *Her long, raven locks shine in the moonlight of hell.*)

SHINTOKU (*Still crouching, hands over his eyes*): They say that my real mother died because she gave birth to me. She wanted good fortune, and so the gods despised her. There was a fire the night I was born. As Mother Bird held me tightly, the fire engulfed us, and Father Bird said,

"Shouldst thou survive, bring forth another child." But Mother said,
"Wouldst thou have me abandon this helpless chick?
Though death ensue, my love for it will never die."
And the grass fire consumed her, and she was burned to death, thus saving my life.
I want to see the face of my sainted Mother.
You who are right behind me, you who I must not see: I want to see your face!
(*Removing his hands that cover his face, he turns around and sees that the person standing right behind him is his* STEPMOTHER, NADESHIKO.)

SHINTOKU: Oh, you are. . .

(*Then his* STEPMOTHER, NADESHIKO, *laughs wildly, and all of a sudden, the voices of the* CHORUS *flow in.*)

Buddha-house and Buddha-words: Four
Corners of the temporal world: More
Holy saint and sacred horse:
Ara-re-ri-uma, of course.

Flowery foam: Rain from an ornamental comb
Robin red-breast
Baby at her breast
Blood-covered breast
Beating her stepchild
Stepmother: Oh, what a lovely boy!
See the lovely baby brother!
Rat-a-tat-tat,
Tat-tat.
Beat that toy
Drum and flute
Happy baby, oh so cute Dancing
Faceless paper dolls
Baby Boy   Pretty boy   Boil the boy   Eat the boy
Grill the boy and eat the boy?
A Demon's mask, ahoy!

Buddha-house and Buddha-words: Four
Corners of the temporal world: More
Holy saint and sacred horse:
Ara-re-ri-uma, of course.

(*Wild laughter, festive music in hell, and a pitch-black shower of cherry blossoms. The* WOMEN *all become* MOTHERS *who dance crazily, and one hundred faceless paper dolls used for weather-control magic* [teruteru-bōzu] *fall from above and writhe in agony.*)

SHINTOKU: Dammit! I've been tricked! Long-Horned Beetle, come out! Come out, and cut these women's hair! (*He cries.*)

(*Slowly, a* LONG-HORNED BEETLE *that is nearly ten feet long appears from the dark. After it walks a few steps toward* STEPMOTHER, *one clap of the wooden clappers is heard, and the nightmare disappears.*)

7. ERASER: SUPPLEMENTAL EDITION

In a vacant lot in Cat Town—or perhaps in a school gymnasium—a boy digs in the ground, burying something. It is STUDENT 2.

Concentrating intently, he does not notice that a WOMAN *appears, standing as close to him as if she were his shadow. One can tell at a glance that the* WOMAN, *with her tousled hair and pale face, is sick.*

WOMAN: What are you doing?

STUDENT 2 (*Caught by surprise but laughing it off*): Hee-hee-hee. Treasure hunting.

WOMAN: Treasure hunting?

STUDENT 2: Yeah. . . . I heard that some guy from India buried a snakeskin wallet around here.

WOMAN: Liar. You were burying something, weren't you?

STUDENT 2: Were you spying on me?

(*The* WOMAN *nods.*)

STUDENT 2 (*Assuming a somewhat defiant attitude*): Since you saw, you didn't need to ask.

WOMAN: Come clean. What were you trying to bury?

STUDENT 2: An eraser.

WOMAN (*Peering at it*): Oh, I see. But why?

NARRATOR: A vacant lot in Cat Town. It is the time of day when the smoke from the bath house chimney has vanished and the howling of dogs is heard. From behind the unknown woman, the pawnshop's gas lamp shines, making her shadow grow longer. Fearing being noticed by others.

STUDENT 2: Don't tell anyone. This is not just any eraser. I used it to erase the first star of the evening.

WOMAN: . . .

STUDENT 2: I also erased a retired used-clothes salesman who set his bulldog on me in the alley. (*Stroking the eraser in his hand.*) This is an eraser that can even rub out humans.

WOMAN: . . .

STUDENT 2 (*In a tearful voice*): See how this slanted part is worn away? That's the part I used to erase my dad. He caught me smoking, and out of the blue, he just smacked me, so last night, while he was sleeping, I rubbed him out, just like this. (*Makes the sound* "goshi goshi," *onomatopoeia for rubbing.*)

WOMAN (*Half in doubt*): Did you erase him from his feet first? Or from his head?

STUDENT 2: I don't remember. I did it with my eyes closed. And (*Choked with tears*) when I got up in the morning, his futon was empty.

WOMAN: Wow!

STUDENT 2 (*Taking out some sheets of blue tissue paper*): Look at this. These eraser scrapings are my dad. *Namu Amida Butsu.*

WOMAN: Listen, young man. (*Very interested.*) I bet that eraser could erase another person, couldn't it?

STUDENT 2: I'm not gonna lend it to you. I'm gonna bury it.

WOMAN: Please, just one person.

STUDENT 2 (*Startled*): What?

WOMAN: There's this woman, she's really sick. It's creating a problem for me. I just don't know what to do.

STUDENT 2: Where is she?

WOMAN: Right in front of you.

STUDENT 2: . . .

WOMAN: It's me.

STUDENT 2: Stop it. That's creepy.

(*And* STUDENT 2 *steps back little by little. The* WOMAN *beckons with her hand.*)

WOMAN: Please . . . please erase. . .

STUDENT 2: No. Keep away from me.

NARRATOR: Moving one of her hands behind her and reaching into the knot of her obi, she takes out a small packet and offers him the money in it.

WOMAN: . . . I'll give you all of this, boy. You can buy a hundred new erasers, OK?

STUDENT 2: I've made a decision. I'll never erase anything again. Even if I write something wrong, I'll just leave it that way.

WOMAN (*Fretfully*): What a pigheaded boy! Ten years ago my parents sold me to a brothel to cut down on the number of mouths to feed. I'm just a whore living in a three-mat room, and everyone sniggers and gossips about me. Ever since I left home, having sold the setting sun for a couple of cents, I've been obsessed with death. Ten years just flew right by. Listen, crickets are chirping again, somewhere. In my hometown, they're holding the annual festival right now. (*Covering her mouth, she makes a choking sound and coughs up blood.*)

STUDENT 2 (*Surprised*): You've got TB!

(*In a gust of wind, a thirty-stringed koto is heard from a secret place, and the* KUROGO *chorus chants.*)

The autumn wind blows:
Whose tomb lingers
On my index fingers?

On my index finger,
Holy words I'll write:
To a distant land, take flight.

Namu Amida Butsu
Please fly away
Namu Amida Butsu
Please fly away.
(*Before one notices, in the dark, phantoms of the dead slowly appear, one by one. The* STUDENT*'s* FATHER *is in the front, followed by, for instance, a* FIRST-YEAR MILITARY VOLUNTEER *who was erased because of his attempt to catch a swallow-tailed butterfly, a mentally dim* GEISHA *who was erased while she was embracing a drunken client behind a telephone pole at Shinbashi stop, and a* TEEN PROSTITUTE *wearing a loose blue silk crepe obi and with her hair braided in three strands. Manipulated by the invisible strings held by the* KUROGO, *they approach* STUDENT 2, *extending their arms as if asking for salvation.*)

STUDENT 2 (*In spite of himself*): Oh! I was sure I had erased them all, but . . .

8. THE CURSE OF A STRAW DOLL

A LITTLE GIRL *appears with a straw doll in her hand, looks around to make sure nobody is there, takes out several six-inch nails and a wooden hammer.*

So sad again today, so blue
Hammering nails into a straw doll
This doll I love the most, it's true
Hammering nails into a straw doll
(*Saying "Big Brother!" the* LITTLE GIRL *decisively sticks a six-inch nail into the forehead of the straw doll! A* DWARF BOY [ISSUN-BŌSHI] *rolls in doing somersaults. The* LITTLE GIRL *watches him with delight, then hammers in another nail. The* DWARF *jumps and does another somersault. Without being noticed,* DUPLICATES OF THE LITTLE GIRL *appear here and there in the theater. They put straw dolls on the walls and start to hammer six-inch nails into them. The sounds of nails blend into a melody. At its peak, the* DWARF, *who has been jumping around with each hammered nail, freezes. The* LITTLE GIRL, *looking at him murmurs involuntarily, "He's dead."*)
Crescent eyebrows
Like the evening moon
Far past his shoulders
Hair grows so soon.
(*Murmuring or singing these lines,* STEPMOTHER NADESHIKO *appears. She looks around. As if calling out to* NADESHIKO, *a* SOLOIST *sings.*)

Marrying into a village of falling flowers
What mysterious realm of passion flowers?
(*Answering as though speaking a monologue.*)
I dream of—Not the flesh of my child?
I pine for—Why is it so distant and wild?
(*Soloist.*)
Beckoning to him, I nod to my lap
His eyes say yes, but I hear a snap
(*Answering as though speaking a monologue.*)
And he cuts all thirty koto strings,
Throws out the pick and away he wings.

STEPMOTHER: Look, look. These are the parings from my child's fingernails. While still suckling at his mother's breasts, in his childlike way, his fingernails clawed into my breasts, purple, and I, cutting the nails, saving the parings, for twelve years saving them in a black lacquer box, those crescent parings still soft and innocent, looking like the evening moon, when I pick them up, my body weakens. What a pity, to be bought from a freak show tent. Is this evil karma from a former life? The curse of the goddess Kanzeon? You were my firstborn son, but bad luck married me into this house, where you must submit to Shintokumaru as the eldest son—compared with you, my delicate flower, he's like coarse summer grass—And thus you are disinherited.

(*As if talking to the fingernail clippings.*) But don't you worry, Sensaku.

I will cast a Mother's curse on that disobedient, defiant Shintoku, a curse to make him die young. Look! Already written on this memorial plank, the fifteen characters of Shintokumaru's posthumous Buddhist name.

(*Sings.*)
Curse the brat and bless my boy,
Endless devotions will you enjoy
Only you we'll worship, I solemnly swear
Oh Kanzeon, please grant my prayer.

You are these fingernail clippings, rustling like grains of sand in my palm. There was never a morning when you failed to dig into my aching breasts with these crescent-shaped nails. (*Putting them back into the small, black lacquer box, which she ties with red string.*) Don't worry, Sensaku, your older brother Shintoku is destined to die of leprosy soon. (*Taking out a six-inch nail.*) If Shintoku dies, you are certain to be the only heir . . .

All night long at the inn I wait
While the blacksmith forges nails of hate
Dawn in Shimizu will seal his fate,
And blood-red flowers will sate
The gods of hell.

(STEPMOTHER *takes out the wooden grave plank on which* SHINTOKU*'s posthumous Buddhist name is written and raises the hammer in order to pound in a six-inch nail. The blindfolded* SHINTOKU *enters, believing that he is wandering in hell.*)

SHINTOKU:

Pushing onward	A springtime haze	
To the edge of hell, to the end of days	A milestone:	
My mother's hair	Tousled in sleep	Tightly bound
A coal-black heap	Visiting	What have I found?

Who's there? A woman, standing with her back turned to me, here in this unexpected place. From the back, she looks exactly like my biological mother. Could it be? I wonder. . . . By any chance, might you be my mother?

(*Surprised,* STEPMOTHER *hides the six-inch nail and hammer behind her back.*)

SHINTOKU: That scent. (*Approaching her.*) Yes, it is you. (*Sighing.*) At last, I have found you in hell. (*Embraces her.*) All day long, Stepmother bullies me, and I can't sleep a wink at night. Mother, I can't help feeling bitter that you abandoned me when you died.

(*Followed by the* biwa *chanter.*)

Mother, I feel bitter, abandoned when you died.
I cried and cried and cried.
Breastfeeding mother
Or perhaps some other?
Shintoku hugs her oh, so tight
And wonders: will she laugh at his plight?

STEPMOTHER: I see, Stepmother's really horrible, isn't she? (*Disguised voice, disguised voice, disguised voice.*)

SHINTOKU: Yes, Mother. She's a demon. I wonder why Father was infatuated with such a woman.

STEPMOTHER (*Anger wells up in her. But she lets* SHINTOKU *caress her as if she were his wife*): That woman isn't kind to you, is she?

(*Song.*)

Tightly embraced,
When this phantom-faced
Mother into a woman will tumble,
Over a stone, his foot will stumble.

SHINTOKU: Oh, here's a little black box. . . . (*Taking it up and trying to loosen the string.*)

STEPMOTHER (*Revealing her true identity involuntarily*): Stop, Shintoku! Don't touch that box! (*Scolds him.*)

SHINTOKU: Oh, no! That voice!

STEPMOTHER: Yes, this voice is mine! (*When she pulls out her comb decorated with fake* nadeshiko *flowers [fringed pinks], her black hair immediately tumbles down to her shoulders. Surprised,* SHINTOKU *pushes* STEPMOTHER *and tries to run away, but*

STEPMOTHER *fixes him in her keen, hard gaze.*) I feel sorry for you, but I'm doing this for my darling child Sensaku, and so I must bestow on you the curse of leprosy, which will make you into a despised outcast. (*Producing the hammer, she pounds the six-inch nail into the wooden grave plank.*)

(*Song.*)

Shintokumaru is eighteen years old   I hammer the nails, striking eighteenfold
Monthly fairs on the seventh abound   Seven more nails on the seventh I pound
Sorya, one!

(*She drives a six-inch nail into the wooden plank and calls out to* SHINTOKU, *who involuntarily covers his right eye and falls over.*)

Without a break, two!

His eyes become putrid   Leprosy!
His eyes become putrid   Leprosy!

(SHINTOKU, *murmuring "mumumu" as he writhes in pain, now covers his other eye as the roar of a Japanese* taiko *drum comes surging.*)

At seven shrines, hammering seven nails
At the holy sanctum, fourteen nails
Hateful stepchild, twelve more nails

At the burial chamber, twelve again
May your eyes go blind! Twelve more, Amen!
And twelve more nails at the Demon's Fen.

Donate a hoe to the water god's purse
Twelve are the nails of a Mother's curse

(*As* STEPMOTHER *drives in each nail,* SHINTOKU *covers his eyes and writhes. Before one notices it, two, three, and more duplicates of* SHINTOKU *appear. As their numbers increase, they wriggle around.* STEPMOTHER *transforms into a child-eating demon / child-protective goddess* [KISHIMO] *who drives in more and more nails. In response,* KUROGOS *and* LITTLE GIRLS *drive more and more nails into straw dolls.*)

A curse   (*They drive in nails, then call out a meaningless shout.*) Hei-ya!
Black hair   (*They drive in nails, then call out a meaningless shout.*) Hei-ya!
Nail the Bodhisattva   (*They drive in nails, then call out a meaningless shout.*) Hei-ya!
A grave   (*They drive in nails, then call out a meaningless shout.*) Hei-ya!
A red obi   (*They drive in nails, then call out a meaningless shout.*) Hei-ya!
Three thousand miles (*They drive in nails, then call out a meaningless shout.*) Hei-ya!
Because I am your Mother   (*They drive in nails, then call out a meaningless shout.*) Hei-ya!
I drive in the nails   (*They drive in nails, then call out a meaningless shout.*) Hei-ya!

May your eyes be crushed (*They drive in nails, then call out a meaningless shout.*)
Hei-ya!
Stepchild, may you die (*They drive in nails, then call out a meaningless shout.*)
Hei-ya!
Die, die, die! *Namu Amida Butsu*
Die, die, die! *Namu Amida Butsu*
(*With the repeated hitting of nails, meaningless shouts, and blood spewing upward, the multiple* SHINTOKUS *have stopped moving. They lie piled on top of one another.* STEPMOTHER *laughs loudly.*)
The prayers are granted
And the curse is planted
One hundred and thirty-six points of pain
Where the nails were driven, with leprosy in flame.
Crushed are his eyes, he cannot see!
Oh, pitiful Shintokumaru
A blind leper is he.
(*The duplicates of* SHINTOKUMARU, *all of whom have become blind, cover their eyes and leave, seeking dim light.* STEPMOTHER, *drawing herself up to her full height and covering the wooden grave marker with her black hair, sees them off. Far away, human voices mimic mountain doves' "hooo-hooo." Blackout.*)
(*Song.*)
Blood blooms red on a straw doll's head.
Strangled poppies bloom blood red.
That's the language of flowers.

9. THIS CHILD WHOSE CHILD? DEMON'S BAG / DEMON WOMB

NARRATOR: Forensic medicine, a freak show, a little cuckoo.

Fall passes and spring comes, then spring passes and another fall comes. At night, the masseurs pass the time. They listen to the sound of the wind and play with the forty-eight letters of the alphabet song, cutting apart the letters with scissors and rearranging the order. I-ro-ha, i-ro-na-shi—colorful, colorless, yu-ri-re-u-su, ro-ke-n-ya-da-i-ba, ghostly apparitions, a-ra-da-ra-ni, a-ra-da-ra-ni-da-ra-no, abra-cadabra, hi-to-sa-ra-i, kidnapped. Where has Shintoku gone? Is he lost or is he hiding? We saw his face on the front page of the special new-year's issue of *House Lights*.

After Shintoku contracted leprosy and left home, Sensaku became the head of the household. He polished the family altar and arranged the chrysanthemums and lived up to all of his Mother's expectations I-ro-ha-ni-ho-he-do, chi-ri-nu-ru-wo, the scent of blood and letters dead, chi-ri-shi, chi-bu-mi-no, scattered letters writ in blood, chi-no-mi-go-ya , a babe at breast tossed out.

(On the temporary stage in the middle of the auditorium, two MABIKI WOMEN *are working a threshing machine with their feet. Dusty smoke is rising in thick clouds. Perhaps they have just tossed an illegitimate child into the threshing machine—a rather long dance scene—. A little away is sitting a* MIDDLE-SCHOOL STUDENT *with his mouth wide open. His scalp is infected with ringworm.)*

MABIKI WOMAN 1: Whose child is this? A demon's bag, a demon womb.
MABIKI WOMAN 2: Break the bag, let the water flow
MABIKI WOMAN 1: I don't want to see its father's face.
MABIKI WOMAN 2: Smash it before it's born.
MABIKI WOMAN 1: Hush, hush, the cat's place
MABIKI WOMAN 2: A fifteen-year old girl
MABIKI WOMAN 1: Deceived by sugared words, telling her, "how lovely!"
MABIKI WOMAN 2: Crying and feeling bitter
MABIKI WOMAN 1: Abandoned like the obi he bought her
MABIKI WOMAN 2: That he sold to a pawnshop
MABIKI WOMAN 1: And never redeemed.
MABIKI WOMAN 2 *(Looking into the threshing machine)*: This child is so quiet, it's not even crying.
MABIKI WOMAN 1: Well, it's time
MABIKI WOMAN 2: To kill it by threshing it.
MABIKI WOMAN 1: Buddha's towel
MABIKI WOMAN 2: Is Indian red
MABIKI WOMAN 1: We tried to dye it red but failed:
MABIKI WOMAN 2: The straw doll

(They step on the machine's foot trestle, and again, powdery smoke rises. For a little longer, the sound of the machine is heard going "gittan battan," but suddenly.)

MABIKI WOMAN 1: Oh, something
MABIKI WOMAN 2: Got stuck
MABIKI WOMAN 1: An obi or a sleeve?
MABIKI WOMAN 2: Or the baby's head?
MABIKI WOMAN 1: Why don't you look inside?
MABIKI WOMAN 2: Not me. You do it.
MABIKI WOMAN 1 *(Looks inside.)*
MABIKI WOMAN 2 *(Looks inside.)*

(Song.)

What crying babe is this? Abandoned child,
Cursed with Grandpa's warts, to be reviled?
Or is it cursed with Grandma's red-stained jowls?
Who powdered its face and oiled its head? And still it howls.

Anonymous Father left a flower
Anonymous Father left a flower

MABIKI WOMAN 1: Someone's inside.

MABIKI WOMAN 2 (*Touching the threshing machine and trying to turn it over*): Heavy...

MABIKI WOMAN 1 (*Helping her*): It's so heavy that it'll need more than just a little shove to move it.

(*The two of them use all their strength to turn over the threshing machine. From inside the machine*, STUDENT 2 IN ARMY UNIFORM *tumbles out.*)

MABIKI WOMAN 2: Oh! (*Jumps.*) It's all grown up!

MABIKI WOMAN 1: Impossible! This can't be the same child. It's someone else.

MABIKI WOMAN 2: Someone else? (*To* STUDENT 2.) Who are you?

STUDENT 2 (*Stands up quickly and salutes her*): No one, ma'am. Just a human being who's been erased.

MABIKI WOMAN 1: What?

STUDENT 2: No one else can see me, ma'am. I'm a man who erased himself with an eraser.

MABIKI WOMAN 2 (*Laughs*): You may think you were erased, but...

MABIKI WOMAN 1: We can see you clearly.

MABIKI WOMAN 2: One star on your uniform means that you're a lowly, new recruit.

MABIKI WOMAN 1 (*Touches him*): You don't look well, soldier.

STUDENT 2 (*Strongly*): Liar. You can't see me.... I'm not here, not in this place!

(*From far away, we hear the sound of marching military boots approaching, going "za-kku zakku."*)

MABIKI WOMAN 1: Hear that? They're coming to get you.

MABIKI WOMAN 2: You shouldn't be idling your time away in a place like this.

STUDENT 2: Liar! Nobody can see me.... It's not possible.... I'm not going anywhere. I'm not the same as them.... I've become an erased man, an invisible soldier, the scrapings of an eraser. (*Screaming.*) Help! Help!

(*Music. The sound of a bugle fades in and, at its peak, fades out.*)

10. A KIDNAPPING BY THE LIFE-MOTHER

(*With accompaniment by mechanical-sounding music that goes "kara-kuri," like metal strings.*)

Hey, hey, hey! — The spinning wheel of fate. — Raven on a string: see him gyrate

Shintoku the leper

Where might he abide? — Where can he hide? — Wandering the world so wide.

Kara-kuri, kara-kuri, kara-kuri-battan

Stepmother, Father, and Son — At home they remain — They never complain

They polish the altar each day
Ni-ichi-tensaku, one, two   The abacus counts anew   Cloud Nine, Seventh
Heaven, Hallelu!
If a card blows away   In this Family play   Autumn's here to stay.

Kara-kuri, kara-kuri, kara-kuri-battan

Shintoku the leper   How does he manage?   His eyes crushed and bandaged?
A pilgrim on the pathway to truth
Ringing his bell   Did he fall in a well?   Or leap into hell
On the railway tracks   In a tragic climax?

Namu Amida Butsu
Kara-kuri, kara-kuri, kara-kuri-battan
(*With a broom in her hands,* STEPMOTHER NADESHIKO *appears. At her feet, arranged like a miniature landscape in a box, is a house, a telegraph pole, and the family altar.*)

STEPMOTHER (*Staring down at them*): Look, look, this is my house. It's almost evening, and the lamp is lit. Sensaku is coming home from school. And behind the telegraph pole, disguised as a traveling medicine salesman, waits a kidnapper. A movie poster is blown over by the wind. Sensaku stops.
(*Suddenly, she sweeps the house, the telegraph pole, and so on, with her broom. The house and the telegraph pole are destroyed and swept away as if they were trash.*)

Darkness falls. It's just an ordinary autumn day.
(*Picking up a handful of soil and scattering it over the stage.*)
Look, look, this is real soil
Should I drive in the stakes, is it worth the toil
To raise the show tent once again?
Mustard flowers   Fatherless children
Just like the old days, when I was little
And I couldn't stop crying, the scales were so brittle
Snake scales. I must be crazy, how pitiful.
(*Spreads the soil, vocalizing a sound to represent this.*)
(*Spreads more soil, again vocalizing a sound to represent tossing or spreading it.*)

Where is Sensaku? He's later than usual today.
(*Slowly, like a phantom, the back entrance of the sideshow tent begins to be visible. Echoes of* jinta *[typical sideshow brass band music] can be heard, and the* ATTENDANT *in charge of customers' footwear is cleaning up.* ISSUN-BŌSHI [DWARF MAN] *goes this way and that with a portable clay cooking stove fired by charcoal, from which rises the black smoke of grilling a small fish.* AIR-PUMP MAN *is counting coins.*)
(STEPMOTHER NADESHIKO *comes closer to* SENSAKU, *who is peeking inside through a torn curtain, and touches his shoulder gently.*)

STEPMOTHER (*Her voice is heard from offstage*): So this is where you've been, Sensaku.

(SENSAKU, *surprised, turns around.*)

STEPMOTHER (*Only voice*): You didn't come home, even though it was late, so I've come to pick you up.

(*Walking a few steps while holding* SENSAKU.)

STEPMOTHER: Are you hungry? (*Taking out a package of rice balls. An especially hairy arm is visible.*)

(SENSAKU *nods, feeling scared.*)

STEPMOTHER (*Unwrapping the package carefully*): Then, eat! (*All of a sudden, she crams a rice ball as hard as a stone into* SENSAKU*'s mouth.*)

SENSAKU: Ah, ouch! You'll break my teeth! (*Screams.*)

(PERFORMERS *in the sideshow freak tent pass by, doing kabuki somersaults in the air.*)

STEPMOTHER: Ha ha ha. (*Starts to laugh in a low voice.*)

SENSAKU (*An idea suddenly strikes him*): Oh, I know who you are . . . !

STEPMOTHER: You guessed it. I'm Shintoku, your brother.

Your mother's curse turned me into a leper. Look, see how my skin is peeling off in patches. I have a human face but an animal's body. When night comes, you should see how my lovely scales glisten!

SENSAKU (*Breathing roughly*): Why did you come back, Shintoku?

SHINTOKU: To pet you and pamper you. I put on this mask to disguise myself as my stepmother, the one who cursed me and threw me out, and now I've returned. How do I look? Don't you think this red crepe kimono is rather fetching on me?

(SENSAKU *steps back.*)

SHINTOKU: Now, Sensaku dear. Don't run away. Come over here and I'll tell you something nice.

(Biwa *narration comes in.*)

Lacking friends, I live in gloom.
With my red lacquer comb, I groom
The cuckoo's feathers,
But they always fall out, and that's my doom.

SENSAKU: No, don't come any closer. (*He says this, but his voice is trembling and he cannot move. It's as if he were bound hand and foot.*)

SHINTOKU: Oh, Sensaku, your face is so lovely when you're terrified. (*Comes closer, suggestively.*)

SENSAKU: Don't come near me, I might catch leprosy.

SHINTOKU: Yes, we're brothers. We're one and the same. I will share the joys of leprosy with you. (*Rips off* SENSAKU*'s school uniform and pants. Holding tight to the completely naked* SENSAKU, *he suddenly says.*) Die!

(*Pushes him down.* SENSAKU *falls head over heels and rolls around.* SHINTOKU *dances crazily like a fool. The freak show tent, which had been unlighted, suddenly appears again, and* AIR-PUMP MAN, FEMALE SUMO WRESTLER, *and* LONG-NECKED

WOMAN MONSTER *all start to dance at once. A barrel spinning in the air is manipulated by the feet of someone lying on their back. Miniature bulbs blink on and off. The scene is transformed into a night filled with vampires who have been revived by the sacrifice of the totally nude boy* SENSAKU, *who is like an acrobatic horse in a circus in hell.*)

11. THE RED HOOD OF GANJINBŌ, THE DANCING MONK WHO SUBSTITUTES FOR YOU AT PRAYERS

YANAGITA KUNIO *appears unexpectedly in the dark, removes his hat and bows.*

YANAGITA: Good evening, everyone. How nice to see you again. I am Yanagita Kunio, and this time, I am disguised as the manager of the Tokyo Municipal Lost and Found Office. In case you were wondering, this time I exchanged my fake beard for a mustache like the one Ronald Coleman has, and I added a pair of pince-nez glasses. I'm trying to mimic the cover of the February issue of *Boy's Club.* So I set up this desk and here I wait. Nothing happens except more and more lost items appear. People keep dropping off items they've found; it's a never-ending parade. But not a single person has come in to claim something he's lost.
(*Solo song.*)
Just me and my long lost goods
A dancing monk in a bright red hood
(*Monologue.*)
Lost items lack noses and eyes
Faceless items without alibis
(*Solo song.*)
That bright red hood on the dancing monk
Originates where? My memory's shrunk
(*Monologue.*)
A thirty-watt lightbulb illuminates
A villain's face. He secretly ruminates
On his hiding place in the autumn of eternal rebirth
Lost items, vanished items, abandoned items, never unearthed.

Well, this lost and found storehouse is as big as a heart, and twice as dark. But is it large enough?! Yes, it is. It all depends on your point of view. In other words, depending on when and where you are, you might say that the entire city of Tokyo is a storehouse of lost property.

What's more, it's a cinch to keep the place in order, because there's only one person missing, and that's the person who lost something. Yes, may I help you?
(SHINTOKU*'s* FATHER, *now shrunken in size, enters, riding in a dwarf-size car.*)
YANAGITA: Oh, it's Father!

FATHER (*Perhaps singing in a baritone*): Indeed, Shintoku's father am I.

YANAGITA: That's good.

FATHER (*Perhaps singing in a baritone*): Pray, let me see with mine eye.

YANAGITA: So, you've finally decided, have you?

FATHER (*Perhaps singing in a baritone*): Decided what, my good man?

YANAGITA: To make yourself into a lost item.

FATHER (*Perhaps singing in a baritone; bothered*): Don't be absurd, how can? (*Becoming very serious.*) It's just that I found something, and I thought I should bring it in.

YANAGITA: A lost item?

FATHER: Yes, as a matter of fact, I found this family register. It's the family register of the Oguris, living in 1 chōme, Kameido Kōtō.

YANAGITA (*Flipping through the pages of a thick book, checking facts, and talking to himself*): That can't be right, I'm sure there's some mistake.

FATHER: There's no question about it. This is the Oguri family register.

YANAGITA: But there are 113 households in 1 chōme, Kameido Kōtō, and everyone is duly registered. There's no Oguri family there.

FATHER: Do all 113 households have intact family registers?

YANAGITA: Yes. Not a single one is lost.

FATHER: So, if this Oguri family is registered, you're saying that some other family will be forced out?

YANAGITA: Found items replace those that were lost. They're not additional ones. That's the way things are; it's what we've always been taught.

FATHER: But then . . .

YANAGITA: Then?

(*In the dark, a line of faces representing wooden or stone seals engraved with names* [hanko]. *Various unregistered name seals such as Tanaka, Yamada, Nakagawa, Hiyoshi, Kobayashi, and Kudō begin to sing together.*)

(*Chorus.*)

I don't understand, and yet At sunset
Blue reincarnation sobs, tearful and wet.
A thoughtless father leaves his fatherless child
A twisted body, deformed and defiled.
Another country, countless miles away
Seeking my child, gone astray
The trumpet plays.

(*Sobbing and writhing in the dwarf car,* SHINTOKU'S FATHER *starts to go crazy, crying, "Shintoku!" "Forgive me!" He rolls out of the car and again grows tall. Sniffing around on all fours like a dog, he exits. Then, to the strains of a thirty-string koto, the unregistered seals go this way and that as they look for something. Soon, the strangeness of looking for things that are not lost turns into sadness, and the lost people/lost items that were stored in the storehouse slowly cross the stage and pass through the audience as they exit.*)

YANAGITA: Everyone! This is the final showing of lost property. It's not too late.

If you find the items you lost among those that are here, please hurry back with your seals, because you must sign off with your seal to retrieve them. The storehouse is overflowing with goods. And besides (*Taking off his false mustache and pince-nez glasses*), it's time for me to go back to my original identity as Yanagita Kunio. I will return to my study and continue working on *The Legends of Tōno.*

(*Twitching his limbs as if being manipulated by strings.*) I don't understand, but at sunset, blue reincarnation sobs, everybody, lost items, the world is someone else's lost item, a telegraph pole and a kidnapping, single-minded truth can be found only in the tales told to children by traveling picture-book storytellers, OK, then, good-bye. (*Disappears.*)

12. WHY DO PREGNANT WOMEN WEAR COTTON BELLYBANDS WITH THE SIGN OF THE DOG?

(*Singing to the* biwa.)
Flowing river, destiny-bound
Flowing hair, round a comb bound,
The comb's as high
As the love god's third eye

Homesick again, and feeling bleak,
Such longings make the darkness creak.
A long-horned beetle in its lair
Creakily, squeakily cuts off her hair
(*Po-tto! The sound of a thirty-watt Mazda lightbulb as it suddenly pops on. In the light, we see* FATHER, STEPMOTHER, *and* SENSAKU *facing one another at the dinner table, with bowls and chopsticks in their hands. Behind them—in darkness as black as a long-horned beetle—a black-framed memorial photograph of the supposedly dead* SHINTOKU *in school uniform. On closer examination, we see that the person who appeared to be* STEPMOTHER *is actually* SHINTOKU *in disguise.*)
(*In a singsong manner.*)

SENSAKU: Father, please give me the Mother of the family of Mr. Ieo Mamoru, the Home Protector.

FATHER: I don't have it. Mother, please give me the child of Mr. Kaneno Narukichi, the Money-Tree Man.

STEPMOTHER (*Really* SHINTOKU): Someone has taken one of my cards. Sensaku, please give me the dog from the family of Mr. Kunio Mamoru, the Nation Protector.

SENSAKU: I don't have it. Father, please give me the Mother of the Ieo Mamoru Family.

FATHER: I don't have it. I already told you that I don't have it. Mother, please give me the Mother of Kaneno Narukichi.

(*Then, with a gesture as she flings open the door, another* STEPMOTHER *[the real one] comes in.*)

STEPMOTHER: I've got that card.

SENSAKU (*Startled*): Ah, you?

STEPMOTHER: Sensaku, look, I have four of the same cards. They all are Mother cards!

SENSAKU (*Confused, looking again at* SHINTOKU *disguised as* STEPMOTHER, *who is right in front of him, and murmuring*): Unbelievable. . . .

SHINTOKU (*With a faint smile*): What happened, Sensaku? You look pale.

SENSAKU: Please let me see the cards you have.

SHINTOKU: These?

(*Holding them out. Four cards come falling out of his hands.*)

SENSAKU: They're all Mother cards! Unbelievable! (*Also taking hold of the cards offered by* STEPMOTHER *and looking at them one by one, as if making sure . . .*)

SHINTOKU (*Becoming* STEPMOTHER *through and through*): Sensaku, go and look. Someone seems to have come in the front door.

SENSAKU (*At a loss for words.*)

SHINTOKU: Can't you hear what your mother says?

SENSAKU (*Asking for help*): Father!

FATHER: I can't see. I can't see anything. (*Starts trembling.*)

(STEPMOTHER *and* SHINTOKU *walk closer to each other and look at the blue bottle.*)

BOTH (*In unison*): Oh, no! Not another long-horned beetle, and right here at home, too! What bad luck. . . . (*And as if looking in a mirror, they look each other in the face as if they are looking at the reflection of their own face. They each replace a stray hair.*) Shintoku must have left it. (*Crouching.*) Where has Shintoku been hiding? I thought he died, but since there's another long-horned beetle right here . . . (*Startled, noticing each other.*) Oh, who are you?

SHINTOKU: I am Shintoku's Stepmother, called

STEPMOTHER: Nadeshiko

SHINTOKU: All day long, I avoid other people

STEPMOTHER: But sometimes I think of Shintoku, whom I killed with my curses,

SHINTOKU: And I tenderly recall him

STEPMOTHER: Then I hide my face with a parasol

SHINTOKU: And pick thistles in the graveyard

STEPMOTHER: Plumed thistles, even those with red blossoms

SHINTOKU: Even if compassion burns hotly

NARRATOR:

Together, they sing a single song
Bisected by a filthy curse

STEPMOTHER (*All of a sudden behaving like a young girl madly in love*): Oh, Shintoku, forgive me. I wanted you to love me.

SHINTOKU (*As if he has come to his senses*): But it took me too long to grow up.

NARRATOR: It took him too long to grow up.

Too early to be a child. Too old to listen to lullabies. Too young to sleep in her arms. Even after eighty, ninety, or a hundred years, those couples bound till death, flowery sex, wet with dew, but Mother and Son, the gods cannot forgive.

SHINTOKU (*All of a sudden takes off the other's kimono that he is wearing*): Mother! Please get pregnant with me and give birth to me again!

FATHER (*Dumbfounded by what he sees, he calls out*): Monsters!

(*He tries to run away, grabbing* SENSAKU *by the hand. Since* STEPMOTHER *holds* SENSAKU *tightly,* FATHER *ends up falling and somersaulting out. Slight sound of the sideshow* jinta *music is heard.*)

STEPMOTHER (*To* SENSAKU): There's nothing to fear. You're the only man in this house now. (*And to* SHINTOKU.) Shintoku, it's me. Am I beautiful? (*Acting flirtatiously, looking at* SHINTOKU, *and turning around.*) Don't worry. Shintoku already is dead. (*She says this in a way that makes it clear that she already is insane.*) You are the heir. Look, I have streamers shaped like carp. I bought them just for you, to celebrate. (*Suddenly looking back at* SHINTOKU *again.*) One, two, even three more times if possible, I want to give birth to you, I want to get pregnant with you.

(*Chorus.*)

Milk is scarce　　Sleep is scarce
Lu-lu-lu-lu-bu　　Lu-lu-lu-lu-bu
Milk is scarce　　Sleep is scarce
Lu-lu-lu-lu-bu　　Lu-lu-lu-lu-bu
Milk is scarce　　Sleep is scarce

(SHINTOKU *stares fixedly at* MOTHER *and takes off all his clothes.*)

SHINTOKU: This is Hell!

(*He is crying and embracing her, and all at once,* STEPMOTHER*'s black hair turns snow white. Like an avalanche, the* CHORUS*'s song comes roaring out.*)

Mother　　One
(*Japanese* taiko *drum.*)
Two　　Three
(*Japanese* taiko *drum.*)
Four　　Six
(*Japanese* taiko *drum.*)

(*Emerging from the darkness are a* MOTHER, *another* MOTHER, *and more* MOTHERS. *All wear bright red lipstick and are elaborately costumed as the characters they played. All the characters who have transformed into these various* MOTHERS *engulf the screaming, naked* SHINTOKU, *draw him to them, lick their lips, tear him to pieces, and devour him.*

A sutra of the Kishimo goddess, the sound of pilgrims' bells.

And everything falls endlessly into the labyrinth of the womb; only their voices echo and reverberate against one another, until gradually they all disappear.

A bell tolls once, telling the time.

Go-wong! It echoes, and then a blackout.)

(*In an innocent girl's voice.*)

If this baby cries,   Stuff it in a bag until it dies

(*Chorus.*)

I-ro-ha-ni-ho-he-to,   A, B, C, D, E, F, G
Wind-scattered petals fade, blown from the tree,
Their scent remains: colors for the nose to see
Wind-scattered letters, written in blood   From bloody womb, a baby bud
With skin like snow: To the sea I go,
To make an offering.   At Shimizu in Tosa, where the ocean roils,
And oil boils from the bottom of the sea, to end life's toils.
At Shimizu in Tosa, where life recoils.

Mother   Faceless   A bird summons her chick
Milk is scarce   Sleep is scarce

CURTAIN

Shimizu Kunio, *The Dressing Room*, directed by Suzuki Kan'ichirō, Seinenza, 1978.
(Courtesy of Seinenza)

THE DRESSING ROOM

That Which Flows Away Ultimately Becomes Nostalgia

SHIMIZU KUNIO

TRANSLATED BY CHIORI MIYAGAWA, BASED ON A TRANSLATION BY JOHN K. GILLESPIE

Born in 1934 and educated at Waseda University, Shimizu Kunio began writing for the stage and screen at the beginning of the 1960s. In 1969, he came into his own as one of the major playwrights of his generation after establishing, with director Ninagawa Yukio, the Modern Man's Theater (Gendaijin gekijō), which produced several of his plays. Shimizu first collaborated with Ninagawa on the 1968 production of his play *Such a Serious Frivolity* (*Shinjō afururu keihakusa*). Ninagawa then directed an acclaimed English-language production in Edinburgh and London of Shimizu's play *Tango at the End of Winter* (*Tango fuyu no owari ni*, 1986), starring Alan Rickman, in 1991. Shimizu's *When We Go Down That Great Unfeeling River* (*Bokura ga hijō no taiga o kudaru toki*) won the Kishida Award for best play of 1974. In 1976, Shimizu founded his own troupe, the Winter Tree Company (Mokutōsha), with his wife, actress Matsumoto Noriko. Many of his plays are keen and sensitive portraits of women, like *An Older Sister, Burning Like a Flame* (*Hi no yō ni samishii ane ga ite*, 1978), and are set in a place evocative of his hometown, Niigata, on the Japan Sea. Considered a literary and theatrical link between older, more orthodox *shingeki* plays and those that came afterward, Shimizu's psychologically complex and lyrical dramas intertwine memory, desire, and fantasy in a way that distorts reality without rendering the narrative absurd. Madness and an often frustrated quest for personal identity are dominant themes in Shimizu's plays, concerns found in the works of many of his contemporaries, such as Terayama Shūji. First performed at Jean-Jean Theater in Shibuya (Tokyo) in 1977, *The Dressing Room* (*Gakuya*) is set backstage, where four actresses are preparing for a production of Anton Chekhov's

The Seagull. We soon learn that not all is as it seems and that memory is a faculty that flows beyond the body, literally transcending death.

Characters

ACTRESS A
ACTRESS B
ACTRESS C
ACTRESS D

Darkness. Several mirrors begin to reflect glittering lights as nostalgic music is heard. The mirrors whisper, "Although the tedium of everyday life deceives you at times, do not embrace sadness and rage. For if you tolerate patiently the sad days, you will without fail be visited by happiness again. . . . Your heart always lives in the future, Present entities aimlessly recollect lonely thoughts. Life in this world flows away in an instant. And that which flows away ultimately becomes nostalgia. . . ."

From the silent darkness, ACTRESSES A *and* B *emerge almost imperceptibly and face the mirrors to begin applying makeup. They are intensely involved in the process.* ACTRESS A*'s eyes are for some reason terribly burned, and her vision appears to be blurred.* ACTRESS B*'s neck is wrapped in a white bandage with fresh blood soaking through. The two actresses, completely absorbed in the makeup process, are quite serious but at the same time somewhat comical and even slightly sorrowful. Suddenly,* ACTRESS C *stands up in front of the full-length mirror. She is dressed as Nina in* The Sea Gull. *She holds a lighted cigarette.*

ACTRESS C: I am a sea gull. . . . No, that's not right. I'm an actress. Ah, well. . . .
(*Light slowly grows brighter. It is an ordinary dressing room. She is rehearsing her lines just prior to going on stage.* ACTRESSES A *and* B *are indifferent to* ACTRESS C *and remain involved in their makeup process.*)

ACTRESS C: . . . So, he is here, too. . . . Well, it doesn't matter. He didn't believe in the theater; he always laughed at my dreams, and gradually I too ceased believing and lost heart. And then there was the anxiety of love, the jealousy, the constant fears for my baby. I grew petty, trivial, my acting was insipid. I didn't know what to do with my hands, I didn't know how to stand on the stage. I couldn't control my voice. You can't imagine what it's like to feel that you are acting abominably, I am a sea gull. . . .

No, that's not right. Do you remember you shot a sea gull? A man came along by chance, saw it, and having nothing better to do, destroyed it. . . . A subject for a short story. . . . No, that's not it. What was I saying? I was talking about the stage.

I'm not like that now. Now I'm a real actress, I act with delight, with rapture, I'm intoxicated when I'm on the stage, and I feel I act beautifully. And since I have been here, I've been walking, continually walking and thinking . . . and I think and feel that my soul is growing stronger with each day. I know now, I understand, that in our work—whether it's acting or writing—what's important is not fame, not glory, not the things I used to dream of, but the ability to endure. To be able to bear one's cross and have faith. I have faith, and it's not so painful now, and when I think of my vocation, I'm not afraid of life.

(*Listening.*) Sh-sh! I'm going. Good-bye. When I become a great actress, come and see me. Promise? (*Grasps an imaginary hand.*) It's late. I can hardly stand on my feet. I'm exhausted and hungry. (*Takes a cookie from the dressing table.*) No, no . . . don't come with me. I'll go alone. When you see Trigorin, don't say anything to him. . . . I love him. I love him even more than before. How good life used to be, Kostya! How clear, how pure, warm, and joyous—our feelings were like tender, delicate flowers. . . . Do you remember? Men, lions, eagles, and partridges, horned deer, geese, spiders, silent fish that dwell in the deep, Starfish, and creatures invisible to the eye—these and all living things, all, all living things, having completed their sad cycle, are no more. For thousands of years the earth has borne no living creature. And now in vain this poor moon lights her lamp. Cranes no longer wake and cry in meadows. . . . Oops! It's already my cue.

(ACTRESS C *suddenly does vocal exercises and runs out of the dressing room.* ACTRESSES A *and* B *react for the first time.*)

ACTRESS A: I am a sea gull. . . .

ACTRESS B: No, that's not right. I'm an actress. Ah, well . . .

ACTRESS A: Can you believe she's forty?

ACTRESS B: Look, that idiot forgot her hat.

ACTRESS A: So she did.

(ACTRESS B *stands up, goes over to the hat, picks it up, and puts it on her chair. She then sits on the hat. The hat, of course, is brutally crushed.* ACTRESS C *reenters in a hurry.*)

ACTRESS C (*Searching*): My hat . . . my hat . . . my hat . . . (*Finds it.*) Ah!

(*She approaches the hat and tries to pick it up.* ACTRESS B *plants herself on the hat.*)

ACTRESS C: What's going on here?

(ACTRESS C *pulls at the hat with greater force. Right at that moment,* ACTRESS B *lifts herself up, sending* ACTRESS C *reeling off balance.*)

ACTRESS C: That's it! I will demand a different dressing room tomorrow.

ACTRESS B: I don't care.

ACTRESS C (*Glaring at the area occupied by the two actresses*): Rotten, foul air always hovers around here.

(ACTRESS C *exits in disgust.*)

ACTRESS A: Did you hear that?

ACTRESS B: I heard.

ACTRESS A: She called us "rotten and foul air . . ."

ACTRESS B: . . . that "hovers."

ACTRESS A: Yeah, "hovers around here."

ACTRESS B: We can't be hovering. That sounds disgusting.

ACTRESS A: What do you mean?

ACTRESS B: Well, if something hovers, it's not solid, is it?

ACTRESS A: Either way, it's a useless image.

ACTRESS B: It sounds poisonous more than useless. We "hover. . . ."

ACTRESS A: You are obsessed with "hovering." My pride is beginning to get hurt. That's enough.

(*Short pause.*)

ACTRESS B: Anyway, the hats in style these days are abominable.

ACTRESS A: Well, you certainly didn't make it any better by crushing it.

ACTRESS B: When we were performing, we wore far more elegant hats.

ACTRESS A: When we were performing?

ACTRESS B: That's right.

ACTRESS A: Huh. . . .

ACTRESS B: What do you mean "huh"?

ACTRESS A: You talk like you played Nina in *The Sea Gull*.

ACTRESS B (*Hurt*): I told you before, I had one opportunity.

ACTRESS A: Only one?

ACTRESS B: What about you? You didn't even have a chance to play a gray starling, never mind a sea gull. You used to feel sorry for yourself all the time. "Ah, I was an eternal prompter. . . ."

ACTRESS A: I can say the exact same about you. Don't condescend to me. I don't run my mouth on lies like you do, but I also had an opportunity . . . Lady Macbeth.

ACTRESS B: Oh my, Shakespeare. . . .

ACTRESS A: 'That's right. I was on a tour . . . some town on the Inland Sea . . . Lady Macbeth ate too much smelt, the local fish dish, that morning and had a sudden attack of diarrhea. It was serious . . . she was in a coma by noon.

ACTRESS B: I see. There was your big chance.

ACTRESS A: I had been carrying a lucky charm from Kasama Shrine for my protection. I prayed to that charm . . . hurry up and die! Drop dead now!

ACTRESS B: Despite your prayer, your enemy miraculously recovered in the afternoon.

ACTRESS A: Not really

ACTRESS B: She didn't recover?

ACTRESS A: No . . . by afternoon, I was suffering, too.

ACTRESS B (*Amazed*): You ate the smelt, too?

ACTRESS A (*Nods*): It was destiny. Everyone eats that fish dish in the Inland Sea.

ACTRESS B: I would have done the same. I have never been able to avoid destiny.

ACTRESS A: Definitely! That dish is delicious.

(*Short pause.*)

ACTRESS B: Lady Macbeth . . . I envy you. You had your chance, if only once. I didn't, even though I attended Macbeth performances over forty, maybe fifty times as a prompter.

ACTRESS A: So you know all the lines?

ACTRESS B: Of course I do. I recited them more than fifty times. (*Recites.*) "Hoarse is the raven that croaks Duncan's final approach within my walls. Come, you spirits that guide human thoughts, unsex me here. And fill me, head to foot, full of warrior cruelty! Thicken my blood; block up all access and passage to remorse, that no sudden strings of conscience shake my dark purpose nor soften its dread effect. . . ."

ACTRESS A: Hold on a minute.

ACTRESS B: I was just getting into it.

ACTRESS A: Um . . . is it the postwar version?

ACTRESS B: Postwar?!

ACTRESS A: Well, it's different from the version I remember.

ACTRESS B: How?

ACTRESS A: It's different from the beginning.

ACTRESS B: You mean the whole thing?

ACTRESS A: Yeah. . . . (*Striking a somewhat old-fashioned posture.*)
"The raven himself is hoarse
That croaks the fatal entrance of Duncan
Under my battlements."

ACTRESS B: . . . "the fatal entrance"?

ACTRESS A:
"Come, you spirits
That tend on mortal thoughts, unsex me here,
And fill me, from the crown to the toe, top-full
Of direst cruelty! Make thick my blood;
Stop up the access and passage to remorse,
That no compunctious visitings of nature."

ACTRESS B: . . . "no compunctious"?

ACTRESS A:
"Shake my fell purpose nor keep peace between
The effect and it. Come to my woman's breasts
And take my milk for gall, you murd'ring ministers,
Wherever in your sightless substances
You wait on nature's mischief!"

ACTRESS B: "Nature's mischief"?

(ACTRESS A *stops reciting.*)

ACTRESS B: Go on, please.

ACTRESS A: Excuse me if I'm old-fashioned. I'm much older than you. I'm from an era when one felt "compunctions."

ACTRESS B (*Comfortingly*): I can understand what you mean, in an indirect sort of way.

ACTRESS A: An indirect sort of way?

ACTRESS B: Well, it slightly lacks sensitivity.

ACTRESS A: Now I'm insensitive. I see. That's why I ended my career being a prompter.

ACTRESS B: There you go getting sulky again.

ACTRESS A: You think us "prewar" people are hardheaded and difficult, don't you?

ACTRESS B: Listen, you claim to be an eternal prompter, but weren't you on stage sometimes? I don't mean as Lady Macbeth or Nina. . . .

ACTRESS A: Yes, yes, of course . . . as Nobleman A or Messenger 2 or Gatekeeper 3 . . .

ACTRESS B: But those are all male roles.

ACTRESS A: I know. For some reason I got only male roles. Maybe because there weren't enough male actors around because of the war. I remember . . . I was even cast in Macbeth several times as a boy.

ACTRESS B: A boy? What were his lines?

(ACTRESS A *hesitates.*)

ACTRESS B: What's wrong?

ACTRESS A: It's just . . . my version is old-fashioned,

ACTRESS B: I don't care.

ACTRESS A: I remember . . . I also had a part as a gambler.

ACTRESS B: You mean a punk?

ACTRESS A: Right. In Miyoshi Jūrō's play *Slashed Senta*. Of course, I wasn't Senta.

ACTRESS B: That's a Japanese classic. You don't have to worry about your version being outdated. (*She insists.*)

ACTRESS A: But. . . . (*Suddenly brandishing a backscratcher as a sword.*) "Count me out. In this mortal land, such a manner of gambler should not ever be forgiven. I know that. Yet I insisted on provoking trouble; I want you to know I have no place to escape to or hide in. But please have mercy this night. I wish to be set free. Big bosses, I can make endless excuses because I don't like to kill. I'm not capable of killing . . ."

ACTRESS B: That's great. Is that your line?

ACTRESS A: No, it's Senta's. . . . "Are you hearing me, bosses. I am, as you can see, a wanderer with neither a name nor identity. I'm just another insignificant pawn. However, if you worry about your reputation being ruined when the word gets out that the one who conquered this gambling joint was a wanderer, make me into a thief. I'm a thief. Right, a thief. But I am not about to use this money for my own pleasure . . . dozens of people's lives will be spared by this money."

ACTRESS B: Look, when do you make your entrance?

ACTRESS A: Hush. It won't be long . . . "I beg you bosses, look the other way just for one night. I will complete my task, and turn myself over to you. I am humbling myself. I understand your rage thinking that I'm another bum, but you are wrong. Think of me as a peasant farmer's son crying his heart out. Do not think that you gave me this one night's take, but think you gave it to peasant farmers, and let me go. Big bosses,

I, Senta of Makabe Village, won't forget what I owe you. Wait. . . . (*Looks around and senses danger.*) I don't want to kill. I don't want to destroy life. Can't you understand that?" At that moment, Takijiro of Shimozuma leaps out on stage. . . .

ACTRESS B: Say . . .

ACTRESS A: "Shut up! Sentaro, what are you babbling about? You don't want to kill? Then I will. I'll rip him apart."

ACTRESS B: Is that your role?

ACTRESS A: No.

ACTRESS B: Are we still waiting?

ACTRESS A: I'm already on stage.

ACTRESS B: What? Where?

ACTRESS A: Right around here.

ACTRESS B: Around here?

ACTRESS A: Yes, here. I came leaping out with Takijiro. In the stage direction it said, "Takijiro leaps out. Seven punks rush out with him. All have their teeth clenched and remain silent."

ACTRESS B: Remain silent!?

ACTRESS A: Right. Everyone was clenching their teeth . . . but I had to prompt Senta and Takijiro on top of that, so I couldn't really be faithful to the stage directions.

ACTRESS B: I can see what you mean. (*Clenching her teeth.*) It's kind of hard to prompt doing this.

ACTRESS A (*As if dreaming*): But I loved that play. I liked the beautiful women's roles like Otsuta or Omyo . . . but I was moved by Senta, who gets slashed . . .

ACTRESS B (*Staring*): You don't mean! . . .

ACTRESS A: Mean what?

ACTRESS B: That's why your makeup is . . .

ACTRESS A: What about my makeup?

ACTRESS B: I've been wondering.

ACTRESS A: Wondering what?

ACTRESS B: About your eternal role.

ACTRESS A: And?

ACTRESS B: Is it Slashed Senta?

ACTRESS A: Give me a break! I am an actress. I would like a female role. What about you? What's your role?

ACTRESS B: It's a secret.

ACTRESS A: Well, I know already.

ACTRESS B: No, you don't.

ACTRESS A: It's Nina. *The Sea Gull.* Right on the mark!

ACTRESS B: Wrong.

ACTRESS A: I sensed it when you destroyed that hat. You were as nasty as a mother-in-law.

ACTRESS B: I said you were wrong.

ACTRESS A: "Nina! My darling. . . . I'm Trigorin."

ACTRESS B: Trigorin!?

ACTRESS A: ". . . these wonderful eyes, this inexpressibly beautiful, tender smile . . . this sweet face with an expression of angelic purity. . . ."

ACTRESS B: Stop it! That's creepy. Senta is a far better male role, if you must.

ACTRESS A: No, I won't stop. Forgive me for my old-fashioned interpretation. "Nina, things have taken an unexpected turn, and it appears we are leaving today. It's not very likely that we shall meet again. I am sorry. I don't often meet young girls . . . youthful and interesting. I've forgotten how it feels to be eighteen or nineteen."

ACTRESS B: That monologue suits you well.

ACTRESS A: Be serious. You were also an eternal prompter, weren't you Nina?

ACTRESS B: "Oh, beautiful lake, romantic forest, splendid big sky. . . ."

ACTRESS A: There you go! But I don't recognize the lines. . . .

ACTRESS B: Never mind. I'm going to say what I like. "A beautiful lake romantic forest, splendid big sky. When I stand at the edge of the lake, I am surrounded by majestic and generous nature. But if I could become an actress, I would gladly sacrifice this grand nature and all else."

ACTRESS A: "All else"?

ACTRESS B: "Yes. For the happiness of being an actress, I would endure poverty, disillusionment, the hatred of my family; I would live in a garret and eat black bread, suffer dissatisfaction with myself and the recognition of my own imperfections, but in return I shall demand fame."

ACTRESS A: "Fame . . ."

ACTRESS B: "Real, resounding fame . . .

ACTRESS A: ". . . real resounding fame . . .

ACTRESS B: "My head is swimming."

ACTRESS A: "Nina, I am being called . . . to pack, I suppose. But I don't feel like leaving."

ACTRESS B (*Abruptly raises her head*): "Do you see the house with the garden on the other side of the lake?"

ACTRESS A: "Where? Oh, yes of course."

ACTRESS B: Can you really see it?

ACTRESS A (*Trying to focus with her damaged eyes*): I should be able to!

ACTRESS B: "It belonged to my mother when she was alive. I was born there. I've spent my whole life by this lake, I know every little island in it."

ACTRESS A: "It's lovely here." (*A wig falls at her feet.*) "And what is this?"

ACTRESS B: "A sea gull. Konstantin Gavrilovich shot it."

ACTRESS A: "A beautiful bird." (*Mimes writing something.*)

ACTRESS B: "What are you writing?"

ACTRESS A: "An idea occurred to me . . . a subject for a short story. A young girl like you lives all her life beside a lake; she loves the lake like a sea gull and, like a sea gull, is happy and free. A man comes along by chance, sees it, and, having nothing better to do, destroys it."

ACTRESS B: My . . .

ACTRESS A: A good story, don't you think? Actually, it's quite common. It can easily happen to a young actress like you. (*She gives a mean glance to the white bandage on* ACTRESS B*'s throat.*) Oh, my dear Nina, what has happened to you? That bandage . . . my goodness, the blood has soaked through it. Has someone shot you, too, like a sea gull?

ACTRESS B: Stop it!

ACTRESS A (*Ignoring this, she grabs* ACTRESS B*'s bandage and rips it open*): Look at this! Numerous little cuts on your neck . . . they look like . . . you did this to yourself. How horrible! I don't understand. Why would you do such a foolish thing? For a play? For a man? Or for both?

(ACTRESS B *pushes* A *away.*)

ACTRESS A (*Continues with a cold smile*): But Nina, let me give you one piece of advice. Committing suicide for a man is the lowest thing an actress can do. It's fine for countless men to commit suicide for an actress; it's like receiving awards. But the reverse is the most detestable act an actress can commit. Don't you agree?

ACTRESS B: When are you going to quit lecturing me? All right, I'll admit that I'm not qualified to call myself an actress. You know, you were lucky. Your wounds were made glorious by the war. Weapons factories, women's volunteer corps, air raids . . . the whole society looks on the scars of the war with sweet sentimentality.

ACTRESS A: Just exactly what are you trying to say?!

ACTRESS B: Wow, you are scary.

ACTRESS A: If you have something to say, why don't you just come out and say it!

ACTRESS B: Oh, I have nothing special to say. I just thought we should really think about which scar is better—the one caused by the bombing, or the one caused by the kitchen knife.

ACTRESS A: I see. Beating around the bush is the way of postwar realism.

ACTRESS B: Huh, the sly approach is the way of prewar realism, right?

ACTRESS A: Shut up, you sewer rat!

ACTRESS B: Stuff it, you spiny rat!

(*They throw objects from the dressing table at each other then immediately return to their makeup. A long silence. Frustrated with the results of the makeup, they throw temper tantrums. Long silence.*)

ACTRESS A: Um . . .

(*Pause.*)

ACTRESS A: I'm sure I'm making a big deal out of nothing, as usual, but what the hell is a spiny rat?

ACTRESS B: A spiny rat is just that, a spiny rat.

ACTRESS A: Do they really exist?

ACTRESS B: Exist? Why do you always ask me things in a stinging way? They exist. They are real. They live on Amami Oshima Island.

ACTRESS A: What is their habitat?

ACTRESS B: Potato patch.

ACTRESS A: Potato patch? Not bad. Their environment is no worse than sewer rats'. In fact, their standard of living is higher than sewer rats'.

(ACTRESS B *is mortified.* ACTRESS D *enters quietly. She is younger than the others. She clutches a large pillow to her chest. She stops, looks around the room, and sits in a chair in a corner. She freezes. [As you must know by now,* ACTRESSES A *and* B *are not visible to* ACTRESS D *because they are dead.] They study* ACTRESS D *intently.*)

ACTRESS A: Who is that?

ACTRESS B: I don't know. She looks familiar, though.

ACTRESS A: One of our acquaintances, maybe?

ACTRESS B: What acquaintances?

ACTRESS A: What is she holding? It looks like a pillow.

(ACTRESS B *stands up.*)

ACTRESS A: Leave her alone.

(*Ignoring this,* ACTRESS B *goes up close to* D *and peers at her.*)

ACTRESS A: So what is it?

ACTRESS B: It's really a pillow.

ACTRESS A: Hm . . .

(ACTRESS D *is staring motionlessly at a fixed spot on the floor.* ACTRESS B *squats down directly in front of her.*)

ACTRESS B: She is agonizing over something.

ACTRESS A: Agonizing?

ACTRESS B: Either that or she has a fever. I wonder if she is using the pillow to exorcise something.

ACTRESS A: Exorcise what?

ACTRESS B: Maybe her fever comes down when she clings to the pillow.

ACTRESS A: I've never heard of such a thing.

(ACTRESS B *studies* D *persistently.*)

ACTRESS A: Come on, leave her alone.

(ACTRESS B *turns to leave* D.)

ACTRESS D: Mamma.

(*Startled,* ACTRESS B *stops abruptly.*)

ACTRESS D (*Without taking her eyes off the floor*): Mamma, did you read my letter?

ACTRESS B: Letter!?

(ACTRESSES A *and* B *look at each other.*)

ACTRESS D: I mentioned it in the letter, didn't I? Finally, I've recovered. In our world, talent is of course important, but health is essential. And the best thing for health is sleep. Yes, I consumed sleep. Moorish people have a saying—"A good pillow for a sound sleep." I have taken that philosophy to heart. Mamma, I'm all right now. Really. I'm the perfect picture of health. So don't worry, Mamma.

(ACTRESSES A *and* B *are dumbfounded. They hastily resume their making up.*)

ACTRESS B: Um. . . .

ACTRESS A: Yeah?

ACTRESS B: If you were her mother, would you stop worrying?

ACTRESS A: Probably not.

(*Music is heard from upstage [where the actual stage is assumed to be]. It is the ending of* The Sea Gull. ACTRESS D *raises her head with a start. She moves to the center of the room as if she were acting. The dressing room seems to transform into a stage. A spotlight on* ACTRESS D.)

ACTRESS D: ". . . I'm going. Good-bye. When I become a great actress, come and see me. Promise? It's late. I can hardly stand on my feet. I'm exhausted and hungry No, no . . . don't come with me. I'll go alone. When you see Trigorin, don't say anything to him. . . . I love him. I love him even more than before. How good life used to be, Kostya! How clear, how pure, warm, and joyous—our feelings were like tender, delicate flowers. . . . Do you remember? Men, lions, eagles, and partridges, horned deer, geese, spiders, silent fish that dwell in the deep, starfish, and creatures invisible to the eye—these and all living things, all, all living things, having completed their sad cycle, are no more. For thousands of years the earth has borne no living creature. And now in vain this poor moon lights her lamp. Cranes no longer wake and cry in meadows. May beetles are heard no more in linden groves. . . ." (*Impulsively embraces a robe hanging nearby and leaves in that pose.*)

(*The light fades to black. Pause. From a distance, sound of thundering applause. As it dies, the light in the room returns to normal.* ACTRESS C *returns from the stage.*)

ACTRESS C: Oh, it itches, itches!

(*As she enters, she takes off her wig and scratches her head violently.*)

ACTRESS C (*Continues*): That idiot! I couldn't hear the prompter at all. "Do you remember? Men, lions, eagles, and partridges, horned deer, geese, spiders, silent fish that dwell in the deep, seahorses. . . ." Why do I always stumble on this word? Not "seahorses" but "starfish." . . . Well, it's good enough for today. At least both starfish and seahorses live in the ocean.

(*She notices* ACTRESS D *sitting motionless in the corner, the pillow clutched to her chest.*)

ACTRESS C: Kiiko . . .

(ACTRESS D *nods.*)

ACTRESS C: I didn't even notice you. Why didn't you say something? When did you get here? Are you feeling better?

ACTRESS D: Yes, thank you.

ACTRESS C: Good . . . (*She notices the pillow.*) What's with that thing?

ACTRESS D: Yes, uh, this is really nothing, but I would like you to have it.

ACTRESS C: A gift?

ACTRESS D: That's right.

(ACTRESS C *is taken aback by the filthy, stained pillow that* D *presents to her.*)

ACTRESS C: I appreciate your thought, but, I . . . I have plenty of pillows.

ACTRESS D: Please accept it.

ACTRESS C: No, really (*She pushes the pillow back.*) But I'm glad you are back. That new girl has been prompting for me since you fell ill, but her timing is just terrible. Listen, can you start tomorrow?

ACTRESS D: What?

ACTRESS C: Prompt. For me.

(*Pause.*)

ACTRESS C: What's wrong? You aren't coming back?

ACTRESS D: Look, I... I am completely healthy now.

ACTRESS C: Yes, I know. That's why I'm asking you.

ACTRESS D: I'm sorry to have troubled you for such a long time.

ACTRESS C: Never mind. It was nothing. So, you will prompt for me?

ACTRESS D: Prompt?

ACTRESS C (*Annoyed*): Yes, prompt.

ACTRESS D (*Annoyed*): Haven't you been listening to me? Why don't you understand?

ACTRESS C: Understand what?

ACTRESS D: I am completely healthy now, therefore...

ACTRESS C: Therefore, what?!

ACTRESS D: I want it back.

ACTRESS C (*Unsure*): What do you want back?

ACTRESS D: Well.... (*Slight laugh as if to say "you know."*)

ACTRESS C (*Increasingly uneasy*): I'm taking care of something for you?

ACTRESS D: I wouldn't say "taking care of."

ACTRESS C: Speak up. What do you want back from me?

ACTRESS D: The role of Nina.

ACTRESS C: What?

ACTRESS D: What I'm saying is, I want the role of Nina back.

(ACTRESSES A *and* B *are shocked. They drop their compacts on the floor.* ACTRESS C *also is speechless for a moment.*)

ACTRESS C: Um... Kiiko, do you know what you are saying?

ACTRESS D: Yes, of course. Why won't you acknowledge my health? Don't I look much better?

ACTRESS C: Even if you have recovered completely....

ACTRESS D: I've already apologized for causing you trouble for a long period of time.

(*As* ACTRESS C *searches for words,* ACTRESS D *stares at her.*)

ACTRESS C: You should go back to the hospital. You haven't recovered completely. This is absurd.

ACTRESS D: What's so absurd?

ACTRESS C: Kiiko... the role of Nina was mine from the beginning. And you were my prompter from the beginning. I don't really want to say this, but you are not ready for Nina.

(*Pause.*)

ACTRESS C: OK? Do you understand now?

(*Pause.*)

ACTRESS C: Go home. I'm going out to dinner with some people.

(ACTRESS C *starts to change her clothes.* ACTRESS D, *clutching the pillow, shows no sign off leaving. Mesmerized by the scene,* ACTRESSES A *and* B *have done strange things with their makeup. Suddenly aware how horrible they look, they start fixing their faces.* ACTRESS C *hangs up Nina's costume. She is uneasy with* ACTRESS D*'s glare.*)

ACTRESS D: It's all my fault. I got sick at the height of my career. I wrote many letters to him from the hospital bed. Letters of apology. I feel terrible for the author.

ACTRESS C: You feel terrible for the author?

ACTRESS D: Yes. He wrote such a brilliant role for me.

ACTRESS C: You know who the author is, don't you?

ACTRESS D: Of course I do.

ACTRESS C: He has been dead for seventy years.

ACTRESS D: That's a mere rumor.

ACTRESS C (*Amazed*): A rumor!?

ACTRESS D: I talked to him on the phone the day before yesterday.

ACTRESS C: Talked to who?

(*Pause.*)

ACTRESS C (*Looking at* ACTRESS D *suspiciously*): I'm beginning to see it. Go ahead, Kiiko, you can tell me.

ACTRESS D: Yes. . . .

ACTRESS C: Should I guess it? Maybe the author?

ACTRESS D: You are right.

ACTRESS C: How wonderful that you spoke to the author. I have done Chekhov numerous times, but never once had an opportunity to talk to him. I doubt I ever will. So what did you two talk about?

ACTRESS D: Many things.

ACTRESS C: I see. Many things.

ACTRESS D: Before we hung up, he asked me to get well soon and return to the stage. He said that he is looking forward to seeing me all healthy and on the stage once again.

ACTRESS C: Un-huh.

ACTRESS D: That's why I want to play Nina starting tomorrow.

ACTRESS C: I don't think so.

ACTRESS D: But I'm healthy.

ACTRESS C: It won't work.

(ACTRESS D *holds the pillow out to* C.)

ACTRESS C: What are you doing that for?

(ACTRESS D *continues to shove the pillow into* C.)

ACTRESS C: I told you, I don't want it.

ACTRESS D: It's my favorite. I slept so well. Now, it's your turn . . .

ACTRESS C: My turn? My turn to do what?

(*Pause.*)

ACTRESS C: You are demanding I exchange the role of Nina for this pillow!

(*Pause.*)

ACTRESS C: Where do you get such a mad idea?

ACTRESS D: You must be tired.

ACTRESS C: I'm not.

ACTRESS D: Yes, you are. Very tired. You need rest and sleep for your exhaustion.

ACTRESS C: Stop it! Stop. . . .

(ACTRESS C *grabs the pillow and throws it across the room. It flies in the direction of* ACTRESSES A *and* B.)

ACTRESS C: I have been an actress for a long time, but this is the first time someone insisted I give up a part for a pillow. I've had enough already. I can't waste my time with you. Go home.

(ACTRESS C *sits at the dressing table and starts removing her makeup.* ACTRESSES A *and* B *are curiously looking at the pillow on the floor.*)

ACTRESS B (*Smells the pillow*): It's sweaty

ACTRESS A: I sense her strong determination from it.

(ACTRESS D *approaches the pillow.* ACTRESSES A *and* B *draw back quickly.* ACTRESS D *picks it up and hugs it affectionately.*)

ACTRESS D (*Mumbles*): And I went through the trouble of reserving you a room at the hospital.

ACTRESS C: What did you say?

ACTRESS D: I said I already reserved a room at the hospital.

ACTRESS C: A room at the hospital?

ACTRESS D: Yes.

ACTRESS C: For whom? (*Suddenly realizing.*) You mean for me?

(ACTRESS D *nods.* ACTRESS C *is speechless.*)

ACTRESS D: I really wanted to get a private room for you, but unfortunately they were all taken. But now I think a large room is better. There is a television set, and you will have a lot of people to talk to. Older people often prefer a large room to a private room. You once said that you were terribly lonely living alone because you had no one to talk to. I thought about that, and came to a real understanding. Loneliness is the worst thing that can happen to anyone.

(ACTRESS C *listens in astonishment, her face still half made up.*)

ACTRESS D (*Continues*): If you really think about it, we actresses get so little reward. We sacrifice everything. Day after day we abuse our degenerating bodies, and what we desperately seek always turns out to be an illusion of love. That's why I'm against a prolonged commitment to this harsh profession. We can endure such cruel work only while we are young . . .

ACTRESS C: And you are going to rescue me.

ACTRESS D: I don't mean to be righteous, but it's not just me, you know. Women my age all feel the same way. They don't say anything, but they all want to liberate you soon from this brutal profession. The role of Nina must be particularly hard for you, moving around like a butterfly. I feel awful that I forced you to take over the role because of my illness. I apologize.

ACTRESS C: Kiiko.

ACTRESS D: Yes.

ACTRESS C (*Restrained*): How can I make you understand? You are right about the work being hard. Indeed, we sacrifice so much. And the cruelest factor is aging. Year after year your own body goes on betraying you. . . .

ACTRESS D: I know. . . .

ACTRESS C: Just a moment, that's not what I really mean. There is more to it than your physical being. Youth alone will not bring Nina alive. How can I say this? . . . What's important is accumulation, all kinds of accumulation. You know, loneliness is also a type of accumulation.

ACTRESS D: I can't imagine. . . .

ACTRESS C: I don't mean loneliness is an accomplishment. I mean . . . Um . . . I'm confused now. Anyway, I am well aware how heartless this profession is. But I made the choice. Nothing else will do. I don't care how brutal it can get. I will enjoy the savagery all the way. Nothing you can say will make me give up Nina. I will perform it two, three hundred more times! I will perform it when I'm an old hag; I'm hungry for brutality! Oh, I sound ridiculous. I'm not making any sense. What am I saying?

ACTRESS D: See. You are tired.

ACTRESS C: What?

ACTRESS D: I reserved a room for you, you know, at the hospital.

ACTRESS C: Get out!

(ACTRESS D *stares at* ACTRESS C.)

ACTRESS C (*Continues*): Don't make me angrier than I already am. I'm afraid of talking to someone like you . . . please . . . I don't want to be ranting and raving and end up feeling miserable.

(*Pause.*)

ACTRESS C (*Pleading*): I beg you, please, go home. I'm really tired now. I want to be alone.

(ACTRESS D *presents the pillow.*)

ACTRESS C: Stop it!

(*In a rage,* ACTRESS C *picks up a beer bottle and smashes it on* D*'s head. The bottle shatters, and* ACTRESS D *falls.*)

ACTRESS C (*Realizing what she has done*): Kiiko. . . .

(ACTRESS C *runs over and takes* D *in her arms.* ACTRESSES A *and* B *cannot hide their curiosity.* ACTRESS D *pushes* C *away and stands up.*)

ACTRESS C: I didn't mean to. . . . How do you feel?

(ACTRESS D *sways.* ACTRESS C *quickly catches her.*)

ACTRESS C: Are you all right?

ACTRESS D: I . . . I'm healthy.

ACTRESS C: I know.

ACTRESS D: Can I have my pillow?

(ACTRESS C *picks up the pillow and hands it to* D. ACTRESS D *unsteadily starts to leave.*)

ACTRESS C: Where are you going?

ACTRESS D: Nothing is better for fatigue than sleep.

ACTRESS C: Kiiko.

(ACTRESS D *exits, clutching the pillow.* ACTRESS C *sinks down in a chair.* ACTRESSES A *and* B *are looking at* C *nastily. Pause. Suddenly* ACTRESS C *grabs a tissue paper box off the dressing table and throws it across the room. It flies in the direction of* ACTRESSES A *and* B*; they dodge it just in time.* ACTRESS C *keeps throwing anything she can get her hands on.* ACTRESSES A *and* B *run around the room dodging them.*)

ACTRESS C: Don't make me laugh! Jesus! I won't be made fun of by that meager actress! Ha, ha . . . Exchange my role for a pillow? I'm going to laugh so hard I'll burst! Really the nerve! "Women my age all feel the same way. We all want to liberate you from this brutal profession." I don't need to be liberated just because it's the "in" thing to do these days. God dammit!

(ACTRESS C *throws more objects. One of them hits* ACTRESS B.)

ACTRESS B: Shit.

ACTRESS A: Are you all right?

ACTRESS B: Why is everything flying this way?

ACTRESS A: Like she is aiming at us.

(ACTRESS C *pours a brandy and gulps it down.*)

ACTRESS C: Ha. She thinks she can play Nina? A woman with fish-eye lenses for eyes! She is nothing but shine and gloss. . . . If we call that passion and youth, then I say this world is full of nothing but grotesque ghosts. . . . And she is huge. It's one thing to be healthy, but it's another to be an overgrown worthless tree trunk. She does not have the body of an actress. On top of that, she moves slower than a hippopotamus in the zoo. Even it moves faster when entering the water . . . Nina? Sea gull? Ha, ha . . . (*She takes a drink.*) Look at the time. I've wasted so much time. Stupid.

(*She sits at the dressing table and starts applying makeup for going out to dinner. She suddenly stops and stares at herself in the mirror.*)

ACTRESS C: . . . Kiiko, I'm the wrong person to take on. Your pillow doesn't do anything to me. I'm thick skinned. Think about it. I've been acting for twenty years. There is some accumulation in that. You haven't experienced the feeling. That feeling . . . like blood slowly oozing out from the root of every hair. I've lived through it over and over. I don't expect you to understand . . . that sensation of blood leaking out from every pore of your body. It's like you have to choose either stabbing your adversary or choosing your own death. Have you heard a human howl? Not scream or curse, I mean howl. Locked in the bathroom of your own apartment . . . alone . . . five or six hours . . . all through the night . . . it's the cry of a beast . . . when your dried-up throat breaks your voice, you drink water out of the toilet . . . then keep howling. . . . That's how you get a stronger voice. . . . That's accumulation . . . of a nauseating kind. . . .

(*Long pause.* ACTRESS C *lights a cigarette and puts on a record. Music. She stands up and takes off her robe. She is in her slip. She looks at herself in the mirror taking various poses.*)

ACTRESS C: True, I have sacrificed certain things, but I can justify them. I always know what I'm sacrificing . . . the battle is eternal, my soldier in the mirror . . . (*She hoists a glass*) . . . as I sit in twilight late alone by the flickering oak-flame . . . musing on long-pass'd war-scenes—of the countless buried unknown soldiers . . . of the vacant names, as unidentified air's and sea's—the unreturn'd . . . the brief truce after battle, with grim burial-squads, and the deep-fill'd trenches . . . even here in my room—shadows and half lights in the noiseless flickering flames . . . again I see the stalwart ranks on—filing, rising—I hear the rhythmic tramp of the armies . . . (*She laughs.*)

(ACTRESS D *appears, clutching the pillow, and stands silently in the doorway. Her face is pale.*)

ACTRESS A: Look.

ACTRESS B: That pillow woman is here again.

(ACTRESS C *turns off the record player.*)

ACTRESS C: Let's see. . . .

(ACTRESS C *crosses in front of* D *to get her clothes.* ACTRESS D *wants to say something to her, but* C *does not notice. As* ACTRESS C *gets dressed near* D, *she murmurs Nina's monologue, during which* D *tries several times to talk, but restrains herself.*)

ACTRESS C: ". . . I was afraid you might hate me, Konstantin Gavrilovich. Every night I dream that you are looking at me and don't recognize me. If you only knew! Ever since I arrived I've been walking here . . . by the lake. I came near the house many times, but couldn't bring myself to come in. Let's sit down. (*Sits at the dressing table and fixes her makeup and clothes.*) Let's sit and talk. . . . It's nice here, warm and cozy. . . . Listen, the wind! There's a passage in Turgenev: 'Happy the man who on such a night has a roof over his head, who has a warm corner of his own.' I am a sea gull. . . . No, that's not right. (*Rubs her forehead and stands.*) What was I saying? Yes, Turgenev. . . . (*Takes her purse and looks back on the dressing room from the doorway.*) 'And may the Lord help all homeless Wanderers. . . .'"

(ACTRESS C *exits.* ACTRESS D *wants to follow her but remains and watches* C *leave. Long pause.* ACTRESS D *slowly looks around the dressing room.* ACTRESSES A *and* B *are watching* D. ACTRESS D *stops her eyes on* A *and* B. *They stare at each other for a moment. Then* ACTRESSES A *and* B *quickly look away and resume their makeup.* ACTRESS D *slowly approaches* A *and* B.)

ACTRESS D: Good evening.

(*Shocked,* ACTRESSES A *and* B *fall off their chairs.*)

ACTRESS B: Y . . . y . . . you can see us?!

ACTRESS D: Yes.

ACTRESS A: Then, you too are. . . .

ACTRESS B (*To* ACTRESS A): That blow before; it got her good. Poor thing.

ACTRESS D: Excuse me.

ACTRESS A: Yes?

ACTRESS D: May I ask a question?

ACTRESS B: Go ahead.

ACTRESS A: Please.

ACTRESS D (*Looking at their makeup*): Were you here doing this every night?

ACTRESS B: Well . . . yes. Didn't mean to invade your space.

ACTRESS D: Oh, no. I don't mind.

(*Pause.*)

ACTRESS D: . . . I used to feel something.

ACTRESS A: What?

ACTRESS D: I am not surprised at all to meet you. . . . It was never clear, but I always felt your existence.

ACTRESS A: You mean the stagnant air around here?

ACTRESS B: The "hovering" air?

ACTRESS D: No, nothing like that, but I always heard voices . . . silent voices when I came in the dressing room every night.

ACTRESS A: Silent voices?

ACTRESS D: Yes, very low whispers.

ACTRESS B: How pathetic. No matter how hard we try, we can't get away from the curse of being a prompter.

(*Pause.*)

ACTRESS D: Excuse me . . . may I ask another question?

ACTRESS B: Go ahead.

ACTRESS A: Don't make it too difficult, though.

ACTRESS D: Have you been doing this for a long time?

ACTRESS B: Doing what?

ACTRESS D: You know, hanging out in the dressing room. . . .

ACTRESS B: I'm new. She is an old hand. Very old. Look at those scars. They are from the air raids.

ACTRESS D: Oh, my . . . air raids. You mean in World War II?

ACTRESS A (*Offended*): Stop staring at me. You make me feel like a museum exhibit.

ACTRESS D: So have you been coming here ever since then?

ACTRESS A: It's not like I'm obsessed or anything, but there is no other place to go, so . . .

ACTRESS D: You must be tired.

ACTRESS A: What?

ACTRESS D: I can see it now. You are far more tired than she is. (*Indicating* ACTRESS B.)

ACTRESS B: I knew it.

ACTRESS A (*To* ACTRESS B): Shut up.

ACTRESS D: Sleep is best for exhaustion.... This is worn out, but.... (*She holds the pillow out to* ACTRESS A.)

ACTRESS A (*Jumping back*): Keep it. I can't deal with that.

ACTRESS D: You can't deal with a pillow?

ACTRESS A: Right. I have no idea why...

(*Pause.*)

ACTRESS D: Um... isn't it about time?

ACTRESS B: Time for?

ACTRESS D: Time to go on stage....

(ACTRESS A *and* B *look at each other.*)

ACTRESS D: Which play are you doing?

(*Silence.*)

ACTRESS D: Which play?...

(*Silence.*)

ACTRESS D: ... Well?

ACTRESS B: How noisy you are! Chatter, chatter, chatter, chatter.... Can't you ever be quiet? Damn, my false eyelashes came off.

ACTRESS D: I'm sorry

(*Pause.*)

ACTRESS D: ... It's Chekhov, isn't it?

ACTRESS B: Chekhov?

ACTRESS A: Oh, yes. You talked to Chekhov on the phone the other day, didn't you?

ACTRESS D: Oh, you were listening?...

ACTRESS B: OK, let's assume we are doing Chekhov. Can you guess which play?

ACTRESS D: Maybe... *The Three Sisters*?

ACTRESS A: How can we do *The Three Sisters* with just two of us?

ACTRESS D: Are there only two of you?

ACTRESS B: As you can see, at least here in this dressing room.

(*Long pause.*)

ACTRESS D: ... I understand now.

ACTRESS A: OK, what do you understand?

ACTRESS D: You don't have a play, do you?

(ACTRESSES A *and* B *do not answer.*)

ACTRESS D: You just sit here doing your makeup night after night for nothing. You wait here for your turn forever... for the opportunity that will never come. Am I right?

(ACTRESSES A *and* B *remain silent.*)

ACTRESS D: Aren't you embarrassed? I wouldn't stand this misery. I would rather be in a hospital bed.

ACTRESS A: Huh, then go back to the hospital! And take your precious little pillow with you. But your bed isn't there anymore. There is no such thing as sound sleep for you anymore.

ACTRESS D (*Shocked*): Do you think I really lost my bed?

ACTRESS A: If you don't believe me, go find out for yourself.

(*Pause.*)

ACTRESS B: . . . You will soon get used to waiting, too.

ACTRESS A: Yeah, you will be just like us before long.

ACTRESS B: You know, we are not just wasting our time waiting. We keep trying, really We recollect our past accumulations.

ACTRESS A: Just a little while ago, we nearly lost our voices recollecting.

ACTRESS D: What came out of that?

ACTRESS B: All sorts of things . . . you know, we have a lot of accumulations.

(*Pause.*)

ACTRESS D: . . . The long night will begin for me, also.

(ACTRESSES A *and* B *look at each other.*)

ACTRESS A: You will get used to it soon. You can learn from us how to pass time in many ways. . . .

ACTRESS B: It may look sluggish to you, but we have a certain routine . . . right?

(ACTRESS D *suddenly stands up.*)

ACTRESS D: But I still think we should do something.

ACTRESS B: We are doing something.

ACTRESS D: That's not what I mean. I mean . . . we should decide on an agenda . . . you know, to prepare perhaps for the day that will come.

ACTRESS B: What day is coming?

ACTRESS D: We may still get opportunities to go on stage. You never know.

ACTRESS A: Yeah, she (*Indicating* ACTRESS B) had a similar dream at the beginning. But I tell you, it's never going to happen.

ACTRESS D: . . . You really are tired.

ACTRESS A: Stop it!

ACTRESS D: You are definitely exhausted. (*Edges in with the pillow.*)

ACTRESS A: God dammit! You want my role, don't you. I won't let you take it away! What kind of person are you? You don't discriminate in your attacks, huh? You can chase me all you want with that pillow. I won't give up my role. Get out!

ACTRESS B: Um . . . excuse me.

ACTRESS A: What!

ACTRESS B: What are you talking about? Your role hasn't been decided, has it?

(ACTRESS A *is furious. Long silence.*)

ACTRESS D: I'm easily misunderstood. Someone encouraged me that to be misunderstood is an asset for an actress. It was a mistake . . . I don't have the team spirit or the ability to adapt. The fact that I'm misunderstood means that I'm not loved. No one loves me. I'm always alone. . . . I have always been alone and I always will be . . .

ACTRESS B: Wait a minute. Why are you summarizing your life now all of a sudden? Sure, it's hard being misunderstood, but the opposite is just as bad. Everyone always told me how nice I was; for a while even I believed that I was just a nice person. Then it occurred to me that I'm like the air. Air isn't bad, I know. But no one would say "I love you madly" or "I have faith in your talent" to mere air . . . Do you understand?

ACTRESS D (*Stubbornly*): It's OK. I've made my decision already.

ACTRESS B: What decision?

ACTRESS D: From now on, I won't bother you. I will go on by myself. I will wait for the opportunity that may come someday. . . . It must be destiny . . . to spend the long night alone. (*Suddenly breaks into Irina's lines from* The Three Sisters.) "Oh, I'm miserable . . . I can't work; I won't work. Enough, enough! I've been a telegraph clerk, and now I have a job in the office of the Town Council, and I loathe and despise every single thing they give me to do. . . ."

ACTRESS B: Where do telegraph clerk and Town Council come from?

ACTRESS A: It's Irina's line from *The Three Sisters.*

ACTRESS B: Oh, she's started already

ACTRESS D: ". . . I'm nearly twenty-four already; I've been working a long time, and my brain is drying up. I've grown thin and old and angry, and there is nothing, nothing, no satisfaction of any kind. And time is passing, and I feel that I'm moving away from the real, beautiful life, moving farther and farther into some abyss . . ."

ACTRESS A: Hold it.

ACTRESS D: What?

ACTRESS A: I can't deal with this incredible noise. Who gave you permission to take the role of Irina, anyway?

ACTRESS D: Permission?

(*Pause.*)

ACTRESS B: The night is forever long.

ACTRESS A: Right. . . . There is no hope for us of ever seeing days filled with sunshine again.

ACTRESS B: Then it's not a bad idea to change our ways a little.

ACTRESS A: I guess so, since there are three of us now.

(ACTRESSES A *and* B *look at each other and smile.*)

ACTRESS A: You'll be Masha?

ACTRESS B: Then you'll be Olga.

ACTRESS A: It's been a while since I had a female role.

ACTRESS D: Um. . . .

ACTRESS B: Throw out that pillow. You are Irina, just as you wanted.

ACTRESS A: Let's not rush this. We have plenty of time.

(ACTRESS A *gets up and returns with* C*'s brandy. Everyone gets a glass. Brandy is poured.* ACTRESS B *runs to the record player, chooses a record, and puts on the music.*)

ACTRESS A: Toast. To our night—a long night.

ACTRESS B: To our eternal rehearsal.

ACTRESS D: And to our forever lost sleep.

(*The tone of the music changes. The three actresses stand close together.*)

ACTRESS B (*Reciting Masha's lines*): ". . . Oh, listen to that music! They are leaving us . . . we are left alone to begin our life over again. We must live. . . . We must live. . . ."

(*During this speech, the light dims slowly and the three figures begin to look like corpses with pale faces.*)

ACTRESS D (*Reciting Irina's lines*): "A time will come when everyone will know what all this is for, why there is all this suffering, and there will be no mysteries; but meanwhile, we must live . . . we must work, only work! . . . Soon winter will come and cover everything with snow, and I shall go on working, working. . . ."

(ACTRESS A *embraces* B *and* D.)

ACTRESS A (*Reciting Olga's lines*): "The music plays so gaily, so valiantly, one wants to live! Oh, my God! Time will pass, and we shall be gone forever; we'll be forgotten, our faces will be forgotten, our voices, and how many there were of us. . . . (*The three figures start to fade.*) Oh, my dear sisters, our life is not over yet. We shall live! The music is so gay, so joyous, it seems as if just a little more and we shall know why we live, why we suffer. . . . If only we knew, if only we knew. . . ."

(*The dressing room is dark. Then faint moonlight reveals a field of grass. There are countless mirrors resembling tombstones in the field. The mirrors whisper.*)

Glorious Town . . .

Indigent Metropolis . . .

Imprisoned Souls . . .

Transcendent Figures . . .

Transcendent Figures . . .

CURTAIN

Ōta Shōgo, *The Earth Station*, directed by Ōta Shōgo, Tenkei gekijō, January 1985.
(Courtesy of Ōta Mitsuko)

THE EARTH STATION

ŌTA SHŌGO

TRANSLATED BY MARI BOYD

Ōta Shōgo (1939–2007) was a playwright and director as well as a central figure in the *angura* counterculture of the 1960s to the mid-1970s. His career can be divided into three periods. During the first, between 1962 and 1968, he tried working in new *shingeki* theater companies but was not satisfied with the quality of their art.

During his second and major period, from 1968 to 1988, Ōta developed his theater of divestiture through his work as a playwright, director, and head of the Tenkei Theater Company (Gekidan tenkei gekijō, Theater of Transformation). In 1977, he produced the nō-inspired *Tale of Komachi Told by the Wind* (*Komachi fūden*), which makes startling use of silence and stillness and won the prestigious Kishida Drama Prize. In 1981, he produced *The Water Station* (*Mizu no eki*), his seminal play, epitomizing divestiture, and for its performance his company received the Kinokuniya Theater Award in the group category. Ōta led the Tenkei Theater on international tours of *The Tale of Komachi Told by the Wind* and *The Water Station* to Europe, North America, Australia, and South Korea.

In his third period from 1990 to 2007, Ōta became a prominent social force in the arts world, providing emerging artists with venues to showcase their art. He served as the artistic director of the Fujisawa Civic Theater in Kanagawa Prefecture, as vice president of the Japan Playwrights Association, and as a professor at the Kyoto University of Art and Design and the chief editor of its periodical, *Performing Arts*.

The Earth Station is the second of Ōta's groundbreaking works in quietude. In this play, only the Daughters of the Wind actually deliver lines. The other figures remain silent throughout and move at a pace of roughly six and a half feet every five minutes. The free-verse score provides the actors with psychophysical tasks through which silence becomes living presence.

Scenes

1. A Girl
2. A Man Looking at a Tree
3. Two Men
4. One of Three
5. A Flask
6. Four Eyes
7. A Woman in Labor
8. An Empty Can
9. A Burial
10. Two Mouths
11. An Interlude
12. A Man and a Woman
13. Distant Thunder

Characters

GIRL
MAN WHO LOOKS AT A TREE
MAN (A)
MAN (B)
MAN WITH A HUGE LOAD ON HIS BACK
WAITING WOMAN
WOMAN IN LABOR
FIRST HUSBAND
FIRST WIFE
WOMAN WITH AN IRON
OLD WOMAN
SECOND HUSBAND
SECOND WIFE
SISTER
BOY
DAUGHTER OF THE WIND (A)

DAUGHTER OF THE WIND (B)
DAUGHTER OF THE WIND (C)
MAN
WOMAN
MAN WHO TAKES COVER
ANOTHER WOMAN

Main Action | **Minor Action 1** | **Minor Action 2** | **Sound**

SCENE 1. A GIRL

With the dark mountain
in the background
Along the mountain
path alone
A girl walks
In the obscure light
Toward an obscure destination
Carrying three bags

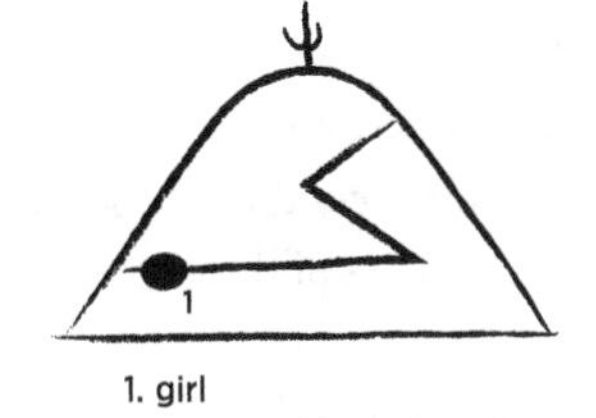

1. girl

SATIE, "GYMNOPÉDIE, NO. 3"

The girl walks

Stopping
The girl's gaze shifts
Crawls up to the dark
mountaintop

SCENE 2. A MAN LOOKING AT A TREE

In a shaft of light
On the top of the mountain
of debris
A single tree and a lone man

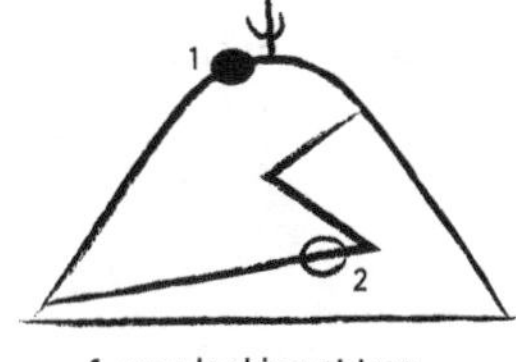

1. man looking at tree
2. girl

At a stunted tree with frail
branches
The man looks
As if at a towering big tree

Still dark
Up the mid-slope of the mountain

Main Action	**Minor Action 1**	**Minor Action 2**	**Sound**
With his baggage on his back	Climb the shadows of two men		
The man lies down			
The reclining man daydreams Of a breeze passing by the towering trunk			
Then looking at the stunted tree He drinks from the spout Of the kettle at his side The man sees the approaching shadows of the two men	The two men approach the mountaintop		
From the cheek of the man looking at the tree Fades the breeze by the towering trunk			
Arising The man regards the watching eyes	Looking for a place to rest The men look around		
Casting a distant look At the stunted tree where no wind blows The man departs			
Over the mountain He fades			
	Walking along the mountain path The girl stops		

Main Action	Minor Action 1	Minor Action 2	Sound

SCENE 3. TWO MEN

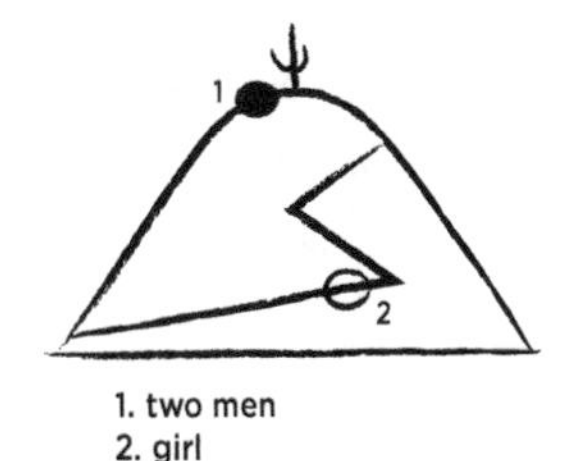

Main Action	Minor Action 1

Lowering his baggage man (b)
  sits down
On the upturned furniture
Protruding from the junk pile
Man (a) sits down beside
  man (b)	

	By the path
Their shoulders touch	The girl sits down

Man (b) inches away
Man (a) slides into
  the space left by man (b)

Shifting his weight man (b)
  moves away

Man (a) senses the rock
Man (b) feels the rock

Man (b) quietly
Without being noticed
Shifts back to his original position

Their shoulders touch

With the widening perspective
  before them their eyes
Graze over the mountain of debris
Then turn to the far distance

With bated breath
Man (a) waits for man (b)'s reaction
In the direction of man (b)'s gaze
Man (a) looks and on to the
  view again

Main Action	Minor Action 1	Minor Action 2	Sound
The look on their faces as they confront each other			
Releasing his breath man (b) stretches out his legs Releasing his breath man (a) stretches out his legs			

SCENE 4. ONE OF THREE

The girl
Takes out children's playthings
From her luggage
Dolls music boxes and toys

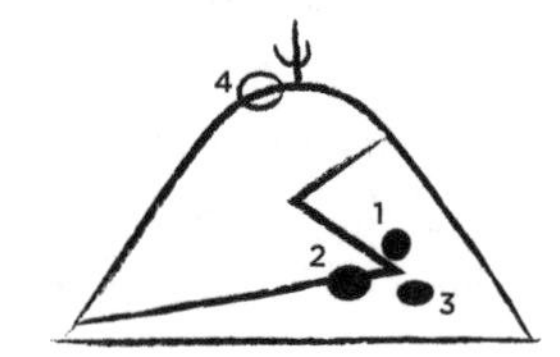

1. waiting woman
2. girl
3. man with a huge load
4. two men

Looking fondly at each
one by one
She throws them away
into the junk pile

SATIE, "GYMNOPÉDIE, NO. 3"

On top of a car half-protruding
From the rubble
A woman waits

Sunken in the junk
A man with a huge load on his back
Is lying down

Watching the girl from behind
the waiting woman stands
Near the man with a huge load
the girl discards
Music boxes and dolls

From the playthings
Tearing her eyes away standing up
The girl walks off

Main Action	Minor Action 1	Minor Action 2	Sound

Following the girl with
their eyes
The waiting woman the man
with the huge load

SCENE 5. A FLASK

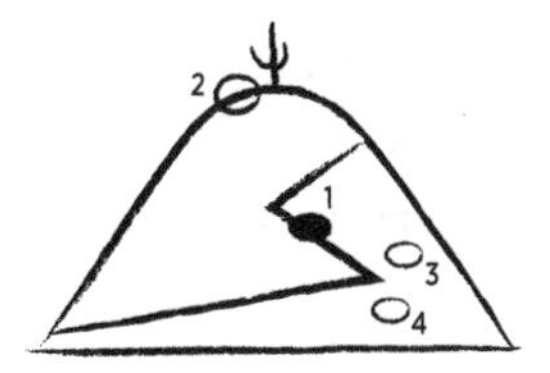

1. woman giving birth and girl
2. two men
3. waiting woman
4. man with a huge load

From a dark crevice in
the rubble appear
A woman's bare legs hands
neck
And face contorted with
labor pains

The girl walks by the
suffering woman

The girl's faltering steps

The woman breathing heavily

Stopping the girl steps
From the path onto the junk

The woman senses the
girl's presence

The woman's hand
stretches out
To the girl's flask

The girl clasps the flask tight
Reaching out the woman
looks up
The girl looks into her eyes

Her eyes and hands move
away from the flask

Main Action	Minor Action 1	Minor Action 2	Sound
The girl's hand turns the cap of the flask Shows it to the woman			
From the cap along the arm To the girl moves the woman's gaze			
Holding the cap the girl's hand Reaches out to the woman The woman's hand clutches the cap The girl brings the flask close			
The face of the woman holding the cap contorts The body writhes The girl is bewildered The woman's eyes open her teeth clench The girl looks away			
The woman breathes with her whole body			
And relaxes	In the hand of the man with a huge load		
	The music box starts to play		MUSIC BOX MUSIC ↓
Offering the flask the girl's hand		A married couple come along the foot of the mountain	|
Pours water into the cap		The waiting woman looks at the music box	|
In the junk the drinking woman The girl watches			↓

Main Action	Minor Action 1	Minor Action 2	Sound
Raising the flask to her lips		Putting the music box down	
The girl drinks gazing up at the sky		The man with a huge load listens	

SCENE 6. FOUR EYES

Main Action	Minor Action 1	Minor Action 2	Sound
The married couple put down their luggage at the foot of the mountain			
Sitting down The husband leans against some junk	Breathing calmly	1. married couple 2. old woman 3. two men 4. woman giving birth and girl 5. waiting woman 6. man with a huge load	
	The woman and the girl		
The wife leans against the husband			
Breathing deeply their bodies Cast afar their eyes	Her belly large The woman lies down on her back		
To shoes stretches the wife's hand			
She takes off her shoes			
Her hand traces a course along the husband's knees Cast afar his eyes	Looking toward the lying woman Gently the girl waits		
Inside his coat The barefoot wife enters			
The couple turn toward the sky			

Main Action	Minor Action 1	Minor Action 2	Sound
The wife as if pushed by the wind Steps into a small hollow The husband turns to her			
Inside the hollow Crawling up the sky her eyes Undoing her bodice her hands			
Discarding his coat Undoing his shirt the husband approaches	Nearby an old woman huddles As if asleep		
In the hollow of the rubble His hands grip her hair, her knees			
Reaching behind she grabs his hair Grappling striving against each other			
Slowly like plants the two bodies intertwine			SATIE, "GYMNOPÉDIE, NO. 3"
Stretched out her bare legs Toward the sky are directed Two pairs of mammalian eyes			
Their breathing calms	Her gaze shifts From their bodies		
Reflected in the two pairs of piscine eyes The starry night the ocean depths	To the pregnant woman		

Main Action | **Minor Action 1** | **Minor Action 2** | **Sound**

SCENE 7. A WOMAN IN LABOR

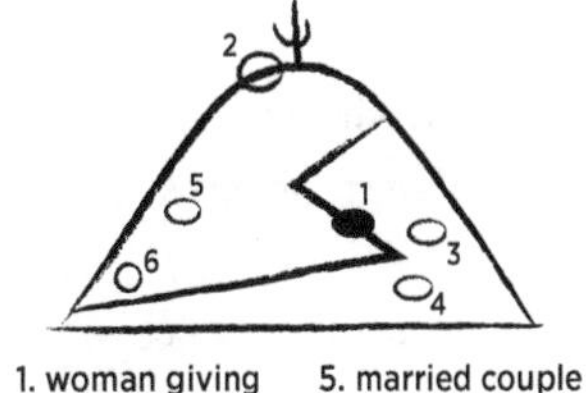

Main Action	Minor Action 1	Minor Action 2	Sound
From the woman's prostrate body a moan escapes The girl looks at her The woman's hands and legs stiffen Teeth clench	The far-off gaze of the married couple Focuses nearer		
The old woman's gaze shifts from afar to the woman Whose body trembles			
With her handkerchief		In front of the waiting woman	
She wipes her face		Stands up the man with a huge load	
Swift as a shadow	From the hollow in the junk		
The old woman approaches umbrella in hand Looks down on the twisting body of the woman	To their luggage The married couple return		
Grabbing the hair Of the writhing woman Stuffing a handkerchief into her mouth The old woman crouches by her legs			
The woman's breath and low moan			

Main Action	Minor Action 1	Minor Action 2	Sound
Crouching between her legs The old woman scolds			
Paralyzed with fear The girl averts her eyes			
The woman's deep voice			
The sound of flesh being slapped The sound of flesh being slapped			
Toward the silence The girl looks back	Passing along the path Above the woman giving birth		
The old woman's face Emerges from between the woman's legs	The man with a huge load		
The motionless woman			
The old woman sits down With a black cloth bundle in her lap The woman raises her upper body Her eyes on the old woman then to the sky			
The old woman holding the black bundle Leans on her umbrella and goes up the path			

Main Action	Minor Action 1	Minor Action 2	Sound
Wrapping around her waist The white cloth that covered her creeping out of the hollow The woman pursues the old woman			
The girl alone The empty hollow			
Climbing up the path the old woman The woman clambers after her	The two men near the summit Stand up		
		Passing in front of the married couple Who are leaning against the junk A woman with an iron	

SCENE 8. AN EMPTY CAN

Main Action	Minor Action 1	Minor Action 2	Sound
With luggage in hand man (a) heads off Man (b) rises and looks back At the empty spot Where he had sat	The woman with an iron walking alone Looking toward her the waiting woman Midway on the path She stops	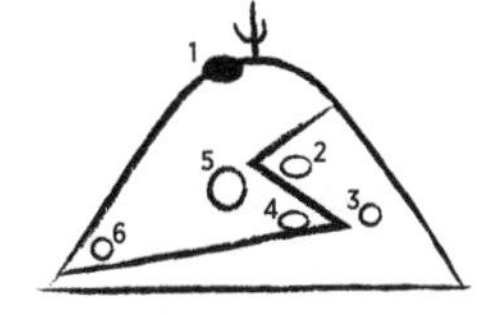 1. two men 2. man with a huge load 3. waiting woman 4. woman with iron 5. woman giving birth, old woman, girl 6. married couple	
Picking up from near his feet A can He holds it above the vacant spot and stares at it			
Man (a) watches man (b)'s actions			

Main Action	Minor Action 1	Minor Action 2	Sound
Having looked at the can Man (b) throws it away Hunting around Finds a battered pot tosses it onto the vacant spot			
Man (a) looks around Finding an old shoe moves it To the place where he had sat			
The two men look at the battered pot and the old shoe			
Throwing away the old shoe From nearby man (a) collects a bucket and other objects From what is lying around into the pot Man (b) adds odds and ends			
The two men stare at the small heaps They have made			
	By the path	Up the path	
Face to face their eyes meet Then shift to afar and to the mountaintop	With the load on his back Sits the man	Climbs the woman with an iron	
They head for the top			
Their bodies and luggage	A married couple come up the path		
Disappear over the top			

Main Action	Minor Action 1	Minor Action 2	Sound
			SATIE, "GYMNOPÉDIE, NO. 3"
	SCENE 9. A BURIAL		
	The hand of the girl looking	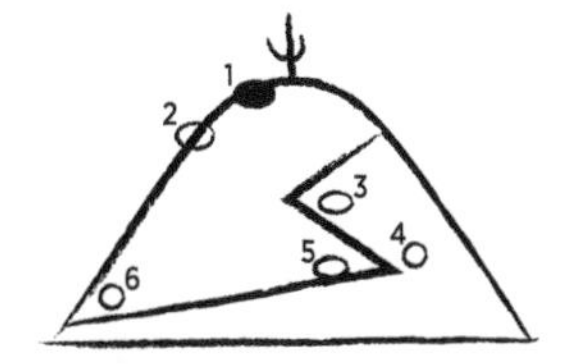 1. woman giving birth, old woman 2. woman with iron 3. man with a huge load 4. waiting woman 5. girl 6. married couple	
The old woman and the woman who gave birth	At the empty hollow		
At the base of the frail, withered tree on the mountaintop	Her hand passes along her leg	The woman with an iron	
	And into her skirt	In a corner of a junk pile	
The old woman from the refuse Digs up empty bottles, pots, and other objects She scoops out a small hole		Puts down her baggage	
The bundle is buried	Reaching the top The married couple		
The woman's mouth	Glance at the two women	Another married couple come along the path	
Gapes open darkly			
The bundle is	In the corner of the girl's eye, the married couple		
Covered with bottles, pots, and pans	The girl's hand	The woman with an iron	
	Emerges from her skirt	To the opened luggage	
The old woman listens to the sound of the wind The woman stands pale by the wasted tree		Her attention is drawn	
		Men's underwear Children's party outfits	

Main Action	Minor Action 1	Minor Action 2	Sound
		Her own blouse Smiles appear and fade At the clothing With a faraway gaze the woman looks Into action the woman's hands Iron the clothes	

SCENE 10. TWO MOUTHS

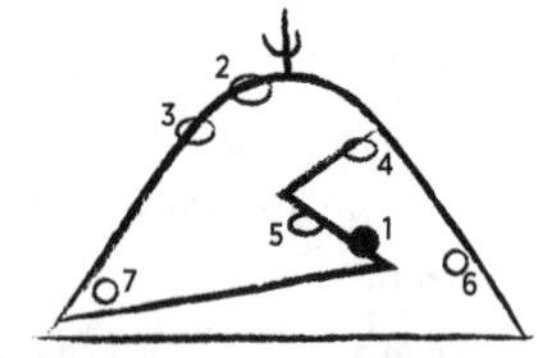

1. married couple
2. woman giving birth, old woman
3. woman with iron
4. girl
5. man with a huge load
6. waiting woman
7. man

On the junk by the path
The married couple put down
their luggage and sit

Lighting a cigarette
the wife

The husband stretches
toward her cigarette

The curling smoke

He reaches for her hand
And draws it near

He stands up
And is riveted to the ground

She stands up
And is riveted to the
ground

He sits down
She remains rooted
to the spot

Main Action	Minor Action 1	Minor Action 2	Sound
He observes her			
She is unable to move			
He stands up			
The two are petrified			
She sits down			
She squats	A lone man		
And calls for help	Comes along the path at		
	the foot of the mountain		
He cannot help			
From the wife he			SATIE, "GYMNOPÉDIE, NO. 3" ↓
cannot help			
He moves away			
Moving away			
His body presses against	Along the way		
the junk			
	He stops		
In the clutter			
Shouting out his mouth			SILENT SCREAMS
opens wide			
Calling for help			
Shouting out her mouth			
gapes open			
Between their voices			VIVALDI, PICCOLO CONCERTO ↓
A faint line of affinity			
To the husband in			
the junk			
The wife attends			
In the junk			
They embrace lightly			
A wind gently passes			↓ ↓

Main Action	Minor Action 1	Minor Action 2	Sound

SCENE 11. AN INTERLUDE

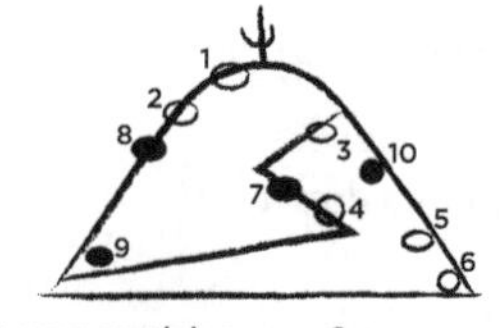

Shrouded in darkness
stands
The somber mountain
of debris
The people scattered
on it
Beckoned by the gently
passing wind
Their faces floating in
the air
Their gazes cast afar

The man with a huge
load stands up

Below him
A girl in summer
attire appears
Out of a fridge

Peering at his sister
From behind the man
is a boy in a straw hat
Looking back the man
with a huge load sees

His boyhood
Squatting under the
summer sun

The man approaches
the boy
Looking at the man
the boy withdraws

(Minor Action 1:)

Out of old sewing machines
and cabinets
Emerge the daughters
of the wind
Following the boy with
their eyes

Main Action	Minor Action 1	Minor Action 2	Sound
Descending the path The boy takes out a whistle and puts it to his lips	Whispering muttering Daughter of the wind (a) My mother too went flower viewing She went flower viewing and started thinking having many thoughts		↓
Trying to blow the whistle	Being blown by the wind being blown by the wind		
He sees in the distance his sister	And so she started having many thoughts Daughter of the wind (b) She must've, she must've, she must've had many thoughts		
Mirror in hand she is putting on makeup	Daughter of the wind (c) Washing the pots and pans looking at the bottom of the pans		
For the first time	(a) Sitting still in the three-mat room next to the storage room / (b) Feeling easy in the dark / (c) Feeling the coolness of the tatami mats		
He watches her doing her face	Three daughters— Yes, yes / (b) My mother, too / (c) My grandmother, too / (b) Twisting her body / (c) Twisted with regrets Daughters of the wind (a, b) Yes, yes / (c) Feeling, "I'm sad" / (a) Feeling, "I'm lonely / (b) Laughing, "never mind" / (c) Laughing		
Finishing up she puts on high heels	(a) Laughing / Three daughters— Yes, yes / (c) Washing the tub / (a) Washing one's breasts / (b) Holding one's breasts		

Main Action	Minor Action 1	Minor Action 2	Sound
Looks at herself in the mirror	(c) Breasting it out against father / (a) Talking with father at the riverbank / (b) Picking flowers / (c) Picking one's nose		
	(a) Biting into a plum		
She notices the boy heading her way	(b) Reciting a prayer		
Rebuffed by her stare	Three daughters— Yes, yes		
He halts	(b) Reciting a prayer genuflecting / (c) Reflecting oneself in a mirror		
	(a) Looking with all one's hate / (b) With all one's love / (a) Yes, yes with all one's love / (c) Washing the rice / (a) Sharpening the knife		
She hides the mirror and high heels	(b) Giving someone the smallpox / (c) Being given to delusions / (a) Feeling, "this is enough"		
He approaches	Three daughters— Yes, yes feeling, "this is enough"		
	(b) Wringing out the washing / (c) Carrying it on one's back / (a) Yes, yes carrying a child on one's back / (b) Hitting the child on one's back		
She edges back	(c) Then being hit back by the grown child		
	Three daughters— Yes, yes		
He pursues	Daughters of the wind disappear into the debris		
She runs down the path			
He watches her go			
At the boy from afar Peers the man with a huge load			

Main Action	Minor Action 1	Minor Action 2	Sound
Looking away			
Beginning to climb the path	Again ironing the clothes		
the man with a huge load			
	The woman with the iron		
The boy descends the path	As before		
	Motionless the waiting woman		
The wind dies			
Climbing up the path			
to the top			
To the top			
And over and beyond fade			
The departing shadows			
The woman who gave birth			
The girl			
The married couple			
The man with a huge load			
At the summit			
Alone the old woman leans			
against the tree			

SCENE 12. A MAN AND A WOMAN

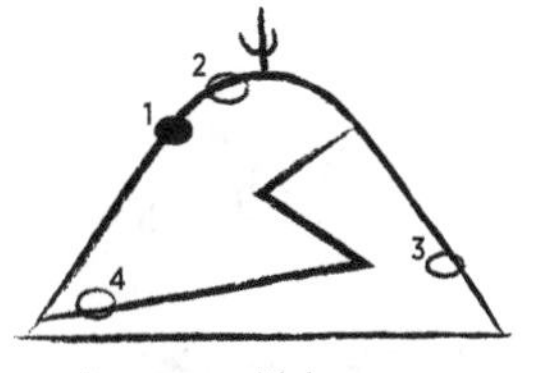

1. woman with iron and man
2. old woman
3. waiting woman
4. man

Main Action	Minor Action 1
Walking along the path	
to the peak	
In the corner of the	
man's eye	
A woman ironing	
He passes by	
	Coming along the foot
	of the mountain a man
He stops	
In the visual range of the	
man looking back	
The woman continues to iron	

Main Action	Minor Action 1	Minor Action 2	Sound
Stepping over the rubble The man approaches her			
She stops ironing			
Near her the man sits down She feels his presence behind her			
She takes up her ironing again	By the path		
He looks away	He rests		
Standing up he reaches for his luggage			
Again By her he sits down She is on guard			
The man's hand touches her hand that holds The motionless iron			
His hand pulls The iron held by the woman			
To his chest Her hand resists Forces clash			SATIE, "GYMNOPÉDIE, NO. 3" ↓
The woman bites his hand Retrieving the iron she finds herself In his lap			↓
At the speed of light Time passes			↓

Main Action	Minor Action 1	Minor Action 2	Sound
His hand moves over her body	Again up the path		
	He walks		
As if years have passed			
The two motionless bodies meet		At the foot of the mountain a woman appears	
As if years have passed			
The man and woman face each other			
He reaches out for his luggage			
She peers at her reflection in the flat bottom of the iron			
He looks back			
Baggage in hand she stands up			
Walking as if years have passed			
To the summit head the man and woman			

SCENE 13. DISTANT THUNDER

Main Action	Minor Action 1	Minor Action 2	Sound
On the roof of a car half-protruding from the debris		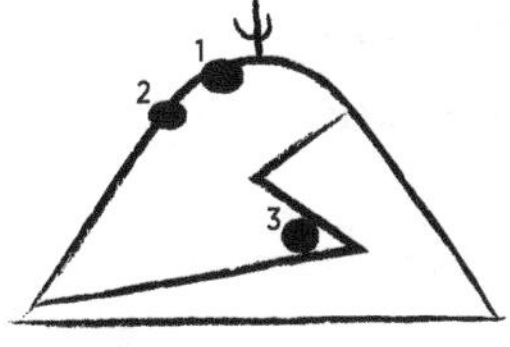	
Sits the waiting woman			
In the direction of her gaze is the shadow of another woman			
From the car			
Leaning forward the waiting woman			

Main Action	Minor Action 1	Minor Action 2	Sound
			SOUND OF THUNDER
On the approaching woman			
The waiting woman's eyes fasten			
The other notices her	Toward the sound raising his eyes	Toward the distant thunder	
	For the source of the sound	The old woman looks	
From afar	He searches		
With eyes wide open the two stare at each other			
Throwing away the luggage	In the direction of the thunder	On the mountaintop	
The woman runs forward to her	He looks	She stands up	
Welcoming the waiting woman			
Kneeling down			
Stretching out their arms			
Their hands touch each other's cheeks	At the sound of thunder		
	He covers his head with a coat		
Toward the thunder			
They turn their gaze	Crouching in the hollow		
	He prepares to avoid the rain		
Eyes smiling			
Facing each other the two women			
Undressing			
They welcome the rain			
	At the mountaintop		
Discarding shoes	The old woman and the withered tree		

Main Action	Minor Action 1	Minor Action 2	Sound
Stripping to undergarments They wait for rain Toward the approaching thunder Side by side the two women			SATIE, "GYMNOPÉDIE, NO. 3" THE END

Inoue Hisashi, *Living with Father*, directed by Uyama Hitoshi, Komatsuza, May 1999.
(Photograph by Yakou Masahiko)

LIVING WITH FATHER

INOUE HISASHI

TRANSLATED BY ZELJKO CIPRIS

A contemporary of playwrights such as Kara Jūrō and Terayama Shūji, in his Christianity and his "old left" politics Inoue Hisashi (1934–2010) nonetheless had more in common with an earlier generation of *shingeki* playwrights. His appeal also has been more solidly mainstream than that of any of the other dramatists featured in part IV. Partially raised by French Canadian Catholic priests in a Sendai orphanage, he shared with Terayama and Hijikata Tatsumi a strong allegiance to the unique culture of Tōhoku Japan. After graduating with a degree in French literature from Sophia University in Tokyo, Inoue began to write comedy skits for Atsumi Kiyoshi (later the star of the popular "Tora-san" movie series) at an Asakusa strip club. In 1964, he made a name for himself as the script writer for *Bottle-Gourd Island* (*Hyokkori hyōtan-jima*), a popular children's puppet show on NHK, Japan's national television network.

Inoue was a prolific writer of fiction, drama, and essays. His first work for the stage, *Japanese Bellybuttons* (*Nihonjin no heso*, 1969), was followed by as many as sixty plays over the course of his career, including *The Great Doctor Yabuhara* (*Yabuhara kengyō*, 1973), *Makeup* (*Keshō*, 1982), *Headache, Stiff Neck Higuchi Ichiyō* (*Zutsū kakatori Higuchi Ichiyō*, 1984), and *Mokuami Opera* (1995). One of Inoue's last plays was *Suite Massacre* (*Kumikyoku gyakusatsu*, 2009), about the 1933 police murder of the leftist writer Kobayashi Takiji. Inoue frequently used humor, music, and Brechtian techniques to critically explore Japanese history. In 1979, he won the Kinokuniya Theater Award for two quasi-biographical

---

The translator would like to thank Shoko Hamano for her great help in both translating the Hiroshima dialect of the original and obtaining permission to publish this translation.

dramas, *Serious Japan: General Nogi* (*Shimijimi Nihon: Nogi Taishō*) and *Kobayashi Issa*. In 1984, he founded his own theater troupe, the Little Pine Company (Komatsuza), to produce his plays. But Inoue was equally prolific as a novelist, winning numerous awards, including the Yomiuri Literary Prize in 1981 for *People of Kirikiri* (*Kirikirijin*, 1981), about a fictional place in Tōhoku that declares independence from Japan. *Living with Father* (*Chichi to kuraseba*, 1994) combines Inoue's interest in Japanese history and regional identity (in Japanese, the whole play is in dialect) in a drama about a survivor of the atomic bomb in Hiroshima and her relationship with her father.

AUTHOR'S PREFACE

When I bring up the subject of Hiroshima and Nagasaki, an increasing number of people say, "It is wrong to dwell on having being victimized, because the Japanese of those days also victimized Asia." The second part of this view is certainly accurate. The Japanese did victimize all of Asia. However, I will never accept the first part of the statement because I believe that the two atomic bombs were not merely dropped on the Japanese; they were dropped on the entire human existence. The bomb victims of that time who were burned by the infernal flames represent people throughout the modern world who cannot escape from the existence of nuclear weapons. I write as one among six billion human beings, not out of a feeling of victimization, but rather out of a conviction that it would be a greater wrong to pretend ignorance of the inferno that I know. Perhaps my life will be over when I finish writing about Hiroshima and Nagasaki. This work is the first in that series. Please take a look.

1

Music and darkness slowly envelop the auditorium. After a while, a far-off rumble of timpani sounds from somewhere. Distant lightning flashes.

Soon a hastily built house nearly as ramshackle as a hut emerges into view, illuminated by the lightning. It is five thirty in the afternoon on the last Tuesday in July 1948. This is the house of FUKUYOSHI MITSUE, *on the east side of Hijiyama in the city of Hiroshima. The layout, in sequence starting with stage right, consists of a kitchen; a six-mat living room furnished with a folding tea table, among other items; and an eight-mat room containing a book table and a bookcase. The eight-mat room also has a closet.*

There is a sound of wooden clogs in the entranceway that is visible to the rear of the living room, and MITSUE *rushes in. She is twenty-two, wearing an old-fashioned white blouse and neat, splashed-pattern work trousers, and is clutching, instead of a handbag, a shopping bag with a wood-slat opening. As she steps into the living room, lightning flashes again.* MITSUE *stumbles onto the mats still clutching her shopping bag, then covers her eyes and ears with her hands.*

MITSUE: Papa, I'm scared!

(*The closet door glides open, and* TAKEZŌ *speaks from the upper half.*)

TAKEZŌ: This way, this way. Come into the closet, Mitsue, quickly.

(TAKEZŌ *is wearing a white open-neck shirt with a national civilian uniform. He has covered himself with a seating cushion to ward off thunder and tosses a cushion to* MITSUE, *too.*)

TAKEZŌ: Why are you dawdling? Put the cushion over your head and quickly hide down here.

MITSUE (*Startled, but happy*): Papa, you're here after all.

TAKEZŌ: Of course I am. I'm here whenever and wherever you tell me to be. What else could I do?

MITSUE: But it's absurd that I'm so frightened. I can hardly believe it.

TAKEZŌ: What are you babbling about? This way, quickly . . . (*A flash of light.*) See, it's coming!

MITSUE (*Crawling into the closet*): Papa!

(*Lightning and thunder are receding into the distance. The conversation heard from the upper and lower halves of the closet is interwoven with the thunderclaps.*)

TAKEZŌ: Let it flash and thunder as much as it likes! With Papa and the closet and the cushion as your three allies, now you are all right.

MITSUE: But I'm twenty-two already. A real adult doesn't get all scared every time there's thunder. It's embarrassing. It really makes me angry.

TAKEZŌ (*Decisively*): It isn't your fault.

MITSUE: I don't know. . . .

TAKEZŌ: It's true, isn't it, that until a while ago you were a tomboy in the women's junior college athletic club, running around the sports grounds without any worry, even when it thundered.

MITSUE (*Nodding emphatically*): There were only three club members, so I was in charge of everything from sprint to long distance. I was so busy I didn't mind thunder or anything else.

TAKEZŌ: Why did you, who were so brave, get to be so scared and jittery?

MITSUE: I'm not sure. I can't help it.

TAKEZŌ: And since when did you get like that?

MITSUE: I guess since about three years ago.

TAKEZŌ: Since that atomic bomb, right?

MITSUE: Is that it?

TAKEZŌ (*Nodding*): Do you know Nobu from the Tomita photo shop?

MITSUE: He often took pictures of us.

TAKEZŌ: A very good photographer, one of the best in Hiroshima.

MITSUE: He was always doing questionable things, along with you, Papa.

TAKEZŌ: Questionable?

MITSUE: Those days you let the army officers use our whole inn as their gathering place, so there were a great many things that they brought, and—

TAKEZŌ: There were. The closets were filled with rice and saké, canned salmon and canned beef, cigarettes, and caramels. You lost your mama when you were still a baby, poor girl, so Papa was making sure that even if you didn't have a mother's love, you had everything else. . . .

MITSUE: When you hooked some ladies with the rice and cigarettes, took them to a hot spring, and they were enjoying the bath, Uncle Nobu sneaked up on them to take the photos that he showed to the officers. And then . . .

TAKEZŌ (*Interrupting*): That Nobu is now selling third-rate sweet potato jelly at the market in front of the train station.

MITSUE: I know.

TAKEZŌ: Why can't a highly talented photographer like Nobu make a living without acting like a black-market operator?

MITSUE: It's his punishment for taking photos of naked ladies.

TAKEZŌ: Be serious and listen.

MITSUE: Sorry.

TAKEZŌ: Nobu says that ever since then, whenever a magnesium flashbulb goes off, in his mind he vividly sees the moment of the atomic flash, as if seeing a brilliantly taken photo, and it terrifies him so much that he quit photography. In other words, both Nobu and you get shaken up because bursting magnesium and lightning look a lot like the atomic flash.

MITSUE: Is that right.

TAKEZŌ: That's right. There's a reason for your feeling shaken up, so you mustn't feel ashamed of it. In fact, it is all right for those who have been exposed to the atomic explosion to be rattled by any flash of light, even that of a lightning bug. Indeed, that is the right of those who have been bombed.

MITSUE: Is there such a right?

TAKEZŌ: If there isn't, I'll make it. One can almost say that if there are any bomb victims who are not rattled by thunder, they're probably impostors.

MITSUE: That's going a little too far.

TAKEZŌ: Well, that's true. . . . (*He creeps out to the veranda and peers into the sky.*) Oh, good. The sun is out.

MITSUE (*Crawls out a little for a look*): Indeed.

TAKEZŌ: The thunder seems to have gone off toward the sea at Ujina.

MITSUE: That's a relief.

(*Reassured, she stands up and brings an earthen teapot and cups from the kitchen.*)

MITSUE: There's barley tea I made before going to the library this morning. Shall we have some?

TAKEZŌ: A good idea.

(MITSUE *pours out two cups and drains hers at a gulp.* TAKEZŌ *raises a cup to his lips but puts it down without drinking.*)

TAKEZŌ: I cannot drink it.

MITSUE: Oh, is that right?

(MITSUE *drinks* TAKEZŌ*'s tea, too, with pleasure.* TAKEZŌ *looks on intently.*)

TAKEZŌ: Good heavens!

MITSUE: What is it?

TAKEZŌ: The bean-jam bun. A little while ago Mr. Kinoshita gave you a bean-jam bun at the library. I sure hope it didn't get crushed.

MITSUE: Oh no.

(*From the shopping bag she was protectively clutching a few minutes ago,* MITSUE *extracts an object wrapped in newspaper and gently unwraps it. The large bean-jam bun has managed to survive intact.*)

TAKEZŌ (*Wonder struck*): It's impressive!

MITSUE: It's from the market in front of the station.

TAKEZŌ: That is an outstanding bean-jam bun, hard to get these days.

MITSUE: Mr. Kinoshita, too, stopped in his tracks the instant he spotted it. He couldn't move past it, as though he were tied to it, so he bought one, but his legs still seemed heavy so he turned back to buy another and was finally able to resume walking at his regular pace.

TAKEZŌ: It certainly packs that much power.

MITSUE: Then Mr. Kinoshita came up to me at the library's checkout desk, and said, "I cannot eat both, so you eat one, Miss Fukuyoshi." (*She breaks it in two.*) Let's eat.

TAKEZŌ: Remember, I cannot eat it.

MITSUE: Oh, that's right, isn't it.

(*While eating,* MITSUE *wraps the remaining half in paper.* TAKEZŌ *swallows hard as he watches, then recovers.*)

TAKEZŌ: The young Mr. Kinoshita who gave you that, he was saying that he is a new teacher in the local college of art and science, right?

MITSUE (*Nodding*): Starting this September he will be an adjunct faculty member of the physics department.

TAKEZŌ: Adjunct faculty?

MITSUE: He'll be an assistant professor.

TAKEZŌ (*Nodding repeatedly*): I saw him wearing milk-bottle glasses and always carrying a big briefcase. And he spoke very calmly, so I was pretty sure he's quite an intellectual.

MITSUE: Until the year of the bomb, he was an instructor at the industrial training institute of the navy arsenal in Kure. He was a naval technician, a lieutenant.

TAKEZŌ: For a navy man, he is rather down-to-earth.

MITSUE: I guess there are various types in the navy. After the war ended, he says, he was a graduate student for two years at his old school, Tōhoku Imperial University, and returned here this month, at the beginning of July. He says that soon after the atomic explosion, he spent a whole day walking the red earth all around the burned-out ruins here in Hiroshima.

TAKEZŌ: How old is he, I wonder. (*Guessing.*) Twenty-nine?

MITSUE: Twenty-five. It says so on his library card.

TAKEZŌ: And you're twenty-two, so it's a good match.

MITSUE (*Smiles for an instant but is soon swept by anger*): What are you saying? Mr. Kinoshita is just a library visitor.

TAKEZŌ (*With conviction*): Someone who's just a visitor would not give you a bean-jam bun.

MITSUE: This is stupid; enough already. Well, time to prepare dinner. Will you be staying, Papa?

TAKEZŌ That is up to you.

MITSUE: Well then, help me clean up over there.

(MITSUE *puts on an apron and begins to wash a wooden lunchbox.* TAKEZŌ *also puts on an apron and takes out a duster but remains quite idle.*)

TAKEZŌ: Returning to the topic: Mr. Kinoshita gave you a bean-jam bun because he likes you. You need to be clear on that.

MITSUE: Papa, you're looking for too much meaning in that bun.

TAKEZŌ: It is a meaningful bun. It's just that you don't have the courage to read its meaning.

MITSUE: Mr. Kinoshita gave it to me as an expression of thanks. That's all.

TAKEZŌ: Are you sure?

MITSUE: Papa, you're impossible!

(MITSUE *comes to the living room and speaks in a formal tone.*)

MITSUE: Please come here a moment and sit down. . . . Four days ago, last Friday in the early afternoon, a person came in, and it was Mr. Kinoshita. He said: "Do you have any materials related to the atomic bomb? When I went to city hall, I was told to ask at the library." Normally, I would simply answer that we don't, but there was something intense about Mr. Kinoshita's voice. So I explained to him: "The Occupation forces are extremely wary of people gathering materials related to the atomic bomb. Even if we had any such materials, making them public is forbidden. And also, as one of the victims of the bomb, I am doing my best to forget that August. There is no material in that August for a story, or a picture, or a poem, or a novel, or a study: In an instant, people's entire world turned into nothing. That is why we aren't collecting any materials. Not only that, but if any materials remain, we would get rid of them. I have also burned everything that reminds me of Father." . . . The bean-jam bun was simply to thank me for that, and nothing more.

TAKEZŌ: There are two checkout desks side by side at the library, with a young female staff member sitting at each.

MITSUE: Right, Miss Takagaki and me. What about it?

TAKEZŌ: Ever since the atomic explosion, you've become an entirely different person, a silent and unsociable girl whose eyes are always downcast. About the only time you smiled was after coming home. On the other hand, Miss Takagaki is said to have a cheerful personality.

MITSUE: So what are you trying to say?

TAKEZŌ: Why didn't Mr. Kinoshita address the approachable Miss Takagaki but instead the unsociable you? That is important. It stands to reason that he would normally go to Miss Takagaki.

MITSUE: He's free to go to whomever he likes.

TAKEZŌ: That's what I'm trying to say. Mr. Kinoshita is not only outstanding but wise. You were always a good-natured and bright girl, a talented woman who graduated second from the top in her college. Mr. Kinoshita saw your true nature at a glance and became interested in you. This is the hidden meaning of the bean-jam bun.

MITSUE: Go on saying crazy things as much as you like. (*She starts toward the kitchen.*) Stay there and keep up the silly talk for days. I've heard enough.

TAKEZŌ: What is the one additional meaning hidden in the bean-jam bun?

MITSUE: Please stop talking about the bun.

TAKEZŌ: This is of the highest importance for you, and so I must pursue the bun's meaning to the end.

MITSUE: Your showing up here all of a sudden and talking silly has given me a headache.

TAKEZŌ: In the final analysis, you like Mr. Kinoshita, too. You two have fallen in love at first sight and will soon be committed to each other. You are tough on the outside but sweet on the inside. Your heart is like the bun.

MITSUE (*Shouts*): That is impossible! . . . I've forbidden myself to fall in love with anyone.

TAKEZŌ: If you didn't care about Mr. Kinoshita, you would have refused on the spot to accept the bun.

MITSUE: Silence at all times! That is the library's principal rule. Do you think I could have held a back-and-forth discussion at the checkout desk? "Thank you very much for the other day. Please have a bean-jam bun." "I'm afraid I can't." "Don't say that. Please take it." "Accepting a bean-jam bun is forbidden by the regulations." . . . The library director and the manager and Miss Takagaki next to me were all pricking up their ears. There was nothing I could do other than silently accept it.

TAKEZŌ: You are going to meet Mr. Kinoshita tomorrow. You've arranged to meet during the noon break by the thousand-year-old pine near the library.

MITSUE: I thought of refusing, but . . .

TAKEZŌ: You mean you could not hold a back-and-forth discussion at the checkout desk.

MITSUE: True, so I just nodded.

TAKEZŌ: There, then . . .

MITSUE: Papa, just wait and see. Tomorrow I will flatly refuse, and tell Mr. Kinoshita not to speak to me again.

TAKEZŌ: Why do you always think about everything backward? There's nothing wrong with your liking Mr. Kinoshita. You like him, and he likes you. If you and he can be together, you'll be happy. This is the true meaning of the bun Mr. Kinoshita gave you.

MITSUE: It's wrong for me to be happy. So don't talk about it anymore.

TAKEZŌ: I am here as a cheerleader for your love, so I'm not going to back off so easily.

MITSUE: Cheerleader?

TAKEZŌ: That's right. Think about it. I started showing up at your place last Friday, the day you caught sight of Mr. Kinoshita coming into the library, and your heart unexpectedly skipped a beat. Am I right?

MITSUE (*Recalls*): . . .

TAKEZŌ: From that skipped heartbeat my body was created. Again you saw Mr. Kinoshita walking toward the checkout desk, and you gently sighed. Am I right?

MITSUE (*Recalls*): . . .

TAKEZŌ: From that sigh were created my arms and legs. Further, you wished quietly for that person to come up to your desk.

MITSUE (*Recalls*): . . .

TAKEZŌ: From that wish was created my heart.

MITSUE: Papa, have you been hanging around here lately intending to make me fall in love? (TAKEZŌ *beams.*)

MITSUE: Love is wrong. I can't fall in love. Don't torment me anymore.

TAKEZŌ: You mustn't suppress your heart so harshly. You'll end up living a flat, flavorless life.

MITSUE: Stop badgering me. I'm busy. I have to prepare dinner. Preparation for tomorrow is waiting, too. We have something called the children's summer-break story club, where for ten days our library staff tells stories to children. Every day, thirty or forty children gather in a cool and breezy pine grove in Hijiyama. Every one of the children likes the sound of our voices and of the wind sweeping through the treetops. They're all looking forward to it, so I must get thoroughly prepared.

(MITSUE *starts vigorously chopping cabbage.* TAKEZŌ *watches her for a while, then withdraws toward the entranceway, cleaning up as he goes.* MITSUE *continues to chop energetically. . . . It slowly grows dark.*)

■

2

Amid music, the eight-mat room quietly emerges, dimly lit by a thirty-watt electric bulb. . . . Mosquito-repelling smoke wafts along the veranda.

One day has passed, and it is Wednesday, after eight in the evening. Under the lightbulb, MITSUE, *wearing a white blouse and work trousers, is writing something with a pencil at the book table.*

Having finished writing, MITSUE, *glancing at the text sideways, begins "the story." It is still in its early stages, and she reads it tonelessly, penciling in corrections from time to time.*

MITSUE: Our Hiroshima has been known since ancient times as "the beautiful city on the water that embraces seven rivers." Those seven rivers merge in the northern outskirts into a single river called the Ōtagawa. I used to go every week with my friends from the Japanese literature class out to the villages that line the Ōtagawa and enjoyed hearing the old stories that were told throughout the region. To tell the truth, we liked even more being treated at the places we visited to such delicacies as soybean-flavored oyster stew, rice with matsutake mushrooms, and devil's-tongue basted with bean paste, and so we enthusiastically roamed all around. The story I will tell you now is one of the old stories we were told at that time by an old villager. If I remember correctly, we heard it over broiled trout.

(*Clearing her throat.*) Now, in a mountainous place not far from the Ōtagawa there lived a grandpa and a grandma. Because grandpa was a greedy lazybones, a useless fellow who never worked, grandma did everything by herself—from doing laundry and gathering firewood to broiling trout—and so they eked out a living.

One day Grandma, who had gone out trout fishing, felt terribly thirsty so she drank a mouthful of water from the river. Lo and behold, all the wrinkles instantly vanished from her face. She drank another mouthful, and her back straightened up. She drank yet another mouthful, and turned into a dazzlingly beautiful young woman. After hearing about this from Grandma, who hurried home to tell him what happened, Grandpa exclaimed, "Why should only you become young again, Grandma? I'll show you what a handsome young buck I'll become: I won't be outdone by you!" So saying, he flew out of the house and vanished. Night came but he still did not return. . . .

(*The rumbling sound of a mixing bowl is heard from the kitchen.* TAKEZŌ, *a twisted towel wrapped around his head and wearing an apron, is grinding up small dried sardines, snatching up a fan from time to time to swat at mosquitoes.*)

MITSUE: Papa?

TAKEZŌ: Ah, it's hot every day.

MITSUE: You're here.

TAKEZŌ: Of course I am. It's been one whole day since I saw you last.

MITSUE: Can you do something about that rumbling? It's bothering me and making it difficult to practice. (*Enters the kitchen and switches on the light.*) What are you doing?

TAKEZŌ: Making bean paste mixed with dried sardines, naturally. Look at how fine I've ground up these sardines.

MITSUE: How did you know I wanted to make bean paste with sardines?

TAKEZŌ: There were the sardines, and there was the bean paste, so it was easy to guess.

MITSUE: . . .

TAKEZŌ: Now we put in all the bean paste. (*From a bowl at the side, he chucks the bean paste into the mixing bowl and resumes grinding.*)

TAKEZŌ: And then we add finely chopped red pepper. (*To* MITSUE.) Red pepper, red pepper.

(MITSUE *picks up chopped red pepper from a small nearby dish and puts it into the mixing bowl.* TAKEZŌ *expertly grinds it up.*)

TAKEZŌ: One serving coming up of bean paste with sardines, a famous specialty of our Fukuyoshi Inn.

MITSUE (*Tastes it*): Mm, it's good.

TAKEZŌ: Papa hasn't lost his knack, eh? So how does the story you were just telling continue? What happened to greedy Grandpa?

MITSUE (*Nodding*): Grandma, worried that Grandpa hasn't returned even after nightfall, picks up a lantern and goes out to meet him. What does she find at river's edge but a greedy-faced baby bawling his lungs out.

TAKEZŌ: That won't be popular with children these days. It's too subtle.

MITSUE: It doesn't have to be popular.

TAKEZŌ: But of course it would be better if it were a little more interesting. I know, this is how you should change it. (*Narrates.*) Grandpa doesn't return even after nightfall. He's vanished. Grandma, worried, picks up a lantern and goes out to meet him. What does she find at river's edge but a pair of dentures, nothing else.

MITSUE: . . .

TAKEZŌ (*Surprised at his lack of success*): Greedy Grandpa drank too much rejuvenating water. So he passed beyond being a baby and disappeared.

MITSUE: Even *I* can see that much.

TAKEZŌ: I think they'll laugh more than at the way yours turns out.

MITSUE (*Shouts*): It's wrong to tamper with the story! Stories told us by earlier generations are to be transmitted to later generations faithfully, just as they are. That was the way of the Folklore Study Group at our Hiroshima Women's Junior College.

TAKEZŌ: Didn't the group catch hell from the prefectural school inspector six years ago? You were told, "It's wartime, a time of crisis, what's studying old stories good for? If you have so much free time, work in a factory." I think the group broke up by the end of 1942.

MITSUE: But the group's original spirit lives on in me even now.

TAKEZŌ: Today at noon you said the same thing when you were quarreling with Mr. Kinoshita.

MITSUE: It wasn't a quarrel, it was a discussion.

TAKEZŌ: But the folks who came to the Hijiyama pine grove because its coolness makes it ideal for napping were startled awake by your loud voice.

MITSUE: I'm telling you it was just a discussion.

(MITSUE *returns to the eight-mat room and tries to memorize the manuscript.* TAKEZŌ *is dividing the bean paste with sardines and packing it into two containers [earthenware, with lids].*)

TAKEZŌ: I hear it was the atomized tile that first got Mr. Kinoshita interested in the atomic bomb.

MITSUE: Yes, that's what he said.

TAKEZŌ: That year, at the end of August, Mr. Kinoshita had to go home to Iwate Prefecture for a while, so he came from Kure to Hiroshima and, while waiting for his train, wandered all around the burned-out ruins. Noon came, and so he sat down in Ōtemachi District, around where a temple used to be, and opened his lunchbox. It was then he felt a piercing pain in his backside as something sharp penetrated the expensive cloth used for making navy officers' trousers.

MITSUE: There was an atomized tile at the spot where he sat down.

TAKEZŌ: Taking a look, he saw the tile was covered with what looked like standing thorns. Every one of them was jutting in the same direction. These were no doubt made in a flash of heat, incredibly high heat, which instantly melted the surface. What a hell of a bomb. He must understand this bomb. He must find out what on earth took place in this searing heat. So thinking, Mr. Kinoshita headed toward the station, picking up pieces of atomized tiles all along the way.

MITSUE: He said that, too.

TAKEZŌ: You kept one of those atomic tiles, I believe.

(MITSUE *lowers a cloth-wrapped bundle from the top of the bookcase.*)

MITSUE: I didn't keep it; Mr. Kinoshita forced it on me.

(TAKEZŌ *takes it and unwraps it atop the book table. Inside is a flat confectionery box made of paper.* TAKEZŌ *raises its lid and freezes. The confectionery box contains an atomized tile [two inches by two inches], a warped bottle for medicine, and several shards of glass.*)

MITSUE (*Takes them out for him, but with great reluctance*): Fragments of glass extracted from the bodies of bomb victims.

TAKEZŌ: Cruel.

MITSUE: Atomic tile.

TAKEZŌ: Needle-sharp.

MITSUE: Bottle for medicine, warped by the heat.

TAKEZŌ: Terrible.

MITSUE: Mr. Kinoshita says that at his place, there are dozens of beer bottles bent into the same strange shapes, and saké bottles twisted as round as horns. There's also a stone lantern with its melted surface turned to bubbles, and a large clock whose hands are burned into its face. . . . Because of those things, Mr. Kinoshita is being driven out of his lodgings, though it's less than a month since he moved in.

TAKEZŌ: Really?

MITSUE (*Nodding*): Whenever he comes back carrying the materials, his landlady says "Bringing in such stuff is creepy. I'll have to charge you more rent because you're sure to break the floor with it soon." She keeps making disagreeable remarks. The dinner the day before yesterday, when he brought in atomized tiles in a petroleum can, was especially bad. There was less rice in his bowl and fewer ingredients in his soup, too.

TAKEZŌ: Coldhearted.

MITSUE: That's why Mr. Kinoshita asked me today, "I have an unreasonable favor to ask you. I couldn't have you keep the atomic bomb materials in the library, could I?"

TAKEZŌ: Can't you?

MITSUE (*Shaking her head emphatically*): If General MacArthur said yes, it would be a different story. I felt bad about refusing on the spot so I asked him to let me think about it for a day. So tomorrow I'll have to meet him over the lunch break. What a troublesome visitor.

TAKEZŌ: Hand me a handkerchief.

MITSUE: What? . . . Here.

(TAKEZŌ *starts wrapping a container of bean paste with sardines using* MITSUE*'s handkerchief.*)

TAKEZŌ: I've put Mr. Kinoshita's share of the bean paste with sardines into this pot, so take it tomorrow and give it to him.

MITSUE: Papa, you are awful . . .

TAKEZŌ: For some reason, men cannot resist a woman's handkerchief.

MITSUE: You meddler. I'm telling you not to make a fuss over imaginary things.

TAKEZŌ: In that case, you can give it to your manager.

MITSUE: The manager's wife is very jealous, so I wouldn't want to cause a misunderstanding.

TAKEZŌ: In that case, you'd better give it to Mr. Kinoshita after all.

(MITSUE *angrily puts it on the book table.*)

MITSUE: Please don't do this again.

TAKEZŌ: Forget about that, and try to remember instead what started the argument with Mr. Kinoshita.

MITSUE: This is what Mr. Kinoshita finally said: "To explain your own experience of the bomb to the children, couldn't you create a good story using my atomic materials?"

TAKEZŌ: Mr. Kinoshita is a person of wisdom.

MITSUE: I told him I couldn't. Because we deeply believe that stories are not to be tampered with.

TAKEZŌ: That again. I can more or less understand sticking to the stories you've gathered yourselves, but . . .

MITSUE: But Mr. Kinoshita kept pressing these materials on me and wouldn't give in at all, so I finally yelled, "I can't do what I can't do." That's what happened.

TAKEZŌ: Wait. I've just had a brilliant idea.

MITSUE: Ah, that's your specialty, Papa, and synonymous with unreliability. Whenever you have a brilliant idea, you start a new business, or make a pass at some ladies, or spend the fortune Grandpa left you on anything other than our little inn . . .

TAKEZŌ: Even if I'd increased that fortune, it all in the end would have been turned into ashes by the bomb. You might say I was farsighted.

MITSUE: That's a truly disrespectful thing to say about people who worked with all their might.

TAKEZŌ: I know. But you realize you'll end up quarreling endlessly because you insist on telling the stories you gathered. How about putting the information about the atom bomb into stories that everyone knows? That will delight Mr. Kinoshita.

MITSUE: The summer-break story club is intended for children.

TAKEZŌ: I know. So you tuck the atom-bomb information into well-known stories like those of Momotarō the Peach Boy, or the battle between the monkey and the crab, or Issun Bōshi, the one-inch warrior.

MITSUE: How do I do that?

TAKEZŌ: It's your job to think how to do it.

MITSUE: The Occupation army's eyes are all over the place. Papa, it's because you don't realize the army's power that you talk so nonchalantly.

TAKEZŌ (*With a flash*): I've got it again . . .

MITSUE: I have to memorize the stories. You don't have to stay any longer, but please come again.

TAKEZŌ (*Undaunted, grandly*): That's it. Because it's storytelling that you'll do, wind will come up to you as you speak and scatter your words in all directions of the compass. Your words will sweep through the hearts of the good children, rise up on the wind into the sky, and become a rainbow. No evidence will remain. The Hiroshima wind that blows through Hijiyama will be your ally.

(*While speaking,* TAKEZŌ *inserts young Kinoshita's atomized materials into the two lower pockets and one upper pocket of his apron.*)

TAKEZŌ: Don't know if this will be useful to you or not, but listen. (*The story begins.*) Issun Bōshi, the one-inch warrior. . . . Everyone knows Issun Bōshi, who arrived in the capital city of Kyoto by sailing there in a tea bowl. To rescue a princess from a demon, he jumped into the red demon's mouth and, using a sewing needle as a sword, pricked all around the inside of his stomach and finally got the demon to surrender. A strong fellow. Definitely strong. But the Issun Bōshi of Hiroshima is stronger yet.

MITSUE: Issun Bōshi of Hiroshima?

TAKEZŌ (*Nodding emphatically*): "Fukuyoshi Mitsue's Apron Theater" begins!

MITSUE: Apron Theater . . .

TAKEZŌ (*Nodding again*): Putting the apron pockets to good use, you can really boost the stories. Now, up to the point where he leaps into the red demon's stomach, it's the same, but beyond that it's very different. (*Returning to the story.*) Issun Bōshi of Hiroshima, who has jumped into the red demon's stomach (*Pulling out the atomized tile from the apron's lower-right pocket and raising it high*), presses this atomized tile against the demon's underbelly. "Hey, you demon. Take the wax out of your ears and listen up. What I'm holding is an atomized tile from Hiroshima. You know that on that morning of that day, in the sky six hundred yards over Hiroshima, there exploded something called an atomic bomb. A second after the explosion, there arose a fireball whose temperature was twenty-two thousand degrees Fahrenheit. Hey, do you understand what kind of temperature twenty-two thousand degrees is? The temperature of the sun is eleven thousand degrees, so on that day six hundred yards over Hiroshima, there rose two scorching, scorching suns. With two suns appearing low overhead for one to two seconds, everything on the ground—people, birds, insects, fish, buildings, stone lanterns—instantaneously melted. Every single thing bubbled up and melted. Roof tiles melted, too. On top of that, the bomb blast swept in. The bomb blast: at four hundred yards per second, faster than sound. Blasted by its atomic wind, the melted tiles all grew ragged, then they cooled and jutted with jagged thorns, like pillars of frost. The tile is now a grater for radish, nay, a flowerbed of spikes. With these terrible jags, I will grate your liver to shreds. Rub-a-dub, rub-a-dub, rub-a-dub, rub-a-dub." And he strikes the red demon who rolls around, pale with agony.

(MITSUE *is frightened.* TAKEZŌ *pulls the medicine bottle from the lower-left pocket and raises it.*)

TAKEZŌ: At once, Issun Bōshi of Hiroshima pulls out a twisted medicine bottle that was warped by the melting heat. "Hey, you demon. Now I am going to plug up your butt-hole from the inside with this atomized medicine bottle. Drop dead from constipation for all I care."

(TAKEZŌ *takes a shard of glass from the upper pocket and raises it high.*)

TAKEZŌ: "Hey, you demon. This is a shard of broken glass that pierced a human body. That bomb blast blew to pieces the glass of all the Hiroshima windows and stuck the splintered glass into human bodies (*The voice turning tearful*) till people looked like hedgehogs. . . ."

MITSUE (*Unawares, clutching her left upper arm*): Stop!

TAKEZŌ: "With this terrible glass knife, I will cut your liver and guts to ribbons. . . ."

MITSUE: Enough!

TAKEZŌ: What an inhuman thing they dropped. Human beings piled up two suns on top of their fellow human beings. (*Putting away the mixing bowl and other utensils.*)

Adding atom-bomb material to a story may be too painful for the people of Hiroshima after all, no matter what kind of story it is. This has to be kept in mind. I wanted Mr. Kinoshita to be pleased with you, but what I've done is wrong. My brilliant idea was not so good after all.

(*He disappears into the back of the kitchen, carrying the cleared-away objects.*)

TAKEZŌ: As a present to Mr. Kinoshita, for tomorrow please just give him the bean paste with sardines.

MITSUE: Thank you for all your help. (*She looks, but he is not there.*) . . . Papa? Papa. . . .

(*It slowly grows dark.*)

■

3

Amid music, it is raining.

The growing brightness reveals the same place on the following day, Thursday, shortly after noon. Rain is dripping from the ceiling, the raindrops accurately intercepted by four or five bowls and teacups placed around the living room, and six or seven more in the eight-mat room. On the stage-right edge of the living room stands TAKEZŌ, *a small pan in hand, a large pan and a rice-cooking pot at his feet. Wearing the expression of a laboratory supervisor, he is on the lookout for rain leaks in the two rooms.*

He discovers a new leak at the borderline between the living room and the eight-mat room. Humming what sounds like a children's song, TAKEZŌ *deftly threads his way among the bowls and teacups as if playing hopscotch and places the small pan where it is needed.*

TAKEZŌ: Last night's rain was an intelligent rain. It fell during the night and stopped in the morning.

(*He returns to his original position. Very soon he spots another leak over the book table off in the eight-mat room and sets out carrying the rice-cooking bowl.*)

TAKEZŌ: The rain that is falling now is a stupid rain. It started falling in the morning and didn't stop even at noon.

(*He moves the book table and puts the rice-cooking bowl in its place but is at a loss as to where to put the book table. He pauses a while holding it.*)

TAKEZŌ: Rain, rain, won't you stop, your father's a scoundrel, your mother's a trollop.

(*He returns to his original position. As he searches for a place to put it, he catches sight of a piece of stationery and an envelope on the tabletop. He lowers the table, sits down in front of it, and reads the address on the envelope.*)

TAKEZŌ: "Mr. Kinoshita Tadashi, Esquire. Care of Mrs. Takizawa. Second block in Kogomori. Town of Fuchū. Greater Hiroshima." Mr. Kinoshita Tadashi, Esquire? . . .

(*He grins from ear to ear. Then he reads the letter.*)

TAKEZŌ (*Aloud from time to time*): "Please excuse this hastily written letter. Thank you for regularly patronizing the city library. . . . I am always busy when you visit . . . (*A raindrop falls on his head. He covers his head with a large pan to ward off the rain.*) I am writing to you because this is an important matter. . . . The atom-bomb material that you have collected. . . . If my place is acceptable. . . . I live alone so there is room. . . . The roof does leak somewhat, but. . . . It is unbearably hot these days. . . . Please take good care of yourself. . . . Yours"

(MITSUE *returns. She is in the entranceway, shaking off the rain from her oilpaper umbrella.*)

TAKEZŌ: Back already?

MITSUE: Ah, Papa?

TAKEZŌ: Yes, I'm making myself at home. It's barely past noon, what happened?

MITSUE: The story club got washed out by this rain.

TAKEZŌ (*Nodding*): If it wants to rain so much, it should rain during the night. Poor children. . . . Did you forget something?

MITSUE: No, I left early.

TAKEZŌ: Do you feel sick? (*Panic-stricken.*) Don't tell me you're feeling nauseated? And also dizziness, ringing in the ears, constipation, diarrhea. . . . Is it still the radiation sickness?

MITSUE: I've no sign of it these days.

TAKEZŌ: Well, that's good . . .

MITSUE: The only thing that keeps on hurting is this. (*Lightly holding her upper left arm.*)

TAKEZŌ: Well, that's a relief. (*Cheered up.*) Maybe that stubborn wretch of an illness has been chased away at last.

MITSUE: That's what it makes you think and you feel relieved, then it suddenly strikes you from behind, so you cannot relax until you die.

TAKEZŌ: Mm, it is a troublesome thing you're burdened with. . . . Well, will you look at that!

(*Stepping out to the veranda, looks up at the sky.*)

TAKEZŌ: Thank goodness! At long last it stopped raining. If it rained any longer, I'd have run out of things to catch it with. I could hardly drag the bathtub out here.

(*He puts away five or six bowls and teacups from places where the leaks have stopped, unfolds the tea table, and makes space to sit down.*)

TAKEZŌ: So did it go well?

MITSUE: Did what go well?

TAKEZŌ: Bean paste with sardines. Was Mr. Kinoshita pleased?

MITSUE: Ah, the bean paste with sardines . . .

TAKEZŌ: Didn't he say it's his favorite?

MITSUE: I haven't given it to him yet . . .

(*She pulls out from her shopping bag a package wrapped in a handkerchief and places it on the tea table.*)

MITSUE: Here it is.

TAKEZŌ: What is it doing here?

MITSUE: I didn't go to Hijiyama.

TAKEZŌ: Why?

MITSUE: Well, it was raining, and . . .

TAKEZŌ: You had your umbrella.

MITSUE: The path was muddy so I might have slipped.

TAKEZŌ: Your clogs have good supports.

MITSUE: The real reason . . .

TAKEZŌ: What is it?

MITSUE: I thought it'd be wrong to meet Mr. Kinoshita . . .

TAKEZŌ: That again. If you keep on repeating the same thing, people will end up laughing at you.

MITSUE: So I was repairing books in the workroom.

TAKEZŌ: You can still make it in time, can't you?

MITSUE: Before long I saw Mr. Kinoshita walking from Hijiyama toward the library. I thought it'd be wrong to meet him, so I left work early.

TAKEZŌ (*Trembling*): If it were a long time ago, I'd smack you one!

MITSUE: Papa, it's better this way. It's wrong for me to love a person.

TAKEZŌ: If you act so hard on yourself, you'll be all broken up later.

MITSUE: I'm telling you I'll be all right. Don't talk about it anymore.

(MITSUE *begins to clear things away.*)

TAKEZŌ: You shouldn't make a fool out of the cheerleader.

MITSUE: What are you upset about?

TAKEZŌ: You shouldn't be deceiving me with silly lies. Are you going to insist that you don't love Mr. Kinoshita?

MITSUE: I'm saying that . . .

TAKEZŌ: It's stupid of me to ask you. (*Pointing to the envelope and the stationery on the book table.*) "Esquire." This title of politeness clearly reveals your feelings.

MITSUE (*Shaken for a moment, but then*): All women write that way.

TAKEZŌ: Could you write to just any visitor: "I live alone so there is room . . ."

MITSUE: That was just a joke. I intended to throw it away. Please give it back.

TAKEZŌ: If you don't need it, I'll throw it away.

MITSUE: Papa, you're wicked . . .

(TAKEZŌ *puts the envelope and the stationery into his trouser pocket.*)

TAKEZŌ: Why is it wrong to love a person? You're certainly not a stunning beauty who bowls men over with her looks. Half the responsibility for that is my own. But a closer look shows that you have respectably pleasant features, and that is to my credit.

MITSUE: What are you talking about.

TAKEZŌ: In other words, since Mr. Kinoshita likes it, your face will do.

MITSUE: I'm telling you that isn't the problem.

TAKEZŌ: Is it perhaps the radiation sickness? Is it wrong to love someone because you don't know when the sickness might strike?

MITSUE (*After nodding*): And yet Mr. Kinoshita said that if that happens, he will take care of me with all his might.

TAKEZŌ: Well, you two are further along than I thought. (*With a flash.*) I know, you are worrying about the baby who will be born. Because it certainly does happen that radiation sickness is passed down to babies.

MITSUE (*After nodding*): If that happens, we'll think of it as fate and do our best to bring up the child . . .

TAKEZŌ: Are those Mr. Kinoshita's words too?

MITSUE: In a roundabout way, that is the sort of thing he said.

TAKEZŌ: Roundabout or shortcut, that you two can discuss things in such detail. . . . I am shocked.

MITSUE: That's all the more reason why it's wrong for me to meet Mr. Kinoshita.

TAKEZŌ: So then the better it goes, the worse it gets?

MITSUE: Yes, you could say that.

TAKEZŌ: If you don't straighten this out for me, I'll really get mad. The story's gone upside down from last Monday to next Sunday, turning somersaults and tumbling end over end, so I have no idea what is what.

MITSUE (*Assuming an unusually formal tone*): Please take a seat here.

TAKEZŌ: All right.

(TAKEZŌ *spontaneously sits down facing* MITSUE.)

MITSUE: There were many people instead of me who should have become happy, so I can't push them aside and become happy. For me to become happy would be an unforgivable offense to such people.

TAKEZŌ: What people are you talking about?

MITSUE: People like Fukumura Akiko, for example . . .

TAKEZŌ: Fukumura . . . That girl?

MITSUE (*Nodding*): We were together throughout high school and college. Our last names start with the same Chinese character for "fortune," since Akiko was Fukumura and I Fukuyoshi, so we sat together for eight years and were also on the same sports team. We were together so much that some people called us "Two Fortunes."

TAKEZŌ: Good thing they didn't decide to be polite and call you "Miss Fortunes."

MITSUE (*Putting up with it*): At college, we started the Folklore Study Group together. Akiko was president, and I vice president. It was also the two of us who, after talking it over, decided on the basic policy that the stories are not to be tampered with.

TAKEZŌ: That's why you were so insistent.

MITSUE: That's right.

TAKEZŌ: You were always competing on grades, too.

MITSUE (*Shaking her head*): Running a race was one thing, but I didn't even once outdo Akiko in studying; I was always number two. This may be your fault, Papa.

TAKEZŌ: Don't throw such an arrow at me out of the blue.

MITSUE: Above all, she was beautiful, praised as a beauty at both high school and college.

TAKEZŌ: Wasn't it her mother who was the real beauty? Running a sewing school and being a widow besides—I don't know why but whenever I came face to face with her, I got tongue-tied.

MITSUE: That's why you sent her a letter, didn't you, along with rice and cans of salmon and beef. "To Madame Fukumura Shizue, from Fukuyoshi Takezō. Might I request the honor of your company in enjoying the night view of cherry blossoms on Hijiyama this spring?"

TAKEZŌ: How do you know about that?

MITSUE: Akiko showed it to me, saying, "'Madame' is a bit odd, isn't it."

TAKEZŌ: Odd, is it?

MITSUE: It's a word women tend to use.

TAKEZŌ: Such things shouldn't be made public. A deceptively wicked widow she turned out to be.

MITSUE: She treated me as kindly, as if she were my real mother.

TAKEZŌ: So she should have become your real mother. All she needed to do was to change a single character of her name, from Fukumura to Fukuyoshi.

MITSUE (*Letting that go, switches to a formal tone*): Akiko is the one who should have become happy.

TAKEZŌ: But why?

MITSUE: She was more beautiful than I, a better student than I, more popular than I, and she also saved me from the bomb.

TAKEZŌ: Saved you from the bomb?

MITSUE (*Nodding emphatically*): It's thanks to Akiko that I'm still alive.

TAKEZŌ: You're talking nonsense. There was no one in our garden at that time but me and you. Where was Akiko?

MITSUE: She saved me with a letter.

TAKEZŌ: With a letter? . . .

MITSUE: Akiko was a teacher then at the Second Prefectural Girls' Junior High. She took her third- and fourth-year students to an airplane factory in Mizushima, in Okayama Prefecture. I'd received a letter from Akiko the previous day and was so happy I spent the whole night writing a reply to her. And then that morning, thinking I'd mail it on the way to the library, I was holding the thick letter and walking through the garden toward the wooden gate in the back . . .

TAKEZŌ: As I recall, I was on the veranda. I'd filled a half-gallon bottle with unpolished rice and was pounding the rice with a stick to make it white. I saw you walk near the stone lantern, so I called out, "Take care of yourself" . . .

MITSUE (*Nodding*): I turned around at the sound of your voice and waved to you. It was then that I saw a B-29 beyond our roof and also saw something shining. "Papa, B dropped something."

TAKEZŌ: "It's strange there's been no air-raid warning." Saying that, I stepped down into the garden.

MITSUE: "I wonder what it dropped. Maybe it's propaganda flyers again." As I watched, my fingers loosened and I dropped the letter at the base of the stone lantern. "Oh, no . . ." I bent down to pick it up. Then all of a sudden the whole world grew pale.

TAKEZŌ: I saw it in full face, the fireball as searing as two suns.

MITSUE (*With pity*): Papa.

TAKEZŌ: Its center was a dazzling white. Around it was a great circle eerily colored a mixture of yellow and red.

(*A brief pause.*)

TAKEZŌ (*Prompting*): And then?

MITSUE: The stone lantern shielded me from the heat rays of that fireball.

TAKEZŌ (*Moved*): That stone lantern. Hmm, it was expensive but worth every yen, to say the least.

MITSUE: If I hadn't received the letter from Akiko, I wouldn't have bent down to the base of the stone lantern. That is why I said that Akiko saved me . . .

(MITSUE *suddenly covers her face.*)

TAKEZŌ: What's wrong?

MITSUE: That morning Akiko unexpectedly returned from Mizushima by the first outbound train.

TAKEZŌ (*Almost speechless*): What . . .

MITSUE: She suddenly needed a set of duplicating-machine items and a thousand sheets of cheap paper for her evening classes, so she came to the school to get them.

TAKEZŌ: What happened then? Surely . . .

MITSUE: She made a quick stop at her mother's place in Nishi Kannon and started out for the school exactly at eight. . . . The bomb struck her near the Senda branch office of the Red Cross.

TAKEZŌ (*Groans*): Ooh.

MITSUE: It was one whole day before her mother found Akiko. But by that time, she had been laid out alongside others on the dirt floor of the rear entrance to the Red Cross building.

TAKEZŌ: What an unfortunate girl.

MITSUE (*Nodding, she sobs*): It seems the back of her work trousers was completely burned off, and her buttocks all exposed, with a little smear of dried excrement . . .

(*A brief pause.*)

TAKEZŌ: That's enough. I think I can understand your feeling that it's wrong to desire happiness as other people do.

MITSUE: . . .

TAKEZŌ: But there is also this way of thinking about it: That you ought to live out Akiko's share of happiness . . .

MITSUE (*Interrupts, shouting*): I can't do that!

TAKEZŌ: Why can't you?

MITSUE: Because of . . . a promise to Akiko's mother.

TAKEZŌ: A promise?

MITSUE (*Nodding*): Something like a promise . . .

TAKEZŌ: What kind of a promise?

MITSUE: When I met Akiko's mother, it was three days after the bomb, the late afternoon of August 9. . . . On the day of the bomb, I ran from Hiroshima to Miyajima and stayed at Mrs. Horiuchi's house until the morning of the ninth.

TAKEZŌ: Mrs. Horiuchi? The name sounds familiar.

MITSUE: The flower arrangement teacher from the time at junior high.

TAKEZŌ: Ah, that old teacher.

MITSUE (*Nods*): . . .

TAKEZŌ: Lucky the good teacher was there.

MITSUE: Encouraged by the teacher, I left Miyajima in the morning and, traveling through a region that smelled like grilled fish, arrived home around noon.

TAKEZŌ (*Sympathetically*): It was burned to the ground.

MITSUE: Crying, I gathered Papa's bones.

TAKEZŌ: You did. Thank you.

MITSUE: After that I went to Akiko's place in Nishi Kannon, but that area, too, was burned to the ground, and Akiko's mother was lying down in a bomb shelter when I arrived. Her back was burned and covered with huge blisters, so she was lying on her stomach looking utterly worn out.

TAKEZŌ: Poor woman.

MITSUE: She was overjoyed to see me, stood up unsteadily, hugged me with all her might, and thanked me for coming. But as she was telling me about Akiko, her face suddenly turned pale, she glared at me, and said . . . (*She cannot say it.*)

TAKEZŌ: What?

MITSUE: "Why are you alive?"

TAKEZŌ: . . . !

MITSUE: "Why is it that you are alive, and not my child?"

(*A brief pause.*)

MITSUE: At the end of the month, she died, too . . .

TAKEZŌ: Look, it isn't much of a consolation to say it, but at that time Akiko's mother was hardly in her right mind to say such a . . .

MITSUE (*Vehemently shaking her head*): It was unnatural that I survived.

TAKEZŌ: What are you talking about?

MITSUE: It's unforgivable that I'm alive.

TAKEZŌ: Don't you ever say such a thing.

MITSUE: Please listen!

TAKEZŌ: I don't want to listen.

MITSUE (*Continues regardless*): Almost all my friends are gone. Miss Noguchi died standing upright in the water tank where she tried to take refuge. Miss Yamamoto died walking, her tongue swollen black and jutting out as though there was an eggplant in her mouth. Miss Katō, who had married soon after graduating, died while breastfeeding her baby. The baby, crying, pressed its face against her breasts, but before long, it too passed to the other world without knowing anything of this one. Miss Otowa, employed at the Central Telephone Office, put her arms around two younger workers who had been immobilized by the bomb and said, "Let's stay here together." I hear she kept on comforting them until she died. Three years have passed since then, but my friends still haven't returned. And then there's you, too, Papa . . . !

TAKEZŌ: You and I came to an agreement a long time ago. Think about it.

MITSUE: No. To have died that day in Hiroshima is natural, to have survived is unnatural. That's why it's strange for me to be alive.

TAKEZŌ: Dead people don't think that way. In fact, I too have come completely to terms with what happened.

MITSUE (*Interrupting*): I have no excuse to be alive. Yet I don't have the courage to die, either.

(*Again it starts to rain.*)

MITSUE: And so I will live as quietly as possible and, when the opportunity comes, vanish from the world. Papa, these three years have been a difficult three years. Please give me credit just for having lived through them somehow.

(MITSUE *stands and moves toward the entranceway.*)

TAKEZŌ: Where are you going?

MITSUE: I left work when I was halfway through repairing books, so I'll go back to the library after all. I don't think Mr. Kinoshita is there any more.

TAKEZŌ: Wait.

(*He takes the envelope and stationery from his pocket and thrusts them at* MITSUE.)

TAKEZŌ: Mail this.

MITSUE: . . . !

TAKEZŌ: By special delivery.

MITSUE: That's absurd . . .

TAKEZŌ: This is an order from Papa.

(*With the envelope and stationery* TAKEZŌ *has forced on her in her hands,* MITSUE *trembles.*)

(TAKEZŌ *discovers a rain leak and once again starts placing bowls and teacups.*)

TAKEZŌ: Rain, rain, won't you stop, your father's a scoundrel, your mother's a trollop. . . .

(*As the rain intensifies, it grows dark.*)

■

4

Soon after the music ends, there comes the sound of a motor tricycle engine accompanied by growing brightness. It is the same place on the following day, Friday, at six o'clock in the evening.

Teacups used by young Kinoshita and the motor tricycle driver remain on the tea table in the living room.

The area from the eight-mat room to the veranda is filled with the atom-bomb material that Kinoshita has just brought.

Placed on the newspaper spread out all over the eight-mat room are cases of melted beer bottles with twisted necks, five or six quart bottles and half-gallon bottles in similar condition, a liquor bottle weirdly warped by the intense heat, a round clock one foot in diameter with hands stopped at eight fifteen, a bride doll with one side burned, and the like. Along the wall at stage left, tea chests, tangerine boxes, and so forth have also been piled up.

In the garden at stage left there are three upper portions of stone lanterns and, mingled in with them is a large head of Jizō, the guardian deity of children, with its face melted. As the revving sound of the motor tricycle's engine soon grows quiet and fades into the distance, MITSUE *steps into the entranceway, still wearing a smile. She takes the teacups into the kitchen, brings a dishcloth, and starts wiping the tea table, but happens to catch sight of Jizō's head, and her smile freezes.*

After a while, she fearfully edges to the veranda and looks at Jizō, then, still barefoot, steps down into the garden and turns Jizō's face toward herself. Her voice, unawares, resembles a scream.

MITSUE: It's Papa on that day!

(*As though in response,* TAKEZŌ *enters from stage right, pounding his shoulders with a blowpipe used to fan a charcoal fire.*)

TAKEZŌ: Did someone call, short or tall, big or small?

(MITSUE *grows even more rigid as she compares Jizō's face with* TAKEZŌ*'s, then abruptly turns Jizō's face away.*)

MITSUE: You were here.

TAKEZŌ (*Nodding*): Old jokes seem to misfire. So, did Mr. Kinoshita say he'll bring more atomic material?

MITSUE: He told me this is exactly half of it.

TAKEZŌ (*Impressed*): He's collected quite a lot. My word, one can't blame his landlady too harshly.

(MITSUE *slaps at the soles of her feet, then steps up into the house. She finishes wiping the tea table and does various chores in and around the kitchen, but continues to grapple with the newly arisen disquiet.*)

TAKEZŌ: How many miles did that motor tricycle driver say there are between Mr. Kinoshita's lodgings and here?

MITSUE: He said it's exactly three miles one way, with six traffic signals and one railway crossing.

TAKEZŌ: In that case, even with the time it takes them to load up at the other end, Mr. Kinoshita should be back here in thirty or forty minutes. At that time, right after greeting him and thanking him for coming again, offer him a bath.

MITSUE: A bath . . .?

TAKEZŌ (*Displaying the blowpipe*): On a hot day like this, a bath is a treat that can't be beat.

MITSUE: You've heated up a bath?

TAKEZŌ: I have.

MITSUE: You think of everything. . . .

TAKEZŌ: I didn't spend twenty years as a widower for nothing. Well then, does Mr. Kinoshita like his bath water piping hot or lukewarm?

MITSUE: How would I know that?

TAKEZŌ: Good point. In that case I'll just make it moderately hot, but after the bath, you'll need to offer him something cold.

MITSUE: I've bought a bottle of beer.

TAKEZŌ: That's good. But for the driver, cold water will do. On a day like this, even cold water is a treat.

MITSUE: I've also bought several pounds of ice.

TAKEZŌ: You'll need to have the driver leave early. Make sure he doesn't stay too long.

MITSUE: He said he has something else to do next.

TAKEZŌ (*Relieved*): That is good. You'll also need to have a new towel.

MITSUE: I've bought it.

TAKEZŌ: You'll need soap.

MITSUE: I've bought that too.

TAKEZŌ: A pumice stone . . .

MITSUE: I've bought it.

TAKEZŌ: A loofah sponge . . .

MITSUE: I've bought it.

TAKEZŌ: And a man's bathrobe . . .

MITSUE: I've . . . I won't buy that.

TAKEZŌ (*Nodding*): If you had a man's bathrobe, it would be slightly disreputable. As you're no doubt aware, it's still much too soon to be scrubbing Mr. Kinoshita's back, so don't do it. This, too, has to do with reputation.

MITSUE: Papa, don't you need to put in more firewood?

TAKEZŌ: I know. So, what is the treat for dinner?

MITSUE: Bean paste with sardines and beer.

TAKEZŌ: That's good.

MITSUE: A salad of little sardines.

TAKEZŌ: Good, good.

MITSUE: Rice flavored with soy sauce.

TAKEZŌ (*Licking his lips*): And with the rice comes what and what and what?

MITSUE: Shaved burdock, julienned carrots, and fried bean curd.

TAKEZŌ: Very good.

MITSUE: And for a finishing touch, melon.

TAKEZŌ (*With a sigh*): Now I feel like eating too.

MITSUE (*Gazing at* TAKEZŌ): If you ate, I would be happy, too, Papa.

TAKEZŌ (*Abruptly*): Will you be able to take a summer vacation?

MITSUE: A summer vacation?

TAKEZŌ: Just now as he was leaving, Mr. Kinoshita mentioned it. "If you can take a summer vacation, come with me to Iwate. I'd like to go back home once before the new semester starts in September. If I brought you along, my parents would be delighted."

MITSUE: If I wanted to take a summer vacation, I suppose I could.

TAKEZŌ: Then by all means go.

MITSUE: I've long wanted to go to Iwate. It's where Miyazawa Kenji is from.

TAKEZŌ: Who is this Kenji?

MITSUE: Someone who wrote children's stories and poems. His books are popular at our library, too. I like poems.

TAKEZŌ: What kind of poems?

MITSUE: The morning of eternal farewell, January on the Iwate railway, the song of travel among stars. . . .

TAKEZŌ: Oh, travel among stars.

MITSUE (*In a lofty tone*): "Scorpion with its red eyes, Eagle with its wings outstretched, the blue-eyed Little Dog, the shining coil of Snake. . . ." It's a poem that names many constellations.

TAKEZŌ: I wrote a poem about stars when I was in elementary school.

MITSUE: Did you really?

TAKEZŌ (*In a lofty tone*): "It's night again tonight, and I, counting stars, nod drowsily to sleep. Three stars, four stars, seven stars, eleven stars. Up above, sparkle stars, down below, burglars rustle, in the forest . . ."

MITSUE: . . . !

TAKEZŌ: I have to go check up on the fire for the bath, so I'll leave out the rest. I recall it was marked good and put up on the classroom wall. (*Starts to leave.*) Mr. Kinoshita's inviting you to go to Iwate is a kind of marriage proposal. You understand that. "In the forest, owl tramps, at the temple badger drums, pon-poko-pon . . ."

(TAKEZŌ *exits stage right, brandishing the blowpipe.* MITSUE *makes sure that he has left, steps down into the garden, and gazes again at Jizō's face. Soon she makes up her mind. With a firm tread, she steps up into the house, takes a large cloth wrapper out of the closet, and begins to wrap her personal belongings.* TAKEZŌ *enters from stage right.*)

TAKEZŌ: Mr. Kinoshita needs a shave, so you need to have a razor.

MITSUE: I will not keep anything like a razor in the house. So many of the bomb victims used razors to cut the arteries in their necks and die. There also were people who died thrusting their hands into bathtubs and slashing the veins in their left wrists.

TAKEZŌ (*After observing* MITSUE): You seem to be packing. And it doesn't look like the kind of packing for a summer vacation journey to Iwate.

MITSUE (*Nodding*): I'm thinking of asking Mrs. Horiuchi to let me help her teach flower arranging. If I leave the house soon, I ought to be able to catch the 7:05 train for Miyajima.

(*Having finished packing,* MITSUE *runs up to the tea table, lays out a sheet of stationery, and takes up a pencil.*)

TAKEZŌ (*With restraint*): Mr. Kinoshita will be coming back, so reconsider that plan. Whoever heard of inviting a person and then throwing him out? That would be very rude.

MITSUE: I'll leave this letter in the entrance where it's easily noticed, so you don't need to worry.

TAKEZŌ: What about the feast you've gone to the trouble to prepare? Will you leave it to rot and feed the flies?

MITSUE: I'll have him eat it by himself. That's what I'll write to Mr. Kinoshita.

TAKEZŌ: What about the bath? Will you write him to please feel free to take a bath?

MITSUE (*Nodding*): And then I'll write . . . (*Briefly staring into space and thinking.*) On the way out, please close the shutters, lock the door, and leave the key with the neighbor. And for the final line: I will continue to take care of the valuable materials. But please forget about me. In haste . . .

TAKEZŌ: You will quit the library?

MITSUE: I guess so.

TAKEZŌ: That same troublesome sickness is starting up again.

MITSUE: No it isn't!

TAKEZŌ: No, it's a sickness. (*Steps up to the veranda.*) My existence arose from the heartbeat in your breast, from the heat of your sigh, from the faint glimmer of your desire. And so I cannot allow you to write such a letter.

(TAKEZŌ *takes the pencil away from* MITSUE.)

MITSUE: Give it back, that's a precious pencil. Akiko had the same kind. It was in the pocket of my trousers when the bomb exploded and so it survived.

TAKEZŌ: You're sick. There's even a name for your disease. Its symptoms, exhibited by those who survived while their friends died, are stubborn feelings of unforgivable guilt over being alive. The name of the disease is "victimitis." (*Breaks the pencil, then in a vigorous tone.*) I understand your feelings well. But you're alive, and you must go on living. That's why the sickness must be cured quickly.

MITSUE (*Shaking off her hesitation*): Papa, the person toward whom I feel unforgivably guilty really is you.

TAKEZŌ (*Incredulous*): What . . . ?

MITSUE: Of course, I feel guilty toward Akiko and my other friends, too. But by focusing on my guilty feelings toward them, I covered up what I had done . . . I am a despicable daughter who abandoned her father and ran away.

(*She jumps into the garden and, using all her strength, picks up the head of Jizō.*)

MITSUE: You had terrible burns on your face that time, Papa, your face was melted like this Jizō. And I abandoned you like that and ran away.

TAKEZŌ: That story was settled a long time ago.

MITSUE: I thought so, too. That's because until a little while ago, I didn't remember even fragments of what happened that time. But when I looked at this Jizō's face just now, I remembered it clearly. I'm a daughter who deserted her father in a sea of flames worse than hell, and ran away. Such a person has no right to be happy . . .

TAKEZŌ: A ridiculous logic.

MITSUE: Papa, do you remember? When I suddenly came to, the house had collapsed on top of us. I didn't know what was happening, but it was something enormous. Thinking I must escape quickly, I kept wriggling and luckily was able to pull myself out. But you, Papa, couldn't move. You were lying on your back, pinned down by pillars, beams, crosspieces, and dozens of other pieces of timber. I screamed with all my might, "Help my Papa!" but nobody came.

TAKEZŌ: Because the same kind of thing was happening everywhere in Hiroshima.

MITSUE: There was no saw, no ax, no hammer. I tried to lift up the wood using pieces of timber as a lever, but it didn't work. I dug at the ground with my fingers, but that didn't work either.

TAKEZŌ: You truly did your very best.

MITSUE: Soon there arose a smoky stench. I looked up, and saw that our hair and eyebrows were smoldering and crackling . . .

TAKEZŌ: You shielded me with your body and countless times put out the flames that were catching hold of me. . . . Thank you. But if you kept on doing that, we'd both be lost. And so I said, "Run away!" You said "No" and didn't move. Back and forth it went on for a while: "Run away," "No."

MITSUE: In the end you said, "Let's play Scissors-Paper-Stone and decide. I'll play the stone so I'll be able to win for sure."

TAKEZŌ: "Ippuku, deppuku, chan-chan-chaburoku, nuppari-kiririn, chan-pon-ge." (*Holds out stone.*)

MITSUE (*Responding with a stone*): Same move as ever.

TAKEZŌ: Chan-pon-ge. (*Stone.*)

MITSUE (*Stone*): A transparent move.

TAKEZŌ: Chan-pon-ge. (*Stone.*)

MITSUE (*Stone*): It's always been like this, ever since I was little.

TAKEZŌ: Chan-pon-ge. (*Stone.*)

MITSUE (*Stone*): With this move you let me win.

TAKEZŌ: Chan-pon-ge. (*Stone.*)

MITSUE (*Stone*): You were sweet and easy, Papa . . .

TAKEZŌ (*Shouts*): Why don't you hold out paper? Don't you understand I'm telling you to win quickly and run away quickly, you little mule. Be a good child and run away. (*Excruciatingly.*) Show Papa one last act of respect. Please. If you still refuse to run away, I'll die right now.

(*A short silence.*)

TAKEZŌ: You understand now. It was by mutual agreement that you survived and I died.

MITSUE: But that doesn't change the fact that I abandoned you. I ought to have died with you, Papa.

TAKEZŌ (*Shouts again*): You fool!

MITSUE: . . . !

TAKEZŌ: How can you be so stupid? Didn't you learn anything in all those years of schooling?

MITSUE: But . . .

TAKEZŌ (*With a slap*): Listen up. That time, as you were crying, didn't you say: "It's heartless, it's horrible, why must we part like this?" . . . Do you remember?

MITSUE (*Faintly nods*): . . .

TAKEZŌ: I said in reply, "A parting like this must never happen again for the rest of eternity, because it's too heartless."

MITSUE (*Nods*): . . .

TAKEZŌ: Did you hear my last words? "Please live out my share of life, too!"

MITSUE (*Nods vigorously*): . . .

TAKEZŌ: That is why I am giving you life.

MITSUE: Giving me life?

TAKEZŌ: That's right. I'm giving you life to have people remember that there were indeed tens of thousands of such heartless partings. Isn't the library where you work also a place to tell about such things?

MITSUE: Huh? . . .

TAKEZŌ: It's your task to tell about the sad things, and the happy things, that human beings have experienced. If you don't understand that, then I won't rely on a fat-headed fool like you any longer. Give me someone else instead.

MITSUE: Someone else?

TAKEZŌ: My grandchild and great-grandchild.

(*After a short silence,* MITSUE *slowly goes to the kitchen, and grips a knife. She looks at* TAKEZŌ *for a while, then picks up a burdock and begins to cut it into thin slices. Before long, she suddenly stops.*)

MITSUE: When will you come next?

TAKEZŌ: That's up to you.

MITSUE (*Smiling for the first time in a long while*): We may not be able to meet for a while.

TAKEZŌ: . . .

(*The sound of a motor tricycle is heard in the distance.*)

TAKEZŌ: Oh no, I forgot to put in more firewood.

(TAKEZŌ *hurries away to the rear, stage right.* MITSUE *calls out toward his back.*)

MITSUE: Papa, thank you.

(*As the sound of the motor tricycle approaches, the curtain swiftly descends.*)

CURTAIN

PART V

THE 1980S AND BEYOND

Japan's economy, society, and culture have seen such change over the past fifty years that the Japanese themselves typically speak of the decades as if they were generations. Thus groups like Kōkami Shōji's Third Stage (Daisan butai) and Kawamura Takeshi's Third Erotica (Daisan erotika) self-consciously signaled their membership in a "third" generation of theater artists in the 1980s. They were following the "first" generation of playwrights and directors, such as Kara Jūrō and Terayama Shūji, who changed the course of Japanese theater in the 1960s, and the "second," 1970s, generation of dramatists, like Tsuka Kōhei and Yamazaki Tetsu. Each "generation" staked out a different identity that was somehow unique to its own time. Nevertheless, we can find some general trends during this particularly turbulent period in contemporary Japanese history.

Since the 1980s, many of *angura*'s (the underground's) innovations in dramaturgy and performance—fragmented narratives; highly physical, metatheatrical, and presentational techniques of acting; and the use of alternative and unusual venues—have become part of mainstream contemporary theater. *Angura* may have lost energy as a countercultural movement in the 1970s as Japan's youth culture became less politicized and more conformist, but the theater grew in artistic influence even as it became more closely aligned with consumer culture. By the 1980s, as many as 300 so-called little theater groups were active in Tokyo alone,

1. Statistics from the 1980s and 2005 are from, respectively, Shichiji Eisuke, "The Mentality of the 1990s in Japanese Theater," in *Half a Century of Japanese Theater*, ed. Japan Playwrights Association (Tokyo: Kinokuniya shoten, 2000), 2:2; and Tadashi Uchino, "Japan's 'Ill-Fated' Theater Culture," in *Half a Century of Japanese Theater*, ed. Japan Playwrights Association (Tokyo: Kinokuniya shoten, 2007), 9:1.

and by 2005, the number of such companies had swelled to 1,600.[1] Performances are typically targeted to young audiences, often in their twenties. At the same time, "little theater" no longer seems an accurate term for many of these groups or productions. Noda Hideki and his Dream Idlers (Yume no yuminsha, 1976–1992), exemplars of 1980s Japanese theater, on one occasion performed before more than 26,000 people in a single day, while a director like Ninagawa Yukio typically stages popular long-run shows in theaters that house more than 1,000. Many contemporary playwrights and actors are celebrities, writing and performing for not only the stage but television and film as well. Indeed, there is now a considerable crossover among the genres, as well as between the traditional and modern theater. Kabuki actor Nakamura Kanzakurō XVIII (1955–2012) starred in modern plays written by dramatists like Matsuo Suzuki and commissioned new kabuki plays by contemporary playwrights like Noda Hideki, Watanabe Eri, and Kudō Kankurō. Even *shingeki*, which seemed on the verge of demise with the deaths of pioneers like Senda Koreya in 1994, Sugimura Haruko in 1997, and Takizawa Osamu in 2000, has won a second life by commissioning plays from Betsuyaku Minoru, Hirata Oriza, and other contemporary "post-*shingeki*" playwrights. Theater, especially in Tokyo, has perhaps never seemed so healthy.

DEVELOPMENTS IN THE 1980S THEATER

In modern times, theaters in Japan have had to rely almost exclusively on the box office or private subscriptions for financial support (traditionally, only the nō theater received official patronage), but in recent years, public funding for the performing arts has grown considerably, despite the economic downturn of the past twenty years. The New National Theater, devoted exclusively to modern theater and opera, opened in Tokyo in 1997. (The National Theater was opened in 1966 to showcase traditional performing arts.) In the same year, Suzuki Tadashi established—with considerable support from the prefectural government—the Shizuoka Performing Arts Center (SPAC), about an hour west of Tokyo by bullet train. Since the 1980s, organizations like the Saison Foundation (established 1987), the Japan Arts Fund (1990), and the Performing Arts Development Project (1996) have helped promote international tours of Japanese performing arts groups. Regional development under the Liberal Democratic Party during Japan's economic boom years in the 1980s led to the building of many new theater and concert halls across Japan, a boom that lasted until the end of the twentieth century.

Although the history of modern Japanese theater, particularly since 1945, has been essentially a history of Tokyo theater, one notable trend since the 1980s has been the growth of regional theater groups and playwrights. Suzue Toshirō, Matsuda Masataka, and Tsuchida Hideo have been based in Kyoto. After the triple disaster of March 11, 2011, Okada Toshiki abandoned his native Yokohama and moved to Kumamoto, far from the threat of earthquakes and nuclear contamination. Hasegawa Kōji hails from, and still practices theater in, Hirosaki, at the northern tip of Honshū. Still, some places, like Osaka, are facing hard times now as local governments begin to cut arts funding.

Other positive trends have been the increasing presence of women and minorities in the Japanese theater since the 1980s. The contribution of female playwrights to the contemporary Japanese theater is discussed in greater detail by Yoshie Inoue in this volume, and the groundbreaking work of women like Kishida Rio (1950–2003), Kisaragi Koharu (1956–2000), Nagai Ai (b. 1951), Watanabe Eri (b. 1955), and the collective of playwrights who call themselves Ichidō Rei, from the company Blue Bird (Aoi tori), bear noting here. (*Poison Boy*, which Kishida coauthored with Terayama Shūji, is translated in part IV.) Even though contemporary theater has not created a strong feminist discourse in Japan, the sheer number of female playwrights, as well as all- or mostly women troupes, active in Japanese theater since the 1980s, is indicative of an erosion of ingrained patriarchal structures. At the same time, the ethnic Korean presence, which had its origins in the theater, is growing throughout Japanese culture. For example, Tsuka Kōhei's impact on 1970s theater was followed by the work of other Korean *zainichi* (Japanese-born) playwrights, like Chong Wishing and Yū Miri, and directors for stage and screen, like Kim Sujin and Yang Sogil. There also has been increasing collaboration among Japanese and other Asian theater artists. Kishida Rio worked with the Singaporean director Ong-Keng Sen on productions of *King Lear* (1994) and a postcolonialist version of *Othello*, called *Desdemona*, in 1999. Playwright Hirata Oriza translated into Korean his own play, *Citizens of Seoul* (1989), about Japan's 1910 annexation of Korea, for a production in Seoul in 1993, and has since worked regularly with Korean playwrights and directors on joint productions.

Japanese theater has never seemed so vibrant or international. Mitani Kōki, heir to Inoue Hisashi for capturing mainstream audiences, has been immensely productive as a writer of comedies and musicals for stage, television, and screen. (The name of his company, Tokyo Sunshine Boys, is a tribute to his hero, Neil Simon.) Yet despite the enormous popular success of post-1980s playwrights like Mitani, Keralino Sandorovitch, and Matsuo Suzuki, many have bemoaned the triumph of mindless entertainment and the death of art in contemporary Japanese theater.[2] *Angura*'s promise in the 1960s for theater to enter the public discourse and be a voice for change failed to materialize as succeeding generations capitulated to the status quo, and the artists, in order to survive, needed more and more to pander to commercial imperatives. At the same time, Japanese society has become increasingly conformist, conservative, and isolationist. The worsening economy and the growing instability of Japanese politics have only exacerbated this general trend, which started in the early 1970s. Youthful energy and innocence, qualities typical of 1980s theater, hardly made up for a general lack of interest in social issues or the world beyond or for a chronic sense of historical amnesia.

2. Ōta Shōgo's comments on contemporary theater are in Yamaguchi Hiroko, "Japanese Drama from Late Shōwa to the Early 21st Century: Reflections of a Tumultuous Era," in *Half a Century of Japanese Theater*, ed. Japan Playwrights Association (Tokyo: Kinokuniya shoten, 2008), 10:1.

The superheated economic growth seen in the 1960s culminated in the boom economy of the 1980s, a time when Japan was (in the words of Ezra Vogel's best-selling book) "Number One" and seemingly could do no wrong.[3] It was a dreamlike decade, when the real estate value of metropolitan Tokyo exceeded that of the entire United States; easy money was made on the stock market; and life in Japan, especially in its capital, seemed like a nonstop party. All the members of this "third" generation of theater artists were born after the war, and very few had ever suffered real deprivation. The sense of festivity, prosperity, and entitlement, in sync with the global postmodernist sensibility of that time, informed the frenetic, noisy theater of playwrights like Kōkami Shōji (b. 1958) and Noda Hideki (b. 1955): light, speedy, ironic, narcissistic, and celebratory. The counterculture had split into numerous subcultures, and inspiration for creative works tended now to come more from new media like television, *manga* (comics), and anime (animation) than from any preexisting theatrical tradition, political stance, or life experience. Noda and the Takarazuka Revue (as we shall see in part VI) based their hit plays on popular graphic novels.

Although not directly involved with the theater culture of this period, two novelists and an artist, all named Murakami, have defined the aesthetic of the past few decades in Japan: Murakami Haruki (b. 1949), for a cool, hipster insouciance that barely masks a heartfelt quest for identity in narratives that confuse fantasy with reality; Murakami Ryū (b. 1952), for his portraits of the contemporary city as a dystopia, filled with crime and sadomasochistic sex; and Murakami Takashi (b. 1963), artist of the aesthetics of "Superflat," in which surface is everything and the categories separating high and popular cultures have collapsed. Allusions to pop culture and in-jokes, a nostalgia for innocence and childhood, an avoidance of psychological depth or "serious" issues, and yet occasional hints at more unsettling anxieties all lurk behind what Kara Jūrō called the "happiness syndrome" of Japanese theater in the 1980s.[4] At the same time that the contemporary theater critic Tadashi Uchino described Kōkami Shōji's landmark, the *Godot*-inspired play *Trailing a Sunset Like the Dawn* (*Asahi no yō na yūhi wo tsurete*, 1981) as "an easy distortion of Beckett's metaphysical 'nothing is to be done' principle into 'everything is OK as it is,'" he labeled Noda Hideki's work of this period as "a kind of subcultural Disneyland."[5] Meanwhile, other groups, like Kawamura Takeshi's Third Erotica, began to explore the darker side of middle-class Japanese anomie in such works as *Nippon Wars* (*Nippon sensō*, 1984). This rather dystopic view was perhaps more familiar to Westerners than to most Japanese: after all, 1980s Tokyo was the inspiration for the near-future cityscapes of Ridley Scott's film *Blade Runner* and William Gibson's cyberpunk novel

3. Ezra F. Vogel, *Japan as Number One: Lessons for America* (Cambridge, Mass.: Harvard University Press, 1979).
4. Quoted in Nishidō Kōjin, "Radicalism in the Theater of the 1980s," in *Half a Century of Japanese Theater*, ed. Japan Playwrights Association (Tokyo: Kinokuniya shoten, 2002), 4:8.
5. Tadashi Uchino, *Crucible Bodies: Postwar Japanese Performance from Brecht to the New Millennium* (Salt Lake City: Seagull Books, 2009), 87.

Neuromancer. But even those riding the crest of Japan's prosperity at the time knew that it had to end, and many felt a sense of spiritual emptiness at the bottom of the "Japanese economic miracle."

The 1980s were a turning point for both Japan and the world. The explosion of radioactive gases from the Chernobyl nuclear reactor in Ukraine in 1986 revived fears of a nuclear apocalypse. The death of Emperor Hirohito in 1989 coincided with the fall of the Berlin Wall and marked the end of an era, which some have called the "short twentieth century," for both the Japanese and the West. Soon thereafter, Japan's bubble economy burst, and the Soviet Union fell. The first Gulf War in 1991 marked the end of Cold War politics and the beginning of new, more chaotic global tensions. In 1990, a new religious cult, Aum Shinrikyō, entered candidates into the national election for the House of Representatives. Five years later and just two months after an earthquake devastated the Kobe region, this cult poisoned thousands of people with sarin gas in the Tokyo subway system.

CHANGES IN THE 1990S

Perhaps as a result, the Japanese have called the 1990s a "lost generation," and with continuing unemployment, increasing economic disparity, homelessness, and the dissolution of the old guarantees of lifetime careers, the first decade of the new millennium seemed to hold out little promise of improvement. Japan's population ages while the country is reluctant to accept immigrants; the national debt rises while the tax base decreases. As the country's economy sank into the long slide from which it has still not recovered, the news was—and remains—filled with bizarre crimes, indiscriminate murders, senseless suicides, shocking cases of domestic violence, family neglect, and school brutality.

The chief effect of these new economic and social stresses on Japan in regard to a new theatrical vision was a sudden return to realism and an attention to well-crafted, literate drama. It was as if Japan had woken up with a hangover after the long party of the bubble economy. One of the first playwrights to write in this vein was Iwamatsu Ryō (b. 1952), who has worked for some of Japan's finest and most popular actors. He first teamed up as a dramatist in the late 1980s with Emoto Akira and the Tokyo Battery Company (Tokyo kandenchi, established 1977), leaving this company in 1992 to become the playwright and director for Takenaka Naoto. Iwamatsu's desultory dramas have focused on the banal lives of feckless characters. *Futon and Daruma* (1988), one of his signature works, won the Kishida Kunio Award for best play of that year. Kara Jūrō compared Iwamatsu to a "perverted Kubota Mantarō," referring to Kishida's contemporary, a prewar dramatist of everyday lyricism.[6] Indeed, a kind of eerie realism verging on the absurd pervades the work of Iwamatsu and a number of other playwrights who began writing in this manner,

6. Quoted in Shichiji, "Mentality of the 1990s in Japanese Theater," 4.

including Suzue Toshirō, Matsuda Masataka, and Hirata Oriza. A stark contrast to the noisy, high-energy comedies that had become staples of 1980s Tokyo, such works were quickly dubbed "quiet theater." If the theater of Japan from the 1960s to the 1980s had been extravagant, exuberant, or even overwhelmed by its own unabashed inventiveness, much of the theater of the 1990s was turning out to be austere, minimalist, constrained, lacking in dramatic flourishes, and wary of making grand statements or attempting to use theater as a vehicle to push any ideological "message."

The most articulate spokesperson for this style of theater in the past two decades has been Hirata Oriza, who won the 1995 Kishida Kunio Award for *Tokyo Notes*, first performed the previous year and one of the works featured here. In his appropriately named collection of essays on theater, *Cities Do Not Need Festivities* (*Toshi ni wa shukusai wa iranai*, 1997), Hirata wrote:

> Most life has nothing whatever to do with what theater in the past has liked to portray but is grounded instead in quiet and uneventful moments. . . . We exist as human beings, and that in itself is amazing, even dramatic. Daily life contains all sorts of rich and complex elements: it can be entertaining, touching, funny, even stupid. What I want to do is distill from all those complicated elements an objective sense of time as it is lived—quietly—and directly reconstruct that on the stage.[7]

More than perhaps any dramatist of his generation, Hirata has a sense of his place in the history of Japanese theater and what makes his work different from what has come before it.

Some critics, however, have taken Hirata and his contemporaries to task for a conservatism that is both ideological and aesthetic. The characters in "quiet realist" plays avoid conflict, their motives remaining opaque sometimes even to themselves. In the avoidance of emotional display is also a reluctance to commit oneself to another person or ideal, which is indicative of the sense of disengagement that many Japanese now feel.

Something of this emotional detachment is also present in the theater's new dynamics in the current generation of playwrights and directors. The 1960s generation was characterized by a number of charismatic patriarchs—notably Kara Jūrō, Suzuki Tadashi, Terayama Shūji, and Hijikata Tatsumi—who gathered about them tribe-like troupes of younger enthusiasts eager to put into practice their masters' ideas. Typically, the "company style" of such theater was branded less by rigorous training or tradition than by the personality of their leader and creator. For most of the twentieth century, modern Japanese theater—with the notable exceptions of such mainstream companies as Asari Keita's Four Seasons Theater (Gekidan shiki) and the Takarazuka Revue—was characterized by its inspired amateurism. Playwrights and directors like Kara, Suzuki, and Noda Hideki were not

---

7. Hirata Oriza, *Toshi ni wa shukusai wa iranai* (Tokyo: Banseisha, 1997), 182.

HIRATA ORIZA

Actors need something on which to ground their delivery of dialogue. The basis for dialogue in *shingeki*, which tried to directly import modern Western theater, is a character's mental state and emotions. A *shingeki* actor interprets the script, finding sadness, for instance, and expressing the emotion of sadness. It was mainly this modernist approach that the emerging underground or little theater movement in and after 1960s opposed. It claimed that psychology and emotions are not the only driving forces for the way that humans speak. The key words for this movement are "body," "unconsciousness," "passion," "instinct." We can therefore see that the transition from *shingeki* to underground theater and little theater has been a transition from logos to pathos and eros.

On the other hand, one can say that the basis of traditional theater, like nō and *kyōgen*, is history. From the age of two or three, nō performers are drilled, without any logical explanations whatsoever, in movement, gesture, and voice projection. The basis of training in nō is that it is the way they've been doing it for six hundred years. That may sound preposterous, but it really is not. All ineffective forms of expression have been eliminated over the course of time, leaving only the present forms [*kata*] for movement and speech.

So I would say that the basis for traditional theater is ethos, or custom. Then what are the grounds for the new theater trend in 1990s? . . . The one thing that makes the new theater that appeared in the 1990s different from former trends is its consciousness of others and the surrounding environment. With only logos, pathos, or eros, we can envisage only one facet of human subjectivity. While we human beings speak as subjects, as individuals, what we say is also being dictated to us by our environment. How do we express ourselves under these circumstances? This focus, I think, has been one of the major achievements of 1990s theater.

FROM HIRATA ORIZA, "KYŪJŪ-NENDAI ENGEKI TO WA NANIKA?" (WHAT IS JAPANESE THEATER IN THE 1990S?), IN *ENGEKI NYŪMON* (*AN INTRODUCTION TO THEATER*) (TOKYO: KŌDANSHA, 1998), 183–85.

classically trained in established theater schools—such institutions are still a rarity in Japan—but typically were drawn to the theater in extracurricular club activities at university. So, too, was Hirata, but increasingly, even playwrights like Noda and Hirata are straying from the older tribal model of creating theater with their own companies toward a model of workshops and shifting casts of actors, new for every production. Some critics have seen in this new model a growing distrust of group dynamics and a reluctance to

HIRATA ORIZA

When we carry out the act of speaking, we do so all the while being implicitly aware of the extent to which the other person understands what we say, the size of the room, the number of people listening, the amount of ambient noise, and so on. So while we are expressing ourselves, we are also being dictated to by our environment. For an actor, the most important element of his environment is the other actor, but other elements like the set, lighting, and costume all come into play, determining the conditions under which the delivery of dialogue takes place.

FROM HIRATA ORIZA, *ENGI, ENSHUTSU (ACTING AND DIRECTING)* (TOKYO: KŌDANSHA, 2004), 133–34.

form close relationships in Japan, a remarkable trend in a society that traditionally has placed so much value on a sense of belonging.

The difficulty of social interaction and the prevalence of increasingly antisocial syndromes in Japan today—*otaku* (nerd) culture and *hikikomori* (shut-ins)—are treated in another work featured here, Sakate Yōji's *Attic* (*Yaneura*, 2002). Sakate has been one of the most politically active playwrights of his generation, not afraid to tackle contemporary social or political issues or to examine critically Japan's recent history. His works nonetheless are typical of the revival of well-written and well-wrought plays after a period in which performance was privileged over text. To that extent, Sakate and many of his contemporaries (Nagai Ai, among others) may signify the resurgence of ideals of drama as literature as well as the mirror of society that *shingeki* had espoused more than a half century earlier.

Not all significant works in the past two decades have been well-made plays, however. Japan's avant-garde has also given birth to various forms of physical theater in which spoken dialogue is attenuated or even absent, as in Ōta Shōgo's work. Many theater practitioners and critics have noted that one of the signal characteristics of modern culture in Japan is an estrangement of language from the body. Various styles of theater since the 1960s have attempted to address, if not resolve, a sense that contemporary Japanese are, mentally and physically, divided selves. Since the 1980s, this trend has produced a number of powerful and even violent performance styles that straddle the worlds of dance and multimedia performance art, such as Miyagi Satoshi's Ku Na'uka, Shimizu Shinjin's Theater of Deconstruction (Gekidan kaitaisha), the Kyoto-based collective Dumb Type, and the Osaka-based company Ishinha (Reformers' Group). Some feel that the future of

Japanese theater can now be seen not so much in dialogue drama as in the world of dance, which in the past twenty years has departed from *butō* and is now attempting to capture the essence of what it is to be human in the technologized world today. The relationship of language to the body will always be a central theme and challenge for practitioners of live theater, and in the work of playwrights like Okada Toshiki, audiences in Japan and, increasingly, abroad can see the difficulties that we all face in negotiating body and soul.

M. CODY POULTON

Noda Hideki, *Poems for Sale*, directed by Noda Hideki, sis company, February 2002.
(Photograph by Aoki Tsukasa)

POEMS FOR SALE

NODA HIDEKI
TRANSLATED BY MARI BOYD

Award-winning Noda Hideki (b. 1955) continues to enjoy a high profile as a playwright, a director, an and actor. His work falls into two periods: the first from 1976 to 1992, with his Dream Wanderers theater company, and the second from 1993, mainly with his Noda Map production company.

In the first period, Noda became famous for his "theater as a sport" approach to performance, dazzling the audience with high-speed, complex spectacles that celebrated "boyhood." His major productions, such as *The Prisoner of Zenda Castle* (*Zenda-jō no toriko*, 1981) and *Here Comes the Wild Beast* (*Nokemono kitarite*, 1984), are characterized by zany wordplay, rapid-fire delivery, and frenetic movement. On his first overseas venture, Noda took the latter play to the 1987 Edinburgh Festival, sparking a concern over language barriers, which in turn has affected the trajectory of his artistic endeavors.

A significant turning point in Noda's career was the year he spent in London, beginning in late 1992. Workshops, especially with the Théâtre de complicité, galvanized his interest in physical theater, collaboration, and dramaturgical methods to transcend linguistic transmission difficulties. In late 1993, he founded Noda Map, at which he tried his hand at kabuki and opera as well as devising his own plays. Thematically, his plays have moved beyond the child's dream world to social issues such as nationalism, colonialism, sexuality, and crime. They are darker in tone and more steadily paced; they also rely less on verbal playfulness. Major full-length works include *Kill* (*Kiru*, 1994) and *Pandora's Bell* (*Pandora no kane*, 1999).

Besides his spectacular main-stage shows, Noda has produced short experimental plays using simple props, minimal sets, and small casts playing multiple roles. Included in this group are his international collaborations—*The Red Demon, Akaoni* (1997), *The Bee* (2008), and *The Diver* (2009)—and also *Poems for Sale* (*Uri kotoba*, 2002), the work translated in this anthology.

Poems for Sale is a one-hander with five roles. Produced by the sis company at the Spiral Hall in Tokyo in February 2002, it addresses, head-on, female desire, both erotic and otherwise. In doing so, it provides a revisionist view of the much idolized poet Takamura Kōtarō (1883–1956) and his relationship with his wife, Chieko (1886–1938). The celebrated marriage of true minds and passions is shorn of its romanticism as Chieko is shown to devolve into insanity. The paralleling of the personal events leading to her collapse and the increasingly jingoistic radio broadcasts suggests that the couple's relationship is a synecdoche for the emperor's with his people.

In his second period, Noda deliberately changed his dramaturgy because he wanted to reach a global audience. He knew that his earlier work was nearly impossible to get across to a non-Japanese audience, given its heavy dependence on Japanese wordplay on both local and structural levels. To date, Noda has devised three plays with non-Japanese versions: *The Red Demon, Akaoni* has been produced in English, Thai, and Korean; *The Bee* and *The Diver* he cowrote in English with British playwright Colin Teevan and subsequently wrote the Japanese text himself. The latter two, in particular, indicate the highest point in Noda's development as an intercultural theater artist. Taking heed of his new script-making approach, we have chosen *Poems for Sale* for this anthology because, unlike his first-phase plays, it loses little in meaning and style when rendered into English and also is a good example of his second-phase experimentation.

Characters

CHIEKO
MAID, speaks in a heavy northeastern dialect
KŌTARŌ
HIRATSUKA RAICHŌ
IMAGAWA BUN SELLER

SCENE 1. CYCLING

A bicycle bursts through a paper-paned partition. Riding the bike is CHIEKO, *who is screaming something while she pedals around the stage. She then drives her bike right through another paper-paned partition and exits.*

The sound of the bicycle crashing, followed by another even louder noise. From upstage, CHIEKO *enters pushing the bicycle.*

CHIEKO: Of course I'll take a tumble when I start something new like this. No one's ever been able to ride a bicycle perfectly from the very beginning. You fall off. Falling off is part of riding a bicycle. The Chinese characters for bicycle mean "a vehicle that falls over by itself spontaneously." You see, Mother. Owowowowowow. You keep falling off, and in a hundred years what do you find? Women riding bicycles. Not just riding them, Mother. The day will come when lots of middle-aged women will be riding bicycles near train stations and getting in *everyone*'s way. Hey lady, you're not supposed to go up that way on your bike. Oh, she's knocking things over, she's hanging things on the handlebars. Oh, something is dripping. Nooo! You mustn't let stuff drip from your bike. Everyone's going to wonder what it is. What is it that's dribbling off your bike? Hey lady! Lady! When the day comes, you middle-aged women'll be grateful to me. I fall off today and the future of Shimo-Kitazawa[1] is guaranteed! . . . (*She sits down in place.*) Mother, let me and all women practice full blast until we drop dead. I'm going to practice this summer. I will. I really will, I really will till I drop dead. If that isn't enough, no one will make the grade! . . .

SCENE 2. THE MAID

CHIEKO *suddenly stands up. She transforms into another identity—that of her own* MAID.

MAID (*In a northeastern accent*): She's a tough cookie, this one is. And she's only a teenager. What do you make of her? I'm the maid that stayed with her almost until she died, but I can't make heads or tails out of her. Her maiden name's Naganuma Chieko; her married name's Takamura Chieko, or to make things really easy to understand, she's the wife of the poet Takamura Kōtarō. She's the Chieko in *Chieko's Sky*, Kōtarō's famous collection of love poems. In my home dialect, Chieko is pronounced "tsarf koh," which, with a lot of imagination, sounds like tough cookie. Ohey ohey. Oh ho, it's weird. Chieko eventually goes mad and dies. I can't explore the mind of a cuckoo, but at least as the one closest to her I can tell you what I saw.

1. Today Shimo-Kitazawa is a trendy night spot with several well-known little theaters.

SCENE 3. THE VALEDICTORY SPEECH AT COMMENCEMENT

The MAID *goes back to where* CHIEKO *was sitting, and now* CHIEKO *bows repeatedly.*

CHIEKO: I beg you. I beg you. Please, please, let me go to the Fukushima School of Higher Education for Women. . . . Oh so you won't let me go to school after I've abased myself this much. . . . All right. I'll burn down the house. Yes, this house. Just kidding! Educated women don't commit acts like that. Uneducated women set houses on fire. Uneducated women also cry. They cry over anything and everything. I'm so lonely, owow wehh. Oh that hurts, owowo behh. I wanna sleep, owow wehh. I'm on top of the world, owowo behh. I'm miserable, owow wehh. I can't walk, owowo behh. This picture is so bee-yu-ti-ful, owow wehh. Whatever it is, owowo behh. She says, "The dog . . . !" and bursts into tears. "The dog . . . !" What about the dog? "The dog . . . !" "What?" "The dog . . . !" What's this about?" The girl says, "The dog . . . !" and simply goes on crying. She doesn't make any sense, the stupid thing. That's because she doesn't have any education. Are you going to be happy with that? What if I became like that and cried out, "The dog . . . !" Dear Father, we have plenty of money, enough to fill a wine cellar. What? Women burdened with unnecessary education are impertinent? Father, please look at me carefully. Am I impertinent? I'm pretty good stuff, you know. You've done a fabulous job of bringing me up. . . . This isn't working. Professor? Professor Kawamoto. . . . Please explain to him. Tell him how education is necessary for young women of the future. Right . . . yes, yes. . . . That's exactly it, Professor. You speak so well . . . uh-huh, uh-huh, right on the mark. That's exactly what I wanted to convey. . . . "The dog . . . !" and they squawk. That's it. "The dog . . . !"

(CHIEKO *transforms into the* MAID.)

MAID: That's how Chieko left Mount Atatara[2] behind and matriculated at the Fukushima School of Higher Education for Women.

(CHIEKO *is a freshman. At incredible speed she turns into a senior about to graduate. She reads the address for the graduating class.*)

CHIEKO: We are gathered here today at our commencement. This has been made possible entirely through the thoughtful guidance of our respected principal as well as our dedicated professors. How can we express our fervent gratitude for the love and care that we have received? And do we through our own puny limitations dare forget the precious teachings that we have had the fortune to imbibe here? In departing from this garden of learning, we hope to retain in our hearts the daily instruction we have received so that we may be instrumental in the elevation of society in beauty,

2. Mount Atatara is in Fukushima Prefecture in northeastern Japan.

harmony, and happiness. As educated modern women, we hope to grow in pride as graduates of this blessed school and contribute to a higher and nobler destiny.

Naganuma Chie, Valedictorian of Fukushima School of Higher Education for Women, March 15.

(*To her parents.*) I beg of you this one and only favor of my life. Please let me attend a women's college in Tokyo. I know. I should be thankful for having been able to attend a school of higher education for women. But everyone says that it's a waste if the valedictorian at commencement doesn't continue her education. The Fukushima School of Higher Education for Women isn't enough. . . . Who says? Everyone says so. I can hear the chorus as I walk the streets. The people in town are chanting, "What a waste!" "What a waste!" like a mantra. It's a new religion. It's kinda scary walking around town when you might be assaulted by this "what a waste-ful" religion. When I graduate, I promise to return home and marry. I beg you to let me go . . . This isn't working. I'll have to depend on that old favorite—"The dog . . . !"

MAID: This is how Chieko yet again got her own way and was able to enter a women's college in Tokyo.

(*The* MAID *switches on a radio. Music is heard. At a small coffee shop called IN.*)

SCENE 4. A TENNIS MATCH WITH HIRATSUKA RAICHŌ

CHIEKO *is drawing a very large painting. She is totally focused on the canvas for a while. She makes a gesture indicating that she notices someone nearby.*

CHIEKO: Oh, who me? Huh? Yes, of course I know who you are. You're Hiratsuka Raichō.[3] Raichō. You are an upperclassman, just one year ahead of me. Uh-huh, I was asked to draw one for the upcoming cultural festival. Yes, that's right. I started learning oil painting when I entered this college. But it's the first time for me to paint such a big painting. . . . Thank you very much. I believe that painting begins with sketches, ifyouplease ifyouplease ifyouplease. Oh, I am very honored. We all put you on a pedestal and idolize you. Honored? What did you say? On their back? I don't know what you are talking about. What is it? What is "on your back"? Huh? —Wait a moment. What for? I don't like this. Huh? Lesbians? I've heard of them. Women who, um, you know. Huh? Lesbians' backstroke? The backstroke? You're saying that if I were a lesbian—a butch—and I slept with you kinda like this . . . What would I do? You said just now that I'd be the butch. Yeah, I'd want to put my arm around you, so I'd stretch my arm like this. Huh? What if you were also

3. Hiratsuka Raichō (1886–1971) was a writer, journalist, political activist, and pioneering Japanese feminist. She was the founder of Japan's first feminist journal, *Bluestockings* (*Seitō*, 1911–1915), whose motto was "In the beginning, woman was the sun."

butch? Well, you'd put your arm around me, then I'd follow suit. You would bring your arm around me again, and in reaction I'd do the same like this, and Raichō, I . . . oh, I am doing the backstroke . . . Sports? (*Modestly.*) I'm not really very good at physical activities. Huh? You want me to be your tennis partner? I'm just a novice tennis player. But if you are willing to have me as your partner, youknow youknow youknow . . .

(*They begin to play tennis. At first* CHIEKO *defers to* HIRATSUKA *and does not hit the ball boldly, but as the match progresses, she begins to forget whom she is playing with. At first she speaks weakly.*)

CHIEKO: Right . . . right . . . here goes . . . Wow! Nice serve . . . Here . . . hah! Now take that! Huh? That was in? Just on the line? . . . Okay, got it . . . Here goes! . . . Take that! . . . Arghh! . . . Dargonit!! . . . Woowee! . . . Oof!

(CHIEKO*'s rapid-fire tennis play shifts into slow motion, and* CHIEKO*'s speech turns into the* MAID*'s monologue.*)

MAID: Neither party gave way in that day's game. Their furious "backstroke" tennis went down in the history of the women's college. How often in a lifetime does a person get into fights? Whatever she did, in the end Chieko would get herself into a fight. Once her spirit was ignited, she wouldn't quit until she won.

(*Like viewers at a match, the* MAID *follows the movement of the ball, swinging her head from right to left and back again. The* MAID *transforms back into* CHIEKO *and swings the racket in a much wilder way than earlier.*)

CHIEKO (*Suddenly stops playing*): What is the matter? Do you give in? Surely not. You can't give up. Tennis isn't a fight. Huh? Oh, Raichō, you are just as powerful.

(*Glowing with pride,* CHIEKO *is pleased to shake hands with* HIRATSUKA.)

MAID: Even this Chieko, though, is beaten by life.

(CHIEKO *suddenly prostrates herself in front of her parents.*)

CHIEKO: I beg you. I truly and sincerely beg you. Please let me stay in Tokyo. I want to paint. There are paintings I want to paint. . . . God, this isn't working. "The dog . . . !" . . .

MAID: Needless to say, Chieko's parents already knew that she would never heed their wishes. Chieko's skill at sketching was incredible.

SCENE 5. LIFE AT ART SCHOOL

A canvas of a tall, imposing nude man is set against the upstage wall. With the painting in the background, CHIEKO *is painting a nude male model.*

CHIEKO (*Tries to draw realistically*): Remove your hand. Never mind. How can I draw with your hand in the way . . . What? Why should I have to shade it over? Come on show me. I said, show me! Darn it. You have balls, haven't you? Take your hand away. THAT hand! You really don't have the balls for being a model! (*Forcing the model to remove his hand,* CHIEKO *takes a good slow look.*) Mmm, you do have balls. (CHIEKO *finishes the painting.*)

MAID: Having finished her painting to her satisfaction, Chieko went and showed it to Nakamura Fusetsu,[4] the instructor at the art school.

MAID-AS-NAKAMURA: Who did this painting? (*Out of sheer pride,* CHIEKO *did not speak up.*) You did? The sketch is not bad. (*Silently,* CHIEKO *smiled inwardly.*) But this coloring is unhealthy. As long as the lights and shades of color match the picture, it doesn't matter if, for instance, you used all yellows. But you should avoid unhealthy-looking colors. This emerald green doesn't work. Your sketching skills are exceptional, but there's a problem with your color palate.

MAID: Chieko was truly silenced by Nakamura's criticism. Everyone thought that Chieko was in silent rebellion. But the one reason she did not speak up was that she believed that she was color blind.

CHIEKO: Watanabe Fumiko,[5] is the sky you are looking at and the one I am looking at the same color? You know, we assume that we are seeing the same thing, but there's no evidence of that. Feeling the same pain, one person might exaggerate and go "Owowowowow!" while someone who has lost an arm may just say "Oof." Colors may be like pain. Some may feel the May breeze to be yellow; others may feel it to be light green. It's not only a matter of color; humans change according to light and shade. Do you get me? I look like this when light hits me from this angle. Everyone believes this is me. But from another angle (*Shining a flashlight from below*), I look like this. (*Under the original lighting.*) I haven't changed, but I look totally different. See? I am exactly the same as before, but (*Turning on the flashlight at herself from below*) I look different, right? I look different, right? I look different, right? Argh!

SCENE 6. FIRST LOVE

MAID: Looking ghastly different, she happened to make eye contact with Miyazaki Yōhei,[6] the man she falls in love with.

CHIEKO (*In a daze*): What? Who is that? The guy looking this way. Watanabe Fumiko, don't you know who it is? (*With a fearful look.*) The guy I made exchange glances with

---

4. Nakamura Fusetsu (1866–1943) was a Western-style painter and calligrapher.
5. Watanabe Fumiko (1886–1977) was a Western-style painter noted for floral designs.
6. Miyazaki Yōhei (1889–1912) was a Western-style painter and illustrator who married Watanabe Fumiko and changed his name to Watanabe.

when I was looking "different." Miyazaki Yōhei? Miyazaki Yōhei... Miyazaki Yōhei. He's at the same art school? Huh? Is he really that famous? Is he really that talented? Oh, oh no, he's coming this way... This spot? Oh, er well is it? Watanabe Fumiko. Is this spot open? It seems to be. Go ahead..... Gee, where did you hear of my name? Huh? No, no I don't. What is your name? Oh, really..... Bye now. (*Miyazaki Yōhei appears to leave.*) Huh? What was that about? Watanabe Fumiko, I'm not interested in him. My mind is set on painting. What's the matter, Watanabe Fumiko? What?! He's cool? That man just now? Weeell, I don't know. Huh? Interested in me? That guy Miyazaki is? I don't think so, Watanabe Fumiko. Don't rag me, Watanabe Fumiko. Don't you dare rag me!

MAID: As most of us know from experience, falling in love is hard to distinguish from stalking prey.

(*Standing in an uncertain light,* CHIEKO *is waiting for someone.*)

CHIEKO (*Someone appears*): Good-bye... (*She is waiting again for someone.*) Good-bye... (*Then her body language indicates obviously that she is waiting for Miyazaki.*) Oh... Excuse me... ah... (*She just watches Miyazaki leave.*) It's Miyazaki Yōhei and Watanabe Fumiko together.

MAID: In this way Chieko's first love ended as simple stalking unnoticed by anyone.

CHIEKO: Watanabe Fumiko, you—. You and your cute girly voice...

MAID: There's nothing wrong with putting on a cute girly voice. A woman with a broken heart cannot understand that.

(CHIEKO *stands in front of a canvas with brush and palette in hand.*)

CHIEKO: Miyazaki Yōhei and Watanabe Fumiko are engaged? For starters, it's weird that an artist would get married at all. Me?! (*Laughs loudly.*) You've got to be kidding. I haven't fallen in love, let alone thought of marriage. I declare: Oil painting is my life. I must paint... Wehhhhh... (*She cries for some length of time.*)

Pride should be thrown out without ceremony. When you're a kid, you have embarrassing moments or miserable times when your chest tightens up. Pride is for tossing away... Blehhehh...

SCENE 7. FIRST ENCOUNTER WITH KŌTARŌ

MAID: Even if you fall asleep miserable with yourself, the despair of youth, unlike cheap liquor, doesn't carry over to the next day. If you sprinkle water on a thirsty soul, it will regain vigor. On that destined morning, the green sun must have shone on the potted gloxinia the color-blind Chieko had. In "The Green Sun" Takamura writes, "It doesn't matter if you draw the sun green. Art enjoys absolute freedom."[7]

7. "The Green Sun" (1910) was Takamura Kōtarō's manifesto on the issue of individual and national identity in modern art.

(*Carrying the potted gloxinia,* CHIEKO *visits* KŌTARŌ*'s studio accompanied by her friend Yanagi Yae.*)[8]

CHIEKO: The one with a large chinquapin tree. . . . Oh, that one? That house? . . . Is it really all right, Yae? You may know him, but I've never met him before. Huh? Of course, I'm nervous. You see . . . You know, Takamura Kōtarō was an honors student at the Academy of Arts. Everyone's heard about him. After he came back from Paris, I read "The Green Sun." "It doesn't matter if you draw the sun green. Art enjoys absolute freedom." I was encouraged. Huh? A failure? How? An innocent idealist? . . . Nowadays? In rebellion against his privileged upbringing, he's now living on the fringe of humanity.

(*She stands at the entrance of* KŌTARŌ*'s atelier.*)

Excuse me . . .

MAID: Deciding not to make the same mistake she made with her first love, Chieko resorted to a girly strategy.

CHIEKO: Excuse me . . . Excuse me . . . Excuse me . . .

(*The moment she met* KŌTARŌ. *A pause.*)

MAID: With a completely silent Chieko in front of himself, Kōtarō talked clumsily on his own.

(*Opening a window, the* MAID *transforms into* KŌTARŌ *seated and talking ineptly on his own.*)

KŌTARŌ: The rain has let up. I hadn't noticed. (*Looking outside the window.*) I went to buy some water this morning. On rainy days, water is heavy. The lemons I bought at the same time were light. The heaviness of water, the lightness of lemons. The anxious wait for the girl of one's dreams . . . oh, sorry.

(*He moves to a different spot and sits down.*)

After the rain, the daisies were stuck all over the lawn like tacks. The grass looked just like the carpeting that fallen cherry blossoms make.

(*He again sits down in a different spot.*)

The freshness after showers reminds me of the terminal station at the far end of the line. Sorrow and a sense of drama permeate the air. Mist rises and someone comes running this way. Ahh, excuse me. I've been babbling on all by myself. What's this? Did you draw this? Is this color called emerald green? I'd like to see your other pictures, too. Oh? *Bluestockings*? Is this the cover of that famous journal edited by Hiratsuka Raichō? I see, then you must be a "new woman."

(*He pulls out a briefcase.*)

This briefcase is new. When something new starts, the container has to be new too. Haven't you had such an experience?

(*From his briefcase, he pulls out a sheet of copper, a sheet of tin, cellophane tape, and paper and begins to make all kinds of things.*)

---

8. Yanagi Yae was a friend of Chieko's at Japan Women's University, as well as being a magazine editor and the wife of the painter Yanagi Keisuke.

I can't foresee what I will start now I'm back in Japan or what will happen here. However, new materials are sure to show new forms of expression. (*Saying so, he presses the sheet of copper to his face.*)

Copper expresses silence.

(*He puts down the copper sheet and picks up the tin sheeting.*)

This tin speaks.

(*After making various sounds with the tin sheeting, he puts it down and picks up the paper.*)

Paper talks, too.

(*He makes different sounds with the paper. Then he stretches out the cellophane tape and makes it zing.*)

Cellophane tape is a rapping comedian.

(*He pulls out the cellophane tape and sticks it to various things, enjoying the sound it makes.*)

I found all these new materials outside Japan. When I returned to Japan, the first thing I felt was that people here made me feel ticklish. I find the fact that I am Japanese ticklish, not irritating. Merely ticklish.

MAID: Hearing him criticizing her people, she felt negated, too. For the first time she felt like retorting.

CHIEKO: Japanese make you feel ticklish? What about Westerners, then? Do they tickle your funny bone? Ticklish, tickle-shit? A joke? What? Who is always joking? Are you talking about yourself or about Westerners? . . . Let's take it again from the beginning. In a nutshell, what are Westerners? Are they people who tell good jokes? For example, could you tell me a good joke? Right. Huh? A person in the throes of death has only five minutes left to live. Uh-huh, and what happens? He asks the doctor, "How should I live out the shrinking remainder of my life?" The doctor replies, "You can boil an egg." . . . Is that an amusing answer? Huh? Westerners roll over laughing about this? I'm taken aback. Excuse me? Kōtarō, I guess my blood flows slowly through my veins. I'm not exactly that fast on the uptake. Huh? . . . A poet? Who? Me? What I said? My blood flows slowly . . . (*To herself.*) I may have won some points for that. Kōtarō was beaming ecstatically. Right, here goes. I'll launch a concerted attack on him. Kōtarō, this is what I think. The human brain is a pathetic organ, but the human heart is as cruel as April . . . (*She waits for a response.*) . . . A hit! Maybe.

MAID: It was not Chieko alone who fell in love at that moment. Around the time this couple started living together, I took a peek at Kōtarō's journal.

(*The* MAID *sneaks into* KŌTARŌ*'s study and reads his journal out loud.*)

MAID: "The love stories that have been written about men and women may all be lies." "I choose love with you. Writing this far, I have discovered the perfect circle of love in the word 'love.' Ah the cruelty of perfection." "Watching you as you talked, I felt that you inhabited a child's world. A child's world is always dominated by sight and smell.

Think of a child opening a box of caramels. Like this, like this, she opens the box like this. The world is all eyes and nose for her. That's a happy world. You inhabit it."

SCENE 8. CHIEKO'S MARRIAGE

CHIEKO: Excuuuse me. . . . I have an important matter to discuss with you. It may not be something that you need to hear . . . (*She stops with her mouth open.*) . . . I can't say it after all. I'm shy. How shy? For example, even if there's a foreigner sitting next to me who's using an ashtray as his soy sauce dish, I would just watch in silence. Huh? I'm not being mean. I simply cannot speak up. Strangely I become convinced that that, too, is possible and I can't point out his mistake to him—excuse me, that little saucer you have there is really an ashtray. Tomorrow I'm going to leave Tokyo and go back home. . . . In fact my family wants me to consider a marriage offer. Why do you want to know? . . . His name is Terada Saburō. He's a doctor.

MAID: Capturing a man's attention by intimating an offer of marriage is a tried and tested method by young women. On top of that, when the man hears the potential competitor is a doctor . . . The thought "My rival is a doctor" rising in the man's heart has been the same for more than a hundred years. Thus started the best-read collection of Japanese love poetry, *Chieko's Sky*.

just can't stand
your going away . . .

like bearing fruit before flowering
like budding before seeding
like spring coming right out of summer
please don't do
such an absurd unnatural thing
just the thought of a stereotyped husband
and you who write in a round hand
is enough to make me cry
getting married? Why you—
you who are timid like a bird
capricious as a great wind?
just can't stand
your going away . . .

how could you so easily
how shall I say? . . . well . . .

feel like selling yourself?

. . .

("TO SOMEONE," FROM *CHIEKO'S SKY*)[9]

MAID: What's more, this was not a poem to begin with. It was from a letter Kōtarō had sent Chieko. Having sent the letter, Kōtarō went off to Cape Inubō[10] to do some sketching. What would you do if you received a letter like this from a man? Traditional women would have waited in mesmerized expectation. But Chieko was a "new woman." She chased after him all the way to the cape.

SCENE 9. CAPE INUBŌ

MAID: At the top of the cape, Chieko maneuvered a coincidental meeting with Kōtarō, who was on his way down from his sketching.

CHIEKO: . . . Oh? Hey? Oohey oohey oohey? Kōtarō, isn't it? It's me. Chieko. To meet you at a place like this is almost like a premeditated coincidence. I thought of sketching the evening sights of Cape Inubō. Huh? I'm staying at the Gyōkeikan Inn Woweee. You're kidding. That's an increeeedible coincidence. We're really staying at the same inn?! Ahhh . . .

MAID: The implication of Chieko's "Ahhh" becomes clear when you take a peek at Kōtarō's journal.

(*The* MAID *again sneaks a peek from* KŌTARŌ*'s journal kept in his desk.*)

JOURNAL: "The long, long eternal kiss ends in a flash. That is the miracle of love." "I don't think you were looking at the sea any longer. Since then you have been within a two-inch radius of me, practically as close as if we were the same person. We overlapped as if we were concentric circles. We looked at the same things, we felt the same feelings, we laughed at the same things, we ate the same food. Almost thirty years of age, we loved like high schools kids each time our eyes met. At the Gyōkeikan we swore to talk right through the night and, after half an hour, fell asleep at the same time. That was a 'concentric' sleep, the happiest sleep in the world."

When people are deeply in "concentric" love, they are apt to encounter crude, angular people. The following day on the way back from sketching at the cape, they came across a rough-looking middle-aged woman selling Imagawa buns.

(*A woman toasts buns, and her weird body language indicates that she has them under her observation. After a while, she daringly calls out to them.*)

9. Unless indicated otherwise, this and all other quotations from Takamura's Chieko poems in this play are from *Chieko's Sky*, trans. Soichi Furuta (Tokyo: Kodansha International, 1978).

10. Cape Inubō is a scenic spot located near Chōshi city in Chiba Prefecture. *Inu* is the Japanese word for "dog."

IMAGAWA BUN SELLER: Hey guv'nor, are you from Tokyo? (*To passersby.*) Guv'nor, guv'nor—this is the way we address people around here. There's no one who doesn't know me, and that means there's no one I don't know, either. The two of you there, guv'nor, don't try double suicide. It's no use trying to hide it. I can see it in people. They all say the same thing. That they have no such intention. . . . But I can see through any faking. In Cape Inubō I teach little children how to read and write. I also take care of all the dogs. In this area when kids and dogs see me, they come up to me. (*A dog passing by runs off quickly.*)

IMAGAWA BUN SELLER: Huh? Are you going back already? I haven't finished talking. Where are you staying? The Gyōkeikan? In that case, I can show you a shortcut. Aren't you lucky? Come along, this way. This route is faster. Huh? You can see it from here? Trust me. Oh, that's right. Yeah, My studio is nearby. I guess I hadn't told you that I'm an artist. Come on by. (*Enters.*) I built this studio. This is the kitchen. (*She keeps glancing at the walls.*) What? You noticed? I drew all these pictures. Those are haiku by the pictures. Can you read them? My brushstrokes are stylized. Hey, guv'nor, guv'nor! You should know, this is my studio. It's not a thoroughfare. You like this place. You really like this place . . . (*She sighs as if this is a problem.*) This is a problem. Everyone wants my artwork . . . I pretended not to know who you are, but I do. You're Takamura Kōtarō, aren't you. I've seen you somewhere, too. Don't worry, I have no interest in gossip. I'm an artist. Mr. Takamura, you've contributed some poems to a literary magazine recently. They weren't so hot. (*Reads in a sugary voice.*) "I don't like your going away??" Writing stuff like that, you're such a little rich boy. I would write, "If you act like a little rich boy, I'll become someone else's darling." An artist would understand what I mean, right guv'nor?

(*The* IMAGAWA BUN SELLER *exits upstage and enters as* CHIEKO.)

CHIEKO: That Imagawa bun seller at Cape Inubō. She was funny, wasn't she, Kōtarō? She was making out that she was an artist, but she was the epitome of the worldly wise. She lives in a totally different world from us. Why do people become like that? The biddy's studio was like a road. Some old men going home from a drinking party passed through one by one as if it were a thoroughfare. They went through, though they had not been invited. Didn't you think that was weird? The long line continued as if the old men were emerging from their graves in the ocean. The long row of elders marched in a wide circle then seemed to go back to the watery burial site. The presents they got at the party looked like gifts for the dead. Watching them it was easy to understand that life is only about birth, living and dying. They were like that. But we will never become like them. We have nothing to do with the march of the dead heading for their final resting place.

(*The sound of a radio is heard, and one radio appears in the darkness.*)

RADIO: For the past five days, the Japanese flag has been lowered to half mast in honor of the death of the Meiji emperor. Stage performances and music have been forbidden until noon today. Entertainment districts have also been voluntarily closed for the past five days. This evening when the state funeral and the period of national mourning are to end, an incident symbolic of the nation's love for the emperor has occurred. General Nogi Maresuke committed suicide in honor of our ruler. Together with his wife, he followed the emperor in death. It is an extremely painful act yet to be celebrated as an expression of the Yamato spirit . . . (*Sound of static.*) . . .

When the whole nation is in mourning, "Is this 'Love at a Beautiful Seashore'" scandal permissible? According to the woman owner of an Imagawa bun shop in that locale, "The beautiful woman seemed so young and lovable. I wondered where she could be going, at which point I noticed a young man walking down from the top of the cape. Their eyes met, and joining hands, they walked off to the inn by the seashore. I intuitively knew who they were . . . Guv'nor!" This couple were none other than Takamura Kōtarō, the son of the renowned sculptor Takamura Kōun,[11] and Naganuma Chieko, the woman painter and Bluestockings Society member.

SCENE 10. THE SECULAR WORLD

Seven years have passed.

CHIEKO: Seki, what are you going to do? You are pregnant, you miserable girl. What's worse, this Komiya guy has a wife and kids, right. Why did you act as if you're in a cheap love story? He may be a disciple of Natsume Sōseki,[12] but he is a notorious playboy. I won't forgive you. Break up with him. If you promise to terminate your relationship with him, I'll put in a good word for you at the women's college so that you can become a foreign exchange student at Harvard University. But breaking up with Komiya is the condition. What are you saying? When you are young, an artist without any income seems to shine brilliantly. It's almost as if not drawing an income is a sign of talent. But that's only when you are young. Unlike real artists, the fake ones soon show their true colors. They lose out to the poverty of life. Huh? The dog . . . ?! What's that about? The dog . . . ?! What about it? What? I don't follow. Why are you saying that? What you're saying is beyond me . . . Footloose and fancy-free? Who is? I am? Look, I'm married to Kōtarō. As artists, we acknowledge each other's talents and cherish each other in this conjugal relationship and . . . Huh? Secret? I don't hide anything from him. But I don't want to burden him with your problems, you know. I don't want to soil our pure artistic life together with the odors of the secular world. Oh come on, I can tell him whenever I want. Kōtarō and I are leading a liberated life

11. Takamura Kōun (1852–1934) was a sculptor and the father of Kōtarō.

12. Natsume Sōseki (1867–1916) was best known for his novels *Kokoro* and *I Am a Cat* (*Wagahai wa neko de aru*) and is considered to be the foremost Japanese novelist of the Meiji era (1868–1912).

style. . . . Hi, Kōtarō. Huh? I'm not scolding her. We're just exchanging views. Seki wants to study at Harvard. Huh? There's no particular reason, right Seki? You don't have any major problems, right? You look healthy. If anything you've gained weight. Well, out with it. Is there a special man in your life? Of course I think it's all right. Whoever it is, as long as you like him. You know, Seki . . . Oh really, Kōtarō. You shouldn't praise your own wife like that. You feel grateful? Don't be silly. I am content with this life. I'm proud of it.

(*Saying that,* CHIEKO *sets the meal on the table. It is indeed a poverty-stricken dinner. Sliced cabbage is piled up on all the dishes. Sitting at the table,* KŌTARŌ *recites a poem.*)

KŌTARŌ:

drenched
in a heavy downpour driven by storm
I bought a pound of rice
that cost me 24½ cents
five dried mackerel
a piece of salted radish
red pickled ginger
eggs from the chicken coops
dried laver like hammered steel
fried fish cakes
soused bonitos
scalding water
we devour our supper like hungry demons
. . .
our supper
bears a more violent force than the storm
our after-supper fatigue
awakens in us a strange carnal passion
makes us marvel at our whole bodies
flaming up in the downpour
this is our supper, the supper of the poor

("SUPPER," FROM *CHIEKO'S SKY*)

CHIEKO: Fantastic. With your power of expression, any and every dinner table will become plentiful. Huh? Of course not, Seki. I'm full now. "Is this all you eat every day?" What are you saying? This is our supper. What? Don't talk about the family. It's all right, Kōtarō. The Naganumas are as well-off as usual. Stop talking about our kid brother, Seki. He's prone to dissipation, but when he reaches the appropriate age, he'll become the head of the family. It's all right, Kōtarō, you don't have to worry about such things . . . uh-huh, go ahead with your work upstairs.

(*Her attitude indicates that she is watching* KŌTARŌ *climb up the stairs to his studio.*)

Seki, you talk too much. What if Kōtarō picks up on what's happening? Now don't tell him that our family business is on the decline. It's embarrassing. Huh? I have never considered this lifestyle poverty-stricken. Whenever Kōtarō finishes a poem or a sculpture, he happily calls out "Chie, Chie" and shows me his artwork. That look of happiness on his face is. . . . Ahh, yes, just as I said.

(CHIEKO'*s attitude indicates that she is watching* KŌTARŌ *come down the stairs. He is carrying a sculpture called "catfish." She reads.*)

. . .

catfish!
even if we run out of coals for the fireplace,
would you rather be devouring some enormous dream beneath the ice?
the chips of cypress wood are my kin
Chieko is not afraid of poverty.
catfish!

("CATFISH," FROM *CHIEKO'S SKY*)

CHIEKO: Do you understand, Seki? (*With the unfinished piece "catfish" in her hands.*) Just as Kōtarō writes, I must not be so poor of heart as to be fearful of poverty. (*The radio comes on.*)

RADIO: Today, the sixth, the whole nation arose in celebration of the Taishō emperor's enthronement. When the emperor left the gate of the Imperial Palace on an official visit to Kyoto, the grassy plot in front of Nijū Bridge was reserved for students gathered to give the emperor a rousing send-off. The road between Nijū Bridge and Tokyo Station was filled with crowds of men and women who wanted to see the ceremonial parade. Convertible streetcars decked with flowers drove through the streets of Tokyo, and a portable shrine was carried around with much fanfare . . . (*Static.*) . . . .

Is a scandal permissible when the whole nation is in celebration over the emperor's enthronement? The pregnancy of Hiratsuka Raichō, the head of the Bluestockings Society, has been confirmed. In the face of reports of her pregnancy during her cohabitation with her younger lover, Okumura Hiroshi,[13] she declared, "I will never become pregnant." However, this time she confessed that "I have come face to face with the difficult problem of bearing and caring for a child."

Raichō is undeniably pregnant; Harada Satsuki[14] is giving birth in July; and Odake Kazue[15] is to be a mother soon. Bluestockings, the supposed home to the "new woman" (of Japan), is in the family way.

---

13. Okumura Hiroshi (1891–1964) was a Western-style painter and jewelry designer and the husband of Hiratsuka Raichō.
14. Harada Satsuki (1887–1933) was a novelist whose best-known work is *To a Man from a Woman in Prison* (*Gokuchu no onna yori otoko ni*, 1915).
15. Odake Kazue (1892–1966) was a painter, journalist, and member of the Bluestockings Society for nine months until she fell ill.

(*Against the background of the radio broadcast,* CHIEKO *is scolding Seki, who has returned from Harvard.*)

CHIEKO: I told you a thousand times to break up with him. What are you going to do, Seki? I put in a good word for you at the women's college so that you were able to go to Harvard. But you corresponded with Komiya all the time and hardly did any study at all in the United States. You ended up in debt and told the creditors that when Kōtarō's father visited, he would pay up. That's called fraud. Why did you abuse the good name of Takamura? I never said that. How could I say such a thing to Kōtarō? Now pay attention. You keep your mouth shut. I'll take care of this. . . . I don't know. Keisuke? Mother goes on too much about how he's the eldest son . . . Seki, leave well alone, OK? You mustn't tell Kōtarō about that, either. I'll take care of this. . . . Mother, I'll take care of this. I'll take care of this. I'll take care of this. I have to take care of this. In his poems, I'm not like this at all.

(*She goes to another spot and lies down.*)

Huh? Er, sorry. Kōtarō? This has come at a busy time for you. It's all right. I'm suffering from water retention in the pleura. It's a case of pleurisy. Huh? You've finished the pamphlet? . . . Customers can buy your sculptures regularly, then. It's a distribution system for sculpture. It's a great idea. You create what you want to make and buyers purchase only what they want. With that income, you can open your one-man show in New York. It's an artist's dream. You don't have to cater to popular demand. Huh? What do you mean? . . . I see, if that's what you want, that might be better for my health, too. You'll go with me, right? I'll go back to my parents for a while. To where I can see Mount Atatara.

SCENE 11. BIRTHPLACE AND THE MINISTRY OF EDUCATION ART EXHIBITION

that's Mount Atatara,
that glistening there the River Abukuma.

as we sit quietly like this,
only the rustle of pine trees from long ago
blows dim-green through our somnolent heads.
let's stop hiding from that white cloud that looks down
on the joy of holding hands, burning quietly
amid these vast fields and mountains of early winter.
. . .

that's Mount Atatara,
that glistening there the River Abukuma.
this is your birthplace,
. . .

("BENEATH THE TREES," FROM *CHIEKO'S SKY.*)

CHIEKO: I'm glad I came back. Looking at this mountain cheers me up. Kōtarō, you don't look so good. Huh? So what? Who cares about a mishap like that? Everyone acknowledges the worth of your art. It's just that the distribution system didn't work out. It's too bad. We are artists. We can't expect making money to be easy for us. Huh? Why are you looking at that? I just painted it for kicks. Huh? . . . Have I shown you my paintings? Haven't I? I didn't realize that. Just that one time right, when we first met, I showed you the cover design for the *Bluestockings* journal. It's the first time since then, I guess. Eh? For the Ministry of Education Art exhibition? This? Impossible. It's just a practice piece. It won't ever pass. You think so? You think the sketching is well done? Really? A winner? Eh? No, no, it would never win special honors. Impossible . . . OK. I'll do it. The Ministry of Education Art exhibition. I don't even have to be accepted. But I will submit the piece, because you praise it to the skies.

SCENE 12. REJECTED

CHIEKO, *out of breath, enters running as if she has just arrived.*

CHIEKO: Special honors: Takamura Chieko, Takamura Chieko, Takamura Chieko. (*Appears to be resigned at not finding her name.*) Special honors, second level: Takamura Chieko, Takamura Chieko, Takamura Chieko. (*Searches for her name but cannot find it.*) Honorable mention: Yoshio Takai, Takagi Kazunori, Takagi Kaede, Takada Seiton, Takahashi Akio, Taka . . .
(*She goes home.*)

(*Reaching home, she speaks extremely brightly.*) I'm back. Oh, were you waiting for me. Kōtarō. Huh? It didn't work out. Too bad for me. Don't worry. I didn't expect anything to begin with. . . . Thank you. That's right. I'm content with your praise of my sketches. Yes, that's right. I know. It doesn't mean that the best is always recognized. After all, I hadn't tried all my might to make a fine painting. It's just one of the many I painted when I was back at the old home, so rejection is a matter of course. That's right. I'll take up the challenge again. There's next year and the year after that. If

I were a winner the first time round, I'd turn into an insufferable brag. I'll paint again. I can always paint again . . .

(*She stands in front of the canvas. She holds a brush.*)

What is it, Kōtarō? "Chie, Chie." I can hear you calling me again. Have you finished an art piece? Eh? A sculpture? Or is it a poem today? Uh-huh, it's OK. This is a good time for me to take a break, too. Show me. I'd like to read it.

(*She reads.*)

when women cast off accessories one by one
why is it they become so beautiful?
. . .
when you stand in silence
you are indeed a creature of God.
now and then I am secretly amazed that
you get prettier and prettier.

("YOU GET PRETTIER AND PRETTIER," FROM *CHIEKO'S SKY*)

CHIEKO: Thank you. It's not as if I'm throwing out accessories out of my own choice . . . Huh? You have another poem?

(*She reads.*)

my dearest other half
possessing all my trust
sharing the innermost torment of my flesh
. . .
you were born for me
You are mine
I have you I have you

("WELLSPRING OF LIFE")

CHIEKO: Thank you. I was born for you. . . . Huh? There's more?

(*She reads.*)

I feel my own pain as if it were yours
I feel my own pleasure as if it were yours.
I rely upon you just as myself
I feel my own growth as your growth
I believe I'll never leave you behind
No matter how fast I walk, and feel easy

("US," FROM *CHIEKO'S SKY*)

CHIEKO: This is me. Right, I'll do my best. This is who I am.

SCENE 13. A YOUNG WOMAN MODEL

MAID: Chieko's pride had been severely damaged by the art exhibition's rejection. What about the effect of Kōtarō's poetry? "I believe I'll never leave you behind / No matter how fast I walk, and feel easy"... had the impact of a heavy body blow. Wasn't Kōtarō being rough with her? The fear she had not felt until then, that she might very well be left behind by him, arose in her mind. It was just then that the other incident happened.... I cannot forget that day Chieko shared with me.

(*Concerned about the studio upstairs,* CHIEKO *cannot stop looking that way. She realizes that the* MAID *has noticed her concern.*)

CHIEKO: Ohh, you've caught me peeping. Why don't you sit down.... What do you think? I know that his sex drive is stronger than most men's. "Woman is aflame with lust. I am aflame with lust. Together we blaze with desire. We burn like geothermal fires...." That sex-crazed man is upstairs with a young naked female model every day. The model's a seventeen-year-old named Yuriko. He's left out from the *Chieko's Sky* collection his poems about lust. The words he doesn't want people to know, the words that don't sell, he keeps locked up in his drawer. Now listen, you mustn't blab about this, if you're a faithful maid...

(*Saying that,* CHIEKO *sneaks* KŌTARŌ*'s journal out of the desk drawer and surreptitiously reads it, just as the* MAID *had done before.*)

Here it is. He's been pretending to write poems only for me.

A seventeen-year-old girl
Strips off her clothes as soon as she arrives
Ah what a lovely creature of early May
With the easy freedom of nature,
Like a wild hare
Its ears stand up as it crouches down on a platform
...
Ahh, as Rodin wrote in his journal
"nothing can replace youth"
The youth of all phenomena
The youth of humankind
The eternal youth that lurks in art
...
Taking some clay in my hand,
My heart trembling with an exaltation close to envy,
At the body of a seventeen-year-old that moves like a living hare
I gaze as if to devour it
I gaze at it.

He gazes as if to devour it. That man is even now gazing as if to swallow a seventeen-year-old.

(*Saying so,* CHIEKO *sneaks upstairs and listens outside* KŌTARŌ*'s studio. He does not come out for a long time.* CHIEKO *descends and whispers to the* MAID.)

Never mind. Just shout out his name in an extra loud voice. Just do as you're told. You are in my employ, aren't you!

MAID: Yes. Master! Master!

(CHIEKO *peeks into the back. Upset by the premonition that* KŌTARŌ *will come, she sits down where she is and pretends to be mad.*)

MAID: I saw everything. From the viewpoint closest to Chieko. I saw her for the first time acting mad just to attract Kōtarō's attention. She was not crazy from the beginning. She only pretended to be. That's what I believe.

CHIEKO: I'm all right. I'll pull myself together. I'm the wife of an artist. I am an artist. I should do some oil painting.

SCENE 14. THE COLLAPSE OF THE NAGANUMA FAMILY BUSINESS AND FOUR DEATHS

TELEGRAM 1: Father died.

TELEGRAM 2: Chiyo died.

TELEGRAM 3: Grandmother died.

TELEGRAM 4: Mitsu died.

(CHIEKO *reads the telegrams and picks up her brush again. An announcement from the radio comes on.*)

RADIO (*Despite the static, some information can be discerned*): A fire started in Twin Pines, Fukushima Prefecture, and burned down the southeastern part of the district.

CHIEKO: Keisuke, you are the eldest son of the Naganuma family. You are hopeless. You can't be overwhelmed by a fire. I cannot afford to be called back home each time there is an emergency.

(*The radio comes on.*)

RADIO: Today before noon, a great earthquake hit Tokyo. The damage is extensive. Tokyo now looks like a vision of hell.

CHIEKO: Mother, I'm going to go back to Tokyo. Huh? Don't depend on me so much.... You want Kōtarō to sell liquor? He's not the right person for business. Show me the ledger. Half the customers are getting their liquor free. Your way of doing business is just like Keisuke's. I, I'll take care of this.

SCENE 15. CHIEKO SWITCHES FROM OILS TO WEAVING

CHIEKO *decisively breaks her brush. She starts to weave.*

CHIEKO: It's all right. You don't have to worry about anything. I can't stay focused on oil painting. Weaving I've enjoyed since childhood. In addition, textiles sell. Huh? You've written another poem. . . . That's wonderful.
(*She reads.*)
—in silence, I handle clay.
—rattling the loom, Chieko weaves.
—a mouse runs for a peanut dropped on the floor.
—a sparrow snatches it away from him.
. . .

("KINDS COHABITING," FROM *CHIEKO'S SKY*.)

MAID: . . . I'm only a maid, but I got angry with Kōtarō's optimistic poetry. For the first time I talked to Chieko of my own accord. . . . Hey, Mrs. Chieko, the master is a selfish beggar. He has you weave while he kneads clay in silence. The only ones who weave and really suffer in this world are you and the crane. Why do his poems always order you about?
(*She reads.*)
do not let the clay in the workshop freeze
Chieko
however empty the kitchen is in the evening
do not forget to stoke up the coals in the fireplace
should the blankets in the bedroom be thin
pile cushions over them.
do not let the clay in the workshop freeze
in the cold dawn.
. . .
Even if New Year's should feel hollow
Chieko
do not forget to stoke up the coals in the fireplace

MAID: Shit, this is, you know. . . . Hey. Before you tell the missus what to do, why don't you shovel some coal yourself. (*To* CHIEKO.) Aren't you getting the raw end of the deal? Even if he writes beautiful poetry about you, your life is sucked into his. He's the one that's developing and growing, and once he reaches the top, he'll leave you and go on, on his own. Aren't you afraid of that? That's why I'm raving and ranting for you. Challenging the beauty of *Chieko's Sky*, I'll take up arms against that poetry and spit out some vulgarities. The job of a maid is like that. We wash, clean, take out the garbage, scrub the toilets; we take care of the lowest level of living. What you didn't want to do since childhood, I've been covering for you. But the day Chieko had to say what had to be said, what should happen? She indeed spoke up.

SCENE 16. THE BANKRUPTCY OF CHIEKO'S FAMILY AND OF HER PRIDE

CHIEKO: . . . (*She has turned pale from the notice she has received.*) Kōtarō, I'm sorry I didn't tell you earlier. My family has gone bankrupt.

(*The sounds of an auction can be heard. The furniture on stage is sold off piece by piece. From the radio, the news of the death of the Taishō emperor is heard. That radio, too, is carted off.*)

MAID: . . . The name and prosperity of her own family line was the one advantage Chieko had over her husband. When the family business went bankrupt, her pride collapsed.

SCENE 17. SCOLDING HER MOTHER

CHIEKO *is writing a letter to her mother.*

CHIEKO: Mother, it's no good going on and on. I won't help you this time. If you just complain and don't take responsibility for your own affairs, you can't make it in this world. You should be troubled by your own problems. A woman who has no assets or vocation—what right does she have to ask for financial support? "A woman who has no assets or vocation" —that's what I have been reduced to. It doesn't matter how many years I study, I can't produce a single painting. What's the difference between that Imagawa bun seller of long ago and me? That biddy I laughed at claimed to be an artist . . . No, I don't sell Imagawa buns . . . but I do weave . . . No. In my mind a kaleidoscope of colors and images are swirling around. But when I face the canvas, I become afraid of mixing and placing colors . . . Do you know why? Why are you silent? . . . Kōtarō would always praise my sketches . . . He would . . . But . . . but . . . what? . . . He never praised the colors I used . . . So you knew. My emerald green and Kōtarō's green sun were totally different. His was merely theoretical. My colors were a true reflection of what I saw . . . No. It can't be that he and I were looking at different things. I have to be the Chieko he writes poems about—Chieko, the concentric circle. I have to be a woman who, unsurprised by poverty, "casts off accessories one by one" and "becomes prettier and prettier." I have to follow without getting left behind. I'm losing it fast. Look after me well, OK. I'm afraid. I'm afraid I'll disappear if I'm not looked after . . . I'm afraid, I'm afraid. . . . What? (*Notices* KŌTARŌ.) What is it?

Right . . . I was talking to myself again? Sometimes I was talking in the Fukushima dialect? . . . I'm probably still upset over my mother's pleading for a loan. But I'm all right now. I feel well. When I've spat out my thoughts, I feel better. I'll rewrite my letter to my mother.

(*Pushing her bicycle, she goes down the hill.*)

Mother, Yesterday we both were sad. But you must never be defeated by worldly fate. We must not die. We must live. We must do our best to live. See, Mother, right now, we must stick with it till we keel over—all of us together. I will do my best this summer. I will, I shall. Until I fall down. If that is not enough, then we all will crumble together.

(*The bicycle falls over by itself.*)

I was the one who fell over. A year later, I attempted suicide.

SCENE 18. THE VOICE OF MADNESS

CHIEKO: Huh? Where are you going, Kōtarō? To the Sanriku District? You're going to go from the Kitagami River to the seacoast and float on the triangular waves? You want to feel the swinging of the ocean. Huh? You're going to be away for a whole month? Alone? That's all right. It's come up quite suddenly, hasn't it? . . . No? You've wanted to go off on your own for the past year? . . . What? I'll be OK . . . I won't be . . . I mean it's just a month, right? It'll pass in a flash. What? I could paint while you're away? As a change of pace? I suppose. You're right, Kōtarō. Painting might be more restful than medication. I'll give it a try. . . . How can I possibly paint? It was what I most wanted but couldn't do. Why does Kōtarō push me in that direction now? There's no way I can paint. I'll tell him. There's no way I can paint. There's no way I can paint.

(CHIEKO, *maid-like, plants herself in front of* KŌTARŌ *confrontationally. But gradually* CHIEKO *transforms back into her usual self.*)

You know, when you return, let's visit Ueno and Asakusa together. They were my old haunts when I was gloating over becoming an artist. When I was vibrant and designed the cover page of the *Bluestockings* journal . . . What? Has Kōtarō left already?

(*In the silence,* CHIEKO *positions her easel.*)

How many days have passed since Kōtarō left on his northeastern journey? (*Facing the canvas.*) . . . There's no way I can paint. You don't have a flair for color. You're no good. You're no good. . . . The sun is going down. . . . It's already dusk. You don't have a sense of color. You're no good. You're no good. You'll die soon. . . . I'm simply exhausted. I want a deep, deep sleep. I'd like to travel to the celestial country.

(*She takes some Adalin sleeping pills.*)

SCENE 19. AN AVALANCHE OF MADNESS

CHIEKO (*In a Fukushima accent*): When I came to, I was there. The me that has always served Chieko . . . Huh? What do you think you're saying? I was always doing the talking. It's true. I was talking in the Fukushima dialect . . . What's happening? Where am I? You can build a fence, but it's easy to clear. Fences are for climbing over, easy-peasy. Kōtarō, I know. You can't get your work done because you have to take care of me. I know . . . Serves you right . . . Serves you right . . . Serves you right. I'm saying it serves you right, Kōtarō! I was underwater until now.

(*Shaking herself.*) Citizens of Tokyo, gather here! Collect in front of me! You know full well that it's rude to stare at me and grin like that. The emperor is ill! Subjects and citizens of this nation. Gather here! War is about to begin. How dare you grin at me. Serves you right. Serves you right! Serves you right! Kōtarō! Kōtarō! Kōtarō. Kōtarō. Kōtarō. Kōtarō, Kōtarō. (*Toning down a bit, she looks for* KŌTARŌ.) Kōtarō. Kōtarō. Chieko? Kōtarō? Chieko? Kōtarō? Chieko? Kōtarō? Aren't the two of you coming out here? Where have they gone? Huh? . . . (*Looking hard and long.*) You are? Really? Ahh, Kōtarō! Kōtarō, right. (*She has become childlike. She is being led by* KŌTARŌ.) Where are you taking me? If you say so, that might be better. Oh that's right. This is the same as coming down with pleurisy and going to Mount Atatara? I enjoyed it. I enjoyed that time. I enjoyed it.

(CHIEKO *enters a hospital room.*)

Hey where's Kōtarō? He's coming back? Where'd he go? . . . I see. I'll wait for him here.

(*Quiet.*)

The day after I entered the hospital, I gave up on Kōtarō, and having lost my ticket back to the human world, I started making paper-cut pictures—Luscious red and ripe persimmons; gentle, delicate wild flowers; insects lovingly detailed— I conjured up an innocent world as if I was opening a box of caramels in front of my very eyes. I had only myself to face, and embracing myself gently, the drama of my life in this world came to an end.

SCENE 20. DEATH

A screaming figure in the hospital, CHIEKO *is reading out loud* KŌTARŌ*'s journal. Mad words stream from her mouth.*

CHIEKO: Citizens of Tokyo, gather here! I went to the hospital and saw Chieko after a period of five months. Her condition was not good, and she has weakened a great deal. . . . I saw Chieko after five months. I saw Chieko after five months. I saw Chieko after five months. Kōtarō, who used to travel all the way to distant Kujūkuri Beach once a week, did not visit Chieko at her hospital, near Minami-Shinagawa in Tokyo, for five whole months. *Chieko's Sky,* famous as an unusual love story told in verse, was written by a man who, at the end, abandoned his wife in a hospital for five months. Citizens of Tokyo! This is a protest against *Chieko's Sky.* During those five months, Kōtarō started a correspondence with a woman poet. To a woman Chieko knew nothing of, he sent his writing about his wife. Citizens of Tokyo! To add insult to injury, Chieko was fed the apples that the woman poet sent him in consolation for his suffering. Chieko, in other words I, die in front of Kōtarō who visited after five months. Nonetheless, according to this poet, even I, miserable as I am, die a beautiful death.

you had yearned for a lemon so long
your clean teeth bit fresh
into the lemon taken from my hands
on a sad white light bed of death
a topaz-colored scent arose
a few drops of heavenly lemon juice
suddenly restored lucidity
your blue limpid eyes smiled a little
how healthy your strength was gripping my hands
though there was a storm in your throat
on such a brink of life as this
Chieko became the Chieko of long before
and drained a lifelong love in one moment
then for an instant
drawing a deep breath as once you did
on a mountain top long long ago
your organ stopped
behind a vase of cherry blossoms in front of your picture
today I shall place a cool shining lemon again

("LEMON ELEGY," FROM *CHIEKO'S SKY*)

Will I be able to die so elegantly? On the brink of death, I have to be in love. For a moment I regained my senses and stared at Kōtarō. Smiling slightly I gave one deep breath.

(CHIEKO *closes her eyes. At the same moment, the radio begins to blare out a series of news items from the beginning of World War II to the Imperial Rescript on Surrender. The relationship between* CHIEKO *and* KŌTARŌ *may have been analogous to that of the people and the emperor. Slow fade-out.*)

CURTAIN

Hirata Oriza, *Tokyo Notes*, directed by Hirata Oriza, Seinendan, March 1998.
(Photograph by Aoki Tsukasa)

TOKYO NOTES

HIRATA ORIZA

TRANSLATED BY M. CODY POULTON

Born in Tokyo in 1962, Hirata Oriza is one of Japan's leading playwrights and directors. His first book was an account of an around-the-world trip he made by bicycle while still a high-school student. He began writing plays for his theater company, Seinendan, in his first year at International Christian University, and as an undergraduate, he spent a year in Korea in the 1980s, signaling an abiding interest in Korean language and culture that began long before it became fashionable in Japan. His sympathies for the Korean people are reflected in his first major play, *Citizens of Seoul* (*Seoul shimin*, 1991), which is set in 1910, the year of Korea's annexation by Japan. With its restrained focus on the everyday lives and conversations of ordinary people, this work was one of the first of what critics called the "quiet dramas" (*shizuka na geki*), which marked a shift in the 1990s away from the boisterous and festive nature of 1980s Japanese theater toward a new, sober realism. Hirata, however, prefers to call his new dramatic style "contemporary colloquial theater." Since the early 1990s, Hirata's plays have been performed abroad, and many of his works have been translated into several foreign languages. He has also collaborated with Korean, Chinese, French, and Belgian directors and theater companies in productions of his work. A prolific writer and critic of contemporary social problems and cultural policy, Hirata also has been active in academic and political spheres.

As its title suggests, the play excerpted here, his most famous work (it was awarded the Kishida Kunio Award in 1995) is an homage to Ozu Yasujirō's classic film *Tokyo Story* (*Tōkyō monogatari*, 1953), about an elderly couple who go to Tokyo to visit their children. Like Ozu, Hirata is interested in the dissolution of the Japanese family, traditionally considered the microcosm of Japanese society as a whole. Here, however, the parents are absent, and we are presented with an awkward reunion of the children and their spouses in the lobby of a Tokyo art gallery that is exhibiting the works of Jan Vermeer, which have been rescued from a war-torn Europe. Written in 1994 but set ten years in the future, the work is a commentary on Japan's dubious role in international affairs. At the same time, like Vermeer's paintings, the work is both a manifesto and a wry critique of the realist impulse.

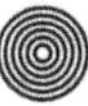

Characters

AKIYAMA SHINYA, the eldest of the Akiyamas
TOKIKO, Shinya's wife
YUMI, the second eldest
YŪJI, the third eldest
YOSHIE, YŪJI's wife
IKUE, the second youngest
SHIGEO, the youngest
HIRAYAMA EMIKO, curator
MITSUHASHI MIYUKI, donor of paintings
ONO KUNIKO, lawyer
SAITŌ YOSHIO, friend of MITSUHASHI's
KUSHIMOTO TERUO, curator
KINOSHITA TAKASHI
NOSAKA HARUKO
HASHIZUME MIKIO
TERANISHI RIKA
ISHIDA EISUKE
SUDA NAO
MIZUKAMI FUMIKO, college student
WAKITA YURIKO, college student

Note: The numbers assigned to each scene are guides for rehearsal and otherwise have no special function or meaning.

Time: May 2004.
Place: The lobby of an art gallery.

A corridor leads directly from stage left to the exhibition rooms. Upstage right is a staircase leading to a mezzanine. The staircase rises in the direction of stage left. The stage area is probably in one corner of the gallery building, a small space connecting the ground and second floors.

Three sofas (A, B, C), *seating three persons each, are arranged on the stage perpendicular to the audience. In this script, each seat is referred to as* 1, 2, 3, *starting from upstage. Farther upstage is another sofa* (D), *set parallel to the audience. The seats are referred to as* 1, 2, 3 *from stage right to stage left. Cylindrical ashtrays are set between seats* A3 *and* B3 *and between seats* C1 *and* D3. *Beside* D1 *is a wastepaper basket in a matching design and a magazine rack.*

Although not on stage, a toilet is located offstage down the corridor leading to the exhibition rooms. Apparently, there is a vending machine located at the top of the stairs.[1]

YOSHIE: You know Yuji won't buy any toys for Tarō with batteries.

YUMI: How come?

3.1.2

YOSHIE: If the toy needs batteries, then it stops working when the battery runs out, and then the kid won't play with it.

(ISHIDA, EISUKE, *and* SUDA NAO *enter from stage right.*)

YUMI: Ah.

YOSHIE: But kids like stuff that moves.

ISHIDA (*Entering*): Yeah, but—

YUMI: How old's Tarō? Three?

SUDA (*Entering*): Uh huh.

YOSHIE: Three and a half.

ISHIDA (*Entering*): But monks drink. They always have.

YUMI: Ah. Well, then.

SUDA (*Entering*): I know that.

YOSHIE: Yeah.

ISHIDA: So, it's not exactly a lie, right?

---

1. This scene starts at the end of 3.1.1, after a conversation in which Yumi tells her sister-in-law Yoshie about her father's aversion to battery-operated toothbrushes.

SUDA: Yeah, but it's too weird, that story.

(YOSHIE *moves to* A1.)

ISHIDA: You're getting kinda red, you know.

SUDA: Huh?

ISHIDA: In the face. (*Sits at* C3, *facing stage left.*)

SUDA: Naw.

ISHIDA: You been drinking?

SUDA: 'Course not. (*Sits at* B3.)

ISHIDA: Oh.

SUDA: What're you talking about? We've been together all along.

ISHIDA: You're, uh, getting redder and redder.

SUDA: Oh shut up.

ISHIDA: Beet red.

SUDA: Shut up I say.

ISHIDA (*To* YUMI): She's red, isn't she.

YUMI: A bit, I guess.

ISHIDA: There you go.

SUDA: You're embarrassing me.

YUMI: So, Tarō's in kindergarten already.

YOSHIE: Yep.

(*A long pause.*)

ISHIDA: Want a coffee?

YUMI: Did you see the photos? His entrance ceremony.

SUDA: No thanks.

ISHIDA: OK.

YOSHIE: Yeah.

YUMI: Dad was so excited, you know.

YOSHIE: Sorry for making him come all the way to Tokyo.

YUMI: No problem. He's not busy.

YOSHIE: Really.

YUMI: Really. Time flies, eh?

YOSHIE: Will you come again next year, Yumi?

YUMI: Yeah, well, probably.

YOSHIE: You'll be coming when? Around this time, May?
YUMI: Not sure. Maybe the summer.

YOSHIE: Ah.

YUMI: I'll come when the galleries are doing something good.

YOSHIE: Ah. I see.

YUMI: Why?

YOSHIE: Nothing special.

YUMI: What?

YOSHIE: Nothing. (*Looks at* SUDA.)
(*A long pause.*)

YOSHIE: Guess we'll be getting more pictures, eh. Lots of 'em.

YUMI: Uh huh.
(*A long pause.*)

YOSHIE: So long as Japan stays out of the war.

YUMI: Ah, yeah.

(ISHIDA *stands.*)

SUDA: Huh? You going?

ISHIDA: Just fooling. (*Sits.*)

SUDA: What're you doing?

ISHIDA: Nothin'. Not bad, eh? A place like this, for a change.

SUDA: Uh huh.

ISHIDA: You know, at night, I fly around in the plane, just looking. From the sky.

SUDA: Uh huh.

ISHIDA: It's pitch black, and all you can see are the searchlights going round and round.

SUDA (*Pausing*): You scared?
ISHIDA: Nah, not us.

SUDA: That so?

ISHIDA (*Twirling his arms around like searchlights*): Like this.
(*A long pause.*)
SUDA: What's that?
ISHIDA: The searchlights.

SUDA: Thought you were a snail for a sec.

ISHIDA: Na.

(*A long pause.*)

ISHIDA: Wouldn't say it was pretty, mind you.

SUDA: Hm.

ISHIDA: You know, Berlin. It's a big city.

SUDA: Uh huh.

ISHIDA: All pitch black. Like everyone was holding their breath.

SUDA: Ah.

ISHIDA: Dead quiet.

SUDA: Uh huh.

YOSHIE: I knew he was a crybaby, but I didn't know he hated corners.

ISHIDA: I fly round like this, just watching. But can't see anything, 'cause it's dark.

YUMI: Huh?

(*A long pause.*)

YOSHIE: Yuji. Being a crybaby.

ISHIDA: They say air raids are scary. If you're on the ground, that is.

YUMI: Oh.

SUDA: Oh—

(*A long pause.*)

(*A long pause.*)

YUMI: Something happen with you and Yuji?

SUDA: Let's go.

3.1.3

YOSHIE: No, we're fine.

ISHIDA: OK.

SUDA: . . .

ISHIDA (*Makes to stand*): What?

SUDA: Been sixty years exactly since Saint-Exupéry died, so I heard.

ISHIDA: Eh?

SUDA: Died in a plane over the Mediterranean, he did. In the war.

ISHIDA: Oh yeah. *Night Flight*, wasn't it? *Vol de nuit.*

SUDA (*Cutting in*): Read a lot about airplanes when you were away.

ISHIDA: *Vol de nuit*? or *Vol au vent*? Which was it now?

SUDA: "Love is to join, to share."

ISHIDA: What's that?

SUDA: That's what he said before he died.

ISHIDA: I ain't gonna die.

SUDA: . . .

ISHIDA: It's not like we're at war or anything.

SUDA: In that case, let me join you.

ISHIDA: . . .

SUDA: I'll join you.

ISHIDA: Sixty years?

SUDA: Uh huh.

ISHIDA: That's almost a life span.

SUDA (*Pausing briefly*): Uh huh.

ISHIDA (*A longer pause*): Sixty years, and humans aren't any better.

SUDA: . . .

ISHIDA: Dead loss, eh?

SUDA: Uh huh.

ISHIDA: Your face is red.

(*A long pause.*)

SUDA (*Stretches and lays her hands on* ISHIDA*'s lap*): A snail.

ISHIDA: Yup.

(SUDA *grinds her fists into his lap.*)

ISHIDA: Stoppit! That's an erogenous zone.

SUDA: Dummy.

(*A long pause.*)

SUDA: Let's go. (*Stands.*)

ISHIDA: OK. (*Pause. She also stands.*)

SUDA: Go to any art galleries in Berlin?

ISHIDA: Nope.

SUDA: How come?

ISHIDA (*Exiting*): There's a war on.

SUDA (*Exiting*): Didn't you just say you weren't at war?
ISHIDA (*Exiting*): Yeah, well, we're not fighting, but some folks are.
SUDA: Same thing, surely.
(*The two exit stage left.*)

3.2.1

A fifteen seconds' pause.

YOSHIE: I might not be able to see you next year, Yumi.
YUMI: Huh? How come?
YOSHIE: . . .
YUMI: Going somewhere, next year?
YOSHIE: I might not be able to see you again, ever.
YUMI: . . .
YOSHIE: He burst into tears the other day. Yūji.
YUMI: Huh?
YOSHIE: Said he'd fallen in love with another woman.
YUMI: Eh?—
YOSHIE: I was the one who wanted to cry.
YUMI (*Pausing*): Hm.
YOSHIE: I feel like my battery's run out.
YUMI (*Pausing*): But, there's Tarō to think about.
YOSHIE: . . .
YUMI: I'm really terrible these days. It's like I take pleasure in other people's misfortune.
YOSHIE: No, surely not.
YUMI: Oh well.
YOSHIE: I feel like I'm letting down your Mum and Dad.

YUMI: Hm?—
YOSHIE: They were so sweet to me.
YUMI: Don't you worry about my parents.
YOSHIE: No, I just can't help but thinking, what am I gonna say to them?
YUMI: Does Shinya know about this?
YOSHIE: No, I don't think so.
YUMI: That so?—
YOSHIE: I think—
YUMI: Uh huh.
(*A long pause.*)
YUMI: I'm feeling kind of hungry.
YOSHIE: Uh huh—
YUMI: You must be hungry too. You didn't have much for lunch.
YOSHIE: Yes.
YUMI: What d'you usually do for lunch?
YOSHIE: Uh, well—
YUMI: You eat alone, I bet.
YOSHIE: Well—yes.
YUMI: Aren't you lonely?
YOSHIE: I pack the lunches.
YUMI: Hm?—
YOSHIE: One for Yūji, one for Tarō, and one for myself.
YUMI: One for yourself too?
YOSHIE: Uh huh—
YUMI: To eat at home?
YOSHIE: Sometimes I go to the park.
YUMI: Ah—
YOSHIE: It's a nuisance making lunch just for yourself.
YUMI: Ah—
YOSHIE: Guess I'm just lazy.
YUMI: Um—
YOSHIE (*Pausing*): You know, we're a family, so it's better we all eat the same thing.
YUMI: Ah—

3.2.2

(IKUE *enters from stage right.*)

IKUE: I'm back.

YUMI: Ah—

YOSHIE (*Cutting in*): So, how was it?

IKUE: I've had my fill, I think.

YOSHIE: Uh huh.

IKUE: From now on, you can call me a connoisseur.

YUMI: A gourmand, more like it.

IKUE: Huh?—

YUMI: Gourmand. You know, food.

IKUE: Not.

YUMI: Shinya and the others are here.

IKUE: Yes, I saw them.

YUMI: Really—

IKUE: Said they'd be along in a minute. (*Sits at* A2.)

YUMI: Ah—

(*A long pause.*)

(HIRAYAMA *and* ONO *enter from stage right.*)

YUMI: What d'you do for lunch?

HIRAYAMA: Hey, they're gone.

IKUE: Never skip it.

ONO: Uh huh.

YUMI: D'you pack one, or eat out?

HIRAYAMA: Wonder where they got to.

IKUE: Depends—

ONO: Probably still looking at the pictures.

YOSHIE: A gourmand.

HIRAYAMA: Ah.

IKUE: Am not!

ONO: Shall we go this way?

YUMI: D'you mean you pack lunch sometimes?

HIRAYAMA: Ah, yes. (*Starts walking to stage left.*) Does Ms. Mitsuhashi like paintings?

IKUE: Guess I don't.

ONO: Well, I don't think she dislikes them. Why? You worried?

YUMI: Figures.

HIRAYAMA: No, not exactly, but . . .

IKUE: What I mean is, sometimes I eat out, sometimes in the company canteen.

(HIRAYAMA *and* ONO *exit stage left.*)

YUMI: The canteen can't be any good.
IKUE: It's not that bad, really.
YUMI: That so?
IKUE: It's quite good, actually. We have a lot of choice.
YOSHIE: What d'you do for lunch, Yumi?
YUMI: Me?
YOSHIE: Yeah—
YUMI: Well, I pack one, usually.
YOSHIE: Ah—
YUMI: You know, I used to make one for Dad, one for Shigeo, and one for myself. Three in all.
YOSHIE: Ah—
YUMI: Then, when Shigeo moved here, only had to make two. Whole lot easier.
YOSHIE: Uh huh—
YUMI: Shigeo and Dad have quite different tastes.
YOSHIE: Oh, I see.
YUMI: Uh huh.
IKUE (*Speaking at the same time as* YUMI): Dad likes oily stuff.
YOSHIE: Oh—
IKUE: Shigeo goes for something light.
YOSHIE: Surely it's the other way around.
IKUE: Uh uh, not our family.
YUMI: Yūji'll eat anything, right?
YOSHIE: Uh, yeah—
YUMI: Middle children aren't picky.
YOSHIE: Ah—
IKUE: That's right. I eat anything too.
YUMI: What about eggplants? You won't eat those.

IKUE: Ah—
YUMI: You eat 'em now?
IKUE: Well, it's not normal to eat eggplants.
YUMI: What're you talking about?
IKUE: Normal people don't eat purple food.
YUMI: You're too weird.
(*A long pause.*)
YUMI: So Shigeo moved to Tokyo, then Dad retired, so I figured I didn't have to make lunches anymore. It's like I was doing it for Dad and Shigeo, never for myself.
YOSHIE: But it wasn't like that, was it.
YUMI: No.
YOSHIE: Naturally.
YUMI: Still, I surprised myself.
YOSHIE: Hm?—
YUMI: I started fixing up some really fancy lunches. Just for myself.
IKUE: You always were a bit of a fuss-pot.
YOSHIE: She used to make lunches for you too, didn't she, Ikue.
IKUE: Not really. Mum was still in good shape then.
YOSHIE: That so.
IKUE: Uh huh—

3.3.1

(HIRAYAMA *and* ONO *return from stage right.*)

YUMI: That's right.
IKUE (*Cutting in*): Mum was fast. At cooking, anything.

ONO: Huh?

YUMI: I can be fast too, if I have to.

HIRAYAMA: They're not here—

IKUE: Hey, you never could do the dishes and the cooking at the same time.

ONO: They'll be back, I guess.

YUMI: Could so!
(*A long pause.*)

HIRAYAMA: Yes, well—

YOSHIE: I'm a lousy cook.

ONO: Well, let's wait then.

YUMI: Surely not.

HIRAYAMA: Yes—

YOSHIE: Really. I'm so disorganized.
YUMI: No kidding?

ONO: Sorry. (*Sits at* C3.)
HIRAYAMA: Don't mention it. (*Sits at* B3.)
ONO: Nice work.
HIRAYAMA: Huh?
ONO: I mean, you must like what you do.
HIRAYAMA: Yes, well—
ONO: Been here long?
HIRAYAMA: Ever since I got out of graduate school.
ONO: Ah. (*Pause.*) Do any painting yourself?

YOSHIE: Hey, Yumi, why don't you ask her, you know, about—?

HIRAYAMA: Uh, no, not at all.

YUMI: Huh?

ONO: Never tried?

YOSHIE: You know, what you said back there, when we were looking at the Vermeer.

HIRAYAMA: I just like looking at pictures.

YUMI: Ah—

ONO: Ah—

IKUE: What? What?

3.3.2

HIRAYAMA: I guess.
(*A long pause.*)

YOSHIE: I don't quite know how to explain it.

YUMI (*Cutting in*): Don't bother—

YOSHIE: You know, she's kind of technical, Yumi.

HIRAYAMA: What about you? D'you like pictures?

IKUE: Oh—

ONO: Uh, yes. Looking.

YUMI: Enough already—

YOSHIE (*To* HIRAYAMA): Uh, excuse me?
(*A long pause.*)

HIRAYAMA: Who, me?

YOSHIE: Yes—

HIRAYAMA: Yes?

YOSHIE: You work here, right?

HIRAYAMA: Yes.

YOSHIE: Is it OK to ask a question?

HIRAYAMA: Why, sure. Please.

YOSHIE: There you go—

YUMI: Yeah, but—

HIRAYAMA: Please. Not sure I can answer you, but—

YUMI: Um, well, is it true Vermeer had eleven kids?

HIRAYAMA: Huh?

YUMI: It's, uh, just something I read?

HIRAYAMA: Is that so?

YUMI: Yes—

IKUE (*Cutting in*): I'll say she's technical—

YOSHIE: That's not it—

HIRAYAMA: Sorry, but my specialty is contemporary art, so I'm not sure I can give you a good answer—

YUMI: Oh—

HIRAYAMA: I'm studying up on that right now. You know, Vermeer, etc.

YUMI: Uh, sorry.

HIRAYAMA: Not at all. We weren't expecting them. Fact is, I *am* a curator, I ought to be able to answer these questions.

YUMI: Ah. Lots of work for you, I guess.

HIRAYAMA: Yeah, well—

YOSHIE: Um, did they have cameras in those days?

HIRAYAMA: Huh?

YOSHIE: Cameras. Said on the plaque that they used them for painting.

HIRAYAMA: Oh, they weren't like our modern cameras. Just a lens, no film.

YOSHIE: Oh—

HIRAYAMA: As I say, I'm not an expert in this area, but I could call out somebody who is.

YUMI: No, please—

HIRAYAMA: There's a fellow called Kushimoto on staff who's an expert in that period. If you don't mind—

YUMI: No, really, please—

HIRAYAMA: Are you sure?

YUMI: Yes. (*Pause.*) But, they don't look like they were painted by somebody with eleven kids.

HIRAYAMA: Ah—

YUMI: They're supposed to be everyday scenes, but they seem strangely tranquil, don't you think?

HIRAYAMA: Now you mention it—

IKUE (*Cutting in*): Wow!

YUMI: Shut up.

HIRAYAMA: Not that I'm an expert—

YUMI: Uh huh—

HIRAYAMA: Did you notice the light from the windows?

YUMI: Yes—
HIRAYAMA: You can only see
the spots where the light strikes,
sort of highlighted.
YUMI: Yes.
HIRAYAMA: That's how he cuts out
the world, maybe. From everyday life.
YUMI: Ah—
HIRAYAMA: Everything else is
in shadow.
YUMI: Ah, yes—
HIRAYAMA: Anyway, that's my
impression.
YUMI: Ah hah.
IKUE: Cool!
YUMI: Shut up, will you?
YOSHIE: She was talking about
something more complicated earlier.
IKUE: Eh?—
HIRAYAMA (*Speaking at the same
time as* IKUE): And what was that?
YUMI (*Cutting in*): Was not.
YOSHIE: Some kind of drafting
method that transcended
photographic realism, something
like that.
IKUE: Wow!—
YUMI: Did not. I was reading it out
from the guidebook, surely.
(*A long pause.*)
HIRAYAMA: You're family?
YUMI: Uh, yes. This one's actually
my sister-in-law.
HIRAYAMA: Ah.
YUMI: Sorry for bothering you with
such strange talk.
HIRAYAMA: Not at all. I learned
a great deal.
YUMI: Not at all—

3.3.3

(YŪJI *returns from stage left.*)
YŪJI: Sorry to keep you waiting.
YUMI: Ah—
YOSHIE (*Cutting in*): Ah—
YŪJI: Shigeo not here?
YUMI: Not yet.
YOSHIE: What about Shinya and Tokiko?
YŪJI: Back in a sec. (*Sits at* D2.) Buying postcards.
(*A long pause.*)
YUMI (*To* HIRAYAMA): My brother.
HIRAYAMA: Ah—(*To* YŪJI.) Hello—
(YŪJI *nods.*)
YOSHIE (*Pausing briefly*): She was explaining the pictures.
YŪJI: Uh huh.
(HIRAYAMA *stands.*)
YUMI: Thank you very much.
HIRAYAMA: Not at all. (*Turns toward stage right.*)
YŪJI (*Pausing briefly*): How's Pop?

ONO: Well done.

YUMI: Well, Dad's fine, but Mum, you know—

HIRAYAMA: Not at all—

YŪJI: Ah—
YUMI: Her nerves.
YŪJI: Hm. Let's talk about that later.
YUMI: Really, we don't have to.
YŪJI: Why?
YUMI: We hardly ever have dinner together. You don't want to spoil it.
YŪJI: But surely we can't avoid the topic.
YUMI: Why not?

3.3.4

(SHINYA *and* TOKIKO *enter from stage left.*)

YŪJI: Ah!—

SHINYA: Shigeo not here?

YOSHIE: How was it?

YŪJI: Not yet—

TOKIKO: Good, I guess.

SHINYA: What's he up to?—

YOSHIE: Wasn't it.

YŪJI: No idea—

TOKIKO: Uh huh.

(YŪJI *stands and goes to* D1. SHINYA *and* TOKIKO *sit at* D2 *and* D3.)

YOSHIE: Good, eh? To look at pictures. Sometimes.
(HIRAYAMA *looks at* YUMI.)

YUMI: How're you and those corners now?

YŪJI: Huh?

YUMI: Corners. You're sitting in one.

YŪJI: Oh—

SHINYA: Now you mention it.

YŪJI: That was a long time ago.

YUMI: How 'bout Othello?

YŪJI: Nah, still can't stand the game.

IKUE: Hates dice, too.

YOSHIE: Oh—

YŪJI: Heard Mum's nerves are bad, eh?

HIRAYAMA: They're taking their time.

SHINYA: Yeah.

ONO: Uh huh.

YŪJI: You knew?

HIRAYAMA: You've got other things to do, I suppose.

SHINYA: Well, *we* went back at New Year's.

ONO: Not this afternoon. Nothing scheduled after this.

YŪJI: Oh, yeah—

HIRAYAMA: Ah.

YOSHIE: Sorry we didn't make it.
SHINYA: No, I didn't mean *that.*
YUMI: You're an only child, aren't you, Yoshie?—
YOSHIE: Yes, but (*To* TOKIKO) so are you. Right, Tokiko?
TOKIKO: Ah, but—
YOSHIE: Besides, my folks are in Tokyo.
SHINYA: You can make it this summer, can't you?
YŪJI: I guess.
SHINYA: Bring Tarō.
YŪJI: Yes.
YOSHIE (*Speaking at the same time*): Is Mum as bad as that?
YUMI: She's fine, really. Same as always.
YOSHIE: Really?
(*A long pause.*)
YUMI: Change the subject, shall we?
SHINYA (*Pausing briefly*): What subject was that?
YUMI: Nothing—
YŪJI (*Speaking at the same time*): We were talking about the folks. You know.
SHINYA: Oh—
YUMI: You know, we hardly ever see each other, like, so let's talk about something else.
YŪJI: Something else? Like what?
YUMI: Something fun. Like, where you went, what you saw.
YŪJI (*Pausing*): Nothing there. To talk about.
YUMI: Eh?—
YŪJI: Nothing's happening. Even in Tokyo.
YUMI: I'm not talking about Tokyo in particular—

SHINYA: Well, everybody's busy.
(*A long pause.*)
SHINYA: Kinda boring just talking about work.
YUMI: No, work's fine. Anything.

HIRAYAMA: Care for a coffee?

SHINYA (*Quickly*): That so?

ONO: Uh, no, I'm fine.

YUMI: Sure. We hardly ever see each other, so it's fine, isn't it? To talk about work, anything. Just so we know what everybody's up to.

HIRAYAMA: OK.

IKUE (*Quickly*): I write computer programs all day.
YUMI: Hm.
IKUE: That's it—
YUMI: . . .
YŪJI: Job, family, all the same, really—
YUMI: Is it, I wonder—
YŪJI: At least, when it comes to spoiling one's dinner.
IKUE: Sorry. We're not much of a family—
YOSHIE: No, really—
TOKIKO: But we envy you guys. Lots of brothers and sisters—
YOSHIE: Yes—
SHINYA (*Cutting in*): It's kinda hard to talk, you know, when you hardly ever see each other.
YŪJI: Yeah.
YOSHIE: No problem, really, if you talk only about fun stuff.
YUMI: Yeah.
YOSHIE (*Quickly*): If you just look at the spots where the light strikes.
YUMI: Ah—
IKUE: Everything else is pitch black.
YOSHIE: That's right.

IKUE: Is that what she meant earlier?
YOSHIE: No, something else, I think.
IKUE: Oh.
YOSHIE: Nothing.
SHINYA: What's all that about?

(YUMI *and* HIRAYAMA *exchange glances.*)

YUMI: Nothing.
YOSHIE: Yes.
(*A long pause.*)
YUMI: Ah, you know what? You should've seen Yoshie back there. Sneezed on the Vermeer.
YOSHIE: Not on the picture.
YUMI: Like this—"honk!"
YOSHIE: Did not!
YUMI: Isn't that how Yoshie sneezes? "Honk!"
YŪJI: Oh—
YOSHIE (*Cutting in*): Do not.
YUMI: What if you got spit on the picture?
HIRAYAMA: Ah, yes, well—
YUMI: That'd be awful, wouldn't it?

4.1.1

(KUSHIMOTO *enters from stage right.*)

HIRAYAMA: We haven't run into that problem before—
YUMI: Ah—

KUSHIMOTO: Huh, what're you up to?

(*A long pause.*)

HIRAYAMA: Ah, we were waiting for Ms. Mitsuhashi—

IKUE: Yumi, why don't you ask her something more decent?—

KUSHIMOTO: That heir to the collection, Ms. Mitsuhashi?

YUMI: Leave me alone. (*To* YOSHIE.) Right?

HIRAYAMA: Yes—

(YOSHIE *smiles.*)

KUSHIMOTO: So?

HIRAYAMA: So, no problem, really.

KUSHIMOTO: Look, the lawyers and tax accountants can be a bloody nuisance but you gotta play tough. The point is to make her donate the whole collection, lock, stock, and barrel.

HIRAYAMA: Uh, this is Ms. Ono. Their solicitor—

TOKIKO: Nice blouse.

KUSHIMOTO: O-oh—

YOSHIE: Think so?

ONO: Ono.

TOKIKO: Uh huh. Suits you.

KUSHIMOTO: Kushimoto. Curator.

YOSHIE: Thanks.

ONO: Hi.

HIRAYAMA: She was here when you came for me, remember?

KUSHIMOTO: Oh. Was she?

HIRAYAMA: Yes.

KUSHIMOTO: Play tough, eh?— (*Hits his own head.*) What the hell—

ONO: Easy does it.

KUSHIMOTO: Same to you—

HIRAYAMA: Uh, uh, excuse me, this is Kushimoto, the gentleman I mentioned?

YUMI: Oh—

HIRAYAMA: He's an expert in Dutch painting.

YUMI: Oh. Yes—

HIRAYAMA: Please, go ahead, ask him anything.

YUMI: Why, uh—

KUSHIMOTO: Can I help?

HIRAYAMA: Please—(*Urges* KUSHIMOTO *to sit down.*)

KUSHIMOTO: Well—(*Sits at* C1.)

HIRAYAMA: Please—

YUMI: Yes—

HIRAYAMA: She was asking about, uh, the camera obscura.

KUSHIMOTO: Ah—

HIRAYAMA: Nothing I know about.

YUMI (*Shifts in her seat to face stage right toward* KUSHIMOTO): Sorry.

KUSHIMOTO: Ah, not at all.

YUMI: . . .

KUSHIMOTO: So, what would you like to know?

YUMI: Uh, what should I say?

HIRAYAMA: The camera, tell her.

KUSHIMOTO: Ah, well. It's called a camera, but it's not like the cameras today, there's no film so, of course, no picture to develop.

YUMI: I see—

KUSHIMOTO: Just a box about this size—camera obscura means a dark box, y'see?—with a lens on front here, and you peer in here, and you can see the object here. The light comes in from this direction.

YUMI: . . .

KUSHIMOTO: Same as looking through the finder in our cameras. Twin lens reflex.

YUMI: But that's the same as just looking at it with the naked eye, surely.

KUSHIMOTO: Yes, but pictures make three-dimensional things two-dimensional, right?

YUMI: Yes—

KUSHIMOTO: So, the picture is distorted somewhat. Do you follow?

YUMI: Yes—
KUSHIMOTO: You project your picture through the lens, right? Then, what they did, I guess, was trace it.
YUMI: Oh, I see—
IKUE: Really, Yumi?
YUMI: Yes, I think so.
KUSHIMOTO: They could actually project images through the lens onto a flat surface, like a wall or a sheet of paper.
YUMI: Oh—
KUSHIMOTO: To look at things through a lens was really quite a feat in those days.
YUMI: . . .
KUSHIMOTO: The seventeenth century was, like, the beginning of the modern era. You had Galileo and his telescope, and the microscope, and, I mean, you could use a lens to look at things you couldn't see otherwise. All sorts of things, little things, the universe even. Well, that was the point of view on things—not like, say, God's perspective, but different. In any case, Holland was the center for the development of lenses back then. The Dutch philosopher Spinoza whiled away his time polishing lenses, speculating about God and the universe and all that. Just polishing his lenses like this, and when he looked through the lens it was like he could see the whole world. It was, well, rather a nice time to live, don't you think?

4.1.2

This section begins during KUSHIMOTO*'s speech, around "The Dutch philosopher Spinoza. . . ."*

(SHIGEO *enters from stage left during* KUSHIMOTO*'s speech.*)

TOKIKO: Ah, there you are!—

SHIGEO: Sorry—

SHINYA: Hey—

SHIGEO: Sorry I'm late.

TOKIKO: We just got here ourselves.

SHIGEO: Oh—

(*A pause.* KUSHIMOTO*'s speech ends.*)

YUMI: Well—

SHINYA: I see—

(*A pause. Everyone looks at* SHINYA.)

SHIGEO: Sorry I'm late.

YUMI: Sure are.

SHIGEO: Er—

IKUE (*Cutting in*): You're late! You're late!

SHIGEO: Sorry.

YUMI: We ate already. Full course, everything.

SHIGEO: You're kidding.

IKUE: Really! Really!

SHIGEO: What's with the girls? In a bad mood, eh?

(*There is nowhere for him to sit, so he seats himself on the wastepaper basket.*)

SHINYA: Well—I.

YUMI: What're you talking about? Girls—you sound like an old man.

IKUE: Old man!

SHIGEO: No, I'm not.

(KUSHIMOTO *looks at* HIRAYAMA, *who makes the V sign.* KUSHIMOTO *also makes the V sign back, but more modestly.*)

YUMI: Typical.

SHIGEO: I miss something?

YOSHIE: Not really.

ONO: Quite something, isn't he?

IKUE: Look at him! Always runs to Yoshie for help.

HIRAYAMA: Well, he is the expert, after all.

SHIGEO: Do not. Come off it.

ONO: Yes.

IKUE: Don't spoil him, now.

KUSHIMOTO: Not at all—

YOSHIE: I won't.

KUSHIMOTO: I'll go get some coffee.

SHIGEO: Why not?

HIRAYAMA: Ah, thanks.

SHINYA: Well. Shall we go?

KUSHIMOTO: Coffee OK?

SHIGEO: Going already?

ONO: Oh, uh, thanks.

SHINYA: After all, we were all waiting for you.

KUSHIMOTO: What about you, Hirayama?

SHIGEO: Sorry.

HIRAYAMA: Yes, please.

SHINYA: How's work?

KUSHIMOTO: Right then.
(IKUE *touches* YOSHIE*'s shoulder.* YOSHIE *turns around.*)

SHIGEO: Busy, busy.

SHINYA: Oh.

SHIGEO: That's why I was late today.

SHINYA: Glad to hear it—

TOKIKO (*Speaking at the same time*): He does look like a businessman now.

SHINYA: That so?

YŪJI (*Speaking at the same time*): Business good, I guess.

SHIGEO: Oh that reminds me, we're gonna make a part for your company.

YŪJI: Eh? What?

SHIGEO: Something for a guided missile. (*Mimes with his arms a guided missile.*)

SHINYA: What's that? A bamboo shoot?

SHIGEO (*Miming again*): Something to go with a guided missile. Some kinda liquid crystal part for it or something.

YŪJI: Something, something. Still don't get what you're talking about.

YOSHIE: Having fun?

YUMI: Uh huh.

SHIGEO: But that's what it is.

YŪJI: Oh—

SHIGEO: But ya know, it's kinda sad. We're just a subcontractor.

YOSHIE: Eh?—

SHIGEO: What I mean is, all our workers are refugees from Russia and what have you.

YOSHIE: Ah—

SHIGEO: Making weapons to kill the folks back home.

TOKIKO: Ah—

YŪJI: Could be the other way round, though.

SHIGEO: Huh?

YŪJI: Maybe you're making weapons to protect them.

SHIGEO: Ah, well—

YŪJI: We're selling to both sides, so ya never know.

SHIGEO: Yeah, but it's like, ya know, a metaphor.

YŪJI: Metaphor? What the hell of?

SHIGEO: Well—

(YUMI *takes out her camera and walks toward stage right.*)

YUMI: Look this way. (*Takes a picture. To* HIRAYAMA.) Why don't you get in the picture?

HIRAYAMA: Uh, no, uh, I—

YUMI: *Please.*

HIRAYAMA: Well, shall I take one of you all?

YUMI: No, I took one already.

HIRAYAMA: I'll take one with you in it.

YUMI: No, I'm fine. (*Pause.*) Really.

HIRAYAMA: You sure?

YOSHIE: In that case, I'll take one of you two. (*Referring to* HIRAYAMA.)

YUMI: Uh—

YOSHIE: Allow me—

YUMI: Well. (*To* HIRAYAMA.) Please.

HIRAYAMA: Well then—(*Stands with* YUMI.)

YOSHIE: Here goes. (*Takes a picture.*)

HIRAYAMA: Thanks—

YUMI: Thanks—

(*A long pause.*)

YUMI: Shall we go?

SHINYA: We're going.

YOSHIE: Uh huh—(*Stands.*)

SHIGEO: OK. (*Pause.*) Hey. I'm stuck.

SHINYA (*Speaking at the same time as* YOSHIE): OK—

TOKIKO: What're you doing?

YUMI: Let's go—

SHIGEO: I'm stuck.

(*It appears he cannot disengage his buttocks from the litter basket.*)

IKUE: OK.

TOKIKO: No kidding!

SHIGEO: Ah, I'm free.

IKUE: Wise up.

SHIGEO: Sorry.

SHINYA: Twit.

YUMI: Thank you.

SHIGEO: Y'know, I once sat on the toilet with the seat up—got stuck. Thought I was gonna die.

HIRAYAMA: Don't mention it.

(KUSHIMOTO *returns with four cups.*)

KUSHIMOTO: Sorry to keep you waiting.

ONO: Thanks.

KUSHIMOTO: Here—

HIRAYAMA: Thanks—

SHINYA: Go on home, why don't you?

SHIGEO: Sorry.

YUMI: You're not going to war, are you?

SHIGEO: Nah, not into that.

YUMI: But everybody's going, these days.

YOSHIE (*Starting to exit*): Yeah.

YUMI (*Starting to exit*): Men seem to get a charge out of stuff like that.

YOSHIE (*Exiting*): Some do, don't they?

(*The six family members exit stage left.*)

4.1.3

(KUSHIMOTO *sits at* C1.)

HIRAYAMA: Quite the speech there.

KUSHIMOTO: Nah—

HIRAYAMA: These days, even the visitors are getting to be experts, so we really gotta know our stuff.

ONO: Ah—

HIRAYAMA: And these pictures came on us all of a sudden.

ONO: So, how many have you got now?

HIRAYAMA: Seventy-four, so far.

ONO: That many.

HIRAYAMA: Yes, we'd really like to put up the collection once it's been donated, but, well, it might be a while—

ONO: So I heard.

HIRAYAMA: Sorry about that.

ONO: Not at all. Well, can't do much about the war, eh?

HIRAYAMA: That's easy for you to say.

ONO: I guess—

KUSHIMOTO: I suppose one can't, after all.

(*A long pause.*)

HIRAYAMA: You were into that, weren't you, Mr. Kushimoto.

KUSHIMOTO: Hm?

HIRAYAMA (*Quickly*): Some antiwar movement. Before you came here.

KUSHIMOTO: Well, not much of a movement, really.

HIRAYAMA: Not involved anymore?

KUSHIMOTO: Nope. Washed my hands of it.

HIRAYAMA: But they're still at it, aren't they? Those guys out there.

KUSHIMOTO: Yeah, well—

(KINOSHITA *enters from stage right, and sits at* D1.)

HIRAYAMA: So, what about them?

KUSHIMOTO: Yeah, well, even those who are fighting can't tell friend from foe anymore.

ONO: I guess not—

HIRAYAMA: Oh, yeah—

ONO: It was real hot there for a while, wasn't it? The antiwar movement.

KUSHIMOTO: Yes.

ONO: You were part of it then, I suppose?

KUSHIMOTO: Yes, well, till about five years or so ago.

ONO: Ah—

KUSHIMOTO: Dropped out of it a bit early.

(*A long pause.*)

ONO: Yes, well, what with all the people, goods, and cash pouring in puts Japan in kind of an awkward place, doesn't it?

KUSHIMOTO: Place? Japan never took a position from the start.

ONO: Oh.

KUSHIMOTO: Yes, well, you know Kästner's story, "The Zoo Conference"?

HIRAYAMA: What? Oh, yes.

KUSHIMOTO: You know, there's this ostrich who sticks his head in the sand so he doesn't have to look at the mess the humans have got themselves into.

HIRAYAMA: Is there now?—

KUSHIMOTO: Strauss. The ostrich's name.

HIRAYAMA: Ah—

KUSHIMOTO: That ostrich is rather like an artist peering into an camera obscura, don't you think?

HIRAYAMA: Oh, really?

KUSHIMOTO: Like this. (*Mimes peering into a box.*) Only seeing what he wants to see, composed just the way he likes.

HIRAYAMA: Uh . . . huh—

(KINOSHITA *exits stage right.*)

KUSHIMOTO: Eh?—

ONO: Ah—

KUSHIMOTO: I mean, that's me.

HIRAYAMA: Huh?

KUSHIMOTO: I'm like the ostrich with his head in the sand.

HIRAYAMA: Oh, but if you were, then surely we're all like that.

KUSHIMOTO: Maybe that's the case. Still—

HIRAYAMA: Kind of serious today, aren't you, Mr. Kushimoto?
KUSHIMOTO: I am?
HIRAYAMA: Yes—
KUSHIMOTO: Sorry.
HIRAYAMA: That's OK.
KUSHIMOTO: Sorry.
ONO: No, not at all.
HIRAYAMA: I'll go look.
ONO: Huh?
HIRAYAMA: For Ms. Mitsuhashi and Mr. Saitō.
ONO: I'll join you.
HIRAYAMA: Better you stay here, in case we miss each other.
KUSHIMOTO: Shall I go instead?
HIRAYAMA: No, I'll go. Besides, you don't know them.
KUSHIMOTO: You're right.
HIRAYAMA: Back in a bit.
KUSHIMOTO: Uh huh.
HIRAYAMA: Keep her company.
KUSHIMOTO: Uh huh.
(HIRAYAMA *exits stage left.*)

4.1.4

KUSHIMOTO: You know, looking at the universe through a telescope doesn't mean the universe is looking back at us.
ONO: . . . ?
KUSHIMOTO: The pictures to be donated—how much are they worth altogether?
ONO: Well, I guess that depends on their evaluation.
KUSHIMOTO: Yes—

ONO: If they weren't given away, the estate taxes would be in the millions, I guess.
KUSHIMOTO: Ah—
ONO: But nobody's buying art right now, to be frank with you.
KUSHIMOTO: And what's your cut in this?
ONO: Huh?
KUSHIMOTO: How much do you get out of this deal?
ONO: I'm on salary.
KUSHIMOTO: You know our director'd do anything for good pictures.
ONO: What're you trying to say?
KUSHIMOTO: Not that I mean to stir up anything. But, you know, I just want to make sure that everything's nice and clear.
ONO: You should watch what you say.

(KINOSHITA *enters from stage right with a cup of coffee. He sits again at* D1 *and drinks the coffee.*)

KUSHIMOTO: Sticking one's head in the sand, trying not to see the world, peering into a dark box, you know—chances are if a person does stuff like that, she'll get something in her eye instead.
ONO: Uh—

(HASHIZUME *and* TERANISHI *enter from stage left.*)

KUSHIMOTO (*Cutting in*): Ya can't always see just what you wanta see.
ONO (*Quickly*): Uh, I think you'd do well to be more careful of what you say to a lawyer—

HASHIZUME (*Entering*): That so?—

KUSHIMOTO: Just a warning, that's all.

TERANISHI (*Entering*): Uh huh, well, seems so.—

ONO: . . .

HASHIZUME (*Entering*): Hm—
TERANISHI (*Entering*): Seems so, anyway.—
HASHIZUME (*To* KUSHIMOTO): Ah, hello.
KUSHIMOTO: My, my.
HASHIZUME: Well, hello—
KUSHIMOTO: Hey, you in Tokyo now?
HASHIZUME: Yeah—
KUSHIMOTO: Well—
HASHIZUME: Thought I might run into you here.
KUSHIMOTO: Well, you should've dropped into the office to see me.
HASHIZUME: Yeah, but, it wasn't like I had any business or anything—

KUSHIMOTO: Ah, 'scuse me—an old acquaintance—

KUSHIMOTO: Yeah, but, you know—

ONO: Go right ahead.

HASHIZUME: But—

KUSHIMOTO: Sorry.

HASHIZUME: Mr. Kushimoto—we were both in the antiwar movement.
TERANISHI: Ah. (*Sits at* A1.)

(ONO *takes out a memo pad and begins making notes.*)

HASHIZUME: She's, uh, my fiancée.
KUSHIMOTO: Ah—
HASHIZUME: We're getting married this summer.
KUSHIMOTO: That so? Congratulations. (*Moves over to* B1.)
HASHIZUME: Thanks.
KUSHIMOTO: How's your Dad?
HASHIZUME: Ah, he died.
KUSHIMOTO: Oh.
HASHIZUME: Yeah—
KUSHIMOTO: Oh—
HASHIZUME: Sorry. That's why I went home.
KUSHIMOTO: Yes, ah, well—

HASHIZUME (*Cutting in*): Sorry I had to chuck it all, right in the middle.
KUSHIMOTO: No, fact is we all split up anyway. Would've been the same if you stayed.
HASHIZUME: Ah, well—
KUSHIMOTO: Yeah.
HASHIZUME: What about you, Mr. Kushimoto? Out of it now?
KUSHIMOTO: Yeah, well—
HASHIZUME: Is that so?—
KUSHIMOTO: What about you?
HASHIZUME: Same here.
KUSHIMOTO: Ain't easy, eh?
HASHIZUME: Uh uh.
KUSHIMOTO: Care for a coffee or something? In the office.
HASHIZUME: No, we're fine here.
KUSHIMOTO: Ya sure?
HASHIZUME: Uh, we're thinking of going back to Fukushima, once we're married.—
KUSHIMOTO: That so?
HASHIZUME: My Mum's hired somebody to look after the field Dad left, so, thought we'd take it over.
KUSHIMOTO: Not a bad idea.
HASHIZUME: Yeah, Mum told me I wouldn't get conscripted 'cause of the farm. Come home, she said.
KUSHIMOTO: Ah—
HASHIZUME: That's all they ever talk about now, back home, in the country.
KUSHIMOTO: Well, we hear the same thing. You know, businessmen will be the first to get conscripted and so on.
HASHIZUME: Kinda pathetic though, at my age, you know. But if it makes my mother happy. . . .
KUSHIMOTO: Well.

HASHIZUME: Yeah, well, she's into organic farming and stuff—

KUSHIMOTO: Hey, that's all right. Got a good reason, eh?—

TERANISHI: But, you see, it was kind of a hobby with me.

KUSHIMOTO: Send me something you've grown, will you?—

HASHIZUME: Sure—

(HIRAYAMA, MITSUHASHI, *and* SAITŌ *enter from stage left.*)

4.2.1

KUSHIMOTO: What're they growing?

HASHIZUME: Quite a variety, I think. Cucumbers, potatoes—

ONO: Ah, found 'em, I see.

KUSHIMOTO: Not bad—

HIRAYAMA: Yeah, just over there.

TERANISHI: Come visit us.

MITSUHASHI: Sorry.

KUSHIMOTO: Thanks, I'll do that. Go that way on business sometimes.

HIRAYAMA: Don't mention it.

HASHIZUME: Do, please.

MITSUHASHI: So, finished your business? (*Sits at* C2. SAITŌ *sits at* B2.)

(KUSHIMOTO *shifts over to accommodate* SAITŌ *next to him.*)
(*A long pause.*)

ONO: Yes, well, more or less.

MITSUHASHI (*To* HIRAYAMA): Well, in that case, please take good care of the paintings.

HASHIZUME: Be seeing you, then.

HIRAYAMA: You sure? There's nothing else?

KUSHIMOTO: Are you going?

MITSUHASHI: No—

HIRAYAMA: We *are* talking about quite a sum here. Sure you're not rushing into this—

MITSUHASHI: No sense hanging on to them.

HIRAYAMA: That may be so, but—

MITSUHASHI: Uh, please try to put up as many as you can.

HIRAYAMA: Yes, of course—

MITSUHASHI: It's good for the paintings to be seen.

HIRAYAMA: Yes.

MITSUHASHI: Well, thanks again.

HIRAYAMA: But—

ONO: Ah, I'll be in touch later about the paperwork.

HIRAYAMA: Yes, of course, but— (*A long pause.*)

MITSUHASHI: Anything else?

HASHIZUME: Just thought I'd come say hello.

KUSHIMOTO: Well, thanks.

HASHIZUME: I'll be in touch.

KUSHIMOTO: Uh, yes.—Here, I'll give you one of my cards. (*Offers him a business card.*)

HASHIZUME: Got a card even, eh?

KUSHIMOTO: You bet.

HASHIZUME: Maybe I should get some saying "Farmer."

KUSHIMOTO: Good idea—

HASHIZUME: I'll let you know when we move back home.

KUSHIMOTO: Please do.

HASHIZUME: Well, then—

KUSHIMOTO: I'll see you off.

HASHIZUME: Don't bother—

KUSHIMOTO: To the door, at least—

HASHIZUME: Sorry to catch you at work and all.

HIRAYAMA: Surely you needn't have to rush with this?

KUSHIMOTO: Nah, this ain't work. Not at all.

MITSUHASHI: When I saw the paintings here, I just felt like it.

HASHIZUME (*To* TERANISHI): C'mon—

HIRAYAMA: Yes, well—

(HASHIZUME *and* TERANISHI *exit stage left.*)

ONO: Your name's Kushimoto, right?

KUSHIMOTO: Hm?

ONO: Uh—

KUSHIMOTO: Yes.

ONO: What you were saying earlier, that you never know with people—

KUSHIMOTO: Hm?

ONO: That the universe isn't watching us through a telescope.

KUSHIMOTO: Did I say that?

ONO: Yes.

KUSHIMOTO (*Pausing briefly*): Yes, well, I guess I meant, if only we could all see ourselves. From a distance, I mean.

ONO: . . .

KUSHIMOTO: If you'll excuse me— (*Exits stage left.*)

CURTAIN

Sakate Yōji, *The Attic*, directed by Sakate Yōji, Rinkōgun, May 2003.
(Photograph by Ōhara Taku)

THE ATTIC

SAKATE YŌJI
TRANSLATED BY LEON INGULSRUD AND KEIKO TSUNEDA

A contemporary of Hirata Oriza and a member of the post-1960s "fourth generation" of playwrights, Sakate Yōji (b. 1962) is notable for writing and directing plays that are pointed commentaries on modern life. In 1981, as a student at Keiō University, he joined Transposition 21 (Ten'i 21), a theater company founded by Yamazaki Tetsu, a second-generation playwright and former member of Kara Jūrō's Situation Theater, who taught Sakate how to use theater as a tool to address contemporary issues. Sakate established his own company, Phosphorescence Troupe (Rinkōgun), in 1983, reacting against the apolitical and consumerist trend so typical of the theater of Japan's bubble economy. His work helped chart the return to more sober themes and the well-crafted dramaturgy indicative of the late 1990s. An early work about Japan's lesbian community, *Come Out* (*Kamu auto*, 1987), signaled Sakate's reputation as a critic of modern Japanese mores. *Tokyo Trial* (*Tōkyō saiban*) and *A Dangerous Story* (*Kiken na hanashi*), both first staged in 1988, satirized Japan's legal system. *Breathless* (*Buresuresu*, 1991), which addressed the Aum Shinrikyō cult some four years before its devastating terrorist attack on the Tokyo subways, won the Kishida Kunio Award. His 1993 play, *Capital of the Kingdom of the Gods* (*Kamigami no kuni no shuto*), deals with the Irish-Greek-American writer Lafcadio Hearn's sojourn in Matsue in the 1890s. In the same year, Sakate staged *Epitaph for the Whales* (*Kujira no bohyō*), about the decline of Japan's whaling industry; both plays are part of Sakate's ongoing series of "contemporary nō" plays. *The Emperor and the Kiss* (*Tennō to seppun*, 1999), which won the Yomiuri Literature Prize, is set during Japan's occupation and addresses issues of censorship and Emperor Hirohito's responsibility for the war. *The Attic* (*Yaneura*, 2003), an excerpt from which is translated here, won the Yomiuri Literature Prize and is one of Sakate's most frequently performed works. Set in a tiny attic, it is a series of vignettes with different characters who explore with great wit the claustrophobia of contemporary Japanese life, with its crushing pressures to fit in, perform, produce, and consume.

Characters

OLDER BROTHER
YOUNG MAN
YOUNG WOMAN
GIRL
BOY
YOUNG MAN WITH A BLUE CAP
YOUNG MAN WITH A RED CAP
MAN WITH CRUTCHES
UME
TAKE
MATSU
GENTLEMAN
ANCHORPERSON
WOMAN
MAN WITH A CAP
MOTHER
TEACHER
LADY
PEOPLE 1, 2, 3, 4, 5
PROMOTER 1, 2
FORMER ATTIC DWELLER 1, 2, 3
PEOPLE IN DISGUISE 1, 2, 3, 4
PACKED PEOPLE 1, 2, 3, 4

KID'S ROOM

GIRL *is lying in a sleeping bag.* BOY *pokes his head into the Attic.*

BOY: Hello.
GIRL: . . .What is it?
BOY: Your mom told me you were here.

GIRL: Don't ask her.

(GIRL *shuts the door.*)

BOY (*Offstage*): It's brand-new.

GIRL: What?

BOY (*Offstage*): This is an expensive Attic kit, isn't it.

GIRL: I don't know.

BOY (*Offstage*): Was it easy to set up?

GIRL: Yes.

BOY (*Offstage*): Did you do it yourself?

GIRL: Of course not. It's included in the price.

BOY (*Offstage*): Your head is facing north, isn't it? That's not good.

GIRL: What?

BOY (*Offstage*): I saw your pillow.

GIRL: . . . I don't care, asshole.

BOY (*Offstage*): You have your own bedroom. Why did you put it on the balcony?

GIRL: It's none of your business.

BOY (*Offstage*): She told me you are climbing up and down the tree in the garden to this balcony.

GIRL (*About her mother*): Big mouth.

BOY (*Offstage*): . . . Living on a tree. What are you? A gorilla.

GIRL: Leave me alone. I'm sick of it. (*She makes a thumping noise with her legs in the sleeping bag.*)

BOY (*Offstage*): Is that because you don't want to see your family?

GIRL: There's nothing strange about it. In the Philippines, or other swampy areas in Asia where people live on the water, they build bamboo cabins on the water, a floating house kind of thing. We learned about it in social studies.

BOY (*Opening the small door, he giggles*): Tee hee. . . .

GIRL: Why are you laughing?

BOY: Your mom asked if I was your boyfriend.

GIRL: No kidding. (*She is angry.*)

BOY: She said this was the first time a boy had visited you.

GIRL: I'm going to kill you.

BOY: May I come in?

GIRL: Shut the fuck up!

BOY: I'll give you a massage. I'm pretty good. You're always so stiff. I've wanted to give you a massage for a while.

(*Without coming out of the sleeping bag,* GIRL *kicks* BOY, *who is trying to come in.*)

BOY: I always massage my grandma's neck and shoulders. . . .

GIRL: No. I don't want you to.

(*She kicks him once more. He bends down, looking hurt.* GIRL *worries a bit.* BOY *suddenly takes out a Polaroid and takes a picture of her. While she flinches from the flash,* BOY *comes in.*)

GIRL: What do you think you're doing?

(GIRL *kicks* BOY *more and takes the camera from him. She kicks him furiously, trying to push him out.* BOY *squats and resists.*)

GIRL: What are you doing here?

BOY: . . .

GIRL: I said, what are you doing here?

BOY: I'm not going to ask you why you stopped coming to school.

GIRL: What are you talking about?

BOY: It's been almost a month now.

GIRL: There's no reason, asshole.

BOY: Maybe there's nothing special about being a shut-in.

GIRL: Am I a shut-in?

BOY: . . .

GIRL: How can you be so sure of that just because I don't go to school?

BOY: Am I wrong?

GIRL: I can't judge that myself.

BOY: So you are a pseudo shut-in.

GIRL: What do you mean pseudo?

BOY: It means you're not a perfect shut-in. . . .

GIRL: Pseudo. (*She hates it.*)

BOY: . . .

GIRL: Why did you come here?

BOY: I wanted to give you something.

GIRL: What?

BOY: You read books, don't you? When you're staying somewhere like this?

GIRL: No. I don't want it.

BOY: It's a gift.

GIRL: There's no occasion.

BOY: It's an encouragement gift. (*He puts a book on the floor.*)

GIRL: For what?

BOY: A sympathy gift.

GIRL: Am I sick or something? Sorry, but I'm physically stronger than you.

BOY (*Answering "Am I sick or something?"*): No.

GIRL: I'm mentally sick, then? (*Opens the book.*) Oh, I get it. You think I should read the biography of a great person and think about myself? (*Throws down the book.*) I don't believe this, it's *The Diary of Anne Frank*!

BOY: It's a good book.

GIRL: Have you read it?

BOY: Yeah.

GIRL: I don't want a secondhand book. I've already read it anyway. Everyone's read *The Diary of Anne Frank*.

BOY: You confine yourself in here like this, but the truth is you're waiting for someone to invite you to come out. And that someone is me.

GIRL: Watch it!

BOY: I mean, I thought I could be your Peter.

GIRL: No! (*Disgusted.*)

BOY: Remember that time the math teacher left us to study on our own, and the class made fun of us by making me sit beside you in front of the blackboard, and they held a "wedding ceremony"?

GIRL: Don't remind me.

BOY: I was pissed off, but to be honest, I felt a little happy, too.

GIRL: The biggest humiliation of my life. They put me in the same category as you.

BOY: I was embarrassed and wanted to escape. I never thought the teacher would go along with it and make a speech as a wedding guest.

GIRL: Don't bring up that bitch.

BOY: I could have escaped, actually. If I'd been alone, I would have run away. But I thought it would hurt your feelings if I left. . . .

(BOY *crawls up to* GIRL *and holds her down. She can't move because she is in the sleeping bag.*)

GIRL: No, no, no!

BOY: Can I kiss you?

GIRL: Wait a minute.

BOY: Can I, if I wait a minute?

GIRL: Well. . . .

BOY: Kiss.

(GIRL *comes out of the sleeping bag and pins* BOY *to the floor. She beats him.* BOY *starts crying.* GIRL *fumbles in* BOY*'s bag and takes out a tiny tape recorder and a microphone.*)

GIRL: Just as I thought.

BOY: . . .

GIRL: . . . This isn't your idea, is it?

BOY: I'm sorry.

GIRL: I see. Takeda, Ogami, all those bastards. They told you to be nice to me and kiss me and bring back a recording or pictures to prove it, right? Get a life.

(BOY *cries.*)

GIRL: You can go now.

BOY: . . .

GIRL: Go.

BOY: Are you going to report this to the school?

GIRL: Do you want to me to?

BOY: . . .

GIRL: Tell them you kissed me.

BOY: . . .

GIRL: Tell them you fucked me.

BOY: . . .

GIRL: Tell everybody you fucked the Gorilla. Should I record something? Moan or breathe heavily? Maybe I could roar with ecstasy and beat my chest? Garrrr!

BOY: . . . Stop it.

(BOY *covers his crotch with his hand.*)

GIRL: What the hell? Do you have a hard-on? Do you? Why on earth?

BOY: Damn it damn it damn it damn it damn it!

(BOY *moves his hand and begins to masturbate.*)

GIRL: Stop it!!! You're crazy! Pervert! Creep! Flasher! Freak! Yuk! Don't look at me. Get away. . . . Do you know what you're doing? What? Are you trying to show it to me? Gross. Germ. Slowpoke. Puke. No, don't look at me. Scum. Asshole. Don't look. Don't look at me!

(BOY *comes.*)

GIRL: Japan will be ruined. Someone like you will casually go to college, join a company, grow up, get married, and you'll tell your kids, "When I was young, blah, blah, blah." Someone like you, who doesn't even deserve to live, bragging shamelessly, like you were someone you aren't. It won't work. It was exposed long ago. Japan will be ruined. And it's your fault. You'll be killed. I'll kill you. I'm going to kill you no matter what!

(BOY *creeps away.* GIRL *shuts the door and locks it, and takes the microphone that* BOY *left.*)

GIRL: . . . At the sound of the tone, the time of my life will be, fifteen years, three months, twenty-six days, fourteen hours, and thirty minutes. Pip, pip, pip, po. . . .

BLACKOUT

HAY FEVER

There is a futon and a blanket in the Attic. YOUNG WOMAN *is putting on her underwear.* YOUNG MAN *is still naked.* YOUNG WOMAN *brushes something off her body. There is no trace of postcopulation listlessness in her.*

WOMAN: You brought pollen in here again.

MAN: . . . Pollen?

WOMAN: It's all over.

MAN: That's impossible. I sealed it up. Just as I was told.

WOMAN: It stuck to your body.

MAN: I took off all my clothes and took a shower before I came in.

WOMAN: It was deep inside your body.

(WOMAN *pulls a stuffed animal out from under the blanket.*)

WOMAN: I can't believe you bought this. The baby isn't even born yet. I see. The pollen was on this.

(WOMAN *hits the doll, and it says something. It's the kind of toy that talks each time you hit it.*)

WOMAN: . . . Go down, quickly.

(MAN *goes down out a small trapdoor and puts on his clothes. We can see only his face now.*)

MAN: We should have bought a house with a loft if you were going to buy something like this.

WOMAN: We can use it as a nursery.

MAN: If you want a private room for yourself, you better say so first.

WOMAN: . . . (*She drops the stuffed doll.*)

MAN: And why did you get a used one anyway.

WOMAN: Someone gave it to me. A guy who looks like you.

MAN: Me?

WOMAN: We brought it home on our minivan. We stopped at a motel, but we didn't do anything in the room. When we went back to the van, I made love with him. With the guy who looks like you.

MAN: No kidding.

WOMAN: Hmm.

MAN: I know you're kidding.

WOMAN: How? How do you know? Did you follow me? Did you watch me with a hidden camera?

MAN: Maybe.

WOMAN: I haven't be able to use my cell phone lately. You're interfering with my phone, aren't you?

MAN: How?

WOMAN: Some kind of device.

MAN: Never heard of such a thing.

WOMAN: There is.

(WOMAN *pulls out a catalog from under the blanket. She hands it to* MAN, *who reads aloud.*)

MAN: . . . Silent Master. A cellular phone communication-jamming device. It deters the cellular phone communication by interfering with radio waves.

WOMAN: It makes the cell phones useless so that the people who shut themselves into their rooms are forced to come out.

MAN: This is a device to block calls in the theater, in case someone forgot to switch off their phone. Nobody uses it in their house.

WOMAN: Enough. I can't live with you. Do you understand. . . . Just give me the money to raise the baby.

MAN: Are you leaving me?

WOMAN: We've come to an agreement.

MAN: You call this an agreement?

WOMAN: I realized that I'll have nothing to do if I quit my job. No job, no money, nothing to live for. That'll be my life. I can see it when I see my parents. They have nothing. Nothing. Do you understand?

MAN: Is that why you shut yourself in?

WOMAN: Babies shut themselves in their mother's womb, don't they? Human beings are like that from the beginning. . . . What about dinner?

MAN: . . . Why not go out once in a while. What would you like?

WOMAN: Korean barbecue. Of course Korean barbecue. You always ask me, and you know my answer. I want to eat Korean barbecue. If I don't, my blood will get thin. Right. It's your fault. You always make me eat beef.

MAN: I'm infected with mad cow disease. I went mad because I ate too much beef. I'll admit it. Satisfied?

WOMAN: You didn't let me go to the seminar on disinfecting beef?

MAN: It's a waste of money.

WOMAN: We have to use some money, it's for the baby.

MAN: It's crazy to be obsessed with a seminar like that.

WOMAN: How can you make love with a crazy woman?

MAN: You are sick.

WOMAN: Yes. I'm sick. It's infectious. It's an infectious disease. You have to quarantine me. Keep me in a barn until I die a slow death.

MAN: You aren't cattle.

WOMAN: If not, I'm your pet. You're waiting for me to get sick. You'll give the baby only cheap hamburgers and make him sick, too. Make his brain shrink so he's easy for you to keep.

(MAN *disappears out the trapdoor.*)

MAN: . . . You don't need to worry about the baby.

WOMAN: Don't open the window. The baby will be allergic.

MAN: Don't talk about the baby.

WOMAN: I'll deliver a fine calf.

MAN: I called the obstetrics. . . . You aren't pregnant.

WOMAN: You liar.

MAN: Who's the liar?

WOMAN: . . . Don't open it.

(*Cherry blossom petals are coming in through the trapdoor.*)

BLACKOUT

THE DIARY OF ANNE FRANK

GIRL *is standing with a book in her hand. She is talking into a small tape recorder. Beside her is a half-full backpack.*

GIRL: I've read *The Diary of Anne Frank.* I think the years from age twelve to fourteen are the stupidest years of one's life. People of this age are stupid and they think they're somehow different from everyone else, or they just hate grown-ups. Anne is the same. . . . I think Anne Frank was lucky. Anne was forced to live in hiding, but I think it forced her to think and feel a lot of things. Because I live a carefree life in peaceful Japan, it's hard for me to imagine the life she was forced to live. I mean I have some of the same thoughts as Anne, like "Why are grown-ups so stupid?" or "I'm an independent individual," but we definitely are different. The difference is, Anne was happy to hear about the plan to assassinate Hitler, and I'm looking forward to seeing a show on TV. Anne was fed up with potatoes because there was nothing else to eat, and I have an argument with my mother about whether to eat rice or bread for breakfast. Anne felt happy by the window, in the sunshine, and I . . . Do I ever feel happy? . . . Maybe not. Even if I do, it's because of something trashy. I can't even remember it now. . . . What's the city of Amsterdam like? Anne gained eighteen pounds and four inches during the first three months she was in hiding. Even if you live with your breath held, your body grows. Even if you have to use a chamber pot because you can't flush the toilet when someone is downstairs, you can dream. Anne wanted to be famous. She wanted to be a Hollywood star. She wanted to be a writer. She decided the title of her first book would be *Hiding.* "When I'm writing, I can forget everything. Sadness disappears and new courage wells up." . . . Is that true?

Just before the Allies came to save them, the Gestapo found the secret door, and they were taken to the concentration camp at Bergen-Belsen, where she died in the barracks. What would she say if she saw the Israelis slaughtering the Palestinians? . . . I don't want to write about myself. Definitely not. My life is too ugly. I can't help it. We live in different times and in different countries. But at least I'm free. I'm sure I am. I keep my stuff in a backpack so I'm ready to leave and start on a journey anytime. I wish I could live every day as if it's the day before a trip.

BLACKOUT

THE ROOM OF ABSENCE

The room is full of red light, with an island of white light from a desk lamp. There is a sheet that looks like it used to be white. We hear the sound of wind blowing through a hollow. MIDDLE-AGED WOMAN *and* OLDER BROTHER *come in.*

WOMAN: Don't touch anything. He'll notice the slightest change.

OLDER BROTHER: What's that noise?

WOMAN: Air purifier. He's really taking care of the conditions in here.

(MIDDLE-AGED WOMAN *holds out her hands to the white light of the desk lamp as if warming her hands at a bonfire.* OLDER BROTHER *looks at the space.*)

WOMAN: I don't think he'll be back for at least another four hours. He went for a drive, and he's doing his shopping, too. It'll take some time. He goes out only once a month.

OLDER BROTHER: Thank you. I need some time to just look at the scene and get an impression of the actual situation.

WOMAN: I don't know what to do. I have no choice but to turn to professionals for help. . . . A lot depends on what kind of people they are. The last one was far from professional; he was playing with my son. Betting on horses, playing games, just messing around. I confronted him and found out that he didn't intend to help him go out at all. He actually used to shut himself in.

OLDER BROTHER: I see. . . .

WOMAN: Have you doing this for a long time?

OLDER BROTHER: No.

WOMAN: What I mean by that is that the people with experience are not always so good.

OLDER BROTHER: . . . I see.

WOMAN: Sorry for babbling on. I don't usually have anyone to talk to about my son.

OLDER BROTHER: When did he get this Attic?

WOMAN: . . . About two years ago now, I guess.

OLDER BROTHER: It wasn't ten years ago?

WOMAN: No.

OLDER BROTHER: I heard your son had put together his own Attic years before Attics became a fad.

WOMAN: Did you?

OLDER BROTHER: It was on the Web, with your son's address.

WOMAN: It was a lie.

OLDER BROTHER: I know that now. This Attic is a ready-made model you can buy on the Internet. Your son didn't build it.

WOMAN: He couldn't have done it.

OLDER BROTHER: I had great expectations that he might possibly have invented the Attic. . . .

WOMAN: Well, my son lies more often that he tells the truth. Actually, it's no exaggeration to say that he rarely tell the truth.

OLDER BROTHER: When did he start using the second floor?

WOMAN: We gave him a bedroom up here when he was in second grade. And we gave him the entire second floor when he was in the eleventh grade.

OLDER BROTHER: Do you come upstairs?

WOMAN: Less than once a year.

OLDER BROTHER: He told you not to come upstairs?

WOMAN: Yes.

OLDER BROTHER: . . . I heard that Japan has the world's highest percentage of children who have their own rooms.

WOMAN: More than the USA?

OLDER BROTHER: Yes. In the USA, parents usually let their kids think it's their room, but the room doesn't actually belong to them. If a parent knocks on the door, the kids have to let him in. That's an absolute rule without exceptions. If guests stay in the house, the kids have to give up their rooms for the guests. That's the father's authority as the captain of a ship called home.

WOMAN: . . . I see.

OLDER BROTHER: I got this all from a book.

WOMAN: His father ran away. He was scared of his son's violence.

OLDER BROTHER: Does he beat you?

WOMAN: . . . Yes. He behaves exactly the same as his father did when he was drunk.

OLDER BROTHER: What makes him violent?

WOMAN: The first time he beat me, he said he didn't like the way I washed his clothes. . . . After that, there was no rhyme or reason. When he gets angry, he says things like, "Why did you have me?" and that's enough of a reason for him. When I forgot the day that the new issue of the *manga* magazine *Shonen Jump* came out, he threw a burning newspaper into the living room.

OLDER BROTHER: He's violent only at home, right?

WOMAN: He had a job, but it lasted only three months. I don't think he can find anyone to beat in the outside world.

OLDER BROTHER: In most cases of domestic violence, the family can't do anything. If antisocial behavior is involved, there are ways for us to deal with it.

WOMAN: Is it too late, then?

OLDER BROTHER: It is essential that we change his environment. We recommend that you to commit him to a private rehabilitation facility.

WOMAN: Will he be all right?

OLDER BROTHER: He'll feel better when he's around fellow patients. The rehabilitation facilities have programs to enforce a well-regulated life and to master vocational skills so that patients can return to society. You can visit them. You'll see the truth in what I say when you observe them. Professionals are working there to rehabilitate adults who shut themselves in.

WOMAN: How much do they pay you as a finder's fee?

OLDER BROTHER: . . .

WOMAN: It's all a business, isn't it?

OLDER BROTHER: This is not the time for saying things like that.

WOMAN: I don't have any money.

OLDER BROTHER: . . .

WOMAN: I'll deal with him somehow as long as I'm alive. There's no age limit on being an insurance salesperson.

OLDER BROTHER: . . . What is your real problem?

WOMAN: . . .

OLDER BROTHER: I promise I'll keep your secret.

WOMAN: . . .

OLDER BROTHER (*He indicates the fourth wall*): It looks like something was erased with benzene; there are lots of traces of graffiti. "Despair," "Death," "Future." . . . Small letters all over the wall. Is it your son's handwriting?

WOMAN (*She squints at it*): No.

OLDER BROTHER: There's someone else, then.

WOMAN: Not my son. Someone else.

WOMAN: . . . Yes.

OLDER BROTHER: A friend is staying with him?

WOMAN: He doesn't have any friends.

OLDER BROTHER: How long has this person been here?

WOMAN: I don't know. I don't even know if my son is here. There is a bathroom next to his room, and he can come upstairs directly from the kitchen door. Sometimes I don't see him for days.

OLDER BROTHER: Does he ask you for food?

WOMAN: Sometimes.

OLDER BROTHER: Sushi, for example. If he orders sushi, how many people does he order for?

WOMAN: Enough for two, plus extra. . . . But he always ate a lot.

OLDER BROTHER: Did he buy this Attic to shut in this other person?

WOMAN: You mean he keeps someone here?

OLDER BROTHER: Yes.

WOMAN: . . . My son is a monster.

OLDER BROTHER: . . .

WOMAN: I'm afraid of his jump-kick. I never know when he's going to jump and kick me, so I always have to be on guard. . . . But if I leave, he'll die. I'm his slave.

OLDER BROTHER: You and your son aren't the only parent and child in the world. If your child was taken away, you'd look for her forever.

WOMAN: They might give up, thinking she was abducted by the North Koreans.

OLDER BROTHER: . . .

WOMAN: If they really look for her, they'll soon find her. There are very few people who would do a thing like this, except my son.

OLDER BROTHER: Are you saying they haven't searched hard enough?

WOMAN: . . . Please don't make me say things like this.

OLDER BROTHER: . . .

WOMAN: . . . Please leave now. I was wrong to ask for your help.

OLDER BROTHER: I don't mind. I'm not really interested. What I really want to know is who invented this Attic. I'm looking for the person who created this.

WOMAN: It's just a toy house. . . .

OLDER BROTHER: Even if you aren't interested in what's going on, you should have figured out something by now. You might have peeked into the room while he was taking a shower. He told you to go buy sanitary napkins. You should have noticed that the noise from upstairs wasn't made by single person.

WOMAN: . . . I heard a voice on the day before the festival in February.

OLDER BROTHER: A voice?

WOMAN: "In with the demon, out with fortune" . . . A girl's voice. Ever since I heard that voice, if I wake up in the middle of the night I can't fall asleep again. I can't even breathe. I hear the voice, "in with the demon, out with fortune." . . .

OLDER BROTHER: I'm leaving now.

WOMAN: . . .Why?

OLDER BROTHER: You know only too well what you need to do.

WOMAN: . . .

(MIDDLE-AGED WOMAN *smiles faintly.*)

BLACKOUT

MOUNTAIN HUT

Sound of a snowstorm. MAN WITH A BLUE CAP *dressed like a mountain climber is sitting in the Attic. The small door opens. Snow blows in.* MAN WITH A RED CAP *dressed like a mountain climber comes in hurriedly.*

RED CAP: Ooh, thank god. . . . (*Notices* MAN WITH A BLUE CAP.) Excuse me.

BLUE: . . . Welcome.

RED: I didn't expect a heavy snowstorm like this. I was worried for a while. Were you heading for camp 5?

BLUE: You, too?

RED: I guess we got lost, huh?

BLUE: Yeah, completely.

RED: Are you alone?

BLUE: I suddenly found myself alone.

RED: Me, too. I usually take the lead, and this time, I showed off and went so fast that I got separated from the others. It happened once before, too.

BLUE: Did they let you go? They should have noticed, since you were in front.

RED: Well, I often break off to relieve myself, you know, defecate—So they didn't care. I usually catch up with them later.

BLUE: It would be embarrassing if they found you pulling down your pants.

RED: Right. I always tend to be loose in the bowels. . . . And it was cold.

BLUE: I see.

RED: I don't like to defecate in the snow. . . . Don't worry, I'll go out when I have to. . . . Phew, I'm feeling warmer now, but I wish there were a fire or something. Well, it'd be strange if there was a fireplace in a hut like this. It's a good idea though, to use an Attic kit as a mountaineering shelter.

BLUE: I wonder how they got it up here.

RED: I heard that they hung it from a helicopter and just dropped it. It's pretty light.

BLUE: . . . Lodge and loft are similar, don't you think?

RED: Pardon?

BLUE: When I was a child, we had an Attic in our house. We called it the loft. And I always called it the lodge by mistake.

RED: Lodge and loft.

BLUE: They sound similar, don't they?

RED: It's easy to get into the habit of that kind of mistake.

BLUE: Yeah.

RED: But this is really a lodge.

BLUE: It's a loft, and it's a lodge.

RED: It's a lodge, and it's a loft.

BLUE: . . . So it was you.

RED: What?

BLUE: . . . I felt someone calling me.

RED: I don't think it was me. I wouldn't yell out loud at the time like this. It's a waste of energy and strains your windpipe, too. Perhaps it was just your imagination?

(*The small door opens as if blown by the wind.*)

RED: It's cold. (*He closes the door.*)

BLUE: The hinges are broken.

RED: I wonder if they've arrived at the camp. . . . I was thinking only of myself. What should I do if they all got lost?

BLUE: They might all come to this Attic.

RED: There isn't enough room.

BLUE: What should we do?

RED: . . . We can make an igloo.

BLUE: Sounds nice. An igloo. We can drink hot toddy and eat mandarin oranges in it. . . .

(*The small door opens again. A* WOMAN *is standing in the snow. She is wearing a white coat.* MAN WITH A RED CAP *goes to close the door. He is surprised to see* WOMAN IN WHITE.)

BLUE: . . . My team?

RED: No. (*Calls out.*) Come on in. (*To* MAN WITH A RED CAP.) Let's make some space. I'll go over there.

(WOMAN IN WHITE *comes in.* MAN WITH A RED CAP *moves to the side of* MAN WITH A BLUE CAP.)

BLUE: You look so pale. . . .

RED: Are you all right?

(WOMAN *nods.*)

RED (*To* MAN WITH A BLUE CAP): Don't you have anything that would give her energy? Some chocolate or an energy bar?

BLUE: Whiskey would be good, too. (*To* WOMAN.) You'll be warm soon. (*To* RED.) I've recovered my spirits since I came in, too, right?

WOMAN: . . . (*She is trembling and huddles in the corner.*)

BLUE: You are all right now. There's nothing to worry about.

RED: . . . Were you in an accident?

WOMAN: . . . (*She shakes her head.*)

RED: You got lost, then?

WOMAN: . . . (*Nods.*)

RED: Are you a student? Which mountaineering club are you in?

WOMAN: . . .

RED: Say something. A silent girl in white. You look like some sort of snow ghost.

(MAN WITH A RED CAP *takes her hands. She doesn't say anything.*)

RED: Well, good thing you're real. Your hands are so cold. Do you want to use my body warmer?

BLUE: . . . Did you hear that?

RED: What?

BLUE: Someone is calling from far away.

RED (*He listens*): . . . I can't hear anything.

BLUE: . . . I'm sure someone is calling.

RED: Really?

(BLUE *goes out.*)

RED: Hey. . . . It's dangerous out there right now.

(RED *tries to follow him, but* WOMAN *doesn't let go of his hands.*)

RED: What are you doing?

WOMAN: Don't go.

RED: You're strange. You are being very strange.

WOMAN: You're the one who's being strange.

RED: . . . What do you mean?

WOMAN: . . . Who were you talking to?

RED: What do you mean? He was . . . a man with a blue hat.

WOMAN: There wasn't anybody here.

RED: . . .

WOMAN: Nobody was here. But the door opened just now, and a kind of white mist or something went out. . . .

RED: No. . . .

WOMAN: . . . I've heard about this. Survivors who see ghosts.

RED: I'm not a ghost.

WOMAN: Me, neither. . . .

(*The snowstorm is blowing in the dark.*)

BLACKOUT

MOTHER AND SON

A room scattered with garbage. MOTHER *opens the door and peeps in.* SON, *who was asleep under the blanket, wakes up and sees* MOTHER.

MOTHER: . . . How can you sleep so much? Are you ill?

SON: . . . I didn't know you were there.

MOTHER: When you're asleep, your face looks like it did in the old days.

SON: Old days?

MOTHER: When the three of us slept together in that small room.

(SON *yawns.*)

MOTHER: Have you stood up lately? You look shorter than you did before.

SON: Mammals are quadrupeds. Our internal organs aren't really situated for walking upright.

MOTHER: I gave birth to you as a healthy and normal baby.

SON: Did you really give birth to me?

MOTHER: Yeah.

SON: Somehow I find that hard to believe.

MOTHER: You haven't washed your face in a while, have you. It's scruffy. . . . You should wash your face every morning. A little habit like that can change people. Shall I run a bath?

SON: It's a waste. I haven't moved. I haven't broken a sweat.

MOTHER: . . . Why not check into some sort of facility? At least then you'll wash your face every morning.

SON: It would be compulsory.

MOTHER: It is compulsory for human beings to wash their face every morning.

SON: I don't mind washing my face every morning, but I don't like to clean toilets.

MOTHER: Don't knock it till you've tried it.

SON: I think I'd do well in a place like that. But when I come back, I'll be like this again. I don't need to bother. I already know.

MOTHER: For appearance's sake, you should at least say hi to the neighbors.

SON: It's actually weirder if someone like me greets them.

MOTHER: Don't go out empty-handed. It's too obvious that you're unemployed.

SON: There's nothing I can do about that. "Shutting yourself in" can be a way of saying no to work.

MOTHER: Those who don't work don't eat.

SON: Left to their own devices, the Russians weren't going to work, so they introduced communism and created a system to force them to work.

MOTHER: Really?

SON: The first person to ever shut himself in was a Russian, wasn't it? A nineteenth-century anarchist named Oblomov.

MOTHER: What's an anarchist?

SON: Something that's not good. Nothing that starts with "an" is any good.

MOTHER: May I come in?

SON: Yes.

(MOTHER *pretends to come in through the small door but pushes a stuffed animal through instead. It is an ambush, and* SON *hits the stuffed animal with a slingshot.*)

SON: . . . How did you know?

MOTHER: How long have I been your mother?

SON: I won't do anything.

MOTHER: I object to violence.

SON: I'm fed up with it.

MOTHER: Really?

SON: I don't want to touch anyone.

MOTHER: . . .

SON: People change, you know. When I was a kid, I didn't mind touching anything, frogs or crayfish. But now I don't even want to touch a beetle.

MOTHER: I thought you had reverted to childhood, but you can't do what a child does now.

(MOTHER *comes in and finds instant noodles, canned food, packets of cornflakes, and a variety of junk food under the blanket.*)

MOTHER: You've got everything here. It's like some kind of store.

SON: I wish my home were a convenience store.

MOTHER (*Points at a spot under the blanket*): You have something growing there.

SON: Indoor cultivation. Bean sprouts, radish sprouts, and alfalfa.

MOTHER: Oh?

SON: You can grow them all the same way. I'm going to try blueberries and leeks next.

MOTHER: Sounds like you have a lot of time to kill.

SON: I'm looking for a way to support myself.

MOTHER: Uh-huh.

SON: There are certain jobs you can't do without shutting yourself in. Actually, Mom, I'm thinking of making my living on the Internet, pretending I live abroad. I'm going to take a law exam, too.

MOTHER: Oh?

SON: There's also a publishing company interested in my "shut-in" lifestyle, and I'm writing an autobiography.

MOTHER: You can't write a book. You don't even read the newspaper.

SON: Has the world changed that much?

MOTHER: Kitano Takeshi is the prime minister.

SON: You're kidding.

MOTHER: Amazing thing is, it sounds true.

SON: Is there a war going on somewhere?

MOTHER: Yes.

SON: I wish there was a war here, too.

MOTHER: Why?

SON: Everything would be burned away and cleared.

MOTHER: . . . Maybe I'm happy. Usually, a boy finds a girlfriend, gets married, has his own kids, grows up, acts his age, and he doesn't give a damn about his mother. Then the mother feels empty. She quickly goes senile. I didn't have time for it. I had a lot of things to do for you.

SON: You're speaking in the past tense.

MOTHER: . . .

SON: I thought you were in the hospital.

MOTHER: I was.

SON: You were?

MOTHER: Why didn't you visit me in the hospital?

SON: . . .

MOTHER: I think I'm going to vanish.

SON: Vanish?

MOTHER: Vanish.

SON: How?

MOTHER: It's a secret.

SON: Shall we die together?

MOTHER: No.

SON: Why?

MOTHER: Never.

SON: I don't want you to die now. I need you to return a video. It's overdue.

MOTHER: Again?

SON: I've seen the detective movie and the samurai movie, but I haven't seen the war movie yet.

MOTHER: I can't. I already did it.

SON: . . . When?

MOTHER: Half an hour ago.

SON: That's not fair, going by yourself. That's not fair.

MOTHER: . . . It can't be helped.

SON: . . . No, it can't, can it?

BLACKOUT

VISIT

GIRL *is typing on a laptop computer, using a bare bulb as a desk lamp. There's a knock at the door.*

TEACHER (*Offstage*): Hello. It's Haruyama, your teacher. . . . May I come in?

GIRL: Yes, please.

(TEACHER *comes in, indicates the computer.*)

TEACHER: Homework?

GIRL: No.

TEACHER: Is this an Attic?

GIRL: . . . Yes.

TEACHER: I've always lived in company-owned houses or apartments. I didn't know what an Attic was like.

GIRL: So you wanted to come in.

TEACHER: Yeah.

GIRL: Wanted to experience how it feels, shutting yourself in?

TEACHER: What are you talking about? It's just a routine home visit. It's soundproof, isn't it. You could play video games as much as you like.

GIRL: I don't play games.

TEACHER: I'm sorry.

GIRL: . . .

TEACHER: I came to apologize to you. I was thoughtless.

GIRL: What are you talking about?

TEACHER: The "wedding ceremony." I was thinking it could be a trauma for the rest of your life. . . .

GIRL: What's a trauma? Some kind of animal or something?

TEACHER: . . .

GIRL: Stop talking about it. I don't care, I just think it was stupid.

TEACHER: Yeah. But I guess Takeda and Ogami thought you would feel closer to the other kids in the class. . . .

GIRL: That's a lie.

TEACHER: . . . Why don't you come to school?

GIRL: I'm aware of this phenomenon of "shutting yourself in," but I'm not like that. I don't go to school because I don't like school. That's all.

TEACHER: Grown-ups don't get to take time off like this.

GIRL: If you aren't allowed to do it when you're grown up, all the more reason I should do it now, don't you think? If I don't go to school again, my parents and the school administration will talk and I'll graduate anyway, isn't that right? It's compulsory education.

TEACHER: How do you know that?

GIRL: You can learn a lot on the Internet. If you write a good report on my grades and conduct, I can pass the high school entrance exam, too.

TEACHER: Your test scores are always high.

GIRL: I have great confidence in your ability to do this.

TEACHER: What about extracurricular activities? Is it just the astronomy club?

GIRL: There are only three members.

TEACHER: You should think how the other two members feel now.

GIRL: You can't see any stars in Tokyo anyway.

TEACHER: Don't you want to talk with your friends?

GIRL (*Indicates the computer*): I chat with a lot of people. There are grown-ups, too, and it's cheaper than talking on a cell phone. Basically I feel more comfortable when I'm alone. That's all.

TEACHER: . . . I can't say this to anyone but you, but I actually feel the same way.

GIRL: What?

TEACHER: I like to be alone. The happiest time of my life was when I shut myself in, cramming for the college entrance exam.

GIRL: That was your happiest time?

TEACHER: Yes.

GIRL: Grow up.

TEACHER: No I'm still in my adolescence.

GIRL: How can you say that?

TEACHER: Someone said that young people today reach their adolescence at the age of twenty and grow up fully at thirty.

GIRL: You're over thirty.

TEACHER: I can't sleep very well lately. Even when I do sleep, I feel as if I'm on a stretcher being carried to an ambulance.

GIRL: Really? There's a rumor you take naps in the infirmary.

TEACHER: It's true. I'm no good. I've lost my confidence. I'm the lowest of the low.

GIRL: I don't. . . .

TEACHER: You don't agree with that, or you don't deny it?

GIRL: . . . I don't agree with that.

TEACHER: Say it clearly. Say, "No, you are not."

GIRL: . . .

TEACHER: I'm bullied, too. Do you think bullying is just between kids?

GIRL: I'm not bullied.

TEACHER: You are! Face it! If it's not bullying to nickname a girl "Gorilla," I don't know what is.

GIRL: . . . It's cruel to gorillas.

TEACHER: There's bullying among teachers, too. The principal makes me rewrite my papers again and again. He says I should make the event schedule plan by the second. When I complained that it's meaningless, he got furious and reported to the board of education that I have a problematic personality. It's been going on for years. It's affecting me physically. I can't wake up in the morning, and I lost my voice.

(TEACHER *rolls up her sleeve. There are razor scars on her wrist.*)

TEACHER: Look. I have to either retire or kill myself. I've got so many scars that I have to wear long sleeves even in the summer. I can't believe anything anymore. I want to stay in a room and be still. Please let me shut myself in.

GIRL: It's pretty weird for a teacher to shut herself in.

TEACHER: Is it weird?

GIRL: . . . Weird.

TEACHER: I know what you mean. Whatever I do, people say I look strained. I think so, too. When I speak, everybody senses I'm being forced to speak. Kids know it. That's why. That's why I took part in the mock "wedding ceremony." I was bullied into it.

GIRL: Let's stop talking about it. It's not like I was in some sort of living hell after they did the "wedding ceremony."

TEACHER: I'm the one who should get married. I want to get married and retire and finish this.

GIRL: You can quit.

TEACHER: I don't want be a loser.

GIRL: Is it a matter of winning or losing?

TEACHER: Why do you study? To be a winner in life, right?

GIRL: . . . That won't get you anywhere. Where there's a winner, there's a loser.

(TEACHER *lies down and weeps.*)

GIRL: I'll show you something.

(*She covers the bulb with a bowl. It's dark in the room. Small spots of light through holes on the bowl project on the wall.*)

TEACHER: . . . What?

GIRL (*Points at the wall*): That's the Milky Way . . . Ursa Major.

TEACHER: . . . A planetarium?

GIRL: The Northern Hemisphere in summer.

TEACHER (*She finds something*): Cassiopeia.

GIRL: Where's Scorpio?

TEACHER: . . . There!

(*The stars blur and fade out.*)

BLACKOUT

RETURNEE

YOUNG MAN *is hanging from the ceiling stretching his body. He looks as if he is floating in the air.* LADY *is speaking.*

LADY: Kasper Hauser was found in Nuremberg, on May 26, 1828. He was a wild man with a simple felt hat. He looked like he was sixteen or seventeen years old. He had been kept in a dungeon since he was born, never saw the sunshine, fed only water and poor-quality bread. He was forced to sit down for long periods of time. His bones were deformed.

YOUNG MAN: When I was taken into protective custody, the muscles in my legs had become so weak I couldn't even walk.

LADY: He couldn't speak, but he wasn't an idiot. Doctors examined him and said that he was close to being an innocent young child.

YOUNG MAN: I was in the hospital for a year, and I came back home after fifteen years.

LADY: Strangely enough, he had peculiar abilities. For example, he could distinguish different kinds of metal just by touching them.

YOUNG MAN: Since then, I have gradually been getting well. Well enough to listen to music and take walks in my neighborhood.

LADY: He got an education, learned language and common sense, but he could never believe in religion and loathed priests and clergymen.

YOUNG MAN: I attended my community's coming-of-age ceremony and got a driving license, too.

LADY: He once asked a professor who was teaching him, "If there is a god almighty, can he turn back the clock?"

YOUNG MAN: Now I've recovered from the aftereffects and am working on rehabilitating socially.

LADY: Once, he was attacked by someone who cut his face.

YOUNG MAN: I can't remember anything about the time I was confined.

LADY: And on December 14, 1833, he was stabbed to death by a stranger in a small park in Ansbach. No one knows for sure who confined him in the first place.

YOUNG MAN: The only thing I faintly remember is that the TV was always on. Someone turned up the volume, and I could hear the voices. They were always detective movies, samurai movies, or war movies.

LADY: . . . What is the most enjoyable thing for you now?

YOUNG MAN: I like to hang like this and stretch my body at night.

LADY: Where are you hanging?

YOUNG MAN: The Attic of the world.

LADY: What are you doing, hanging there?

YOUNG MAN: I'm on watch.

LADY: What are you watching?

YOUNG MAN: The whole world.

LADY: What do you hear?

YOUNG MAN: The sound of the earth spinning.

LADY: . . . Ladies and gentlemen, does this young man shut himself up in the universe of the night? No, he doesn't. This young man is spying on people's private lives through the knotholes on the ceiling and listening to private conversations. He has become the phantom of the Attic.

(*We hear the noise of people. It sounds like a large number of whistles rather than people's voices. Sometimes we hear words.* PEOPLE *appear one after another.*)

PEOPLE 1: Someone is spying on me from the Attic. For about three years now.

PEOPLE 2: The ceiling board in the closet was loose, and you can go up and down through it.

PEOPLE 3: He remodeled the Attic without my permission and built a room up there.

PEOPLE 4: There are lots of knotholes as if it had been eaten by insects. . . .

PEOPLE 5: He was staring at me. Holding his breath.

PEOPLE 1: My life leaked out.

PEOPLE 2: He comes down while I'm out and eats the food in my fridge.

PEOPLE 3: He pissed all over there.

PEOPLE 4: He swapped my brand-new electric appliances for secondhand ones.

PEOPLE 5: He swaps everything for fakes.

PEOPLE 1: He's trying to see if I notice it.

PEOPLE 2: These clothes I'm wearing now are cheap imitations that look exactly like the real thing. I can tell by the texture.

PEOPLE 3: . . . My dog and my kid have changed, too.

PEOPLE 4: I'm the only real thing.

PEOPLE 5: He is going to confine me in the Attic and take my place, too.

PEOPLE 1: . . . My neighbors are all changed.

PEOPLE 2: Get out.

PEOPLE 3: Get out.

PEOPLE 4: Get out of the Attic.

PEOPLE 5: Get out.

(YOUNG MAN *is pulled down by* PEOPLE.)

YOUNG MAN: We strongly protest the unreasonable persecution of the Attic users.

(YOUNG MAN *is carried away by* PEOPLE. OLDER BROTHER *appears and watches.* ANCHORPERSON *appears.*)

ANCHORPERSON: Since the Attic regulation passed both Houses, the Attic Club went underground and continues the illegal distribution of the banned Attic. Despite investigations by the authorities, the Attic kit hasn't disappeared from Japanese society and is still out there even today.

(*The* ATTIC PROMOTERS *enter.*)

PROMOTER 1: The Attic is a culture. Especially the original Attic. It is the Japanese invention that is valued all over the world.

PROMOTER 2: It's all right to use it because we bought it. Isn't that right?

(PROMOTERS *are pushed back by* PEOPLE, *who have appeared again.*)

OLDER BROTHER: The question is, who is making the Attics?

ANCHORPERSON: Elephant Brand, Yanmar, and the copy company in Taiwan stopped producing them.

PEOPLE 1: We should focus on the originals.

(PEOPLE *wearing a sign "Former Attic Dweller" stand side by side.*)

FORMER DWELLER 1: I used to be an Attic dweller. But now I drink milk everyday.

(*He drinks a bottle of milk, with his arms akimbo.*)

FORMER DWELLER 2: If there wasn't an Attic, I would never have dreamed of shutting myself up.

FORMER DWELLER 3 (*He is naked except for the sign*): I healed myself by streaking.

ANCHORPERSON: . . . Now I've sneaked into an Attic boycott meeting.

(PEOPLE IN DISGUISE *appear.*)

DISGUISE 1: Even if people are allowed to own Attics, I think we need a registration system.

DISGUISE 2: I demand the wholesale arrest of distributors and the prohibition of sale.

DISGUISE 3: Protect our children.

DISGUISE 4: Attic parties are the most extreme decadence.

DISGUISE 1: This is a revival of dungeons.

DISGUISE 2: My neighbor hid their good-for-nothing child in one.

DISGUISE 3: Attics speak of the darkness of the human mind.

DISGUISE 4: They are possessed by evil spirits. We must keep praying.

DISGUISE 1: They're for sex. How can you think otherwise?

DISGUISE 2: In a small space like that, there is only one thing you feel like doing.

DISGUISE 3: There are people who held wedding ceremonies in them.

DISGUISE 1: I have never seen anything more immoral than the Attic conference. They livened things up by trying to see how many people could get into an Attic at once. It was the most repulsive thing I've ever seen.

ANCHORPERSON: How many could get into one?

(PEOPLE *are packed in an Attic.*)

PACKED PEOPLE 1: Exactly thirteen.

PACKED PEOPLE 2: I respect the *Guinness Book of Records* for rejecting their application.

OLDER BROTHER: I'm looking for the person who invented all this.

PEOPLE: . . .

OLDER PEOPLE: Haven't you found him yet? The person who manufactured the original Attic?

(PEOPLE *disappear in back of the Attic. The sound of an elevator door opening. The back wall of the Attic that closed a moment ago slides open again from the center. There is darkness and no one is there.* OLDER BROTHER *jumps into the darkness. The sliding doors close.*)

BLACKOUT

ELEVATOR

The sound of the elevator doors opening. The back wall of the Attic slides open from the center. OLDER BROTHER *comes in.* MAN WITH A CAP *is waiting in front.*

MAN: . . . Going up.

(*There is a "ping" sound and then the sound of the elevator going up.* MAN WITH A CAP *takes out a cushion from the ceiling space and offers it to* OLDER BROTHER.)

MAN: Please have a seat. Which floor do you want?

BROTHER: Is this an elevator?

MAN: Yes, sir.

BROTHER: Why this shape?

MAN: I don't understand what you mean, sir . . . ?

BROTHER: Was this like this originally?

MAN: Is there a problem, sir?

BROTHER: People usually stand in an elevator.

MAN: It's more comfortable to sit. (*Offers tea.*) Would you like some tea, sir?

BROTHER: What great service.

MAN: They serve meals on airplanes, don't they? Which floor do you want?

BROTHER: Who remodeled it to look like this?

MAN: I don't know.

BROTHER: You didn't do it, then?

MAN: I'm an elevator man.

BROTHER: Not an elevator girl?

MAN: I am a man.

BROTHER: Why don't they have a girl?

MAN: Most drivers of vehicles are men.

BROTHER: Leaving room on elevators for the girls.

MAN: This is my job, sir.

BROTHER: They usually have a girl on an elevator.

MAN: Could you tell me which floor you want?

BROTHER: How many floors are there?

MAN: Aren't you getting off?

BROTHER: How many?

MAN: I'm telling you I'll go to any floor you want, asshole.

BROTHER: You actually are operating it, then.

MAN: We are going up and up now.

BROTHER: Just go up as high as you can.

MAN: Is that what you want?

BROTHER: Yeah.

MAN: . . . I'll take you there.

(MAN WITH A CAP *pushes a button, and the machine roars. The elevator suddenly accelerates upward.*)

MAN (*Looking up*): It's picking up speed.

BROTHER: Just go ahead.

MAN: . . . Go, go, go. Don't hold back!

BROTHER: Go the whole way.

MAN: I don't want anyone to go higher than me!

BROTHER: How high are we going?

MAN: To the top, of course.

BROTHER: The top?

MAN: I've told you over and over that we are going up.

BROTHER: Go to the highest point.

MAN: Very well, sir.

(*Sudden brake noise and the sound of the elevator stops. The back door slides open. There is a darkness spreading in the back. The sound of water dripping. Wind blows. We hear air noise from far way.*)

MAN: The top floor, sir.

BROTHER: . . . Where are we?

MAN: The top floor.

BROTHER: What's on the top floor?

MAN: The top floor is just under the roof. What is just under the roof?

BROTHER: An Attic?

MAN: Yes.

BROTHER: It looks like there's nothing here.

MAN: . . .

BROTHER: All right. Get off.

MAN: . . .

BROTHER: You are dismissed.

MAN: I can't get off.

BROTHER: You can't?

MAN: This is an Attic.

BROTHER: Why can't you get off?

MAN: We went up and down, but this is still an Attic.

BROTHER: . . .

MAN: If you want to leave, please go this way.

(OLDER BROTHER *goes out into the darkness in the back.*)

BROTHER: . . . It's so dark I can't see anything.

MAN: Watch your step.

BROTHER: It's slippery. It's like a cave.

(OLDER BROTHER *calls out.*)

BROTHER: Hey!

(*His voice echoes. The echo dies out, and we only hear the dripping sound of water as though we are in a limestone cave.* OLDER BROTHER *lights his lighter.*)

BROTHER: What's over there?

MAN: I don't know.

(OLDER BROTHER *steps into the darkness and disappears. Then we hear his voice.*)

BROTHER: . . . Who's there? . . . Don't hide. Come on out.

(OLDER BROTHER *holds up his lighter to the space. He comes downstage.*)

BROTHER (*Stares*): They're all drawings—Murals?

MAN: They say the first human graffiti was on cave walls.

BROTHER: . . .

MAN: The sun has never reached this cave.

(*The flame of the lighter flickers in the wind. . . .*)

BROTHER: Horses, reindeer, bears. . . . They look alive.

MAN: Ancient people knew the drawings on the cave walls would look alive when they were lit with a flickering flame.

(OLDER BROTHER *is staring at* MAN WITH A CAP.)

MAN: People leave behind evidence of their lives.

BROTHER: Who are you?

MAN: . . .

BROTHER: Are you the man in the drawing?

MAN: There is something else on the wall that isn't a drawing.

(OLDER BROTHER *finds something engraved in a corner of the murals.*)

BROTHER (*Reads*): The day you choose to be alone is as long as a year you spend adrift.

MAN: . . . What is it?

BROTHER: My brother. My brother wrote this for a collection of essays in high school.

MAN: Why not draw something yourself?

BROTHER: . . .

MAN: If there is something you've lost, draw it all over the wall.

BROTHER: . . .

BLACKOUT

CARDBOARD HOUSE

The evening casts a red light on a cardboard house. The house is the same size as an Attic. Or the walls of an Attic are covered with cardboard. There is a bicycle horn hanging on the wall. MAN WITH CRUTCHES *comes.*

CRUTCHES: Hello—Hello.

(*He waits for a while, but nobody replies. He tries the horn. One wall is taken away from inside, and we can see into the house. . . . A lot of furniture, kitchen tools, blankets, and so on fill the house. Almost everything necessary for human life is there. But everything is old and shabby. We can see that it was originally an Attic, but because the back wall is also covered with cardboard, it isn't as tightly sealed up as the original. A blue plastic sheet covering the crevices rattles. A curtain is waving in the wind. It was* TAKE *who took away the cardboard wall.* UME *is toasting dried sardines on a portable kitchen stove. They sit face to face at a small table with an electric foot warmer, sipping a glass of Japanese saké.*)

TAKE: . . . Welcome.

UME: What is it?

CRUTCHES: I was told to warn you. It's the consensus of the community.

TAKE: Is it?

CRUTCHES: We'd like to ask you to leave because you're spoiling the beauty of the riverbank.

UME: How did you set the criteria for beauty?

CRUTCHES: I don't know. I can't live in this town if I rebel against the neighborhood association. I'm just telling you what was decided.

TAKE (*To* UME): He is just doing what he's told.

CRUTCHES: Kids are scarier than the neighborhood association. They're so worked up that there isn't much they won't do. (*He takes a look.*) They're seeing how things work out around here now, too.

TAKE: They stole empty cans right out of my hands the other day.

UME: You can get eight yen per can at a recycling shop.

CRUTCHES: They kicked and broke my crutches, too. . . .

UME: I see you every once in a while. You've had those crutches for some time now.

CRUTCHES: . . . Yes.

UME: Why can't we stay here? There are lots of stalls on this riverbank.

CRUTCHES: This isn't a stall.

UME: If stalls are all right, we'll sell something.

CRUTCHES: What are you going to sell?

TAKE: We'll serve tea. The smallest café in the world.

UME (*Offers the glass to* MAN WITH CRUTCHES): Or do you prefer saké? We could call it the "3.3 Square Meter Bar."

CRUTCHES: There's no room for customers.

UME: How about a pachinko cash-in booth?

TAKE: A box seat for the fireworks festival.

UME: A ticket booth.

CRUTCHES: Tickets for what?

UME: If you want a ticket to the other world, I'll give you a discount.

(MATSU, *who has been sleeping under a blanket, wakes up.*)

MATSU (*Still half asleep*): . . . A messenger from the other world?

TAKE: Another of the last surviving human beings is here.

CRUTCHES: Are human beings going to become extinct?

MATSU: Yeah, yeah.

UME: The world is coming to an end.

CRUTCHES: I hadn't noticed.

UME: Look at that.

CRUTCHES: What?

UME: You can see the clouds around Mount Fuji from here.

CRUTCHES: I can't see Mount Fuji itself.

TAKE: On a clear day you can.

UME: . . . The clouds are glimmering gold.

MATSU: Yes, they are.

CRUTCHES: Are they?

UME: They always shine that way the evening before a disaster.

CRUTCHES: Disaster?

UME (*Nods*): Years ago, before the ANA crash. Before the big Hanshin earthquake, before the day the Aum cult spread the sarin gas in the subway, and the day before 9/11. . . .

CRUTCHES: You can predict things that happen in the United States as well?

UME: I've lived on this riverbank for ten years. I always know, on the evening before when something is going to happen.

CRUTCHES: Then tell it to the people.

UME: I can't do that. These events are inevitable destiny.

CRUTCHES: What do you do, then?

TAKE: Providing is preventing.

(TAKE *opens a small door on the ceiling and pulls down a cloth bag.*)

UME: We are taking all possible measures to control the crisis.

TAKE: We've secured emergency provisions.

UME: We've got a shelter, too.

CRUTCHES: A shelter?

UME (*Displaying a radio*): We can cope with any kind of crisis as long as we stay in here.

TAKE: Earthquakes, lightning strikes, fire, my father, anything.

UME: We can even cope with a nuclear war. It can withstand the explosion and keeps the radiation away, too.

CRUTCHES: Really?

UME: It's the latest model shelter.

CRUTCHES: It wasn't built that way.

MATSU: Well, I don't care if I die.

UME: The Deva god will protect us.

CRUTCHES: The Deva god?

UME (*Looking at the drawing on the wall*): Our guardian god here.

CRUTCHES (*Peers at the drawing*): Does it look like a Deva god?

TAKE: He's carrying a fishing rod. He's that fishing freak from the movies.

(MATSU *looks at* MAN WITH CRUTCHES *and bursts into tears.*)

MATSU: . . . The other day, my son visited me for the first time in twenty years. He's about the same age as you. He glared at me.

TAKE: You should be kind to the elderly.

MATSU: Get out.

CRUTCHES: . . . I've notified you.

TAKE: Be careful tomorrow.

UME: Come visit us again.

(MAN WITH CRUTCHES *exits.*)

TAKE: . . . People cooled to us after we moved into this place.

UME: They don't like us living in here.

TAKE: It was abandoned; why shouldn't we?

(*The Attic suddenly trembles.*)

TAKE: Earthquake.

UME: It's all right. It's quake proof.

MATSU: . . . It's the kids.

TAKE: They climbed on the roof.

UME: It can handle the weight of the kids.

TAKE: It can handle an elephant stepping on it.

(*It seems that the Attic was lifted up and then thrown down.*)

UME: They threw us in the river.

TAKE: . . . We're floating.

UME: Don't panic. We'll float.

MATSU: Oh!

TAKE: We're sinking!

UME: Didn't you say this was the latest model . . . ?

(*The water comes in from the crevices. They are sinking. The sound of bubbles. The three of them are swaying in the water.*)

BLACKOUT

FACTORY

The sparks are coming from a grinder grinding an iron frame. What we thought to be the sound of bombing and explosions is actually the sound of hammering and construction. We are inside a small factory. It's where the Attics are manufactured. There is an Attic that is put on a worktable for someone to work on. It's almost competed except the back and front walls. MAN WITH CRUTCHES *is working with the grinder.* MAN WITH A CAP *is lying in the Attic. He is drawing something in a corner of a wall with a brush tied to the end of a rod.* OLDER BROTHER *is standing in the corner.* MAN WITH CRUTCHES *stops working.*

CRUTCHES: How did you find us?

BROTHER: . . .

CRUTCHES: You're the first person to discover that this is the place where the Attics are made.

BROTHER: Is that so?

CRUTCHES: Are you going to rat on us? . . . Do you want money?

BROTHER: I didn't know what I would do when I found the manufacturer. . . . Now I know. I just wanted to know who it was.

CRUTCHES: It is as you see it.

BROTHER: Just you and your partner?

CRUTCHES: Yeah.

BROTHER (*To* MAN WITH A CAP): Are you drawing something?

CAP: . . .

CRUTCHES: Sorry, but he can't speak or sit up.

BROTHER: It's his job to draw the trademark to complete the product. He also puts in the plugs and turns on the switches.

(MAN WITH A CAP *is using another rod now, taking a dust cloth, touching the tools in the factory, and the like.*)

BROTHER: . . . Are you brothers?

CRUTCHES: An accident. Ten years ago.

BROTHER: . . .With your older brother?

CRUTCHES: He's my younger brother.

BROTHER: . . .

CRUTCHES: We liked bicycles. We often built them by ourselves. We might be the best double riders in the world.

BROTHER: . . .

CRUTCHES: I don't remember my first love, but I remember his.

BROTHER: . . . What is the Attic Hunter?

CRUTCHES: I heard that they call it that.

BROTHER: Is it his self-portrait?

CRUTCHES: It was originally a room for him. We made it the perfect size for him to lie inside.

BROTHER: . . . Doesn't he use one?

CRUTCHES: Looks like he can't be satisfied with his drawings.

BROTHER: How long are you going to continue making them?

CRUTCHES: Until he finishes the last one.

BROTHER: . . .

CRUTCHES: When we were kids, we wanted to make a time machine. Then we could go anywhere and see anybody. But a time machine is dangerous. We might not be able to come back. . . . There is only one way to call for help.

BROTHER: What is it?

CRUTCHES: Draw a large version of this picture.

BROTHER: Then what happens?

CRUTCHES: My brother comes to help me.

BROTHER: . . .

CRUTCHES: That's the rule we made a long time ago.

(MAN WITH A CAP *pushes a buzzer on the factory wall with a long rod.*)

CRUTCHES: Done. . . . This is the last one.

CAP: . . .

(MAN WITH A CAP *bushes another buzzer with the long rod.*)

CRUTCHES (*Listens to the buzzer*): It isn't perfect yet.

BROTHER: . . . I'll take it.

CRUTCHES: . . . All right.

BROTHER: Can I go in?

CRUTCHES: Go ahead.

(OLDER BROTHER *enters the Attic. He sits beside* MAN WITH A CAP. OLDER BROTHER *draws a large version of the Attic Hunter. Lights fade out. Deep darkness covers the space.*)

BLACKOUT

MEMORY

Drops of water are dripping, drawing intricate patterns like a cobweb. The sound of wind blowing through a hollow. We can see two vague shadows in the deep darkness. One of them is OLDER BROTHER. *The other is* MAN WITH A CAP. *He looks like a young man dressed for climbing mountains. We hear faint voices from the darkness.*

MAN: . . . Looks like we're lost.

BROTHER: Yeah.

MAN: What shall we do?

BROTHER: Don't panic at a time like this. Look 360 degrees around you, and you'll find a clue.

MAN: That's just like you.

BROTHER: I should retire soon.

MAN: Why?

BROTHER: I can't take a long vacation. I'm not a student anymore.

MAN: . . . I'm sure we can find the way back.

BROTHER: Don't you ever get lost?

MAN: . . . When I get lost, I listen.

BROTHER: What do you hear?

MAN: . . . Sound of the wind. Sound of water boiling in the kitchen. Sound of a railroad crossing. Sound of an old electric fan. And the sound of you spinning the globe. The sound I heard while I was hiding in the Attic with you.

BROTHER: . . . I see.

MAN: Do you remember?

BROTHER: Yes, I do.

MAN: Really?

BROTHER: If I get lost in the future, I'll go back there.

MAN: . . . Haven't you noticed yet? This is it.

BROTHER: Where are you?

MAN: I've been in the same place all along.

BROTHER: . . .

MAN: My favorite place in the world. The top of the world. The secret base for adventure. The place we promised where we'd meet each other again whatever happens.

BROTHER: . . . Then I've arrived at last?

MAN: . . . Yes, you have.

(*The darkness deepens. . . . Only the sound of the wind remains.*)

CURTAIN

Okada Toshiki, *Five Days in March*, directed by Okada Toshiki, chelfitsch, March 2006.
(Photograph by Yokota Tōru; courtesy of precog)

FIVE DAYS IN MARCH

OKADA TOSHIKI

TRANSLATED BY AYA OGAWA

Okada Toshiki (b. 1973) is a playwright, director, and novelist. His work for the stage is a unique marriage of performance art and the hyperreal colloquial dialogue innovated by older dramatists like Hirata Oriza. A native of Yokohama, Okada collaborated with the dancer Tetsuka Natsuko to establish in 1997 their own theater company, chelfitsch, which is baby talk, the playwright explained, for the English word "selfish." The distinctively spasmodic gestures and contortions of Okada's performers bear no relation to the text or action being related, thereby signifying a gap between word and deed. This is similar to the gap in modern life between thought and action that Miyagi Satoshi, director of the Ku Na'uka Theater Company, also uses in his bunraku-like productions. Although words no longer seem to reflect our true feelings, our bodies betray us in many subtle ways. Okada's dramaturgy, for which he credits Bertolt Brecht's *Verfremsdungseffekt* (alienation effect), marks a division between the fictional story or drama spoken by his characters and the actual presence of the actors enacting it. Despite the shock appeal of his physical performance pieces, Okada is still a consummate storyteller and a keen critic of contemporary society. His plays are made up of monologues and dialogues about Japan's disaffected young people and their awkward place in a country beset by economic and political challenges. The language is slangy and idiomatic, a startlingly realistic record of the way that young Japanese men and women speak today and an accurate reflection of their present preoccupations and anxieties. Works like *Enjoy* (*Enjoi*, 2006) and *Free Time* (*Furī taimu*, 2008) address the phenomenon of "freeters," twenty-somethings forced to work in the shadow economy of contract and part-time jobs because the postwar system of lifetime employment no longer exists. *Five Days in March* (*Sangatsu no itsukukan*), which won the Kunio Kishida Award for best play of 2004, is set during the previous year, during the invasion of Iraq, when Japan once again was forced to reassess its dubious role in international affairs. Against a backdrop of antiwar demonstrations in the streets of Tokyo, a couple uses sex as a way to connect to each other and to the world that they feel they cannot find in politics or any other social activity.

SCENE 1

ACTOR 1: So, I'm thinking we're going to start this Five Days in March thing, but on the first day, well, first of all, I'm thinking we'll kick off with setting this story in March 2003, but when he woke up in the morning, this is kind of the story about this man named Minobe, but he was in a hotel when he woke up in the morning, and he thought like, why am I in a hotel, and on top of that there's like this woman, who the hell is she I don't know this chick, and he's all thinking like she's asleep and stuff, and like, but he remembered right away, oh that's right last night, like, oh yeah last night I got totally wasted, and I remember now, this must be the love hotel in Shibuya, he remembered right away. . . . And so I'm thinking we're going to do the story of the real day 1, oh last night I was in Roppongi, like, um, Roppongi because back in March 2003 was before they made like Roppongi Hills, that's where we wanna start this story, but now Roppongi station is like totally when you're coming up from the subway and when you get above ground, you know how you're going downhill if you want to come toward Azabu, back then right where the Hills are now there's like a pedestrian bridge, but around there, it was a normal, back then, it was still like a normal straight path you could walk right, that's about the time of this story I'm thinking about, this story takes place, but over there, there's like this club with live music, and I'm thinking about starting this story when he went to this club to hear some music, but I was thinking I would talk about how so the live music there was really great but, and also, I mean I say also, but I'm thinking I'll talk about how there was this girl he met that day at the club, and he kind of just afterward with this girl totally hooked up with her or like and, not only that but went crazy and hooked up without any protection and stuff but before that, or like, first off he went to the club on day 1 of the five days in March but like (*By this moment,* ACTOR 2 *has entered.* ACTOR 1 *indicates himself and* ACTOR 2 *as he continues*) that day, the two of them, man and man, went to the club, see, that, um, there were two men who were like going to go to Roppongi right, so that's where it starts with the two men, that's how the story starts . . . The way that road goes downhill toward West Azabu was, around that area where before you get to the part where the slope gets seriously way steep, there's a club that's basically facing the main drag, this pretty minor band from like Canada was playing that night, and the reason why they went to see something like that was because, well, but that club had really awesome music, like that was really awesome, man, actually it was just one of the two of the guys who thought that it was "a really awesome club" and was like "totally really moved, like honestly it wasn't like I had high expectations or anything like that, but while I had left my guard down and wasn't expecting anything special, the music was like unexpectedly really awesome, and I was seriously totally moved," they were drinking beer at that moment, but that club was or, rather, that day there was a one-drink minimum, so that's why they were drinking beer or, rather, the music had finished already ,and they were just hanging out after and he'd already drunk his one drink so his second drink was, he was on his second beer, but "But there's this, that music probably, on the level of skill, that and wasn't really, probably if I were thinking along the good-to-lame spectrum, because I'm not really knowledgeable about music, really, so this isn't a professional you know so, but it was pretty much, completely lame probably, this thing of performance or like, yeah, but that's what I was thinking while I was listening to the music and feeling moved, but" and that was like not necessarily the first time I'd thought that but "the importance of that kind of thing in the end is *not* about technique and stuff is, like in live music is like that and, in a way everything has something of that, I think, but I thought that was admirable, or like not admirable but more, that thing itself, that thing in and of itself is, probably really important, was what I was thinking or like, that's what I think, yeah, you understand what I'm saying? Am I drunk, and has what I've been talking about perhaps been complete nonsense?" I asked, and "Nah, I get it," was what she said, so "Oh, this girl might actually get it," I thought, and "but I guess it's pretty obvious, for her to be at a club like this is pretty, I mean, she'd have to have that kind of quality to know about this kind of club," is what I thought, actually, and convinced myself in that moment, kind of

ACTOR 2: Remember he said that there were two men and that one of them had hooked up on day 1, right, but to be accurate it was actually pretty late at night, so really it was the second day, that's the story, but, I mean, the day of the hook-up,

ACTOR 1: And then the chick said like "For me the songs or like the music or like the songs, were good but, they were good but, you know, how in between he made those intros, wasn't that super awesome? I was really impressed" she said, and I was like "Oh wow you understand English, I don't understand any of it, huh, then you understood what that the guy was saying, it was like about Iraq, right, that's about all I could catch but," and she was like "Yeah, he was talking about Iraq and stuff, the thing is what he was saying was, um you know, like he came to Japan, right, and he's staying in a hotel, right, and that's like in Shibuya, where he's staying, so this morning he got up early to take a walk because he was in Japan after all, so he first he thought Akihabara, he thought he'd go there first but then, like, in like Shibuya, he ran into the protest coming through, and then so he kinda joined up with it together and marched."

ACTOR 2: Oh really

ACTOR 1: And then like, of course, it was the first time I ever participated in a protest in Japan, but, like, protests in Japan are interesting, unique, really unique, the vocalist, he kept saying,

ACTOR 2: Oh really

ACTOR 1: That was like interesting, and stuff like that, was what he was saying, there were some people who were playing music on their, like, boom box while they were marching, and stuff like that, and there were a few people were singing along to that music, and stuff

ACTOR 2: Yeah, oh really

ACTOR 1: Yeah

ACTOR 2: You really understand English, were you, like, in America or abroad somewhere?

ACTOR 1: Huh, yeah, sort of

ACTOR 2: Study abroad program?

ACTOR 1: Oh, yeah, right study abroad sort of

ACTOR 2: Oh really

ACTOR 1: Also on home stay and stuff

ACTOR 2: Oh really, huh, where did you go?

ACTOR 1: Huh, America

ACTOR 2: "Oh really," he said and then, "Huh, if you were in America, then it must be like, you wanna fuck?" he said, and the two of them just cabbed over to Shibuya and disappeared . . . that's how that story went and the other guy, named Azuma, who was with Minobe that night, didn't have anything as palatable as what happened to Minobe happen to him at all, in fact, after the music was over, the trains had stopped running too, so he couldn't get home so, or, like, he could have made it home if he'd rushed but, like Minobe, has suddenly disappeared, he thought, and, like, he started to feel like well, whatever and stuff, he picked up some chick, so he wandered around till morning in the Roppongi area, but that story just now was what happened on the morning of day 5 when Azuma and Minobe met up again, at a diner, at the break of dawn, that's when he'd heard this whole story, no, Minobe ended up staying in the love hotel with that girl for three days straight, spending the whole entire time in Shibuya apparently, but so this story is what Azuma heard from Minobe when they met up after those three days but, "Did you guys stay in the same place for the whole three days?" he asked and

ACTOR 1: Yeah

ACTOR 2: Huh, that's like, don't they get suspicious, do they care? or like, you can do that kind of thing, huh?

ACTOR 1: Nah, you can do that sort of thing, or like I didn't know either, but we did,

ACTOR 2: "Oh really, you'd never spent several nights in a love hotel before?" of course, I'd only ever stayed single nights myself,

ACTOR 1: Nah, probably in love hotels like probably anything is a go, right, you can do anything as long as you pay . . . like in the guidebooks for, like, foreigners, but super poor foreign tourists they say that the love hotels in Japan are these super cheap hotels, and there're a lot of foreigners who stay in them a lot, she was saying

ACTOR 2: Oh really

ACTOR 1: She did the whole foreign exchange thing and went to America in high school or something, and, like, you know, that guy was talking between songs at the concert that night, she could tell me everything he was saying,

ACTOR 2: "Oh really, so she could speak English"

ACTOR 1: "That like guy, the vocalist, the hotel he was staying in Japan was in Shibuya but, with the other band members, and they all went out to like take a walk in Shibuya, or was it with everyone or just that guy alone, I'm not sure about that but, and then you know that antiwar protest, he saw it, and then he kinda joined up with it and marched"

ACTOR 2: Oh really, he joined up, so you can join up with those that casually?

ACTOR 1: "I don't know but, and then protests in Japan are like, maybe in foreign countries the police don't really follow them like glue, I don't know, but anyway in Japan they're practically like surrounded by the police, and the protest marches are under watch by them, not exactly but they follow them, and that's what was really interesting about Japanese protests, was the story, apparently, not interesting but like particular"

ACTOR 2: You can just slip in that easily into those protests, huh?

ACTOR 1: "Nah, it might be that that one happened to be an open protest, maybe, I don't know but, also they were playing songs on their boom box and stuff" is what she was said

ACTOR 2: Oh really

ACTOR 1: Yeah, so, isn't that amazing? You understand English, did you go abroad to like America or somewhere? I asked, and then she said like "Yeah sort of," study abroad? I asked and then she said like "Oh yeah, right, sort of study abroad," oh really, I said, and because I think girls who speak English are kinda hot and then she said like "I studied abroad but aside from that I did home stays several times and stuff" oh really, huh, so where'd you go? I asked, and she said like "Huh, America" oh really, I said . . . and then seriously I don't remember a single thing after that, that's how his story went, this guy Minobe really didn't remember anything but "Wait, seriously, you don't even remember screwing, isn't that fucked up?" Azuma asked him but he said, "Nah, it's not exactly that I don't remember, I mean I have an image of doing it but I'm not sure when that was, it might have been the girl before," and Azuma told him, "That really is fucked up," and Minobe agreed, "Seriously, it's such a waste not to remember," but like that's not what he meant by fucked up, you know, and then when he woke up he thought like, "why am I in a hotel," and on top of that there's like this woman, who the hell is she I don't know this chick, and he thought like, "she's like asleep" and that's what, but actually he does quickly remember, that's what ends up happening but (*He exits.*)

SCENE 2

ACTOR 3 (*Entering*): So, from here, the story turns over to day 1 of the Five Days in March for Azuma, who got separated from the Minobe guy, but, from the night of day 1 to the morning of day 2, nothing like the hook-up that Minobe had was happening for Azuma or anything, but he was just waiting for the first train with no activity till morning and was apparently just wandering around Roppongi kinda aimlessly, but actually, for Azuma, there was a possibility at the club or like, Azuma that night was secretly, to be honest Azuma thought there was a girl who was maybe going to come to the club, and apparently, there was maybe a chance that Azuma could maybe hook up with that chick, but in the end that girl didn't show up, so after the concert he was like "Oh Minobe's taken off" and "Oh the trains have stopped running—what the heck am I gonna do by myself till morning?" Azuma thought, so then that's where I thought we'd start, but "I might as well get out of here" is where he left the club, but even as he left, there was this lingering thought in his mind, "Oh—that girl, person didn't show up I guess" and like "the Roppongi night is really cold," and stuff like that was what was going through his mind, but Azuma hadn't told Minobe, "There was maybe this kind of girl who might come" or anything, but he talked to me about it a lot, and that's why I'm able to talk about it, because I'd listened to him so I know, but I had met up with Azuma in the evening of the day after the concert, and I had a little, we met up because I needed to return the money I had borrowed from Azuma, and so now we're going to do when I heard that story from Azuma, that's the thing we're going to do now,

ACTOR 2: Nah, really that's not it

ACTOR 3: Oh yeah

ACTOR 2: Nah, or like, that person was a little, nah, really, there was this like "I'm gonna pass on this one" thing, well definitely as a woman's, OK, OK, as a girl's, nah, but really, it wasn't at all like I was thinking about whether this person like "I wonder if she'll be there" or like, there was no, this kind of, feeling of the chemistry or anything, in fact just the opposite, the opposite or like,

ACTOR 3: Opposite

ACTOR 2: "Opposite, opposite, but it might not have even been the opposite or anything," this guy, um, remember there was the concert, well about two days before that, really . . . "We just met at a movie theater so it's like, I mean we did chat a little bit for some reason but, already though, just from that little chat it was really like 'whoa,' like truly, I'm sorry but please, thanks—but no thanks, or like, I don't know what to say you know"

ACTOR 3: So she was the kinda girl who was not at all your type

ACTOR 2: Nah, or like well, yeah, her appearance was see, so-so, cute, cute or like, what is it, kinda, well it doesn't really matter but, but it's not like, "I can't because she's cute," I mean, it's not like I'm not into ugly girls or anything OK, but it was totally, what is it, nah, first of all really, we met at the movie theater and just chatted a little and there was totally an aura like "whoa" really like . . . (*By this point,* ACTRESS 1 *enters.* ACTOR 2 *indicates* ACTRESS 1 *as he continues.*) This is the girl here, the person I had secretly been thinking "she might show up," I was talking about this person see, but, um, to explain who she is, it, and also, why I even knew about the concert that night, which was like "hey, pretty obscure" that was the thing I was going to talk about next, but and that is related to this person also but, . . . I think I said earlier that the band playing the concert today was a Canadian band, but right now they're totally, in fact there's this wretchedly minor movie from Canada, it's flopping pretty badly actually, I went to see it right, nah, I, really like to go see movies that I hear is totally a dud, or like, to tell you the truth the more a movie flops to the extent that it doesn't even inspire rumors about how bad it is, the more interested I am, to actually go and watch a movie and to like experience "Wow, it's true, this is pretty bad," and stuff, I know that's cynical of me, but it's kind of a hobby of mine, so then to get to the point, the music for that movie was made by the band we went to see today, there was that, right, so then at the movie theater there were some flyers for the concert, live performances in Roppongi on such-and-such day, it announced, and it was like, through that connection I kind of, in the end, felt compelled, I mean the substance of the movie itself was really run-of-the-mill, kinda, "the story of an adolescent girl and blablabla" sort of, "who cares" kind of a movie,

ACTRESS 1: It was the sort of "who cares" kind of, totally, yes

ACTOR 2: And you couldn't really say "but at least the music was good" either, but (ACTRESS 1 *lurches*) nobody's going to this concert, I thought (*To* ACTOR 3), it's like weird right, for her to act like she had the chair pulled out from under her here

ACTOR 3: Yeah.

ACTOR 2: That movie was like, it was a late show you know, that started at 9 o'clock, so then you can't get inside until like around 8:45, or maybe it's later, fifty past, so it was really cold, because it's winter, and I was standing at the entrance of the movie theater wearing my coat but, oh, but the reason why I was standing was that, that day I had two advance tickets to that movie, but the other person was, or like well, she was basically like this, my girlfriend, but she said something like "Sorry, I just can't get out of work after all" and couldn't come is what happened, so I was like "Oh yeah? Drop dead," and so then what am I going to do with this extra ticket, was the thing, and so that eventually turned into I'll sell it to someone who doesn't already have a ticket and who's going to buy a ticket at the theater, or it didn't turn into, but I decided that's what I'd do, and so then the first person to show up was, well, her, I asked, "Oh did you come to see the movie?" right, "Do you have a ticket?" is what I said, oh I kind of don't really know, but I thought maybe she mistook me for a weird, you know, I mean weird, you know, you know, I don't even know but, I said "Nah, excuse me, today I was planning to come with a friend, you see, so these two tickets, I bought them, right, but like so then the other person kind of couldn't make it, it turns out, so I have one extra ticket," I said, "So, if you like, or like, I'd be really happy if you'd buy my advance ticket," but then because she looked young I said, "But maybe, um, are you a student, because if you are, then the student price ticket you can buy at the box office downstairs might be cheaper, so buying my ticket would be, in that case, you know," but then she said, "Oh I'm not in school now or anything," so then it was like, "Oh really" and then it was like "I was going to buy a ticket at the door, so I'll buy it," so then, well, I sold it, so that's like, . . . so then well, we were talking a little until the movie started, "Do you watch a lot of movies," "Oh, yes, I guess I do," kind of stuff, and then well we watched and it was over, and then it was like "OK then" . . . (*To* ACTOR 3) so then afterward she kinda, keeps talking to me, or like, kinda, she tried to leave the movie theater with me, you know, saying stuff like "How did you like it? What did you think of it?" and when I said "Nah, it was kinda, well, a normal girl's coming-of-age kinda, yeah, like, who cares kind of movie, wasn't it" she said something like "Oh yes, it was kinda the sort of 'who cares,' totally, yes," and then she found that flyer and said like "Oh, they're like playing a concert!" and "Oh, it's a concert of, oh, a concert by the band that did the music for the movie, and that was like, oh, this is tomorrow and the day after isn't it, it is, they're doing it, wow, maybe I'll go," and you know her saying "maybe I'll go" was a total lie, coming out of her mouth like that,

ACTOR 3: Yeah

ACTOR 2: So then she's like "So do you want to buy the soundtrack and have a good listen for one?" like, for one? what's "for one," I thought like,

ACTRESS 1: So do you want to buy the soundtrack and have a good listen for one?

ACTOR 2: Um, but I don't know about soundtracks—maybe it's just me, but, I don't know, it's kind of like soundtracks are never played for long, or, pretty generally speaking, aren't soundtracks all sort of like that?

ACTRESS 1: Oh, yes, it's like I might totally know what you mean, it's like I totally feel it,

ACTOR 2: Uh, it's just, I think there's this thing with soundtracks, or is it just me, of generally getting bored of listening to it pretty quickly, what do you think about that, I'm pretty, as far as generalizations go,

ACTRESS 1: Yes, there is totally that, yes

ACTOR 2: Yes, there was this time I realized that, and since then, I've been trying out this not buying any soundtracks thing,

ACTRESS 1 (*To the audience*): "Uh-huh, Yes I know what you mean, I think that's so like, such a good point, yes," isn't this guy totally awkward, I mean I am too so, and that's why I felt this really comfortable feeling with him, like it pulled on my heartstrings, like really, you might be like what do you mean heartstrings, but when I met him, there was this, he just seemed pure, but also, whenever I felt that way toward someone, in the past, they always had a girlfriend, and there was this thing like I thought, so this time's probably the same, so there was that, and then I was like fuck it, I'm just gonna take him, I didn't really know why, I felt so like forceful, but I said (*To* ACTOR 2), "Oh, so I guess I shouldn't buy this soundtrack, huh?"

ACTOR 2: Oh uh but, you should just get it, why not?"

ACTRESS 1: Ah—yes, well isn't there this thing like everybody's got their own taste or, yeah, taste, right? So there's this depending on who you are, it might be OK to buy soundtracks.

ACTOR 2: Uh-huh.

ACTRESS 1: Yes, um, so do you want to go to the concert with me, day after tomorrow?

ACTOR 2: Uh, the day after tomorrow, you mean the band from the movie?

ACTRESS 1: Yes.

ACTOR 2: Oh—but if it's the music from that movie, this movie fell flat, even in the reviews and stuff

ACTRESS 1: Oh, but when you actually see it, it's totally, yes

ACTOR 2: So like the music from the movie's probably just as lame

ACTRESS 1: Yes the probability is pretty high, I'd say

ACTOR 2: Oh but like for me, there's actually enjoyment in going to see flops

ACTRESS 1: Oh really?

ACTOR 2: Yeah, I mean I don't know.

ACTRESS 1: Oh, um, well I like totally lucked out today but, I was so stupid—I should've bought advance tickets, but I didn't and I just showed up here, and it was like super lucky to be able to get this sweet ticket, that would've been like are you out of your mind prices at the door, so I mean I'm totally like thank you so much, you know

ACTOR 2: Yeah—

ACTRESS 1: Whoa, but if you had an extra ticket today, weren't you planning to take a date, actually, uh—is that like, I'm sorry, um, but can you tell me your name, only if it's OK, I mean if you don't want to you can just forget it but I feel like, won't you tell me your first name, or it could even just be a nickname—it'd be fine if you want to just call me Miffy, but.

ACTOR 2: Uh—

ACTRESS 1: Yes even like your handle, or whatever would be cool, I'm just asking because there's like I don't know what should I call you thing, um, oh, is this too weird of me, it's really, is there a wigged out feeling like are you like "oh my god how'd I get stuck with this crazy girl" what can I do, like, um, um, how about I'll just give you a name, I'm really sorry I'll just choose a really convenient name, is that all right?

ACTOR 2: Uh—

ACTRESS 1: So let's say Mr. Sato, yes, Mr. Sato, you have a girlfriend, right? Like, oh wow, yes, um, it's totally like, is there a like, the silence is deafening, you know, exactly like, there I've gone and done it again, or like, oh my god I wanna die like, Sato, like, yes, actually, I'm, you know those fake food displays you know what I'm talking about at restaurants, you know not the high-end restaurants, but more like family-type cafeterias, you know, where there's this thing where they have the fake curry and ramen and pancakes, stuff from the menu on display, you know, they're called like dummies or samples or, so that's what I make at work

ACTOR 2: Oh really?

ACTRESS 1: Yes, so is it OK if I ask you to make a final decision, not like about what we were talking about before but

ACTOR 2: Uh, yes

ACTRESS 1: And what I mean by final, is that like you really have to pick just one option, there's like three options for me, all right, um, Option 1: Mr. Sato will give me his address

ACTOR 2: Uhhhh—(*He exits.*)

ACTRESS 1: Option 2: Mr. Sato gives me his e-mail; Option 3: Mr. Sato give me his cell phone number, though it could be your home number too, or are you like "whoa, no way to any of those" or what do you think, are you like "no way" to all of them?

SCENE 3

ACTRESS 1: Yes, anyway that's kind of the way that the young girl failed in her conquest or like sunk even before even getting to the conquest, or like, just sunk, like suicide bomb BOOM, or like, you've really gone and done it again, arg arg arg, you really can't ever leave the house again for the rest of your life, kind of, it's better if you just don't go out like, you have no place on Earth, really I think I really just want to go to Mars and like, but Miffy did succeed in getting Sato's address actually, although it's not certain whether it was his real address, but Miffy was thinking "I'll write a letter from Mars," even though she was pretty sure "If I were to write a letter from Mars I'd have to address it, and I think there's a pretty big chance that that address is probably fake," but she also imagined, "But even if it runs out to be an unknown addressee, it probably wouldn't be returned all the way to Mars, or like if it were returned, then that would just confirm what I'd predicted, though still, the shock would be pretty great, but mailing from Mars there's a part of you that's like whatever happens to that letter you'll never know, and another part that's like you'll never have to find out that the address was fake and the letter never reached him, Mars is psychologically healthy," like Miffy did you blow yourself up at the movies, and afterward, Miffy, she lives with her Mom and Dad in their house right now, but she has her own room and she lives there by herself, but when Miffy came home after blowing herself up she got online at home, Miffy has her own Web site, but she wrote on her journal from her computer, "Today was an absolutely important day in my life, and the reason why is that, today, I decided that I am definitely going to Mars, something happened that made me realize clearly that I can no longer remain on Earth, although I had suspected this vaguely for a while up till now, but today it's like I really felt it, and what it was that triggered this was something that I cannot write down in detail here, but in one word, I had done it, again, to a mistaken person, and on top of that he turned out to be a really awkward guy, and probably, or like most definitely he thought I was some weird chick, although he himself was the weird one, and I was even weirder than him so, it was really, I've done it again or like, that's why even though I already knew that nobody wanted me to remain on Earth any longer, I had today, furthermore, increased the number of people who thought I should not be on Earth by one person, of my own accord, that's why I was like I should really go to Mars, if I remain on Earth any longer, the number of that kind of people is only going to grow to amazing heights I thought, and I just discovered the other day that there's this thing, apparently, this summer, Mars is going to be closer to Earth than it has ever been, apparently, so I did have the thought that this would be good timing for me to get to Mars, and so I'm secretly making plans and stuff, but when I write posts on my home page about how I really want to get there soon, and I always write these entries in my study, but I mean though it's called a study, it's not as if I actually study there anymore of course, but for me, even though I'm not studying, since my childhood it was, I mean my study, but when I was a kid I studied quite a lot actually, I was among those who actually liked studying quite a bit, but of course I was just a kid, but there's a sense that I feel quite nostalgic for that part of me, or it's a very precious part so, from my point of view, this room should still be referred to as the study, and that's how things are but, to my parents I just call it my room, like normal, but like now, when I'm updating my home page or writing in my diary like this, or reading comic books, or drawing comics, which in fact at times has been the case, since I still do stuff like that in the study, but when I am doing stuff like that in the study, there are times when suddenly I begin to feel like this study is this kind of small spaceship, and like the study is tearing away from the rest of the house and becomes independent and, well, is flying but, I mean it's this tiny little spaceship in the vast outer space and, it's really the air and stuff that's so quiet, transparent or like, the sense of solitude or something is at this really great feeling of, what is it, I'm filled with the feeling that what I love the most is being all alone by myself after all, and if I open the door, in zero gravity, the airless air of outer space would come seeping in, and there's this feeling that if I pull the curtain away from the window right now, there would definitely be the view of the universe, and it's this intense feeling sometimes, and in those moments I am, no matter what anyone else says, free, or like I'm wishing I could always have that feeling you know, or like I totally feel that way, but I should just get carried away by it and really get whisked off to Mars just like that or like, because Earth is all like, there's a war starting, and China's all messed up with this SARS thing, and Earth is all like gonna run out of oil in a few decades, they're saying, but I would still, thinking logically, totally be alive, hello, like, on the one hand, Earth and stuff is, I think it's kind of done, it's already game over, they say that if you breathe the air in areas where they've blown up dirty bombs and stuff you totally get cancer, or like dirty bombs are not cool or like that's why Earth is finished already on so many levels, really, Mars and stuff is way more, I mean I don't think it has to be Mars either but Jupiter and stuff, but definitely we'd be better off thinking about how to seriously escape from Earth to another, like a star somewhere or a planet, starting now, really, for sure, everybody! I tend to get overwhelmed by thoughts like that actually, or like . . . whoa, it's kind of like, I just thought as I was writing in this diary but, after all, I kind of suddenly fell for this person I met at the theater today, man, or so then I swear it was this, I completely made the wrong move-type-deal, I mean even this diary entry is wrong you know, or like I know this, but I'm doing it anyway, and that's around where I have a hyperactive personality" and stuff, and when Miffy wrote this and uploaded it, it was March 20 or 19 at like three in the morning or something, right when there was about thirty-one hours left in the forty-eight-hour countdown where the U.S. demanded Hussein's abdication from Iraq, and if this abdication didn't take place within forty-eight hours a war was going to break out, but well this is enough about Miffy,

SCENE 4

ACTRESS 2 (*Enters*): This is a separate story but, this story well takes place after more than thirty-one hours have passed and the war had actually started, there's this woman named Yukki, and on March 20 she was, um, so the war on Iraq began on March 20, but at that moment I had some errands to run down at Shimokita so I was by nearby Shibuya station, a little bit in front of the turnstiles for the Inokashira line, but at that moment, there was like, from the station you can see that building with the glass facade right, from there, what is that? there was a huge swelling noise coming from there, like what *is* that noise, was coming from there, and it turned out to be a protest, but I was just watching from there, but around that time, right around that time, there were tons of marches in places like Shibuya, like pretty frequently, and this Yukki was, during that whole time in that area, she was staying at a fancy hourly hotel, near Dōgenzaka, in Shibuya, for five days straight, but

ACTOR 3: Um, now we're going to do the story about how Minobe woke up in the morning, and there was some woman he'd never seen before, but from the point of view of a woman named Yukki,

ACTRESS 2: At the beginning like on the first day and stuff, it was right after we met right, so we totally had sex like a bunch of times, without any rest between, maybe just talk a little and then right away, next round, kind of, but after about three times, you know he gets tired, right, and just falls asleep, so, I think like maybe I'll sleep, too, then, so I go to sleep, right, and about two hours go by, right, even though really I don't know if it's been two hours or what, but you know the rooms in those places don't have windows, so when you wake up in those kinds of places, you can't tell at all, but then like he woke up and then he like starts touching me again, so I woke up, and as we're kind of groping each other, it's kind of like another round, or like so this kept going on for two whole days, but after a while I couldn't tell any more what time it was on which day and in one of those moments, I mean I had a watch but I hadn't looked at it, like I was not looking at it on purpose, like aren't there times you think you want to be surprised?

"Oh, it's only the second day, I thought it was already about the fourth day" and it was like totally, a time warp . . . after we did it, we'd talk, right, looking at the ceiling, right, and then, it'd be after the second or like the third time, oh, no wait, it was totally more, it was after like the tenth time, but, and this was totally hysterical, he said like "A while ago we, you know, the first time," he said like "we got carried away and didn't use anything, huh," he said and "do you think it's OK?" like he says this after all this time, I thought it was pretty hysterical but, hm? OK? Is he talking about STDs? Or babies? It turned out to be babies, but we'd done it easily more than ten times, and not only had we never used anything any of those times, but, right, you know how those places only have two condoms, they only have two, and of course if you want, you can pay additional for more, . . . but anyway they only come with two, right, you know, that's the convention, but like why is it two, do they have some data about the national average being two, or not two but twice?

Those kinds of places, I mean, if you buy additional ones, they're probably expensive, the Matsukiyo pharmacy would definitely be better, we agreed on that, so we did it two more times, using the guys that came with the room, which, that itself is also pretty hysterical, but and then we went outside once, and when we asked the person at the hotel, we want to leave and come right back, they were like, that's fine, so it was totally OK so, "I thought it wouldn't be OK, but apparently it's fine," "Oh really? Then let's go outside," and we went out, and when we looked at the time, it was the morning of the third day, like ten o'clock or something, really I thought it'd be around the evening of the second day, but, then when I said that, he was also thinking "Oh I was thinking it was about that too," and I was saying like "I, you know how once in a while it's not at all the time that you thought it was, I really love that," and he was thinking like oh really, and said like, "It's kinda, right, like a time warp, which makes me pretty happy," and she was thinking oh really, and then first off, we went shopping at Matsukiyo's and bought about three dozen but, it was pretty unlikely by that time for us to use up all three dozen, totally like in the end, during the second half, our pace totally fell off and, and then, right, we were like, wait a second, have we gone through two whole days without eating anything? and then we were kind of like, "oh yeah, I totally forgot about that," like aren't we really just a couple of beasts? which totally cracked us up, and then we were like what should we eat, and in Shibuya on weekdays, you know you see a lot of those lunch buffet places when you're in Shibuya during the day? We were like, let's go to some place like that and stuff our faces so that we can prepare to fuck our brains out when we get back to the hotel, because we are so-called beasts after all, but it was pretty unlikely by that time for us to use up all three dozen, like in the end during the second half the pace totally fell off, but we did use up two dozen.

ACTRESS 1: Yukki and her then boyfriend, well, this guy and Yukki had mutually agreed that they'd be together for five days only, and the two kind of decided that they were going to stick to this restriction, and they spent five days in March together in Shibuya in this love hotel together, but they were really absolutely strict about limiting their fling to those five days and beyond that, they apparently didn't even exchange addresses or phone numbers or e-mail addresses with each other, but the decision to do this hadn't been made at this point, it wasn't until later on this day when they got back to the hotel that they were going to do this, but like they're going to go into detail about that a little later, but like I don't know what the two of them were thinking at this point exactly, but like probably they weren't thinking much at all (ACTRESS 2 *exits*), then this Yukki went with the guy to this 950-yen Indian food buffet they have on Center Street, and she was like "Oh it's a little pricey but whatever," and totally stuffed her face, and she ordered a lassi to boot, which cost extra, 250 yen to boot, and she gave him a sip, and the reason why, even though she was like "Well, it's pricey, but, maybe it's all right," was that she was also really kind of having fun, and was thinking, "Doesn't it feel like we're on a trip? Like even though it's just Shibuya, isn't it fun, like doesn't it feel like we're in a foreign country?" and "I really feel like we're sightseeing, somehow it's so much fun, I was thinking, I mean, here we are in Shibuya, but it doesn't feel like Shibuya, seriously this is such a blast, and then, it felt like we were playing into that feeling of it being Shibuya, but not Shibuya, like, for instance, not leaving the restaurant until we'd eaten so much that it was like 'we can't possibly eat any more!' and then we heard this, uh, crazy mounting noise coming from toward the Shibuya Scramble intersection, we heard a noise that made us go like, what the hell, and that was, wow, precisely when this huge protest was going by, oh, and we were like oh look at the protest and we pulled each other by the hand to get closer and the protest was pretty packed, oh, and the impact of being in the middle of it, live, was pretty raw, I thought, but"

ACTOR 3: And, they were like, oh yeah, what about the war, when the huge vision screen on the Tsutaya building was showing the headlines about how the cruise missile air strike on Baghdad had started, and they were like, "Oh, it's started, after all," and watched the march and stuff for a little bit, and pretty much headed right back to the hotel, but, anyway we're going to do a little bit from the march.

(ACTOR 3 *and* ACTRESS 1 *exit.*)

SCENE 5

(ACTOR 4 *and* ACTOR 5 *enter.*)

ACTOR 4: Oh so now we're going to take it from the protest.

(ACTOR 4 *and* ACTOR 5 *line up side by side and begin walking.*)

ACTOR 4 (*After a while*): Aaaah—

(*After that, they walk for a long time in silence. Then:*)

ACTOR 4: . . . this was like, me and Yasui are friends and we were lined up walking along in the protest and talking, um so just a little background, the two of us were in the line that was totally, to be frank, the line was actually this wide (*Indicates a width of about three intervals*) but Yasui and I were, this is Yasui-kun by the way, off on the side there's this line made up of people who weren't that into it but who were like we're participating in the march too, and that's more of the line that we were in but . . . oh, so, we're going to take it from that one part of the protest again, now,

(ACTOR 4 *and* ACTOR 5 *line up side by side and begin walking.*)

ACTOR 4 (*After a while*): Aaaah—

(*After that, they walk for a long time in silence. Then:*)

ACTOR 4: The lyrics go "You don't have to be Number One," but it's like who the hell are you, you know?

ACTOR 5: Aaaah—

ACTOR 4: I get stuck there listening to that song, you know.

ACTOR 5: Ah—, you're kind of, when it comes to those kinds of thing, but I've thought this before but, you know, you're pretty pure, Ishihara-kun

ACTOR 4 (*After a while*): "Aaaah—"

(*After that, they walk for a long time in silence. Then:*)

ACTOR 4: . . . Um some background here, the type of people who were really into it were, totally way, in the front part but, all totally bloodthirsty and scary, so that's why we had put some distance between us and those types of people, the other day there was this crazy, when you go toward the street along the park, there's the Disney Store, but the other day in front of the store, the entrance of the store is encased all in glass, right, there were these people standing in front, and you know there was the story about how Israel's massacred tons of Arabs, these people were holding photos of corpses of children so that everyone inside the store could see, showing them to everyone inside the store, photos with the faces all totally mutilated like, "whoa, that is disGUSting" kind of photos, and on top of that, shouting into megaphones stuff like, "Hello good boys and girls, look at what is happening to children your age in the Arab world" with those disgusting photos on top of that, and then the store clerks and stuff came running out from the back, one woman was practically crying, saying, "I'm sorry, really, please stop this," but they were all, "Your tears won't save these children's lives!" and pushing the photos of the corpses even more, parading them like a flag, and jacking the megaphone up to twice the volume, there was like this totally overheated shift, which was like, whoa, merciless, those were the kinds of people who were completely at the very front of the line, or the center, raising their voices, but it's like, "RA RA RA," like they use that kind of voice that's like is that the kind of voice you want to use here, like "BRING IT ON" kind of, huh?

Also, the police are always flanking both sides of the line the whole time, like sticking to the side of the protest but, and this kind of pisses me off, for me, even, it pisses me off, but it's like oh, I'm sorry, for those who are super into it, they practically shoulder tackle them down, saying like "Koizumi's dogs" like pretty heated, like oh explosive, like is this OK kind of, does everybody know that, the cops are all black belts in judo, I mean they are, if they know that and still do stuff like that, that's pretty outrageous, I think, here was another war, that's the kind of feeling that was welling up in that place, kind of . . . oh, so we're going to do it again,

(ACTOR 4 *and* ACTOR 5 *line up side by side and begin walking.*)

ACTOR 5: You know, you don't usually get to take a close look at police uniforms that much, but during this protest, you can take a good look, and, there's a lot to observe and it's like, wow, you know

ACTOR 4: Oh the Anna Miller's?

ACTOR 5: Not that the police . . . hey when was it that the uniforms there changed?

ACTOR 4: Ah, . . . Anna Miller's, is, over there by Spain Slope in Shibuya, right?

ACTOR 5: "Oh, right, right"

ACTOR 4: Oh, that place . . . that reminds me, I haven't been to Anna Miller's these days.

ACTOR 5: Did the uniforms change?

ACTOR 4: Uh I don't know, at Anna Miller's?

ACTOR 5: Right

ACTOR 4 (*In surprise*): Huh?

ACTOR 5: . . .

ACTOR 4: Have you been there, to the Anna Miller's on Spain Slope?

ACTOR 5: Or like, I always knew there was an Anna Miller's on Spain Slope, but to tell you the truth, I am, as of yet, I'm an Anna Miller virgin

ACTOR 4: Oh that makes sense, right, right . . . I'm sorry to bring it up. . . . Maybe, you're feeling dejected right,

ACTOR 5: What can you get to eat at Anna Miller's? Is it fast food?

ACTOR 4: . . .

ACTOR 5 (*Blowing his nose on a tissue*): Did Anna Miller's come from America?

ACTOR 4: Oh, I don't know about that

ACTOR 5: There's no slogan shouting here, no, I mean, it's better that way but. . . . They're kind of doing it toward the front of the march but

ACTOR 4: I'm just guessing but, doesn't Anna Miller's seem like a Japanese thing? That kind of cutesy costume is super Japanese. In America it would be the Bud girl

ACTOR 5: I'm allergic to cedar pollen

ACTOR 4: Ah yes

ACTOR 5: Cypress too, both, but, I didn't wear a mask to the protest because I heard a rumor that that's how people mistake you for a serious protester type

ACTOR 4: Ahh—

ACTOR 5: "I've got it pretty bad though right now" is what I said, but at this moment, I was pretty much at my limit, but we happened to be right then, in front of the Hachiko intersection in Shibuya, about to go under the overpass to turn toward Dōgenzaka, and there's a big drug store nearby so I thought I would buy a mask there so, "Can I take off for a second?"

ACTOR 4: Ahh—

ACTOR 5: Hey, I just have to go buy a mask, but

ACTOR 4: Oh that makes sense . . . then I'll wait here

ACTOR 5: You can go on ahead, I'll catch up with you

ACTOR 4: Ahh—

ACTOR 5: Go ahead, I'll catch up with you

ACTOR 4: Ahh—, no I'll wait

ACTOR 5: Oh, really

ACTOR 4: Or like is it better if I went ahead?

ACTOR 5: Or like, it's fine for you to go ahead, I'll catch up with you real quick anyway

ACTOR 4: Or like, huh, is it going to take a long time for you to buy a mask?

ACTOR 5: Nah, it probably won't take long

ACTOR 4: Oh really? How many minutes? About five minutes?

ACTOR 5: Nah, probably not five minutes, I'm thinking

ACTOR 4: Oh really? Then I can wait you know (ACTOR 5 *is like "Oh really?"*), huh, are there like lots of different kinds of masks?

ACTOR 5: Or like you know, there actually are but, I already know which kind to buy, the super solid kind

ACTOR 4: Oh is that right

ACTOR 5: It'll really be done in a second, so it's fine if you just go on ahead, I'll catch up with you right away

ACTOR 4: Oh really

ACTOR 5: Yeah, so I'm gonna go for a sec

ACTOR 4: "Oh, all right then I'll be waiting" and that's it, the explanation about the protest will conclude around here, thank you.

ACTOR 5: Um, actually, there's this person named Suzuki who hasn't yet appeared at this stage in the game, but or, like to be accurate, she actually did appear a little bit back then, but nobody has talked about this person yet, not even saying like "This person is named Suzuki" or anything, but like I will give a general explanation here, but Suzuki is someone with a really flexible body, but the fact that he's flexible isn't that, or like totally irrelevant to, like, the story that I'm trying to tell right now, but before we get into it we were thinking of maybe taking a little break here for about ten minutes, was the plan. . . . Just a second ago I think this guy came out here a little bit who was the guy that after Azuma left Minobe at the club, the next day, Azuma met up with a guy who was his mate from his part-time job, well he was the talked-about or like the guy that we're trying to talk about or like we say talk about, but I don't think it's anything that would really cause a sensation, but anyway well, the thing is that the guy I just mentioned is Suzuki, but, I'm thinking about talking about him now, but before that I think we're going to try to take about a twenty-minute break, but I mean, not think we're going to try but, we are (*He exits.*)

SCENE 6

ACTOR 3 (*Entering*): Um, this is about when Minobe and the girl went back to the hotel afterward and decided to limit their relations to five days, but the girl was the one who said like, "It's like it's totally Shibuya, but it's really fun, kind of like we went on a trip" and "It's like Shibuya, but it's like when you're in a foreign city and there's kind of something there that's really evocative mood-wise and really fun," she said, and Minobe said "Oh really" and then "Oh, but me too, I kind of know what you mean," and by then the two of them were in the hotel but . . . "Isn't this fun?" said the girl, "Nah, it is fun, for real, totally," Minobe said . . . and then, "Hm, honestly, how much like money do you have right now?" Minobe said, "Yeah, by money I mean not just what you have in your wallet but in the bank and stuff," Minobe said, "And by in the bank, I'm not like seriously asking you about all your assets, I'm not asking that at all, but like in your account that you use regularly your regular checking account and stuff, I was just wondering how much money do you have that you could just withdraw, you know," said Minobe, "Cause I'm like a part-timer, but just now I thought like 'whoa' like work, you're not like a full-time employee at some company, are you?" is what Minobe said, "Nah, I'm a part-timer too," she said, "Oh really, huh, are you OK, taking these days off?" said Minobe, "Well it's not really OK, but I'll just find my another job," the girl said, the girl's name was Yukki, by the way, but it's not as if Minobe and that so-called Yukki chick told each other their names, but really names are really unnecessary, "When there's just two people together, even without names, you only have one conversation partner so you really don't need names," is what Minobe was saying but, . . . so then ,"Oh is that right, so you're OK, since you're a part-timer, I'll just do whatever you know so I'm fine . . . but, no, or like, just a thought or like, it occurred to me, until the money runs out, this is totally fun, what we're doing here, now, this way of life or like, I guess it's not really a way of life or anything, but this daily routine like we're on a trip? Living in a hotel? But it'd be difficult to keep doing this kind of thing, or like we can't keep doing this, you know," is what Minobe said, "Or like I wonder how long the two of us are going to continue doing this kind of thing is like the, until when are we going to do this, is like, huh, honestly, what do you think? I kind of, out of the blue, said the two of us, and we've really just met and look at where we are but, I mean I'm totally fine with it, but Is this OK? Like, don't you have a boyfriend? I mean, it's none of my business but" is what Minobe said, "I was thinking we should talk about these things a little bit, not like that, but yeah, I was thinking, soon," he said, "Oh, by the way, wait what? I only have about 2,000 yen in my wallet is the thing, but if I go to the bank, there's some left from my job, but even that is only like 30,000, I think, 'cause my job, the twentieth is the last day on the monthly pay cycle, so right now is exactly the most difficult time you know," said Minobe, and then she was also pretty much on the same wave length, and the girl was also a part-timer so, but her payday was the twentieth, so financially she had quite a bit in her bank account, but it's not as if then she could go out and spend that whole amount, of course, is how the conversation started veering, like oh yeah, you're right, and . . . so in the upshot, the two of them decided, "OK so three more days, including today? Which means two more nights? For a total of five days and four nights," and that was the deal, "Because financially too, that's kind of the limit" was the thing, "Not the limit, but well, a safe amount, if you imagine thinking about this in retrospect, that would be the line," was the thing, "Yeah, maybe that's right, it's kind of a little bit sad, but realistically, you're right" was the thing "But three more days, including today, let's, yeah, spend them together," and then "We stockpiled condoms from Matsukiyo just now, so let's go at it with enough vigor to use them all up" was how their conversation went, but they didn't use up all of them, and after a little bit more than two dozen, that was completely enough on Minobe's side. . . . "Yah, well this is probably my estimation, but" this is what Minobe said to the girl, after one of the times they were having sex, which they did countless times that they really didn't know how many times they did it, they were like lying side by side staring at the ceiling and talking and stuff, right, this was what Minobe said then: "Yah, well, this is probably my estimation, but probably after three days, we'll leave this hotel and each of us'll go back to our lives, but by then, probably according to my estimation, I think that the war is going to be over, maybe that's naive, nah, but honestly, the difference in power is completely off the charts right, and plus remember the Gulf War, which ended right away, right, they go in all at once and totally nail their targets and finished it off right away, yeah, so probably, I'm thinking, it's going to be over. . . . The TV, um, this entire time we've been in this hotel, we've been screwing our brains out, yeah, but we haven't watched TV at all, even though we have one, it's kind of, so you know, if it's all right with you, let's agree that we're not going to watch TV," said Minobe, to which the girl said, "Oh, sure," and Minobe said, "Oh, really, is that cool?" and the girl said "that's fine" but "Oh really? With either of us knowing, three days from now, we'll return to each of our normal lives? And then when we turn on the TV, let's say, we'll think 'Oh the war is over, is that the plan?' I think that's good you know, 'Once it started it was over pretty quickly, maybe that was for the best, in the end,' is what we'll think, and then you'll think like 'oh, it's true, it is over, it's just like that guy said it would be,' and then like 'so were we perhaps like doing it for the whole duration of the war?' and like 'while the two of us were fucking our brains out at this extraordinary pace in Shibuya the war began and ended?' that's like, that kind of thing is totally, think about it that memory will be linked to history, it's quite, wonderful or like, I think that as a memory, there's a high probability that it will be one of those that flash before your eyes before death, I think"

SCENE 7

(ACTOR 1 *and* ACTRESS 2 *enter.*)

ACTRESS 2: Like he was the vocalist and (ACTOR 1: *"Yeah"*) the hotel they were staying at when they came to Japan was in Shibuya so (ACTOR 1: *"Yeah"*) The other band members were also (ACTOR 1: *"Yeah"*) so they were like taking a walk in Shibuya altogether, or were they all together? But then, you know, there were those antiwar protests right, they saw one (ACTOR 1: *"Yeah"*), and so they joined it and marched,

ACTOR 3: Oh really, he joined up (ACTRESS 2: *"Yeah"*), so you can join up with those that casually?

ACTRESS 2: I don't know but, and then he said protests in Japan are like, maybe in foreign countries the police don't really follow them like glue, I don't know, but anyway in Japan they're practically like surrounded by the police, and they have the protest marches under watch, not exactly, but they follow them (ACTOR 3: *"Oh really"*), and that's what was really interesting about Japanese protests, was the story, apparently, not interesting but particular

ACTOR 1: You can just slip in that easily into those protests, huh?

ACTOR 3: Nah, it might be that that one happened to be an open protest, maybe, I don't know but, she said, "also they were playing songs on their boom box and stuff" is what she said

ACTOR 1: Oh really

ACTOR 3: And so then "That's amazing you understand English, did you go abroad to like America or somewhere?" (ACTOR 1: *"Yeah."*)

ACTRESS 2: Huh, Yeah sort of

ACTOR 3: Study abroad? (ACTOR 1: *"Yeah."*)

ACTRESS 2: Oh yeah, right, sort of study abroad. (ACTOR 1: *"Yeah."*)

ACTOR 3: "Oh really," I said, and because I think girls who can speak English are kinda hot and then she said like "I did study abroad, but aside from that, I did home stays several times and stuff" (ACTOR 1: *"Yeah"*) so then I asked, oh really, huh, so where'd you go? and she said like "Huh, America" (ACTOR 1: *"Yeah"*), "oh really," I said

ACTRESS 2: These two . . . men, or like, if you say men, it kinda sounds like formal, it's not like that, but these two, well, guys, that's also weird for me to say but, these two . . . one of them, up until that day had spent five whole days without taking a single step outside Shibuya, he had spent the whole time in a hotel, but by hotel I mean Maruyamacho, but not like Mark City, um, if you go to a city in a foreign country for instance, and you're like, I just spent five days in such-and-such place, there was that feeling, I think, and those five days were extremely, sort of, he'd spent those five days in Shibuya with that kind of feeling, but Shibuya is like, you go there pretty often, normally, even if it's just to change trains, but still it was kind of, during those five days, it was a different from always, a special Shibuya, and we were like, or I was like, "I wonder why it was like that" and like "I wonder why it is, it kinda feels like we're on vacation you know" and "I think it feels like when you go on a trip to a foreign country" the whole time while we were in the hotel, of course it wasn't like we were talking the whole time, but there was a good portion of time spent talking during all those days, I mean all those days it was only five days, but at the hotel, we were in the hotel for most of that time, but what happens is that ultimately, or not ultimately but, gradually we spent more and more time talking . . . at the time we were so full of curry, and we were on our way back to return to the hotel, you know how you go through the Center Street and at the Book First there's that big road off to the left to go to Dōgenzaka, toward the intersection where there's that Don Quixote, . . . right, and so that sensation of "going home" was what we were just talking about, we were really just right at that moment, while we were heading back, at first we were like "I wonder why, it's just the regular old Shibuya but" and "Maybe it's because, even though it is a place we go to a lot like Shibuya, we're doing something like staying in a hotel" I was saying, and then he was saying like "Maybe because there's the war, and the protests, and the commotion? like stuff going on" . . . and then we were saying "there's also something directional" and like "not directional, but" like "that sensation of 'going home' you know," and like "Direction—usually, heading toward Shibuya station from here is the direction you go to go home, right, but it's kind of just to say 'let's go home' and walking in this opposite direction is enough to kinda of, just that is, kind of really, like we are on vacation," I said,

ACTOR 3: Yeah I know, also, though, the war's going on, they're protesting, that kind of commotion? I think that's definitely a part, I was seventeen when the Kobe earthquake happened, and I'm remembering now, at the time I had this strong feeling like

"Why am I in this place listening to this class lecture that's like poo, maybe I'm doing something really bad right now."

ACTRESS 2: Really

ACTOR 3: And now I'll really be thinking "I was twenty-five when the Iraq war started, but 'why am I in this place having sex that's like poo?'"

ACTRESS 2: Really

ACTOR 3: It's not like poo . . . but can I be honest? it's kinda, I am totally, I've used up too much, like, I'm totally raw from chafing

ACTRESS 2: Oh really, is that why you've been moving like that? I was thinking it was the opposite,

ACTOR 3: What? (*To* ACTOR 1.) Like she thought the opposite, that I wanted to do more (*To* ACTRESS 2.) By opposite, you mean you thought I wanted to do it more?

ACTRESS 2: Yeah . . . did we buy too many?

ACTOR 3 (*To* ACTOR 1): But that's like, you don't move like this when you really want to do it, if you did, it would be too obvious, like practically a monkey

ACTOR 1: Yeah

ACTOR 3: And like, when it was decided that we would limit this relationship to five days, I'm trying to remember, but what was the flow that led to that, which one of us suggested it first, like those details, who was it again who suggested it and like

ACTOR 1: You don't remember

ACTOR 3: Yeah, or like it's weird that I don't remember, those kind of touchy subjects, usually I remember normally who said it first and stuff like that is definitely input into my memory, because it's strong, but the fact that I don't remember, I wonder what it means, maybe we both suggested it at once, but there's no way I definitely would have remembered that

ACTOR 1: Azuma was at the diner, he was awakened very early in the morning by a phone call from Minobe saying, "Come to the diner now" so then he went, and he had to listen to this story, Minobe spent, in the end, four nights in Shibuya with a girl, though it seems like there's the three-night version and the five-night version of the story, it actually was four nights, but after those four night they parted ways, and immediately Minobe called up Azuma, you see, "I'm at the diner, so come over," he said, so well he went, because essentially, Azuma has a lot of time on his hands, so when he got there, Azuma had to listen to Minobe's story about how he fucked his brains out for five days and four nights in Shibuya, so that's where I'm thinking we'll pick it up from now,

ACTOR 3: When I woke up in the morning, I was kind of like where the hell am I, and on top of that, there was this, who is this woman next to me, I don't know her, but I remembered right away, oh last night, that's right, . . . having said that, though, there was always this moment of, wait a second where am I? during the second night and the third night, but of course by then, I didn't have the who the hell is this woman reaction, but . . . oh but on the second night, maybe there was a moment, when I woke up for a second, like, but there's someone sleeping next to me, and who is it? but even while thinking that, it was always pretty obvious what was going on, I mean she was asleep right next to me, so the third night or the last night the fourth night the thought really didn't occur to me, like who is this, but maybe up till the second night, there was a subtle moment, wait who is she? . . . so then, and I was pretty proud about this, she's sleeping right next to me. But I didn't lay a finger on her, seriously, during those who is she? moments, even though she was sleeping right next to me in bed, a woman, next to me, just right here, but to like instinctually go to touch her was, well I didn't touch her, and I thought that that was pretty magnificent of me, like wait, underneath it all I'm not just a beast, I'm quite wonderful, because my instinct was to take measures and make sure I was like, oh yeah, I remember this woman before I went to touch her, wow really, I thought I was totally completely magnificent

ACTOR 1: Oh really, what? How long does that kind of state of being like "oh there's a woman net to me but I don't know who it is" (ACTOR 3: *"Yeah"*) how long does that last, how many minutes?

ACTOR 3: Approximately five seconds

ACTOR 1: Oh really

ACTOR 3: "Well yeah, that's about right," he said, "And then when it was decided that we were going to limit this relationship to five days," I'm backtracking a little bit, but "I'm trying to remember how it was that we came to that conclusion like, which of us had first suggested it, like the specifics, where did it come from or like"

ACTOR 1: You don't remember

ACTOR 3: No at the end, I guess last night, we talked about that a little bit, the two of us, "Tomorrow's the end," "Or like it's over in the morning tomorrow, so it's really today," we said, and in that moment, "When it was decided that we should limit this relationship to like five days, what was the train of thought that brought us there?" was how the conversation started going, but we're going to do that part now,

ACTRESS 2: First we were talking about money, "I have only 2,000 yen" he said, and I thought what, why is that all you have? but . . . like at the beginning he asked me "Hey, honestly, how much like money do you have in the bank right now?" and I thought why is he asking me that? but it was because he didn't have any money on him but, "'cause at my job, the twentieth is the last day on the monthly pay cycle, so right now is exactly the most difficult time you know," he said, but sure enough, that day was the twenty-fifth or so of March, sure enough, or around there, but he said, "I have only about 2,000 yen in my wallet, but if I go to the bank, I probably have about 30,000, so afterward we'll divide everything by two, and I'll pay you back," and I was thinking, yeah, obviously, . . . so, because there was this conversation about money, I think we were still at the time like this in the hotel, like we were like this before I knew it, as if we were on vacation, but how much longer shall we do this? that was something we hadn't decided, but both of us, I mean most likely both of us, were not like, let's be proactive about making this decision, but we really should decide pretty soon, we were both thinking, I'm guessing that both of us were, we were both, right, both thinking about it, so then, up until then we hadn't talked about anything like that, but, but the subject of money came up in conversation so, we were like saying, money is so important, how much longer should we do this, we should decide, and then that became a good reason for a break, like this was kind of about the limit for us financially, so we decided on four nights and five days, at the time we were on the third day after the second night, but so then we were like "OK, we have two more nights," and "it'll be the day after tomorrow, on the day after tomorrow, we'll leave here and each of us'll go home, and hey, by then, I wonder whether the war'll be over," we said, "That almost sounds like 'I wonder if Japan won the soccer match today' and not knowing the results and coming home to watch the news all excited, you know?" we said, so then, to get back to the story, the fact that we decided on the five-day limit or like, I was talking about this because of the question of trying to remember who it was that suggested that, but . . . I didn't know but . . . but I don't remember how that conversation started off, but, during that conversation I do, for example I said, "That would definitely be best, and like, that would be better definitely"

ACTOR 3: Yeah . . . nah, I say this because I don't think you'd get mad, but you don't like believe in that, "forever and a day" like (ACTRESS 2: *"No."*) Oh wait it's reversed, "now and forever," kind of thing, I mean do you want that? You don't think that, right, with me, nah really, you can say "no," because the feeling is mutual

ACTRESS 2: No

ACTOR 3: No, but it's like, not as if there's a hierarchy between the forever types and other types, like the forever types definitely do not rank higher, you know (ACTRESS 2: *"Yeah"*), you understand me right

ACTRESS 2: I understand

ACTOR 3: You understand right, but that in itself is amazing, it's pretty miraculous I think, to have spent five super special days with someone who understands these things, really I (*To* ACTOR 1) if everyone understood these kind of things, no one would go to war, I really think that, I thought, but in that moment I didn't think I should say that out loud so I didn't but

ACTOR 1: Yeah

ACTOR 3: So anyway (*To* ACTRESS 2) you understand right, but that's amazing, you know, it's pretty miraculous I think, to have spent five special days with someone who understands these things, really I say super special because, yeah, we were only having sex, that would be one way to look at it, but two dozen plus times, that's not an impressive pace, is it?

ACTRESS 2: No

ACTOR 3 (*To* ACTOR 1): So then (*To* ACTRESS 2), so you're always in Tokyo, right, you live here, mainly

ACTRESS 2: Yeah

ACTOR 3: But I hope we don't see each other again, if it's possible, not even by accident

ACTRESS 2: Yeah

ACTOR 3: We might run into each other . . . but really it would be better if we never did

ACTRESS 2: Yeah

ACTOR 3: I haven't told you anything, my address? Phone number? Cell phone, oh yeah, and e-mail? We haven't even told each other our names. (*He exits.*)

ACTRESS 2: We won't meet again, don't worry, but even more important than whether it'd be OK or not, I mean in the end it was decided that it would be OK but, um, to explain why and how it was decided was, well, for example we might meet again, right, at like the club where we first met and stuff, we were talking about that but he was saying "No, that won't happen," and the reason why was he hadn't come to the club because he wanted to at all, but there was another person who was there with him then, though I hardly talked or anything to that person at all but, he had been invited by that person to the concert, that's why he went, he was totally like "That was amazing, that was amazing" from the moment I met him so I assumed that he was definitely a hard-core fan or something, but that wasn't the case, it was just that he usually never goes to places like that so, it's OK, if you think we might bump into each other at a show, that won't happen probably, so (*She exits.*)

SCENE 8

ACTOR 1: And then, the rest is what Minobe was saying to me at the diner, "what I really wanted to say" he was so kind of, so insistent . . . no, you know what, let's not do that story, so then well let's take the morning of the last day, where the two are like, see you later and finish these five days in March, but this story itself will end in about ten minutes, but even when they left the hotel, it would have been best if, at the entrance to the hotel, like you go right and I'll go left, but in reality, in the end they both needed to get to Shibuya station, so they walked there together, and on top of that, on their way, the man was like "Can we stop by a bank so I can pay you back?" and since the ATM at the bank, which opens at nine, opens at nine, they timed their leaving the hotel so they could be the first people when the machine opened at nine, but then he was like "Can we actually stop by the bank?" and she was like "Oh, OK," so that was that, but and then, when she was wondering which bank, he said like "the Hokuriku Bank" and what? you want to go to the Hokuriku Bank, does such a bank exist in Shibuya, but then, actually there is a very large Hokuriku Bank in Shibuya, in the same building as the Lotteria burger joint, wow I didn't know that, and, and so the man withdrew cash from the ATM, and the woman was waiting outside, and the money was safely withdrawn, a total of 20,000 yen, right, if we split everything in half, so then, OK see you, but, they walked to the station together and then at the station, he said, "Oh I take the Yamanote line," and she said, "Oh I take the Tōyoko line," and so there they were, like, see ya, and then from there he called up Azuma and told him the story just like this, and that's, well, so something like what I just described took place, and then Azuma that day, essentially, Azuma has a lot of time on his hands, but on that particular day he had a bunch of errands that day, so after listening once through to Minobe's story he was like see ya and left the diner and went to Roppongi, again it was Roppongi . . . before the intermission, we said we would tell the story about Suzuki and then we went to intermission, I believe, but a lot of other things got stuck in between, but from here we're finally going to get to that story (*Exits.*)

SCENE 9

(ACTOR 2 *and* ACTOR 5 *enter.*)

ACTOR 2: What we're thinking of doing now is, the story about how Yasui, who was participating in the protest just a while ago, got chewed out, that's what we're thinking of doing but,

ACTOR 5: Yes, "Shibuya is, like geographically speaking, there's the Scramble intersection in front of the Hachikō in front of Shibuya station, and I am really, I'm imagining a map of Shibuya in which the Scramble is the center, but so then, not toward Dogenzaka and not toward where you can see the bus stops on the right, on the right, you should see the way toward Aoyama, but not that way but where you can see bus stops on the left, toward Roppongi Way, or like actually Roppongi Way itself there, if you go all the way, or like, actually for Roppongi Way, it'd be better to make the point of origin not Hachikō but the Moyai statue, that's the better point of origin so, I just realized that now, so if you go all the way down Roppongi Way, straight past Nishi Azabu and stuff, and apparently the club that Minobe and them went to is somewhere along this road but past that, and past Roppongi station for a little bit, is where the American embassy and stuff is, but the protest march came all the way here, though as for the route it took, it might have been, for the march, they came from Dōgenzaka toward Aoyama till halfway and then a right turn in the middle, and around Nogizaka, it might have come this way, but the American embassy is in Roppongi, but the address is, however, in Akasaka, but in front of the embassy, they were crowding around with intense ferocity, some with placards and like shouting 'No More War,' and there are a lot of people who live in that neighborhood. . . . But for the residents, they were doing that kind of thing totally everyday right, also trafficwise, everyday it totally gets backed up and stuff, right, for these people, so it's like, really, they want them to cut it out"

ACTOR 2: Yes

ACTOR 5: Seriously, the stress is totally intense, you know, people who have families with small children, they're there, right, even with cars, some people commute right, there are people who, of course, have babies, you know, although I'm still single myself

ACTOR 2: Yes

ACTOR 5: But this is the place for them to live their normal lives, right, like me, I still get home really late at night, but a normal housewife and stuff is made to listen this everyday, right, even for me, I totally want to rest up on the weekends, but then what happens is that they're making a racket during the day, right

ACTOR 2: Yes

ACTOR 5: You gotta, what do you think, peace or whatever is fine, I mean in the end, it's like after all they're just doing it out of a desire for a dramatic event, don't you think?" this is how he was scolded, and that was the story for (*Indicating* ACTOR 2) Yasui-kun but

ACTOR 2: Thank you (*Exits.*)

SCENE 10

ACTOR 4 (*Enters*): So here's the story about the woman Yukki afterward when he was like "Oh I'm on the Yamanote line," she was like "Oh I'm on the Tōyoko line," as it were, and they were, like see ya, and it ended with good-bye, but after that, but the woman didn't get on the train right away, she kind of wanted to prolong her experience of this different Shibuya, so she was kind of like strolling toward Dōgenzaka, going back where they'd come from, but she was thinking, "Ooh, Shibuya during these last five days was different from always, it was kind of like a familiar town that was unfamiliar, but, but if I get on a train now and take even one step out of here, the next time I come to Shibuya, it'll be the regular old Shibuya," so then she kind of wanted to stay in this Shibuya for a little while longer, that's how she felt, so after she had walked all the way to the station, she turned back and returned all the way toward Dōgenzaka, when for a moment she was like "Oh no maybe it's too late, that sensation, it's already beginning to feel like the normal Shibuya, maybe because I walked all the way to the station," but then she was like oh no, it's OK it still feels like that Shibuya, but, and then she was like, maybe I'll go all the way back to the hotel where they'd been staying, kind of like how a criminal always returns to the crime scene kind of thing, she thought, "So then the hotel is like at the top of this hill, but when I was at the bottom of the hill at the street toward Bunkamura looking up toward the hill toward the hotel, the road was kind of like this with telephone poles along both sides of the road, and at the side of the telephone poles were those trash cans, the big guys, and stuff, I think, and then I noticed at the side of one of the telephone poles there was, what I at first thought was this huge black dog, and the dog was kind of crouched around the telephone pole, and it was like, oh, eating something or like sniff sniffing something, but then, my eyes are bad, I wear glasses, I mean I think that's why, but what happened was that it wasn't a dog, but a human being, and not only that, he wasn't down like this (*On all fours*) but like this (*Squatting*), and it turned out to be like a homeless guy who was taking a shit, so then I, I, no not me but that woman named Yukki, was all like 'Oh' and then that person was like 'Oh' and looking over at me, and our eyes met and we were like 'Oh' and ran away, and I thought, I just couldn't believe it, because that was what, it wasn't like I couldn't believe that someone would take a shit on the street, but that person, that person, the fact that for several seconds, I had looked at that person and believed that it was an animal, even though it was a human being, in the end, I just couldn't believe the fact that I had been looking at a human being and seriously believed that it was some kind of dog or animal, I really couldn't believe it, I thought, I couldn't believe it, right, and then I vomited, I mean I wanted to find a bathroom in a store somewhere, but I couldn't make it in time, so I threw up on the street, and then afterward I felt calmer and I hightailed to the station, but by then I, Shibuya had totally turned back to being normal, but that wasn't even important anymore" that's the way the story went, so now we're going to take it from the final morning of the Five Days in March, where this girl, who's about to go through that, and the guy who was with her, and the guy is withdrawing money at the bank, and the girl is waiting for him, and then that will end Five Days in March. (*Exits.*)

(*Blackout. When the lights come up,* ACTRESS 2 *is standing, wearing a spring jacket.* ACTOR 1 *appears, also wearing a jacket.*)

ACTOR 1: Here. (*Handing her 20,000 yen.*)

ACTRESS 2: Thanks. (*Takes the money.*)

(*The two of them start walking.*)

ACTOR 1: Well see ya, or oh, but I guess we're both going to the station.

(*Both exit. After a while, blackout.*)

CURTAIN

PART VI

POPULAR THEATER

As is often pointed out, histories of modern theater consist of the emergence of innovative and artistic theaters, each kind replacing what has preceded it. In contrast, popular theater is rarely discussed in these histories because it is primarily not innovative, even though it constitutes the mainstream of contemporary theater. Only recently have significant forms of popular theater, such as melodrama in the nineteenth century or musicals in the twentieth century, become the focus of academic theater research. These forms, however, are analyzed mostly from a cultural point of view, not necessarily from the perspective of theater history. But theater always must be popular, since it would not exist without spectators. Furthermore, only in modern times did theater begin to be enjoyed in printed form as well as in performance. Since then, theater has been split into two kinds, an entertainment theater and a consciously artistic theater. The former is popular among ordinary people, and the latter is favored by intellectuals.

In Japan, too, *taishū engeki*, a term equivalent to "popular theater," is new, literally meaning "theater for the masses." One definition of it is "a kind of theater whose ticket prices are relatively low, whose audiences are not inclined to dig out the deep meaning in the play or reveal the knowledge of old theater styles, and whose story or form of expression is easy for those audiences to understand and accept."[1]

---

1. Kata Kōji, "Warai to namida ga nidai shichū: Taishū engeki," in *Dentō to gendai*, ed. Dentō-geijutsu no kai (Tokyo: Gakugei shorin, 1969), 8:96.

Taishū engeki is popular entertainment theater, so it is also commercial theater, which can survive through box-office income and thus does not have to be subsidized by the government. Accordingly, the term *shōgyō engeki* (commercial theater) is used interchangeably with *taishū engeki*. We might say that although both are popular theater, *shōgyō engeki* is for upper-class or upper-middle-class audiences, whereas *taishū engeki* is for middle-class or lower-middle-class audiences. *Shōgyō engeki* is presented in a large theaters located in the central part of major cities, and the tickets are quite expensive. *Taishū engeki* is played in small theaters in the suburbs or small towns for a relatively small admission fee.

POPULAR ENTERTAINMENT IN MODERN JAPAN

Today Japan has several forms of popular entertainment, generally called *engei* (entertainment performance). *Engei* includes *rakugo* (solo recitations of comic stories), *manzai* (a sort of stand-up comedy by two or three players), *mandan* (a one-person talk show), and *kōdan* (a narrative form of traditional stories). These performing arts are usually differentiated from *engeki* (theater). But some *engeki*—such as kabuki, *shinpa*, and *shin-kokugeki* (new national drama)—are considered to be popular entertainments.

Kabuki, a highly refined traditional theater style, is performed almost daily and constitutes a profit-making enterprise under the management of an entertainment conglomerate, the Shōchiku Company. There is no doubt that it is still popular. As noted in the general introduction to this book, kabuki once tried, unsuccessfully, to modernize. But those writers trying to create this new type of kabuki play were not *zatsuki-sakusha*—that is, professional writers employed by theater companies. For example, Tsubouchi Shōyō (1859–1935), a professor at Waseda University, was one of the new kabuki dramatists, whose plays were termed *shin-kabuki* (new kabuki). After Shōyō, Okamoto Kidō (1872–1939), Mayama Seika (1878–1948), Hasegawa Shin (1884–1963), Hōjō Hideji (1902–1996), and Uno Nobuo (1904–1991) are the best-known new-kabuki playwrights. Their plays also are both entertaining and popular. Kidō's *The Story of Shuzenji* (*Shuzenji monogatari*), Seika's *Treasury of the Loyal Genroku Samurai* (*Genroku chūshingura*), and Hasegawa's *A Lone Sword Enters the Ring* (*Ippon-gatana dohyō-iri*) are still frequently performed. Before and during World War II, kabuki troupes even dramatized modern political or military themes in such plays as *Mussolini* and *Three Heroic Human Bombs* (*Nikudan-san-yūshi*).[2] After the war, the most popular new-kabuki play may have been *The Tale of Genji* (*Genji monogatari*), by Funabashi Seiichi (1904–1976), which was an adaptation of the famous classical tale of the same

2. This is wonderfully documented in James R. Brandon, *Kabuki's Forgotten War, 1931–1945* (Honolulu: University of Hawai'i Press, 2009).

title by Murasaki Shikibu.[3] Ichikawa Ebizō (later, Ichikawa Danjūrō XI, 1909–1965) played the main role of the "Shining Prince," Hikaru Genji, and enthralled packed theaters, and especially his female fans, with his good looks and the play's gorgeous costumes and settings. The popularity of kabuki actors increased with the introduction of television, for some kabuki actors also became TV stars. Matsumoto Kōshirō IX (b. 1942) is an example. He has appeared not only in *shingeki* and television dramas, but even in musical plays, such as *The Man of La Mancha* and *The King and I*.

Mishima Yukio (1925–1970) was an exceptional new-kabuki playwright, as he also was a world-famous novelist and the writer of many *shingeki* plays. His best-known plays include *Five Modern Nō Plays*, which are frequently performed in the West, and *Madame de Sade* (*Sado kōshaku-fujin*), which once was directed by Ingmar Bergman in Europe and is considered Mishima's most representative play. But he loved kabuki as well and wrote a number of kabuki plays, among them the one featured here, *The Sardine Seller's Net of Love* (*Iwashi-uri koi no hikiami*), a comedy, unusual for Mishima, and quite successful when performed at the Kabuki Theater (Kabukiza) in Tokyo in 1953.

Shinpa also has been under the management of the Shōchiku Company. As pointed out in the general introduction, most of the early *shinpa* plays were adaptations of popular novels. The *shinpa* play in part VI, *Nihonbashi*, is an adaptation of Izumi Kyōka's novel of the same title. As this one does, many *shinpa* plays have a tragic ending, hence the term *shinpa higeki* (*shinpa* tragedy), referring to a sad, melodramatic story.

In addition, *shinpa* maintained the kabuki convention of using female impersonators (*onnagata*). Although Kawai Takeo (1877–1942), Kitamura Rokurō (1871–1961), and Hanayagi Shōtarō (1894–1965) were renowned *shinpa onnagata*, Mizutani Yaeko (1905–1979) also gained fame as the first great *shinpa* actress. Both actresses and *onnagata* often appeared on the same stage without upsetting the audience.

In the first few decades of the twentieth century, *shinpa* was enormously popular, much more than the traditional kabuki theater. But then after World War II, it began to lose its luster, even though such playwrights as Kawaguchi Matsutarō (1899–1985) and Nakano Minoru (1901–1973) still were popular. Today, *shinpa* is often performed as a vehicle for important kabuki actors or television stars.

Shin-kokugeki is an offshoot of *kokugeki* (national drama), a term coined by Tsubouchi Shōyō. The founder of *shin-kokugeki*, Sawada Shōjirō (1892–1929), was one of Shōyō's disciples. Sawada later joined the Art Theater Company (Geijutsuza), famous for the group's director, Shimamura Hōgetu (1871–1918), and for the actress Matsui Sumako (1886–1919), but he soon founded his own company in order to realize Shōyō's ideas. The company had financial difficulties, however, and was able to survive only by presenting plays about sword-fighting heroes, works like *Kunisada Chūji*. Whereas

3. For an entertaining account of this play, see Samuel L. Leiter, "Performing the Emperor's New Clothes: *The Mikado*, *The Tale of Genji*, and Lèse Majesté on the Japanese Stage," in *Rising from the Flames: The Rebirth of Theater in Occupied Japan, 1945–1952*, ed. Samuel L. Leiter (Lanham, Md.: Lexington Books, 2009), 125–71.

KUBOTA MANTARŌ

[Around 1904 or 1905,] Takada Minoru, Fujisawa Asajirō, and Satō Toshizō, who were experts of *shinpa* since the first performances by the Kawakami company at Asakusaza, were featured at the Hongōza, while at the Masagoza the boss, Ii Yōhō, was leading young and promising actors, such as Murata Masao, Inoue Masao, and Seki Kiyomi. These two theaters were competing from opposite poles. If you would call the Hongōza a pro-government party, the Masagoza could be called an opposition party. Their contrasting stances, however, contributed a great deal to the popularity of *shinpa*. *Shinpa* completely dominated over kabuki during this period. . . .

These actors were concerned not only with plays but also with direction. And soon they created extremely realistic and innovative stage sets, which were called the Hongōza style. Lighting and sound effects were also developed together with scenery. One reason for this was the fact that Takada Minoru and Kitamura Rokurō from Osaka were meticulous on the details of acting. They were not only good actors but also excellent directors, though both were considered to be noisy and fussy actors who invaded even the territory of the playwright. They annoyed even theater critics. It was the time when directors were unknown.

Soon, however, a part of the literary world got interested in Ibsen and the *shingeki* movement, based on Ibsen, took hold. Kabuki was nothing to fight against for those young literary people who were eager to modernize theater. They considered *shinpa* as the real enemy, for *shinpa* audiences were intellectually superior to those of kabuki. (Like the audience of the Tsukiji Little Theater at one time, most *shinpa* audiences were on the level of college students or higher.) Besides, for those reformists who opened their eyes to modern drama with Ibsen and other dramas, *shinpa*'s modern dramas looked only superficially realistic, merely telling stories that did not explore the meaning of life. The reformists criticized this fictitiousness before anything else.

Then, what did our *shinpa* do? That's the point.

Shinpa did nothing.

FROM KUBOTA MANTARŌ, "JO NI KAETE YANAGI-KUN NI" (TO MR. YANAGI IN PLACE OF A PREFACE), IN *SHINPA NO ROKUJŪNEN* (*SIXTY YEARS OF SHINPA*), BY YANAGI EIJIRŌ (TOKYO: KAWADE SHOBŌ, 1948), 2–3, 6–8.

shinpa attracted middle-class female audiences with plays about the sorrowful fates of their heroines, *shin-kokugeki* were popular with younger male audiences. Indeed, the great popularity of *shin-kokugeki* in the 1920s and 1930s led to *onna-kengeki*, plays about female sword fighters, in which a strong female character overwhelms men with her superior fighting skill.

Partly because *onna-kengeki* was *taishū engeki*—theater for lower-middle-class audiences—it tended toward eroticism in the liberal atmosphere of Japanese society after the war and so began to compete with the striptease shows in vogue at the time. Asakusa, the location of the highest-ranking licensed quarters during the Edo period, was the main entertainment district for the *taishū engeki* companies in Tokyo, as Dōtonbori was in Osaka. In addition, before and after the war, many small traveling companies performed plays in the style of *shinpa* or *shin-kokugeki*, including the songs and dances between acts. But then they rapidly lost their audiences to television and gradually disappeared during the 1970s, although a few traveling companies still exist. Sometimes, however, an actor from such a *taishū engeki* company is recognized by his fans, and he rises to sudden stardom in the commercial theater, just as an off-Broadway actor occasionally turns into a Broadway star.

All these popular theaters are, in a way, modern descendants of kabuki. But even more kinds of popular theater emerged under the influence of the Western performing arts. One that attracted intellectual theatergoers was opera. When the Imperial Theater (Teikoku gekijō) opened as the first completely Western-style theater in Japan in 1911, it was intended not only for kabuki and *shingeki* but also for opera. The theater organized its own opera troupe and employed an Italian opera director and choreographer, Giovanni Vittorio Rossi (b. 1867). But opera productions at the Imperial Theater were financial failures, and the opera troupe later disbanded. Rossi remained in Japan until 1918, staging operas at smaller theaters, and he had considerable influence on the future development of the Japanese opera world. The most notable result was the so-called Asakusa opera, which presented shortened and popularized operas and was the precedent for, at the beginning of the Taishō era, the Takarazuka opera.

TAKARAZUKA

The Takarazuka opera (Takarazuka kageki-dan), whose official English name is the Takarazuka Revue Company, was the idea of Kobayashi Ichizō (1873–1957), one of the most successful businessmen in modern Japan. He ran the private railway line running from central Osaka to the hot-spring spa Takarazuka, located in nearby Hyōgo Prefecture. Kobayashi built a huge warm-water swimming pool at the spa so that families would go there by train. Unfortunately, his plan did not succeed, as swimming pools were still new to ordinary Japanese. So Kobayashi had the pool covered and used the space for theatrical performances. In 1913, he organized a song-and-dance troupe of teenage girls,

KOBAYASHI ICHIZŌ

The discussion of employing male actors in Takarazuka started long ago. Already at the time of the founding of the company, Mr. Andō, the composer, insisted on this. If we had decided to have pupils both male and female at that time, such an irregular company as Girl's Opera, a unique art of Takarazuka, would not have been born. And it might have developed into a genuine opera with male and female singers, or have soon failed.

At that time, I was not sure of the success of this enterprise. I was aware of only the economic risks and of the dangerous world of young men surrounding girls, so that I made a secure plan—that is, a girls' chorus group like the Mitsukoshi Boys' Music Group, which was already popular. I thought that the Takarazuka Girls' Chorus Group would be an excellent advertisement for the Takarazuka Hot Spring Resort. This was my simpleminded plan at its inception. . . .

I have no ear for music by nature. I know I don't understand music. But thanks to my fifty-year experience of the customer business, I know whether or not an opera will be a box-office hit or whether or not it will draw an audience, even when I nod off watching it in rehearsal. In short, I have no artistic appreciation, but I have an eye for commercial profit. So when we started this business, I praised Mr. Andō's works but often refused to include them in the repertoire. Mr. Andō complained, saying that an amateur couldn't judge; I understood his feeling. At one time, he ran away and hid himself with all the musical scores he had composed. We were at a loss before opening night. But I have, as a young man, read many novels. I have an ability to make a one-act piece of patchwork from interesting songs out of high-school or college music textbooks. I put together *The Maple Viewing* [*Momiji-gari*] and *Murasame and Matsukaze* overnight. Mr. Andō couldn't stand my barbarism and resigned himself to work for Takarazuka, though he complained about me all the time. He was one of the earliest great contributors to Takarazuka.

FROM KOBAYASHI ICHIZŌ, *ITSU-Ō JIJODEN* (*AUTOBIOGRAPHY OF ITSU-Ō*) (TOKYO: SANGYŌ-KEIZAI SHINBUNSHA, 1953), 235–38.

the Takarazuka chorus troupe (Takarazuka shōka-tai), and the following year he presented his first production: two opera pieces, *Splash* (*Donburako*) and *The Joyful Dharma* (*Ukare daruma*), and a dance piece, *Butterfly* (*Kochō*). They were quite successful, and the Takarazuka troupe continued to present similar attractions to the spa guests. In

1918, Takarazuka went to Tokyo and performed at the Imperial Theater. The next year, a training school, the Takarazuka Music and Opera School, was approved by the government as a private school of education. At the same time, the troupe acquired a new name, the Takarazuka Girls' Opera Company (Takarazuka shōjo kageki-dan). The term *shōjo* (girls) was dropped in 1940, and the troupe's current name has been used ever since. All the members of the company are required to graduate from the school's two-year training course, and they continue to be called "pupils" of the school even after they become members of the company.

In 1924, Kobayashi built a theater with a capacity of four thousand, with the intention of realizing his vision of *kokumingeki* (the nation's theater for the people), reminiscent of Shōyō's *kokugeki* (national drama). But Kobayashi meant to appeal to a broader public than what Shōyō had had in mind. Hence Takarazuka, as an all-girl company, attempted to project an image of being "pure, proper, and beautiful" (*kiyoku, tadashiku, utsukushiku*: the school's motto), lest it be disparaged by the middle class, who at that time regarded actresses as immoral. Kobayashi wanted Takarazuka to perform mainly musical plays, rather than spoken drama, in accordance with his understanding of ordinary people's natural appreciation for traditional Japanese theater. But he believed that the music used should be Western, since the Meiji government's Ministry of Education had decided that the primary schools should have a Western music curriculum.

In any event, the theater's large seating capacity raised questions about Takarazuka's performance style, so a stage director, Kishida Tatsuya (1892–1944), was sent to Paris to seek out a suitable new type of entertainment. The first fruitful result of his study tour was a grand revue, *Mon Paris*, produced in 1927. It was an epoch-making success. In 1930, Shirai Tetsuzō (1900–1983), who also had been sent to Paris, directed another revue, *Parisette*, which was again a huge hit. Takarazuka's future was now firmly established.

Takarazuka is an interesting theatrical enterprise from a cultural, if not strictly artistic, viewpoint. The first production was staged with only sixteen young girls, but today Takarazuka has five troupes: Hana (Flower), Hoshi (Star), Yuki (Snow), Tsuki (Moon), and Sora (Cosmos), each consisting of roughly eighty members. All are run on the star system, in which the top male impersonator (*otokoyaku*) is "the top star" of the troupe and his (her) partner is "the top female role" (*musumeyaku*) player. They play the main roles together as long as they remain in these positions, four or five years on average. They then are replaced by younger stars. Since all the members must remain single, those who want to marry must retire immediately.

Most performers remain at Takarazuka for about ten years. After training at the school, their acting ability is evaluated. But the top stars are selected for their charisma, thereby ignoring the company's almost feudalistic view of the upper- and lower-year pupils, or even their individual performing abilities. The company and each production are governed by the conservative moral attitude of the so-called *sumire* (violet) code—that is, no politics, no religion, and no sex. Until recently, when Takarazuka became a financially independent entity, it had always been under the financial umbrella of the Hankyū

Railway Company, with Kobayashi as the founder. Despite the many ups and downs in its long history, especially during and after the war, Takarazuka has remained popular to the present day.

Takarazuka has ten main productions a year, two per troupe, with each lasting a month. Smaller or experimental productions are staged as well. Usually a production is shown first in Takarazuka city and then in Tokyo, although some troupes go to other cities. There are no guest performers, and Takarazuka players are not allowed to perform in any non-Takarazuka productions, including films and television. Each production usually consists of two shows: one musical play lasting about an hour and forty minutes and one revue lasting about an hour. The performance almost always concludes with a gorgeous and colorfully designed parade of all the players in the production, who walk down a huge staircase at center stage. The top star comes down last, wearing a spectacular costume with feather wings. Once in a great while, the production is made up of only one musical play, and one of these is *The Rose of Versailles* (*Berusaiyu no bara*), the Takarazuka's most important and significant production after *Parisette*. It was first performed in 1974 and became a huge-box office hit. An excerpt from it is translated in part VI.

COMIC THEATER

According to Kata Kōji, Japan has had two kinds of comic, or farcical, popular theater. One is *Soganoya kigeki*, originally based in Osaka, and the other is nonsense or slapstick comedies, which were introduced from the West and performed mainly in Tokyo.

The Soganoya Company was Japan's first commercial comedy troupe, whose principal performers were Soganoya Gorō (1877–1948) and Soganoya Jūrō (1869–1925), both originally low-class kabuki actors. When they established their new theater of comedy in 1904, they pretended to be brothers, though they were not, and soon became very popular. Soganoya comedy (*Soganoya kigeki*) is a uniquely Japanese comedy of manners based on traditional comic and improvisational skits called *niwaka* in Osaka. Whereas Gorō tended toward social criticism of the ruling class, Jūrō wanted only to encourage laughter of the kind that in the 1920s was called "nonsense" (*nansensu*). Before long, they began to perform separately. Gorō eventually began performing in rather moralistic plays praising Japan's traditions and conservative family values. His company was extremely successful, as it was in perfect accord with ordinary people's social attitudes. It was followed by many similar companies, among which the Soganoya Gokurō Company also did very well. Soganoya Gokurō (1876–1940) used actresses instead of *onnagata*, whom the Soganoya Gorō Company still employed.

After Gorō's death in 1948, the Soganoya Gorō Company merged with the Shōchiku Family Theater (Shōchiku katei-geki) and other companies and was led by Shibuya Tengai (1906–1983). This, the Shōchiku New Comedy (Shōchiku shin-kigeki), was enormously successful and remained so under Fujiyama Kanbi (1929–1990), Tengai's successor, until the 1980s.[4]

Another stream of popular comedy, influenced by Western models, also flourished in the Asakusa entertainment district after the beginning of the Shōwa era in 1926. Shortly before then, in 1923, the Great Kantō Earthquake destroyed much of Tokyo, and more than 100,000 people were killed. The theater changed completely. Before the earthquake, kabuki actors had often privately performed modern plays, both domestic and foreign. But after the earthquake, these experiments stopped, and most performers confined themselves to traditional kabuki plays. In 1924, the Tsukiji Little Theater was founded, marking the start of genuine *shingeki.*

After the earthquake, Asakusa opera, too, was supplanted by a kind of vaudeville show, which included song and dance. These performances were based on Western slapstick-comedy films, which a company, the Casino Follies, provided. Enomoto Ken'ichi (1904–1970) was the company's star comedian, and his comic shows were termed *acharaka*, a twisted pronunciation of *achira* (beyond) the sea. Enoken (an abbreviation of Enomoto Ken'ichi) appeared in many films as well, including Kurosawa Akira's first film after the war, *The Men Who Tread on the Tiger's Tail* (*Tora no o wo fumu otokotachi*, 1945), a cinematic version of the famous kabuki play *The Subscription List* (*Kanjinchō*). Before the war, Enoken even played a role in a Japanese adaptation of Bertolt Brecht's *The Threepenny Opera.*[5] Another popular comedian, who competed with Enoken, was Furukawa Roppa (1903–1961). He started his career as a narrator for silent films (*benshi*) and, together with other narrators, founded a comedy company when the talkies took over. His strong point was nonsense comedy, and his company attracted large audiences even during the Great Depression.

In 1932, Kobayashi Ichizō established the Tokyo Takarazuka Company, and in 1934, he opened the Tokyo Takarazuka Theater in Hibiya, in the central part of the city. He eventually bought several theaters in Hibiya, including the Imperial Theater, and created an entertainment conglomerate referred to as Tōhō (an abbreviation of Tokyo Takarazuka), in competition with Shōchiku. Tōhō dominated Tokyo's Hibiya area, and over the years, Tōhō has tried from time to time to hire kabuki actors away from Shōchiku in order to start what has been called Tōhō kabuki. But each attempt failed, and the actors returned to Shōchiku. Thus, today, all kabuki actors belong to Shōchiku, except those in the Forward Advance Theater (Zenshinza), a group of leftist kabuki actors.

Kikuta Kazuo (1908–1973), the most important playwright and producer for Tōhō, was originally a company writer for Furukawa Roppa's group, which eventually came

---

4. For an account of this style of comedy, see Yoshiko Fukushima, "Illegitimate Child of *Shingeki:* Comedy Actor Soganoya Gokurō and His *Nonkina tōsan* (*Easygoing Daddy*)," in *Modern Japanese Theatre and Performance*, ed. David Jortner, Keiko I. McDonald, and Kevin J. Wetmore Jr. (Lanham, Md.: Lexington Books, 2006), 171–87.

5. For more information on Enoken, see Yoshiko Fukushima, "Ambivalent Mimicry in Enomoto Kenichi's Wartime Comedy: His Revue and Blackface," *Comedy Studies* 2, no. 1 (2011): 21–37.

under Tōhō's management. Before the advent of television, Kikuta's radio dramas had been tremendously popular. *On the Hill the Bell Rings* (*Kane no naru oka*) and *What Is Your Name?* (*Kimi no na wa?*) absolutely thrilled the whole nation, which was otherwise severely deprived after the war. Although Kikuta was primarily a writer and producer of popular theater, his best play, *A Port with Flowers Blooming* (*Hana saku minato*, 1943), should be categorized as a *shingeki* play. His longest-running play, *Diary of a Vagabond* (*Hōrō-ki*), had featured the actress Mori Mitsuko (1920–2012) in the main role since 1961. But in 2010, she turned ninety and finally stopped performing. Such loyalty from fans is typical of popular theater.

Today's successors to Kikuta Kazuo are perhaps Mitani Kōki (b. 1961) and Makino Nozomi (b. 1959), although both, unlike Kikuta, preside over their own theater groups as well as write plays for television and commercial theater as freelance playwrights.

Popular theater generally emphasizes the actor more than the text and the surface techniques of acting more than the themes and ideas underlying the text. Although popular theater is very satisfying to watch when performed, it seems shallow when read. Accordingly, the texts for popular theater are rarely retained after production. This is one reason why many popular performances were so rapidly replaced by television programs, whose visual appeal can make a much stronger impression than theater. This also is the reason why we include here only kabuki, *shinpa*, and Takarazuka plays. They may not be great works of art, but at least they are more readable than other forms of popular theater, and they hold up well in competition with television, which today is where the most popular drama in Japan (and, for that matter, all over the world) can be found.

MITSUYA MORI

Izumi Kyōka, *Nihonbashi*, 1920s.
(The Tsubouchi Memorial Theatre Museum Waseda University; courtesy of Nihon haiyū kyōkai)

NIHONBASHI

IZUMI KYŌKA

TRANSLATED BY M. CODY POULTON

By the Taishō era, the novelist and playwright Izumi Kyōka (1873–1939) was as famous for his stories and plays about the demimonde as for his ghost stories, and the former—works like *A Woman's Pedigree* (*Onna keizu*, 1907) and *The White Heron* (*Shirasagi*, 1909)—quickly became staples of the *shinpa* stage. *Shinpa* was a transitional and highly melodramatic form of theater that was modern in its subject matter and, later, its use of actresses. But it still retained many of the conventions of kabuki theater: male specialists for female roles (*onnagata*); the *hanamichi*, a runway going from stage right through the auditorium, which is used for dramatic entrances and exits; and *geza* incidental music, to name a few common features. Through the 1890s to 1910s, *shinpa* adapted, and even stole, a considerable amount of material from Kyōka and other contemporary novelists. By the second decade of the twentieth century, Kyōka himself began writing adaptations of his own fiction and, increasingly, original plays for *shinpa*, just as its star was falling in critical circles to the more modern, realistic *shingeki* (new theater).

Nihonbashi began life as a novel about competing geishas in the demimonde of Tokyo's old downtown, or *shitamachi*, district. In Edo (the old name for Tokyo) days, all roads pretty much led to the "Japan Bridge" of the title, but in Kyōka's time it was losing ground to the more upscale districts of Marunouchi, Ginza, and Hongō. The story involves two geishas, the elegant Kiyoha and the much less elegant, feistier Okō, and two men, Igarashi Dengo, a rough fish merchant who has abandoned his wife and child and ruined his business over love for Okō, and Katsuragi Shinzō, a neurotic professor of medicine who has fallen for Kiyoha because she reminds him of his elder sister, who became a concubine to pay for his education. Okō resents Kiyoha's success as a geisha and steals Katsuragi away. In the scene translated here, convinced that Katsuragi has become her patron (*danna* also means "husband"), she throws Dengo out. The scene shows off Kyōka's gift for portraying strong, passionate, and tragic women: Okō's tirade (*tanka*) against Dengo provides a couple of famous *miseba* (showstoppers), in which, in kabuki style, the actor poses and the audience shouts its praise. This also marks a dramatic turning point in the play. The curious exchange between Okō and her apprentice geisha (*oshaku*) Ochise, in which Okō pretends to be Katsuragi and Ochise becomes Okō, sets up the mistaken identity that leads to Ochise's death. Vowing revenge on Okō, Dengo stabs Ochise because she is wearing Okō's scarlet *kanoko* kimono. Okō then slays Dengo with his own sword and takes her own life, by poison, in the arms of her beloved Katsuragi, who survives but has the blood of more women on his feckless hands. In an act of self-sacrifice not typical of Okō, she asks Kiyoha to look after him.

First published in September 1914 by Shun'yōdō, with beautiful illustrations by Komura Settai, the novel was staged the following March with a script by the leading playwright Mayama Seika. A close look at the stage text (*daihon*) for this first performance reveals, however, that it was the work of several hands. Kyōka's fiction was famous for its lively dialogue and intense dramatic incident, and Seika lifted many of the lines verbatim from the novel for his adaptation. Kitamura Rokurō, an actor whom Kyōka highly respected (he played Okō in the first production), also crafted much of the dialogue. The text translated here is based on Kyōka's own stage adaptation, which he published in 1917, and is found in the *Complete Works of Kyōka*. The famous *shinpa onnagata* Hanayagi Shōtarō made his debut, as Ochise, in the play's first production. *Nihonbashi* is now a standard of the *shinpa* repertoire, and Okō is one of the favorite roles of the leading kabuki *onnagata* Bandō Tamasaburō V. Director Ichikawa Kon's film version, made in 1956, features the brilliant *shinpa* actor Yanagi Eijirō in the role of Dengo.

ACT 3, SCENE 2. THE SECOND FLOOR OF INABA HOUSE

IGARASHI DENGO *is wrapped in a padded jacket tied with a woman's waistband. He has been staring steadily at a fish knife with a wooden scabbard clutched in his hand. He now thrusts the knife into the sleeve of a quilted housecoat rolled up in front of the closet, and leaning back on the bedroll, he throws out his legs, his head hanging down. Then, taking his head in his hands, he glares up at the ceiling. All his actions are abrupt, rough.* OKŌ *adjusts the cushion in front of the hibachi and sits, half facing* DENGO. *She straightens herself, as if about to say something important. The sound of a hand drum can be heard in the distance.*

OKŌ: Go wash your face, why don't you.

DENGO: Heh heh. (*Sneers.*)

OKŌ: Hey, stop using my toothpicks like you'd had breakfast in bed.

DENGO: Heh heh. Who'd you be talking about now?

OKŌ: Oh, you really scare me. You were listening, weren't you?

DENGO: You'd make a man deaf with that racket. You thought I couldn't hear what was going on downstairs? You've got a voice like a gunshot.

OKŌ: Yeah. I thought that seeing as how you've got such a thick skull, you'd be hard of hearing, too. But please go wash your face. There's something else I have to say, if you don't mind.

DENGO: You want to tell me you're sorry 'cause I found out you've had it off with another man? Hey, Okō? (*Sits up.*) I don't have to wash my face to hear that, surely. If it was all just a dream, it'd be one thing, but if you're asking me to wake up and wash my face for this news, you've got another thing coming to you.

OKŌ: You think I'm just going to lie back and take it?

DENGO: If you don't, I hope you're ready for the consequences. You're really asking for it, you know.

OKŌ (*Resignedly*): Go ahead, I'm ready for anything. . . .

DENGO: What I'm saying is, if you don't shut up, I'm not going to leave you in one piece. Bitch! You want to get yourself killed?

OKŌ: I don't know if I've been killed or coddled, spoken my mind or given a piece of somebody else's. Have I loved and been wronged, have I gone through hell? Sometimes I've wanted to spend the rest of my life with him; other times I've just wanted to die. I don't know anymore. Don't ask. Just get out, go home. I've got a good man now.

DENGO (*Rises abruptly*): What? Go home?

OKŌ: Yeah, for good. I'm not letting you in here again.

DENGO: You must be crazy, Okō.

OKŌ: Don't "Okō" me. —You call me crazy? I am *not.* I've never felt so sane as I do right now. . . . The good doctor's diagnosis is that I'm madly in love. Madly in love, you hear? Not crazy. I'll stake my life on it. I'll be kind to strangers—you don't have to wash your face. Listen: Okō of Inaba House has got herself a husband. Mr. Katsuragi is his name. You and I are through.

DENGO (*Suddenly goes limp*): What? A husband? That's all right by me if it's just a husband we're talking about. I got a big heart, so I'll overlook that. I'll be a good boy, or my name ain't Igarashi Dengo.

OKŌ (*Looks away and sighs*): I've said all I can, so just be a good boy and get out. Right now. Stay away and there won't be any more trouble around here.

DENGO: Nah. If that "husband" of yours shows up, what's wrong with my being here? If he drops by without warning, why, I'll just throw this quilt over me and stow away in the clothes closet. That's one of my favorite games from 'way back.

OKŌ: Be my guest. But if you do, we'll be overrun with roaches. So forget your bedroom pranks and just get yourself straight down the stairs and out the door.

DENGO: Okō, try saying that again.

OKŌ: I told you, stop calling me "Okō." —All right, I'll say it as often as you like. —We'll be overrun with roaches if you don't—

DENGO: What do you take me for? Just what do you take me for?

OKŌ: A seal in a bearskin, that's what I take you for. —Listen, you staked your fortune on a boatload of lumber, and you left Hokkaido and swam into that harbor over there and set yourself up in the seafood business for a time. Your fishy friends got you a free pass into the best bars on the embankment, didn't they? And once you'd laid eyes on Kiyoha, well, the sky was the limit for you! Like some mole who'd found the wings of an angel. No doubt you tugged on her sleeve and she tugged back, and before you knew it, your eyes rolled and you fell head over heels for her. What a laugh! . . . If it's somebody Kiyoha threw over, I thought to myself, who cares if he's a caterpillar, or even a cockroach? I'll sew him into the hem of my skirts and wave him in her face just to spite her. And when it happened to be a seal in a bearskin, folks couldn't help but notice. Every tongue in town was wagging. The fact I ended up with you must be one of the seven wonders of the quarter. Better yet, one of the wonders of the world . . . You remember, don't you? When I listened to your story, it certainly wasn't for love. Nor for the money, no . . . I did it just to get even with Kiyoha. When the time comes and I get tired of you, I'll call it off, I said. And you made a solemn promise that it was all right by you, didn't you? You've got no grounds for complaint. I'm tired of you, so let's call it quits. Go on, get out! Go home this minute. And don't ever come back. From now on, the two of us don't even know each other. You understand?

DENGO (*Rubbing his eyes, silently glares at* OKŌ. *Finally bursts out laughing*): Hah, hah, hah! Crazy dame! Hah, hah, hah! What an outburst! I don't have anything to add to that, that's for sure. A regular little fireball, you are. I love it! Hah, hah, hah! You're so cute when you're mad. (*Again he leans back on the bedding, his head hanging down, and throws out his legs. Belying his words, he shakes his legs as if to fan the flames of agony in his heart.*)

OKŌ (*Sharply*): I told you, get out! . . . This is the Inaba House, Okō's place. No, it belongs to Mr. Katsuragi. It's his . . . second residence.

DENGO: I don't give a damn if it's a whorehouse. If I'm in the way, I'll just crawl into the closet. Hah, hah, hah! (*Laughs mirthlessly.*)

OKŌ: What's the point of losing my temper? You're a cockroach, not a man. Just listen to what I have to say. If I'm a real geisha, it doesn't make a damn bit of difference whether I've got a patron, a client, or even a guy on the side. But from this day forward, by the grace of the gods, I'm Katsuragi's wife. (*Sits up.*) I won't have the smell of another man hanging over my house for three blocks around. Do you really think some animal in a housecoat, like some oversexed badger figurine, is the sort of thing I'd decorate my bedroom with? (*Bolts up.*) Look! There's this filthy oaf stinking up my tatami! I don't need your kind in my place. Get out of my way! Just clear off! (*She yanks on the quilt that* DENGO *is leaning against. The knife with its wooden scabbard falls out with a clatter.* DENGO *leaps up, fixing his eyes on it.*)

OKŌ (*Draws back a step*): Hey. Did you have this on you last night?

DENGO: It's for you, bitch. I got a whiff of Katsuragi, you see, and I've made up my mind. If you don't shut up, it'll be this. Understand? (*Draws the knife from its sheath.*) How about it?

(*Kicking up her skirts,* OKŌ *makes for the stairwell.* DENGO *reaches out and pulls her back by her* obi. OKŌ *falls on her haunches, shaking loose the trapdoor over the stairwell, which slams shut. Barred from escape by her own hands, she quietly returns to her seat. Dumbfounded,* DENGO *stands bolt upright.*)

OKŌ: Kill me. Go ahead and run me through.

DENGO: Whore! (*Draws back a step.*)

OKŌ: Kill me! Do it! Run me through! That's what a knife is for, isn't it? Cut me, slash me, right to the bone, a stroke for every letter in Katsuragi's name. How many does that make? (*Counts on her fingers.*) "K" for "kill." "A" for "assassin." "T" for "torture." . . . Who knows how many strokes it takes? But I'll take it! I'll take it as long as I draw breath. I'll watch you engrave his name on my heart. I'll show you how a woman dies! Go on, stab me. (*Edging up to him.*)

DENGO: Uh . . . (*Retreating.*)

OKŌ: If the blade can't cut, I'll take off my kimono. (*Laying her hands on the waistband.*) Is my skin too thick? Shall I take that off, too? How about it, eh, hairy bear? Shall I scrape off my scales for you?

(DENGO *still retreats inch by inch and, as if unaware of his own actions, raises the trapdoor to his shoulders and tumbles down the stairs.* OKŌ *turns around in the direction of the noise, then looks about her. Seeing the cherry blossoms arranged in the alcove and adjusting her dress, she takes a sprig in her hand and steadily gazes at it, smiling faintly.*)

OKŌ (*To the flowers*): There's not a breath of wind, but little cherry blossom, you tremble so.

OCHISE (*Dashing in, embraces* OKŌ): Okō!

OKŌ: Well now. Your lessons over for the day?

OCHISE: Why, you talk as if nothing happened! Okō, I hadn't the faintest idea what to do. We were all huddled together at the bottom of the stairs, at our wit's end. . . . Well, thank goodness you're through with your bear friend, hm?

OKŌ: Just forget about it. I've got something to show you instead. (*From the carefully folded clothes in her dresser, she takes out an undergarment. It has a dappled* kanoko *design on a scarlet and pale blue ground.*) Once—I can't remember when—I met Kiyoha on the way back from Ichikoku Bridge, and she was wearing one just like this. With her black hair and pure white skin it was a little on the flashy side, but it suited her. She cut a real figure, she did. Quite the coquette, I can tell you. Oh, I wanted so much to wear something like that myself, but I'd never have looked good in it unless it was maybe a dinner party and I had a dance to perform. So I thought I'd give it to you, and I placed an order at the tailor's to make up one in a hurry. They brought it over last night. You'll look just right in it. Go ahead, try it on.

OCHISE: But Okō, you'd waste it on me.

OKŌ: You're my kid sister, aren't you? Might as well be. Go ahead, put it on over top. (OKŌ *has* OCHISE *stand, puts it on, and tidies up her appearance.* OCHISE, *blushing happily, stands before the mirror.*)

OKŌ: It looks good on you. (*She says, and then collapses onto* OCHISE'*s lap.*) Okō—

OCHISE: . . . ?

OKŌ: Call me Katsuragi. (*Laughs.*)

OCHISE: Ho ho ho. Madame Katsuragi.

OKŌ: You make me sound like a prostitute. . . . No, *Mister* Katsuragi.

OCHISE: Mr. Katsuragi. . . .

OKŌ (*Impersonating* KATSURAGI, *embraces* OCHISE): Yes? Or, rather (*More gruffly*), yeah? . . . Okō! Let me spoil you, girl.

CURTAIN

Ueda Shinji, *The Rose of Versailles*, Takarazuka kagekidan, 2001.
(Courtesy of Takarazuka Revue Company)

THE ROSE OF VERSAILLES

A Takarazuka Grand Romantic Play

UEDA SHINJI

TRANSLATED BY KENKO KAWASAKI

The Rose of Versailles (*Berusaiyu no bara*) was first performed in 1974 and has remained the greatest hit in the whole history of the Takarazuka Revue Company, an all-female troupe that started to stage theatrical events in 1914. The most recent production of *The Rose of Versailles* was in 2013. (Takarazuka's productions usually are scheduled to run for no more than one month.) So far, more than 4 million people have seen this play.

The Rose of Versailles has more than a dozen variants, depending on the year of the production and the various performances staged by Takarazaka's five troupes. The translation here, of about half the play, is based on *The Rose of Versailles 2001: A Story of Fersen and Marie Antoinette*, which was the script used for the production of Takarazuka's Cosmos Troupe in 2001, directed by Ueda Shinji and Masazumi Tani and published in *A Collection of Takarazuka Grand Theater Performance Scripts* (*Takarazuka daigekijo kōen kyakuhonshū*, 2002).

The Rose of Versailles is an adaptation of a long series of *shojo manga* (girl comics) of the same title by Ikeda Riyoko, published in a weekly magazine of girl comics, *Weekly Margaret, How Appropriate!* in 1972 and 1973. The plot of *The Rose of Versailles* is based on the actual history of the French Revolution (1789–1799), although the main character, Oscar François de Jarjayes, the youngest daughter of General Jarjayes, is fictional. In the play, because the general has no son, he raised and educated his youngest daughter as a son, which allowed her to adopt the outlook of a man. Oscar has served as the royal guard of Marie Antoinette ever since she was married, at the age of fourteen, to the crown prince of France, the future Louis XVI. When Marie Antoinette meets a Swedish noble, Hans Axel von Fersen, they instantly fall in love with each other.

The main story line of *The Rose of Versailles* follows Oscar's fateful life and the forbidden love of Fersen and Marie Antoinette in the stormy times before and during the French Revolution. The various Takarazuka versions are divided into plays about Fersen and Marie Antoinette and those about Oscar and André, who is a grandson of Oscar's nurse and has been secretly in love with her. The excerpt translated here is about Fersen and Marie Antoinette, as the subtitle suggests, although elements of Oscar and André's story also make up part of the plot.

Takarazuka's adaptations are not entirely faithful to Ikeda Riyoko's original *manga*. In this version, for instance, André's death, Oscar's demise, and Fersen's appearance in Marie Antoinette's prison cell are not found in the original work. In addition, some of the characters' names are intended to provide comic relief: Duchesse de Monzette sounds like the word *monzetsu* in Japanese, which means "to faint in agony," and Marquise de Sisina sounds like *shisshin*, which means "a fainting fit." André's grandmother, who serves as Oscar's nurse, is named Marron-Glacé, a reference to the well-known chestnut confection.

There are several reasons why *The Rose of Versailles* became Takarazuka's greatest success. First, Ikeda Riyoko's original comic broke all records in sales of *shojo manga*, thus attracting audiences new to Takarazuka. Second, an important film star, Hasegawa Kazuo, directed the first production, establishing a highly praised stage style with both a presence and a precise form, which was different from and superior to the usual Takarazuka productions. Third, the role of Oscar, a woman who looks like a man, is one of the best created for star performers who portray men in Takarazuka productions. Takarazuka's extravagant production is, of course, perfect for a story about the French court in the rococo period. Finally, the musical hit—from the play known as *Beru bara*, an abbreviation of *Berusaiyu no bara*, the Japanese title of the work—has been regarded as a sort of national anthem for young women.

Characters

HANS AXEL VON FERSEN, a Swedish noble

MARIE ANTOINETTE, the queen of France

OSCAR FRANÇOIS DE JARJAYES (dressed as a man), the commandant of the Royal Guard

ANDRÉ, son of OSCAR's nurse, MARRON-GLACÉ
COMTE DE MERCY, an Austrian count, MARIE ANTOINETTE's guardian
MARIA THERESIA, the queen of the Austrian Empire, MARIE ANTOINETTE's mother
GIRODELLE, a major in the Royal Guard
BERNARD CHÂTELET, a journalist of the revolutionary party
ROSALIE, BERNARD's wife
LOUIS XVI, the king of France

PART I

SCENE 1. PROLOGUE A

With a flamboyant overture, the stage curtain opens. Low over the stage hangs a rococo frame of letters spelling the words "The Rose of Versailles." In front of it, pretty young boys and girls sing and dance.

CHORUS:
Behold, behold, the Rose of Versailles
Behold, behold, the Rose of Versailles
BOY ARISTOCRAT:
So now, let me tell you this tale
A tale of a man and a woman
Drawn together by mysterious ties
Come and listen to
The Rose of Versailles
The Rose of Versailles
The Rose of Versailles
The Rose of Versailles
(*The rococo frame rises.*)

SCENE 2. PROLOGUE B

On the stage is a rococo set with a frame in the center displaying MARIE ANTOINETTE*'s portrait. In front of this,* FERSEN *rises from below on a trapdoor lift, holding the doll Stephan in his arms. He recalls his memories of* MARIE ANTOINETTE *while he sings with great feeling.*

FERSEN:

How could I, how could I
Possibly forget her
She was, she was
Like a rose
Her image still burns
Branding my heart
I still long for her
Wandering helplessly
My world changed
The moment I met her
Her eyes
Her voice
Her soul
My life was tied to hers
When I recall the wasteland that was my soul
I see the image of my love, smiling so sweetly
When I recall the wasteland that was my soul
I see the image of my love, smiling so sweetly

MARIE ANTOINETTE:

A seed born
On the banks of the blue Danube
The memory of a beautiful rose
Blooming on the banks of the Seine
Forever and ever
Unchanging

(*The portrait closes. At the same time both sides of the rococo set transform into portraits of* OSCAR *and* ANDRÉ. *The two of them step out of their portraits and sing.*)

OSCAR:

Love can be so sorrowful
Love can be so painful

ANDRÉ:

Love can be such a torture
Love can be ephemeral

TOGETHER:

Love, love, love
Because of love
There is joy in life
Because of love
The world is one
That is why people are so beautiful

(*The two, still singing, sink into the floor on the trapdoor lift. The rococo frame rises.*)

SCENE 3. PROLOGUE C

The entire stage set is looks like a huge rococo chandelier. FERSEN *and* MARIE ANTOINETTE *take turns appearing stage center. They sing the song "Ai areba koso" (Because of Love). Many beautiful girls dance while they sing. The stage rotates.*

FERSEN:
Love can be so sweet
Love can be so strong
MARIE ANTOINETTE:
Love can be so precious
Love can be so sublime
TOGETHER:
Love, love, love
FERSEN AND MALE ENSEMBLE:
Because of love
FEMALE ENSEMBLE:
Ahh ahh ahh
There is joy in life
Because of love
The world is one
That is why people are so beautiful
SHADOW CHORUS:
Ahh ahh

SCENE 4. THE SCHÖNBRUNN PALACE

April 21, 1774. Vienna, Austria. The Hall of Mirrors at Schönbrunn Palace. The GRAND CHAMBERLAIN *appears.*

GRAND CHAMBERLAIN: Your Majesty Maria Theresia, the comte de Mercy is here to see you.
(*Grand flowery music.* MARIA THERESIA *appears, followed by a lady in waiting. From the other side of the stage, the* COMTE *appears.*)
COMTE DE MERCY: Your Majesty, I have come to offer you my farewell greetings.

MARIA THERESIA: Comte de Mercy, serve me well. From this day forward, I put my daughter's life in your hands.

COMTE DE MERCY: I am grateful for your trust in me. I will do what I can to guard over Her Highness, the princess.

MARIA THERESIA: She is only fourteen. As a parent, it's unbearable for me to marry off a daughter of such tender age, but as the empress of Austria, I must turn a blind eye to those feelings.

COMTE DE MERCY: Your Majesty, I realize this must be hard for you. However, this is the best strategy for ending the long conflict between our Austrian House of Hapsburg and the French House of Bourbon.

MARIA THERESIA: As the empress of Austria, I realize how important goodwill between Austria and France is. However, Marie Antoinette is only fourteen and doesn't adequately comprehend the meaning of this political marriage.

COMTE DE MERCY: Your Majesty, just as you are the empress of Austria first and a mother second, Marie Antoinette is a princess of the House of Hapsburg first and a fourteen-year-old girl second.

MARIA THERESIA: This is the fate of one who reigns over her country. . . .

(*The* CHIEF LADY-IN-WAITING *appears.*)

CHIEF LADY-IN-WAITING: Your Majesty, the princess is ready to depart and has come to bid you farewell.

MARIA THERESIA: So the time for her departure has really come. There are some things left I must tell her before she leaves. Have her come here at once.

CHIEF LADY-IN-WAITING: Yes, Your Majesty.

(*Flowery music. The pretty princess* MARIE ANTOINETTE *enters the stage, embracing her doll Stephan.*)

MARIE ANTOINETTE (*Overjoyed*): Oh mother, look! Isn't this pretty? And it suits me, doesn't it? Oh, I've never worn clothes so beautiful.

MARIA THERESIA: . . . Comte de Mercy . . . look at her . . . such a child . . .

COMTE DE MERCY: Your Majesty, Empress Maria Theresia!

MARIA THERESIA: Marie Antoinette, listen carefully. You're only fourteen years old. You probably have no idea what marriage is like. But I can assure you that it is not as sweet and kind as you expect it to be. From now on, you will be the French dauphine. From the moment you cross the Rhine, you will no longer be an Austrian: you will be French. Please do your best to be beloved by the people of the House of Bourbon and, even more, by all the people of France.

MARIE ANTOINETTE (*In high spirits*): Mother, please don't be worried. I have my doll Stephan. And the comte de Mercy will be with me and I am my mother's daughter. I will become an honorable queen beloved by her people. I will not do anything that would bring shame to the Austrian House of Hapsburg.

MARIA THERESIA: Oh Marie Antoinette. Please be happy.

MARIE ANTOINETTE: Farewell, mother. Farewell, Vienna. Farewell, Austria!

(*Flowery and strong music. On stage, the palace becomes transparent, and a glass carriage pulled by white horses appears.*)

SCENE 5. THE DREAM CARRIAGE

MARIE ANTOINETTE *climbs into the glass carriage, accompanied by flowery music. The carriage starts to move.*

CHORUS:

La li la la lu la la,
La li la la lu la la, La li la la lu la la,
La li la la lu la la, La li la la lu la la,
La li la la lu la la, La li la la lu la la,
(MARIE ANTOINETTE, *overjoyed, starts to sing.*)

MARIE ANTOINETTE:

The light jingling of the tiny bells
My glass carriage glides through the clouds.
I am a bride doll in a dream
Going to France, the country I long to see

CHORUS	MARIE ANTOINETTE:
La la	In a big white palace
La la la	
La la la	The prince of my dreams is waiting
La la la	
Lu lu lu	I am a bride doll in a dream
Lu	
La li la	
La lu la la	
La li la	
La lu la la	

(*The carriage rotates. The stage stops revolving. Many guards line up. Using the trapdoor lift, a thirty-two-year-old* MARIE ANTOINETTE *takes the place of her younger self. She sings.*)

MARIE ANTOINETTE:

A seed born
On the banks of the blue Danube
The memory of a beautiful rose
Blooming on the banks of the Seine
(*The stage set changes while* MARIE ANTOINETTE *sings.*)

SCENE 6. THE PALACE OF VERSAILLES

Spring, 1788. A drawing room at the Versailles palace. The COMTE DE MERCY *appears. He gently calls out to* MARIE ANTOINETTE.

COMTE DE MERCY: Your Majesty . . .

MARIE ANTOINETTE: Oh, my dear Comte de Mercy, I didn't know you were here.

COMTE DE MERCY: Your Majesty, is there something troubling you?

MARIE ANTOINETTE: Comte de Mercy, recently I have often been dreaming of the past, of the day I left my homeland Austria to come to France.

COMTE DE MERCY: I, too, remember that day and you, sweet and naive, as if it were yesterday.

MARIE ANTOINETTE: I left the Schönbrunn Palace in Austria in April when the flowers were blooming, and in a small palace on the banks of the Rhine, everything I had brought from Vienna, the lace, the ribbons, my crucifix, my rings, even my underwear, everything I wore was replaced by things made in France. Even my doll, my one and only true friend, I had to relinquish to you because I was to be the wife of the dauphin of France.

COMTE DE MERCY: Oh yes, that doll. Didn't you call him Stephan? I have kept him all this time.

MARIE ANTOINETTE: Have you really? Do you still have him? How mean of you. Please return him to me.

COMTE DE MERCY: I will, when the time is right.

MARIE ANTOINETTE: But it already has been eighteen years. What have I been doing during all this time?

COMTE DE MERCY: Your Majesty . . .

(*The* DUCHESSE DE MONZETTE, *the* MARQUISE DE SISINA, *the* COMTESSE DE LAMBESQUE, *and* VISCOMTESSE CALONNE, *all followers of* MARIE ANTOINETTE, *enter flamboyantly.*)

DUCHESSE DE MONZETTE: Ah, Your Majesty, here you are.

MARQUISE DE SISINA: Oh Your Majesty, you look pale. Are you not feeling well?

MESDAMES: Your Majesty . . . ?

COMTE DE MERCY: Well, actually . . .

DUCHESSE DE MONZETTE (*Bossily*): Comte de Mercy, you're leaving? Well, then, we will be attending to Her Majesty.

COMTE DE MERCY: But . . .

DUCHESSE DE MONZETTE: Don't you think it would be better if you left?

MARQUISE DE SISINA: Don't you worry about Her Majesty. We will look after her as usual. . . . There now, you may leave.

MESDAMES: There now, there now, good day.

COMTE DE MERCY: Well then. (*Fleeing from the place, although he would prefer to stay.*)

MARIE ANTOINETTE: Comte de Mercy . . .

COMTESSE DE LAMBESQUE (*Flatteringly*): There now, Your Majesty. What shall we do today?

DUCHESSE DE MONZETTE: Oh . . . Her Majesty has been enthusiastic about gambling these days. Isn't that true, Your Majesty . . . ?

VISCOMTESSE CALONNE: Well, Your Majesty, let us play cards as usual. I won't lose today. . . .

(*Each tries to curry favor. Suddenly, we hear* OSCAR*'s voice.*)

OSCAR'S VOICE: Wait. The queen is not feeling well. Please leave, now!

DUCHESSE DE MONZETTE: How rude! Who is it talking to us in such a fashion? Who's there? Show yourself!

(*Lively flowery music.* OSCAR *appears.*)

MESDAMES: Oscar!

OSCAR: Dear ladies, I am Oscar François de Jarjayes, at your service.

DUCHESSE DE MONZETTE (*Cloyingly*): Oscar, we were just . . .

OSCAR: My mission, as captain of the Royal Guard, is to protect Her Majesty the Queen. I won't take orders from anyone concerning Her Majesty, even from the wife of the duc de Monzette!

DUCHESSE DE MONZETTE: My my, but you're just a woman!

OSCAR: No, I am not a woman.

MARQUISE DE SISINA: But you are . . .

OSCAR: From early childhood, I, Oscar, have been raised as a boy in order to protect Her Majesty the queen. When I wear the uniform of the Royal Guard, I am a man, both mentally and physically.

DUCHESSE DE MONZETTE: Oscar!

OSCAR (*Looking at the duchess coolly*): Yes. Is something the matter, Your Grace?

DUCHESSE DE MONZETTE (*Fumblingly*): No . . . I just feel so weak when you look at me that way. I don't know if you're a man or a woman . . . (*Trembling*) but somehow I feel like my body is on fire.

OSCAR: I'm honored, Your Grace.

DUCHESSE DE MONZETTE (*Her body shaking*): Oooh, I think I am going to faint. . . . Well then, Oscar. (*Conceitedly.*) Come mesdames, Let us take our leave . . .

MESDAMES: But . . .

DUCHESSE DE MONZETTE: Oscar commands it. Come, come. . . . Well then, Oscar, I trust you will execute your duties responsibly.

(*The ladies take their leave. Quiet music.*)

OSCAR: Please, forgive me, Your Majesty, for being so forward . . .

MARIE ANTOINETTE: Oscar . . .

OSCAR: I, Oscar François de Jarjayes, have come here today to give you a word of warning. I'm prepared for whatever punishment or reproaches you wish to mete out to me.

MARIE ANTOINETTE: What is it? Have you come to speak your mind again?

OSCAR: Your Majesty, you already know that all those nobles are preying on you and exploiting your court. The more luxurious your life is, the more impoverished the people of this country will become. What should go to the people disappears because it is used up by a handful of heartless aristocrats.

MARIE ANTOINETTE: Oh, Oscar, thank you. I have finally come to realize that myself. Eighteen years ago, when I came to France to be married, the previous king took me under his wing, and I could do whatever I wanted, every day. I so enjoyed those days. Even though I have three children by Louis XVI, I have remained that fourteen-year-old girl up until now.

OSCAR: Your Majesty, I am glad you understand the situation so thoroughly. Now that I know this, I would like to make another request.

MARIE ANTOINETTE: Why so formal? What is it?

OSCAR: Please send Fersen back to Sweden.

MARIE ANTOINETTE: Oscar!

OSCAR: Your Majesty, your relationship with Fersen has become court gossip. The rumors have become even more and more outrageous, and the unscrupulous among the aristocracy have been using these rumors to agitate the malcontents. You are the queen of France. As the mother of the French Empire, I beg you to send Fersen back to Sweden.

MARIE ANTOINETTE: Dear Oscar, you have been protecting me as a member of the Royal Guard since I was fourteen. And I believed that you, more than anyone else, understood my feelings as a woman. I trusted that you would understand because you yourself are a woman, but I see that at some point you lost touch with your feminine side.

OSCAR: Your Majesty . . .

MARIE ANTOINETTE: I'm a person before I'm a queen! And I'm a woman with a beating heart! I'm a woman waiting and wanting to love and be loved just like anyone else. I was born to love him. He is the first man I ever wanted to love of my own free will. Oscar, all the blood in my body surges toward him, and even God can't stop this deep red flower from blooming!

OSCAR: Your Majesty . . .

MARIE ANTOINETTE: I know I'm committing a sin. But still, I cannot send Fersen back to Sweden!

OSCAR: Your Majesty!

MARIE ANTOINETTE: Even if the sun rose from the west!

(*Indignantly,* MARIE ANTOINETTE *leaves. A distressed* OSCAR *is left alone.* MAJOR GIRODELLE *of the Royal Guard appears quietly.*)

GIRODELLE: Commandant . . . you were brave to speak your mind. . . .

OSCAR: Major Girodelle, Her Majesty spoke harsh words to me.

GIRODELLE: What you said was not without good reason. Ever since the queen came to France to be married, you have been at her side to serve her. That's why you may well give her such considerate advice.

OSCAR: I think I understand the queen's sorrow. It is quite palpable to me. However, even if the queen hates me, I must do my duty devotedly, for I am the commandant of the Royal Guard.

GIRODELLE: Commandant . . .

OSCAR: Major Girodelle, my trusted aide-de-camp, let us work together to guard the palace.

GIRODELLE: It's my honor. I'll do my best to help you.

OSCAR: Thank you, Girodelle.

GIRODELLE: Commandant . . .

(*The two shake hands firmly.*)

SCENE 7. A HALLWAY IN THE PALACE OF VERSAILLES

A hallway of the palace of Versailles with beautiful tapestries displayed. FERSEN *appears, trying to be inconspicuous. He sings:*

FERSEN:

Even though I know this love doesn't stand a chance
I'm worn out by love and in love with love
I want to believe you
I want love, eternal
Intense, intense love
Even though I know this love shall separate us one day
Even though I know this love shall separate us one day

(OSCAR *approaches.*)

OSCAR: Fersen . . .

FERSEN: Oscar . . .

OSCAR: What are you doing here, in the middle of the night? What would happen if people saw you here?

FERSEN: Oscar, laugh at me, this man who's blinded by love. I just wanted to see the queen, even if it is from afar.

OSCAR: Don't be a fool! You're a Swedish aristocrat. Don't forget your social standing!

FERSEN: Oscar . . .

OSCAR: You know what a turbulent state this country is in. And you're one of the reasons for it.

FERSEN: Now wait a minute. However blinded by love I might be, I am discreet and can tell right from wrong. Ah, the hardships I have endured . . .

OSCAR: Fersen . . . despite the hardships, your efforts were not enough. You might not have realized it, but even the king has started to notice.

FERSEN: What? The king?

OSCAR: The king is deeply considerate and mild. He says nothing in public, but the rumors have reached his ears.

FERSEN: Oscar . . .

(*Sad music.*)

OSCAR: Fersen, she is the queen of France. You know very well that she can't just give up her throne and come running into your arms!

FERSEN: Oscar . . .

OSCAR: Please go back to your own country! Return to Sweden immediately! It will be for the sake of her happiness.

FERSEN: I won't let you give me any orders!

OSCAR: Fersen . . .

FERSEN (*Laughing coldly*): To try to explain this agony to you, a woman who has relinquished her femininity, would be a waste of time. . . .

OSCAR: Fersen!

FERSEN: If you knew the agony of being in love, you wouldn't be able to say such cruel things to me!

(FERSEN *is angry and leaves.*)

OSCAR: Fersen . . . to be rebuked by you is worse than being rebuked by anyone else. Fersen . . . Fersen . . . I also am in love. . . . it is an unrequited love . . . for you. From the moment we met, at the masquerade ball at the Opera House. . . . But . . . you had eyes only for the queen, even though you didn't know who she was. And I have loyally protected the queen as a Royal Guard from the time she was fourteen. Oh dear God, why did you bring together the three of us, born in different countries, here in France?

(OSCAR *sings sadly as she crosses the silver bridge.*)

OSCAR:

I'm on a pilgrimage of love
I'm on a pilgrimage of love
I'm alone, on unfamiliar terrain
I long for love, wandering aimlessly again today
Farther and farther
Through endless countries
Where is the love I long for?
What is that love I long for?
Looks may be deceiving but
Who can understand this woman's heart of mine

SCENE 8. THE GARDENS

A waterway in the gardens of the Palace of Versailles. A beautiful moon is reflected in the water, and the overpowering scent of trees in early summer envelopes the area. Seductive music. In a pretty little dreamlike boat, MARIE ANTOINETTE *and* FERSEN *embrace.*

MARIE ANTOINETTE: Oh . . . I live only in the shadows of the night. Fersen, at night, I come to life. During the day, I slumber through court rituals and ceremonies. But when the night comes, at last I awaken. When the sun goes down on the horizon beyond the forest, my heart starts to beat faster and my blood starts to course. This is proof positive that I am alive in this world. . . .

FERSEN: My queen, at the masquerade ball at the Opera House, when everyone ignored me and I didn't know what to do, it was you who so kindly spoke to me. That kindness . . . it made me feel so . . .

MARIE ANTOINETTE: I discovered something of myself in you.

FERSEN: My dear queen.

MARIE ANTOINETTE: I am still Austrian. Even though eighteen years have passed, I have not yet been able to become a French woman. Even those subjects who are seemingly obedient think of me as an Austrian woman. So this heart, which I had to protect from such hostility, was moved by . . .

FERSEN: So you had not a moment of peace . . .

MARIE ANTOINETTE: I came to France at the age of fourteen, forced into a political marriage. I believed the prince of my dreams would be waiting for me. However, I was used only to dispel the discord between the House of Hapsburg and the House of Bourbon. And they also wanted my dowry. . . . Can you imagine how miserable I was when I realized this? . . . I wasn't a human being; I was just a tool.

FERSEN: How sad . . .

MARIE ANTOINETTE: It was you who comforted my lonely heart. . . . Fersen . . . Don't leave me . . .

FERSEN: I won't leave you, whatever may happen! Even if we burn in hell as immoral sinners . . .

MARIE ANTOINETTE: Oh Fersen . . .

(*They sing passionately.*)

FERSEN:

Love can be so sorrowful

MARIE ANTOINETTE:

Love can be so painful

TOGETHER:

Love can be such a torture
Love can be ephemeral
Love, love, love,

(*While the two sing their painfully sad song, their boat silently floats through the waterway.*)

[In scene 9, the orphan ROSALIE, *who has been raised in* OSCAR*'s mansion, marries the revolutionary journalist* BERNARD. OSCAR *and* ANDRÉ *gradually start to sympathize with the republican ideology of the revolutionaries, so* OSCAR *requests a transfer from the Royal Guard, which protects the royal family, to the French Guard, which works with the people. In scene 10, the* COMTE DE MERCY, *troubled by trends in public opinion, tells* FERSEN *to go home.]*

SCENE 11. CURTAIN

In front of the curtain, the MARQUISE DE SISINA, *the* COMTESSE DE LAMBESQUE, *and* VISCOMTESSE CALONNE *appear, consoling the* DUCHESSE DE MONZETTE, *who is upset and in tears.*

MESDAMES: Madame Monzette.

(*The* DUCHESSE DE MONZETTE *weeps.*)

MARQUISE DE SISINA: Calm down . . . calm down . . .

DUCHESSE DE MONZETTE: How can I possibly be calm?! Oscar has been transferred from the Royal Guard to the French Guard! The French Guard is different from the Royal Guard, which protects this palace. The French Guard is in charge of keeping the peace in France . . . to transfer to such dangerous post right now . . .

COMTESSE DE LAMBESQUE: So you say, but it's by Oscar's own wish.

DUCHESSE DE MONZETTE: Is that what you think, too?

VISCOMTESSE CALONNE: That's right, indeed. It is not our place to object to her decision.

DUCHESSE DE MONZETTE: And you?

MARQUISE DE SISINA: Madame la Duchesse, our brilliant Oscar must have had her reasons.

DUCHESSE DE MONZETTE: Then, are you saying that Oscar has abandoned us?!

MARQUISE DE SISINA: Oh, don't say that . . .

DUCHESSE DE MONZETTE: But it's true! Her resignation from the Royal Guard means that she abandoned us, the aristocracy!

COMTESSE DE LAMBESQUE: You need to worry, Madame la Duchesse. The French Guard is composed of rough commoners, different from the Royal Guard. Even our capable Oscar will find them uncontrollable, and she'll come back . . .

DUCHESSE DE MONZETTE (*Hysterically*): You! You all say that we should wait till then?! Should we just watch with folded arms our dear, dear Oscar in danger and do nothing at all?! I won't. My Oscar . . . oh, Oscar, Oscar, wherefore art thou Oscar?

MESDAMES: Madame Monzette . . .

DUCHESSE DE MONZETTE: Oh, I'm going to faint away in such agony because I am so, soooo worried.

SCENE 12. THE AUDIENCE ROOM

The audience room at Versailles. There is a distant view of the extensive palace gardens through the window.

FRANÇOISE: Your Majesty. Comte de Mercy has arrived.

(*The* KING *appears with the* COMTE DE PROVENCE. *The* COMTE DE MERCY *and* FERSEN *appear.*)

KING LOUIS XVI: Comte de Mercy. What is it?

COMTE DE MERCY: Your Majesty. Comte de Fersen has come to greet you before his return home.

KING LOUIS XVI: What . . . ? His return?

COMTE DE MERCY: Yes, Your Majesty. Because preparations for his engagement to be married are now completed in Sweden, he has been requested to make his way back home immediately.

CONTE DE PROVENCE: What? An engagement? (*Ironically.*) Ha, ha, ha . . . what amusing news I hear. You're still a bachelor?

KING LOUIS XVI: You can't.

COMTE DE MERCY: Pardon?

KING LOUIS XVI: You really can't.

CONTE DE PROVENCE: My dear brother . . .

KING LOUIS XVI: Fersen, can't you possibly postpone your departure?

FERSEN: Your Majesty . . .

KING LOUIS XVI: The queen will be so sad. She is solely dependent on you. It would not be a problem if the country were at peace, but there is much turmoil now. Would you please give your support to her?

CONTE DE PROVENCE: My dear brother, you know this man and my sister-in-law are . . .

KING LOUIS XVI: What do you say? Is it not possible?

FERSEN: Your Majesty . . . Forgive me . . .

KING LOUIS XVI: Then it really isn't possible, is it?

FERSEN: It is an order from the king of Sweden . . .

KING LOUIS XVI: Yes . . . but we will miss you . . .

FERSEN: Your Majesty . . .

KING LOUIS XVI: May you be happy . . .

FERSEN: I wish Your Majesty the best of health . . . Farewell. (*Leaves.*)

CONTE DE PROVENCE: Brother, how can you be so friendly to him. Why did you speak to such a man? He is . . .

KING LOUIS XVI: I know.

COMTE DE MERCY: Your Majesty . . .

KING LOUIS XVI: Don't embarrass me. Fersen is an agreeable man. Any woman would be attracted to him. . . .

CONTE DE PROVENCE: You knew and still . . . ? You and my sister-in-law are married with three children. And even though your wife is . . .

KING LOUIS XVI (*Interrupting his brother*): Oh, I've just remembered. The door of my room has been creaking since the other day. Let me fix it now. . . .

CONTE DE PROVENCE: Oh brother . . . (*Follows him.*)

(*Calm music.*)

COMTE DE MERCY: Your Majesty . . .

(MARIE ANTOINETTE *appears.*)

COMTE DE MERCY: Your Majesty. Did you hear what His Majesty said . . . ?

MARIE ANTOINETTE: How deeply have I sinned. . . . My king, please forgive me. . . . Not knowing how magnanimous your heart was, I have been . . . I am . . .

COMTE DE MERCY: Your Majesty . . .

(LE DAUPHIN *and* LA DAUPHINE *appear cheerfully.*)

LE DAUPHIN and LA DAUPHINE: Maman!

LE DAUPHIN: Maman, I heard that Oscar is going to Paris. She said she'll let me ride on her horse before she says good-bye. I can go, can't I?

LA DAUPHINE: I want to go with him.

(MARIE ANTOINETTE *holds her two children tightly.*)

MARIE ANTOINETTE: Comte de Mercy. From today, I will sever my ties to the past and protect this Bourbon dynasty. For the king, and for our children . . .

(*Music. Rising.*)

[*In scene 13,* ANDRÉ *sees* FERSEN *off.* FERSEN *lectures* ANDRÉ*—who is suffering from unrequited love for his lord's daughter* OSCAR, *who is of a higher class than he—on the nobleness of love.*]

SCENE 14. OSCAR'S SITTING ROOM

OSCAR*'s sitting room.* OSCAR *is sitting in front of a mirror and having her hair combed by her nurse.*

OSCAR: You know what, nanny?

MARRON-GLACÉ: What is it?

OSCAR: They say that nowadays, it is more honorable among commoners to be called *citoyen* and *citoyenne* than to be called *monsieur* and *madame. Citoyen* and *citoyenne.* Those do not sound bad.

MARRON-GLACÉ: It's none of our concern, what new words are popular with commoners . . .

OSCAR: You are right. I am an aristocrat after all . . .

MARRON-GLACÉ: Yes, indeed. I brought you up as a French aristocrat, a young lady of the House of Jarjayes.

OSCAR: A lady . . .

MARRON-GLACÉ: Yes. It's already late. Good night, Lady Oscar.

(MARRON-GLACÉ *goes out of the room.*)

OSCAR: Oh Nanny, that mirror and comb I leave to you . . . if I go to Paris . . . something may happen that will force me to shed my aristocracy . . .

OSCAR: André . . . André . . . (*Shouts.*)

(ANDRÉ *comes in.*)

ANDRÉ: What's wrong at this time of night . . . ?

(OSCAR *walks toward the window.*)

OSCAR: Oh André. How beautiful these stars are. They are shining as if they are unaware of human despair and the sorrows of this world. Our earthly problems are tiny when seen from the vastness of the universe.

ANDRÉ: When you were a child, you used to say that a glass carriage filled with happiness would come to fetch you from the Milky Way. . . .

OSCAR: What was my happiness . . . ?

ANDRÉ: Oscar . . .

OSCAR: André, I didn't make wrong choices in life, did I?

ANDRÉ: This is not like you. Something is wrong with you tonight . . .

OSCAR: André, I must thank you.

ANDRÉ: Why do you act so formal all of a sudden?

OSCAR: It's not as if I didn't know how you felt about me.

ANDRÉ (*In amazement*): Oscar.

OSCAR: . . . Do you like me?

ANDRÉ (*Camouflaging*): Why are you going into this now? . . .

OSCAR: Be honest with me.

ANDRÉ: . . . I like you . . .

OSCAR: Do you love me?

ANDRÉ: Yes, I love you.

OSCAR: My existence is next to nothing compared with the giant wheels of history. See, I let myself get away with such emotional dependence.

ANDRÉ: Oscar . . .

OSCAR: Yet . . . do you still love me? Will you vow to love me for as long as you live?

ANDRÉ: Do you want me to swear a thousand times, ten thousand times? Do you dare make me utter these words and stake my life on them? I love you! Of course I love you . . .

OSCAR: André, hold me!

ANDRÉ: Oscar . . .

OSCAR: Just this one night I want to be the wife of André Grandier . . .

ANDRÉ: Oscar . . .

OSCAR: I want to be called the wife of André Grandier, to be the wife of the one who carried a torch for me for more than a decade . . .

ANDRÉ (*Hugs* OSCAR *tightly*): I am . . . I'm so glad to have lived to see this day . . .
(*They hug each other tightly and sing an anthem to love.*)

ANDRÉ:
Love can be so sweet

OSCAR:
Love can be so strong

TOGETHER:
Love can be so precious
Love can be so sublime
Love, Love, Love
(*Music. Rising.*)

SCENE 15. CURTAIN

Music. Uneasy and apprehensive. BERNARD *appears in a state of nervous excitement.*

BERNARD (*Shouts*): Rosalie . . . Rosalie . . .

ROSALIE (*Appears*): Yes, my dear . . .

BERNARD: Go to Versailles immediately.

ROSALIE: To Versailles?

BERNARD: You must tell Oscar not to come to Paris.

ROSALIE: Lady Oscar is coming to Paris?

BERNARD: Yes. It seems that Oscar had requested a transfer from the Royal Guard to the French Guard and has been appointed their commander.

ROSALIE: Oh no . . . the Royal Guard guards the palace, but the French Guard is different because they are the peacekeeping troops of France. What was she thinking to transfer at such a time?

BERNARD: Well at last, the French Guard has received its marching orders but there's going to be trouble. Fed up with troops trying to oppress us with brute force, the citizens are arming themselves and gathering to take a stand. This can't possibly end in peace. So the French Guard led by Oscar will be the first line of attack. Oscar's life is at risk. You must go and stop Oscar.

ROSALIE: But . . . but . . . I can't!

BERNARD: Do you want to let her die?!

ROSALIE: No! But given who and what she is, how she must have suffered and agonized over this. . . .

BERNARD: Rosalie . . .

ROSALIE: Darling, if there was ever an end worthy of her extraordinary life, I think there's no other way than to let her do what she believes. Please, darling, let her go where her heart leads her.

BERNARD: Rosalie . . .

ROSALIE: This is . . . this is for her sake . . .

(*Suddenly, gunshots resound in the distance.*)

BERNARD: Oh, those gunshots can only mean . . .

ROSALIE: Darling . . .

BERNARD: Dash it . . . too late . . . Rosalie . . . we must go . . .

ROSALIE: Yes!

(*They leave in a hurry. Music, rising with apprehension and uneasiness.*)

SCENE 16. THE CITY CENTER OF PARIS

A bridge in the city center. ANDRÉ *is pushing back many soldiers of the* FRENCH GUARD.

ANDRÉ: Everyone, wait! We must not act recklessly without an order from our commandant! Didn't we promise? The French Guard in disarray will sow seeds of trouble for the future. A little more patience. Don't move until our commandant comes back!

(*A gunshot nearby.*)

GENERAL DE BOUILLE: You troops! What are you all doing here?! Start the attack now!

ANDRÉ: General de Bouille! We are waiting for the order from our commandant!

GENERAL DE BOUILLE: No need to wait for orders from the likes of Oscar! The battle has begun! I am in charge of the French Guard! I will give the orders!

(OSCAR *appears.*)

OSCAR: Please wait! General de Bouille!

THE GUARDS: Commandant.

OSCAR: Even if you would give the order, General, I, Oscar, am the commandant of the French Guard, and I will not make my soldiers attack!

GENERAL DE BOUILLE: Silence! This is no time to argue with you, a mere woman!

OSCAR: Women have the right to live and the right to make themselves heard!

GENERAL DE BOUILLE: Such impertinence. Do as you please, then! There are plenty of soldiers even without your guards! You'll be sorry for this later . . .

OSCAR (*Taking out her sword and pointing it at* GENERAL DE BOUILLE): My fellow soldiers! Just as the United States of America won independence from England with its own hands, now we, the people of France, under the banner of Liberty, Equality, and Fraternity, have bravely arisen. Don't move! From this moment, I renounce my title of comtesse and forfeit all that comes with it!

THE GUARDS: Commandant!

GENERAL DE BOUILLE: You, how dare you . . .

OSCAR: Silence! If you want to live, close your mouth and listen quietly! Well, my fellow soldiers, make your choice. Will you remain pawns of the king and the aristocrats and point your guns at your own people? Or will you, as free citizens, join the people in this glorious struggle?

THE GUARDS: Commandant . . . we will follow you! Our commandant!

GENERAL DE BOUILLE: You . . . You'll pay for this . . . Come. (*Leaves.*)

(*The sound of gunshots.*)

OSCAR: My brave soldiers. Let us join the people and fight for our homeland. May the exploits of the French Guard live on in history, passed down from generation to generation, for as long as men live!

THE GUARDS: Hurrah!

OSCAR: Load your guns!

THE GUARDS: Yes, sir!

THE PEOPLE: Let us join for the fight! Rahh!

(THE GUARDS *leave in high spirits.*)

OSCAR: André.

ANDRÉ: You were very brave to make up your mind . . .

OSCAR: André! When this battle is over, it will be time for our wedding . . .

ANDRÉ: Oscar . . .

OSCAR: For France . . . let us fight splendidly.

(*Gunshots resound nearby.* ANDRÉ *leaves.*)

OSCAR: Please forgive me, my queen. Oscar has finally betrayed you, despite the profound confidence you had in me. . . . Father, please forgive Oscar's disobedience . . . but someone needs to protect the weak citizens. . . . Farewell to all these yokes of the past . . . Farewell to my youth, never to return . . .

(BERNARD *and* ROSALIE *hasten in.*)

BERNARD: Oscar . . .

ROSALIE: Mademoiselle Oscar!

OSCAR: Bernard, things are as you have heard . . .

BERNARD: Thank you. How . . . how . . .

OSCAR: We shall unite to restore France to its former glory!

ROSALIE: Mademoiselle Oscar. I cannot tell how much the citizens were encouraged by you. . . .

OSCAR: Rosalie. The army is tough! Are you ready . . . ?

ROSALIE: Yes, I am.

(*Suddenly. A bullet hits the bridge girder.* OSCAR *and others lie down.* ANDRÉ *returns.*)

ANDRÉ: Oscar . . . Oscar . . .

(*The sound of gunshots nearby. The citizens run about trying to escape.*)

OSCAR: André . . .

ANDRÉ: Don't come, stay away. The enemy is near. (*A bullet strikes him.*)

OSCAR: André . . .

ANDRÉ: Oscar . . . you must live . . .

OSCAR: André!

ANDRÉ: Just take good care of your life. (*Three shots, and he falls down.*)

OSCAR (*Screams*): André.

(BERNARD *stops* OSCAR *from running to* ANDRÉ.)

ANDRÉ: Oscar . . . Oscar! Where are you?

OSCAR: André!

ANDRÉ: Oscar . . . waving blonde hair . . . blue eyes . . . and looking like the wings of Pegasus . . . makes my heart flutter.

(ANDRÉ *dies in a flood of bullets, his body riddled with holes like honeycomb.*)

OSCAR: Let me go! Let me go! André!

ANDRÉ: Os . . . car.

OSCAR (*Shaking off* BERNARD): André . . .

(*Music. Strongly. Blackout, except for* OSCAR.)

OSCAR (*Forsaking her grief, stands up resolutely*): *Citoyens!* We must not let his death be in vain! We will fight till the end. For Liberty, Equality, and Fraternity . . . *Citoyens!* Let us attack the Bastille first and show our force! *Citoyens!* Forward! (*Almost shrieking.*)

SCENE 17. THE BASTILLE

The set is arranged with the famous painting, The Taking of the Bastille. *The French Guard. A dance number representing the attack by the people. A merciless bullet hits* OSCAR.

ROSALIE: Lady Oscar!

OSCAR: André . . . lend me your hands. The suffering you've borne, I will try to bear it too . . . André . . . André . . . Are you no longer here?

(*A white flag rises in the backstage set.*)

ROSALIE: Mademoiselle Oscar!

BERNARD: Oscar . . . a white flag flies over the Bastille.

OSCAR: Has it fallen at last . . . France . . . Vive la France.

ROSALIE: Noooooooh! Mademoiselle Oscar! (*Cries.*)

(*People are rejoicing at a distance: The Bastille has been taken! In hearing that,* OSCAR *breathes her last. Music. Rising.*)

[*In scene 18,* FERSEN, *who is confined in Sweden, receives word of the French Revolution and learns of* OSCAR*'s and* ANDRÉ*'s deaths from* GIRODELLE. *In scene 19, those who consider* FERSEN*'s attempt to rescue the French royal family to be against Sweden's national interest work against him. In scene 20,* FERSEN *pleads to his king for permission to leave the country because he is willing to risk his life for love. He is granted permission.*]

PART II

[*Scene 1 is the prologue. In scene 2, the courtiers abandon the royal family. In scene 3,* MARIE ANTOINETTE *declares to the people that she will take responsibility as the queen of France. She leaves the palace of Versailles. In scene 4,* FERSEN *asks Austria,* MARIE ANTOINETTE*'s homeland, for help but is refused. From scene 5 onward,* MARIE ANTOINETTE *discovers that she does have ties to her family, but then* LOUIS XVI *is called to stand trial.* MARIE ANTOINETTE*'s aria is featured in scene 6. (Scene 7 is missing in the book.) In scenes 8 and 9,* FERSEN *crosses borders as he makes his way to France.*]

SCENE 10. PRISON

In the prison of the gloomy concergerie. The bells of Notre Dame toll desolately nearby. Alone in the prison, MARIE ANTOINETTE *combs her hair. The door opens with a heavy sound and* ROSALIE *comes in.*

ROSALIE: Your Majesty . . .

MARIE ANTOINETTE: Rosalie . . .

ROSALIE: I brought your dinner . . .

MARIE ANTOINETTE: Oh, it's already night . . . It's hard to tell morning from evening in this dimly lit prison . . .

(ROSALIE *cries.*)

MARIE ANTOINETTE: Please don't cry.

ROSALIE: Your Majesty . . .

MARIE ANTOINETTE: Rosalie. You will be punished if you say "Your Majesty." Call me female convict 280 or Widow Capet.

ROSALIE: No, I won't. To me, you will always be my queen.

MARIE ANTOINETTE: But that puts you in a difficult situation. And think of how it may affect your husband . . . it's already hard for you to tend to me like this . . .

ROSALIE: Your Majesty . . . this is my husband, Bernard.

(BERNARD *appears.*)

BERNARD: Widow Capet.

MARIE ANTOINETTE: Rosalie has been very kind to me.

BERNARD: Not at all. She does what she must do as the warden of this prison.

MARIE ANTOINETTE: . . . Bernard . . . my turn has come, has it not?

BERNARD: Widow Capet.

MARIE ANTOINETTE: Be frank. I know it well. I hear Death's footsteps close by.

BERNARD: Please forgive me. I am powerless. . . . At least, will you please accept your end with the royal dignity . . .

MARIE ANTOINETTE: I understand. I left Versailles with that resolution.

ROSALIE: Please. Partake of some food . . .

(MARIE ANTOINETTE *shakes her head.*)

ROSALIE: You must. You did not eat yesterday, and neither did you eat the day before yesterday. Your body will . . .

MARIE ANTOINETTE: I will be summoned by God soon. At this stage, why should I make an effort to live?

BERNARD: Your Majesty . . . please at least try the soup. Rosalie made it for you with all her heart.

ROSALIE: Your Majesty . . . at least a sip.

MARIE ANTOINETTE: Thank you, Rosalie . . .

BERNARD: Please, Your Majesty.

MARIE ANTOINETTE (*Takes a sip*): Thank you. I can tell this soup was prepared with the warmth of your heart. I am truly blessed till the very end . . .

BERNARD: . . . Widow Capet. The last visitor is here . . .

MARIE ANTOINETTE: Who is it? Who could possibly want to meet a prisoner condemned to die?

(*The* COMTE DE MERCY *comes in when* BERNARD *and* ROSALIE *go out.*)

COMTE DE MERCY: Your Majesty . . .

MARIE ANTOINETTE: Comte de Mercy. You shouldn't be here. . . . If you are seen here, you will be punished.

COMTE DE MERCY: Your Majesty . . .

MARIE ANTOINETTE: I want you, at least, to stay alive . . .

COMTE DE MERCY: I came to return this to you. (*Takes out the doll Stephan.*)

MARIE ANTOINETTE: Stephan . . . (*Hugs it dearly.*)

COMTE DE MERCY: When you came for your marriage from Vienna to Versailles, I took this doll away from you in hopes that you would become an adult as soon as possible . . . but because you grew up . . . Your Majesty . . .

MARIE ANTOINETTE: This doll was me. . . . And I was just a doll myself, my whole life.

COMTE DE MERCY: Your Majesty . . .

MARIE ANTOINETTE: I was scolded by you often. Such a naughty girl I was. . . .

COMTE DE MERCY: Your Majesty . . . please take good care of Stephan from now on . . .

MARIE ANTOINETTE: Thank you. I will talk to this doll as I used to in the past . . . but for how long will that be?

COMTE DE MERCY: Your Majesty . . . (*Tries to kiss the hem of her dress.*)

MARIE ANTOINETTE: Comte de Mercy (*Avoiding him*), it is time to say good-bye. I am glad I was able to see you in the end . . . please take good care of yourself . . .

COMTE DE MERCY (*Unbearably*): Your Majesty . . . (*Leaves.*)

(*Music. Calm.*)

MARIE ANTOINETTE: Everything is over. . . . This is . . . this is all . . . well, my last bit of work is to die with dignity . . .

(FERSEN *appears, enveloped in a black mantle.*)

FERSEN: My Queen . . .

MARIE ANTOINETTE: Fersen . . . Fersen . . . Why? . . . Who let you in here . . . ?

FERSEN: I cannot tell you, for the person will be endangered by doing so . . .

MARIE ANTOINETTE: Am I . . . am I dreaming . . . ?

FERSEN: No. This is not a dream. I have come to save you, Your Majesty . . .

MARIE ANTOINETTE: Fersen . . .

FERSEN: Your Majesty. Everything has been arranged. I, Fersen, promise to guide you outside the country.

MARIE ANTOINETTE: Thank you, Fersen . . . even at the risk of your own life.

FERSEN: Your Majesty . . .

MARIE ANTOINETTE: I am touched, really, to know that there was still a person who cared about me so deeply . . .

FERSEN: Please. Your Majesty . . . the sooner the better.

MARIE ANTOINETTE: Now . . . now I can die in peace . . .

FERSEN: Your Majesty . . .

MARIE ANTOINETTE: Please forgive me . . . since I will not obey you . . . Fersen . . . I am the queen of France. My mother has once told me to not be Austrian but to become a splendid Frenchwoman. . . . I want to honor her words until my last moment. Fersen . . . I am the queen of France, the widow of the king, and a mother of the little dauphin. My dauphin and dauphine, where are they, and how are they doing? . . . I cannot possibly abandon my poor children and escape. I am the queen, but at the same time I am a mother, a very ordinary mother. How can I possibly escape and leave them . . . ?

FERSEN: You are . . .

MARIE ANTOINETTE: Fersen. Please. Let me die, at least on the soil of France where my children are . . .

FERSEN: No! I cannot forsake the person for whom I risked my life!

MARIE ANTOINETTE: Fersen. We have endured so much until this day, have we not . . . ?

FERSEN: Your Majesty . . .

MARIE ANTOINETTE: I beg you. If you still love me, then please let me end my life with dignity as the queen of France. That will be the last proof of your love for me . . .

FERSEN: My queen . . .

MARIE ANTOINETTE (*Strongly embrace each other*): Fersen . . . Thank you . . . thank you . . . (*Puts the doll in his hands.*)

(*Heavy sound of the door opening.*)

MARIE ANTOINETTE: Oh no . . . someone is coming . . . (*They separate.*)

(FERSEN *hides.* BERNARD *appears with a surveillance soldier.*)

MARIE ANTOINETTE: Bernard . . . thank you for your trouble . . .

BERNARD: Widow Capet . . .

MARIE ANTOINETTE: I know. Don't say anything more . . . now . . . Shall we go? . . .

BERNARD: Let me accompany you . . .

(MARIE ANTOINETTE *is about to leave.* FELSEN *loses his self-restraint and steps out.*)

MARIE ANTOINETTE (*Speaking to* BERNARD, *even though her words of farewell seem to be directed to* FERSEN): Bernard! I am deeply grateful for your kindness because till the very end I will be able to be as dignified as the queen of France ought to be, just like a red rose blooming in Versailles.

BERNARD: Widow Capet!

MARIE ANTOINETTE: Yes . . .

(MARIE ANTOINETTE *leaves for the execution ground.*)

FERSEN: Your Majesty . . . (*Tries to run after her.*)

ROSALIE (*Appears and stops him*): No, you mustn't! I beg you . . .

FERSEN: Let me go! Rosalie . . .

ROSALIE: Please let Her Majesty go. Please do not cast a shadow on her smile. For that is the end of the queen of France . . .

(*The people's cheers in the distance.* ROSALIE *bursts into tears and leaves.*)

FERSEN: My queen . . .

(*As if he wishes to have* MARIE ANTOINETTE *hear his song,* FELSEN *sings while weeping.*)

FERSEN:

Love can be so sorrowful,
Love can be so painful,
Love can be so torturous,
Love can be ephemeral

(*The silk gauze in the prison becomes transparent.*)

FERSEN and MARIE ANTOINETTE:

Love, Love, Love

(MARIE ANTOINETTE *slowly climbs up the steps to the guillotine.*)

SCENE 11. THE GUILLOTINE

The guillotine makes use of the grand staircase.

FERSEN: My queen . . . you will live in my heart forever. Forever like the red roses that bloom in Versailles . . .

(*Ascending,* MARIE ANTOINETTE *pauses midway and turns around.*)

MARIE ANTOINETTE: Adieu, Versailles . . . Adieu, Paris . . . Adieu . . . France . . .

(MARIE ANTOINETTE *disappears as she ascends the staircase. Shouts of joy from the crowd.*)

FERSEN: My queen!

(*With this desperate cry,* FERSEN *sinks below the floor on the trapdoor lift. Music rising.*)

BACKSTAGE CHORUS:

Love can be sorrowful
Love can be painful

Love can be tortuous
Love can be ephemeral
Ahhh . . . Ahhh . . .
Ahhh . . . Ahhh . . .
Ahhh . . .
(*In an instant, the grand staircase turns into the stage of the spectacular finale.*)

[*It is customary in Takarazuka musicals to have variously costumed and choreographed dance finales that are not necessarily connected with the story of the play. At the very last comes the Grand Finale, in which main characters in the play appear and sing in gorgeously decorated costumes*:
Scene 12. Finale A (Rockets)
Scene 13. Finale B (Tango of Roses)
Scene 14. Finale C (Bolero)
Scene 15. Finale D]

SCENE 16. GRAND FINALE

MARIE ANTOINETTE:
A seed born
On the banks of the blue Danube
The memory of a beautiful rose
Blooming on the banks of the Seine
Forever and ever
Unchanging
Like humans who are mortal
Even flowers will die some day
Like humans who must say farewell
Even flowers will die some day

LE DAUPHIN and LA DAUPHINE	DOUBLE TRIO CHORUS:
Showing loose wisps of hair	Ahh . . .
waving in the morning wind,	Ahh . . .
The valiant figure vanishes in the distance	Ahh . . .
Hiding the shadows of a hidden sorrow	Ahh . . .
ROSALIE and SOFIA:	
To love and care for someone unforgettable	Ahh . . .
The beautiful white vision	Ahh . . .
Oscar, Oscar	Ahh . . .
Are you the white rose of our hearts	Ahh . . .

OSCAR:

Where is the love I long for	Ahh . . .
What is the love I want	Ahh . . .
Looks may be deceiving but	Ahh . . .
Who can understand	Ahh . . .
this woman's heart of mine	Ahh . . .

ANDRÉ:

Streaming blonde hair
The figure with the blue eyes
Looking like the wings of Pegasus
Makes my heart flutter
Ahh, unforgettable you
I call to the heavens and you answer me not

FERSEN:

How could I, how could I
Possibly forget her
She was, she was
Like a rose

ALL	DOUBLE TRIO CHORUS:
Love can be so sweet.	Sweet
Love can be so strong,	Strong
Love can be precious,	Ahhh . . . precious
Love can be sublime,	Ahhh . . . grand
Love, Love, Love	
Ah, because of love,	Ahhh . . .
There is joy in life,	Ahhh . . .
Ah, because of love,	Ahhh . . .
The world is one,	Ahhh . . .
That is why people are so beautiful	Ahhh . . .

CURTAIN

Mishima Yukio, *The Sardine Seller's Net of Love*, Kabukiza, 1962.
(The Tsubouchi Memorial Theatre Museum Waseda University;
courtesy of Nihon haiyū kyōkai)

THE SARDINE SELLER'S NET OF LOVE

MISHIMA YUKIO
TRANSLATED BY LAURENCE R. KOMINZ

The Sardine Seller's Net of Love (*Iwashiuri koi no hikiami*), the second kabuki play by Mishima Yukio (1925–1970), is by far his most successful and the most frequently performed of any kabuki plays. It is also Mishima's finest work of parody in any theatrical genre. But *The Sardine Seller's Net of Love* is more than just a parody of classical kabuki; it also is a warmhearted romantic comedy that leaves audiences glowing. The text is a tour de force of wordplay couched in classical Japanese. Indeed, Mishima fuses sophisticated wordplay with physical comedy so effectively that audiences understand everything that is taking place on stage.

After *Hell Screen* (*Jigokuhen*), in 1953, the Shōchiku Company left Mishima's choice of material for his kabuki plays entirely up to him. In 1953, thanks in part to a successful revival of the 1698 hit play *The Courtesan and Mount Asama* (*Keisei asamagatake*), Mishima discovered the joys of Genroku kabuki and its "cheerful, refreshing, generous, bright, dialogue-based plays."[1] *The Courtesan and Mount Asama* dates from the Genroku era, from the 1680s to the 1720s, when the first great actors and playwrights created kabuki as a dramatic art, so plays from that era reflect the exuberance and optimism of a great art in its first flowering.

In honor of Genroku kabuki—with its disguises, parodies, and playful love affairs—Mishima created the story of *The Sardine Seller*, borrowing ideas from two medieval tales (*otogizōshi*), one of which contains a parody of *The Tales of the Heike*, in which all the protagonists are animals and fish. Genroku plays

1. Mishima Yukio, "Iwashiuri ni tsuite," Kabukiza program, November 1954, in *Mishima hyōron zenshū* (Tokyo: Shinchōsha, 1994), 869.

proceed at a more rapid pace than do later kabuki, and accordingly, Mishima's play moves quickly from scene to scene.

In the first scene, Mishima creates the "ludicrous environment" essential to comedy, using slapstick, punning, hyperbolic statements made seriously, and easily seen-through disguises.[2] To cite just one example of the delightfully absurd environment he creates: toward the end of the first scene, Sarugenji mounts a horse for the first time in his life. Struggling to mount it, he finds himself facing backward. He says,

> What's this? It's a headless horse! Even poor little sardines have heads. (*He looks behind him.*) It's like a poem with the prelude stuck on the wrong end. (*He struggles to turn around and face forward, finally succeeding.*)

Ignorance this impossible is utterly delightful.

The response to *Sardine Seller* in 1954 was unanimously positive. It is an "unpretentious, charming, stylish, elegant, and large-hearted play that summons loud laughter,"[3] wrote the kabuki critic Toita Yasuji. For Mishima, the play was a joy to write, and the actors could sense his upbeat mood from the first read-through of the script. Fans and kabuki producers were suddenly urging him to give up fiction and become a full-time playwright.

Utaemon and Kanzaburō XVII performed *The Sardine Seller* five times together between 1954 and 1973. Seventeen years passed before Kanzaburō's son, Kankurō (later given the title Kanzaburō XVIII), decided to revive the play in 1990 to celebrate the twentieth anniversary of Mishima's death. Kankurō had never seen his father perform *The Sardine Seller*,[4] but his collaborator in this endeavor, Bando Tamasaburō (who played Hotarubi), had played a minor courtesan in 1973 and remembered much of the staging.[5] Tamasaburō and Kanzaburō XVIII have performed *The Sardine Seller* regularly since 1990, and it is now both one of their favorite plays and a great favorite of audiences all over Japan.

Characters

SARUGENJI, a sardine vendor
EBINA NAMIDABUTSU, his father, a former fish wholesaler, now in retirement
BAKURŌ ROKUROZAEMON, a packhorse driver and horse trader

2. Neil Schaeffer, *The Art of Laughter* (New York: Columbia University Press, 1981), 160.
3. Toita Yasuji, "Shinsen na iwashi," *Engekikai gekihyō*, December 1954, 42.
4. Nakamura Kanzaburō XVIII, interview with Laurence Kominz, January 21, 2002.
5. Bando Tamasaburō, interview with Laurence Kominz, February 13, 2002.

The MASTER of the Gojō Higashinotōin house of assignation
A gardener, really YABUKUMA JIROTA, a retainer of the lord of Tankaku Castle
SAMURAI vassals, really fishmongers
USUGUMO, a courtesan
HARUSAME, a courtesan
NISHIKIGI, a courtesan
TAKI NO I, a courtesan
RANGIKU, a courtesan
HOTARUBI (Flickering Firefly), a courtesan, originally the daughter of the lord of Tankaku Castle
TOMBO (Dragonfly), an apprentice courtesan (*kamuro*) in the service of HOTARUBI

SCENE 1. THE GOJŌ (FIFTH AVENUE) BRIDGE IN KYOTO

Cheerful, rhythmic music plays as the curtain opens, revealing the stage set. Fifth Avenue Bridge is at the center, with the willows of Yanagigawara visible in the distance beyond the end of the bridge. ROKUROZAEMON *enters from stage left, leading a horse, and from stage right a palanquin enters. They enter simultaneously and move to the rhythmic clapping of the* tsuke. *The two have a difficult time passing each other.* EBINA *noisily alights from the palanquin.*

EBINA: Here now, horse trader, what do you mean by this? Your horse is blocking traffic on the biggest bridge in the Imperial Capital. What are you doing?

ROKUROZAEMON: Oh, you're Ebina Namidabutsu, aren't you? You must be the father of the famous sardine seller, Sarugenji.

EBINA: I see you must be one of Sarugenji's friends. I'm so glad I ran into you. (*He pays the palanquin bearers and sends them away. He pats the horse as he speaks.*) My, what a fine chestnut you've got here. He looks like a three-year-old.

ROKUROZAEMON: I've heard that you are retired and wearing priest's robes now but once you were a renowned sardine vendor and, before that, a samurai from the East Country. That's why you have such a good eye for horses. This horse used to be in the stables of a feudal lord, but he injured his hoof and has come down in the world. Somehow I just can't find a buyer for him.

EBINA: I see, I see. That explains why he was too proud to give way in the street. Anyway, I passed on my sardine selling trade to that boy of mine, and I came around to find out how his business is going. Has Sarugenji been doing well?

ROKUROZAEMON: Doing well? Well . . .

EBINA: What are you trying to say?

ROKUROZAEMON: Well, what I mean is . . . Oh, but, look, look! (*He stares intently at the* hanamichi *curtain.*) It's Sarugenji himself. What excellent timing. I'm sorry, I've got some important business to attend to. I hope we can meet again sometime soon. (*He exits stage left, leading the horse.*)

EBINA: What a busy fellow he is.

(Geza *music begins to play.* SARUGENJI *enters from the* hanamichi *curtain, walking as if in a daze. He calls out his sales pitch in a weak, monotonous voice.* EBINA, *on the main stage, shows his anger at the weak voice.*)

SARUGENJI: I'm Sarugenji from Akoji Inlet in the province of Ise. Buy my sardines.

(*He repeats this spiel several times and enters onto the main stage, where he bumps into his father.*)

SARUGENJI: Oh, hello Dad.

EBINA: What do you mean, "hello Dad?" What a pathetic voice. With a voice like that your sardines will rot. Do you mean to sell red-eyed sardines? Why you scoundrel! (*He beats his son with his closed fan.*)

SARUGENJI: Please forgive me, please forgive me! There's a good reason why I'm like this.

EBINA: Nothing should ever interfere with selling your sardines.

SARUGENJI: Please, just listen to what I have to say. (*Music accompanies his monologue.*) It happened in early autumn. It was twilight, and I was selling off the last of my sardines here at the Fifth Avenue Bridge. Suddenly a wicker palanquin went past. Just at that moment a strong breeze blew from the river, and the palanquin's brocade blinds flew open. I caught a glimpse of the lady inside and, with that one look, fell hopelessly in love. Now I yearn for her day and night. Because I'm in despair, my voice has disappeared.

EBINA: I see. So lovesickness is the cause.

SARUGENJI: Yes . . . I feel so ashamed.

EBINA: What a pitiful son you are . . . nothing at all like your father. But it is just as I always taught you. Our guide on the path of love is none other than poetry. After all, as it says in the great book, the purpose of poetry is to "move invisible gods and demons and make sweet the ties between men and women." Even though I am getting on in years, I, Ebina, will assist you, my son, with your love poems. I am with you, heart and soul.

SARUGENJI: Oh, father, I'm so grateful! Buddha be praised! Buddha be praised!

(*He presses his hands together reverently in thanks to his father. There is humorous business as, hands pressed together, he pursues* EBINA, *who backs up in a circle as* SARUGENJI *circles after him. Presently* SARUGENJI *once again falls into a state of depression. He speaks emotionally.*)

SARUGENJI: But the woman I love is so far above me in station, she's dwelling above the clouds. I am just a humble sardine vendor. No, I'm afraid mine is a hopeless love.

EBINA: It might not be an impossible love. What is the name of the woman?

SARUGENJI: I asked about her and found out who she is. She is called Hotarubi and lives in Gojō Higashinotōin.

EBINA: Hotarubi? Hotarubi is a courtesan.

SARUGENJI: Huh?

EBINA: She is called Hotarubi, after the firefly, because she sparkles when night falls. She's a courtesan of great renown, known throughout the city. She truly dwells above the clouds. It must be because I'm such an upright man that I have a son who causes me so much grief.

SARUGENJI: So, does that mean she's a prostitute?

EBINA: Look, there are prostitutes and then there are prostitutes. She does not take customers lower than men of baronial rank. Hmm. I wonder if I can come up with a good plan? (*He ponders as* SARUGENJI *fidgets about in a state of agitation.*) Hey. When you fidget about like that I can't think clearly.

(ROKUROZAEMON *reenters from stage left, slowly leading the horse.* EBINA *sees this and slaps his thigh.*)

EBINA: Yes, I've got it! It's a great plan.

SARUGENJI: You've got it? (*He joyfully slaps* EBINA *on the back and sets* EBINA *coughing.* SAURGENJI *starts rubbing* EBINA*'s back to assist him, but* SARUGENJI*'s awkward administrations are ineffectual, and* EBINA *continues to cough.*)

ROKUROZAEMON: It's that old fellow I talked with before.

(ROKUROZAEMON *ties the horse to a tree, hurriedly takes out a small towel, dips it in the river, and puts it in* EBINA*'s mouth. He then pushes forcefully on* EBINA*'s back as if trying to suppress convulsions.* EBINA *gets angry.*)

EBINA: Hey, what're you doing?! Stop that! Stop it, I'm telling you! Use Kamo River water to cure a cough—you may think it's a miracle drug but it will never work.

SARUGENJI: Father, while you were scolding him, your cough went away

EBINA: You're right. My cough is gone. Why, aren't you the same horse trader I was talking with a little while ago?

SARUGENJI: Aren't you Rokurozaemon?

EBINA: He told me that his chestnut horse had been in the service of a feudal lord and that's given me an idea. Now then, Sarugenji, your most effective strategy is to impersonate a feudal lord. The lords of the nearby provinces—Hosokawa, Hatakeyama, Isshiki, Akamatsu, Doi, and Sasaki—are too well known for it to work. Among the eastern baron, Danjō of Utsunomiya has not yet visited Kyoto. Furthermore, I've heard that he will soon make his first trip here. We're very lucky in our timing You must impersonate the lord of Utsunomiya.

ROKUROZAEMON: And for your horse, use this swift-footed steed.

EBINA: I, Ebina, will lead him.

SARUGENJI: Rokurozaemon, you shall play my chief retainer.

EBINA: And for the attendants and servants to accompany the lead actor

SARUGENJI: Yes, we're fortunate to have fellow fishmongers. We'll have each of our comrades play roles . . . as soldiers, servants, and so on.

EBINA: Speed is of the essence. My son, you are now Lord Utsunomiya.

SARUGENJI: Bring me my horse!

(*The* geza *orchestra plays a lively tune.* ROKUROZAEMON *leads out the horse.* SARUGENJI *has difficulty mounting it. He finally manages to mount; he finds himself facing backward.*)

SARUGENJI: What's this? It's a headless horse! Even poor little sardines have heads. (*He looks behind him.*) It's like a poem with the prelude stuck on the wrong end. (*He struggles to turn around and face forward, finally succeeding.* ROKUROZAEMON *takes the horse by the bit.*)

ROKUROZAEMON: Why you look like a feudal lord...

EBINA: ... In all his splendor. (ROKUROZAEMON *and* EBINA *look at each other. They are amused but pretend to be impressed with* SARUGENJI.)

SARUGENJI: The grasses and flowers on the Kamo River bank soon wither to autumnal brown.

ROKUROZAEMON: At a time like this, firefly hunting is such a pleasure.

EBINA: Now make way ... (*He opens his fan and signals for a change in the stage set*) ... for my sardine-flower lord!

(*The stage revolves.*)

SCENE 2. THE HOUSE OF ASSIGNATION AT FIFTH AVENUE AND HIGASHINOTŌIN, KYOTO

A building with a raised inner room. The back wall consists of sliding doors (fusuma) *gorgeously decorated with paintings of flowers and birds. The area in front of the garden is planted with numerous chrysanthemums. The five courtesans sit surrounding* HOTARUBI*'s apprentice* (kamuro), *a young girl named* TOMBO (*Dragonfly*).

USUGUMO: Tell us, Tombo, is that beautiful lapis jar a gift for Hotarubi?

HARUSAME: I don't know what's inside it, but it must be something quite splendid...

ALL: ... Mustn't it?

TOMBO: Why don't you try guessing what's inside?

TAKI NO I: It's sure to be something delicious.

RANGIKU: In that case I wonder if it's candied persimmons.

TOMBO: No, it's not.

USUGUMO: Oh Rangiku, you just said that because candied persimmons are your favorite treat. Of course you're wrong.

NISHIKIGI: In that case, maybe if we say something we hate, we'll get it right. Harusame, what do you think?

HARUSAME: What I hate the most is exactly what all of us hate.

NISHIKIGI: And what's that?

HARUSAME: Shall I try guessing what's inside?

TAKI NO I: I wonder if you'll guess what it is?

HARUSAME: What I hate the most is . . . of course . . . men.

USUGUMO (*Even though she actually likes men*): I agree with you. I hate men. Just hearing the word "man" makes my head begin to hurt.

NISHIKIGI: Usugumo, you really do have it bad. I agree. Whenever I hear the word "man," I hate it so much that my body begins to shake violently.

RANGIKU: Does that mean it's not candied persimmons in this jar (*She puts her sleeve lovingly over the jar*), but a hateful, hateful handsome man who'll come out like oil from an oil jar?

TOMBO: You're wrong again.

USUGUMO: Since we don't know, let's open it up.

TOMBO: All right, all right. (*She opens the jar, and many beautiful painted shells pour out. Each has a classical poem written on the inside.*)

USUGUMO: Look at all these shells. I wonder if Hotarubi is hinting that all of us courtesans assembled here are like a group of seashells. Her friends will abandon her for this.

HOTARUBI (*From inside the sliding doors*): I'm not comparing you to the shells.

USUGUMO: That voice . . .

ALL: . . . belongs to Hotarubi-san.

(*Music plays as* HOTARUBI *emerges upstage center from a sliding door.*)

HOTARUBI: Usugumo-san, these shells are used in a game that's played for fun. Classic poems are written inside these beautifully decorated shells, see? (*She picks up a shell.*) Verses from old poems are written here, and players enjoy themselves by competing in matching first and last verses of the poem.

USUGUMO: We've had feudal lords and other high-ranking customers, but we've never played the shell-matching game. I've heard that it is about the only thing that princesses have to do to while away their boredom. It seems like an interesting game. Girls, shall we imitate princesses and try playing it this evening?

ALL: That's a fine idea.

(TOMBO *spreads out the shells over a wide area.*)

HOTARUBI: All right, let's begin. (*She reads the first verse of a poem written in a shell.*) "Even though I see you in my dreams, morning after morning you are nowhere to be seen."

USUGUMO: Let's see . . . what was the second verse . . .

ALL: Which shell is it on? (*They hunt among the shells.*)

HOTARUBI: There it is. The last verse is, "If only I could depart my own body."

USUGUMO: Oh, what a depressing poem that is.

HOTARUBI: All right, next I'll read the last verse first: "As the wind blows and blows, they scatter in disarray."

(*When she reads this, a gardener appears in the garden. Sweeping with his broom, he looks carefully at the women inside. All the women are busily engaged in searching for the shell with the matching first verse.* HOTARUBI *suddenly looks into the garden, and her eyes meet those of the gardener. She senses something strange about him, and she stands up, but he quickly exits.*)

HOTARUBI: What a strange gardener. (*She sits down.*) Harusame-san . . . I've never seen that servant before. Who is he?

HARUSAME (*Engrossed in the shell game*): Hmm. It seems like this could be the first verse: "I wonder who that unknown servant is, in the spring rain?" I wonder if this is the matching shell?

HOTARUBI: Yes, I'm quite bewildered. Nishikigi-san, that servant . . .

NISHIKIGI: What servant?

HOTARUBI (*Looking around*): My goodness, he's gone.

NISHIKIGI: Come now, Hotarubi. You started out playing the shell-identifying game, but have you switched to trying to identify your lover's servant?

HOTARUBI: No, not at all.

USUGUMO: This shell-matching game is so upper crust. It's not the right game for courtesans. Let's play a game that's more fun.

(*The* MASTER *of the establishment enters from stage right.*)

MASTER: Now, now, this is no time to be arguing. You've heard that Lord Utsunomiya is coming to visit Kyoto from the East Country. Well, he's already entered the city, and they say he'll pay a ceremonial call on the court this morning. He'll be here soon. There is a lot to do to get this room ready for him. Go to your own rooms and prepare yourselves. Let's show him how beautiful the finest courtesans in Kyoto can be.

(*All the ladies except* HOTARUBI *stand and exit through the sliding doors upstage center.*)

MASTER: There now, Hotarubi. Don't let the girls' thoughtless comment upset you, all right?

HOTARUBI: You're always so concerned about how I feel. I'm so happy that you care.

(HOTARUBI, *too, exits through the sliding doors upstage center. The* MASTER *of the establishment remains alone in the room.*)

MASTER: My, my, good and bad fortune are so completely beyond our control.

(*As he ponders the situation, music begins.* EBINA *enters along the* hanamichi *and stops at the seven-three spot.*)

EBINA: I haven't been to this neighborhood since I took religious vows, but somehow my legs seem to remember the way all by themselves. (*He strikes his legs with his closed fan.*) Hey, legs! Stop walking so happily. You mustn't resist the progress of age.

(*Music begins again.* EBINA *goes onto the main stage. He knocks on the outer gate. The* MASTER *descends and opens the gate.*)

MASTER: My goodness, if it isn't Mr. "Hail to the Buddha" Ebina. What an unexpected visit. Please come in, come in.

(*They both ascend to the main level of the establishment. After* EBINA *enters through the gate and onto the raised stage, a stage assistant removes the gate.*)

EBINA: My apologies for having been out of touch for so long.

MASTER: It has been a long time, and your visit is so unexpected. I thought that weasels never took the same path twice. Where is it that you are going now? Surely you must have taken a wrong turn somewhere and lost your way?

EBINA: Please don't talk like that. You can see that I have taken religious vows, and it would be much worse were I to forget my obligations to the Buddha and the Kannon. One can never do as one pleases in this floating world.

MASTER: At least you're not using your age as an excuse. Always the witty one, aren't you, Ebina?

EBINA: Not at all. Today I'm here as a sort of forerunner for a festival carriage. Recently I went to the East Country on business. While I was there, Lord Utsunomiya approached me with a personal request. He told me that during his upcoming trip to Kyoto he wanted to visit this establishment and meet the renowned Hotarubi. He asked me to arrange everything for him. I just heard that he has already gone to make his formal calls this morning. He'll probably be coming here very soon. I wanted to warn you to prepare for his visit, so I put these old legs in motion and came here to give you some advance warning.

MASTER: Thank you for taking the trouble to come all the way over here, but everything is in readiness for his lordship's visit. So, please put yourself at ease on that score.

EBINA: I'm so relieved to hear you say that. Since all is ready this afternoon, after so long a time apart . . .

MASTER: . . . Let us burn incense to the Bodhisattva, sitting side by side,

EBINA: And intone the Amida Buddha's sutra.

(*A voice shouts from beyond the* hanamichi.)

VOICE: Make way for Lord Utsunomiya!

MASTER: My goodness, his lordship is already here.

EBINA: I think we had better go out . . .

MASTER: . . . and greet him.

(*The two descend to the main stage level and sit there. Music plays.* ROKUROZAEMON *enters, dressed as a senior samurai adviser. He leads numerous lesser retainers. After them enters* SARUGENJI, *seated astride the horse and splendidly attired. He is impersonating Lord Utsunomiya. The horse stops at the seven-three spot.*)

ROKUROZAEMON: This is the establishment at Fifth Avenue and Higashinotōin.

SARUGENJI (*Wobbling slightly in his saddle*): Kyoto looks just as prosperous as I thought it would.

(*The music resumes.* SARUGENJI *enters the main stage, dismounts, and, together with his "senior adviser," enters the establishment.*)

MASTER (*Clapping his hands to emphasize his commands*): His lordship has arrived! Go to the storehouse and get our finest saké cup! The lacquered one, with crickets and autumn grasses on it. Tell the courtesans to come out at once! And bring the saké and dishes that were prepared for his retainers! Quickly, quickly!

(*Inside a voice answers, "Yes, sir!" Lower-ranking* SAMURAI *retainers lead the horse, exiting stage right. From the upstage sliding painted paper doors, the girl apprentice* TOMBO *enters, carrying a lacquer tray with the cricket saké cup on it. She is followed by the courtesans* USUGUMO, HARUSAME, NISHIKIGI, TAKI NO I, *and* RANGIKU. *They sit.* SARUGENJI *stares at them, all agog at their beauty.*[6] EBINA *taps the floor with his fan to warn him to pull himself together. The* MASTER *has* TOMBO *take the cricket saké cup.*)

MASTER: My good Lord Utsunomiya. I am so grateful that you have come from so far away to grace our establishment. To begin, please partake of saké served in our finest cup. Now, is there anyone among my ladies that you had particularly in mind? I would be pleased to present her to you.

(SARUGENJI *fiddles nervously with his saké cup.*)

SARUGENJI: I have long heard of Hotarubi, a courtesan so famous that her name is well known even in the far-off East Country. Which of you is Hotarubi? Since you are all so remarkably beautiful, I can't tell which of you she is.

USUGUMO: Sir, I am that Hotarubi.

SARUGENJI: So, you are Hotarubi? (*He is about to offer her saké, but* EBINA *immediately signals with his eyes for* SARUGENJI *to stop.*)

HARUSAME: No, it is I who am Hotarubi. (EBINA *signals that she is not* HOTARUBI *either.*)

MASTER: Now then, stop your teasing. (*He rebukes the two.*) Your lordship, Hotarubi is not yet with us.

SARUGENJI (*Emphatically*): What? Hotarubi isn't here?

HOTARUBI (*From behind the upstage center sliding doors*): I'm here and will join you right now.

(HOTARUBI *enters to music. All the other courtesans look jealous.*)

(*He is about to stand up to approach her, but* EBINA *and* ROKUROZAEMON *signal him not to stand.*)

HOTARUBI: I am happy to share a drink with you.

(SARUGENJI *is struck dumb with rapture.* HOTARUBI *receives a cup of saké from* TOMBO, *but he just stares at* HOTARUBI, *stupefied.*[7] HOTARUBI *drinks the saké and offers her cup to* SARUGENJI.)

USUGUMO: Truly you barons from the East . . .

HARUSAME: . . . don't let your eyes stray to other pretty flowers.

NISHIKIGI: You rush to pledge your troth with saké.

TAKI NO I: How jealous . . .

---

6. As performed by Kanzaburō XVIII, Sarugenji staggers from girl to girl, enraptured by each one. When he sits down, he struggles clumsily to remove his swords from his sash and place them by his side.

7. As Kanzaburō XVIII plays it, Sarugenji knocks Tombo out of the way before she is able to pour saké for Hotarubi, and pours for her himself.

ALL: . . . we all are!

USUGUMO: But you know, one of the rules of this house is that we courtesans have the right to request that a newly arrived guest perform for us all. How lucky that you are a warrior from the East. You must be skilled in martial arts. Come on everybody, why don't we ask him to recount for us a tale of his brave deeds in battle.

HARUSAME: What a fine idea, Usugumo. Yes, a tale of battle . . .

ALL: . . . is our request for you.

(SARUGENJI, EBINA, *and the "senior retainer" are in a panic.*)

USUGUMO: Attention everybody, attention! A tale of battle . . .

ALL: . . . Is about to begin.

(*Clappers sound to signal the beginning of an independent section of the play. A* jōruri *ensemble is revealed at stage left.*[8] *The* shamisen *player begins his prelude.*)

SARUGENJI: Well, if that's what you'd like . . .

EBINA (*Aside*): This will be painful.

(EBINA *and* ROKUROZAEMON *slump down and cover their eyes and ears.*)

NARRATOR (*Singing*):

He sits in formal position, about to begin the recitation.

SARUGENJI:

And so it came to pass, that near the beach at Akashi,
In a splendid full suit of armor, bound with scarlet cords,
Red Snapper Akasuke raised a great war cry.
"You who flee before me are none other than Ohsuke of the Long Fins
Come back! Return and fight like a fish!"

(SARUGENJI *performs dance and pantomime to the following narration.*)

NARRATOR (*Singing*):

When summoned thus,
Ohsuke of the Long Fins feared to dishonor his name,
And he turned his head around in the waves.
As he approached, Snapper's soldiers drew their bows to the full,
Shouting, "Shoot him through his fin!"
The two heroes fought bout after bout in the surf
Surrounded by Red Snapper's oyster and clam minions . . .
(*Speaking.*)
. . . Who scattered hither and thither in fear.
"Let's grapple again!" shouted Flounder and Snapper,
When a wave threw them both up upon the beach.

---

8. When Kanzaburō XVIII performs the play, there is much comical pantomime by Sarugenji and the *jōruri* chanter as they attempt to communicate about how to perform the battle narration together. This sort of metadramatic conversation between an actor and a musician is almost never done in kabuki plays.

(*Singing.*)
They fought on and on, covered all over in sand.
Suddenly Flounder shouted, "Take this!"
And fitting an arrow to his string he pulled and let fly.
The shaft penetrated deep beneath Snapper's fin
And he writhed in agony.
His vassal, Brother Octopus,
His vassal, Brother Octopus, the Lay Priest,
Cradled Snapper's fish head in his lap and spoke,
(*Speaking.*)
"If you have last words to say while you yet live,
Entrust them to me, the Octopus Priest."
(*Singing.*)
Snapper spoke in tears and stroked his whiskers,
(*Speaking.*)
"My dear wife knows that this is the fate of a war fish,
But my children are still just roe inside her womb—
I so wanted to see my children alive in this world just one time."
(*Singing.*)
Saying this, Snapper tragically expired.
As all the while the salt wind of Akashi . . .
(*Speaking.*)
Resounded with cruel clamor of battle.

ALL THE WOMEN: Well done, well done!

USUGUMO: Yes, but what strange names they are: Red Snapper Akasuke Flounder Ohsuke, and the Lay Priest Octopus. Even among feudal lords and other distinguished patrons, I've never heard names like those before.

SARUGENJI: That battle was my first taste of combat. You were just a little child then, so of course you've heard nothing about it. Now I've fulfilled my side of the house rule, so come, let's share the saké. (*He hands her a saké cup.*)

USUGUMO: I'm happy to drink with you, although I know I'm not the one.

(*They exchange cups.* SARUGENJI, *beginning to feel the effect of the wine, rests his head on* HOTARUBI*'s lap. The girls signal each other with their eyes, and exit, leaving the two alone.*)

HOTARUBI (*Speaking loudly to* SARUGENJI, *whose head is resting on her lap*): Your lordship, your lordship! It seems you've fallen asleep.

(*Musical accompaniment from the* geza *begins.*)

HOTARUBI: I'm embarrassed to admit this, but in this hard life I lead, all the men I've met have been like demons. Now I realize that for the first time I'm lucky enough to be with a kind and charming customer and what happens—you ignore me and fall into a drunken sleep. How can you be so heartless?

(SARUGENJI *mumbles in his sleep.*)

HOTARUBI: My goodness, he seems to be talking in his sleep. I couldn't quite hear what he said, but I think he spoke another woman's name. What a hateful man you are. If you're going to talk in your sleep, at least speak loud enough so I can hear you.

(SARUGENJI *groans.*)

HOTARUBI: What was that? Oh, you've fallen asleep again, haven't you?

SARUGENJI (*Though talking in his sleep, speaking vigorously and clearly*): I'm Sarugenji from Akoji Inlet in the Province of Ise. Buy my sardines!

HOTARUBI: My goodness, that was strange. The baron shouted some sort of vendor's cry. Something about the Province of Ise. I do hope he does it again so I can figure out what he's saying.

SARUGENJI (*In his sleep, but in an even bigger voice*): I'm Sarugenji from Akoji Inlet in the Province of Ise. Buy my sardines!

HOTARUBI: What? I know that. That's the spiel of a sardine seller. Could that mean that ...? Now that I think about it, he does seem to smell a bit like sardines. (*She holds her nose.*) What an unexpected aroma his perfume sachet has. Come now, Sardine Lord, I'd like to ask you some questions. Please wake up!

(*She shakes him awake.* SARUGENJI *opens his eyes, sits up, and speaks in a voice heavy with sleep.*)

SARUGENJI: I was in heaven while I slept, and I'm still in heaven even now that I'm awake. (*He pinches his own cheek.*) I sure hope this isn't a dream.

(*He lies down again on* HOTARUBI*'s lap.* HOTARUBI *slaps him and he sits up.*)

HOTARUBI: Come on, please wake up. Please! You were talking in your sleep so loudly they can hear it all over the city.

SARUGENJI (*Alarmed*): What?! Did you say I was talking in my sleep?

HOTARUBI: Yes, and I want to ask you about what you said.

SARUGENJI (*Trembling*): What do you want to ask me?

HOTARUBI: You're really a sardine seller, aren't you?

SARUGENJI: What? A sardine seller? (*He claps his hand to his mouth.*) Now then, what do you mean by making such an outrageous statement to Utsunomiya no Danjō, renowned baron of the East Country? A sardine seller . . . what might that be? This is the first time I've heard of such thing since the day they cut my umbilical cord.

HOTARUBI: In that case, let me ask you some questions about what you said in your sleep. First, what do you mean by "Akoji Inlet"?

SARUGENJI: Hmm, Akoji Inlet . . . yes. I enjoy poetry and it appears that I've recited poetic places in my sleep.

"At Akoji Inlet, where girls gather wood for salt fires
If you cast your net again and again they will appear."

I was thinking about that poem when I talked in my sleep.

HOTARUBI: All right. But what does "Sarugenji" mean?

SARUGENJI: Hmm. . . . yes, Sarugenji. Oh, I know. It's from the poem,

"Like the willows at Sarusawa Pond, I'll take a strand of tangled hair,
From my sleeping sweetheart as a keepsake."

Even in my sleep, I said I could love none other than you. But you're subjecting me to such a strict interrogation.

HOTARUBI: I have just one last question for you. (*She can no longer suppress her laughter as she continues.*) In your sleep you said, "Buy my sardines," What sort of poetic origin do those words have?

SARUGENJI: Hmm . . . (*He wipes cold sweat from his brow as he mumbles and he attempts to put the words into a poem.*) Now then, the words "Buy my sardines" that I said in my sleep . . .

HOTARUBI: Well?

SARUGENJI: Well . . .

HOTARUBI: Well?

SARUGENJI: Well . . .

HOTARUBI: Yes, well! Tell me what they mean!

SARUGENJI: What those words mean . . . yes, that's right! Long ago, the poetess Izumi Shikibu was about to eat a sardine, the fish called *iwashi.* Just at that moment, the courtier Yasumasa arrived. Izumi was embarrassed and hurriedly hid the *iwashi.* When Yasumasa asked her what she had just hidden, she answered with this poem:
"When one thinks of the nation of Japan, surely none of its people
Have failed to visit Iwashimizu Shrine."

How cleverly she concealed her wish for him to ignore the *iwashi* using the name of the shrine. Yasumasa was impressed. His face revealed his sympathy for her and he answered her poem thus,
"Since it is a medicinal fish that warms the body and improves
one's looks, by all means you should partake."

So it was that a fish go-between secured a love that grew even closer over time. I'm so inspired by this happy love affair that I must have spoken about it in my sleep.

HOTARUBI: There could never be a sardine seller who knows poetry as well as you do. I suppose then that you must be the true Lord Utsunomiya Danjō.

SARUGENJI (*Sighing in relief and rubbing his chest to relax himself*): That's right. I'm Utsunomiya, the genuine article.

HOTARUBI: Then you're not a sardine seller . . . (*She collapses, weeping.*)

SARUGENJI: Why are you crying?

HOTARUBI: Why shouldn't I be crying? I thought you were a sardine seller, and it turns out that you are really and truly the baron.

SARUGENJI: But why would that make you cry?

HOTARUBI: I have good reason to feel the way I do, but until now I've told my story to no one but the master of the house.

SARUGENJI: I want to hear your story, too. Please tell me.

HOTARUBI: Since you are who you are, I guess I'll tell it to you, too.

(Jōruri *music begins to play.* HOTARUBI *dances and pantomimes to the accompaniment of the passages delivered by the* jōruri *narration.*)

NARRATOR (*Singing*):

I will never forget it . . . It was ten long years ago.

HOTARUBI: I was born the daughter of the lord of Tankaku Castle in the province of Ki. When I was a young girl, I climbed to the highest tower and gazed all around at the scenery.

NARRATOR:

Off in the distance, on the high road,
I spied a person carrying some sort of heavy load.
His voice carried beautifully from far away.

HOTARUBI: "Buy sardines! Buy sardines!"

NARRATOR:

This is what he cried.
Suddenly my heart was filled with yearning
And it was as if my soul had left my body in pursuit.
I stole out of the castle through a secret passageway
And rushed off in the direction of the voice.

HOTARUBI: But though I hurried on and on, it was as though a strong headwind blew against me. I could hear his voice, but he got farther and farther away. I wanted to stop him and tell him of my love, but . . .

NARRATOR:

Soon I was in the shadow of the trees
And his voice was drowned out by the cicadas' raucous trill.
I couldn't see anything.

HOTARUBI: Looking about, it was already dusk. I was lost, and as I lay crying, I heard the honest-sounding voice of a tradesman speaking to me offering assistance.

NARRATOR:

But the kind-seeming traveler was a slave trader,
A demon in human guise. He captured me
And sold me straight off to this brothel.

HOTARUBI: I've managed to live on here for ten long years, and although I've become a high-ranking courtesan, I still recall the sardine seller's loud, clear voice.

NARRATOR:

The sardine seller is my one true love.
Day and night I pray to merciful Kannon to lead me to him.
I so want to meet this humble sardine seller
And become his wife. How I long for him.

HOTARUBI: I thought that today the Wheel of Karma had brought me my salvation, but when I learned that you in fact . . .

NARRATOR:

... Are a samurai lord, I realized that
I am doomed to a terrible fate
No matter how long I live on in this useless, floating world.

HOTARUBI: I have no more to say. My lord, I bid you farewell.

(*She pulls out the dagger that samurai ladies always carry and attempts to stab herself.*[9] SARUGENJI *is startled but manages to intervene and physically prevent her from harming herself with the dagger/sword.*)

SARUGENJI: Don't be rash, my lady Hotarubi!

HOTARUBI: No, please let me die!

SARUGENJI: I'm telling you not to go through with it because in truth I am your sardine seller! My robes and swords come from a rental shop. I am of humble birth, and my name is Sarugenji.

HOTARUBI: No, no please don't try to deceive me again. I would rather die!

SARUGENJI: Oh please, don't panic! Stay calm!

(SARUGENJI *himself is in a panic as he shouts these lines, all the while tussling with* HOTARUBI. *The upstage sliding doors open, and* EBINA, ROKUROZAEMON, *and the* MASTER *enter.*)

EBINA: Hotarubi, I heard everything. My son, Sarugenji, is indeed a sardine seller. Because he told me that he wanted so much to meet you, our plan was to turn him into a counterfeit baron. He is a fine young man who loves reading poetry and is himself an excellent poet. And now I have heard from the master all about you and who you are.

ROKUROZAEMON: I am dressed as the lord's retainer, but really I'm a horse trader. The chestnut mare that I couldn't sell was useful to my friend, so I joined in the plot and became a fake samurai.

HOTARUBI: So, are you really the sardine vendor?

SARUGENJI: Yes. I carry my load like this.

(*Using his long sword,* SARUGENJI *mimes carrying a load of sardines around the room.*)

HOTARUBI: Oh merciful Kannon, how can I ever express my thanks. (*She clasps her hands in prayer.*)

SARUGENJI: From today you are my wife.

HOTARUBI (*Embracing* SARUGENJI): Can this be a dream? I'm so happy.

MASTER: But it will cost two hundred pieces of gold to redeem her.

EBINA: This is a real problem.

ROKUROZAEMON: But what can we do ...

ALL FOUR: ... to raise the money?

(*They silently ponder the problem. Presently a lively drum pattern is played in the* geza. JIROTA, *a samurai retainer from Tankaku Castle, enters from stage right. He was on*

---

9. Or, as is currently staged, she uses one of Sarugenji's swords that is lying nearby.

stage earlier in this act, disguised as a gardener. Now he is dressed in splendid samurai robes. He has captured the fake SAMURAI *in* SARUGENJI*'s retinue and tied them one to another, like a string of beads. He leads them onstage by a rope.*)

JIROTA: Princess, I am exceedingly delighted to see that you are in good health. I have witnessed everything from my hiding place in the shadows. I have also captured these false samurai. Now I must beg you to return to Tankaku Castle at your earliest possible convenience.

HOTARUBI (*Speaking like a princess*): Aren't you the gardener who was here earlier?

JIROTA: Yes. My true name is Jirota, and I am a retainer of your clan. Your father and mother ordered me to search for you. I disguised myself as a gardener and sneaked into this establishment to spy it out. We can ascertain your identity for certain using this inscription. If it matches the inscription known to be on the miniature Kannon figurine that the princess had in her possession, then you are the true princess.

HOTARUBI: I have the Kannon figurine right here.

(*She takes a gold brocade packet from her kimono fold and removes a Kannon figurine made of pure gold. She gives it to the* MASTER, *who hands it to* JIROTA. JIROTA *compares the inscription on the figurine with the inscription he has brought with him.*)

JIROTA: Yes, they do indeed match.

HOTARUBI: Since they match, return the figurine to me.

(JIROTA *hands the figurine back to the* MASTER, *who returns it to* HOTARUBI. HOTARUBI *prays to the Kannon once again in thanks, then carefully puts away the figurine.*)

HOTARUBI: Jirota, untie the false samurai.

JIROTA: Yes my lady, but why on earth . . .

HOTARUBI: I ordered you to untie them, so untie them at once!

(JIROTA *grudgingly unties the false* SAMURAI.)

HOTARUBI: Now then, Jirota, since you have urged me to return to the country, I assume that you have brought with you the money necessary to pay off my contract. Am I correct?

JIROTA: Yes, my lady, I have 250 gold coins here with me.

HOTARUBI: Then be a good fellow and pay two hundred gold coins to the master of this establishment.

JIROTA: Yes, my lady.

(*He gives two hundred gold coins in a packet to the* MASTER.)

SARUGENJI: This is wonderful!

HOTARUBI: That's not all. (*She points at* ROKUROZAEMON.) Give the remaining fifty gold coins to this horse trader.

JIROTA: Why on earth should I do that?

HOTARUBI: Do you mean to challenge your master?

JIROTA: No, my lady.

HOTARUBI: Mr. Rokurozaemon, you have just sold your chestnut horse. Bring it here and give it to Jirota.

ROKUROZAEMON: Oh, thank you so much! (*He quickly leaves the building and returns, leading the horse.*)

JIROTA: My goodness, there's no telling what she'll do next.

(HOTARUBI *takes* SARUGENJI*'s hand, and the two descend the steps and approach* JIROTA.)

HOTARUBI: Now then, Jirota, tell me—are my father and mother both well?

JIROTA: Yes, my lady, both are enjoying excellent health.

HOTARUBI: In that case I want you to convey to them what I am about to tell you. I, Hotarubi, am going to marry this sardine seller. It is a wife's commandment that once a woman leaves her parental gate, she must never again return home. In the future I will go with my honored husband to sell sardines in the province of Ki. I will call out, "Buy sardines!" below Tankaku Castle. Please tell my parents that at that time they should stand high on the castle tower and they can see me.

JIROTA: Oh my god! What a calamity—you have turned heaven and earth upside down! Princess! Princess! Please don't go through with this.

(JIROTA *clutches at* HOTARUBI*'s sleeve, but she shakes free.* HOTARUBI *and* SARUGENJI *walk toward the* hanamichi. JIROTA *begins to follow them.*)

HOTARUBI (*To* JIROTA): Kneel before me and move no further. Kneel, I say!

JIROTA: Yes, my lady.

(HOTARUBI *and* SARUGENJI *walk to the seven-three spot on the* hanamichi.)

HOTARUBI: Now then, Lord Genji . . . no, I should say, "husband, dear" . . .

SARUGENJI: Yes, ma'am. (*He bows abjectly.*)

HOTARUBI: What are you doing, my dear? From today we are sardine-selling husband and wife. Please teach me your sales call.

SARUGENJI: All right. Listen carefully. (*He straightens up and calls out in a clear voice.*) "I'm from Akoji Inlet in the province of Ise! Buy my sardines!"

HOTARUBI: Let me try. How about this? "I'm from Akoji Inlet in the province of Ise! Buy my sardines!" (*They repeat it several times before she gets it right. She turns to face the main stage.*) Come on everybody, why not give it a try?

(*On the main stage* JIROTA, *the* MASTER, EBINA, *the false* SAMURAI, *and* ROKUROZAEMON, *who is holding the horse by a rope at stage right, all raise their voices and cry out.*)

ALL: "I'm from Akoji Inlet in the province of Ise! Buy my sardines!"

HOTARUBI: Oh, you all called out so beautifully.

JIROTA: All is lost! I must atone for my failure.

(*He draws his sword and thrusts it toward his abdomen. Everyone except* HOTARUBI *is in a state of shock.* EBINA *runs over to* JIROTA *and discovers that* JIROTA *is uninjured.* EBINA *seizes the sword and inspects it.*)

EBINA: Of course it couldn't cut anything. It's as dull and rusty as a red sardine. Now then, daughter-in-law . . .

HOTARUBI: . . . Mr. Ebina. From now on, as husband and wife, we shall spend our evenings at Akoji Inlet, matching shells and their poems.

SARUGENJI: The dish accompanying our nuptial saké . . .

ROKUROZAEMON: . . . Will be sardines laid side by side, auspiciously leaving the heads and tails on.

MASTER: What good fortune for you to be able to say farewell to the pleasure quarter.

JIROTA: This is all too cruel. (*He sighs dejectedly, and* EBINA *looks at him.*)

EBINA: Yes, today we have seen the secrets of the magnificent art . . . (*The rapping of* ki *sticks begins, announcing the impending end of the play*) . . . of buying and selling merchandise.

(*Drums join the sticks in a lively rhythm as the curtain closes, leaving* SARUGENJI *and* HOTARUBI *still visible at the seven-three spot on the* hanamichi. *The drumming becomes quieter.* HOTARUBI *takes out her Kannon figurine. She unwraps it and prays to it.* SARUGENJI *takes her arm and leads her off, down the* hanamichi. *They exit together.*)

CURTAIN

SELECTED BIBLIOGRAPHY

This bibliography supplements the definitive bibliography compiled by Kevin J. Wetmore Jr., "Modern Japanese Drama in English," *Asian Theatre Journal* 23, no. 1 (2006): 179–205. Most items published before 2006 are listed there.

GENERAL READINGS

Cody, Gabrielle H., and Evert Sprinchorn, eds. *The Columbia Encyclopedia of Modern Drama.* New York: Columbia University Press, 2007.

Eckersall, Peter. *Theorizing the Angura Space: Avant-Garde Performance and Politics in Japan, 1960–2000.* Leiden: Brill, 2006.

Goodman, David G., ed. and trans. *After Apocalypse: Four Japanese Plays of Hiroshima and Nagasaki.* Ithaca, N.Y.: East Asia Program, Cornell University, 1994.

——, ed. *Japanese Drama and Culture in the 1960s: The Return of the Gods.* Armonk, N.Y.: Sharpe, 1988.

Japan Playwrights Association, ed. *Half a Century of Japanese Theater.* 10 vols. Tokyo: Kinokuniya shoten, 1999–2008.

Jortner, David, Keiko I. McDonald, and Kevin J. Wetmore Jr., eds. *Modern Japanese Theatre and Performance.* Lanham, Md.: Lexington Books, 2006.

Kano, Ayako. *Acting Like a Woman in Modern Japan: Theater, Gender, and Nationalism.* New York: Palgrave Macmillan, 2001.

Keene, Donald. *Dawn to the West: Japanese Literature of the Modern Era.* Vol. 2. New York: Holt, Rinehart and Winston, 1984.

Leiter, Samuel L., ed. *Rising from the Flames: The Rebirth of Theater in Occupied Japan, 1945–1952.* Lanham, Md.: Lexington Books, 2009.

Nara, Hiroshi, ed. *Inexorable Modernity: Japan's Grappling with Modernity in the Arts.* Lanham, Md.: Lexington Books, 2007.

Poulton, M. Cody. *A Beggar's Art: Scripting Modernity in Japanese Drama, 1900–1930*. Honolulu: University of Hawai'i Press, 2010.

Powell, Brian. *Japan's Modern Theatre: A Century of Continuity and Change*. London: Japan Library, 2002.

Rolf, Robert T., and John K. Gillespie, eds. *Alternative Japanese Drama: Ten Plays*. Honolulu: University of Hawai'i Press, 1992.

Shea, George Tyson. *Leftwing Literature in Japan: A Brief History of the Proletarian Literary Movement*. Tokyo: Hōsei University Press, 1964.

Takaya, Ted T., ed. and trans. *Modern Japanese Drama: An Anthology*. New York: Columbia University Press, 1979.

Tschudin, Jean-Jacques. *La ligue du théâtre prolétarian japonais*. Paris: L'Harmattan, 1989.

Uchino, Tadashi. *Crucible Bodies: Postwar Japanese Performance from Brecht to the New Millennium*. Salt Lake City: Seagull, 2009.

INDIVIDUAL PLAYWRIGHTS INCLUDED IN THE ANTHOLOGY

PART I. THE AGE OF "TAISHŌ DRAMA"

Izumi Kyōka

Demon Pond, The Sea God's Villa, The Castle Tower. In *Spirits of Another Sort: The Plays of Izumi Kyōka (1873–1939)*, by M. Cody Poulton. Ann Arbor: Center for Japanese Studies, University of Michigan, 2001.

The Ruby (*Kōgyoku*). In *A Beggar's Art: Scripting Modernity in Japanese Drama, 1900–1930*, by M. Cody Poulton. Honolulu: University of Hawai'i Press, 2010.

PART II. THE TSUKIJI LITTLE THEATER AND ITS AFTERMATH

Enchi Fumiko

Kano, Ayako. "Enchi Fumiko's Stormy Days: Arashi and the Drama of Childbirth." *Monumenta Nipponica* 61, no. 1 (2006): 59–91.

Kishida Kunio

Goodman, David G., ed. *Five Plays by Kishida Kunio*. Rev. ed. Ithaca, N.Y.: East Asia Program, Cornell University, 2002.

Paper Balloon, Cloudburst, A Diary of Fallen Leaves, The Two Daughters of Mr. Sawa. In *Five Plays by Kishida Kunio*, edited by David G. Goodman. Ithaca, N.Y.: East Asia Program, Cornell University, 1989.

Rimer, J. Thomas. *Towards a Modern Japanese Theatre: Kishida Kunio*. Princeton, N.J.: Princeton University Press, 1974.

Two Men at Play with Life (*Inochi o moteasobu otoko futari*). In *A Beggar's Art: Scripting Modernity in Japanese Drama, 1900–1930*, by M. Cody Poulton. Honolulu: University of Hawai'i Press, 2010.

Kubo Sakae

Land of Volcanic Ash: A Play in Two Parts. Translated by David G. Goodman. Ithaca, N.Y.: China-Japan Program, Cornell University, 1986.

Zheng, Guohe. "From War Responsibility to the Red Purge: Politics, *Shingeki*, and the Case of Kubo Sakae." In *Rising from the Flames: The Rebirth of Theater in Occupied Japan, 1945–1952*, edited by Samuel L. Leiter. Lanham, Md.: Lexington Books, 2009.

Murayama Tomoyoshi

Weisenfeld, Gennifer S. *Mavo: Japanese Artists and the Avant-Garde, 1905–1931*. Berkeley: University of California Press, 2002.

PART III. WARTIME AND POSTWAR DRAMA

Abe Kōbō

Bolton, Christopher. *Sublime Voices: The Fictional Science and Science Fiction of Abe Kōbō*. Cambridge, Mass.: Harvard University Press, 2009.

The Box Man (*Hako otoko*). Translated by E. Dale Saunders. New York: Knopf, 1974.

Friends (*Tomodachi*). Translated by Donald Keene. New York: Grove Press, 1969.

Iles, Timothy. *Abe Kōbō: An Exploration of His Prose, Drama, and Theatre*. Florence: European Press Academic Publishing, 2002.

Involuntary Homicide, *Green Stockings*, and *The Ghost Is Here*. In *Three Plays by Kōbō Abe*, translated by Donald Keene. New York: Columbia University Press, 1993.

Key, Margaret. "'Destroying the Audience's Alibi': Empathy and Ethics in Abe Kōbō's *Mihitsu no koe*." In *Modern Japanese Theatre and Performance*, edited by David Jortner, Keiko I. McDonald, and Kevin J. Wetmore Jr. Lanham, Md.: Lexington Books, 2006.

——. *Truth from a Lie: Documentary, Detection, and Reflexivity in Abe Kōbō's Realist Project*. Lanham, Md.: Lexington Books, 2011.

The Man Who Turned into a Stick (*Bō ni natta otoko*). In *The Man Who Turned into a Stick: Three Related Plays*, translated by Donald Keene. Tokyo: University of Tokyo Press, 1975.

Shields, Nancy K. *Fake Fish: The Theater of Kobo Abe*. New York: Weatherhill, 1996.

You, Too, Are Guilty. In *Modern Japanese Drama: An Anthology*, edited and translated by Ted T. Takaya. New York: Columbia University Press, 1979.

Akimoto Matsuyo

Goodman, David G. "The Quest for Salvation in Japan's Modern History: Four Plays by Akimoto Matsuyo." In *Modern Japanese Theatre and Performance*, edited by David Jortner, Keiko I. McDonald, and Kevin J. Wetmore Jr. Lanham, Md.: Lexington Books, 2006.

Kaison the Priest of Hitachi. In *The Return of the Gods: Japanese Drama and Culture in the 1960s*, edited by David G. Goodman. Photo reprint ed. Ithaca, N.Y.: East Asia Program, Cornell University, 2003.

Our Lady of the Scabs. Translated by Stefan Kaiser and Sue Henny. In *Half a Century of Japanese Theater*, edited by Japan Playwrights Association. Vol. 7. Tokyo: Kinokuniya shoten, 2005.

Kinoshita Junji

Between God and Man: A Judgment on War Crimes. Translated, with an introduction, by Eric J. Gangloff. Tokyo: University of Tokyo Press, 1979.

Requiem on the Great Meridian (*Shigosen no matsuri*) *and Selected Essays*. Translated by Brian Powell and Jason Daniel, with an introduction by Brian Powell. Tokyo: Nan'un-do, 2000.

Sorgenfrei, Carol Fisher. "A Fabulous Fake: Folklore and the Search for National Identity in Kinoshita Junji's *Twilight Crane*." In *Rising from the Flames: The Rebirth of Theater in Occupied Japan, 1945–1952*, edited by Samuel L. Leiter. Lanham, Md.: Lexington Books, 2009.

Morimoto Kaoru

Poulton, M. Cody. "The Road Taken, Then Retraced: Morimoto Kaoru's *A Woman's Life* and *Japan in China*." In *Sino-Japanese Transculturation: From the Nineteenth Century to the Pacific War*, edited by Katsuhiko Endo, Richard King, and M. Cody Poulton. Lanham, Md.: Lexington Books, 2011.

Zheng, Guohe. "Reflections *of* and *on* the Times: Morimoto Kaoru's *A Woman's Life*." In *Modern Japanese Theatre and Performance*, edited by David Jortner, Keiko I. McDonald, and Kevin J. Wetmore Jr. Lanham, Md.: Lexington Books, 2006.

Tanaka Chikao

The Far Fringes of the Clouds. Translated by John D. Swain. In *Half a Century of Japanese Theater*, edited by Japan Playwrights Association. Vol. 8. Tokyo: Kinokuniya shoten, 2006.

The Head of Mary (*Maria no kubi*). In *After Apocalypse: Four Japanese Plays of Hiroshima and Nagasaki*, edited and translated by David G. Goodman. Ithaca, N.Y.: East Asia Program, Cornell University, 1994.

Mama (*Ofukuro*). In *A Beggar's Art: Scripting Modernity in Japanese Drama, 1900–1930*, by M. Cody Poulton. Honolulu: University of Hawai'i Press, 2010.

PART IV. THE 1960S AND UNDERGROUND THEATER

Betsuyaku Minoru

The Cherry in Bloom. Translated by Robert T. Rolf. In *Alternative Japanese Drama: Ten Plays*, edited by Robert T. Rolf and John K. Gillespie. Honolulu: University of Hawai'i Press, 1992.

The Elephant. In *After Apocalypse: Four Japanese Plays of Hiroshima and Nagasaki*, edited and translated by David G. Goodman. Ithaca, N.Y.: East Asia Program, Cornell University, 1994.

The Legend of Noon. Translated by Robert T. Rolf. In *Alternative Japanese Drama: Ten Plays*, edited by Robert T. Rolf and John K. Gillespie. Honolulu: University of Hawai'i Press, 1992.

The Move: A Play in Six Scenes with a Solemn Epilogue. In *Modern Japanese Drama: An Anthology*, edited and translated by Ted T. Takaya. New York: Columbia University Press, 1979.

Sick (*Byōki*). Translated by M. Cody Poulton. In *Half a Century of Japanese Theater*, edited by Japan Playwrights Association. Vol. 6. Tokyo: Kinokuniya shoten, 2004.

Inoue Hisashi

The Face of Jizō (*Chichi to kuraseba*). Translated by Roger Pulvers. Tokyo: Komatsuza, 2000.

Makeup. Translated by Akemi Hori. In *The Columbia Anthology of Modern Japanese Literature*, edited by J. Thomas Rimer and Van Gessel. Vol. 2, *From 1945 to the Present*. New York: Columbia University Press, 2007.

Yabuhara, the Blind Master Minstrel. Translated by Marguerite Wells. In *Half a Century of Japanese Theater*, edited by Japan Playwrights Association. Vol. 6. Tokyo: Kinokuniya shoten, 2004.

Kara Jūrō

A Cry from the City of Virgins. Translated by Leon Ingulsrud. In *Half a Century of Japanese Theater*, edited by Japan Playwrights Association. Vol. 6. Tokyo: Kinokuniya shoten, 2004.

A Cry from the City of Virgins. Translated by M. Cody Poulton. *Canadian Theatre Review* 85 (1995): 45–65.

John Silver: The Beggar of Love. In *After Apocalypse: Four Japanese Plays of Hiroshima and Nagasaki*, edited and translated by David G. Goodman. Ithaca, N.Y.: East Asia Program, Cornell University, 1994.

The 24:53 Train Bound for "Tower" Is Waiting in Front of That Doughnut Shop in Takebaya (*24-ji 53-pun no "Tō no shita" yuki no densha ga Takebayachō no dagashiya no mae de matteiru*). Translated by M. Cody Poulton. In *The Columbia Anthology of Modern Japanese Literature*, edited by J. Thomas Rimer and Van Gessel. Vol. 2, *From 1945 to the Present*. New York: Columbia University Press, 2007.

The Virgin's Mask. Translated by John K. Gillespie and Paul H. Krieger. In *Alternative Japanese Drama: Ten Plays*, edited by Robert T. Rolf and John K. Gillespie. Honolulu: University of Hawai'i Press, 1992.

Ōta Shōgo

Boyd, Mari. *The Aesthetics of Quietude: Ōta Shōgō and the Theatre of Divestiture*. Tokyo: Sophia University Press, 2006.

Sarachi: A Play. Translated by Robert T. Rolf. *Asian Theatre Journal* 10, no. 2 (1993): 133–62.

The Tale of Komachi Told by the Wind. Translated by Mari Boyd. In *Half a Century of Japanese Theater*, edited by Japan Playwrights Association. Vol. 6. Tokyo: Kinokuniya shoten, 2004.

The Water Station (*Mizu no eki*). Translated by Mari Boyd. *Asian Theatre Journal* 7, no. 2 (1990): 150–83.

Shimizu Kunio

Jortner, David. "Remembered Idylls, Forgotten Truths: Nostalgia and Geography in the Drama of Shimizu Kunio." In *Inexorable Modernity: Japan's Grappling with Modernity in the Arts*, edited by Hiroshi Nara. Lanham, Md.: Lexington Books, 2007.

The Sand of Youth, How Quickly. Translated by Robert T. Rolf. In *Alternative Japanese Drama: Ten Plays*, edited by Robert T. Rolf and John K. Gillespie. Honolulu: University of Hawai'i Press, 1992.

Such a Serious Frivolity. Translated by J. Thomas Rimer. In *Half a Century of Japanese Theater*, edited by Japan Playwrights Association. Vol. 7. Tokyo: Kinokuniya shoten, 2005.

Tango at the End of Winter. Edited by Peter Barnes. London: Amber Lane Press, 1991.

Those Days: A Lyrical Hypothesis on Time and Forgetting. Translated by John K. Gillespie. In *Alternative Japanese Drama: Ten Plays*, edited by Robert T. Rolf and John K. Gillespie. Honolulu: University of Hawai'i Press, 1992.

When We Go Down That Heartless River (*Bokura ga hijō no taiga o kudaru toki*). Translated by J. Thomas Rimer. In *The Columbia Anthology of Modern Japanese Literature*, edited by J. Thomas Rimer and Van Gessel. Vol. 2, *From 1945 to the Present*. New York: Columbia University Press, 2007.

Terayama Shūji

Clark, Steven. "Terayama in Amsterdam and the Internationalization of Experimental Theatre." In *Modern Japanese Theatre and Performance*, edited by David Jortner, Keiko I. McDonald, and Kevin J. Wetmore Jr. Lanham, Md.: Lexington Books, 2006.

Knock: Street Theatre. Translated by Robert T. Rolf. In *Alternative Japanese Drama: Ten Plays*, edited by Robert T. Rolf and John K. Gillespie. Honolulu: University of Hawai'i Press, 1992.

Ridgley, Steven C. *Japanese Counterculture: The Antiestablishment Art of Terayama Shūji*. Minneapolis: University of Minnesota Press, 2011.

Sorgenfrei, Carol Fisher. *Unspeakable Acts: The Avant-Garde Theatre of Terayama Shūji and Postwar Japan*. Honolulu: University of Hawai'i Press, 2005. [Includes translations of *The Hunchback of Aomori*, *La Marie Vison*, *Heretics*, and excerpts from *The Labyrinth and the Dead Sea: My Theatre*]

PART V. THE 1980S AND BEYOND

Hirata Oriza

Citizens of Seoul. Translated by John D. Swain. In *Half a Century of Japanese Theater*, edited by Japan Playwrights Association. Vol. 1. Tokyo: Kinokuniya shoten, 1999.

Sayonara. Translated by Hiroko Hatsuda and Bryerly Long. *Comparative Theatre Review* 11, no. 1 (2011): 22–28, https://www.jstage.jst.go.jp/article/ctr/11/1/11_1_22/_pdf.

The Scientifically Minded. Translated by Hiroko Matsuda and Tim Keenan. *Comparative Theatre Review* 12, no. 1 (2013); 29–118, https://www.jstage.jst.go.jp/article/ctr/12/1/12_29/_pdf.

"*Tokyo Notes*: A Play by Hirata Oriza." Translated by M. Cody Poulton. *Asian Theatre Journal* 19, no. 1 (2001): 1–120.

Noda Hideki

The Bee (with Colin Teevan). London: Oberon Books, 2007.

The Diver (with Colin Teevan). London: Oberon Books, 2008.

Fukushima, Yoshiko. *Manga Discourse in Japanese Theater: The Location of Noda Hideki's Yume no Yūminsha*. London: Kegan Paul, 2003.

The Red Demon Akaoni. Translated by Roger Pulvers. In *Half a Century of Japanese Theater*, edited by Japan Playwrights Association. Vol. 4. Tokyo: Kinokuniya shoten, 2002.

Okada Toshiki

Poulton, M. Cody. "Krapp's First Tape: Toshiki Okada's *Enjoy at 59 E59*." *TDR: The Drama Review* 55, no. 2 (2011): 150–57.

PART VI. POPULAR THEATER

Izumi Kyōka

"*At Yushima Shrine*, a Scene from *A Woman's Pedigree*, by Izumi Kyōka" [translation of *Yushima no Keidai*]. In *A Tokyo Anthology: Literature from Japan's Mega-City, 1850–1920*, edited by Sumie Jones and Charles S. Inouye. Honolulu: University of Hawai'i Press, 2014.

Mishima Yukio

Five Modern Nō Plays. Translated by Donald Keene. New York: Knopf, 1957.

Goodman, David G. "An Aesthetic of Destruction: Mishima Yukio's *My Friend Hitler*." In *Inexorable Modernity: Japan's Grappling with Modernity in the Arts*, edited by Hiroshi Nara. Lanham, Md.: Lexington Books, 2007.

Kominz, Laurence R. "*Steeplechase*: Mishima Yukio's Only Original Nō Play." In *Modern Japanese Theatre and Performance*, edited by David Jortner, Keiko I. McDonald, and Kevin J. Wetmore Jr. Lanham, Md.: Lexington Books, 2006.

Madame de Sade. Translated by Donald Keene. Tokyo: Tuttle, 1971.

Mishima on Stage: The Black Lizard and Other Plays. Translated and edited by Laurence R. Kominz. Ann Arbor: University of Michigan Press, 2007.

My Friend Hitler and Other Plays of Yukio Mishima. Translated by Hiroaki Satō. New York: Columbia University Press, 2002.

Yoroboshi: The Blind Young Man. In *Modern Japanese Drama: An Anthology*, edited and translated by Ted T. Takaya. New York: Columbia University Press, 1979.

Yuya, a Modern Nō Play. Translated by Jonah Salz and Laurence Kominz. In *The Columbia Anthology of Modern Japanese Literature*, edited by J. Thomas Rimer and Van Gessel. Vol. 2, *From 1945 to the Present*. New York: Columbia University Press, 2007.

Takarazuka

Longinetto, Kim, and Jane Williams. *Dream Girls*. Video distributed by Women Make Movies, 1993.

Robertson, Jennifer. "The Politics of Androgyny in Japan: Sexuality and Subversion in the Theatre and Beyond." *American Ethnologist* 19, no. 3 (1992): 419–42.

——. *Takarazuka: Sexual Politics and Popular Culture in Modern Japan*. Berkeley: University of California Press, 1998.

Stickland, Leonie R. *Gender Gymnastics: Performing and Consuming Japan's Takarazuka Revue*. Melbourne: Trans-Pacific Press, 2008.

Yamanashi, Makiko. *A History of the Takarazuka Revue Since 1914: Modern Girl's Culture, Japan Pop*. Folkstone: Global Oriental, 2012.

PERMISSIONS

The editors and publisher acknowledge with thanks permission granted to reprint the following material.

Father Returns, by Kikuchi Kan, translated by M. Cody Poulton. Pages 85–98 in *A Beggar's Art: Scripting Modernity in Japanese Drama, 1900–1930*, by M. Cody Poulton. © 2010 University of Hawai'i Press. Reprinted by permission of the publisher.

The Skeleton's Dance, by Akita Ujaku, translated by M. Cody Poulton. Pages 134–52 in *A Beggar's Art: Scripting Modernity in Japanese Drama, 1900–1930*, by M. Cody Poulton. © 2010 University of Hawai'i Press. Reprinted by permission of the publisher.

A Nero in Skirts, by Murayama Tomoyoshi. Published by permission of Murayama Harue.

Paper Balloon, by Kishida Kunio, translated by Richard McKinnon. Pages 44–55 in *Five Plays by Kishida Kunio*, expanded edition, edited by David G. Goodman (CEAS vol. 51, 1995). Reprinted with permission. Cornell East Asia Series, Cornell University, Ithaca, New York 14855, USA.

The Man Who Turned into a Stick, by Abe Kōbō. *Bō ni natta otoko* © 1969 The Heirs of Abe Kōbō. Reprinted by permission of the Sakai Agency, Inc.

Twilight Crane, by Kinoshita Junji, translated by Brian Powell. Pages 475–90 of *Modern Japanese Literature*, vol. 2, *From 1945 to the Present*, edited by J. Thomas Rimer and Van C. Gessel. © 2007 Columbia University Press. Reprinted by permission of the publisher and Kinoshita Tomiko.

The Little Match Girl, by Betsuyaku Minoru, translated by Robert N. Lawson. Pages 27–51 in *Alternative Japanese Drama: Ten Plays*, edited by Robert T. Rolf and John K. Gillespie. © 1992 University of Hawai'i Press. Reprinted by permission of the publisher and Betsuyaku Minoru.

Two Women, by Kara Jūrō, translated by John K. Gillespie. Pages 293–322 in *Alternative Japanese Drama: Ten Plays*, edited by Robert T. Rolf and John K. Gillespie. © 1992 University of Hawai'i Press. Reprinted by permission of the publisher and Kara Jūrō.

Poison Boy, by Terayama Shūji. Reprinted by permission of Terayama Eiko.

The Dressing Room: That Which Flows Away Ultimately Becomes Nostalgia, by Shimizu Kunio, translated by Chiyori Miyagawa and John K. Gillespie. Pages 200–222 in *Alternative Japanese Drama: Ten Plays*, edited by Robert T. Rolf and John K. Gillespie. © 1992 University of Hawai'i Press. Reprinted by permission of the publisher and Shimizu Kunio.

The Earth Station, by Ōta Shōgo. Reprinted by permission of Ōta Mitsuko.

Living with Father, by Inoue Hisashi. Published by permission of Inoue Yuri.

Poems for Sale, by Noda Hideki. Reprinted by permission of Noda Hideki.

Tokyo Notes, by Hirata Oriza, translated by M. Cody Poulton. Reprinted by permission of Hirata Oriza and M. Cody Poulton.

The Attic, by Sakate Yōji. Reprinted by permission of Sakate Yōji.

Five Days in March, by Okada Toshiki. Reprinted by permission of Okada Toshiki.

The Rose of Versailles: A Takarazuka Grand Romantic Play, by Ueda Shinji. Reprinted by permission of Takarazuka Revue Company.

The Sardine Seller's Net of Love, by Mishima Yukio, translated by Laurence Kominz, from pp. 125–147 of *Mishima on Stage: The Black Lizard and Other Plays*, edited and with an introduction by Laurence Kominz, foreword by Donald Keene, Michigan Monograph Series in Japanese Studies, Number 59 (Ann Arbor: Center for Japanese Studies, The University of Michigan, 2007). Copyright © 2007 the Regents of The University of Michigan. All Rights Reserved. Reprinted with the permission of the publisher. *Iwashiuri koi no hikiami* © 1954 The Heirs of Mishima Yukio. Reprinted by permission of the Sakai Agency, Inc.

Printed in the USA
CPSIA information can be obtained
at www.ICGtesting.com
JSHW061337221123
52606JS00016B/46